PLANT ECOLOGY

McGRAW-HILL PUBLICATIONS IN
THE BOTANICAL SCIENCES

Edmund W. Sinnott, *Consulting Editor*

There are also the related series of McGraw-Hill Publications in the Zoological Sciences, of which E. J. Boell is Consulting Editor, and in the Agricultural Sciences, of which R. A. Brink is Consulting Editor.

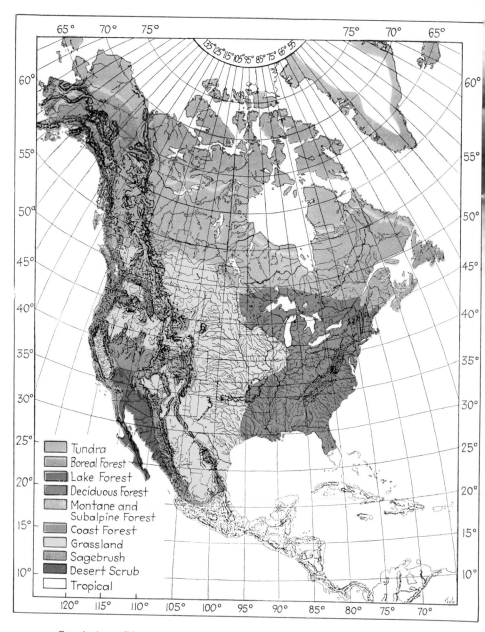

Frontispiece.—Diagrammatic map showing the general relations of the climaxes.

PLANT ECOLOGY

BY

JOHN E. WEAVER
Dean of Graduate College
University of Nebraska

AND

FREDERIC E. CLEMENTS
Ecologist, Division of Plant Biology
Carnegie Institution of Washington

SECOND EDITION

McGRAW-HILL BOOK COMPANY, INC.
NEW YORK AND LONDON
1938

PREFACE TO THE SECOND EDITION

Advances in plant ecology have been rapid during the past decade. Methods of studying vegetation have been improved, the fundamental natural units are better understood, knowledge of ecesis and invasion has been greatly advanced, and reactions and coactions are more fully comprehended. Marked progress has been made in the study of the effects of light, wind, and drought upon vegetation. Experimental evidence has greatly changed the concept of xerophytism; reactions, coactions, and stabilization are much better understood and are now directly applied to problems of conservation.

The new conception of the vast importance of climate and vegetation in soil development has now been generally adopted. The enormous importance of a plant cover in stabilizing soil against erosion by wind and water is more fully realized. Studies of conservation of wild life have been shown to hinge upon an understanding of the vegetation which furnishes food, cover, and shelter for animal life. The heavy toll exacted by erosion on tilled lands must be overcome in the main by farming systems that are in harmony with the environment—the normal climatic and vegetational processes. A fairly comprehensive understanding of Nature's principles and methods has now been attained as regards the processes of plant succession, stabilization of climax vegetation, and the use of plants and plant communities as indicators of what has happened in the past, what is taking place today, and what can be made to happen in the future.

The purpose of the revised edition is to furnish a comprehensive textbook in accord with present-day ecological progress and a guide to workers in the numerous related fields where an intimate knowledge of plants and plant environments, whether natural or modified by man, is fundamental to progress.

In the preparation of the revision the authors have become indebted to several persons for reading portions of the manuscript. Their thanks are due especially to Doctors F. J. Alway, C. E. Kellogg, and H. C. Hanson, and to Prof. T. J. Fitzpatrick and Dr. W. J. Himmel for reading both manuscript and proof.

JOHN E. WEAVER.

FREDERIC E. CLEMENTS.

LINCOLN, NEBRASKA;
SANTA BARBARA, CALIFORNIA,
  January, 1938.

PREFACE TO THE FIRST EDITION

This volume is designed to meet the need for a comprehensive text-book of plant ecology and to furnish a guide to workers in related fields. It is written from the standpoint of development, instrumentation, and experiment. The student of plant production, whether in botany, agriculture, grazing, forestry, plant pathology, or other fields, is beginning to study more thoroughly the intimate relations between plants or groups of plants and their environment. In fact, many of his most important problems deal with the relations of plant to habitat, whether the latter be natural or modified by cultivation, and these can not be satisfactorily solved until these relationships are well understood. In addition, the field of ecology is unique in its fundamental contributions to a general understanding of the plant world upon which man and animals are dependent. This book has been planned to meet these several needs. It is the outgrowth of many years of research and teaching by both authors, and comprehends the general course in ecology given by the first-named author in the University of Nebraska. The subject matter has been repeatedly used by classes and found readily comprehensible; the experiments and exercises have proved workable, and the field work illuminating.

The experiments and exercises for greenhouse and laboratory have been outlined in detail as an outcome of repeated use by classes. More experimental work has been included than the average class will find time to do and, thus, a choice of materials may be had to fit the time and conditions under which the course is given. Field studies have been suggested only in broader outlines. While all of this work is usually done, the details are left to be elaborated for the particular communities available to the student.

The writers are under great obligations to the Carnegie Institution of Washington for the liberal use of text and illustrations from several publications and to Henry Holt and Company for similar permission in connection with "Plant Physiology and Ecology." To a number of students of the first-named author, especially Mr. T. L. Steiger and Miss Theodora Klose, the writers are indebted for certain drawings. The

ix

chapter on Soils has been carefully read by Prof. J. C. Russel, and the entire manuscript by Dr. Herbert C. Hanson. The writers are further indebted to Prof. T. J. Fitzpatrick and Dr. Walter J. Himmel for the reading of both manuscript and proof.

JOHN E. WEAVER.

FREDERIC E. CLEMENTS.

LINCOLN, NEBRASKA;
SANTA BARBARA, CALIFORNIA,
   May, 1929.

TO THE TEACHER

Plant ecology is preeminently a field subject. No type of class work needs more careful planning than does that given in the field. Although the first-named author has taught ecology for many years, he seldom takes a class into the field without making a preliminary visit for the purpose of formulating a detailed plan. When carefully outlined, enough field experience may be gained during 8 to 10 half-day trips to afford a fairly adequate background for study during the winter. To illustrate, at Nebraska the first field trip usually has for its purpose the study of about 10 dominants and subdominants of low and high prairie, respectively, including something of the autecology of each. It is concluded by securing soil samples from the two habitats for water-content determinations.

A second half-day is spent in a brief survey of the important species of areas of upland prairie, tall marsh-grass swamp, and sumac thicket. Measurements of evaporation, humidity, and wind velocity in each community are supplemented by readings from cut-shoot potometers for a part of the period.

A study of salt-marsh dominants, their autecology, distribution in zones due to varying alkalinity, and successional relations from bare area to stabilized prairie, together with the securing of soil samples for later salt-content analysis, occupies another half-day.

Usually an entire day is spent in the forest, where especial emphasis is placed upon the recognition of various kinds of communities, *e.g.* hazelnut-coralberry chaparral, bur oak-bitternut hickory, shellbark hickory, and red oak-linden upland communities, and elm-ash flood-plain forest. Attention is directed toward a study of the conditions of soil, water content, etc. under which each develops; the structure of each community as regards important species, layering, and rate of growth of dominants as determined by an increment borer; the reactions of the community upon light, humus accumulation, and soil structure; and the relations of one community to another in their successional sequence.

The story of a hydrosere, beginning with an examination of submerged and floating plants, including bulrush, cattail, and reed swamp, and ending with the development of sedge meadow into climax prairie, occupies another half-day. Even in so brief a time much may be learned concerning the autecology of the dominants, their adaptations to the

habitat, the community reactions, and the resulting shifting of populations in the processes of development.

A visit to carefully selected rock outcrops affords opportunity for
tracing the several stages of a xerosere. The ecesis and competition
of crustose and foliose lichens are observed; the invasion of xeric mosses
and the disappearance of the lichens; the establishment of pioneer
herbaceous species where a thin soil has been formed; the development
of the xeric herbaceous stage with the deepening of the substratum
and humus accumulation; invasion of shrubs and their profound reactions
resulting in the disappearance of the herbs and later in the invasion of
drought-resistant trees. This includes a study of water- and humus-
content of soil.

At least one-half day is given to learning the method of making list
and chart quadrats and belt transects, usually in open areas. This
includes examination of bisects found along steep roadside cuts or
elsewhere.

One trip is concerned with the problems of grazing; indicators of
various degrees of overgrazing are studied; the vegetation in exclosures,
one to several years old, is compared and succession traced from greatly
overgrazed, weedy, eroded areas to the climax vegetation. Later the
changes as recorded by permanent quadrats, community maps, and
photographs are examined and discussed.

Two stations are established near or on the campus where students
operate hygrothermographs, soil thermographs, atmometers, and anemometers. The instruments are frequently checked and their operation
continued until each student is familiar with all. This also includes the
measurement of light intensities in several habitats. Little time is given
to comparing and interpreting the records until the several factors
measured are studied in detail.

During the field work, soil samples are secured for pH determinations,
various living plants are transferred from field to greenhouse where they
furnish material for the work on ecological anatomy, experiments on
aeration, relative transpiration, length of day, etc. The field work of
spring and summer need not be outlined here. A discussion of the text
should present so many problems concerning instruments, phytometers,
methods of studying vegetation, pollination, life histories, coactions,
indicators, etc., that the question is one of doing what seems most
important and expedient in the time allotted for the work.

Meteorological instruments and apparatus may be obtained from
Julien P. Friez and Sons, Belfort Meteorological Observatory, Baltimore,
Maryland, and Henry J. Green, 1191 Bedford Avenue, Brooklyn, New
York. The more strictly ecological instruments are supplied by Fred C.
Henson, 3628 East Colorado Street, Pasadena, California.

CONTENTS

CHAPTER IV

CHAPTER V

CHAPTER XI

CHAPTER XII

CHAPTER XVIII

PLANT ECOLOGY

CHAPTER I

VEGETATION; ITS ORIGIN, DEVELOPMENT, AND STRUCTURE

Vegetation is the sum total of plants covering an area. It may be a forest with its trees, undershrubs, and herbs and the forest floor with mosses, fungi, and lichens. It may consist of bulrushes, cattails, and

Fig. 1.—A layer of herbs, touch-me-not (*Impatiens*), three-seeded mercury (*Acalypha*), etc., in a young oak-hickory forest.

similar groups of plants growing in marshes, or of algae submerged in water, or of the sparsely spaced cacti, sagebrush, etc., of the desert, or of the crustlike growth of lichens on otherwise bare rocks.

Vegetation is more than the mere grouping of individual plants. It is the result of the interactions of numerous factors. The effects of the plants upon the place in which they live and their influence upon each other are especially significant. When trees develop in an area,

1

they greatly modify conditions for growth by decreasing light and lessening the force of the wind (Fig. 1). Water evaporates less readily from the soil when covered with a mulch of decaying leaves, and the air is more humid under a leafy forest canopy. Sun-loving shrubs and herbs disappear and are replaced by those which thrive in cool, moist, shady places. The trees not only largely determine the kind of plants which grow beneath them but also profoundly influence each other. If densely crowded, they grow tall and straight and usually lose their lower branches

Fig. 2.—Much-branched bur oak about 140 years old which grew for nearly a century in an open area in eastern Nebraska. The tall straight oaks growing around it are only about 50 years old. They have developed since the cessation of prairie fires.

as a result of insufficient light. Under such conditions, many species of trees cannot thrive. Where the forest is open, the branches extend more widely and each individual makes a better development (Fig. 2.) A study of vegetation reveals that it is an organic entity and that, like an organism, each part is interdependent upon every other part.

How Vegetation Originates.—Vegetation arises from the coming together of individual plants and their interactions upon each other. The latter are brought about by the plants modifying the habitat or place in which they live. They cause it to become wetter or drier; they may increase the richness of the soil and decrease the light. In different ways, they make it a fit or an unfit place for various other kinds of plants to grow.

The origin of vegetation may be observed in a fallow field or garden. When all the former vegetation has been destroyed and seeds or other propagules buried too deeply to develop new plants, the area is usually populated very sparsely the first season, mostly with weedy annuals. By the second year, vegetation has greatly increased. In addition to a new crop of annuals, many biennials and even some perennials appear. These increase by both seed and vegetative propagation and, with other plants that have migrated into the new area, soon cover the ground and apparently appropriate all the space. In the struggle for light, water, and nutrients that follows, the annuals, which must start anew each year, show their handicap by disappearing, while perennials, which constantly hold the ground and extend their territory, increase in importance. Some are more successful than others and in time occupy the area more or less exclusively.

An abandoned field or unused road in the Great Plains passes through these various stages and after many years is revegetated with buffalo grass and grama grass.[810] In New England or Kentucky the final vegetation is a forest. Sand dunes are vegetated in a similar way, by the coming together or aggregation of individual plants; so, also, are shallow ponds or dried lake bottoms, talus slopes, mud-covered flats, exposed rock ledges, and, indeed, all bare areas.[339] Just as bare areas are being covered by plants today, so, too, they were vegetated in the past. Plants became grouped in the areas left bare by retreating glaciers, on the wind-blown hills of loess, on the uplifted margins of the ocean, and on the mountain ranges of naked rock. In short, vegetation originated with the appearance of the land mass that it covers.[187,191]

How Vegetation Develops.—The development of vegetation consists of a number of closely related processes so important that each forms a special field for study. All bare areas that are entirely free from seed or other propagules owe their pioneers to *migration* (Fig. 3). This includes all movements by means of which plants are carried away from the parent or their original home. The distance may be short, barely outside the area dominated by the parent, or very great, as often occurs with wind-blown or water-carried germules. The fundamental process is moving the germules—seeds, spores, runners, etc.—away from the old and into the new area.

Migration alone, however, cannot produce vegetation. It is entirely ineffective if the propagules do not grow. The seeds must germinate in the new area, the seedlings grow into mature plants, and these, in turn, must reproduce if the area is to be vegetated. The migrants must make themselves at home, an idea that is expressed in a single term *ecesis*.

After the establishment of the first scattered invaders, the individuals come to be grouped, as a result of propagation, a process termed *aggregation*.

Aggregation sooner or later results in *competition*. The pioneer invaders may grow so far apart that no other plants encroach upon the same territory for water, nutrients, or light, or if they do there may be sufficient for all. In such cases, there is no competition. But when the plants are aggregated so that the demand for energy or materials is greater than the supply, competition begins. There is not enough for all; the stronger suppress the weaker; the latter are dwarfed or die as a result. Competition among plants goes on so quietly that it is usually unnoticed.

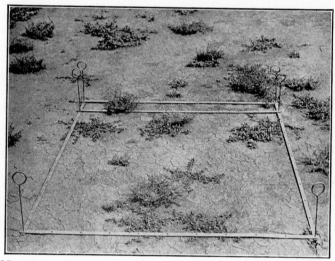

Fig. 3.—Migration of weedy annuals, knotgrass (*Polygonum*) and peppergrass (*Lepidium*), into a tennis court the surface of which had been covered with clay.

Of 10,500 plants of the great ragweed (*Ambrosia trifida*) that germinated and started growth in a single square meter of rich, moist soil, only 192 survived at the close of the season. All but 1.8 per cent died in consequence of insufficient light for making food. None of the survivors was fully developed, for on such a small area there was really only enough light available for the best growth of a few individuals.

When plants grow together and compete for the necessary factors, they profoundly affect or react upon the place in which they grow. Competition results in *reactions*. The area once so fully lighted becomes more or less densely shaded. If it was wet, the large amount of water absorbed from the soil and lost through transpiration makes it drier. If it was dry, the accumulation of humus by the decay of dead roots, stems, and leaves adds to the water-retaining power of the soil. The dry area gradually becomes moister. The vegetation checks the wind movement near the soil where seedlings grow. Owing to the shade, temperature becomes lower and less variable, and the air contains more water vapor than formerly, *i.e.*, it has a higher humidity. Moreover, the soil becomes richer, owing to the accumulated humus and the work of bacteria and fungi, and thus more favorable to plant growth.

The changes in the area are manifold. The vegetation has such a profound effect upon it that conditions for plant growth become very different. While early invaders may be unable to survive because of

Fig. 4.—Grassland that has reached stabilization in eastern Nebraska on a soil similar to that in Fig. 3. Needle grass (*Stipa*) is the most important species; the bushy herb is the many-flowered psoralea.

changed conditions and keen competition, others, which at first grew poorly or could not grow, now find the habitat favorable. Consequently, there is a shifting in the plant population as the developing vegetation modifies the environment. Shrubs may replace herbs in consequence of shading them, if conditions are favorable to their growth. Trees may be able to start under the shelter of the shrubs and, once fairly established, cause the disappearance of their benefactors. But whether herbs or shrubs or trees will be the final type of vegetation is determined by the climate, since the habitat cannot be modified indefinitely.

If the precipitation is meager and evaporation high, only enough water may be present for the growth of drought-enduring grasses and their associates. Such is the climate of the plains. In western Washington and the mountains of Colorado, conditions are favorable to the growth of coniferous forest which is the final stage of development. This is the highest type that the habitat can support under the present climate. The soil becomes no richer, the water content and humidity remain fairly constant, and light, also, is approximately the same. The vegetation is in equilibrium with its climate; it has become *stabilized* (Fig. 4). If it is cut or burned or the area otherwise partially or entirely denuded, the processes of migration, ecesis, aggregation, competition, and reaction, culminating in stabilization, are again repeated. Thus, like all organisms, vegetation arises, develops, matures, reproduces, and may finally die.

In cultivated vegetation, man is the chief agent causing migration. He also determines the density of aggregation and fosters ecesis. Moreover, the thoughtful grower of plants controls in a large measure the degree of competition by the rate of seeding and spacing or by thinning or transplanting. Since the reactions of the vegetation are modified by tillage and invaders largely kept down, stabilization is never reached.

How Vegetation Shows Structure.—Vegetation, like all organisms, not only undergoes development but also possesses structure. The vegetation of a continent, such as North America, is not uniform throughout. Depending upon climate, it is differentiated into large natural units such as forest, chaparral, grassland, tundra, etc. The composition or structure of each type differs from the others. Each of these larger units of vegetation is called a *plant formation*. But no formation is uniform throughout its entire extent. Since the climate is different in various portions of the formation, differences in the vegetation occur.

A grassland climate dominates the region from the Missouri River through Nebraska, Kansas, and Colorado to the Rocky Mountains. Since precipitation, which is one of the most important climatic factors, decreases from 30 inches in the east to 15 inches westward, the true prairie in the region of higher rainfall gives way westward to the vegetation of the mixed prairie. Likewise, the oak-hickory community occupies the drier western portion of the deciduous forest. Such major divisions of a plant formation are termed *associations*.

Practically all vegetation shows more or less striking differences every few feet. Differences in the habitat—here a little drier, perhaps owing to thinner soil, there a little wetter because of a slight depression or greater humus accumulation—are reflected both in the number and in the kinds of plants. Where these differences are continuous, as around swamps or ponds, the structure of the vegetation is clearly shown in *zonation*. A belt or zone of floating plants in moderately deep water is surrounded by the tall, coarse, marsh vegetation of the pond margins, and this, in turn, may be bordered by sedge meadow. Forest margins usually exhibit definite zonation. The trees are bordered by a zone of shrubs and the latter, perhaps, by grassland (Fig. 5). Zonation may result from excessive salt accumulation in depressions. The center of the area may be bare but bordered by zones of various halophytes (salt plants) in the sequence of their tolerance to salt.

In any area of vegetation, usually only a little study is necessary to distinguish the controlling or *dominant species*. The others are either *subdominant* or *secondary*. In a mature forest of beech and hard maple, one may occasionally find a white pine or red oak, but these are present merely because the area is not completely occupied by the dominant beech and maple in the shade of which they cannot grow. In more

Fig. 5.—Zones of grassland, oak scrub, and ponderosa pine in Colorado.

open forests such as ponderosa pine or bur oak, enough light penetrates through the dominant trees to permit a growth of shrubs and below these, in turn, grasses and herbs, while shade-enduring mosses and lichens occur on the forest floor. In fact, the presence and development of these species are controlled largely by the environmental conditions determined by the dominant trees. These various *layers* or vertical zones of plants are closely related to the decrease in light intensity from the primary layer of tree crowns downward. They are another expression of the structure of vegetation. Layering, although not so pronounced as in the forest, also occurs in grassland, and is characteristic of nearly all vegetation. It is revealed aboveground and among the roots as well. In cultivated vegetation it occurs when a nurse crop such as oats is sown with alfalfa or a cover crop in an orchard.

Where conditions change abruptly instead of gradually and zonation is disturbed or incomplete, vegetation exhibits *alternes*. This is illus-

Fig. 6.—Alternation on north and south mountain slopes in Colorado. The north slope is covered with a stabilized forest of Douglas fir (*Pseudotsuga*), the south with oak scrub and scattered ponderosa pines. (*Photograph by G. E. Nichols.*)

Fig. 7.—Alterne of wheat grass in true prairie near Hebron, Neb., resulting from accumulation of wind-blown dust. It is being slowly replaced by other grasses.

trated where shrubs or trees extend up a moist north slope or ravine but do not occur on the drier areas. A series of parallel ridges may each have one type of forest, *e.g.*, ponderosa pine on the warm, dry, south slopes and spruce or fir on the cool, moist, north ones (Fig. 6). Moss-covered rocks or wet sedge lands in an otherwise forested area not only show abrupt differences in the structure of vegetation but also, like the undeveloped meristem in a mature root or stem, indicate an early stage in the development of that particular part. As time goes on, the meristem will become mature tissue, the rock will crumble to soil, the pond will be

Fig. 8.—Society of daisy fleabane (*Erigeron ramosus*) in prairie near Lincoln, Neb., late in June. It contributes a part to the summer aspect.

filled and, like the area occupied by the rock, will support the mature stabilized forest. Final development has merely been delayed (Fig. 7).

Vegetation shows structure not only in the general dominance, *i.e.*, control of water, light, etc., by certain species, but also in local dominance by other species. In early spring in grassland, local areas are conspicuous because of the abundance and vigorous growth of certain herbs which blossom and mature seed. Such *societies* may make maximum demands upon the habitat before the grasses overtop them. By early summer, spring societies are inconspicuous and other societies of taller species are locally conspicuous (Fig. 8). The appearance of the vegetation again changes as summer gives way to fall. This adjustment of species to seasonal changes results in what are called *aspects*. It is another of the several ways in which vegetation shows structure.

CHAPTER II

METHODS OF STUDYING VEGETATION

Structure and development of vegetation and the manner in which these are affected by the factors of the environment should be studied with the same care and thoroughness as are individual plants. Vegetation readily responds to changes in the habitat. If the habitat becomes wetter or drier, better or more poorly lighted, etc., certain species and often whole groups of plants disappear and are replaced by others. Similar changes occur when vegetation is repeatedly mowed, grazed, burned, or cut as in lumbering.[673] In the adjustment to a modified environment, the entire composition and structure of the vegetation may be altered. Such changes are not only of much scientific interest but are also frequently of great economic importance.

The object of range management is to produce the most valuable yield of forage possible and to harvest the crop through the medium of livestock in such a manner that the yield will be sustained from year to year.[566] Also the cover is thus enabled to play its indispensable part in the control of erosion and flooding. It is important to know whether the most valuable forage species are able to reproduce and retain their place under the degree of grazing imposed upon them or are being replaced by less valuable ones. To be sure, this may often be determined in terms of overgrazing indicators, but it usually is not done until the range has been depleted to such an extent that great loss in its grazing capacity and erosion control has been incurred.[771] In reseeding overgrazed range or pasture land or in reforesting burned or cut-over areas, it is so important to know exactly how the herbaceous and tree seedlings are developing or to determine the cause of their failure, that exact methods of tracing the growth of the individual are in constant use.[553] The rate of increase or decrease in the number of poisonous plants on a 'range or the rapidity of distribution of introduced weeds in a pasture can be accurately determined only by careful study.

THE QUADRAT

The quadrat is a square area of varying size marked off for the purpose of detailed study (Fig. 3). It is one of the many unit areas that constitute the whole. By the study of numerous quadrats a knowledge of the structure of vegetation may be obtained. In its simplest form, the

10

quadrat is used in counting the individuals of each species to determine their relative abundance and importance. It is also employed to determine exact differences in the composition and structure of vegetation. By its use, changes in the development of vegetation from season to season and from year to year may be followed and recorded in detail. Although a quadrat includes only a small area of vegetation, it reveals the exact structure of this small part. It is impossible and, in fact, unnecessary to study the whole area with the same thoroughness. A number of quadrats, located with care in places that appear to be different upon careful scrutiny, will reveal the entire range of structure. The quadrat, like any other method, must be used with discrimination, and it should rarely be located at random, except in pure stands of a single species or where large numbers of quadrats are employed.

Kinds of Quadrats.—Quadrats vary in both size and use. The size may vary from 100 square meters to 1 square decimeter. The meter quadrat is used in grassland and most other herbaceous vegetation (*e.g.*, cultivated fields of the smaller cereals, forest floor, etc.). A square decimeter is employed in studying soil-forming lichens and mosses on rocks. Areas of 100 square inches, each square inch marked off separately, are convenient in studying the development of seedlings[172] (Fig. 92). In woodland when trees and shrubs alone are considered or in fields where the plants are large or rather widely spaced (*e.g.*, maize, cotton, or sunflowers), a major quadrat, *i.e.*, an area of 4, 16, or even 100 square meters, is employed.[124]

Quadrats are also named with respect to their use. The *list quadrat* is one in which the species are listed and the number of individuals of each is counted. In the *basal-area* quadrat the basal area occupied by each species is estimated or measured; in the *clip quadrat* the dry weight is ascertained. In practice, it is desirable to restrict the list quadrat to the first, which provides an actual census, and to term the others *basal-area* and *clip quadrats*, respectively. *Chart quadrats* are those in which the position of each plant is accurately indicated upon the chart. *Permanent quadrats* may be of either kind. They are distinguished by the fact that they are marked in such a way as to permit study from year to year. The *denuded quadrat* is a permanent one from which the vegetation has been removed in order that the manner in which the plants reenter may be followed. Frequently, the denudation is partial, only certain species being removed in order to reveal the course and outcome of competition or related processes.

Marking Out Quadrats.—Strips of steel or hardwood, or cloth or steel tapes slightly more than a meter in length and a centimeter wide are used in marking out quadrats. These are furnished with small holes or eyelets a decimeter apart and the ten intervals between the holes are

numbered from left to right. If the second and last holes are 10.5 centimeters from the first and ninth, respectively, the frame will then enclose
exactly 1 square meter. The strips are held in position on the ground
by means of sharp-pointed steel stakes with loops at one end (Fig. 3).
Rigid frames of wood or steel may be employed; the space may easily
be divided into 100 square decimeter areas by means of stout cord

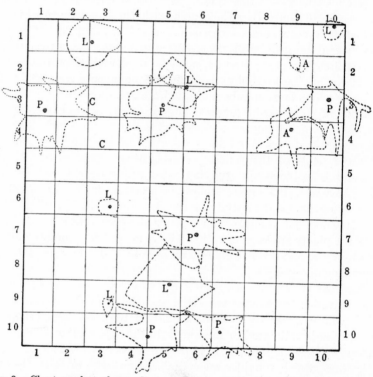

Fig. 9.—Chart quadrat of area shown in Fig. 3. *P*, knotgrass (*Polygonum aviculare*).
L, peppergrass (*Lepidium virginicum*); *A*, prostrate amaranth (*Amaranthus blitoides*):
C, green foxtail (*Setaria viridis*). The dotted lines bound the areas occupied by the tops
of the plants.

In marking out a quadrat, the far and near tapes are always so placed
that the numbers read from left to right and the side ones so that they
read toward the observer. Care must be taken to make the quadrat a
square. In making a chart, a fifth tape is stretched across the quadrat
parallel to the tape on the far side and a decimeter from it. The location of the plants in this decimeter strip is then indicated on the chart.
The outside tape is moved to the next interval, enclosing another decimeter strip which is likewise charted, and so on, thus facilitating the
rapid and accurate mapping of the whole quadrat (Fig. 9).

List or Census Quadrat.—This method consists in counting either the number of plants or stems of each species. The total number of these in the quadrat and the ratio between species are then easily determined. This method is particularly applicable to such communities as western wheat grass, big bluestem, sand reed, ragweed, etc. In listing a quadrat it is usually desirable to start with the bottom decimeter row, which is marked off with a fifth tape, and work upwards. This avoids injury to plants by stepping or lying on them before they are charted. Each square decimeter may be further bounded, if desirable, by means of quadrat pins laid horizontally. Except in cases of unusual difficulty, plants should not be broken or pulled as they are counted.[369]

A series of 30 list quadrats (2 meters square) was systematically distributed in a pasture under a continuous system of grazing and a similar series in one under a deferred and rotation system. These pastures in the wheat-grass (*Agropyron smithii*) type of mixed prairie had been moderately grazed for nine years. In the first pasture an average of 597 stalks of wheat grass per quadrat was found; in the second 912, an increase of 53 per cent. The great difference appeared to be due chiefly to the different systems of grazing.[371]

Data from 70 list quadrats on exposed south and southwest and sheltered north and northeast slopes in the prairies of eastern Washington revealed the fact that the dominant wheat grass (*A. spicatum*) averaged 9 small bunches per square meter on both slopes. A nearly equal distribution of the dominant *Festuca*, 13 and 10 bunches, respectively, also occurred. Most of the subdominants, however, showed a preference for either one slope or the other, and some were confined almost entirely to either the north or south hillsides. The differences in distribution were shown to be due to differences in habitat, a much greater water content and humidity prevailing on the northerly slopes.[963]

In grazing studies, list quadrats are often permanently located in pastures and also in areas protected from grazing. Usually, a record is kept from year to year of only the more important species. In North Dakota, it has been shown that while certain of the best grasses almost entirely disappeared under close grazing, weedy herbs, such as certain sages, which are not eaten at all or only when the other vegetation is very sparse, were greatly increased. At the end of 5 years, they were five times as abundant as in ungrazed or normally grazed areas where they were held in check by the grasses. Not only had they increased in number but also in size and they soon became so abundant that the value of the pasture was greatly reduced.[780]

The principle of the list quadrat is employed in estimating crop yields. In a study of the smaller cereals, the average number of plants per square yard is determined; next, the number of stalks bearing spikes;

then the number of spikelets; and, finally, the number of kernels in spikelets of average size. Such determinations in several places in the field permit forecasting the yield with exceptional accuracy. Studies on the percentage of germination, rate of tillering under different conditions of soil, applications of fertilizers, etc., are accurately made by means of the list quadrat. Similar methods may be used in studies of the eradication or control of weeds including poisonous plants such as loco weeds (species of *Astragalus* and *Oxytropis*), larkspurs (*Delphinium*), death camas (*Zygadenus*), etc., on western ranges. The list quadrat is also regularly used in making disease surveys which deal with the number of rust-infected plants or smutted heads of the cereals.

Making List Quadrats.—Select representative places in newly populated areas where the vegetation is not dense, such as weedy fields, gardens, or other disturbed areas. List all the species in the quadrats together with the number of each. Which species are annuals? Which ones have a longer life? Which is the most important and which is the least important species? Make a list of the kinds and numbers of weeds in the quadrats in a pasture. If possible, list the same quadrats again in spring or fall.

Basal-area Quadrat.—This method consists in estimating or measuring the *basal area* afforded by each species and by the total basal cover of vegetation. The total basal cover or full density in a forest is equivalent to normal stocking. This means less living plant materials on poor soils than on good ones. Similarly, a full stocking of young stands will represent a smaller mass of living materials than does full density for older stands. A common means of expressing the degree of stocking or density of stand is the total basal area at a height of 4.5 feet.[34] This is determined for each species and expressed as square feet per acre (Table 1).

The maximum average basal area (density) in virgin stands of hemlock and hemlock-beech in northern Pennsylvania is about 200 square feet per acre.[554] For a virgin hardwood forest in southern Michigan, it is about 223 square feet,[125] while the average maximum per acre in the cedar-hemlock-white fir type of northern Idaho is about 300 square feet.[424] The basal area in a forest (and consequently the volume) usually increases as the succession progresses towards the climax.

In grassland, obviously it is, in general, impracticable to determine the basal area of each stem or plant. Instead, the total area occupied by the species is determined in each square decimeter of a quadrat and this is recorded as percentage of the entire square meter.

In grassland and forest, but still more in desert, the control exerted by the community is only incompletely expressed by the per cent of basal cover. In true prairie, for example, it seldom exceeds 20 per cent, and in certain types, as tall marsh grass (*Spartina pectinata*), it is usually less than 1 per cent, although the *foliage cover* completely obscures the

TABLE 1.—NUMBER AND BASAL AREA (AT 4.5 FEET IN HEIGHT) OF DOMINANT AND CODOMINANT TREES IN A CHESTNUT-OAK FOREST IN CONNECTICUT BEFORE AND AFTER THE RAVAGES OF THE CHESTNUT BLIGHT*

Species	1910—1911				1924			
	Trees per acre		Basal area		Trees per acre		Basal area	
	Number	Per cent	Square feet	Per cent	Number	Per cent	Square feet	Per cent
Chestnut	153.3	70.5	64.18	76.2	0	0	0	0
Red oak...............	22.0	10.1	9.13	10.8	38.0	28.6	16.45	42.2
Chestnut oak........	22.0	10.1	5.25	6.2	52.7	39.7	14.48	37.2
White oak........	9.4	4.4	1.97	2.3	9.4	7.1	2.07	5.3
Black oak.............	2.0	0.9	0.82	1.0	3.3	2.5	0.94	2.4
Scarlet oak............	8.0	3.7	2.75	3.3	5.3	4.0	3.31	8.5
Sweet birch............	0.7	0.3	0.13	0.2	0	0	0	0
Red maple.............	0	0	0	0	8.7	6.6	0.82	2.1
White ash.............	0	0	0	0	6.7	5.0	0.32	0.8
Hickory...............	0	0	0	0	6.0	4.5	0.29	0.8
Sugar maple...........	0	0	0	0	2.7	2.0	0.26	0.7
Total...............	217.4	100.0	84.23	100.0	132.8	100.0	38.94	100.0

* Korstian and Stickel, 1927.

soil. The essential control in grassland can be adequately expressed only in terms of leafy shoots of crowns in relation to competition for light and especially of root systems in relation to water content of soil.

In using this type of quadrat, the basal cover of the entire vegetation in each square decimeter is first determined. In grassland, estimations are made at or near the soil surface, and until sufficient experience and accuracy have been gained in judging the cover, a frame may be employed to divide the square decimeter into a number of equal parts. However, an error of one unit in a decimeter square results in an error of only 0.01 of a unit in the total for the whole quadrat. The basal cover furnished by each species is also determined in a similar manner. The sum of the percentage cover for the 100 determinations of each species is then ascertained and expressed as a percentage of the total basal cover—*not* the total area of the quadrat. The total basal cover, of course, is the sum of the partial covers of the several species. The data thus obtained give all the necessary information, in terms of area occupied and distribution, for each quadrat.[631]

By this method it has been determined that the total basal cover in the little-bluestem (*Andropogon scoparius*) type of true prairie averages 15.3 per cent. This is an average from 138 quadrats (Fig. 10). Little bluestem furnishes 55 per cent of this total, big bluestem (*A. furcatus*) 24.8 per cent, bluegrass (*Poa pratensis*) 4.7 per cent, and forbs 4.1 per cent. Seven other species contributed all but 1.5 per cent of the remainder.[976] Where grazing results in replacement of the vegetation by the sod-forming short grasses (*Buchloe* and *Bouteloua*), the total basal cover increases to 50 to 80 per cent, which is similar to that in many short-grass areas of the Great Plains.

In open vegetation of semiarid and arid regions, the square meter may be divided into only 25 unit areas.[369] Frequently only the more

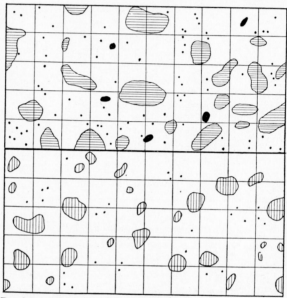

Fig. 10.—Basal area (above) of little bluestem, *Andropogon scoparius*, (horizontal hatch), other tufted grasses (black), and isolated stems of grass or forbs (dots). Half of another square meter (below), showing the basal area of needle grass, *Stipa spartea* (vertical hatch). Total basal areas are 17.4 and 8.7 per cent, respectively.

important species are listed separately and the remainder considered as a group. Often the basal cover is determined at a height of an inch above the soil surface, which approximates the level of grazing. The method is widely used in range and pasture studies.[772]

Where the basal area occupied by each species is measured in each unit area of the quadrat, a listing ruler or listing square is employed. These are calibrated to give the area directly when the average diameter of the bunch or sod mat is determined (Fig. 11).[454,665] The areas are expressed in square centimeters or square inches instead of percentage. The number of isolated stalks and seedlings is also counted. The total area occupied by these stems may be calculated from measurements of the basal area of representative samples of each species. Totals of each species in the quadrat are then secured. Vegetation consisting of small clumps or mats may, perhaps, best be measured by the listing ruler or square; in rather open types of grassland also, this method is very useful. Bunch formers, such as certain species of *Agropyron, Stipa, Balsamorrhiza,* etc., have been recorded over a period of years in the semiarid northwest,

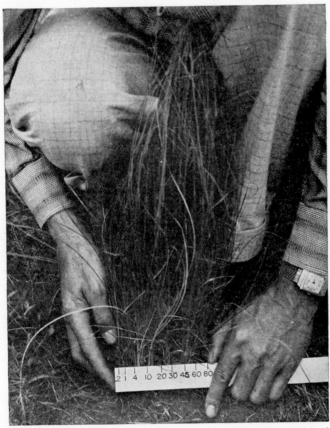

FIG. 11.—Listing ruler showing area scale in square centimeters used in determining basal area of prairie dropseed (*Sporobolus heterolepis*). The average diameter of the bunch is 10 centimeters and the basal area 80 square centimeters.

where plots 5 by 5 meters in area were listed in 1 by 5 meter strips.[665] In this method, measurements replace estimates and in tabulation the data are less complicated. Information is had on the density of each species, the total density, the number of plants of each species present, and the size of each plant growing on the plot.

Basal-area Quadrat.—Select an area where some type of bunch- or mat-forming vegetation is not too dense, such as needle grass (*Stipa*), dropseed (*Sporobolus*), or little bluestem (*Andropogon*), or a bunch form of wheat grass (*Agropyron*). Determine the basal area of each species in a square meter and calculate the total basal area of the vegetation. It may be desirable to clip a few bunches of each species ½ or 1 inch from the ground so that the basal area may be more clearly seen at this level before working in the selected quadrat. What are the chief facts you have learned in this study?

In forests, larger quadrats or sampling areas are required. Basal area is a measurement of a timber stand by the use of which the errors peculiar to measurement by volume are avoided and by which a more adequate picture of the timber is provided than by diameters alone. For these reasons it is in wide use.[63] A basal area of 103 square feet per acre in a 21-year old stand of white pine in New England, for example, was

Fig. 12.—Clip quadrat in the short-grass plains of eastern Colorado.

reduced to 57 square feet by a combination thinning and improvement cutting.[6]

Clip Quadrat.—This method consists in securing the oven-dry weight (100–110°C.) of each species clipped at the soil surface or at a height of one or more inches.[780] The total weight of the vegetation and the weight of that furnished by each species in the quadrat are ascertained. This method not only constitutes a good basis for showing the relationships between species of different growth form, but also gives the forage production by weight. Two clippings may be necessary in order to secure plants of early spring as well as those of late summer.

In experimental pastures, clip quadrats are used in which the vegetation is cut near the soil surface or at various heights to simulate different degrees of grazing (Figs. 12 and 13). This differs somewhat from the actual manner in which the forage is removed, since grazing animals pull and break off flower stalks and leaves neither uniformly nor at the same level. The natural preferences of livestock for certain species and at certain stages of development result in patchy rather than uniform grazing. Moreover, the effects of trampling, natural reseeding of the area, and the accumulation of litter are not the same as under natural grazing.[216] Despite these differences, clip quadrats are useful to show just how much forage is removed under different systems or degrees of stocking, as well as how closely the important palatable plants may be grazed without impairing their growth, vigor, and future productivity. They also disclose the forage yield each year over a period of years, variation in the yield between species, relation cf yield to soil moisture, and probable trends in plant succession under different degrees of utilization.[216,12,260]

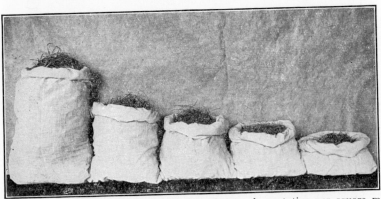

Fig. 13.—Average decrease in the production of natural vegetation per square meter, proceeding westward from eastern Nebraska to eastern Colorado.[967]

In the mixed prairie of North Dakota, the clip method was employed to determine the period of most active growth of the different species and the effect upon growth of the frequent removal of the vegetation as in close grazing. At each clipping the vegetation was weighed and the proportional weight afforded by each of the more important species was determined. It was found that four species produced approximately half of the forage and that, among these, blue grama (*Bouteloua gracilis*) produced a fairly uniform growth throughout the year. Needle grass (*Stipa comata*), like most of the others, gave a light yield toward the close of the season. Two species of sedges (*Carex*) produced the most abundant growth very early in the spring, but the yield rapidly became less with the oncoming of summer. Needle grass disappeared in direct relation to the frequency of clipping, but the growth of grama grass and of sedges in less degree was stimulated by moderate clipping; these persisted, although in a much weakened condition, in quadrats where practically all the other vegetation had disappeared.[780] This striking difference in the response of mid grasses and short grasses is to be ascribed to the fact that clipping removes a much larger proportion of leaves from mid grasses.

By the use of similar methods, it has been found that the ranges of the southwest are often seriously depleted by prairie dogs, which not only eat much the same kinds of grasses as the cattle and in the same order of preference but also in large quantities.[907] However, there is considerable evidence that prairie dogs and other rodents really prefer forbs, a fact correlated with their increase under overgrazing.[908]

Fig. 14.—Development of wheat grass and disappearance of buffalo grass (left) after 3 years of protection from grazing, and persistence of buffalo grass (right) where the cattle have reached over the fence and grazed.

The most important objects sought in the revegetation of native pastures are a continuous, vigorous growth and ample seed production. Clip and grazed quadrat studies in the Blue Mountains of Oregon and the Wasatch Mountains of Utah have shown that the removal of the herbage several times in a season, especially if the first harvest is made a few days after growth has started, seriously weakens the plants and immediately decreases their forage production. For example, plots harvested once each season just before seed maturity yielded more than five times as much forage as those from which the vegetation had been removed four times during the year. Moreover, plants in the latter quadrats became so weakened from starvation that they failed to produce flower stalks and viable seeds.[768] The applications of these results to grazing practice are evident[774] (Fig. 14).

Frequent and early cutting of alfalfa may for a short period increase the yield, but this occurs at the expense of food reserves. The vigor and productivity of alfalfa growing in fertile soil were greatly reduced, weed infestations augmented, and both summer and winter mortality of the plants accentuated by frequent and early removal of the tops.[335,336]

Frequency-abundance Quadrat.—This method necessitates the use of a large number of quadrats, 30 to 50 commonly being studied. They are sometimes 0.5 square meter or less in area. They are located equidistant along several lines extending across the area for study, often several rods apart. Frequency is expressed in percentage calculated by dividing the number of quadrats in which a species occurs by the total number employed. Thus, if a species occurs in 25 of 50 quadrats, it has a frequency of 50 per cent, but frequency alone has very little significance.

For each quadrat an estimate is made of the abundance of each species according to some selected scale. For example, rare = 1 to 4 stalks or plants per quadrat; infrequent = 5 to 14; frequent = 15 to 29; abundant = 30 to 99; and very abundant = 100 and over. Average abundance is then calculated for each species by adding the abundance values and dividing by the number of quadrats in which the species occurred. For example, a forb may be present in 4 quadrats only, with abundance estimates of I, F, F, and A. By adding the numerical values assigned to each of these letters according to the scale $R = 1$, $I = 5$, $F = 15$, $A = 30$, and $VA = 100$, a sum of 65 is obtained. Since the forb occurred in 4 quadrats, the average abundance is 65 divided by 4, or 16.2. An index number of the frequency-abundance of each species on the entire area is then secured by multiplying the frequency by the average abundance, *i.e.*, 8 (per cent) by 16.2, which equals 1.3. For the dominant species the frequency-abundance might be 80 to 100. Various modifications of the general method have been employed.

The frequency-abundance quadrat is given as an example of methods that have come into some use during the last decade or two, primarily by the plant sociologists of Europe. The original methods have now been largely abandoned, and there is likewise much doubt whether the more recent ones have sufficient value to justify the labor involved in the statistical calculations.[663,143,28,29] The application of statistics to the composition and density of a plant community is based upon the assumption that species are distributed through it by chance, *i.e.*, at random, an assumption that appears probable in very few cases, such as a pure stand or family in a habitat exceptionally uniform. It has been shown that frequency depends so much upon the size of quadrat employed as to be without value by itself, and it necessarily invalidates abundance to a high degree when the two are combined. In dynamic ecology, dominance, subdominance, and subordination represent the primary numerical and process relations of component species, and serve as the proper basis for describing communities, measuring yield and reaction, and tracing changes in composition and structure.

In order to secure these values as fully and accurately as possible, it is necessary to combine several methods, such as exclosure, process grid, and permanent quadrat, and preferably also the isolation transect, as described on following pages. The detailed measures and records are obtained by means of overhead views at the upper level of the community and of the basal area, after the quadrat is clipped, to which is added a bisect photograph. From these may be gained definite and objective determinations of total weight as well as the weight of each dominant and subdominant and similar records of height, density, volume, and basal area. All this presupposes the use of the list method and of the permanent quadrat for tracing changes from year to year or from time to time.

Chart Quadrat.—The chart quadrat is employed when a graphic and detailed record of vegetation is required. The position of each plant within the square meter and the areas occupied by bunches, mats, or tufts of grasses, mosses, etc., are determined and recorded upon a chart. This forms at once a record of the present structure and a basis for determining future changes.

The vegetation is mapped on coordinate paper, a square decimeter in size, to a scale of 1:10. Where the vegetation is dense, consisting of a great number of individuals in a small area, a larger scale is often more convenient, one of 1:5 usually being sufficiently large. The chart is made on paper ruled to square centimeters and each square decimeter of vegetation occupies 4 square centimeters on the chart. In making quadrats of forest trees, the scale is 1:100 or 1:500. In this case, the chart remains the same size but it represents a greater area.[184,552]

Mapping is begun at the farther left-hand corner of the chart after the fifth tape has been fastened in place. The plants in the first square decimeter of the quadrat are indicated in their relative positions in the first square centimeter on the chart. Individual plants are indicated by a single letter, usually that beginning the generic name, except where two or more begin with the same letter in which case two letters may be used (Fig. 15). The number of stems from one root is indicated by an exponent with the proper initial unless the stalks are far apart. The areas of 0.5 square centimeter or more occupied by tufts, mats, or bunches of grass, mosses, and large rosettes are outlined and may be indicated by hatchwork. Smaller ones are shown by dots. Dead centers of clumps are outlined by broken lines, and the peripheries of shrubs are projected upon the ground and indicated by dotted lines. When the first decimeter strip is completed, unless a rigid frame is used, the upper tape is moved to enclose a new decimeter strip, and this is repeated until the quadrat is finished. It is often desirable to start with the bottom row and work upward, thus avoiding injury to the plants. If a photograph of the quadrat is to be made, this should be done before the vegetation is disturbed. Data obtained from quadrats should be compiled as soon as possible and in such a way as to be readily available for analysis and study.[591]

Making a Chart Quadrat.—Select an area where the plants are rather widely spaced and chart a square meter of the vegetation. After the method is learned, typical meter quadrats of grassland, forest herbs, and woody seedlings or offshoots, etc., and major quadrats of forest trees should be plotted. In the latter, indicate the

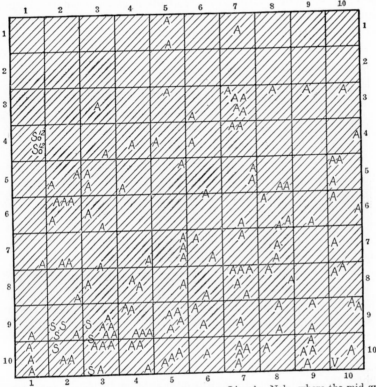

Fig. 15.—Quadrat in an overgrazed pasture near Lincoln, Neb., where the mid grasses have largely been replaced by buffalo grass. Charted June 11, 1924, of the first season of protection from grazing. Left hatch (*Buchloe dactyloides*); *A*, wheat grass (*Agropyron smithii*); *S*, dropseed (*Sporobolus asper*); *So*, wolfberry (*Symphoricarpos occidentalis*), the exponent being the height in inches; *V*, speedwell (*Veronica peregrina*).

diameter of the trees by an exponent following the initial. Write a concise statement as to what information each quadrat gives about the vegetation of the particular area in which it was made, and draw comparisons between the various communities.

Certain modifications of the chart method are often desirable depending upon the object to be attained. Sometimes it is sufficient to determine the area occupied by the more important forage species only. In such cases, bunches or mats of the two or three dominants are charted without reference to subdominants. This may usually be done in only a fraction of the time necessary for making a complete chart. Similar studies in the management of certain forest types such as reproduction of aspen from roots and stumps may be followed with little reference to herbaceous vegetation.[770]

Pantograph-chart Quadrat.—This method requires the use of a pantograph and a planimeter. The pantograph is especially valuable in accurately reproducing the outlines of mats and tufts of vegetation and in locating individual plants where vegetation is not too dense. It consists of a low stand and pantograph arms. Two men are necessary to operate it, but only one need have a knowledge of the vegetation (Fig.

Fig. 16.—Making a pantograph chart of blue grama grass.

16). The operator guides a pointer about the periphery of tufts and bunches, etc., and their size is automatically reduced to scale, often to one-fifth, and recorded in exact position upon the record sheet. The planimeter is an instrument which automatically records the size of an area when its boundaries are traced by the needle. It is used in determining the area occupied by each species shown on the chart, as well as the area of the bare soil.

Changes in the cover of mixed prairie vegetation during the great drought of 1934 have been studied intensively by means of scores of permanent quadrats.[972] The pantograph-chart method was used in mapping the vegetation before, during, and after the drought (Fig. 17). In the little-bluestem type of mixed prairie, *Andropogon scoparius* suffered losses of 50 to 87 per cent where it was ungrazed, and 66 to 96 per cent under moderate grazing. The best type of short-grass sod, where

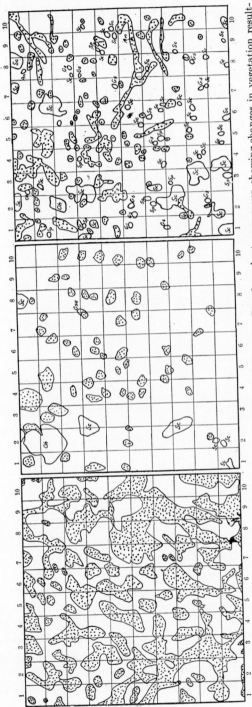

FIG. 17.—A quadrat in west-central Kansas in the open-mat type of *Buchloe-Bouteloua* short-grass cover, showing changes in vegetation resulting from drought. It was charted at three different times. In 1932 (left), before the great drought, 43 per cent of the soil was covered. This was reduced to 8.7 per cent late in 1934 (center). Owing to propagation by stolons of buffalo grass the cover increased to 14 per cent in 1935 (right). Only a few other species occurred. They are indicated by the first letters of the genus and species, *e.g.*, *Oh* is a cactus, *Opuntia humifusa*.

70 to 90 per cent of the soil was covered, showed losses of only 10 to 20 per cent where protected from grazing, although certain native forbs entirely disappeared. Losses in the open type of ungrazed short grass on poorer soil, where the basal cover is normally only 20 to 30 per cent, were 70 to 80 per cent. Where the short-grass cover had been greatly depleted in 1934, numerous small areas of living plants occurred throughout the quadrats.[972] From these sprang stolons of buffalo grass which rapidly reclaimed the bare areas during the moist spring of 1935.[781,782]

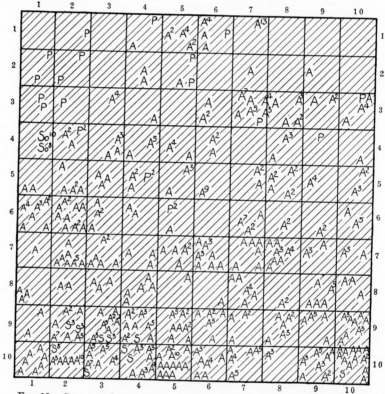

Fig. 18.—Same quadrat as shown in Fig. 15, but charted on May 25, 1925.

Permanent Quadrat.—Any quadrat may be made permanent by marking precisely the position of the original one. This should be done very carefully by means of placing stakes at the intersections of the tapes in the upper left- and lower right-hand corners, just outside the quadrat. Since wooden stakes are not permanent and easily destroyed, $\frac{3}{8}$- or $\frac{1}{2}$-inch round iron pegs, 12 inches long, may be securely driven into the soil so that they scarcely protrude. If the ends are blunt, domesticated animals will not be injured should they chance to step on them. A tall wooden stake securely placed a few paces distant from the iron one where mapping is started, will help in relocating the area. It should not be placed too near the quadrat since it may attract animals and result in unwonted trampling or grazing. The stake should be definitely located with reference to natural or artificial landmarks in order that it may be easily found upon successive visits, since permanent quadrats are usually charted annually over a long period of years.

Permanent quadrats may yield much information even in a single year and often in a few weeks (Figs. 18 and 19). For example, counting and relisting the species in any waste area in spring will usually reveal marked changes in short periods of time. Permanent quadrats in grassland or forest show striking changes as the season progresses. By their use a complete record of the *prevernal* (early spring), *vernal* (spring), *estival* (summer), and *autumnal aspects* of vegetation is secured. Species in flower or fruit are indicated by a horizontal line through the symbol, while a vertical line indicates a seedling.

Permanent quadrats recharted year after year in originally bare areas give the complete story of development. The fate of seedlings, the time required for the survivors to mature and produce seed, the method, rate, and success of vegetative propagation, as well as the length of life of the individual, make an interesting story. One can see how the plants have aggregated; follow the invasions of new migrants; trace ecesis; gain much information about competition and how it results in the appearance of new species and the disappearance of others; with proper instruments, determine the changed conditions within the habitat resulting from reactions of the developing vegetation; and finally, discover how it all ends in stabilization. Permanent quadrats in the path of retreating glaciers in Alaska are yielding many data on all these processes and should reveal much of the history of glaciated parts of those states that were once covered with the ice sheets.[187,191]

Quadrats in such dynamic areas as sand dunes, river bars, or flood plains, or on the border line or *ecotone* between two plant communities, such as shrub and grassland, often show remarkably rapid changes, and many of the principles of ecology are illustrated by a comparison and interpretation of the charts from permanent quadrats. The initial stands and resulting percentages of certain grasses and legumes from year to year under different methods of grazing are determined in this way.[398,259] Permanent quadrats have also been used successfully in studying composition and change in submerged aquatic vegetation.[120]

The importance of a knowledge of the life history of the individual and under what conditions the seed will germinate and the seedling become established cannot be overemphasized. Forests are composed of individual trees and ranges of species of grasses and other herbs, all of which must germinate, grow, mature, and reproduce unless vegetation is to disappear. By studying these communities and the way in which they are affected by various degrees and types of grazing, a system of management has been worked out for native grazing lands. By means of this system they have been fully revegetated and the range main-

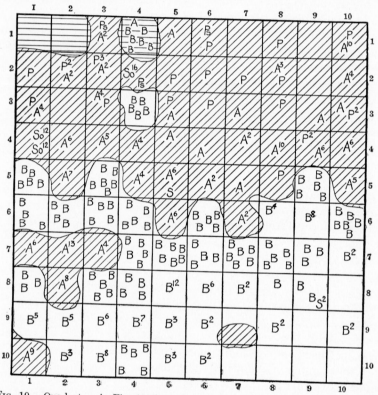

FIG. 19.—Quadrat as in Fig. 15 charted on June 4, 1926. Left hatch or B (*Buchloe dactyloides*), the exponent indicates the number of stems or unit clumps; A or unhatched area, wheat grass (*Agropyron smithii*); horizontal hatch or P, bluegrass (*Poa pratensis*); Ps, panic grass (*Panicum scribnerianum*); rest of legend as in Fig. 15.

What was the dominant species in 1924? Count the number of wheat grass stems in the three lower rows of quadrats 1(Fig. 15) and 2, and calculate the percentage increase under protection. Determine the percentage increase in the rest of the quadrat. Compare the percentage of the area dominated by buffalo grass in 1924 and 1926. From how many of the unit areas has buffalo grass been shaded out? Is it losing its hold elsewhere? Are any of the other species of importance? Has the wheat grass increased its abundance in the four upper decimeter rows during the 3 years? Will the future vegetation in this quadrat be mid grass or short grass?

tained in a high state of productivity without the loss of the forage crop for a single year or the presence of a forest-fire risk as a result of the non-removal of the herbaceous vegetation.[768]

Results in reforestation are scarcely less marked. An exact record of the fate of the tree seedlings, losses due to rodents, winterkilling, frost heaving, damping-off, etc., can be had only by a detailed study of representative areas. Changes in the development of the herbaceous and shrubby vegetation by which one group of plants replaces another, a process called *plant succession,* and the effects of this on the tree seedlings are studied in detail. Such knowledge is indispensable to the proper management of the forest.[668]

A Study of Permanent Quadrats.—Select and permanently mark out quadrats in one or more of the places suggested in the preceding paragraphs, or very carefully rechart permanent quadrats where the previous composition of the vegetation has been recorded. These should be visited and recharted once or more each year, the several charts studied and compared, and explanations suggested for the changes that have taken place.

Denuded Quadrat.—It is frequently desirable to remove the vegetation by burning, flooding, or generally by a more profound disturbance, such as removing the surface soil with its roots, rhizomes, seeds, etc. The permanent quadrat thus becomes a denuded one. In partially denuded quadrats, only certain species of grasses and forbs are removed or a portion of the area denuded.[171] Denuded quadrats may be used in experimental sowing or planting and are especially desirable in connection with artificial regeneration. It is a reliable method of determining rate of invasion and establishment of vegetation on badly depleted ranges; quadrats may be placed in areas entirely or nearly denuded by grazing animals.

The practice of burning pastures and ranges has been widespread, in order to render green feed available earlier in the spring, to destroy weeds, and to get rid of old vegetation on areas so lightly grazed during the previous season that there is danger of poor growth and uneven utilization. The expediency of this procedure has been investigated in Kansas by means of denuded and clip quadrats. The experimental plots were burned annually either in late fall, early spring, or late spring, and other areas were fired on alternate years. This was done when the soil was moist, in order to avoid too great injury to rootstocks and crowns of plants. Each burned area contained an unburned control plot. Yields from large samples of mature vegetation were obtained by clipping in early October.

It was found that burning decreased the yield of vegetation. The yield was least on plots burned late in the fall and intermediate on those burned in early spring, while that from the plots burned in late spring most nearly approached the yield of the controls. Over a period of 6 years, the yield averaged approximately 48 per cent more than that of the plot burned in late spring, and 88 per cent more than the plot burned in late fall. A thorough analysis of a large number of meter quadrats listed three or four times annually showed that the plant population was greatest on plots burned in late fall and least on those burned in late spring.   Plots burned in late fall and early spring also had a greater number of plants than the unburned plots.

The greater population of the fall-burned plots resulted mainly from an increase in the number of stems of *Andropogon scoparius*.   While late burning in fall caused a successional trend in favor of the little bluestem, in plots burned in late spring the change was toward the coarser grasses, mainly *A. furcatus*.[12,337]   *Poa pratensis* increased on all the unburned plots but was either decreased or eliminated in all the burned ones.   Elsewhere the burning of bluegrass pasture has also been found to be harmful.[334]   However, quadrat results in burned areas of chaparral, mesquite, and some sagebrush show that fire tends not merely to maintain the scrub but actually to increase it at the expense of the grasses.   The effects of forest fires, burning brush land, and disposal of slash after lumbering as well as the growth of subsequent vegetation upon the reproduction of the forest, are all studied with a high degree of accuracy by the quadrat method.[547]   Clip quadrats have also been used in studying the production of submerged vegetation.[1010]

Since growth of twigs of shrubs occurs mainly from terminal and lateral buds, a different method of determining the relationship between the extent of grazing or browsing of the current season's growth and the subsequent plant vigor must be employed. The method of removing all or part of the current growth by clipping has been employed.   If the total twig growth accessible to livestock is eaten year after year, ultimately the shrub will lose its vigor and slowly die.   But if a portion of the twig remains there will be several buds unharmed from which renewed growth may occur the following year.   In such studies the green and dry weights of leaves and twigs are also determined.[634]

Method of Photograph Charts.—While the charting of quadrats by hand or by pantograph is regularly in use, the camera has been employed for a number of years and promises to become a general method when its marked advantages are recognized.[188]   Chief among these are its enormous saving of time, increased accuracy owing to elimination of the personal equation, and a visual record in three dimensions (Fig. 20).   A fourth feature that may prove equally important is the possibility of enlargement up to a meter or more; in the case of enlarged negatives, two successive photographs may be superimposed and illuminated, thus permitting the direct demonstration of changes in composition and density.   If a large camera is utilized, such as a 6.5- by 8.5- or 8- by 10-inch size, the details are sufficiently clear so that the film negatives may be superimposed without enlargement.   Another advantage is seen in the fact that a ruled screen may be placed just in front of the film and thus do away with frames or tapes.   Color plates may be used for certain purposes.

A simple and inexpensive apparatus for overhead photography consists of a light wooden arm that screws on to the tripod and carries a tilting camera top at the free end. For a 4- by 5-inch camera, this arm is approximately 30 by 6 by 0.5 inches and is sufficiently long to bring the lens directly above the center of the quadrat. For the most convenient operation, a wide-angle lens, such as Bausch & Lomb Protar, series V, is desirable, since this enables one to focus on a meter quadrat at a ground-glass distance of about 3 feet. A larger camera may be used with the regular lens, or a

Fig. 20.—Overhead photograph of balsamroot (*Balsamorrhiza*), etc., at Logan, Utah. The total area within the grid is 3 square meters. (*Courtesy of B. Maguire.*)

standard with heavy base is utilized for moving the camera to the height required. A stepladder with camera arm also serves as a crude but fairly satisfactory device (Fig. 21). By varying the equipment or height, a milacre quadrat may be brought into a 4- by 5-inch size, and even larger areas may be covered. It is obvious that an airplane photograph is merely an overhead view on a grand scale.

Kinds of Quadrats to Employ.—The investigator will discover that each of the methods has certain advantages and disadvantages. The results secured by one method of listing or charting are not comparable to those secured by any other method.   The purpose of the quadrat and the nature of the vegetation are major factors in determining the method or methods to employ.[885],[530]   Likewise, the time required for the different methods is an important consideration.   If the purpose is to determine changes in the vegetation from year to year, various kinds of permanent quadrats may be used.   It is far better to make a few chart quadrats carefully than a large number hastily.   If the vegetation consists chiefly of large and well-defined mats or bunches, a combination

Fig. 21.—Inexpensive apparatus for overhead photography.   (*Photograph, courtesy of Soil Conservation Service.*)

of the pantograph-chart and list method may be very desirable.[368]   If it consists chiefly of smaller areas or a mixture of small clumps or mats and species with single or few stems, then the basal area combined with the list method appears to be preferable.[369]

The best size of quadrat to use is also a matter of importance.   It should be large enough and enough quadrats should be made to give reliable results.   These factors vary with the type of vegetation.   Studies in the mixed prairie dominated by wheat grass have shown that the most suitable size in this type of vegetation is one not less than 1 square meter in area and preferably 2 square meters lying adjacent to each other.[370]   In scrub and chaparral, a milacre (4 square meters) is the most convenient.   Investigations in deciduous forest indicate that areas of 4 square meters are the most suitable size where the forest vegetation is analyzed as a unit. Smaller quadrats are desirable for herbaceous layers and larger ones for trees.[124] In a quantitative study of the weed flora of arable land, it has been determined that the meter quadrat is a more efficient unit than similar areas 5 meters long and 0.2 meter wide, or 5 squares, each 0.2 square meter in area.[854,142]

THE TRANSECT

It is frequently desirable to know just how vegetation varies with changing environment, such as is caused by slope exposure or other irregularities in topography or soil, or to determine how one community of plants gives way to another. This may best be ascertained by a transect, which is a continuous narrow strip that gives a cross section of the vegetation. Transects are indispensable in studying zones, alternes, and transitions of all kinds. They are always made at right angles to the extension of the zones or ecotones.

Belt Transect.—The belt transect is a strip of vegetation of uniform width and of considerable length. The width is largely determined by the character of the vegetation, just enough being included to reveal its true structure. In close herbaceous vegetation, the usual width is 1 decimeter, but it varies from 1 to 10 meters in woodland. The 1-meter transect is employed if the shrubs and seedlings of the forest floor are included, but if mature trees only are mapped, the 10-meter transect is best. The length of the transect is determined by its purpose. It may be made permanent by marking the boundaries at intervals with stakes. In staking a belt transect in grassland, two tapes are employed to mark out the strip of desired width. The distance between them is uniform throughout, and they are held in place by quadrat stakes. The plants are recorded as for the chart quadrat, except that an interval of a centimeter is left between the successive portions of the strip in order that they may be cut and pasted or readily copied on a sheet showing the topographic outline. This should be drawn to scale.

The belt transect shows a definite range of vegetation, and by making it permanent and recharting at suitable intervals, changes in the vegetation along the line of the transect may be readily detected and measured. The factors causing the differences in the plant cover should also be determined wherever possible. The limits of zones may be shown on charts of belt transects by single cross lines.

Portions of a transect in the prairie of eastern Nebraska extending from the top of a gravelly hill to its lower slope are shown in Fig. 22. Because of differences in soil and slope exposure, marked differences in vegetation occur. The grama grass on the crest is the same species that is so abundant in the dry, short-grass plains; the bunch grasses on the upper slope indicate a less arid situation and, like the bluestems of the lower slope, are typical of great expanses of grassland in eastern Nebraska, Kansas, and Dakota.

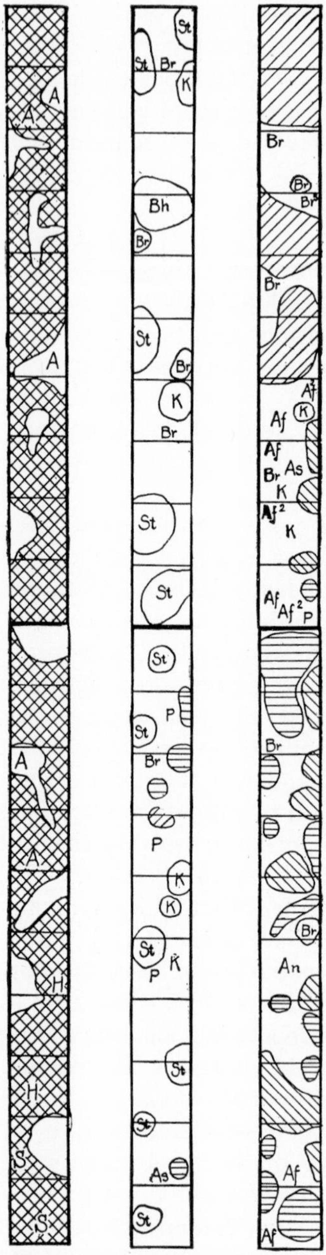

Transects are used in determining the influence of trees upon other plants, especially as affected through water content and light. About the roots of ponderosa pines in Arizona, for example, the soil is drier and the vegetation much sparser than in soil where roots are not present. Conditions for reforestation are thus modified within a radius of 30 to 40 feet from the trees and even beyond the zone of root activity.[668] Transects several meters wide, extending from windbreaks composed of rows of trees into fields of cereals, alfalfa, and other crops, reveal a decreased production in the area of root competition and shade. If the transect is extended beyond this, however, the beneficial effects of the windbreak are usually shown in the yield being increased to an amount that more than compensates for the loss near the trees.[43] However, this influence usually disappears at a distance of 6 to 12 times the height of the trees.

Making Transects.—Make a belt transect 3 to 5 meters long at right angles to the zones

FIG. 22.—Portions of a transect 1 decimeter wide (each 2 meters long) from the top of a steep hill (left), from its southeast slope (center), and from its base (right). The gravelly loam at the top, with a water content of 5 to 18 per cent, is dominated by blue grama (*Bouteloua gracilis*), also common on the Great Plains. The sandy loam half way down the slope, water content 13 to 30 per cent, is dominated by needle grass (*Stipa*) and June grass (*Koeleria*), both characteristic of upland prairie. The silt loam soil at the foot of the slope and only 200 feet from the hilltop, with a water content of 17 to 40 per cent, is dominated by the bluestems (*Andropogon*) which require more water. *A*, western ragweed (*Ambrosia psilostachya*); crosshatch, blue grama (*Bouteloua gracilis*); *H*, sunflower (*Helianthus rigidus*); *S*, dropseed (*Sporobolus asper*); *St*, needle grass (*Stipa spartea*); *Br*, slender grama (*Bouteloua curtipendula*); *K*, June grass (*Koeleria cristata*); *Bh*, hairy grama (*Bouteloua hirsuta*); horizontal hatch or *P*, Kentucky bluegrass (*Poa pratensis*); right hatch or *As*, little bluestem (*Andropogon scoparius*); left hatch or *Af*, big bluestem (*Andropogon furcatus*): *An*, Indian grass (*Andropogon nutans*).

about a pond or including the transition area (ecotone) between two different communities such as scrub and woodland, etc. Locate areas where the vegetation changes abruptly due to differences in slope, depth of soil, grazing, burning, or for other causes, and mark out and plot a belt transect of appropriate length and width. Belt transects 5 to 10 meters wide and including only the trees should be plotted from the top of a forested, steep hill or bluff to a flood plain below, including a part of the latter. Point out the differences shown by the transect, indicate the dominants in each area, and suggest reasons for the change in structure.

The transect or strip method is commonly used in studying forest trees. These transects are often 1 chain (66 feet) wide and are run along parallel lines established with compass and tape within the area when the study is begun.[554] The trees are divided into size classes and only those of larger size (4 inches or more in diameter breast high, *i.e.*, 4.5 feet) are counted, measured, and recorded on the transects. The tally should be kept separately for each 0.1-acre plot or chain length along the lines. The numbers and kinds of smaller trees are determined over smaller areas, perhaps only one-tenth as great, and a large number of meter quadrats are employed in studying the herbaceous and shrubby vegetation. Milacre quadrats are often used; these are 6.6 feet on a side and contain 4 square meters. If they are distributed at 0.5- or 1-chain (33 or 66 feet) intervals along parallel strips 2.5 to 10 chains apart, they give a sample of 0.1 to 0.8 per cent of the total area. This has been found to give satisfactory values for percentage of area stocked and average number of seedlings per acre.[356] Size classes are arbitrarily selected depending upon the vegetation:

Size Class Designation	Size
1. Small reproduction	0.0 to 0.9 foot high
2. Medium reproduction	1.0 foot high to 0.9 inch D.B.H.
3. Large reproduction	1.0 to 3.5 inches D.B.H.
4. Small trees	3.6 to 9.5 inches D.B.H.
5. Large trees	9.6 inches or over D.B.H.

The abundance and frequency of the dominant trees, the numbers of size classes in which each species is represented, and the basal area of the dominants in square feet per acre are usually determined. These data for each species may be shown by means of Lutz's phytographs (Fig. 23).

The phytograph makes possible the graphic representation of several measurements simultaneously, thereby furnishing an integrated picture of the relationships between the several measurements. Though it gives an impression of "mass effect" of the several factors, yet any particular factor is readily isolated for study. The method is valuable not only in studying the status of the various species composing the forest type but also in comparing different types of forest.[419] Phytographs may be used in comparing other data concerning plants or modified for direct comparison of evaporation, wind movement, etc., in different habitats or change in the stand, site factors, and growth of trees resulting from thinning, selective cutting, etc.[6]

The belt-transect method has been used very successfully for recording the composition of tropical rain-forest and especially for commercially important trees. The belts are of sufficient width (66 feet) and frequency (1.25 miles apart) to include 1 per cent of the area.[294] In fact, the method has long been used by American foresters, although they make an optical estimate of the width of the area cruised and record the number and size of merchantable trees instead of mapping them.

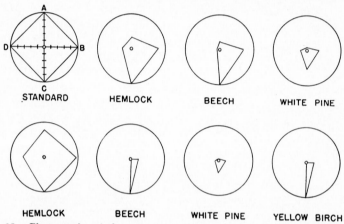

Fig. 23.—Phytographs of the most important species in the hemlock-beech forest (upper row) and hemlock forest (lower row) in north-central Pennsylvania. AO = per cent abundance (each division represents 20 per cent). BO = per cent frequency (each division represents 20 per cent). CO = number of size classes represented (each division represents a size class). DO = basal area in square feet per acre (each division represents 40 square feet of basal area). (*After Lutz.*)

Isolation Transect.—These transects are frequently used in grazing experiments. They usually consist of two strips, each 300 feet long and 20 feet wide with a protected strip between as a control (Fig. 24). One is grazed, the other ungrazed. In the major installation on the Santa Rita Range Reserve in Arizona, the length is 1,100 feet, comprising two 50-foot strips, one protected against cattle, the other against cattle and rodents, while the control units occupy the middle lengthwise. At the end of each year, one unit of ungrazed area is opened and one of the grazed units closed. Hence, after a few years, a history of the development of vegetation as affected by 1, 2, 3, or more years of grazing may be seen, as well as its development for a similar series of years under protection. Thus, the influence of climatic cycles in terms of annual variations in density and volume may be measured. The central strips of these transects may be protected against cattle only or much better against both cattle and rodents. Experimental exclosures of various types have been established in all the grassland associations during the past decade. In conjunction with various types of clip, burned, and seeded quadrats, they have been of great value in confirming field interpretations.[160,371]

In reseeding depleted ranges, exclosures 15 or 20 rods long and 1 or 2 rods wide are sometimes maintained. These plots, which are usually located in an open wind-swept area, are heavily seeded and the seed carefully worked into the soil. Under favorable rainfall, the resulting cover produces a good seed crop in a year or two; the seeds find lodgment on the adjoining depleted areas and in two or three seasons young plants may be seen radiating from these central colonies.[772]

EXCLOSURE AND ENCLOSURE

These are practically identical in as much as they are fenced areas of varying size and shape.[155] The primary difference between them is reflected in the terms, the exclosure keeping out one or more species of animals and the enclosure restricting them to a definite area. In this respect, any pasture is an enclosure, but technically it qualifies as such only as definite experiments or checked observations are carried out in it. The chief purpose of the exclosure is to provide protection against plant-eating animals, mainly stock and rodents, and thus permit experimental study of the processes of natural recovery or artificial regeneration. The enclosure as a pasture affords the opportunity of determining carrying capacity, and the course of overgrazing, as well as a scale of overgrazing indicators. It is also employed to measure the coactions especially of rodents and grasshoppers upon native species.

Exclosures for protection against cattle are usually from 1 to 10 acres in extent and are best fenced with steel posts and four to five strands of barbed wire (Fig. 25). Those against rodents are much smaller, usually less than an acre, owing to the smaller size of the animals and the greater expense and labor of fencing these with hardware cloth. In the original installation on the Santa Rita Range Reserve in Arizona, each exclosure contained two units of equal size, the one "cattle-proof," the other "total

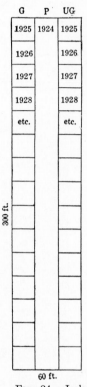

Fig. 24.—Isolation transect consisting of a series of units *G* closed from grazing on the years indicated; a protected, ungrazed strip *P*; and a series of ungrazed units *UG*, some of which were opened for grazing on the years indicated.

protection," excluding both large rodents and cattle. In the case of mice and other small rodents, birds, or insects, cages of fine-mesh hardware cloth are employed. In grazing experiments, the series of enclosures is well illustrated by those at Mandan, N. D., in which the respective sizes are 30, 50, 70, and 100 acres, each pasture stocked with 10 head of cattle.[780] For the detailed study of rodent effects upon cover, enclosures rarely need to be an acre in size, and 50 to 200 feet square are preferred dimensions. The fencing must completely exclude the one or more species to be studied, a purpose that demands sinking the netting or

Fig. 25.—Exclosure transect established by the Soil Conservation Service in overgrazed mixed prairie near Colorado Springs, Colo.

hardware cloth a foot or two in the ground and providing a strip of tin or galvanized iron to prevent climbing over.

In order to express the results secured by exclosures and enclosures in quantitative terms and to employ them in regulating grazing and directing recovery or regeneration, the extensive use of quadrats and experimental plots or grids is imperative. The grid is a series of rectangular plots placed side by side, with or without a buffer strip, and designed to furnish evidence as to the course and outcome of the various processes to which the particular cover is subject. A complete series will include one or more plots devoted to clipping, burning, eroding, denuding, pulling, scraping, grubbing, and sowing and transplanting in pure stands and competing mixtures. They include measuring runoff and erosion where slope is concerned, but a single process or any combination may be selected in accordance with the set of conditions or the objectives sought.

The plots have been as small as 1 square meter, but rectangles 1 by 3 meters or 2 by 6 meters, or often much larger, yield more representative results. In effect, each is a short transect of permanent quadrats, to be staked, charted, and averaged in evaluating the actual or potential role of the processes concerned. In the case of clipping to simulate grazing, the yield of forage is not merely measured and analyzed, but the effect of time or season, frequency and intensity upon species and life forms is likewise determined. Life forms in particular exhibit quite unlike responses to the season and severity of burning, and burn plots are indispensable to the initiation of projects that involve the eradication of weedy annuals, such as bromes, half-shrubs like burroweed and snakeweed, or taller shrubs, sagebrush, etc. Grasses not only respond in a different manner from forbs as to clipping and grazing, fire, and competition, but tall, mid and short grasses, sod forms and bunch forms all behave differently under these processes. Denuded plots are helpful in anticipating the rate and course of secondary succession in abandoned fields, and sown or planted ones have even greater usefulness in indicating the methods to be employed wherever it is desirable to hasten or replace the natural processes of succession.

THE BISECT

The structure of vegetation with regard to the relative height and lateral spread of plants and the interrelation of one plant to the other is important. It is equally essential to understand the relative position, depth, and extent of underground parts. Such information may be gained by the use of the bisect. It is essentially a line transect along which a trench has been dug to a depth greater than that of the deepest root systems. The underground parts such as rhizomes, corms, etc., as well as the roots of each plant, are isolated and the position and extent of each carefully measured and plotted to scale on coordinate paper. The whole root system, so far as it can be represented in one plane, may be drawn, but if the vegetation is at all dense, only that part occurring in the first 4 inches of the trench wall need be represented. This method reveals the form of the root systems of different species and shows their relationships to each other and to different layers of soil, etc. Without an exact knowledge of these facts, an understanding of the structure and economy of a plant community is incomplete. While the belt transect shows the structure of vegetation in two dimensions, the bisect supplements this by showing the third[965] (Fig. 26).

It is often unnecessary to chart the root system of every species. Frequently the dominants alone will suffice. It is best to measure and draw or photograph the shoots to scale first, for they are often more or less disturbed while excavating the parts underground. The work of making

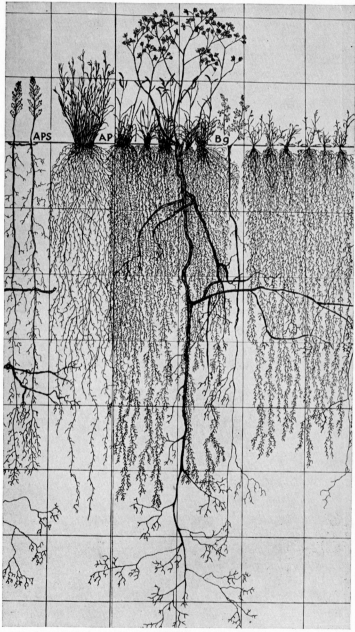

Fig. 26.—Bisect in mixed prairie at Hays in west-central Kansas. Each square is 1 foot in length. Buffalo grass on the right; *Bg*, blue grama grass; *Ap*, wire grass (*Aristida purpurea*); and *Aps*, western ragweed. The large legume in the center is *Psoralea tenuiflora*. (*After F. W. Albertson.*)

a bisect chart is usually lengthy and laborious and especially so where deep root systems are involved, but the results obtained fully warrant its use. A few examples will best reveal its value.

On the Great Plains, under 17 inches annual rainfall, great differences in the type of vegetation are found on level lands within a radius of a few miles. Certain areas are covered with the short buffalo (*Buchloe*) and grama (*Bouteloua*) grasses, others with tall bunches of bluestem (*Andropogon*) and other herbaceous vegetation, while certain areas are characterized by extensive growths of wire grass (*Aristida*), a species of intermediate height. Bisects revealed the fact that the short grasses grow in silt loam so compact that surface runoff frequently causes the loss of over one-third of the precipitation. Usually, the surface 12 to 18 inches of soil alone are moist, and absorption by grass roots is largely confined to this layer. But in the sandy soil where the bluestem grows, practically all of the rainfall is absorbed, the soil is moist to depths of 4 to 5 feet, and to this depth it is penetrated by the deep roots of the tall grasses and other herbs. In the semisandy wire-grass areas, water penetration and root depth are intermediate. Thus, the causes underlying the distribution of the three communities were clearly revealed and much information made available for an intelligent understanding of the behavior of crop plants when grown in these areas.[808]

Bisects have been made in fields of the smaller cereals in loam soils from the Missouri River to the Rocky Mountains and in three grassland communities. Westward, with decreasing rainfall, the plants are much shorter and the roots decrease in length from about 7 feet to approximately 2 feet. The plants, moreover, show a strong tendency to grow in clumps or bunches, in this respect resembling some of the native grasses which form a sod in moist situations but grow in bunches in dry places.[966]

Vegetation in the Wasatch Mountains develops from a mixed grass and weed stage, dominated by needle grass (*Stipa*) and yellowbrush (*Chrysothamnus*), into a growth of the sod-forming wheat grasses (*Agropyron*). Why the yellowbrush gives way to the wheat grass is clearly revealed by the bisect. The dense sod formed by the roots and rhizomes of the wheat grass and the consequent vigorous absorption prevents the moisture from penetrating deeply. The deeply rooted yellowbrush, quite unfitted to compete with the grasses in the surface soil, succumbs as a result. This illustrates the course of a plant succession which is of much economic importance. Wheat grass produces a large amount of forage and is especially well suited to the grazing of cattle and horses. Close grazing tends to destroy the wheat-grass cover and permits the growth of the needle grass and yellowbrush as well as a considerable variety of palatable weeds that are associated with these and are especially valuable for grazing by sheep and goats. Thus, the range, once the history of its vegetation is understood, can be held by judicious management in the most desirable stage of its development.[771]

Bisects through the dense mass of vegetation in a swamp show, for example, that cattails (*Typha*), arrowheads (*Sagittaria*), and smartweeds (*Polygonum*) secure light at different levels and that their rhizomes and roots occupy different levels in the soil.[819]

Three rather clearly defined root layers are evident in prairie. Some species absorb entirely from the surface foot or two of soil. Others extend their roots to depths of 3 to 5 feet, while some nongrassy herbs are branched but little in the surface foot or two but absorb water and solutes from depths between 2 and 15 feet. Clearly, a shallow-rooted grass and a very deeply rooted wild rose are carrying on their activities rather independently and with very little competition although they may grow on the same square foot of soil. The principle applies quite as well to cultivated crops as to natural vegetation.

CAMERA SETS OR TRISTATS

In temperate climates, the study of vegetation must be largely made during the growing season and time is often the limiting factor. The tristat method consists of repeatedly photographing the same area of vegetation. Three stakes are driven into the ground and one leg of the tripod placed on the top of each. The picture is taken in exactly the same direction each time with the camera at the same height. It gives a record of the development of the vegetation throughout the season and from year to year.[190,843] Such photographs are not only quickly made but also bring out characteristics and illustrate features that do not lend themselves readily to description or measurement. The improvement of depleted range lands, for example, is marked by the appearance and spread of certain palatable species. Conversely, the deterioration caused by overgrazing is marked by the disappearance of these species and a simultaneous increase in weeds. These changes may take place so gradually that even the trained investigator must have permanent records for comparison. They are best followed by permanent quadrats, but photographs showing the density and character of the vegetation are highly valuable.[188] By obtaining such a series of photographs from plots representing the area as a whole and by comparing them, a panorama of the change may be brought before the eye.[878]

The method is readily applicable in tracing the spread or decrease of poisonous plants, weeds introduced from centers of infection, shrubs introduced into grassland, rate of deterioration of fields of alfalfa, clover, or other crops, revegetation of denuded or bare areas, and, indeed, most of the phenomena concerned with a dynamic study of plants.

RING COUNTS

The age of a tree, shrub, woody vine, or half-shrub and sometimes that of an herb may be determined by counting the annual rings of the aerial or subterranean stems. In many plants, such as pines and spruce, the annual growth is marked not only by the bud scars but also by the whorls of branches. Many valuable data may be obtained in regard to the general climate as indicated by rate of growth as well as in regard to local environment under which the plant lives. The method of ring counts is important in determining the successive stages of developing vegetation and especially the sequence of dominants and subdominants.

Fig. 27.—Cross sections of three 20-year-old bur oaks from typical oak forests along the Missouri River. The largest, 4.5 inches in diameter, is from southeastern Nebraska where the precipitation is 33 inches; the smallest, 2 inches, from northeastern Nebraska, precipitation 23 inches; and the second from an intermediate station. The trees were 40, 25, and 18 feet high, respectively.

Trees usually invade grassland under cover of xeric (dry-habitat) shrubs, and other species, including shrubs, follow the trees because of their ameliorating effect on climatic conditions. Where trees overshadow shrubs on forest borders and doubt arises as to the sequence of invasion, ring counts usually reveal that the more xeric shrubs were the pioneers (Fig. 27).

It is sometimes of great importance to know the age of newly built islands, sand bars, or flood plains. Ring counts afford a reliable method. In 1919, 100 years after a treaty with Spain had fixed the south bank of the Red River as the boundary line between what are now the states of Oklahoma and Texas, oil was discovered underlying certain lands which had apparently been added to the south bank by deposit but possibly by a change in the course of the river's channel. A dispute between the two states followed, involving millions of dollars. Each claimed the oil lands. It thus became necessary to establish with certainty just where the south bank of the river was located 100 years earlier. By counting the rings of numerous and well scattered elms and other trees in the valley, as well as by a study of the rate at which the vegetation on the flood plain developed to a stabilized or climax condition, it was found that the oil lands had been on the Texas side of the river for more than 100 years.[804]

The close relation between actual rainfall and that calculated by means of the yearly growth rate of trees is shown in Fig. 28. Marked resemblances are found in certain individual rings over a wide range of the country in which climate is the only common factor. Thus, exceptional smallness in one ring (formed in 1851) has been found in trees over an area 750 miles wide, being shown by sequoias in California,

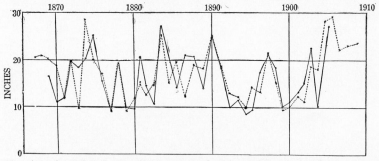

Fig. 28.—Actual rainfall (broken line) compared with rainfall calculated from growth of trees in Arizona. (*After Douglass.*)

ponderosa pines in New Mexico, and Douglas firs in Colorado. By a study of cross identification of ring groups bounded by growth rings formed during years of marked peculiarity, it has been possible to tell the date when trees were felled.[246] The records of ponderosa pines in the southwest have been extended back in a continuous series to 11 A. D. by the aid of beams from prehistoric ruins.[250] They have made possible the dating of 100 ruins (pueblos and cliff dwellings) scattered over northern Arizona and New Mexico and the southern edges of Colorado and Utah.[249]

During 1918, an enormous seed crop of ponderosa pine on the Colorado plateau was followed by a year of precipitation unusually favorable to the growth of the seedlings. This coincidence had not occurred before for a period of 25 years. It will result in the repopulation of the area by an even-aged forest.[668,672] Ring counts in even-aged Douglas-fir forests of Oregon and Washington give us the date of previous burns and that of the new growth resulting. From ring counts on sagebrush and other desert shrubs, it seems clear that reseeding takes place only periodically and during especially favorable years (Fig. 29).

FIG. 29.—Reproduction cycle of Engelmann spruce (*Picea engelmanni*), in Colorado

FIG. 30.—Section of a tamarack tree from a Minnesota swamp. Because of poor aeration in the wet peat it had reached a height of only 10 feet in 49 years. The swamp was drained in 1918, indicated by *x*, after which the tree grew 10 feet higher in the 7 years before it was cut down. (*After Zon.*)

In measuring width of annual rings, several precautions need to be taken. Trees growing in well lighted, constantly moist habitats show a complacent growth, with rings all or nearly all the same size. Those growing with a limited water supply are more sensitive to rainfall and the ring width varies widely. A suppressed tree may, moreover, have smaller rings in a favorable season than a dominant one in a poor season.[248] Where poor aeration and not water is the limiting factor to growth, as in beech trees in central Germany, the annual rings are widest during dry years (Fig. 30). Occasionally, a double ring is formed, when, for some reason (*e.g.*, frost, caterpillars eating the leaves, etc.), growth is interrupted and again resumed during the same year.[32] Double rings frequently occur in certain warm climates, as in Arizona, with two seasons of rainfall. Further, it must be recalled that the growth rate of trees decreases with age. The ponderosa pines of the dry Colorado plateau of northern Arizona have been shown, when corrections have been made for these factors, to represent the rainfall with an accuracy of 85 per cent.[247]

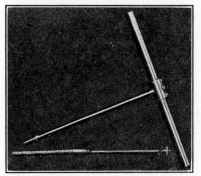

Fig. 31.—Increment borer and core 4 inches long from 27-year-old oak.

In practice, stumps resulting from lumbering or clearing are usually available in woodland, but often the trees must be felled as needed. The increment borer, which removes a small core of wood from circumference to center without injuring the tree, obviates this difficulty (Fig. 31). Since trees often grow more rapidly on one side than on the other, if better lighted or watered, borings should be made in two radii. The holes should be closed with wooden pegs driven firmly into the tree, to prevent infection by fungi, etc. A study of annual ring width has been made on oaks in Missouri,[726] beech in Indiana,[242] long-leaf pine in Florida,[542] eastern hemlock in New England,[556] and western white pine in Idaho.[570]

Determining the Age of Woody Plants.—Examine the stumps in a cut-over area. Are the trees of even age, *i.e.*, did most of them start at nearly the same time after a previous cutting or fire? Making allowance for the growth of the seedling to the height of the stump, in what year did the group (or a particular tree) germinate or start from sprouts? Is the width of the annual ring about the same for the different trees of the same species? Compare the rate of growth of those on a hilltop and in a ravine. Are there any rings that are especially narrow or wide? What was the date of this dry or wet year? Does any tree show narrow rings abruptly followed by wider ones such as would occur if it were suddenly better illuminated as a result of the falling of an older tree? Examine a mixture of young trees and tall shrubs, and determine if possible which were in possession of the area first.

In standing timber, employ an increment borer to determine the age and width of rings of a densely shaded (suppressed) tree and a well lighted one of the same species or of one growing in a dry habitat and another equally lighted growing in a moist one.

THE BURN SCAR

Much information about the life history of a forest may often be obtained by a study of scars caused by fire. Not only the time of the fire but also its severity, the direction from which it came, and the extent of the burned area may be ascertained. *Surface fires,*[887] which usually consume only the grasses and other herbaceous vegetation, may result in *ground fires* that burn more slowly down into the litter and mold,

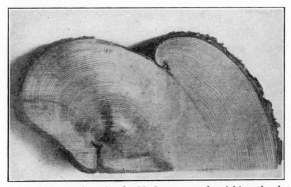

Fig. 32.—Section of the heal edge of a double-burn scar, furnishing the dates of two successive fires, Long's Peak, Colo.

often following tree roots underground. They are much hotter and usually kill all trees and other vegetation.[940] Often they are limited to a few acres in extent.[831] *Crown fires* race through the tops of trees at a high rate of speed, killing practically all vegetation in their path and usually leaving the soil in a sterile condition.[698]

Fires leave their traces on the woody plants perhaps as bark scars, more often as wood scars, and, especially on the edges of burns where the fire has died down, as heal scars, *i.e.*, wood scars that have healed over.[554] The time of a fire may be determined by counting the number of rings of wood put down since the burn scar was formed. Sometimes the burn scar may be double or even triple and thus give the dates of successive fires (Fig. 32). The direction from which the fire came is revealed by the side of the trees which was burned, and the extent of the area burned is coincident with the trees bearing scars, unless the fire became more destructive and killed all of the plants. In such areas, it is necessary to determine the age of the oldest trees, shrubs, and herbs, both standing and fallen, which have come in since the fire. If the growing season was not over when the fire occurred, root sprouts will show one more annual ring than trees and perennial herbs starting from seed which germinated the following spring. In order to secure the first annual ring of trees, it is necessary to cut the seedling or sapling at the ground line or even below the ground line on steep slopes.[152]

Burns have a pronounced effect upon the composition and development of a forest. In the coniferous forests of the west, especially at high altitudes, they are almost invariably populated with lodgepole pine (*Pinus contorta murrayana*), a forest weed tree which grows very rapidly, reproducing by seed at the age of 6 to 12 years and dominating the area until other pines, firs, or spruces grow up and shade it out. Repeated burns may result in an area being rather continuously occupied by lodgepole pine, a very inferior commercial type of forest. This is the case in much of the Rocky Mountain Park region, where at least 13 burns have been determined as occurring between 1707 and 1905.[152] The cambium of trees with thin bark like the white cedar (*Thuja plicata*) is much more easily killed by heat than a tree with thick bark like tamarack (*Larix occidentalis*). Differences in fire-resisting qualities of various shrubs also occur. Hence, a fire may greatly change the composition of a forest both by direct destruction of part of the plants and by altering the environmental conditions, especially light, for invaders.[888] The origi nal structure may often be determined by a study of adjacent, similarly located, unburned areas. That the history of the past aids in the present methods of forest management and their relation to future development needs scarcely be indicated.

THE RELICT METHOD

In ecological usage, a relict is a community or group of plants, rarely an individual, which has been left behind by the disappearance or modification of an earlier vegetation, usually a climax.[160] They may have survived climatic change and accompanying migration of the climax, as illustrated by oak-hickory forest in Texas and Oklahoma in a present grassland climate. Even more numerous are the relicts due to general disturbance by man in the form of clearing, fire, overgrazing, draining, etc. The pine woods of the coastal plain regularly exhibit relicts of the original deciduous climax, while today grasslands are nearly everywhere disturbed areas in which only fragments of the primitive cover still persist. Likewise, fragments of vegetation characteristic of swamp or bog may clearly indicate a former wet area.

The relict method combines observation, scrutiny of scientific reports and records, experiment and interpretation, but its essential feature is the search for areas continuously protected against disturbance. In grass· land, such areas are found more or less continuously along fenced railways (and frequently along unfenced ones also) in spite of an increase in burning and cultivation; they are common features of highways not too much widened and recur as hayfields and in cemeteries, schoolyards, rocky hills, and other situations somewhat withdrawn from grazing or cultivation. Forest exhibits a similar general relation, but logging and fire have destroyed the primeval stand in all but the most remote valleys or coves, or in national parks and similar reserves. With respect to climatic relicts, sand is one of the chief equalizers, because runoff is almost nil and loss by evaporation is greatly reduced by a mulch of dry sand. Tall grass has persisted for thousands of years in the extensive sand hills of Nebraska and Kansas, and deciduous woods even longer in the sandy soils of Oklahoma and Texas. The surrounding hard land supports chiefly mid and short grasses.

Scientific reports and herbarium specimens that antedate the period of general disturbance by man are invaluable in determining the presence and composition of the original climax. The report on the forests of North America for the Tenth Census bears witness to the nature and extent of the pine-hemlock climax before the greater portion of it had been logged off.[778] The Hayden surveys of the western territories rendered a similar service in connection with the mixed prairie, and the photographs leave no question of the earlier dominance of mid grasses. The advance of the tall Andropogons over much of the true prairie is attested by scientific accounts of its composition, written fifty to a hundred years ago,[829,707] and similar records as to the Pacific prairie of California are likewise in existence.

Experimental proof that relicts belong to an existing climax is most readily secured in grassland by means of exclosures against grazing and a considerable number of such demonstrations have been made, in the mixed prairie especially. This proof is reenforced by the evidence from clip quadrats that mid grasses, notably *Stipa*, disappear under frequent cutting, while short grasses and sedges are much less affected. Because of their longer life span, similar evidence is difficult to secure in forests, but it is not impossible when fire and logging can be eliminated.

Once the relict nature of a particular community has been determined, it is a simple matter to explain its origin and role in most instances of disturbance. In fact, the explanation is supplied by the proof itself when it is obtained by means of exclosures and competition cultures. However, the most convincing demonstration is that afforded by isolation transects in the mixed prairie, where one series of annual units is being reclothed with mid grasses at the same time that the other is grazed down to short grass. Even with shrubs and trees, the final outcome of the competition between seedlings of the dominants may be forecast from a quadrat study extending over 5 to 10 years.

THE METHOD OF POLLEN ANALYSIS

From the relict as a living indicator of past events in climate and vegetation, it is but a short step to fossil leaf, stem, or pollen grain and. from these, to the fossil animals that lived upon plant food. The subject that deals with the climaxes and climates of the past is called *paleoecology*. It is obvious that it has to do with the same causes and processes and

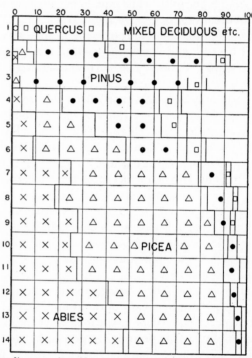

FIG. 33.—Pollen diagram of an Ohio bog. Depth in feet is shown at left and percentage scale at top. Proportions of the four genera, fir (*Abies*), spruce (*Picea*), pine (*Pinus*), and oak (*Quercus*), are shown at each level as they occur. Any remainder is designated as "mixed deciduous," and is composed mostly of hickory (*Carya*), birch (*Betula*), and other deciduous trees. It has been variously estimated that 200 years are required to form 1 to 12 inches of peat. The sequence of vegetation with change of climate appears to have been fir-spruce, spruce-pine, pine-oak, and oak-mixed deciduous forest. (*Redrawn from Sears.*)

much the same materials as present-day ecology, and equally evident that the one is incomplete without the other. However, for our purpose it is sufficient to discuss briefly the microfossils or fossil pollen, which supplement relicts in furnishing a picture of the immediate past.[514,706,219a] This method of pollen analysis has recently come into general use wherever peat bogs are found and there is some evidence that it will have wider applications.[301]

The technique of pollen analysis comprises the following steps: (1) collection of samples from different depths or layers in peat bogs, swamps or alluvial deposits; (2) preparation of material for examination; (3) identification of pollen grains; (4) calculation of percentages; (5) expression of results in diagrams or spectra. In America, collections are made usually with a Davis peat sampler at regular depth intervals of 6 inches or so, the number of complete cores being determined by the size or nature of the bogs.[800] A small sample for treatment is taken from the middle of each segment and boiled in 10 per cent potassium or sodium hydroxide, or other macerating solution.[326,268] This may be done on a slide, or larger portions may be treated and centrifuged; in either case the material may be stained as desired and mounted permanently. The tree pollens are those of most significance and for the most part these are readily identified. As a rule, 100 to 200 grains from each of two or more slides are counted and the amount for each genus is given as a percentage of the total tree pollen. The fluctuations in amount for each are then expressed by a vertical curve or as shown in Fig. 33.

Though there are several sources of error in pollen analysis, notably as to quantities and their expression, the general values are high, and the method is an indispensable adjunct to those of climatic seres, climax, and succession, chiefly of course, for events during postglacial time. In Sweden and northern Europe generally, the major outcome has been to verify the earlier evidence of climatic pulsation and the mass migration of climaxes, though it has reduced the number of stages from five to three. In North America, a similar modification of views has taken place and the later opinions are in harmony with the European.[303,801] In accordance with this, postglacial time is divided into three periods, respectively, of rising temperature, maximum warmth, and falling temperature, marked by corresponding shifts of boreal, pine, and hardwood forests, with an accompanying invasion of the prairie climax from the west during the warm-dry maximum.

EXPERIMENTAL VEGETATION

In the study of vegetation, many problems arise as to the causes of the particular plant distribution and the resulting structure. Measurement and comparison of the factors of the habitat usually throw much light upon the probable causes, but the answer can be made positively and decisively only by trying it out with the plants in question.[73,173] Much has been written, for example, about the causes for the treelessness of the prairies, but the question remained unanswered until seedling trees were grown and their fate studied. It has been shown by experiments extending throughout many years, that in eastern Nebraska, because of drought, trees cannot grow on the upland in competition with the grasses, even when planted in favorable small seedbeds. They are likewise unable to grow in low prairie because of the dense shade of the tall grasses.[675] Fire, too, has been shown to be fatal to tree seedlings but much less harmful to grasses.[172]

The reason upland prairie species cannot grow in tall marsh-grass (*Spartina*) swamps has been shown by transplanting large blocks of sod. Species that are not killed by deficient aeration, as shown by yellowing of leaves and rotting of stems, soon die as a result of shading. Ability to grow in alkali or acid soils may be tested in a similar manner. Forests offer excellent opportunity for determining the behavior of plants under different degrees of shading. Experimental areas in a desert valley, in an oak grove on the mid-slope of an adjacent mountain, and in the coniferous forest at its crest were each furnished with seeds or transplants of species from each of the three habitats. The experiment has yielded much direct information on the dissemination of species and barriers to ecesis.[558] Rodents, grasshoppers, and other animals often effectively prevent the successful invasion of plants from one community into another, although the fitness of the species for its native habitat may possibly be less than for the new one.

Extensive tests in seeding depleted ranges with native forage plants have been conducted in various portions of the country, many introduced species being used. Although the tests in the southwest were largely unsuccessful, ranges in less arid climates have been greatly improved. By use of over 600 reseeding experiments, directed by one forest ecologist using various cultivated grasses and other herbaceous forage plants, good results have been obtained in mountain meadows, irrigated field, and similar moist situations.[666,767] Not only the best species for sowing (timothy, Hungarian brome grass, rye grasses, Kentucky bluegrass, and redtop) were ascertained, but also the best season for sowing, the best method of scattering and planting the seed, and the causes of failure were fully determined.[772] However, on the open ranges of the Great Plains and the southwest, success in seeding has been rare and it will be secured only by proper preparation and other aids to establishment.

Growing ordinary crops in a new country or new crops in a region long under cultivation is really a type of experimental vegetation. Much has been done to improve agriculture along such lines, as, for example, the introduction of winter wheat and alfalfa from the dry portions of Eurasia and of the sorghums from Africa into the drier portions of the United States. But only a beginning has been made when compared with the possibilities.

Importance of Field Experiments.—The importance of field experiments cannot be overestimated. Often a simple experiment requiring little or no special apparatus throws much light upon problems of vegetation.[445] If, however, the problem demands, there should be no hesitancy in securing the needed apparatus and transporting it into the field. The experimental method simply means the observation of processes under controlled conditions. The nature and extent of the control will vary widely according to the end to be accomplished (Fig. 34). The fencing of an area against rodents, the cutting of a ditch to divert the water supply ordinarily received after heavy rains by one area to another, the supply of extra water to vegetation in times of drought, or the addition of fertilizers are examples of field experiments which have given valuable results.[278,292,1007]

Why regeneration of beech woods in England and Scotland is so poor was determined by fencing small areas. From some areas, rabbits were excluded; from others, both rabbits and birds; and from still others, field mice as well. By placing beechnuts in each exclosure both on the surface and within the forest litter, it was found that rabbits ordinarily ate very few seeds, birds secured only those on the surface, but mice destroyed almost the entire supply, except a few overlooked in the duff. This simple experiment established the fact that, in a large measure, mice are responsible for the failure of the rejuvenation of beech forests.[961]

Fig. 34.—Relative growth of a native sunflower (*Helianthus rigidus*) in competition with prairie grasses (right) and in a quadrat where these competitors had been removed.

An exact knowledge of the amount of damage done to the range by rodents and especially of the rate and degree of recovery of the various types of vegetation after rodents have been eradicated has been obtained in a similar manner. Exclosures were made against rodents and cattle, against cattle alone, and against cattle where rodents had been killed. Clip quadrats from these as well as from enclosures inhabited by jack rabbits and others inhabited by kangaroo rats showed the heavy toll of vegetation taken by these pests, a matter of grave importance, especially in times of drought[907,908] (Fig. 35).

The experimental grid is an invaluable method for disclosing the processes in action on a particular range or grazing type, tracing their effect upon the cover, and measuring the reactions and coactions of the latter. This method is practically indispensable in giving advance information as to species and methods for sowing and transplanting, and hence should be installed in all major exclosures at the outset.

Experiments need by no means be confined to native vegetation. Many ecological processes may be conveniently studied in a garden, orchard, or grove, and it should be kept clearly in mind that what man calls agriculture is, in a large measure, the making of an environment more or less suitable to crop plants. Fundamentally, the growth and functioning of the plant depend upon the nature of the environment

Fig. 35.—Wheat grass from clip quadrats; (left) where both cattle and prairie dogs have been excluded, (center) where cattle only have been excluded, and (right) on the open range. Grand Canyon, Ariz. (*After Taylor and Loftfield.*)

and the adjustment to it and not directly upon cultural practices. The latter only modify the relation of the plant to the environmental complex.

FIELD SURVEYS AND MAPPING

Just how to begin the study of vegetation may usually be decided by the object in view. In general, a preliminary survey or reconnaissance precedes intensive work in any particular area. This is true whether all the communities in the region or only certain ones are to be studied. Such a survey gives a general knowledge not only of the various types of vegetation but also of the conditions under which they occur and enables the investigator to choose typical areas for more detailed study. It is evident that a thoroughgoing survey will combine intensive and extensive methods in the highest possible degree. Every local area or community is but a fragment or modification of some unit of a climax and can be understood and placed in its natural relations only by a wide acquaintance with the climax. While the usual limitations as to time and funds, as well as knowledge of vegetation, render it necessary to begin with detailed analysis locally, this must be supplemented by wider survey before the details can be properly interpreted. The local study is a matter of painstaking examination step by step through two or more years. This is accompanied by a motor reconnaissance through as large a portion of the territory as can be managed, and this examination demands constant and adequate stops at intervals of a few miles, or whenever the composition changes, in order to secure details for comparison. At its best, motor survey will traverse every available section line, or road, but in prairie and often in woodland, parallel transects a mile apart are usually sufficient, while in desert scrub and sagebrush a greater interval is permissible. Finally, wherever it is feasible,

Fig. 36.—Airplane view of burned-over area (lightly colored, left) and chaparral-covered foothills (darker) near San Antonio Heights, Calif. White lines on the ridges are firebreaks. (*Photograph, courtesy of 23rd Photo Section, Air Corps, U. S. Army.*)

both kinds of survey should be supplemented by airplane observation and mapping, a task that is being met more and more by federal agencies[1000] (Fig. 36).

Mapping in some form and on the proper scale is a desirable, if not indispensable, adjunct of every survey. Motor mapping is particularly adapted to tracing the boundaries of vegetational units or of species, since it is the sole method that combines extensive and intensive values. In regions of bold relief, the technique of the U. S. Geological Survey in mapping topography is applicable to vegetation where topographic sheets exist or can be made available. In the case of scrub and forest, the mapping can best be done by airplane, when the importance warrants the cost, as is the case at present in the great public projects in erosion and flood control and other problems of conservation. Great improvement in the technique of photographing and interpreting air pictures is certain, and it is probable that special types of planes like the helicopter or autogyro will permit much greater refinement. However, even at its best, the airplane can be regarded only as an adjunct or extension of a proper ground survey.[122]

Both surveying and mapping must deal adequately with the structure and development, as well as the spatial relations of the climax or some portion of it. Fragments of the original climax are invaluable as the background for this and must be diligently sought in order to recognize and evaluate the changes everywhere wrought by succession, disturbance, or cyclic fluctuations, such as a series of years of excessive precipitation or of drought. For this the relict method is indispensable, and in grassland or scrub, motor trips should be routed along railways as a regular procedure. It must be clearly understood that nearly all the vegetation "on the ground" today has been more or less modified and hence the closest observation is required to make sure of recognizing the various units, their relationships, and stages of development.

The mapping of a suitable area furnishes excellent experience with extensive vegetation, especially if a considerable number of communities are encountered, for the relations of these have to be closely studied in order to present them on a map. A general idea of the broad features of vegetation will have to be formed. This focuses the attention upon particular problems and compels one to make a decision about the vegetation studied. It must first be determined what plant communities are to be mapped, their extent, transition into other communities, etc. In this way, the larger communities should be distinguished, recorded, and characterized, and their relation to topography, exposure, and soil type determined in a general way. Typical examples of each community must be rather thoroughly examined, their more important species listed, and the main features of their structure determined. In such work, it must be clearly kept in mind that the aim is to get a general idea of the whole area. Detailed work in any community will follow as a natural sequence.

Aside from the map, complete field notes should be taken and a very valuable supplement to these are photographs not taken at random but to illustrate typical vegetation. These greatly help when it comes to rewriting the field notes in connected sequence. The amount of detailed information obtained and the accuracy of the mapping will vary, of course, with the size of the area under study.[898]

Community Maps.—Much may be learned about the structure and development of individual communities by making a large-scale map of a relatively limited area. Such maps represent the details of the vegetation of a small area on a large scale. They are made by dividing the area for study by means of cross tapes into units usually a meter square.

The boundaries of small, well defined, uniform communities can be plotted to within 3 inches of their actual position and the position of large, isolated, individual plants or clumps of vegetation definitely located. Much of the detail of the actual structure of the vegetation may be shown by means of appropriate symbols. These should be so simple that the map may be readily interpreted. Crosshatching or distinctive shading may be used and transitional areas shown by the overlapping of the two kinds. It is well to trace the original chart in ink and to keep it for reference, since the chart method reaches its greatest usefulness only when the area is permanently marked and changes occurring from year to year are recorded (Fig. 37).

Many situations warrant permanent mapping, but it must be understood that the chart in itself is of little value unless it is a characteristic sample of the detailed structure of a widely distributed community. It should show some definite distribution of vegetation in relation to habitat or be of use in solving some problem in the development of vegetation, etc. For example, the distribution of communities or zones about marshes or lakes may be correlated with water content, or those in saline areas with salt.

Methods have been devised for mapping low shrubs or woody seedlings in range management and in investigations on watershed protection, etc. They are used to obtain exact data on the character and extent of the cover of shrubs, successional change, rate and period of growth in the brush type and the influence of grazing, browsing, and fire upon the plants.

The gridiron method* consists of subdividing the plot with strong cord into squares of convenient size, usually 1 or 2 square feet, and mapping the crowns of the shrubs on coordinate paper of a suitable scale, after determining their location, by measurements, within the squares.

The more recent coordinate method consists in establishing the boundaries of a plot, 4 by 25 feet, with flat steel surveying tapes held at a height (which is adjustable) slightly above the level of the shrubs. Four strong steel stakes, 3 to 5 feet in length, are used, one at each corner. A light but strong metal crossbar engages the side tapes and is suspended by them. The crossbar is first placed at the end of the parallel tapes. The mapper looks perpendicularly down at the shrubs and determines just where the edges of each individual intersect the crossbar. After establishing these points on cross-section paper, on which the boundaries of the plot have previously been drawn to scale, the crossbar is advanced

---

* For a description of the much more complicated traverse or plane-table method, see references 634 and 694.

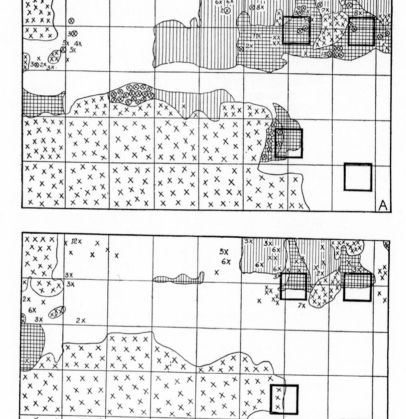

Fig. 37.—A, an area 42 by 25 feet in an overgrazed pasture at Lincoln, Neb. It was marked off in 5-foot squares and mapped in June, 1924, one month after excluding the cattle. x, shrubs, mostly wolfberry (Symphoricarpos). x with circle indicates those starting in 1924. The number of individual stems is indicated only outside the areas dominated by shrubs; vertical hatch, bluegrass (Poa pratensis); crosshatch, buffalo grass (Buchloe dactyloides); unmarked areas, wheat grass (Agropyron smithii). The positions of four quadrats are indicated by squares.

B, same area at the end of the third growing season, August, 1926.

Has bluegrass increased or decreased its territory? Has buffalo grass extended its area anywhere? What is replacing it in a large measure? Note that the shrubs have extended their front only slightly and not uniformly. By counting the squares, or more accurately by placing a heavy cardboard under the map and using a planimeter, ascertain the percentage decrease of bluegrass and buffalo grass and the increase of wheat grass. All three grasses formed dense sod in which only a few other species occurred.

0.5 foot and all points of intersection at the second position are plotted. The outline of each crown between the two points upon it is then drawn, after which the crossbar is again advanced as before. The height of each shrub is determined and the data are recorded within the outline of the crown on the map. Thus low shrubs may be rapidly mapped and the data quickly compiled.[694] Shrubby areas may be permanently charted and again recharted at 5-year intervals.

The total cross-sectional foliage area occupied by each species of shrub in the plot may be determined either by a planimeter, or where cross-section paper is used, the squares and parts of squares enclosed by the outlines of the crowns may be counted. The coordinate method may also be used in mapping low shrubs in woodland and forest. The mapping of crowns of forest trees on permanent sample plots is accomplished by projecting the periphery of each tree vertically upon the forest floor. One method is to employ a bob on a line held by a pole at various points on the periphery of the crown. Delimiting the areas occupied by large forbs with spreading crowns in studies in prairies, pastures, and range lands may be accomplished by modifications of the preceding methods.

In the study of succession, community charts are often indispensable. By their use, the changes from year to year, such as the shifting of ecotones following invasion of one community and the disappearance of another, may be traced in detail. By this means, changes are permanently recorded, the time element determined, the causes of change often automatically revealed, and a record obtained the accuracy of which cannot be impugned. This greatly supplements the study of change by inference, *i.e.*, piecing together the course of development from the various kinds of communities found in the region.

CHAPTER III

PLANT SUCCESSION

As vegetation develops, the same area becomes successively occupied by different plant communities. This process is termed plant succession. Within a region, the same final or climax stage results from this series of successive stages whether they start in open water, or solid rock, or on denuded land. Successions beginning in ponds, lakes, marshes, or elsewhere in water are termed *hydrarch*, and the different stages of the series or sere constitute a *hydrosere*.[184] Although the movement from initial stage to climax is usually continuous, when one group of dominant plants reaches its maximum the change is clearly marked. This is especially true when one life form, such as that of floating plants, gives way to another, such as reeds and rushes. The stages and the processes operative in bringing about plant succession in the various seres will now be examined.

A HYDROSERE

Submerged Stage.—Near the shores of a lake or, perhaps, throughout its extent, if the water is less than 20 feet in depth, may be found many species of plants growing entirely submerged. These are the pioneers of the hydrosere. Prominent among them are several species of flowering plants such as water weed (*Elodea*), pondweeds (*Potamogeton*), hornwort (*Ceratophyllum*), and naiads (*Najas*). These grow at various depths, mostly rooted in the muddy or sandy bottom, depending somewhat upon the species but especially upon the clearness or turbidity of the water. They often form dense masses of vegetation. Submerged buttercups (*Ranunculus*), bladderworts (*Utricularia*), and eelgrass (*Vallisneria*), together with numerous algae, varying in size from microscopic forms to the herblike *Chara*, help to fill the water more or less completely with a tangled vegetation. The vegetation forms rather open patches in some places but a continuous, tangled, aquatic garden in others. Indeed, the density of growth of some of these submerged plants is sometimes so great, especially in late summer when they are fully grown, that boating may become difficult if not impossible.

The growth of this submerged vegetation year after year has a very marked effect upon the habitat. Material eroded by streams and transported into the lake is deposited about the plants because they form a direct obstacle to its advance, and especially because they slow down the currents. Moreover, when the plants die their remains sink to the bottom where, because of insufficient oxidation, the vegetable debris and the dead animals associated with it are only partially decomposed, forming a mass of humus which cements the mucky soil together, making it firmer. The result of these reactions brought about by the submerged plants is to shallow the water by building up the bottom of the lake. Obviously, this process is disadvantageous to the present occupants and ultimately there are formed a suitable water depth and a rich substratum for invaders.

Floating Stage.—Where the water is only 6 to 8 feet deep, various species of floating plants begin to invade the area occupied by the pioneer,

FIG. 38.—Water lilies (*Nymphaea polysepala*) in a lagoon, illustrating the floating stage of a hydrosere.

submerged plants. They migrate mainly by rhizomes from their stronghold in the shallower water. Chief among them are various water lilies (*Nymphaea, Castalia*), numerous pondweeds (*Potamogeton*), and smartweeds (*Polygonum*), although many others may occur. Usually, several species are associated, sometimes only two, and often a single representative covers large areas (Fig. 38). All are rooted in the mud. Nearly all have rhizomes, sometimes several feet in length, or stems rooting at the nodes, while the petioles or stems, varying in length with the depth of the water, permit the broad leaves to float on the surface.

At first, the floating plants are intimately associated with the submerged species, particularly those that grow best in the shallowed water.

But as the invaders increase in numbers, gradually spreading year by year, their leaves occupy more of the water surface and the light for submerged plants is decreased. These must migrate into deeper water. Frequently, the masses of unattached floaters, such as duckweeds (*Lemnaceae*), water hyacinth (*Eichhornia*), etc., cover the surface and aid materially in reducing the light. Because of the dense tangle of stems, much water-borne soil is deposited in the floating-plant zone, while the debris formed by the decay of these rather massive species rapidly builds

Fig. 39.—Three dominants of the reed-swamp stage, reed (*Phragmites communis*), bulrush (*Scirpus validus*) in blossom on left, and cattail (*Typha latifolia*).

up the substratum. Spring freshets may, wholly or in part, wash away this accumulated material, in which case the floating stage persists for a long time. But usually the soil-building process goes on so rapidly that within a few years at least the shoreward margin of the floating-plant zone can be invaded by swamp plants. Water that is too shallow is distinctly unfavorable to floating species, and this community, even if uninvaded, would ultimately make the habitat so unfit for itself that floating plants would disappear.

Reed-swamp Stage.—With the continued shoaling of the water, invasion becomes possible for plants that root at the bottom and are partly submerged but whose foliage is raised above the surface of the water. The tall bulrush (*Scirpus validus*), cattail (*Typha*), and reed (*Phragmites*) may invade the territory occupied by the floating plants where the water is 1 to 4 feet deep. The bulrush usually grows in the deepest water, sometimes in excess of 6 feet, and reeds in the shallowest, but they are often intermixed (Fig. 39). All have large, much-branched rhizomes, and where establishment of seedlings is unsuccessful, invasion is still possible. Associated with them or in similar habitats are other bulrushes, bur reeds (*Sparganium*), wild rice (*Zizania*), etc. Like the preceding plants, their tall stature and dense, sodlike growth exert a controlling influence. Obviously, the floating plants are at a great disadvantage as regards light. As the reed-swamp community develops, they largely or entirely disappear, moving outward into deeper water in the wake of the submerged species.

The reaction of the reed-swamp plants is not only to shade the surface of the water but also to build up the lake shores by retaining the sedimentary materials washed into the lake and by the very rapid accumulation of plant remains. Not only is the plant population much denser than before but also mechanical tissues, which resist decay, are much more highly developed in plants with aerial organs. Thus, the water depth is gradually decreased.[72] Many secondary species such as arrowheads (*Sagittaria*), water plantain (*Alisma*), sweet flag (*Acorus*), smartweeds (*Polygonum*), etc., aid in bringing these reactions about and ultimately in making the habitat less fit for most species of the reed-swamp stage.

Sedge-meadow Stage.—The cattails, bulrushes, etc., develop less vigorously with a lowering of the water level, and other species invade their territory. Favored by an increasing amount of light, as the former occupants disappear, they gradually change the reed swamp into a sedge meadow. Numerous carices (*Carex*), rushes (*Juncus*), and spike rushes (*Eleocharis*) form, with their tough, tangled rhizomes and slender, copious roots, sodlike mats of vegetation (Fig. 40). The soil gradually becomes too dry for plants of the preceding community but is still very wet in spring and early summer when it may be covered with several inches of water. But later in the season, this surface water disappears and the soil may be merely saturated, the water level sinking a few inches below the surface. Varying degrees of wetness may be found depending upon the progress of development and irregularities of topography (Fig. 41). Islands of bur reeds or cattails may persist in depressions for a long time as relicts of the old community and indicators of a former swamp. Many species of forbs occur intermixed with the patchwork of the *Eleocharis-Carex-Juncus* complex. Examples of these are mints (*Mentha, Teucrium*), marsh marigold (*Caltha*), blue flag (*Iris*), bedstraw (*Galium*), water hemlock (*Cicuta*), cotton grass (*Eriophorum*), and bellflower (*Campanula*). All react upon the habitat by binding water-carried and wind-borne soil, accumulating plant debris, and transpiring enormous quantities of water.[995] The spike rush alone may add a few

Fig. 40.—Spike rush (*Eleocharis palustris*) characteristic of the sedge-meadow stage of a hydrosere. The plants are about 18 inches tall.

Fig. 41.—A sedge meadow of spike rush (*Eleocharis*) bordered by a bulrush or tule (*Scirpus validus*) swamp in the background.

millimeters of humus each year. Finally, the marshy sedge meadow becomes too dry for these water-loving plants (*hydrophytes*) to thrive. They are gradually replaced by species of another community. In dry climates, this may be grassland or some other xeric climax; but in more moist ones, woodland.

Woodland Stage.—When the lowland has been built up to an extent where the soil is saturated perhaps only in spring and early summer, certain species of shrubs and trees may appear. Those that can tolerate waterlogged soil around their roots will be the pioneers. Various species of shrubby willows (*Salix*), dogwoods (*Cornus*), buttonbush (*Cephalanthus*), and other hydrophytic shrubs, propagating rapidly and through considerable distances by rhizomes, may form dense thickets. These, with alders (*Alnus*), tree willows, and cottonwoods (*Populus*), come to occupy more and more of the area. These woody plants react upon the habitat by producing shade and by lowering the water table both by further building up the soil and by vigorous transpiration. The drier, shaded soil is a very uncongenial place for sun-loving, sedge-meadow species, which gradually disappear, extending their territory into the zone of the receding reed swamp. Simultaneously, shade-enduring or tolerant herbs replace them, growing among the trees and shrubs.

Climax Forest.—As humus accumulates and the moist soil becomes filled with bacteria and fungi and other organisms which enrich it, many other trees may invade. Mixed forests of alder, willow, cottonwood, hackberry (*Celtis*), elm (*Ulmus*), ash (*Fraxinus*), oak (*Quercus*), and hickory (*Carya*) with their accompanying characteristic shrubs and herbs may result. But as the trees become denser in the drier, better aerated soil and the forest canopy more closed, many species, especially the pioneers, find difficulty in reproducing their kind since their seedlings are intolerant, *i.e.*, cannot grow in shade. After a few generations, only the most tolerant species may survive and a rather pure forest of oaks and hickories may develop. If the even more shade-enduring sugar maple and beech are present, they may replace the oaks. The sorting of the tree populations, however, has been no more marked than that of the herbs and shrubs. Plants of medium requirements for water (*mesophytes*) have replaced the hydrophytes. The subdominants of the climax-forest community are, moreover, all tolerant of shade. Their density, as well as their very existence, depends, in many cases, upon the control exerted upon the habitat by the dominant trees.

Thus, the area once covered by deep water becomes transformed into a forest, a phenomenon clearly conceivable when one follows the actual processes of development. The various stages—submerged plant, floating plant, reed swamp, sedge meadow, woodland, and climax forest—are merely cross sections of a continuous development made with reference to certain points where, because of more or less pure dominance, change is most apparent. This whole developmental process in action may be found about lake margins where each stage is shown as a definite zone. The stages in the present horizontal sequence from shallow water to marginal forest become arranged in a vertical sequence as the bottom of the lake is built up, forest forming the top stratum. In forests that have developed in undrained bogs, where largely because of deficient aeration the plant remains only partially decayed, borings have revealed a complete series from a forest community to submerged plants.[725]

To Study the Development of a Hydrosere.—Examine the shallow water and shores of lakes, ponds, or marshes for the characteristic plants of the hydrosere. Make a list of the dominants belonging to each stage of development. Examine the roots and rhizomes of some of the floating species if possible. How do the plants adjust themselves to different depths of water? What free-floating forms have you seen? Cut sections of the leaves and stems (including rhizomes) of cattail, bulrush, and other plants of the reed-swamp stage in the field and ascertain how they are adapted to live in wet soil with a deficiency of air about the underground parts. Are the rhizomes of the various species at the same level in the soil? Can you make out whether or not the roots are much branched? Do the plants all receive light at the same level? How are they adapted for growing so close together? Are there any relict or "left-over" reed-swamp plants in the sedge-meadow stage or other indications that the area was formerly wetter? Dig into the soil and see if you can find remains of reed-swamp species. Why do the dominants of sedge meadow grow in such dense clumps? Are they also adapted to grow in wet soil? Trace the succession from the wet meadow to the climax stage. The water level should be determined by digging holes in the soil occupied by the early medial stages, and the water content determined in each zone (p. 207).

A XEROSERE

Successions initiated on bare rock, wind-blown sand, rocky talus slopes, or other situations where there is an extreme deficiency of water are termed *xerarch*, and the different stages of development constitute a *xerosere*. A xerosere occurring in the same climatic climax as a hydrosere will end in a similar mesophytic community.

Crustose-lichen Stage.—On the smooth surface of a bare rock, regardless of its kind, few plants are able to become established owing to the extreme deficiency of water and nutrients, great exposure to the sun, and extremes of temperature to which they are subjected. Crustose lichens alone are usually able to grow in such situations. They flourish during periods of wet weather and remain in a state of desiccation for very long periods during drought. The fungus living parasitically upon the enmeshed terrestrial algae secures its carbohydrates from the host which, in turn, is protected by the crustlike fungus growth from extreme drought.

The rapidity with which these sponge-like organisms absorb water from rains as well as the large amount they can retain may be shown by dropping water upon them from a pipette. Mineral nutrients are obtained by the secretion of carbon dioxide which with water forms a

weak acid that slowly eats into the rock into which the rhizoids sometimes penetrate for a distance of several millimeters. Nitrogen is
brought in by rain or by wind-blown dust. Thus, all the life requirements of these simple, crustlike species are met.[339]

Migration on to distant rocks takes place either by wind-carried
spores or lichen fragmentation, *i.e.*, *soredia*. Thus, species of *Rhizo-
carpon*, *Lecidea*, *Rinodina*, and *Lecanora* come to colonize these bare
areas and play an important part in converting the rock into soil. Not
only do they exert an influence at the contact of thallus and rock, but
also the corroding effect of carbonic acid and perhaps other secretions

Fig. 42.—Lichens and mosses on a granite boulder, showing the early stages of a xerosere.

extends beyond the thallus margins during moist weather. This permits
slow extension of the thalli or furnishes starting places for new ones
(Fig. 42). Thus, lichens help corrode and decompose the rock, supple-
menting the other forces of weathering, and by mixing the rock particles
with their own remains make conditions possible for the growth of other
vegetation. The rapidity with which a minute amount of soil will
form is controlled very largely both by the nature of the rock and by the
climate.[299] On quartzite or basalt in a dry climate, the crustose-lichen
stage might persist for hundreds of years.[190] But on limestone or sandstone in a moist climate, sufficient change to permit the invasion of
foliose lichens may occur within a lifetime.

Foliose-lichen Stage.—Foliose lichens, *i.e.*, those attached to the
substratum at a single point or along a single margin, appear as soon as a
little soil has accumulated (Fig. 43). On the more weathered portions
of the rock and in depressions or other slightly less exposed situations,

they slowly replace the crustose forms. Their expanding leaflike thalli may completely overshadow the latter. Thus, cut off from the source of light, the crustose species may die and decay. About the foliaceous invaders, water has a better chance to collect and to be absorbed, evaporation is greatly decreased, wind- and water-borne lichen fragments and dust particles lodge, and humus is more rapidly accumulated because of its less rapid oxidation. The acids produced by the living and decaying plants are constantly eating farther into the rocks. Indeed, it is probable that the change from crustose to foliose lichens is a change of habitat as great as happens anywhere in the sere, although too minute in extent to be impressive. After the crustose forms give way to various foliose

Fig. 43.—A foliose lichen (*Gyrophora*) growing on a rock. (*Photograph by Fink.*)

species (such as *Dermatocarpon*, *Parmelia*, *Umbilicaria*, and others), a new type of invader appears.[279]

Moss Stage.—As soon as sufficient amounts of soil have accumulated in the minute crevices and depressions in the rock, xerophytic mosses begin to appear. These are commonly species of black moss (*Grimmia*), hair moss (*Polytrichum juniperinum*, *P. piliferum*, *P. commune*), and twisted moss (*Tortula*). They may have migrated long distances by wind-blown spores. Their rhizoids compete with those of the foliose lichens for water and nutrients and the erect stems often exceed the latter in height. The power of withstanding desiccation is almost as marked among these pioneers as among the lichens.[594] They and the more exacting foliose species may occur simultaneously, or, indeed, the mosses may sometimes precede foliose lichens.[183]

Soil rapidly accumulates among the erect stems as the plants, dying below but continuing growth above, build up the substratum and constantly increase their area. The depth of soil under the cushionlike moss mats, often an inch or more, contrasted to the thinner layer under the foliose lichens and the hard substratum under the crustose forms can best be realized by inserting a knife blade into a rock surface occupied by each. Sometimes, fruticose lichens, especially *Cladonia* and *Stereocaulon*, with the mosses overtop the foliose forms which are unable successfully to compete with the invaders. At the same time that they yield to the mosses, they more completely invade the area of the crustose forms. Frequently, all three stages may be found on a single rock surface, the pioneers occupying the most exposed places.

Herbaceous Stage.—The soil-forming and soil-holding reactions of the mosses are so pronounced that the seeds of various xerophytic

Fig. 44.—Early herbaceous stage of a xerosere. The plants growing in the shallow, rocky soil are a drought-enduring bluegrass (*Poa*), knotweed (*Polygonum*), and woolly plantain (*Plantago*).

herbs, especially short-lived annuals, are soon able to germinate and the plants to mature, although the first generations, because of the drought and sterility of the soil, may make only a stunted growth. Their roots continue the process of corroding the rock, and each year the humus from their decaying remains enriches the soil. Gradually, biennials and perennials begin to invade, ever increasing in numbers as the habitat becomes more congenial (Fig. 44).

The processes of rock disintegration and humus and nutrient accumulations are greatly accelerated as the tangled network of roots increases and the soil becomes shaded. Evaporation and temperature extremes are decreased, humidity slightly increased, and drought periods shortened.

The bacterial, fungal, and animal populations of the soil increase and conditions gradually become less xeric. The intensely xerophilous, shallow-rooted wire grass, poverty grass, and dwarfed specimens of bluegrass (species of *Aristida*, *Festuca*, and *Poa*) with mullein (*Verbascum*), alumroot (*Heuchera*), and rock ferns are supplemented in their invasion by many drought-enduring mustards, cinquefoils (*Potentilla*), goldenrods (*Solidago*), and many others. The reactions brought about by the new community, especially the reduced light, are distinctly detrimental to the mosses and fruticose lichens which gradually become fewer in number.

Shrub Stage.—On the soil thus prepared by the pioneer lichens, mosses, and herbs, woody plants find conditions possible for growth. Shrubs may start from seed or invade from adjacent areas by rhizomes. In such invasions, snowberries (*Symphoricarpos*), sumac and poison ivy (species of *Rhus*), and ninebark (*Physocarpus*) often dominate. Thickets of leafy shoots from the underground tangle of rhizomes overtop and shade the herbs, and, when the shrubby growth becomes sufficiently dense, the former possessors of the land find the habitat so modified that growth becomes almost or quite impossible. The herbaceous population largely disappears. Among the numerous stems, the falling leaves find lodgment and wind-blown snow accumulates. Massive networks of roots fill the soil. The deepest of these continually corrode the rocks and pry open their pores and crevices. Wind movement is retarded and humidity is higher above the decaying leaf mold covering the shaded soil, from which surface evaporation is greatly reduced. All these conditions, coupled with the enriched soil with its greater capacity for holding water, furnish an excellent nursery for tree seedlings, and trees may now begin to appear.

Climax Forest.—The first species of trees are relatively xeric. The pioneers are widely spaced, and the hard conditions of life are reflected in their stunted growth. But as weathering processes continue and the soil deepens, trees increase in both number and vigor. A forest of bur oak and bitternut hickory may develop. With increasing shade, the light-demanding shrubs fail and other more tolerant and mesophytic ones replace them under the protection of the leafy tree canopy. A new herbaceous vegetation develops in the forest shade, indicating a more humid atmosphere and a moister and richer soil than had heretofore prevailed. This is quite in contrast to the once bare rocks.

The accumulated mold of generations of forests worked over by an ever increasing host of soil organisms furnishes a more constantly moist soil and other conditions favorable to a more mesophytic forest. The bur oak–bitternut hickory forest may be replaced by the red oak–shellbark hickory community. Once established, the invaders become controlling. Their shade is so dense that the bur-oak and bitternut-hickory seedlings grow poorly or die. Only tolerant species, such as ironwood (*Ostrya*) and elms (*Ulmus*), can live in this new forest. Once more the shrubby and herbaceous populations shift, the less tolerant following the former community in its invasion of the shrubs. The most tolerant, supplemented by other invading mesophytes, constitute the layers of the climax mesophytic forest.

Thus, in the xerosere as in the hydrosere, the habitat has changed from one of extreme to one of medium water relations, and the vegetation, at first adapted to xeric or hydric conditions, respectively, has developed into a mesophytic forest. The climax forest may be dominated by hard maple and beech if the climate is conducive to the growth of these trees; or it may be characterized by Engelmann spruce and alpine fir if the succession occurs at the higher elevations in the Rocky Mountains.

To Study the Development of a Xerosere.—Examine the development of vegetation on a rocky ledge or other outcrop or on very thin, stony soil, etc. Determine the power of the crustose lichens to absorb and hold water when it is dropped upon them. Is there any evidence that they are increasing their area of occupation? Find places where foliose lichens are replacing them. By scratching the rock with a knife blade, determine the depth of loosened materials under crustose and foliose lichens and under xeric mosses that have replaced them. Determine the power of the cushion of moss to absorb and hold water. What parts of the moss plants are alive? Where do the pioneer herbs first appear? Make a list of some of the most important ones. Does the sere end in grassland or is there a shrub stage? What are the most important shrubs? How do they propagate? Examine their underground parts in relation to the underlying rock. Trace the succession to the climax of the region. Determine the water content in each stage of the sere where sufficient soil occurs to afford representative samples, discarding all large rock particles.

FURTHER STUDIES OF SUCCESSION

In the preceding paragraphs the outlines of processes that require long periods of time for their completion have been sketched, the successions on rocks usually being longer than those in water.[486] Moreover, only two typical successions have been outlined. Others occurring in sand, in bogs, and elsewhere will now be considered together with certain other phenomena fundamental to an understanding of this developmental process.[189]

Viewpoints of Succession.—The successive waves of plant populations —crustose lichens, foliose lichens, mosses, herbs, shrubs, and trees— each, in turn, holds possession of a habitat and produces its profound influences upon it. Beginning slowly, increasing to a maximum, and then gradually receding, the plant populations of each have made conditions fit for the next community but often less fit for their own continuation. This is true for both hydrosere and xerosere. This is one viewpoint of succession. The process may also be viewed as a change of life forms,[304] the lichen life form being replaced by the higher type of moss life form, and this by the herb, shrub, and tree in regular sequence. Fixing attention on the changes in the habitat, one finds the rock becoming less and less dry, the lake area with a diminishing water content, both approaching the medium condition of mesophytism. A study of vegetation as a developing organism comprehends all three points of view in a connected whole.

Other Successions on Rock.—Xeroseres do not always occur in the exact sequence described. On talus slopes, for example, the interstices between the coarse, loose rock fragments may furnish a habitat in which the seeds of herbs or even shrubs or trees may germinate and the

FIG. 45.—Succession on a gravel slide in the Rocky Mountains. The most important species are a parsley (*Pseudocymopterus*) and a borage (*Krynitzkia*) in the foreground.

seedlings successfully ecize (*i.e.*, make a home). This happens long before the lichens and mosses on the rock surfaces have had sufficient time to form even a thin soil. The rapidity of colonization and development, aside from climate, depends, in part, upon the nature and degree of the physical and chemical erosion of the rock fragments and partly upon how much humus is carried down by the rain from the decaying surface vegetation. On a talus slope composed of fine gravel intermixed with coarse sand, succession is rapid.

Herbs usually play the pioneer role, binding the loose soil, forming mats on its surface, adding humus, and otherwise producing a suitable habitat for shrubs and trees (Fig. 45). Vast areas in the mountains are regularly forested in this way, gravel slide with its sparsely placed herbs giving way to grass- and herb-covered half-gravel slide into which shrubs invade only to be replaced later by forests of pine, fir, spruce, etc., depending upon climatic control.

A shrub or heath community may result from several types or lines of succession which converge into it. Not infrequently, while crustose and foliose lichens are aiding in weathering the rock surface, fruticose lichens, mosses, and crevice herbs are forming humus in the clefts of the rock, while in depressions on the same rock mass, where water stands part of the time, mats of sedges, etc., may flourish and similarly build up soil. Finally, the shrub vegetation of the rock surface coalesces with that of the crevices. The rock pool also adds its quota, mostly of similar species,

Fig. 46.—A falling tree exposing the substratum of boulders upon which vegetation has laid a deep blanket, part of which is now a living mat of moss. (*Photograph by W. L. Bray.*)

all forming a dense mat of shrubby vegetation quite covering the rocky substratum[184] (Fig. 46).

Successions in Sand.—Extensive successional studies have been made on the sand dunes about Lake Michigan.[201,300] The prevailing westerly winds blow the beach sand into dunes which almost continuously fringe the eastern and southern borders of the lake. The vegetation, at first extremely xeric, culminates in a mesic maple-beech forest.

Extensive beach dunes cannot be formed, since one wind destroys what another builds, unless the plants, which are obstacles compelling the wind from the lake to deposit its load, continually increase in size. Such plants must be pronounced xerophytes or be able to endure partial burial by the sand or continue to thrive when much of the sand has blown away and the underground parts are partially exposed.

Embryonic Dunes.—The most successful dune formers are marram grass (*Ammophila*), wheat grass (*Agropyron*), sand reed (*Calamovilfa*), willows (*Salix*), sand cherry (*Prunus*), and cottonwoods (*Populus*). All have great powers of vertical elongation as the sand piles up about them and some of the grasses and shrubs propagate extensively by rhizomes which, with the tangle of roots, bind the sand. The dunes may reach a height of 10 feet or more (Fig. 47).

In low places where the wind blows the sand away to near the water level, cottonwoods may germinate and grow rapidly forming a new

Fig. 47.—An embryonic dune with the sand reed (*Calamovilfa longifolia*) holding the sand. (*Photograph by G. D. Fuller.*)

obstacle for the wind-blown soil. No vegetative propagation takes place nor can new individuals start in the dry sand. Cottonwood dunes are consequently the highest and steepest. The trees may become almost buried but are still able to survive.

Wandering Dunes.—As the embryonic dunes become larger and higher, conditions for sand accumulation become more favorable. But the dune-holding plants have grown farther from the water level each year. Cottonwoods are relatively short-lived and no new trees can replace the old ones, once the dune is formed. Gradually, the wind begins to reshape the dune, the plants lose their hold, and the dune begins to wander. The wind blows the loosened sand into great dunes or series of dunes which have a long, gentle slope toward the lake but a steep leeward side. It sweeps up the windward slope carrying or rolling the sand along until the crest is reached, when the sand rolls down the leeward side. The crest of dunes is often higher than the forests over which they may slowly but irresistibly advance (Fig. 48). They move forward only a few inches or, at most, a few yards each year but always forward.[204] The old vegetation is entirely covered, but as the dunes advance the remains of buried forests may be uncovered.

Arrested Dunes.—Vegetation appears to be unable to capture a rapidly moving dune, although xerophytes may grow upon it. But as the dune wanders farther from the lake, perhaps a mile or more, the force of the wind is decreased, usually by other dunes being built up between it and the beach. Vegetation commonly gets its first foothold at the base of the lee slope about the outer margin of the dune or dune complex.

Fig. 48.—Advance of a dune over forest and swamp, Dune Park, Ind. (*Photograph by G. D. Fuller.*)

Here there is abundant soil moisture as well as protection from the wind. Plants may creep up the slope by vegetative propagation. Marram grass and other xeric pioneers are among the first to appear. They are followed by a dense growth of shrubs, dogwood (*Cornus*), willows (*Salix*), choke-cherry (*Prunus*), and grape (*Vitis*). A mesophytic forest dominated by linden (*Tilia*) rapidly replaces the shrubs but is, in turn, replaced by the climax maple and beech.

On the long windward slopes, which make up about nine-tenths of the dune area, the succession is quite different, probably owing to the action of the drying winds. The pioneer herbs of the embryonic dunes, many of which grow on the shifting dune complex, are succeeded by a shrub stage, consisting largely of xeric evergreens especially shrubby and prostrate junipers (*Juniperus*) and bearberry (*Arctostaphylos*). Conditions become less severe under cover of the shrubs, and a coniferous forest develops. Jack pine (*Pinus banksiana*) is usually the first tree to appear. It may be followed by red pine (*P. resinosa*) or the latter may be the pioneer where the jack pine is absent They are succeeded by climax forests of white pine (*P. strobus*) in the Great Lakes forest formation. In the deciduous forest climax the white pines are replaced by oaks. Black oak (*Quercus velutina*) commonly appears first, but it is succeeded by forests of white oak (*Q. alba*). Finally, the sere culminates in a maple-beech climax.[302]

Succession on River Bars.—When sand or silt is deposited in a river as bars or islands, colonization and succession usually occur rapidly. This is due to relatively favorable soil. Trees with light, wind-blown seeds or fruits, such as willows and cottonwoods, are often the pioneers. These are regularly followed, if the island is built up, by more tolerant species such as elms, ashes, linden, etc., in the development toward the climax forest.

Succession in Bogs.—The hydrosere in bogs is different from that in ponds and lakes. A bog is an area of wet, porous land of which the soil is composed principally of partially decayed vegetable matter so loosely consolidated and containing so much water that the surface often shakes or quakes when one walks on it.[226a] Bogs are different from ponds and lakes in being undrained. This results in deficient aeration and the concomitant conditions of a poor bacterial and fungus flora and, often, of acidity. Bogs are most abundant in the glaciated portions of the north temperate zone where precipitation is great and regularly distributed, evaporation low, runoff small due to undrained glacial basins, and where a rather long summer season affords conditions conducive to vigorous growth.[320,531]

The earlier stages of submerged and floating plants may be quite the same as for ordinary swamps, but medial and later stages are different. Instead of a process of filling up the depression, the bog is usually bridged over with a mat of vegetation which culminates in a forest. The third stage in development usually consists of a floating sedge mat which grows inward from the periphery of the bog over the open water. This is composed of various sedges, *e.g.*, *Carex filiformis*, rushes, etc., usually with much-branched, light, buoyant rootstocks. A tangle of roots arises from the nodes and extends into the water. Each year the mat extends farther outward, as new shoots grow from rhizome tips, and its older parts increase in thickness. Where the floating mat has reached a thickness of 18 to 24 inches, it may even support the weight of a man.[329] Sometimes the water willow (*Decodon*) plays a similar role.

Various mosses, especially peat mosses (*Sphagnum*), find excellent conditions for growth about the moist tufts of sedges, etc. They retain water like an enormous sponge, dying below and growing above. Numerous shrubs such as cranberries (*Vaccinium*), leather leaf (*Chamaedaphne*),

Labrador tea (*Ledum*), poison sumac (*Rhus*), and bog rosemary (*Andromeda*) are characteristic of the subsequent stage. These are accompanied by numerous herbaceous species among which are pitcher plants (*Sarracenia*), sundews (*Drosera*), orchids, various ferns, buckbean (*Menyanthes*), and many others.

Succeeding the shrubs are characteristic swamp trees such as tamarack (*Larix laricina*), black spruce (*Picea mariana*), and white cedar

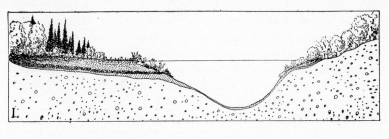

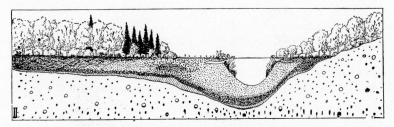

Fig. 49.—Diagram illustrating stages in the origin of peat deposits in lakes from open water with submerged plants to the climax forest. (*After Dachnowski. Reproduced by permission from Geological Survey of Ohio, Bull.* 16.)

(*Thuja occidentalis*). In the Great Lakes forest, white pine is the climax stage (Fig. 49).[219]

Variation in Stages and Dominants.—A study of succession in many lakes and ponds or on numerous rock outcrops, etc., shows that variations occur in the number of stages as well as in the dominants of a given stage.[153] In the seres just outlined, the usual stages have been described and representative dominants have been used to illustrate each stage. Some reed swamps may be entirely dominated by wild rice (*Zizania*), just as certain rock ledges may be clothed with a xeric herbaceous vegetation that may include none of the preceding communities. But the general sequence of stages is the same whether the succession occurs in Maine or in New Mexico.

Seres on primary areas, *i.e.*, those previously unoccupied by plants, are designated as primary or *priseres;* those on secondary areas such as lumbered, burned, flooded, or otherwise denuded ones are termed *subseres.* Since soil is already formed in subseres and germules usually on the ground, succession nearly always takes place much more rapidly. Usually, only the middle (medial) and final stages need be repeated. Succession after lumbering in a deciduous forest may consist simply of a shrub stage followed by the climax forest which has reproduced by sprouts from the bases of the stumps. In burned, coniferous forest, a liverwort-moss stage may be quickly replaced by one of herbs and this, in turn, after only 2 or 3 years, by shrubs, which are soon followed by trees.[862] Thus, the number of stages varies greatly. In subseres there may be only 3 or 4 or fewer. Among priseres, the number is usually greater, sometimes 10 or more.

The initial stages of primary seres are marked by extreme physical conditions and by correspondingly specialized life forms. Such primary areas as open water, rock, dune sand, etc., occur throughout the world. The life forms produced by them are likewise universal and are usually highly mobile. Consequently, the pioneer aquatics of water areas, the lichens and mosses of rocks, the xeric grasses of dunes, and the halophytes of salt areas consist of much the same species throughout the Northern Hemisphere. Hence, the initial stages of water, rock, dune, or saline seres may be nearly or quite identical in widely separated regions. Some of the medial and the final stages of each are determined by the particular climatic climax under which they occur. From the extreme nature of primary areas and the plants in them, initial stages persist for a long time, largely because of the slowness of reaction and the incomplete occupation. Primary areas differ much in these two respects. The greatest duration is found in the initial stages of a rock sere. The stages of a water sere follow each other more rapidly, and those of a dune still more rapidly, though the extent of the area plays a part.

As a consequence of almost universal use and misuse by man, subseres in every possible stage of succession constitute the most abundant of all communities.[517] They occur most frequently in the form of the sub-climax (*i.e.*, next to the last stage), partly because this persists for a longer period than earlier stages and partly because it is quickly restored among trees and shrubs that form root sprouts, as well as among the closed-cone pines.[439] In regions long settled, subseres form practically the entire cover of vegetation, apart from cultivated fields, and even these exhibit the first stage after the annual harvest. Old fields, logged and burned areas, roadsides, and the roadbeds of railways furnish the great majority of subseral communities, but these are also typical of other kinds of disturbed places. In all instances, they possess definite indicator values, not only as to the agent and degree of disturbance, but likewise as to the course and rate of succession, and the possible methods and objectives in restoration.

In addition to the subsere, there exists a miniature succession or *serule*, which resembles it in some respects. This occurs in fallen logs, decaying stumps, leaf litter, bodies of dead animals, offal, etc. It comprises minute or microscopic organisms for the most part, especially bacteria, molds, pore and gill fungi, sow bugs, spiders, and insects. Such successions are characteristic of forest in particular, where they serve to return all fallen matter to the soil through the medium of decay and decomposition.

Classification of Seres.—Seres are classified primarily upon the water content of the initial area in which they develop. With priseres, the extremes are marked and the quality of the water content also frequently becomes controlling. Consequently, hydroseres in saline areas are distinguished as (salt) *haloseres*. Moreover, while the surface of rocks and of dune sand may be almost equally dry, the differences of hardness and stability result in very dissimilar seres. These are distinguished as (rock) *lithoseres* and (sand) *psammoseres*, respectively. In subseres, extreme conditions of water content are rare or they persist for a brief period only (Fig. 50). Hence it is sufficient to recognize but two subdivisions, hydrosere and xerosere.

Prisere
  Hydrosere
   Halosere
  Xerosere
   Lithosere
   Psammosere
Subsere
  Hydrosere
  Xerosere

A Study of Other Types of Succession.—If access can be had to gravel slides, sand dunes, river bars, road cuts or fills, etc., the successions should be worked out as fully as time permits. Subseres occurring in abandoned fields or gardens, cut-over areas, etc., should also be studied. Such seres may be found, at least in miniature, almost anywhere in disturbed places.

The Climax.—Developmental processes have been going on for so long a time that on soils long formed the major portions of the area are usually covered with the stabilized or climax vegetation. The initial and medial stages of succession may not be much in evidence. But they are found everywhere in sufficient abundance to give the complete story of the way in which vegetation has helped reduce into soil the solid rock of mountains, emerged ocean margins, or glacier-swept areas. In the rocky wastes of the mountains, on eroding cliffs and gravel-strewn talus slopes, this story is most vividly portrayed. The building of ponds, lakes, lagoons, and marshes into dry land, just as it is taking place today, has occurred on an enormous scale in the past. This is shown by accumulations of peat and earth-covered seams of coal.

While the general sequence of a sere is the same nearly everywhere, the degree to which it can develop, *i.e.*, the climax community in which it ultimately terminates, is determined by the climate. Had the hydrosere described (p. 60) occurred in the grassland climax of Dakota or Kansas, shrub and woodland communities would have been eliminated and the sedge-meadow stage would have given way to prairie. In the Pacific Coast forest climax, the xerosere would have passed from the shrub

Fig. 50.—Subsere alternes in New Mexico due to the removal of sod for adobe houses, showing three stages of a subsere.

stage to one of ponderosa pine followed by Douglas fir (*Pseudotsuga*) and tamarack (*Larix*) and possibly culminated ultimately in a forest of white cedar (*Thuja*) and hemlock (*Tsuga*).

While the climax is permanent because of its entire harmony with a stable habitat, the equilibrium is a dynamic one and not static. Superficial adjustments occur with the season, year, or cycle. Annuals of the desert may be present in millions one year and absent the next. During a year or series of years of unusual moisture or drought, certain dominant grasses may seem to prevail one season and another species or group the following year. But these modifications are merely recurrent or indeed only apparent. While change is constantly and universally at work, in the absence of civilized man this is within the fabric of the climax and not destructive of it. Man alone can destroy the stability of the climax during the long period of control by its climate. He accomplishes this by fragments in consequence of destruction that is selective, partial or complete, and continually renewed.[162,688]

Subclimax.—Every complete sere ends in a climax when a point is reached where the occupation and reaction of the dominants or dominant are such as to exclude the invasion of other dominants. Frequently, however, the climatic climax is not developed on all the areas within the climatic control. The development of vegetation may be arrested in the subfinal (next to last) stage of the succession as a consequence of repeated burning, cutting, grazing, flooding, and other causes. This imperfect stage of development, in which the vegetation is held indefinitely either by natural or by artificial factors, other than climate, is termed the *subclimax*.* It is the stage immediately preceding the climax in all complete seres, both primary and secondary. In contrast to the original climax areas, those occupied by subclimaxes are relatively small, the chief exceptions being those resulting from fire or from logging and fire combined. Subclimaxes are, however, often exceedingly numerous.

Subclimaxes of "jack pines" result from fire, or lumbering or clearing followed by fire. These are chiefly species with closed cones that open most readily after fire. For example, extensive subclimaxes of jack pine (*Pinus banksiana*) occur in the lake forest. Similar areas dominated by pure stands of lodgepole pine (*P. murrayana*) are frequent in the Rocky Mountains, while long-leaf pine (*P. palustris*) and loblolly pine (*P. taeda*) play a similar role in the "piney" woods of the Atlantic-Gulf states. The characteristic subclimaxes of the boreal forest are composed of aspen (*Populus tremuloides*), balsam poplar (*P. balsamifera*), and paper birch (*Betula papyrifera*), either singly or in various combinations. Aspen also forms a notable subclimax in the Rocky Mountains, for the most part in the subalpine forest.

Prisere subclimaxes are regular features of bogs and muskegs throughout nearly the entire extent of both boreal and lake forests. Where pines are absent in the region of the deciduous forest, post oak and blackjack oak may constitute a subclimax. Subclimaxes in grassland are composed largely of tall grasses, as tall marsh grass (*Spartina pectinata*) in true prairie and giant wild rye (*Elymus condensatus*) in mixed prairie. Chaparral constitutes a fire subclimax where it extends beyond its proper climatic limits into the montane or even subalpine zone. Woodland is frequently reduced to scrub by fire, and the scrub often persists wherever repeated fires occur (Fig. 51). Even where fires cease after the settlement of a region, scrub subclimaxes may persist for a long time

---

* Where development is arrested and held indefinitely at some earlier stage, it is defined as a *serclimax*, such as the Everglades of Florida, the cypress-gum swamps of the Gulf Coast, and the tule marshes of California.

because of the more or less complete removal of the forest. Long-continued overgrazing has reduced the portion of the mixed prairie, often designated as "short-grass plains," to an apparent subclimax, but actually a community resulting from disturbance, the mid-grass layer having almost entirely disappeared.

Preclimax and Postclimax.—The formations of a continent stand in a definite climatic relation to each other, best seen in miniature on the slopes of a high mountain range. An effective change in climate will cause each one to replace the next but without disturbing their essential arrangement. A shift in the direction of greater rainfall will permit the more mesophytic to replace the less mesophytic throughout the series, while a swing toward less rainfall will favor the more xerophytic com-

Fig. 51.—Chaparral subclimax in California due to fire. The pines are relicts of a former forest.

munity at each line of contact. For example, the woodland formation of the southern Rockies, consisting of junipers, pines, and oaks, lies above the grassland to which it is postclimax but below the montane forest of ponderosa pine and Douglas fir to which it is preclimax. Likewise, the alpine tundra of the high Rockies is preclimax to the subalpine forest below timber line. The latter is postclimax to the tundra but preclimax to montane forest which has the climate (water-evaporation-temperature complex) more favorable to growth.

This relationship is true not only for altitudinal distribution but also for latitude. At the onset of the glacial period the arctic tundra migrated southward, slowly replacing boreal forest. The boreal forest encroached upon the lake forest and the latter pushed far southward into the territory of the deciduous forest. With the retreat of the glaciers under the

influence of a warmer climate, the reverse movement occurred.   Thus
each of these formations plays a double role.   It is a preclimax to its
more mesophytic neighbor and a postclimax to its more xerophytic one.
This is true also of the associations of a formation.   Mixed prairie, for
example, is preclimax to true prairie but postclimax to the desert plains.
Under the fairly static conditions of a major climatic phase the movement
of climaxes or associations is only a potential one.   Studies of past
climates and community migrations show, however, that during moist
periods of long duration the deciduous forest extended far westward into
the grassland formation, which in turn encroached upon the deserts.
Conversely, during similar dry periods, deserts have encroached upon
grasslands, and the latter have advanced far into bordering forests.

   In order to understand the present distribution of plant communities,
the student of vegetation must know something of what has happened
in the past.   A unit of vegetation by itself represents but a segment of
the dynamic flow of processes.   The great climatic changes of the past
have everywhere left relict communities that bear either a preclimax or
postclimax relation to the surrounding climaxes of the present day.
These may occur either between climaxes or entirely within one or the
other.

   A relict is a community or fragment of one that has survived some
important change.   It often appears to be an integral part of the existing
vegetation.   Thus hemlock (*Tsuga canadensis*) constitutes relict groups
in the maple-beech forest of the eastern United States.[296]   Tall bluestems
(*Andropogon*) are relicts in the sand hills of Nebraska, and certain other
grasses are relicts in the desert scrub of Death Valley.   The term is also
applied to the individual or the species, as in successional stages, but in
nearly every case a community of some degree is concerned.   Relict
communities indicate the operation of a compensatory or protective
feature.   Compensation for reduced rainfall, in the case of the dry phase
of a great climatic cycle, may be provided by altitude, by northerly slope
exposure, or by sandy soil.   Elevation or a barrier may protect local areas
of vegetation from general flooding or lava flows, or modify the force and
direction of the wind which causes the drifting of sand or the running of
fire throughout the community as a whole.   Relicts may also be due to
human agencies such as fencing (exclosures), fire lines, etc., but by far
the greater majority of these are caused by topographic features such as
altitude, slope exposure, ridges, or valleys (Fig. 52).   For example,
deep narrow gorges of central western Oklahoma still harbor relict forests
of deciduous trees, of which sugar maple (*Acer saccharum*) may be the
chief dominant.   Likewise, paper birch (*Betula papyrifera*) has been
relict in deep canyons of northern Nebraska since the retreat of the ice
following glaciation.

Preclimax.—Preclimaxes are most clearly marked where two adjacent formations are concerned, such as prairie and forest. Examples are seen in the grassy "openings" and oak savannas of the deciduous forest, and in the so-called "natural parks" which are grassy areas along the margins of montane forest. They are also well developed on dry slope exposures in the Rocky Mountains. Here the compensation is afforded by a local climate due to more direct insolation; in the preceding examples usually by a sandy or rocky soil. Preclimaxes of desert shrubs have been left stranded in mixed prairie- and desert-plains grassland by the

Fig. 52.—Relict mixed prairie in eastern New Mexico.

recession of the last great dry phase of climate. Creosote bush and sagebrush are examples. Usually, however, these species have profited by the overgrazing of grasses to extend across a territory much larger than that in which they are now climax. These preclimaxes must be distinguished from subclimaxes. In subclimaxes, when the disturbing factor is removed, reaction of the vegetation leads to the entry of the climax dominants with a change in plant populations. In preclimaxes, compensation by local factors is rarely if ever to be overcome within the existing climate, short of man-made disturbance.

Within the same formation, the more xeric associations or consociations are preclimax to the less xeric ones. This is the general relation between oak-hickory and beech-maple associations of the deciduous forest; the oak-hickory occupies the warmer, drier sites, produced by insolation or type of soil, in the beech-maple forest.   In the montane forest of the Rocky Mountains, the consociation of ponderosa pine is preclimax to that of Douglas fir.   A similar condition recurs in all forests where there is more or less segregation of the dominants into consociations.

Postclimax.—Major examples of postclimaxes are provided by valleys, especially gorges and canyons, long and steep slope exposures, and by extreme soil types.   As a general rule, postclimax relicts are much more abundant than those that represent preclimaxes.   This is due, in part, to the large number of valleys, sand hills and sandy plains, and escarp-

Fig. 53.—Postclimax of scrub and woodland in the prairie climax in North Dakota.   The shrubs are buffalo berry and serviceberry; the trees, elm, ash, and bur oak.

ments in the grassland especially.   Postclimaxes of oak-hickory and their flood-plain associates, elm, ash, walnut, etc., are characteristic features of true and mixed prairies (Fig. 53).   They extend far westward in major valleys but are limited as outliers on ridges and sandy stretches near the eastern edge.   The compensation of the last two habitats is usually so incomplete that the postclimax is typically reduced to the savanna type.

The Cross-Timbers of Texas are postclimax on sandy soil surrounded by climax grassland.   A similar savanna forest occurs northward in Oklahoma, mostly consisting of post oak and blackjack oak.   With decrease of rainfall the trees dwindle at first to 4 or 5 feet in height and finally to dwarfs only "shin" high, known locally as "shinnery."   With these are associated tall grasses such as big bluestem, sand reed, etc., forming a postclimax in the mixed prairie. Farther northward the oaks are absent and the tall grasses form a typical postclimax that extends on sandy soil into Canada.

The compensatory influence of sand is still sufficient to permit an abundance of such low bushes as New Jersey tea (*Ceanothus*), lead plant (*Amorpha canescens*), sand sage (*Artemisia filifolia*), and *Yucca*, as well as depauperate hackberry and aspen. In the vast sand-hill area of Nebraska, the tall-grass postclimax attains its best development, which is assumed to reflect the climate when the prairies were occupied by the bluestems and their associates some millions of years ago. The gradual decrease of the rainfall to the present has led to the tall grasses finding refuge in all areas of edaphic compensation, not only in the sand but likewise on foothills and in valleys.

Postclimax savanna woodland is an almost universal feature where forest, woodland, or chaparral touches grassland. It results from the fact that shrinkage under slow desiccation, which has occurred since Cretaceous time, operates gradually upon the density and size of individuals. Thus, savanna is derived from the reduction of the aspen community of the boreal forest along the southern edge. On the western borders along the front ranges of the Rockies, postclimax savanna of pines extends outward along streams, escarpments, or plateaus with higher rainfall, far into the mixed prairie. Savanna is derived from the woodland or chaparral on the western and southern borders. Here mesquite (*Prosopis juliflora*) forms a widespread postclimax savanna that often resembles a true woodland climax.

Disturbance Climax.—The most frequent examples of this community result from modification or replacement of the true climax, either as a whole, as by cultivation, or in part, as in the practice of grazing. It may also result from a change in the direction of succession. Disturbance climaxes or *disclimaxes* are nearly always the result of disturbance by man or domesticated animals. In some cases disturbance and the introduction of alien species act together to produce a community with the general character of the original climax. This is well illustrated by the almost complete replacement of the bunch-grass prairie of California by wild oats and brome grasses (*Avena-Bromus* disclimax). A similar replacement by downy brome grass (*Bromus tectorum*) has taken place over large areas of the Great Basin. An even more striking phenomenon is the steadily increasing dominance of Russian thistle (*Salsola*) over range and crop land in the west. All cultivated crops, whether fields of rice, maize, alfalfa, or wheat, are to be regarded as disclimaxes.

The short-grass plains represent a reduction of the mixed prairie due to overgrazing, supplemented by periodic drought. Over most of this area, mid grasses, such as needle grass (*Stipa*) and wheat grass (*Agro-*

pyron), etc., are still in evidence, though often reduced in abundance and stature, but in some areas they have been practically eliminated. Similar though less extensive disclimaxes characterize short-grass pastures in true prairie and both pastures and ranges in the coastal prairie of southern Texas. The grasses concerned here are species of grama grass (*Bouteloua*), buffalo grass (*Buchloe*), and curly mesquite (*Hilaria*).

In mixed prairie, continued overgrazing results in the fragmenting of the short-grass sod and permits the dominance of prairie sagewort (*Artemisia frigida*) or snakeweed (*Gutierrezia*). Similar disclimaxes of sagebrush (*Artemisia tridentata*) in the west and southwest and creosote bush (*Covillea*) in the southwest result from grazing. "Towns" of prairie dogs and kangaroo rats often represent more or less extensive disclimaxes. In range lands disclimaxes of various species of cacti (*Opuntia*) occur widely, the plants possessing the double advantage of protective spines and ready propagation.

Other grass disclimaxes are produced the world over as a result of grazing, or of burning and grazing combined, and they persist just as long as these disturbances recur.[60,61,177] The range lands of the Wasatch Mountains in Utah pass through various stages of development, which culminate in a cover of wheat grasses (*Agropyron*) to constitute such a disclimax. Coniferous forest, preceded by chaparral, constitutes the true climax. When the cover of wheat grasses, which have formed a turf excluding most other plants, is broken by destructive grazing or otherwise, both deep-rooted and shallow-rooted species can successfully invade. Thus the yellowbrush-needle grass (*Chrysothamnus-Stipa*), which constitutes the *mixed grass and weed stage*, becomes established. Where the turf-forming wheat grass is permitted to redevelop, it again completely occupies the area, entirely replacing the yellowbrush and needle grass. So completely do the roots occupy the soil that practically all of the water is absorbed in the surface foot, and deeper rooted plants die. On the bunch type of wheat-grass land they may persist as subdominants.

Further overgrazing of the yellowbrush-porcupine grass community, which includes considerable bluegrass (*Poa*), fescue grasses (*Festuca*), and scattered stands of the relict wheat grasses, causes the invasion by a still earlier stage. This is characterized by brome grasses (*Bromus*), beardtongue (*Pentstemon*), sagewort (*Artemisia*), yarrow (*Achillea*), etc., and is designated as the *second or late-weed stage*. These invaders are turf-forming perennial weeds. Associated with them are various short-lived, perennial herbs, many of which propagate only by seed. Continued heavy grazing, which not only destroys the perennials but also permits soil erosion, depletion of humus, and heavy leaching of nutrients, results in a very open plant cover largely consisting of annual weeds.

Thus, the *first or early-weed stage* characterized by lamb's-quarters (*Chenopodium*), tansy mustard (*Sophia*) knotgrass (*Polygonum*), etc., replaces the second or late-weed stage.

By judicious range management the subclimax wheat-grass disclimax, which is especially well suited to the grazing of cattle and horses, may be indefinitely maintained. Slight overgrazing produces the highest type of development of the mixed-grass and weed stage which, because of its large variety of palatable plants, is probably the most desirable, all classes of stock considered, and especially so for sheep. Thus, the intensity of grazing determines the disclimax stage of development. The principle is applicable to pasture lands generally.[771]

Repeated flooding of lowlands makes conditions favorable to the growth of wild rice (*Zizania*) and many other hydric plants which furnish excellent food for wild ducks, geese, and other game. Such disclimaxes may be indefinitely maintained. In New England, disclimaxes of cranberry swamps may be maintained by properly regulating the water level with much more profit than permitting the natural development of forest. By judicious burning, blueberry scrub may be held as a disclimax.[640]

Selective cutting not infrequently initiates disclimaxes, as may the similar action of such other agents as epidemic disease. The most dramatic example is the elimination of the chestnut (*Castanea dentata*) from the oak-chestnut canopy, but of even greater importance has been the extreme reduction and fragmentation of the lake forest through the overcutting of white pine.

There is an increasing need for the experimental study of succession.[245] A thorough understanding of successional phenomena in forests, pastures, ranges, abandoned fields, etc., is of the utmost importance in properly pursuing the several lines of industry concerned and in conserving the national resources.

CHAPTER IV

THE UNITS OF VEGETATION

The climate over an extended area of land, such as a continent, is usually very diverse and conditions for plant growth correspondingly different. Distance from the ocean, differences in latitude and altitude, etc., all profoundly affect precipitation and temperature as well as other climatic factors. Vegetation responds by its distribution into groups, each of which is in close equilibrium with its particular climatic complex. Such major groups as forest, grassland, and desert have long been recognized.

The Formation.—The plant formation is the major unit of vegetation. It is a fully developed or climax community of a natural area in which the essential climatic relations are similar or identical. Each formation is a complex and definite organic entity with a characteristic development and structure. It is a product of the climate and is controlled by it.[154] The deciduous forest of the east, the coniferous forest of the Great Lakes region, the tundra of the far north, and the grassland of the central west are examples. Every formation is delimited by climate. The rainfall and evaporation of the Ohio Valley region are very different from those of the prairie plains. The temperature of forest-covered mountain slopes is quite unlike that of the alpine meadow above timber line. A climate marked by a moderately long, warm, fairly humid summer, which is favorable to trees with deciduous leaves, and by winters during which the surface soil is frozen and absorption retarded will be characterized by a deciduous forest.

While the greater portion of a climatic region is occupied by the climax vegetation characteristic of it, many areas in which new or denuded soils occur show various stages of development. In the deciduous forest climax, for example, marshes may be populated by cattails and dry ridges by shrubs. But these are only stages in the development of the vegetation. When the annually accumulating plant debris with its admixture of water- and wind-borne soil builds up the marshy lowland, trees will ultimately occupy the area, because the climate is congenial to trees. When the decaying roots, stems, and leaves of the shrubs, etc., add enough humus to cause the soil of the eroding ridge to hold more water, it too will become forested (Fig. 54).

Thus like other but simpler organisms, each climax has its own growth and development, in terms of primary and secondary successions. A formation arises, grows, matures, and finally dies. The formation, moreover, is able to reproduce itself, as may be seen after fire, lumbering, or other catastrophe to the vegetation. It also has evolved during geologic time out of a preceding climax, and with profound change in climatic control it will be replaced by a new formation.

This developmental point of view is exceedingly important, since it furnishes a dynamic working basis for the classification of vegetation.[642, 897]

Fig. 54.—A boulder in a coniferous forest of New York on which the soil blanket has become heavy enough to support approximately climax forest vegetation. (*Photograph by W. L. Bray.*)

Climaxes, however, are characterized by a high degree of stability to be reckoned in thousands or even millions of years. The midcontinental grassland climax evolved 20 to 30 million years ago as a consequence of change in climate resulting from the uplift of the Rocky Mountains. The deciduous forest climax is much older. Climaxes display superficial changes with the season, year, or cycle, but even successive years of abnormal rainfall or unusual temperatures have little or no permanent effect upon their composition and structure.

The major divisions or units of the vegetation of a continent are the highest expression of vegetation possible under a particular climate, grasses, sedges, and lichens in tundra, scattered shrubs in sagebrush desert, and dense jungles of trees, shrubs, and lianas in the tropics. Consequently, the formation is designated as a climax or climax formation.* The climax is not merely the response to a particular climate, but is at the same time the expression and indicator of this climate. The visibility, continuity, and fixed nature of the plant community are peculiarly helpful in indicating the fluctuating limits of a climate. The vegetation integrates the climatic factors and expresses them in terms of food manufacture, growth, and life forms.

Dominants.—The visible unity of the climax is due primarily to the dominants or controlling species. All of these belong to the same life form. In prairie and steppe this is the grass form, *i.e.*, the climax dominants are all grasses and sedges. Sedges are especially characteristic in tundra. The shrub life form characterizes the three scrub climaxes of North America, *viz.*, desert, sagebrush, and chaparral. The tree appears in three subforms, coniferous, deciduous, and broad-leaved evergreen, to typify the corresponding boreal, temperate, and tropical climates. Just as each stage in succession has its temporary or seral dominants, so too each formation has its climax dominants. Many are major dominants that range throughout and bind the associations of a climax; others are more or less closely confined to one association and hence characterize it, while still others are more limited and hence of lesser importance. Thus eight species of grasses, including blue grama (*Bouteloua gracilis*) and western wheat grass (*Agropyron smithii*), occur very widely in the grassland formation. White pine (*Pinus strobus*) occurred throughout the much decimated lake forest formation. Likewise, numerous oaks (red, black, white, bur, scarlet, and others) and many hickories (shellbark, mockernut, bitternut, and pignut) range more or less throughout the deciduous forest climax.

The dominants of related associations for the most part belong to a few common genera. There are a dozen species of needle grass variously distributed as dominants in the grassland, such as *Stipa spartea* in true prairie, *S. comata* in mixed prairie, and *S. pulchra* in the California prairie. In deciduous forest, oak (*Quercus*), hickory (*Carya*), and maple (*Acer*) are the great genera. Many species of the sage genus (*Artemisia*) occur in the sagebrush formation, and various species of firs (*Abies*) and pines (*Pinus*) are found in the associations of the subalpine forest. Thus, most of the dominant genera extend throughout the formation, although usually represented by different species.

Each formation is named after two of its most widely spread and important dominants. Examples are the cedar-hemlock (*Thuja-Tsuga*) or coast forest climax and spruce-larch (*Picea-Larix*) or boreal forest climax (Fig. 55). A complete list of the climaxes of North America is

---

* This term is occasionally used for emphasis, since climax and formation are exact synonyms. The word "climatic" is sometimes added for the same purpose, but as the root of the term indicates, every climax is climatic in nature.

given on page 481, and an idea of their relative extent may be gained by an examination of the Frontispiece.

More than a century ago when Lewis and Clark set out upon their memorable journey across the continent of North America (1803–1806), they were the first to traverse the great climaxes from deciduous forest in the east through the vast expanse of prairie and plain to the majestic coniferous forest of the northwest. At this time the oak-hickory woodland beyond the Appalachians was almost untouched by the ax except in the neighborhood of a few straggling pioneer settlements, and west of the Mississippi hardly an acre of prairie had known the plow. Nearly

FIG. 55.—Climax forest of Douglas fir (*Pseudotsuga taxifolia*) in Colorado.

the whole area of each climax was then occupied by the dominant species. With the advent of civilization, there followed great destruction of natural communities by fire, by lumbering, and by clearing land for cultivation. This has added greatly to the difficulty of drawing exact boundaries between formations. Such difficulties may be appreciated when it is realized that developmental studies have not yet determined whether or not all of the climatic areas are actually occupied by the type of vegetation which they may ultimately support. Part of the area covered by chaparral, for example, may have a forest climate, the trees being held in check by repeated fires. Sagebrush and desert scrub may exist under a grassland climate in part, the grasses having largely disappeared as a result of severe overgrazing during times of drought.

In delimiting climates and climaxes, the plant is the ultimate criterion, and climatic measurements must be interpreted in terms of plant growth.

From the human standpoint, eastern Washington and central Kansas possess distinct climates, but in terms of wheat production and grassland vegetation, they are very similar. Likewise, the winter in Saskatchewan is long and the summer short, while in Texas just the reverse is true. But the short growth-period of grama grass fits into the short summer of Saskatchewan as readily as it does into the early summer of Texas, with the result that this dominant covers large areas in both.

The Association.—Every climax formation consists of two or more major subdivisions known as *associations*. These are climax communities associated regionally to constitute the formation. The number of associations in a particular formation is naturally determined by the

Fig. 56.—Detail of the oak-hickory association. A society of May apple (*Podophyllum*) occurs on the forest floor.

number of subclimates within the general climate of the formation. Each association is marked by one or more dominants peculiar to it (Fig. 56). Often there are also differences in the rank and grouping of those dominants that range throughout the formation. For example, the portion of the grassland formation between the deciduous forest climax and the Rocky Mountains consists of true prairie in the best-watered eastern part, mixed prairie in the area of intermediate rainfall, and desert plains in the very arid southwest. Each of these constitutes a separate association. Two dominants of true prairie are *Stipa spartea* and dropseed (*Sporobolus heterolepis*); two of mixed prairie are needle grass (*Stipa comata*), and buffalo grass (*Buchloe dactyloides*); while grama grass (*Bouteloua rothrocki*) and triple awn (*Aristida divaricata*) are examples of dominants in the desert plains. Moreover, blue grama grass (*Bouteloua gracilis*), which ranges throughout these associations, is of very minor importance in true prairie but of major rank in the mixed prairie and of intermediate value in the desert plains. Ponderosa pine and Douglas fir constitute an association of the montane forest formation in the Rocky Mountains and sugar pine–white fir a second association in the Sierra Nevada–Cascades of the far west.

An association is similar throughout its extent in physiognomy or outward appearance, in its ecological structure, and in general floristic composition. To illustrate: The mixed-prairie association is similar everywhere in having an upper story or layer of mid-grass dominants and a lower one of short, mat-forming grasses. Needle grass, wheat grass, or June grass overtops the buffalo grass and grama grass or sedges of similar, low-growing habit. These, like many subdominant legumes, composites, etc., range throughout the association.

The Consociation.—Every association consists of several dominants, sometimes ten or more. In its typical form the consociation is constituted by a single dominant, but as a matter of convenience the term is also applied to areas in which other dominants are but sparingly present and hence have no real share in the control of the community. Thus, in true prairie a dominant such as little bluestem (*Andropogon scoparius*), needle grass (*Stipa spartea*), or wheat grass (*Agropyron smithii*), may control more or less exclusively or dominate an area to such an extent that it is far more important than any of the others. Accordingly, within the true prairie association there occur little-bluestem, needle-grass, and other consociations. It is convenient to refer in the abstract to each major dominant of the association as a consociation, though with the realization that it may occur more frequently in mixture than by itself (Fig. 57). In this sense it may be considered a unit of the association, though the actual area of the latter is to be regarded as divided into definite groupings of dominants or faciations.

The consociation is plainly expressed over a considerable area only when the habitat factors, especially water content of soil, fluctuate within the limits set by the requirements of a dominant. This is well illustrated by the consociation of ponderosa pine (*Pinus ponderosa*) in the lower part of the montane forest formation. In the Rocky Mountains, forests of nearly pure ponderosa pine occur over great areas; others support extensive forests of Douglas fir (*Pseudotsuga taxifolia*). These represent two consociations of the montane forest formation. The former extensive stands of nearly pure white pine (*Pinus strobus*) in the region of the Great Lakes were representative of the pine consociation of the pine-hemlock association. A consociation is also well demarked when the other dominants are not found in the region. An example is the Engelmann spruce (*Picea engelmanni*) consociation in the Front Range of Colorado, its usual associate, alpine fir (*Abies lasiocarpa*), being absent from the district. It sometimes happens that one dominant occupies an area so completely as to exclude the others simply because it invaded first, although the habitat was equally suitable to all.

The consociation dominants of an association fall into a more or less regular series as regards factor requirements, especially water content, and consequently often exhibit zonation. For example, in mixed prairie, western wheat grass (*Agropyron smithii*) often occupies swales and lower slopes, and needle grass (*Stipa comata*) the upper slopes and ridges. Likewise, in the rolling topography of the true prairie, each

Fig. 57.—Consociation of red oak (*Quercus borealis*).

dominant recurs constantly in the proper situation, little bluestem on the slopes, prairie dropseed or needle grass on the drier ridges and levels, and big bluestem on the lower slopes and well drained lowlands. Thus, each of these consociations is regularly fragmented in nature. Where areas of intermediate factor values occur, there is an intermingling of the dominants.

The Faciation.—This is the concrete subdivision of the association, characterized not by pure dominance but by the grouping of dominant or controlling species. Except for the fragments of the several consociations (where complete or nearly complete dominance of one species occurs) and for seral stages, the entire area of the association is composed of its various faciations (Fig. 58). On the Great Plains three of the several groupings of dominants that constitute faciations are needle grass-blue grama, needle grass-wheat grass-buffalo grass, and blue grama-buffalo grass. Each faciation corresponds to a particular regional climate of real but small differences in precipitation, evaporation, and temperature. In general, temperature appears to play the leading part in the arrangement of grassland faciations, since they really fall into a sequence determined by latitude or altitude. A similar disposition is seen in the three major faciations of the oak-hickory association, characterized respectively by a northerly, a southerly, and a central overlapping group of species of oaks.

The Society.—Within the area of vegetation under the control of a dominant or group of dominants, *i.e.*, within the consociation or faciation,

Fig. 58.—Faciation of *Stipa pennata* and *Hilaria jamesii*, Peach Springs, Ariz.

certain subdominant species may exert local control. The many-flowered psoralea (*Psoralea floribunda*) is often so abundant in the little-blue-stem consociation that for a time it overtops and almost obscures the grasses. The same is true of the daisy fleabane (*Erigeron ramosus*), ground plum (*Astragalus crassicarpus*), and numerous other forbs (Fig. 8). These local communities are called *societies*. A society is a community characterized by one or more subdominants, *i.e.*, species of different life form from those of the regional dominants. The latter strongly influence and sometimes largely determine, especially by shading, the rest of the species belonging to the association.

The species forming the society are very abundant over portions of an area already marked by the dominance of consociation or faciation. That is, the society is a localized or recurrent grouping of subdominants within a general dominance. In grassland, a society is usually conspicuous for only a part of the season. While the dominants such as needle grass, wheat grass, or buffalo grass are present and controlling at all times, *Psoralea*, *Erigeron*, and *Astragalus* are conspicuous and play an important role in vegetation only at certain times of the year. They are subdominant or subordinate to the grasses, depending largely on the factors, such as water content, in excess of that required by this dominant life form.

Societies in forests are found only beneath the primary layer of trees, and their subdominance is obvious. Their development and abundance are largely determined by the amount of available light and moisture. They may attain much prominence when the canopy is not too dense. Such societies as gooseberries, witch hazel, jack-in-the-pulpit, and strawberries are illustrative. In forest and woodland, societies consist of herbs, shrubs, and even species of small trees; in grassland, of forbs and half-shrubs. Particular societies are not confined to a consociation or faciation, but may occur widely throughout the association. They may extend more or less uniformly over wide stretches or be repeated wherever development or physical factors permit.

Two kinds of societies may be distinguished, one in seasonal *aspects*, the other in *layering*. The most casual observation shows that in a climate with well marked seasons, different species of an association make their most vigorous growth, flower, and fruit at different periods of the growing season. A little study reveals that the species tend to fall into rather distinct groups, the flowering of each group giving a distinct *aspect* to the association. Aspect societies are usually most conspicuous and best developed in grassland. Four distinct aspects occur in true prairie from early spring to autumn. Thus, in eastern Nebraska, certain sedges (*Carex*), prairie cat's-foot (*Antennaria*), and prairie windflower (*Anemone*) stand out conspicuously during April against the brown background of dry grasses and herbs. They constitute the early spring or *prevernal aspect*. Each species forms an aspect society. During May, the purple and blue of societies of ground plum (*Astragalus*), the massive cream-colored racemes of false indigo (*Baptisia*), and the bright yellow heads of *Senecio*, with many other spring or *vernal* societies, add tone to the landscape. But by June most of these have waned and the prairies until late July are characterized by extensive summer or *estival* societies of many-flowered psoralea (*Psoralea*), daisies (*Erigeron*), niggerhead (*Echinacea*), lead plant (*Amorpha*), rose, and many others. Then, again, the scenes are shifted. The purple of the *autumnal* societies of blazing stars (*Liatris*) is mixed with the yellows of goldenrods (*Solidago*) and sunflowers (*Helianthus*). These with the asters and numerous other species mark the end of the growing season.[976]

Seasonal aspects are determined primarily by the seasonal march of habitat factors, of which temperature and length of day are the most important. So far as the plants themselves are concerned, they may be in evidence throughout the entire growing season, but they give character to the matrix of vegetation only during the period of flowering. In grassland and desert, they are often more striking than the dominants themselves, sometimes owing to large size but chiefly as an effect of color and abundance. There are usually three aspects in mixed prairie and two major ones—those of winter and summer—in desert and desert plains. Both arctic and alpine tundra, because of the short growing season, usually exhibit but two aspects. In woodland the number and character

Fig. 59.—Layer society of dog's-tooth violet (*Erythronium*) in the early spring aspect of the oak-hickory forest at Lincoln.

of aspect societies depend largely upon the nature of the canopy. In deciduous forest the flowery aspect societies regularly belong to spring and autumn when foliage is either developing or disappearing (Fig. 59). Characteristic forbs of spring are bloodroot (*Sanguinaria*), spring beauty (*Claytonia*), dog's-tooth violet (*Erythronium*), violets (*Viola*), columbine (*Aquilegia*), squirrel corn (*Dicentra*), and many others. Autumnal societies include *Aster, Solidago, Eupatorium, Helianthus, Silphium, Verbesina,* and various other composites.

Layer societies are best developed in forest with a canopy of medium density. Under the most favorable conditions as many as five or six may be recognized. In such forests there are usually two stories of shrubs, an upper and lower, often much interrupted. Tall, medium, and low-forb layers occur, and below them a ground community of mosses and liver-worts, lichens and other fungi, and usually some delicate annuals. They are not usually continuous but more or less interrupted, largely depending upon the amount of light passing through and between the crowns of the trees and, in part, upon soil moisture and other factors. Because of the low light intensity, a single layer of low herbs alone may occur in climax forest, especially of conifers, and even this may be lacking in dense chaparral. Three layers of forbs occur in true prairie, one near the soil, a second at the midsummer level of the grasses or just above it, and a third, consisting of taller plants, which distinctly overtops the grasses. Layers are almost lacking among the widely spaced dominants of sage-brush and desert scrub, but otherwise occur in the majority of associations.

The units of climax vegetation are arranged below in their proper sequence or rank. Here are included the corresponding seral units, which characterize vegetation in the process of development towards the climax.

CLIMAX	SERAL
Climax or Formation	
Association	Associes
Consociation	Consocies
Faciation	Facies
Society	Socies
Aspect	Aspect
Layer	Layer
	Colony
	Family

The Associes.—The associes is the developmental equivalent of the association. This name is used where the community is not permanent but is replaced by another in the process of development or succession. A group of floating plants such as pondweeds, water lilies, and water shield form the associes of the floating stage. A community of cattails, bulrushes, reeds, etc., represent only a temporary stage of development, *i.e.*, the reed swamp or amphibious associes. As the pond shallows, they will be replaced by other kinds of plants. In the hydrosere of the decidu-ous forest, the typical stage just preceding the climax is that of the flood-plain associes (Fig. 60). It is composed of elm, ash, walnut, hackberry, sycamore, sweet gum, poplar, willow, etc. The swamp associes of the lake and boreal forests consists of tamarack, black spruce, and arbor-vitae. Following fires in the boreal and northern forests of the Rocky Mountains, the aspens and birches form associes covering thousands of square miles. Likewise, an associes of two or more species, such as dog-wood, sassafras, persimmon, papaw, witch hazel, cherry, black locust, etc., occurs widely in the deciduous forest area. On the flat, poorly drained lands of southwestern Ohio and southern Indiana in the developing maple-beech climax, the pin oak–red maple–sweet gum associes is the initial forest stage. It is followed by an intermediate associes of white oak–pin oak–shellbark hickory. The last developmental stage, just preceding the maple-beech climax, is the white oak–beech associes.[83] The subclimax of the deciduous forest xerosere is constituted for the most part of species of oak, forming an eastern, a southeastern, and a western associes.

FIG. 60.—An associes of walnut (*Juglans*) and elm (*Ulmus*) on a flood plain.

The Consocies.—In an associes (developmental association), each dominant may occur singly to form a consocies (developmental consociation). This often happens when the habitat offers just the proper conditions for it or when the other seral dominants have failed to reach the area. The reed swamp furnishes an excellent illustration. Thus, there occur vast areas of marshy land dominated almost entirely by bulrush, cattail, or reed. The bulrush thrives in the deepest water, cattails in intermediate depths, and the reed in the shallowest. Likewise, the floating associes may be represented over considerable areas by a single dominant or consocies of water lily, duckweed, or water hyacinth. Certain trees of the southeastern United States, such as bald cypress and tupelo gum, often dominate swamps in pure growth. Forest flood plains are locally dominated by elms, or willows, or walnut, each representing a consocies. The tamarack swamp of the northeastern states and Canada is a well known consocies, as are also the vast stretches of jack pine or aspen (Fig. 61). Abandoned fields in the forest-cleared areas of Oklahoma are rapidly claimed by a consocies of persimmon as are cut-over forests in Illinois and Iowa by hazel brush. Pin oak in almost pure stands, with a ground layer of sedge which is often covered by shallow water in spring, is an important consocies in the flat lands of Ohio and Indiana as is also red maple. Once the development of vegetation is understood, many dominants will be found to be relatively transient. For example, sand-binding grasses on dune areas which are being forested furnish examples of associes with their consocies, as does also the shrub stage which usually precedes the trees.

Fig. 61.—Consocies of aspen (*Populus tremuloides*).

The Facies.—This is the developmental unit of the associes character-ized, as is the faciation of climax vegetation, by the grouping of domi-nants. In a habitat of considerable range of factors—depth of water in a swamp, for example—various combinations of two or three dominants constitute facies. Sedge swamps of cattail and bur reed or of bulrush and wild rice are examples. Pondweed and floating smartweed, water shield, and spatter dock are examples of facies in the floating associes. Groupings of elm–ash–walnut, box elder–poplar–willow, and sweet gum–sycamore are facies of flood plains and poorly drained lands. Facies of sumac (*Rhus*), blackberry (*Rubus*), and *Sassafras*, or of persimmon (*Diospyros*) and *Sassafras* are common about margins and openings in deciduous forest. Two well marked facies of the oak-hickory preclimax are post oak–blackjack and bur oak–shellbark hickory, the two groupings forming the western associes.

Seral terms apply to postclimax vegetation as well as to preclimax. For example, in the sand hills of Nebraska certain tall grasses such as sand hill's bluestem, big bluestem, Indian grass, sand reed, tall panic grass, etc., form various groupings or facies in the mixed-prairie climate. Likewise, a consocies of big bluestem extends far up the moist valleys of mixed prairie. The mesquite-acacia associes illustrates the invasion of trees into the grassland climate of the arid southwest, as a result of breaking the hold of the grasses by continued overgrazing.

The Socies.—Societies of developmental communities, such as arrowheads, water plantain, lobelias, or mints in reed swamp, are termed socies. Communities of phlox, buttercups, and water leaf (*Hydrophyllum*) in

Fig. 62.—Socies of an evening primrose (*Anogra albicaulis*) in a fallow field.

forests on flood plains or poorly drained till plains are properly designated as socies, a term which at once denotes temporary instead of permanent subdominance. Seral societies are often poorly developed in the initial stages of both hydrosere and xerosere, where the dominants are relatively few. In medial and subfinal stages they may equal the climax communities in abundance and development. For example, the tall-grass associes of sand hills is often quite as rich in socies as is the climax true prairie in societies. Likewise, the preclimax stage of the several great forest types may equal the latter in the wealth of subdominants of each season and layer, and the actual communities are often very much the same. Many ruderals (weeds) form socies on roadsides, and in fields and pastures (Fig. 62). Bindweed (*Convolvulus*), smartweeds (*Polygonum*), and foxtails (*Setaria*) are examples in cultivated soil, ragweeds (*Ambrosia*), marsh elders (*Iva*), and goosefoots (*Chenopodium*) in waste places, and ironweeds (*Vernonia*), goldenrods (*Solidago*), and vervains (*Verbena*) in overgrazed pastures.

The Family.—In nearly bare or recently populated areas such as railway embankments, alluvial deposits, abandoned fields, etc., the vegetation frequently consists of groups of individuals belonging to a single species. Such a community of ragweeds, sunflowers, stinging nettles, etc., where all the individuals belong to a single species, is a family (Fig. 63). While the family often springs from a single parent plant,

Fig. 63.—A family of knotweed (*Polygonum majus*) on a talus slope.

this is not necessarily so. It may consist of only a few individuals or it may extend over a large area as Russian thistles in abandoned fields during very dry years. The family, however, is usually a small unit and is especially typical of early stages of development, rarely being found in stabilized vegetation, except where local disturbance has occurred, *e.g.*, a family of wire grass (*Aristida*) on a gopher mound, or of *Marchantia* or *Funaria* in the ashes from a brush pile.

The Colony.—As the individuals of a family become more numerous, usually adjacent families merge, or germules from one family may invade another at some distance. Sometimes two or more species may enter a bare area simultaneously. In either case, such an initial community is termed a colony (Fig. 85). Colonies are practically always a consequence of invasion and, therefore, like families, are characteristic of early vegetational development. Colonies of ruderals occur in neglected gardens or on lowlands subjected to periodic overflow, colonies of sand binders on wind-formed dunes, and colonies of fireweed (*Epilobium*) and hair grass (*Agrostis hiemalis*) are frequent in burned woodland, etc. Usually they are easily identified, since they occur in bare areas or open vegetation. When they occur in stabilized vegetation, it is usually where a small bare area permits invasion. If two or more invaders populate the bare area, the community is a colony; if only one, it is a family. While a clean field of corn represents a family, a weedy one is a colony. Both family and colony are developmental and no corresponding climax units occur.

To Outline the Major and Minor Communities of a Region.—After a number of field trips in which examples of each unit of vegetation have been examined, make a summary list of the plant formations and associations visited, the associes studied, and typical consociations and consocies observed. What are some of the more important societies? Name some developmental societies or socies encountered. What species form families and colonies in the region and under what conditions?

The Study of Communities.—It must not be supposed that one can distinguish the units of vegetation of any given area offhand or by superficial examination. The major difficulty in the analysis of vegetation is its great complexity, but it discloses a definite pattern when analyzed from the developmental point of view. The study of a local area of vegetation should always be supplemented so far as is feasible by examining that of adjacent regions. Only in this way is it possible to gain a broad viewpoint for a proper interpretation of the local communities. Until sufficient examination has been made by means of ecological methods to warrant placing any area of vegetation in a particular formation, association, or faciation or to designate certain parts as families, colonies, or societies, each should be called a community, a term which implies no definite rank. Moreover, all ecological investigators have not given the same rank to equivalent units of vegetation. This has resulted often from the limited area studied, *i.e.*, its relations to adjacent major units were not determined, or sometimes from the fact that the studies were made in transitional areas. Moreover, in countries long occupied by civilized man, the natural vegetation is represented by the merest fragments.

There are seldom sharp lines of demarcation where one of the communities of higher rank merges into another. They usually overlap forming a mixed community. Such transitional areas are termed *ecotones*. In level country where conditions are fairly uniform, *e.g.*, between true and mixed prairie, the ecotone may be broad and indefinite. But on mountains or steep hillsides or in the associes of saline areas, or about lakes or ponds, etc., communities may be very definitely delimited. By careful and extensive study, it is always possible to analyze the vegetation of a region, and to determine its natural communities and their dynamic relationships. A study of the mass of vegetation making up the community, called *synecology*, necessarily focuses attention upon the individual species of which it is composed. It is one of the best ways of suggesting the most important problems presented by the component species, *i.e.*, problems of *autecology* or the ecology of the individual.[176,416,617] However, neither species nor community can be understood by itself but only in relation to other species and adjacent communities.

Finally, it should be emphasized that an understanding of the natural relationships of the vegetation, together with a knowledge of the environment, and the structure, and indicator significance of each community, furnishes a fundamental background for determining its proper uses or the use of the land it occupies for grazing, farming, forestation, conservation, wild life, or other economic practice.

CHAPTER V

INITIAL CAUSES OF SUCCESSION

Having gained a general view of succession, the universal process by which formations develop, the causes may now be studied somewhat in detail. The development of a climax formation consists of several essential processes. Every sere must be initiated and its life forms and species selected. It must progress from one stage to another and finally must terminate in the highest stage possible under the climatic conditions present. Since succession is a series of complex processes, it follows that there can be no single cause for a particular sere.

The processes causing succession may be distinguished as initiating or *initial causes*, continuing or *ecesic causes*, and stabilizing or *climatic causes*. Initial causes produce the bare area or destroy the original population in areas already vegetated. The deposition of sediment as alluvial fans at the mouth of a river illustrates the former; and the wandering sand dune covering a forest, the latter. Ecesic causes produce the essential character of vegetational development, *i.e.*, the successive waves of plant populations. They have to do with the interaction of vegetation and habitat and are directive to the highest degree. Climatic causes determine the nature of the climatic climax, *i.e.*, where the succession will end. They likewise have a profound effect in determining the population from beginning to end, the number and kinds of stages, as well as the reactions of the successive stages. While the process of succession in the tropics is similar to that in temperate regions, the plant populations are often very different. Clearly this is due to climate.

Initial causes of succession are those which produce a new or denuded soil upon which invasion is possible. Seres originate only in bare areas or in those in which the original population is partially or wholly destroyed. It is a universal law that in all bare places new communities arise, except in areas which present the most extreme conditions of water, temperature, light, or soil. Of these there are few. Even fields of ice and snow show algal pioneers, rocks in the driest deserts bear lichens, caves contain fungi, and all but the saltiest soils permit the entrance of halophytes. From the standpoint of succession, water is the most important of bare habitats, and it is almost never too extreme for plant life. Seaweeds grow and fruit abundantly in arctic waters at temperatures of about 32°F., and various algae invade hot springs where the temperatures are as high as 180°F.

Habitats are either originally bare or bare by denudation. The former are illustrated by water, land produced by rapid emergence, such as islands, continental borders, etc., lava flows, deltas, and dunes. Denuded habitats arise in the most varied ways and are best exemplified by bad lands, flooded areas, burns, and fallow fields. The essential difference between the two is that the originally bare area has never borne a plant community and is, therefore, physically different in lacking the effects of reactions caused by successive plant populations. Not only must the initiating process produce a new area capable of promoting ecesis but it must also furnish it with physical factors essentially different in quantity at least from the adjacent area. Otherwise, the new area would quickly be controlled by the association at hand and soon made an intrinsic part of it.

Treated from the standpoint of the nature of the agent or process producing bare areas, the causes may be grouped as *topographic, e.g.,* erosion and deposit; *climatic, e.g.,* wind, fires caused by lightning, etc.; and *biotic, i.e.,* produced by man or other organisms.

Topographic Causes.—All the forces which mold land surfaces have one of two effects. They may add to the land or take away from it. The same topographic agent may do both, as when a stream erodes in its upper course and deposits a delta at its mouth or undercuts one shore and forms a mud bank or sand bank along the other. In similar fashion, a glacier may scoop out a pond or a lake in one region and deposit the material as a moraine in another. The wind may sweep sand from a shore or blowout and heap it up elsewhere, or it may carry dust from dry lake beds or flood plains for long distances and pile it in great masses of loess. Gravity in conjunction with weathering removes the faces of cliffs and accumulates the coarse material in talus slopes at the base.

Bare Areas Due to Erosion.—The chief topographic causes producing bare areas are erosion and deposit. Erosion is the removal of the soil or rock by the wearing away of the surface of the land. The agents of erosion are water, wind, gravity, and ice (Fig. 64).

Important areas laid bare through erosion by water are gullies, ravines, valleys, sand draws, washes, flood plains, river islands, banks, lake shores, crests and slopes, and bad lands and buttes. In all, the success of initial invasion depends upon the kind of surface laid bare and the water content as determined by the surface, the slope, and the climate of the region. The form and nature of the area itself are unimportant except as they affect these factors.

Characteristic bare areas due to wind erosion are dunes and sand hills, particularly the blowouts. Related to these are the strands from which the dune sand is gathered by the wind, and the plains of rivers, lakes, and glacial margins from which sand hills and loess deposits have been formed. Abandoned fields are also subject to wind erosion.

Gravity produces bare areas by pulling down materials freed by weathering (Fig. 65). Crumbling and slipping are universal processes on

Fig. 64.—Erosion and deposit in a young ravine in the bad lands of Nebraska.

Fig. 65.—Bare areas due to the action of gravity, canyon of the Yellowstone River, Yellowstone National Park.

the steep slopes and crests of hills, along stream banks, lake shores, and seashores everywhere. Landslides in mountains as well as heavy snowslides often produce extensive bare areas. From their hardness, instability, or dryness and the steep or vertical faces, areas thus produced are usually among the slowest to be invaded.

Bare areas are produced on wind-swept shores by the grinding and pushing action of ice. Fine illustrations are to be found in the region of the Great Lakes. Bare areas are also formed along the margins of glaciers, usually in conjunction with water erosion. The extreme conditions which rock invaders must meet in the Rocky Mountains and Sierra Nevada are often the direct outcome of glacial scourings in the past.

Bare Areas Due to Deposit.—Bare areas are often due to deposit, the agents being running water, ground water, wind, glaciers, ice and snow, gravity, and volcanoes.

Among bare areas due to deposit by running water, flood plains and channel deposits such as sand bars and alluvial cones and fans are perhaps

Fig. 66.—Sand bars due to deposit in streams.   North Platte River in Nebraska.

most familiar (Fig. 66). Other deposits such as deltas and beds of lakes are often extensive. Along the shores of large bodies of water, waves and tides produce such bare areas as beaches, reefs, bars, and spits.

Characteristic deposits from ground water are made by mineral springs, especially hot springs, and geysers. Travertine or tufa is formed from water highly charged with lime and is deposited in lakes of dry regions as well as from spring waters and their streams. Siliceous sinter or geyserite is typical of the areas about geysers where it arises by deposition from the hot siliceous waters, through the action of algae. Both travertine and sinter are rock and exhibit the general relation of rocks to succession, the first colonists being algae and lichens. Salt may be deposited from spring waters, as in salt basins, or by the water of lakes in arid regions where evaporation exceeds the inflow. In moist and semiarid regions, the salt crust is usually thin and, hence, readily dissolved or weathered away, permitting halophytes to enter and begin the succession. In arid regions, on the contrary, the deposits are thicker, and removal by weathering or solution is nearly impossible, so that extensive areas, in Utah and Nevada for example, remain absolutely sterile under present conditions.

The principal wind deposits are sand, chiefly in the form of dunes, loess, and volcanic dust. Of these, dunes, both inland and coastal, are much the most important at the present time (Fig. 67). The wide distribution of dunes and their striking mobility have made them favorite subjects of investigation and there is probably no other initial area and succession of which we know so much. Inland dunes of the Great

Fig. 67.—Sand hills showing blowouts.

Plains are called sand hills. In spite of the irregularity of the topography of dunes, they affect succession by virtue of instability and water relations and not by form. Sand hills, deep hollows or blowouts, and sandy plains all show the same development, regardless of their difference in form. In all of these the controlling part is played by the sand-catching and sand-binding plants, usually grasses, which act as pioneers. The chief reactions are the fixation of the sand, gradual accumulation of humus, and decrease of evaporation and increase of water content. Loess, while covering enormous areas in the valleys of the Mississippi, Rhine, Danube, Hoang-Ho, and other rivers, is not in process of formation today. Deposits of volcanic dust are infrequent and localized and cover relatively small areas. They are unique in the suddenness and completeness with which the area is covered and in their absolute sterility.

Glaciers, ice, and snow are agents that often cause extensive deposits. Glaciers have been of the greatest importance in the past, although today their action is localized in the mountains and polar regions, as is also that of snow and ice. They deposit materials showing all possible degrees of variation. The enormous blocks of rock deposited by glaciers present an extreme condition for rock succession; the till sheet proper of clay mixed with sand and pebbles offers an area prepared for a higher type of colonists. All intermediate conditions occur.

Bare areas due to deposit by gravity such as talus masses and slopes are universal at the base of cliffs, shores, banks, etc. The initial conditions for succession are often very like those of the cliff or bank above. The chief change is one of density or coherence. Hence, the lichens or cleft plants of a granite cliff or wall are usually found in the talus as well, even when this is disintegrated to the stage of coarse gravel. Talus derived from soils such as sand or clay or from rocks which decompose readily presents typically more extreme conditions as to water content and stability than the fragmenting area. Here the initial stages are new and unlike those at the top of the cliff or bank. Whether they will be hydric or xeric is determined by the location of the talus and its resulting water content.

Volcanoes produce bare areas by deposits of lava, of cinders so called, of ash or dust, and of sinter. The deposits of ash may be local, sometimes reaching depths of 50 to more than 100 feet, or scattered widely by the wind; coarser materials—cinders, rocks, and enormous stones—are also blown from craters in great quantities and fall near the cone or upon its slopes. The lava and mud expelled from volcanoes flow in streams from the crater. Rivers of lava have been known to reach a length of 50 miles and a width of ½ mile. In flat places, the stream spreads out and forms a lava lake which hardens into a plain. Mud volcanoes are small, geyser-like structures which discharge mud. They build up small cones, which are usually grouped and cover considerable areas. The deposits due to volcanoes or geysers regularly result in the destruction of vegetation, but this effect may be produced in consequence of the emission of poisonous gases, steam, hot water, hot mud, or fire blasts or the heating of the soil. Such bare areas are characteristic features of Yellowstone National Park.

All volcanic deposits are characterized by great sterility.[340] They are usually small in extent and, hence, easily accessible to migrants. The seres on volcanic deposits have been little studied, but it is known that they are relatively long. This is particularly true of lava, though climate exerts a decisive effect as is shown by the invasion of lava fields in Iceland[651] and Java.[269]

Other physiographic causes of bare areas are earthquakes and possibly also the rapid elevation or subsidence of the land.[154]

Climatic Causes.—Climate may produce new areas for succession through the destruction of existing vegetation. This destruction may be complete or partial. When it is complete or nearly so, a bare area with more extreme water conditions is the result. The factors which act in this manner are drought, wind, snow, hail, frost, and lightning. In addition, evaporation, which is the essential process in drought, produces new areas from water bodies in semiarid and arid regions. It may have the same effect upon periodic ponds in humid regions. Evaporation may merely reduce the water level to a point where ecesis of hydrophytes is possible, or it may continue to a point where islands, peninsulas, or wide strips of shore are laid bare to invasion. Finally, the lake or pond may disappear entirely, leaving a marsh, a moist or dry plain, or a salt crust.

The action of drought in destroying vegetation and producing areas for colonization is largely confined to semiarid and arid regions. In humid regions it is neither frequent nor critical, while in desert regions it is the climax condition to which vegetation has adapted itself fully or nearly so. The usual effect is to produce a change in existing vegetation, but in regions like the Great Plains it sometimes destroys vegetation completely. As a rule, the destruction operates upon cultivated fields, simply freeing the area somewhat earlier for the development of a ruderal or weed stage, especially when the wind enters to produce soil drifting. In native vegetation the complete destruction of a community is rare.

The wind acts directly upon vegetation in producing bare areas due to "wind throws" (Fig. 68). Areas where trees have been blown down by the wind are frequent in some regions but usually are of limited extent. They are most apt to occur in pure stands of such trees as balsam fir, spruce, and lodgepole pine. Wind throws are frequent in mountainous regions where the soil is moist and shallow. The action of the wind chiefly affects the tree layer and tears up the soil as a consequence of uprooting the trees. It is supplemented by evaporation, which destroys the shade species by greatly augmenting their transpiration at a time when the water content is being diminished by the drying of the soil. As a consequence, wind throws often become completely denuded of vegetation. In the case of a completely closed forest, the fall of the trees amounts to denudation, since occasional saprophytes are often the only flowering plants left.

Bare areas may be due to snow, hail, or frost. Those due to snow are restricted largely to polar and alpine regions. An abnormal fall or unusual drifting may cause the snow to remain in places regularly exposed each summer. After a winter of less precipitation or a summer of unusual heat, the drifts or fields will melt, leaving a bare area for invasion. The effect of frost in producing bare areas by destroying the plant population is almost negligible but the denuding action of hail is often very great. In some parts of the Great Plains, destructive hailstorms are so frequent that they have caused the abandonment of farms and sometimes whole districts. It is not infrequent to see the fields so razed by hail that not a single plant is left alive. Native species often suffer great damage, especially broadleaf forest and scrub, but the effect rarely approaches denudation. As with frost, the effect upon cultivated plants is very much greater than upon native vegetation.

Fig. 68.—Wind throw in a pine forest in Minnesota.

The role of lightning in causing fire in vegetation has come to be recognized as very important. The majority of lightning strokes do not set fire to trees or other plants and the attendant rain usually stops incipient burns. Even under these conditions, forest fires have actually been seen to start from lightning and the number of such cases in the aggregate would apparently be large.[360] In regions where thunderstorms unaccompanied by rain are frequent, as in Montana and Idaho, lightning is the cause of numerous, often very destructive, fires (Fig. 69).

Bare areas may result indirectly from climatic factors. These are due almost wholly to the effect of physiography in exceptional cases of rainfall, of runoff due to melting snow, or of wind-driven waters. In all three the process is essentially the same. The normal drainage of the area is overtaxed. The flood waters reach higher levels than usual and are ponded back into depressions rarely reached. Moreover, they cover the lowlands for a much longer period. The first condition forms new water areas for invasion. Since these are usually shallow and subject to evaporation, the development in them is nearly always short. In the lowlands, the vegetation of many areas is washed away, covered with silt, or killed by the water, and the area is bared for a new development. This is, of course, essentially what must have occurred at the end of each period of glaciation.

Biotic Causes.—With few exceptions, plants rarely play the role of initial causes. The reactions of plant communities on the habitat are

Fig. 69.—An old "burn" in eastern Washington. Typical of the destruction by fire of coniferous forests of the northwest. (*Photograph by Palmer.*)

of paramount importance but plants rarely destroy vegetation and produce bare areas. The reverse is true of man and animals. They are initial causes of great frequency and widespread distribution, but only a few have a definite reaction upon the habitat. Their activities may be grouped as follows: (1) activities which destroy vegetation without greatly disturbing the soil or changing the water content; (2) activities which produce a dry or drier habitat usually with much disturbance of the soil; and (3) activities which produce a wet or wetter soil or a water area.

Bare areas are sometimes due to destruction of vegetation alone. Ant areas in arid regions are, perhaps, the best examples of clearing by animals without soil disturbance (Fig. 70). The primary activities by which man produces denuded areas are burns and clearings. Clearings result, for the most part, from lumbering or from cultivation. In all kinds of burning and clearing, the intensity or thoroughness of the process determines whether the result will be a change of vegetation or the initiation of a new sere. The latter occurs only when the destruction of the vegetation is complete or so nearly complete that the pioneers dominate the area. Lumbering consequently may not initiate succession unless it is followed by fire or other process which removes the tree seedlings and destroys the undergrowth. Most fires in woodlands completely denude the burned area, but surface fires and top fires may merely destroy

Fig. 70.—Bare area 3 to 4 feet in diameter due to ants. Note the invasion of sunflowers, etc., about the periphery of the bared area and the better growth of the vegetation resulting from an increased water supply. Eastern Colorado.

a part of the population. Fires in grassland practically never produce bare areas for colonization. Poisonous gases from smelters, factories, etc., sometimes result in complete denudation, although the effect is usually seen in changes in the vegetation. Cultivation normally results in complete destruction of the original vegetation. In new or sparsely settled grassland regions, the wearing of roads or trails produces a characteristic denudation with little or no soil disturbance.[810] Complete denudation by animals is only of the rarest occurrence, except where they are restricted to limited areas by man. Severe overgrazing and trampling by stock are examples. Complete destruction by parasites usually occurs only in the case of annual crops.

Bare areas may result from a dry or drier soil. These occur chiefly where there is a marked disturbance of the soil. The latter affects the water content by changing the structure, by changing the kind of soil, as from clay to sand or gravel, or by both methods. These results may be produced by removal, by deposit, or by the stirring of the soil in place. Roads and railroads are universal examples. In surface or "strip" mining for coal or iron, large areas are laid bare, the raw subsoil brought to the surface, and sometimes, also, materials which upon oxidation produce extreme acidity.[215] Gravel pits and deposits formed by dredging and draining are other examples. The removal and deposit of soil by animals are confined to the immediate neighborhood of their burrows, the homes of ants, etc. In some places, such as densely populated prairie-dog towns, the burrows are sufficiently close to produce an almost completely denuded area. Insignificant as most areas of this sort are, they give rise to real though minute seres of much value for successional studies in communities otherwise little disturbed.

Bare areas may occur as a result of increase in water. Draining and flooding may bring two different areas (*e.g.*, a pond and a valley) to the same condition for invasion. The habitats produced by both are similar in having a wet soil, capable of colonization only by hydrophytes, except in areas where drainage is reenforced by rapid or excessive evaporation. This is true of canals and ditches as well as of the areas actually drained or flooded. It is unimportant whether flooding, for example, is brought about by the diversion of a stream of water or the construction of a dam. It is equally immaterial whether the dam is built by man or by beavers. The essential fact is that the water content will be excessive and that the pioneers will consist of hydrophytes.

To Study the Initial Causes of Succession.—In the course of the field work, give careful attention to the kinds of bare areas in your region and the causes for their production. Make a list of all of the bare areas you have seen. What cause or causes operate most widely in producing bare areas in the regions that you have studied?

CHAPTER VI

MIGRATION, ECESIS, AND AGGREGATION

It has been seen how the field of action for the development of plant communities has been prepared by the various initial causes. But it seems clear that, regardless of the kind or extent of the bare area, succession will not occur unless other causes are at work. The real causes of the development of vegetation, *i.e.*, the paramount causes of succession, are the responses or adjustments that the successive communities make to the habitat. Development is due to biotic reactions. The causes that produce the successive waves of populations are migration, ecesis, aggregation, competition, and reaction. To them is due the rhythm of succession as expressed in the rise and fall of the successive populations which constitute the several stages in any sere and terminate in the climax. Thus succession is always progressive.

MIGRATION

Migration begins when the germule leaves the parent area and ends only when it reaches its final resting place. It may consist of a single movement, or the number of movements between the two places may be many, as in the repeated flights of fruits with wings or pappus. The entrance of a species into a new area or region will often result from repeated invasions, each consisting of a single period of migration and ecesis. This is well illustrated by the invasion of the Russian thistle (*Salsola pestifer*). It was introduced into South Dakota in 1874 with imported flaxseed. By 1888, there were enough plants in the Dakotas to have it reported as a weed. Ten years later, it was found in all the area east of the Rocky Mountains, from the Gulf of Mexico to Saskatchewan.[328] Evidence of past migration is shown by the fact that where suitable places for particular groups of plants occur (*e.g.*, swamps, rock outcrops, etc.), they are nearly always found growing there.[871] Germules of various kinds find their way into communities but only a very few find suitable habitats not already overcrowded in which they can ecize. It is only by the process of migration that the plants of any stage in a sere are brought into the new area.[723]

To Determine What Propagules Have Migrated into a Bare Area.—Select a bare area such as a flood plain, talus slope, or fallow field. Remove enough of the surface soil from an area of 2 square decimeters to fill a 4-inch flowerpot. Place under conditions favorable to growth. When the seedlings of the first crop have been

117

counted and identified, remove them. Pour out the soil, mix it thoroughly in order to permit dormant seeds to germinate, and grow another crop. Repeat the process until no more seedlings appear. Record the total number of species and individuals.

The four factors entering into migration are *mobility, i.e.,* the ability of a species to move out of the parent area, *agent* (wind, water, etc.), *distance,* and *topography.* These are not always present in every case of migration, but, as a rule, each factor plays some part. The value of mobility to the plant is dependent upon the presence of proper agents for causing movement, and the operation of these two factors is much affected by distance and topography.

Mobility.—Mobility indicates the power of the plant for movement. Among terrestrial plants it is indicated chiefly by the size, weight, and surface of the disseminules, especially those carried by wind and water. A small, light seed or fruit with a wing, such as elm or birch, is much more mobile than a large, heavy, smooth one, such as the walnut. Man and animals distribute fruits for so many reasons and in so many ways that the only test of mobility, in many cases, is the actual movement. This is especially clear in a study of many weeds of cultivated fields which owe their migration wholly to their associates, *i.e.,* cultivated crops. Although mobility depends primarily upon devices for bringing about dissemination (hooks, plumes, etc.), the number of seeds is also an important factor. It is increased by abundant seed production, first, because among the larger number of seeds or fruits some may get out of the parent area, and, secondly, because of their correspondingly smaller size.

Mobility is most marked in those plants which are themselves motile such as bacteria, diatoms, volvox, etc., or possess motile spores as among some of the green algae. On the other hand, it is little or not at all developed in flowering plants with large, heavy seeds or fruits. The range is extreme, from the almost immobile offshoots of lilies, which move by growth, to the nonmotile but very mobile spores of fungi, which are blown about by the wind. There is no necessary correspondence between mobility and motility. The latter is practically absent in terrestrial plants, and, in spite of its importance among the algae, it plays a relatively small part in migration.

Mobility depends not only on the nature of the device for dissemination and upon the number of germules produced but also is greatly influenced by the position of seed or spore with reference to the action of the distributive agent. Winged fruits, for example, are nearly confined to trees or shrubs or high-climbing vines. They would be much less mobile if borne near the soil.

The relation of mobility to succession is obvious. Fireweeds, among the earliest pioneers in bare land areas, and especially in denuded ones, have very mobile germules. The spores, soredia, and gemmae of lichens, liverworts, and mosses are microscopic in size and broadly disseminated by wind. The early herbaceous pioneers are grasses and herbs with small seeds and fruits, well adapted for wind carriage, as in hair grass (*Agrostis*

Fig. 71.—Fireweed (*Epilobium*) in a burned area in Idaho.

Fig. 72.—Pioneer willows and cottonwoods on a sand bar in the Missouri River. If the bar is built up these will be replaced by elms, linden, etc.

hiemalis) and fireweed (*Epilobium angustifolium*), or mobile by virtue of association (*i.e.*, moved by man with his crops), as the mustards (*Brassica* and *Lepidium*) and goosefoot (*Chenopodium*) (Fig. 71). The sequence of shrubby species is determined partly by mobility, as berry-producing shrubs (*Rubus*) in burns and willows (*Salix*) in lowlands (Fig. 72). Likewise, cottonwoods (*Populus*) and birches (*Betula*), which have light, wind-blown seeds, are everywhere woodland pioneers. Rapid occupation of a new area depends upon mobility, but in permanent occupation it is much less important. Fireweed may soon occupy a burned forest area, but it does not occur in the reestablished climax.

Organs of Dissemination.—Plants differ much with respect to the organ modified or utilized for dissemination. Such modification, while it usually affects the fruit or seed alone, may act upon any organ or upon the entire plant body. Special modifications are usually developed in connection with spores and seeds, and mobility is most marked in species of this sort. It is much reduced in the various offshoots such as rhizomes, stolons, and root sprouts and in plant bodies, at least in terrestrial plants, notwithstanding a few striking exceptions, such as the tumbleweeds. Plants may be grouped as follows with reference to the part distributed:

Spore Distributed.—This group includes all plants possessing structures which are called spores, *viz.*, algae, fungi, liverworts, mosses, and ferns. Spores rarely have special devices for dissemination but their minute size makes them extremely mobile. In general, spores are more readily and widely distributed than are seeds or fruits. They are blown about like the dust. Tropical islands, for example, are notable for their fern population.

Seed Distributed.—This group comprises all species of plants in which the seed is the part modified or disseminated. Seeds are not very mobile except when they are minute or are provided with wings or hairs. They are, however, as a group more mobile and more widely distributed than fruits, largely because of their smaller size.

Fruit Distributed.—The modifications of the fruit for distribution exceed in number and variety all other modifications for this purpose. Many structures which are commonly mistaken for seeds belong here. Such are the achene (of sunflowers, and other composites, etc.), caryopsis (of wheat and other grasses), perigynium (of sedges), and utricle (of chenopods and amaranths), etc.

Offshoot Distributed.—To this group are referred all plants that produce lateral shoots, such as root sprouts, rhizomes, stolons, etc. When new buds are thus carried from several to many feet from the parent plant, *i.e.*, out of the area under parental influence, the results may well be regarded as migration rather than aggregation. The migration of such plants is very slow, but it is usually effective, since the new plant is nourished by the parent until it becomes fully established (Fig. 73). It plays a small part in the colonization of new areas, being almost negligible in comparison with the migration of free parts such as spores, seeds, and fruits, especially in large areas.

Plant Distributed.—This group includes submerged and surface water plants, both motile and nonmotile, and those land forms in which the whole plant, or at least the aerial part, is distributed, as in tumbleweeds and many grasses.

Modifications for Migration.—Plants may be arranged in several groups according to the nature of the device by which migration is brought about. The perfection of the device determines the success of the agent, as is well seen in those modifications which increase the surface for wind carriage. Saccate fruits may be membranous and

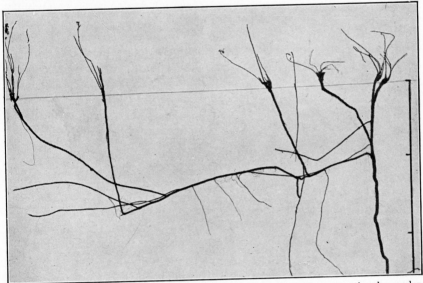

Fig. 73.—A wild rose (*Rosa arkansana*) showing the method of propagation by underground offshoots. Scale in feet.

serve for wind distribution, as in ironwood (*Ostrya*) and bladder nut (*Staphylea*), or impervious and air containing, as in sedges (*Carex*), water lily (*Nymphaea*), etc., where they serve for water transport. Many plants have winged, margined, or flattened fruits and seeds, such as are found in maple (*Acer*) and birch (*Betula*). The vast majority of the samaras of elm, maple, ash, etc., fall near the parent tree. This is often also true of the seeds of conifers. A careful transect study of the flight of seeds of the spruce and the fir showed that practically all of them landed within a distance equal to two or three times the height of the tree. Where isolated seed trees are left standing, as in lumbering operations, the distance to which the seeds may be carried is greatly increased.[411,440] Fruits and seeds with long silky hairs, as fireweed (*Epilobium*) and cotton (*Gossypium*), are termed comate. The parachute, as illustrated by the dandelion (*Taraxacum*) and other ligulate composites, represents the highest degree of mobility that has been obtained by special modification. Achenes with chaffy or scaly pappus, as those of niggerheads (*Echinacea*) and sunflower (*Helianthus*), are only slightly mobile but plumed fruits, such as clematis and pasque flower (*Pulsatilla*), are highly mobile. Many grasses, such as wild oats (*Avena*) and needle grass (*Stipa*), are provided with awns which serve for distribution by water or animals or by creeping movements. Mobility of a few fruits is brought about by attachment by spines, as in sand bur (*Cenchrus*) and ground burnut (*Tribulus*). Hooks and barbs which serve for attachment, as in cocklebur (*Xanthium*) and beggar-ticks (*Bidens*), afford many species a high degree of mobility. The number of pioneers which possess fruits with spines or hooks is significant. Fleshy fruits are scattered in consequence of being swallowed, especially by birds, the seeds usually being protected by a stony envelope which enables them to resist digestion. Various other devices occur.

Migration.—In the fall of the year, make a careful survey of a bare area that is being populated and classify the plants (1) as to the organ utilized in migrating into the area and (2) the nature of the device by which migration was brought about. Identify and classify 50 or more propagules of plants common to your region upon the basis of modifications for migration. The relative efficiency of some of the various migrating devices should be determined.

Distance of Migration.—The distance of migration is a direct consequence of the perfection of the device. Hence, the latter is of first importance in selecting the migrants which are moving toward a new area. It thus plays a large part in determining what species will enter as pioneers as well as the stages in which others will appear. The comate seeds of fireweed, aspen, and willow may be carried several miles in such quantities as to produce dominance. In secondary areas especially, dominance is directly dependent upon the number of viable seeds which enter and, hence, upon the migration device. If seeds or one-seeded fruits migrate singly (*e.g.*, maple, elm), the resulting individuals stand separately. Dominance results only from the movement of large numbers. Where germules travel in groups, as tumbleweeds (*Salsola*, *Cycloloma*) or cockleburs adhering in mats, the new area is at once dominated by families.

Interaction and Work of Agents.—Many fruits migrate readily even when the devices for migration are not greatly perfected. This is due to the fact that they avail themselves of two or more agents, either by means of two distinct devices or because of their behavior on drying. In the ground cherry, the bladdery fruit is rolled over the ground by the wind and then the seeds are scattered by birds and rodents. *Pilobolus*, a dung-inhabiting fungus, discharges its mucilaginous masses of spores upon adjacent weeds and grasses, where they cannot grow. But when the vegetation is eaten by animals, the spores pass unharmed through the alimentary tract and are deposited in a suitable substratum for germination and growth. Needle grass, stork's-bill, and other plants with sharp-pointed, twisting fruits are carried by attachment to animals and blown by the wind in tangled clusters, the two agents often alternating many times. The wild balsam apple (*Micrampelis*) is a frequent pioneer in denuded areas along streams. The fruits are blown by the wind, floated by streams, and even carried by attachment, while the seeds, in addition to being forcibly expelled, are carried by water.

Although the possibilities of the interaction of two or more agents in nature are great, actual instances of it are not frequent except where the activities of man enter into the process. Seeds and fruits are frequently blown by the wind into streams by which they are carried away. As a rule, however, parts adapted to wind distribution are injured by immersion in the water, and the number of plants capable of being scattered by the successive action of wind and water is small. As a general rule, plants growing in or near the water, if modified for migration at all, are adapted to water carriage. Species that grow in exposed grassy or barren habitats are, for the most part, wind carried. Those found in the shelter of forests and thickets are usually scattered by animals, though the taller trees and shrubs are generally wind distributed by reason of exposure to the upper air currents. There is seen to be a certain amount of correspondence, since hydrophytes are usually water carried, shade plants are borne by animals, and the majority of sun mesophytes and xerophytes are wind distributed. In each group, however, are numerous exceptions to the rule, owing to migration into various types of habitats.

Influence of Seed Production.—The chances of migration depend, to a large degree, upon the number of fruits, seeds, or spores produced. A large seed production increases the movement of a mobile species. Seed production of a species bears a general relation to its power of invasion. The latter is expressed more exactly by the efficient seed production, which is the total number of fertile seeds left after the usual action of destructive agents. The number of seeds produced by a tree of limber pine (*Pinus flexilis*) is large, but the efficiency is almost nil. The toll taken by nutcrackers, jays, and squirrels is so complete that no viable seeds were found in hundreds of mature cones examined. Of two species with equally good devices for distribution, the one with the larger number of seeds is the more mobile. Even in immobile plants, seed production increases the few chances of movement.

The viability of seeds is greatest in typical many-flowered (polyanthous) species, such as grasses and composites, which produce but one seed per flower.   This is shown by the large number of successful invaders, *i.e.*, weeds produced by these groups.   The movement of abortive seeds, of course, is of no benefit to the species.   Fertility is often low in plants with many-seeded (polyspermous) flowers due to the lack of fertilization or to competition between the ovules, *e.g.*, evening primrose (*Oenothera*).

The periodic variation in seed production is a factor of much importance, especially in trees and shrubs.   This is due to the fact that birds and rodents consume practically the entire crop of seeds of conifers, oaks, beech, etc., during poor seed years.   The efficient production is high only during good seed years, and the invasion of such species is largely dependent upon the occurrence of such years.

Position of Disseminules.—The position on the plant of the part disseminated, *i.e.*, its exposure to the distributing agent, plays a part in mobility.   In the majority of flowering plants, the position of the inflorescence gives a maximum of exposure, but in many plants special modifications are developed to place spores or seeds in a more exposed position.   The height of the inflorescence or capsule from the ground or above the surrounding plants aids in increasing the distance to which the seeds or spores are carried in the first flight.

The most perfected device of this kind is found in such composites as the dandelion, prairie cat's-foot (*Antennaria*), etc., in which the stalk stretches up after flowering is completed.   By the time the involucre expands to release the fruits, the flower stalk has often grown to several times its original length.   The movements in fruits of various plants often serve to place seeds and fruits in a better position for dissemination. In certain composites, the involucral scales are reflexed at maturity, thus loosening and lifting the achenes.   A somewhat similar result is obtained in such grasses as *Stipa* and *Aristida* by the twisting of the awns. In many mosses, liverworts, and puffballs, the spores are sifted out through slits or teeth, or the whole spore mass is elevated and held apart by the mass of elaters or threads.   In most cup fungi, the spores are driven out of the cup by tensions within, caused, in some cases, by the sudden change of glycogen to sugars with a corresponding sudden increase in osmotic pressure.

Role of Migration Agents.—It is significant that the agents which carry migrules, *viz.*, wind, water, gravity, glaciers, man, and animals, are also initial causes of bare areas.   Thus, the force which produces an area for succession also brings the new population into it.   Often the two processes are simultaneous, especially in denuded habitats.   Water as a migrating agent brings to new water or soil areas chiefly those germules which can be gathered along its course.   Thus, it is evident that a new area with an excess of water will be provided, for the most part, with water-borne migrules and that the viable ones will practically all be of this kind. The action of wind is broader, but it is clear that initial areas due to wind are found only in wind-swept places, which are, of course, where the wind will carry the largest load of migrules. An extremely close connection is found also in talus slopes due to gravity, for the majority of the species are derived from above. The universal prevalence of ruderals in denuded areas due to man's activities is sufficient evidence of the direct relation here.

Methods of Migration.—The possibility of migration depends primarily upon the action of distributing agents.[723] In the absence of these, even the most perfected modification is without value, while their presence often brings about the movement of the most immobile plants. As to method of migration, the following groups are distinguished:

Water.—This group comprises all plants distributed by water whether in the form of ocean currents, tides, streams, or surface runoff. As regards streams and runoff especially, the nature of the modification is of little importance, provided the disseminules are impervious or little subject to injury from water. The action of water upon seeds, however, practically eliminates all but hydrophytic or ruderal species in water or wet areas, though this effect is doubly insured by the difficulties of ecesis.[257] The high-water stage following spring floods is often marked by rows of seedlings. The same is true of the shores of ponds and lakes. The chief species are water, shore, and bottom-land plants. On newly formed islands, frequently water-borne plants are found on the margins and those transported by wind in the interior.[345,346,794]

The coconut, which is often seen floating on tropical waters, and which until recently has been cited as a classical example of long-distance water distribution, loses its viability within a few days due to water infiltration.[180,181] The seeds of certain hydrophytes, such as the arrowhead (*Sagittaria*), and the mermaid weed (*Proserpinaca*), have been shown to have retained their vitality after lying in mud covered with water for 7 years.[850] Motile plants, or those with motile cells, as well as submerged forms and unattached floaters, such as duckweeds (*Lemnaceae*), belong entirely to this group.

An instructive example of ocean currents as agents of dispersal is afforded by the floras of the two types of mangrove forests. The eastern mangrove has a rich flora very uniform along the coasts of East Africa, India, and Malaya. The western mangrove has a poor flora, the important species being the same on the western coast of Africa and the east coast of tropical America. The two types have no species in common. Distribution throughout the two regions has been entirely by ocean currents. It has been shown that the mangroves and their associates of the western region are all capable of floating in the sea for at least 2 months and that all could be carried by the main equatorial currents from West Africa to South America. In the mangroves, the fruits are viviparous and it is the seedling which is carried.[347,856]

Wind.—The group of wind-distributed species includes practically all terrestrial plants in which modifications for increasing the surface of the seed or fruit have been greatly developed or in which the part carried is minute.[722] Sacklike, winged, hairy, parachute, pappose, plumed, and some awned seeds or fruits are the various types of modifications for wind distribution. Whatever the device, the greater the surface exposed in proportion to the weight the more resistance it offers to falling through the air and the farther it may be carried by the wind. Milkweeds, thistles, willows, and dandelions increase the surface enormously without materially increasing the weight. The fruit of the dandelion is kept aloft indefinitely in a breeze of only 2 miles per hour. The seeds of orchids and many ericaceous plants are as fine as particles of dust, the former often weighing only $\frac{1}{500}$ milligram. These, like spores, rise into the upper currents of air and may travel hundreds of miles.

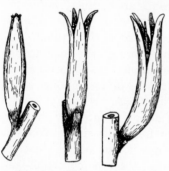

FIG. 74.—Three stages in the splitting of the capsule and dispersal of the seeds of an evening primrose (*Oenothera biennis*).

On the island of Krakatau, whose vegetation was entirely destroyed by a volcanic eruption in 1883, the first plants were thallophytes and bryophytes from wind-blown spores. The first vascular plants to appear in abundance were ferns, whose spores are readily scattered by the wind. The distance to the nearest island not affected by the eruption is over 12 miles, and the distance to the coast of Java is about 25 miles. Fifteen years after the eruption, 53 species of seed-bearing plants had reached the island. Of these, it was estimated that 60 per cent, chiefly shore forms, were brought by ocean currents, 32 per cent by wind, and 8 per cent by animals.[244,269]

Plates of gelatin exposed from airplanes at high altitudes collect spores of many fungi, including those of wheat rust and other disease-producing organisms.[597,877] The rapid spread of the chestnut blight (*Endothia*) throughout the range of the host within a few years is an excellent illustration of the efficiency of the wind as an agent in spore distribution.[397] Most epiphytes, whether lichens, mosses, ferns, or seed plants, such as orchids and bromelias, have wind-blown disseminules. The wind often plays an important role as migrating agent in shaking the stalks of plants with dehiscent fruits, such as evening primrose, and thus causing the seeds which are unmodified for transport to be scattered some distance from the parent plant (Fig. 74). In wind-swept areas, such as prairies and plains, many plants or inflorescences migrate for miles as tumbleweeds, scattering the seeds as they go.   Such are Russian thistle (*Salsola*), tumbleweed amaranth (*Amaranthus graecizans*), species

Fig. 75.—A group of tumbleweeds, Russian thistle (*Salsola pestifer*), left; winged pigweed (*Cycloloma*), center; and salt bush (*Atriplex hastata*).   The largest is nearly 4 feet in diameter.

of *Atriplex*, witch grass (*Panicum*), hair grass (*Agrostis*), etc. (Figs. 75 and 76).   The wind is the most efficient agent of migration but, at the same time, the most wasteful.   Most of the migrules are carried to areas already so thoroughly populated that the newcomer cannot ecize.

Animals.—Animals distribute seeds in consequence of attachment, carriage, or use as food.   Dissemination by attachment has been specialized to a high degree.   The three types of contrivance for this purpose are found in spinose, hooked, and glandular or gelatinous coated seeds or fruits.   Distribution by ingestion and that by carriage often play a striking part on account of the distance to which the seeds may be transported.[65]   The one is characteristic of fleshy fruits and the other of

Fig. 76.—Tumbling panicles of hair grass (*Agrostis hiemalis*) left, and witch grass (*Panicum capillare*).

nut fruits.   The destructive action of seed-eating animals, particularly birds and rodents, is often completely decisive.   So complete is the destruction of seeds in certain instances, notably in forests of lodgepole pine, that the appearance of certain species is possible only where the rodent population is driven out or destroyed. This is confirmed by the almost uniform failure of broadcast sowing in reforestation, as well as in other methods of sowing when the birds and rodents are not destroyed. In a single squirrel cache, 4 or 5 bushels of cones are often found, and in years of good seed production, sometimes as many as 15.[501] Foresters have practically abandoned seeding and now reforest or afforest areas by means of transplants grown in nurseries.[947] The destruction of seed is a factor of great importance affecting invasion.

Distribution of plants by animals is often very efficient, since each species of animal usually frequents a certain type of vegetation. The usual way for such trees as walnuts, hickories, and oaks to migrate is by animal carriage. Nearly all may be eaten, but some, buried in the forest or near its margin, are overlooked. Most forest animals seldom venture far into grassland; neither do prairie animals usually frequent woods. The rapid spread by birds of shrubs and vines with edible fruits to planted groves is common.[702] Some birds may carry small seeds from one marsh to another in the mud on their feet or feathers. If the seed or fruit has a mucilaginous coat, such as certain species of *Juncus* and others, these may adhere to their feathers.[347] Mistletoe, a parasite on trees, often of considerable economic importance, is disseminated by birds. After eating the enveloping fleshy rind, the slimy seeds which frequently stick to their bills may be wiped off upon the branches where they are perched and, hence, in places suitable for germination.[396,679] Certain seeds with oily or albuminous appendages are often distributed by ants, *e.g.*, wild ginger (*Asarum*), bloodroot (*Sanguinaria*), etc.[986]

Man.—Distribution by man has no necessary connection with mobility. It acts through great distances and over immense areas, as well as near at hand. It may be intentional, as in the case of cultivated plants, or unintentional, as in thousands of native and foreign species. Ships carry the migrules over the oceans, and trains and automobiles scatter them over the land. Wagon trails through the prairies were lined with ruderals. More than half of our weeds have been introduced from Europe by the continual shipment of agricultural and horticultural products.

Gravity.—Gravity is an agent of migration in hilly and mountainous regions, where seeds and fruits regularly reach lower positions, either by falling from bank, cliff, or rock or, more frequently, by the breaking away and rolling down of rock or soil masses. In this process, nearly always, large quantities of seeds are destroyed. Dissemination by this method is necessarily local, though it plays an important part in rock fields and gravel slides of mountains, especially in the case of immobile species.

Glaciers.—Transport by glaciers is of slight importance at the present time, because of their restriction to alpine and polar regions where the flora is poorly developed. In considering the migrations of the glacial epoch, however, distribution by glaciers is an important factor.

Growth.—The mobility of species disseminated by the growth of offshoots is extremely slight and the annual movement relatively insignificant. Solomon's-seal (*Polygonatum*), strawberries (*Fragaria*), and sumac (*Rhus*) are examples. The certainty of migration and ecesis is so great, however, and the presence of offshoots so frequent in terrestrial plants that growth plays an important part in migration in the local

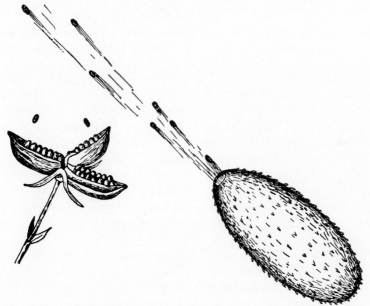

Fig. 77.—Fruits of violet (*Viola elatior*) and squirting cucumber (*Ecballium elaterium*) discharging their seeds. (*Redrawn from Kerner and Oliver.*)

communities. They produce very effective mass invasions such as cattails into ponds and shrubs into grassland.

Propulsion.—Dissemination by mechanical propulsion, though it usually operates through short distances, is important on account of its cumulative action from year to year. All species of this group agree in having modifications by which a tension is established. At maturity this tension suddenly overcomes the resistance of sporangium or fruit and throws the enclosed spores or seeds to some distance from the parent plant. After sporangia of ferns dehisce, the annulus springs back suddenly and releases the spores when it has attained a certain degree of desiccation. Movements of the teeth of mosses are also hygroscopic.

Often the teeth curve back and open the capsule in dry weather, but when moist they quickly bend up and close the entrance. Propulsion by turgescence occurs in a large number of fungi where the tiny spores or spore masses are hurled a distance of many feet.[438,956] The squirting cucumber forcibly ejects the seeds because of turgidity within the fruit[475] (Fig. 77).

Agents of Migration.—Make a careful survey of the plants found in an isolated community, such as a grove or thicket surrounded by grassland. Classify them in accordance with the agent that has probably brought them into the area. What is the nearest station from which the fleshy fruits of the various trees, shrubs, and herbs might have been carried? Complete the study on page 122 by adding the probable agent of migration after each of the species listed.

The Direction of Migration.—The direction in which a migrant moves is determined by the agent concerned. While migration tends to radiate

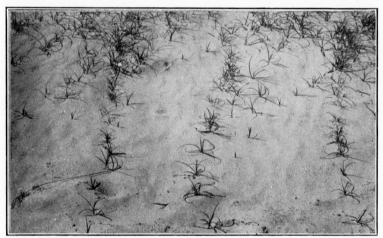

Fig. 78.—Linear migration of a sedge (*Carex arenaria*) on a sand dune.

in all directions from the parent group, as illustrated by the action of winds which blow from any quarter, it often becomes more or less *determinate* (Fig. 78). Where there are constant winds, for example, it is somewhat definite, the exact direction being determined largely by the fruiting period of the species concerned. The migration of plants along water courses is an excellent example of determinate migration. The position of invaders with reference to the original home does not necessarily indicate the only direction of migration, since seeds are regularly carried to places in which they cannot ecize.

In general, migration is *radial* or *indeterminate* when it is local and *unilateral* or *determinate* when more general. The local movement of plants carried by animals takes place in all directions, while their distant migration follows the pathway of migratory birds or mammals. Distribution by man is determinate when it takes place along commercial routes or highways. In ponds, lakes, or other bodies of standing water, migration usually occurs in all directions, but in ocean currents and streams it is determinate except for motile species. Dissemination by gravity and glaciers is local and definite, but propulsion is entirely indeterminate. Migration by growth is equally indefinite, but it produces a radiate movement away from the parent mass, while propulsion throws germules into the mass as well as away from it. Distant migration may take place by means of water, wind, animals, and man, and it is, in some degree, determinate, since these agents act in a definite direction over great distances. On the other hand, local migration is indeterminate, as a rule, except in the case of streams, glaciers, and slopes. The direction of migration is thus seen to be controlled by the distributive agent. The distance is determined by the intensity and duration of the agent as well as by the nature of the area through which it acts.

In succession, local migration is primarily responsible for the population of new areas. Nearly always, effective invasion in quantity is local. Forest and scrub usually extend their areas slowly, working out from their margins. When migrants travel long distances, they are apt to be too scattered to become controlling. This undoubtedly holds true for the great migrations following glacial invasions where populations of tundra, grassland, and forest moved hundreds of miles. They were apparently only the gross result of repeated local movements, acting in the same general direction through long periods.

If the germules arrive too soon, that is before the habitat is suitable to their growth, e.g., seeds of trees on moss-covered rocks, migration is entirely ineffective. The same holds true after the sere has passed into a stage of development so that the habitat is unsuitable to their growth. To modify the course of succession, migration must be followed by ecesis.

ECESIS

Ecesis is the adjustment of the plant to a new home. It consists of three essential processes, germination, growth, and reproduction. It follows migration and sooner or later results in competition. Ecesis comprises all the processes exhibited by an invading germule from the time it enters a new area until it is thoroughly established. Hence, it really includes competition, except in the case of pioneers in bare areas. The germination, growth, and reproduction of a plant growing among others are the same as those of an isolated individual except that those of the former take place under conditions modified by the neighboring plants. Hence, it will be clearer if ecesis is considered first and competition subsequently.

Ecesis is the decisive factor in invasion. Migration without it is wholly ineffective. In fact, migration is usually measured by the number of plants that ecize in an area rather than by counting the germules that have arrived. The relation between the two is most intimate. Migration, if followed by ecesis, results in the establishment of a new center from which further migrations may occur, and so on.

The time of year in which fruits ripen and migration occurs has a marked influence upon the establishment of a species. Seeds which ordinarily pass through a resting period are often brought into places where they germinate at once and perish because of unfavorable factors or because competing species are too far advanced. Spores and seeds capable of immediate germination may likewise be scattered at a time when conditions make growth impossible. The direction and distance of migration are decisive because the seed or spore is carried either into a habitat sufficiently like that of the parent to secure establishment or into one so dissimilar that germination is impossible or at least is not followed by growth and reproduction.[357] The rapidity of migration has little influence except upon conidia, gemmae, etc., which have not much resistance to drying. The number of migrants is likewise important since it affects the chances that germules will be carried into bare areas where ecesis is possible. Willows, for example, may colonize a new channel deposit if the wind carries the seeds to the new area which is much like that of the parent one, in sufficient numbers, within the few weeks before they lose their viability. They must be carried at the right time, in the proper direction, and a sufficient distance, with enough rapidity, and in large numbers. Thus, each of these factors plays an important part.

In unattached aquatic forms, *e.g.*, algae, water hyacinth, etc., the growing part or plant is usually disseminated, and ecesis consists merely in being able to continue to grow and reproduce. It is quite certain because of the similarity of aquatic habitats. In dissemination by off-shoots, the conditions are somewhat similar, and ecesis consists of growth and reproduction alone, since the offshoot grows under the same conditions as the parent plant.

Ecesis occurs only when a migrant enters a new place in which it germinates, grows, and reproduces. Plants may migrate into an area without germinating; they may germinate and then disappear; they may germinate and grow without reproducing; or they may complete ecesis by reproducing either by flowers or by offshoots or both[883] (Fig. 79).

Germination.—The first critical process in ecesis is germination. Germination is the emergence of the root and the unfolding of the first leaf or leaves which may or may not be cotyledons. The seeds of some species of *Oxalis* germinate soon after leaving the capsule, and in viviparous plants (*e.g.*, mangrove) the embryo continues in a state of uninterrupted development from the outset. Others, like the willow and cottonwood, retain their power of germination for only a few days. But even when conditions of moisture, temperature, and oxygen supply are favorable, the overwhelming majority of seeds lie dormant for a few months or at least until the growing season following their formation.

Dormancy and Delayed Germination.—When a seed does not germinate immediately upon leaving the parent plant, it is said to be in a state of dormancy. Dormancy is not confined to seeds, [916] however, but is also characteristic of many offshoots such as rhizomes, bulbs, tubers

Fig. 79.—Migration and germination of great ragweed (*Ambrosia*) in cracks in soil of a river bank.

etc.[231,233,234,895] Dormancy may extend over a period of only a few days or weeks as in the seeds of the elm, cottonwood, and willow, which do not withstand desiccation, or it may persist for years as in certain legumes, mints, and snapdragons. It is usually more pronounced in seeds produced in late summer or autumn.

Dormancy is much more general among native than among cultivated plants.[644] Frequently, the latter show none, and under favorable conditions their seeds will germinate before leaving the parent plant, *e.g.*, wheat in the shock. Wild oats (*Avena fatua*) and cultivated oats (*A. sativa*) both produce seed in summer. Unless artificially stored, the latter germinates at once, and upon the advent of cold weather the crop is frozen. The wild oats lie dormant, but germinate the following spring. Man, by his methods of seeding and harvesting, has unintentionally selected plants the seed of which germinate readily, since only those seeds that germinate soon after sowing mature plants for harvest. Thus, throughout the centuries of agriculture those races of plants that did not germinate readily were largely eliminated. The causes of dormancy are many. Some of them lie within the seed, others are due to the external environment.

External Causes of Dormancy.—When seeds mature in late autumn, the temperature may be too low for germination; or the temperature at the time of seed ripening may be too high, as among cool temperate species growing in the desert.[41] In fact, at ordinary summer temperatures, many seeds will not germinate but remain dormant until death overtakes them.[4,373] Lack of a sufficient water supply is another common cause. On the Great Plains, fall-sown wheat often fails because of drought to germinate until spring.[364] An insufficient supply of oxygen may prevent germination, as when seeds upon ripening fall to the bottom of a pond. Frequently, they are covered with earth to such a depth that a supply of oxygen is practically excluded. Here they may lie dormant for long periods and germinate only upon being brought to the surface.[210]

On an area planted to woodland, seeds of certain mustards and plantain lay dormant for 20 to 40 years before finally producing seedlings. Ten years after tilled land had been sown to pasture, the sod was again broken. This resulted in the germination of 16 species of weeds that had lain dormant.[87] Where seeds have been buried at a depth of 3 feet in open bottles in moist sand for a period of 50 years, 5 out of 22 species remained viable.[222,223] Seeds of many land plants have been shown to lie dormant in mud covered with water for a period of several years.[230] Many coniferous seeds retain their viability best when stored at low temperatures in sealed containers.[40] Delayed germination may occur in forest or in highly manured gardens if the organic matter is decaying rapidly and evolving much carbon dioxide and the oxygen supply is low.[476,918] It is a notable fact that when a forest is cut over or burned, many seeds which have found conditions unfavorable for germination, rapidly produce seedlings (Fig. 80). Temperature, water content, and oxygen supply may all be involved.

The seeds of a few species, *e.g.*, bluegrass, certain varieties of tobacco, mistletoe, and mullein, will not germinate in the absence of light or at least germinate better when illuminated.[209,431,625] The cause of dormancy in many such seeds has been found to be complicated with other factors such as temperature, nitrogenous compounds, enzymes, and after-ripening. Light may alter the seed coat in relation to its permeability to water or oxygen but the actual effects of light are not well understood.[211a,310]

Thus, the control of the habitat is twofold. It determines whether the seed will germinate immediately or during the season. If germination is delayed, it determines whether or not conditions will permit the seed to remain dormant but viable for several years. Habitats which are most favorable to germination are least favorable to dormancy, and, conversely, those which allow seeds to persist through long periods are inimical to germination. In many seeds, of course, the surface layer favors germination, and deeper layers promote dormancy.

Internal Causes of Dormancy.—The failure of seeds to germinate under favorable external conditions is often due to certain characteristics of the seed or fruit coats or of the embryo.[214] The more important causes are as follows; sometimes a combination of two or more occurs:[869]

Fig. 80.—Reproduction of Douglas fir in Washington from seed stored in the forest floor. (*After Hofmann.*)

Seed Coats Impermeable to Water.—One of the commonest causes of dormancy is the exclusion of water from the seed because of the impermeability of the seed coat or ovary wall. Many water plants such as *Nelumbo*, mints, and legumes are examples of this type. This character, however, is not peculiar to any particular group. In some species, all of the seeds are "hard" and impervious to water; in others, only some of them. Since no absorption takes place even when the seeds come in contact with water, germination cannot occur until the seed coat is made permeable. This may be brought about by a natural, slow deterioration of the seed coat or artificially by abrading or removing it.[890] The former agencies, such as freezing and thawing, bacteria and fungi, may require a period of several years. Naturally, when a crop of alfalfa or clover is sown, it is advantageous to have all of the seeds germinate at about the same time.   It not only requires less seed, but also competition with weeds is much reduced and a crop ripening evenly is the result. Hence, the seed coats are usually abraded or scarified mechanically, thus greatly increasing the percentage of germination, although the vigor of the seedling is sometimes decreased.   Small lots of seeds may be treated with acids or alkalies or the coats abraded by stirring them vigorously with sharp sand.[365]   Heating the seeds, *e.g.*, alfalfa, to a high temperature (85 to 90°C.) not only increases permeability to water and increases germination but also, at the same time, kills many of the accompanying seeds of weeds.[551,876]   Intense freezing also promotes permeability.[119]

Effect of Impermeability of Seed Coat on Germination.—Select 12 fully matured seeds of the previous year's crop of honey locust (*Gleditsia*) or Kentucky coffee tree (*Gymnocladus*).   Cut through the seed coats of 5 of the seeds with a file and place with 5 others in a glass of water, saving 2 for a check on size.   Change the water and examine from day to day for a week and state results.   From a lot of unscarified seed of sweet clover (*Melilotus*) or alfalfa (*Medicago*), select 50 that are well developed and a similar number from the same lot after they have been scarified.   Place them in a moist chamber on wet blotting paper.   Count and remove those that have germinated each day for a period of 10 to 14 days.

Seed Coats Impermeable to Oxygen.—In a second class of seeds, dormancy is due to the exclusion of oxygen.   The seed coats or fruit coats enclosing the seeds are either impermeable to oxygen or at least do not permit it to diffuse into the embryo in sufficient amounts to promote germination.   This is the cause of dormancy, as may be readily shown in the case of the cocklebur (*Xanthium*), either by injuring the seed coat, by increasing the oxygen pressure, or, more simply, by removing the coat.[849,917]   The same agencies that cause hard seed coats to become permeable to water also gradually reduce the impermeability of seed coats to oxygen.   Many grasses, composites, and other plants belong to this group.[846]   Subjection to a high temperature (120°F.) for a period of time increases the permeability and breaks the dormancy.

Seed Coats Mechanically Resistant.—In other species, water and oxygen can be absorbed, but only a small amount of water enters the seed since the expansion of the embryo is limited by the seed coats.   In water plantain (*Alisma plantago*), for example, the embryo swells and presses against the restraining walls with an imbibition force of about 100 atmospheres but cannot rupture them and is thus unable to germinate.[213]   The seeds of black mustard (*Brassica nigra*), shepherd's-purse (*Bursa bursa-pastoris*), peppergrass (*Lepidium*), and pigweed (*Amaranthus retroflexus*) belong to this class.   These may lie dormant in the moist soil for many years, although if brought to the surface the seed coats more readily decay.   This explains why they are such persistent weeds in fields and in gardens, occurring even in those that have been kept free from weeds for a number of years.[92,94] When cultural operations bring the seeds to the soil surface where conditions are favorable to germination, they immediately produce a crop of seedlings. Likewise, seeds of many water plants, such as arrowheads (*Sagittaria*), pondweeds (*Potamogeton*), bur reed (*Sparganium*), etc., may lie dormant in the mud for many years, the resistance of the fruit walls to embryo expansion being the chief cause, though oxygen relations may sometimes be involved.

Imperfectly Developed Embryos.—In some seeds, the embryo is not completely formed when separation from the parent plant occurs. In certain seeds, it is little more than a fertilized egg, and all gradations from these few-celled embryos to nearly or completely developed ones may occur. In certain plants indeed, such as *Ginkgo*, under cultivation in Europe, fertilization does not take place till after the seed has fallen. In others, development of the undifferentiated embryo proceeds slowly in the detached seed through autumn and winter and is completed just before germination in spring. Plants belonging to this general group are dog's-tooth violet (*Erythronium*), buttercup (*Ranunculus*), many orchids, and holly (*Ilex*).

Embryos Requiring Acidity.—Certain seeds with fully developed embryos fail to germinate even when the seed coats are removed and they are placed in an environment ordinarily suitable to germination.[740] This type of dormancy is due to lack of acidity and until the proper degree of acidity is developed or artificially supplied, the seeds will not germinate. In the hawthorn (*Crataegus*), for example, this after-ripening process requires 1 to 3 months, the acidity of the embryo increasing as after-ripening proceeds. This may promote water absorption and affects metabolism, particularly enzyme activity, which is essential in the processes of digestion, assimilation, and respiration.[255,869] The seeds of many plants belong to this group.[374] Conspicuous among them are red cedar, hard maple, peach, linden, apple, and ragweed.[212] Such seeds may be germinated at once by removing the seed coats and immersing the embryos in a weak acid.[653] A rather low temperature (about 40°F.) is generally favorable to the development of acidity and explains why seeds that are layered, *i.e.*, placed under a thin layer of soil out of doors during winter, germinate much sooner than those kept at room temperature. Layering is a long-established horticultural practice.[211,463] Much more work must be done to devise good methods of germinating seeds and producing seedlings from many of even the most common horticultural plants.[1031]

Longevity of Seeds.—Little is known about the normal period of viability of seeds under the usual conditions of natural sowing.[331] When the seeds are thoroughly dried and stored in a dry place, they may retain their viability for a long time.   High temperature hastens loss of viability. Seeds of many cultivated plants rapidly decrease in viability; others slowly over 5 to 15 years.[731]   Seed corn, for example, is usually selected from the current year's crop.   As a rule, the seeds of many native species remain alive at least 5 to 10 years and a few may, under favorable conditions, lie dormant 25 to 50 years.[54,68]   Legumes, water lilies, mallows, and mints are especially long lived.[273]   There are a few authentic records of some seeds germinating after being stored 100 years, and *Nelumbo nucifera* gave 100 per cent germination after lying for more than 200 years in moist peat.   But seeds germinating after long periods of dormancy are rare.[650]   Hard-coated seeds are especially long lived.   During prolonged storage the proteins of the seed are gradually coagulated or changed into insoluble forms.   Hence, when the seeds are planted the proteins do not become soluble nor will the seeds grow.[209]

It has been seen that the germination is postponed in a variety of ways and the vitality of the seed retained over a long period of time. The longevity of a seed combined with dormancy is a means by which the offspring of a single parent or the seeds of a single year may go on germinating throughout a series of years.   This may be a real advantage inasmuch as some of the germinating seeds may find conditions favorable to growth and reproduction.[344]

Rate of Germination.—The germinative power of the seeds of forage plants in Oregon has been determined.   Both those of the high mountain and lower ranges were tested.   Germination was affected by both altitude and slope and by the vigor of the plant, those weakened by overgrazing producing less viable seed.   Seed viability decreased with altitude. Species of the higher ranges (above 6,500 feet) gave an average germination of 28 per cent; those at lower elevations, 45.   In general, the more weedy species gave a higher percentage of germination than the more desirable forage grasses.[768,1007]

Experiments with a large number of prairie species show that the amount of viable seed produced varies greatly from year to year.[171,441,611] Seeds of 42 species were studied.   Most were subject to deep dormancy during the greater part of the year, germinating best in spring.   Important grasses gave 10 to 20 per cent germination; a few yielded over 40 per cent.   That of most forbs was below 15 per cent, although in some species it was regularly at least 50 per cent.[70]   Certain range grasses yield 70 to 97 per cent germination.[305]   Extensive experiments under way in the Soil Conservation nurseries should yield valuable information on germination.

Extended experiments among cultivated, annual crops show that large, well developed seeds often give a higher percentage of germination and greater yield than smaller ones.   Similar relations probably hold true for native plants.[585]

Depth of Germination.—Successful germination usually occurs only at the proper depth, with the exception of bare areas with wet or moist surfaces. A few species have the peculiar property of being able to plant themselves when they germinate on the surface, but the rule is that seeds must be covered with soil to permit ecesis. This is particularly true of seeds on a forest floor covered with a thick layer of leaves or needles, which prevent the root from striking into the soil. There is, doubtless, an optimum depth for each species, which varies more or less with the habitat. Too great a depth prevents the seedling from appearing altogether or causes it to appear in such a weakened condition that it quickly succumbs. The former condition may lead to dormancy, germination occurring only after the area has been cleared or burned.

The effect of depth of planting and its relation to the size of seed have been shown as follows in the case of conifers.[412]

TABLE 2.—GERMINATION AND ESTABLISHMENT IN RELATION TO DEPTH OF PLANTING

Species	Depth of planting, inches	Per cent germinating	Per cent appearing aboveground
Ponderosa pine (*Pinus ponderosa*)	1.00	82	82
	4.00	36	0
Douglas fir (*Pseudotsuga taxifolia*)	0.50	93	93
	4.00	17	0
Western hemlock (*Tsuga heterophylla*)	0.25	96	96
	1.25	42	0
Western red cedar (*Thuja plicata*)	0.12	78	78
	1.00	26	0

It was also found that the seeds of conifers lie dormant in the forest soil for a period varying from 3 years in hemlock to 6 in white pine (*P. monticola*) and Douglas fir, and those of the yew (*Taxus*) for 8 years.[411] Recent studies, however, are contradictory.[440] These data throw much light upon the source of seedlings following lumbering and burning. In many parts of the west, where a single fire has destroyed the mature forest, the natural restocking has been prompt, uniform, and complete. But after the seeds in the forest floor have germinated and fire again occurs before the trees reproduce, the area must be artificially reseeded. In other cases, reproduction from seed deposited in the duff cannot be depended upon.[515] In lumbering, it is a common practice to leave three or four large coniferous trees standing on each acre to insure the scattering of seeds throughout the area.[676,920] This is in striking contrast to cut-over hardwood areas where oaks, hickories, and other deciduous trees sprout vigorously from the stumps which retain their power of propagation for many years.

Experiments with prairie species showed that depth of planting has a pronounced effect upon germination and establishment. With the grasses, a depth exceeding 0.5 to 1 inch was distinctly detrimental, except in the needle grasses (*Stipa*) which plant the seed deeply by means of hygroscopic awns. Most of the grasses, as well as the composites. did best at a depth of 0.12 to 0.25 inch.[171]

Effect of Depth of Planting upon Germination and Establishment.—Secure viable seed from three or more native plants including a grass, a legume, and a composite. Plant the seed at various depths so as to determine the best depth for maximum germination and establishment. Use loam soil in good tilth and water daily, if necessary, especially those cultures where the seeds are shallowly planted. Is there any relation between depth of planting and size of seed?

Fate of Seedling.—The crucial point in ecesis is reached when the seedling is completely free from the seed coat and is thrown upon its own resources for food and protection. Even before this time, invading seedlings are often destroyed by birds and rodents, which pull or dig them up for the food supply still left in the seed coats. The tender seedlings are often eaten by the smaller chipmunks, and sometimes coniferous seedlings seem to be pulled up or bitten off in mere wantonness.[676] In farm practice, rows of corn may be missing for some distance due to the work of gophers and squirrels. Flocks of crows also do great damage. In regions where overgrazing occurs, the destructive action of animals is very great, especially in pasturing sheep, although this may be partly offset by their planting of seeds. Some toll is taken by damping-off fungi, such as *Pythium* and *Fusarium*, in moist, shady soils, but these are, perhaps, never decisive except under artificial conditions.[358,384]

Among most herbs, the greatest danger arises from excessive competition, especially in the dense aggregation typical of annuals. For example, in one experiment involving 3 square meters and 31,500 seedling great ragweeds (*Ambrosia trifida*), less than 400 plants (1.2 per cent) reached maturity. The direct effect is often due to lack of water, although light frequently plays an equally important part. Many attempts have been made to reseed the more arid, sparsely vegetated range lands to cultivated plants. Nearly all of the trials ended in failure, due to deficient soil moisture, lack of proper depth of planting, or suitable seed. On mountains or semihumid lands throughout the west, the results were partially successful. The seed was sown broadcast and usually worked lightly into the soil or trampled in by sheep. The most drought-enduring species such as Hungarian brome grass ranked among the first in the successful seeding, which, in some instances, reached 60 per cent. Naturally, the best results were obtained in the less arid portions of the area. Drought, lack of success in competition with the native species, and overgrazing were among the chief causes of failure.[767,772]

Seeds of prairie species sown on the soil surface during a period of several years gave a slightly higher percentage of germination and establishment in mixed prairie than in true prairie or short-grass plains. The number of species showing some germination was 79, 76, and 45 per cent in the above sequence, respectively. The annual precipitation at the several stations in the same order is 23, 28, and 17 inches. The establishment of the seedlings, however, was only 14, 9, and 11 per cent. The differences were due partly to water relations but largely to soil

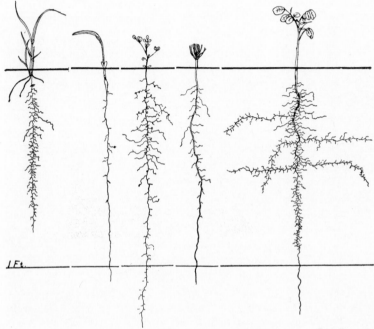

Fig. 81.—Seedlings of dropseed (*Sporobolus asper*), blazing star (*Liatris punctata*), sweet clover (*Melilotus alba*), ponderosa pine (*Pinus ponderosa*), and black locust (*Robinia pseudacacia*). The grass is 44 days old, the sweet clover 63, and the rest 75.

structure, the soil at the true-prairie station becoming quite hard and cracked upon drying. Where the same kinds of seeds were planted at the proper depth in small, denuded areas, germination decreased with rainfall, being found among 85, 59, and 21 per cent of the species, respectively. Of these, 27 per cent became established in true prairie, 21 per cent in mixed prairie, and none in the short-grass disclimax.

Even a short period of drought after germination is often disastrous. Another critical period especially for grasses is that of tillering when the transpiring surface is rapidly increased. Simultaneously, new roots appear. Unless the surface soil is moist, these cannot absorb, and the plant is literally holding to life by a single thread.　Mortality at this time is often very great[171] (Fig. 81).

With the seedlings of woody plants, the cause of greatest destruction is drought in midsummer or later.　This is the primary factor in limiting the ecesis of many conifers, though the "heaving" action of frost is often great or even predominant.[349]　The root system is often inadequate to supply the water necessary to offset the high transpiration caused by conditions above the surface of the soil.　It is, moreover, too short to escape the progressive drying of the soil itself.　In open places in

Fig. 82.—Ponderosa pine plantation, 11 years old; Lolo National Forest, Montana.　(*U. S. Forest Service.*)

the Rocky Mountains, such as parks, clearings, etc., the late summer mortality is excessive, often including all seedlings of the year.　On the forest floor itself, it is considerable or even decisive in places where a thick layer of dry mold or duff increases the distance roots have to penetrate. Following destructive forest fires in the Rocky Mountain region, in 1910, nearly 3,000 acres of forest were seeded broadcast and over 10,000 acres by hand corn planters.　Various native species were used.　So great was the toll of drought, frost heaving, fungi, cutworms, etc., that the result was absolute failure in practically all cases.[947]　After years of such experiences, the conclusion has been reached that the only dependable way of getting new forest crops started on denuded forest lands is to transplant seedlings of well developed 2- or 3-year-old nursery stock[501] (Figs. 82 and 83). Direct seeding, however, is sometimes employed.[828]

In deserts, seedling mortality is very high. Studies on the paloverde (*Parkinsonia*), a leguminous tree in the deserts of Arizona, showed that it was 89 per cent during the first 16 months and 97 per cent at the end of the third year.[834,840]

Growth.—Growth is the second stage in ecesis. If the seedling establishes itself, it is fairly certain that it will develop. This seems to be the usual result with herbaceous plants, though there are some exceptions among trees and shrubs. Even though conditions become

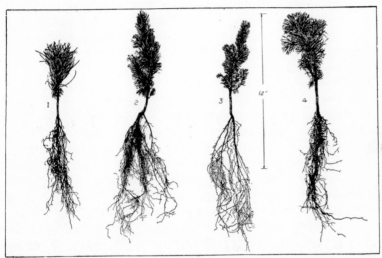

Fig. 83.—Typical development of lodgepole pine, blue spruce, Norway spruce, and western white pine grown in a forest nursery in Utah. The seedlings are grown two or more years in the seedbed and then usually one year in the transplant bed before they are transplanted in the field. (*After Korstian, U. S. Forest Service.*)

more extreme, the old plant is usually better able to resist them. Since the water relation is often decisive, the rate of root development and the distribution of roots in the deeper, moist soil are extremely important. Roots often grow at the rate of 0.5 to 1 inch per day, and even seedling grasses, trees, and other plants have remarkably extensive root systems. Light may be an equally important factor, but once the seedling is established it usually is able to endure much shading. Among woody plants, seedlings are notably tolerant of shade when contrasted with their demands later in life.

With increasing size of individuals, the demands become correspondingly greater. Hence, growth causes an increasing competition. Out of this competition some species emerge as dominants, reacting upon the habitat as regards light, water, nutrients, etc., in such a controlling way as to determine the conditions for growth of the other species in the community. Others represent an adaptation to conditions caused by the dominants and always play a subordinate part. This is well illustrated in the development of forests. The growth of shrubs and herbs on the forest floor is held in check because of the reduced light. A third behavior is shown by those species or individuals ordinarily capable of becoming dominants in some stage of the sere (*e.g.*, bur oak in linden forest) when they appear tardily or reproduce under unfavorable light intensities. The growth is diminished and the plant becomes suppressed. In forest and thicket, suppression increases from year to year and usually results in death, either through the low photosynthetic rate or in consequence of the attacks of insects or fungi. While suppression reduces the normal development of the plant, often causing it to become tall, spindling, and poorly rooted, its most important effect lies in inhibiting reproduction.

Reproduction.—The invasion of a bare area is made possible by reproduction or seed production in the neighboring communities. The duration of each stage in the resulting sere is the consequence of the excess of reproduction over immigration of other species. Mosses, for example, dominate a rocky outcrop only so long as they reproduce more abundantly than other invading species are able to do. Reproduction is consequently the final measure of the success of ecesis. In terms of succession, at least, ecesis occurs only when a species reproduces itself, and thus maintains its position throughout the stage to which it belongs. In the case of annuals, clearly there is no ecesis without reproduction, although they may appear and disappear finally in a single season. Even among perennials, there are few species that can maintain themselves in an area by vegetative propagation alone. Since bare areas are rarely invaded by means of vegetative propagation, complete ecesis in them must rest upon reproduction.

Ecesis in Bare Areas.—The bare area shows a selective action upon the germules brought into it. This is exerted by ecesis, for only those plants adapted to the conditions of the particular bare area, *e.g.*, soil, water, rock, can ecize. The essential nature of such areas is found in their water relations. The two extremes for ecesis are water and rock. The first is impossible for plants whose leaves live in the air and light; the latter, for those whose roots must reach water. The plants which can ecize in such extremes are restricted in number and specialized in character, but they are of the widest distribution, since the habitats in which they can grow are universal. From the standpoint of ecesis, succession is a process which brings the habitat nearer the optimum for germination and growth, and thus permits the invasion of an increasingly larger population. Primary successions are long because the physical conditions for growth are, for a long time, too severe for the vast majority of migrants as well as for the rapid increase of the pioneers. Secondary soils such as abandoned fields, burns, etc., afford more or less optimum conditions for germination and ecesis. They are invaded and stabilized with corresponding rapidity.

AGGREGATION

All sterile, bare areas owe their pioneers to migration. But after the ecesis of the first invaders, the development of families and colonies

Fig. 84.—Simple aggregation of the seedlings of bugseed (*Corispermum*) about the parent plant.

is due primarily to aggregation, the process by which germules come to be grouped together. This coming together of individual plants gives rise to the innumerable groups of varying rank which taken together make up vegetation.

Simple Aggregation.—The simplest form of aggregation is the grouping of germules about the parent plant. It is independent of migration. The simplest examples of this process occur in such algae as *Gloeocapsa* and *Tetraspora*, in which the plants resulting from fission are held together by a sheath of mucilaginous materials. The relation of the plants is essentially that of parent and offspring, even when the parent disappears regularly, as in the fission algae, or sooner or later, as in annuals. Practically the same family grouping occurs among most terrestrial forms, flowering plants especially, where the seeds of a plant mature and fall to the ground about it (Fig. 84). Although in the falling of seeds there is often some movement away from the parent plant, it cannot properly be regarded as migration unless the seed is carried beyond the sphere of influence of the parent. Simple aggregation increases the individuals of a species and tends to produce its dominance, while migration has just the opposite effect.

The size and density of the family group are determined by the manner of reproduction and especially by the number of seeds produced. The character of the family is also affected by the height and branching of the plant and the position of the seeds upon it. The family will be small and definite in species whose fruits or seeds are immobile, the seeds falling directly beneath the plant (*e.g.*, sunflowers, ragweeds). A similar group is often produced by offshoots (*e.g.*, false Solomon's-seal, nettle) when they do not carry the new plants too far from the original one. Aggregation at once gives rise to competition between the aggregated individuals, and upon the outcome of this depends their adjustment or establishment.

If the fruits or seeds are mobile, the degree of aggregation in the family is correspondingly decreased, since the seeds are carried away from the parent. Very mobile forms such as the dandelion rarely produce families for this reason, and this is often true also of plants which produce few seeds. Annuals occur more frequently in families, owing to the large number of seeds and the frequent absence of devices for migration. Many perennials also arrange themselves in families, especially those that are immobile or migrate by means of underground parts.

Lack of dissemination promotes the grouping of parent and offspring into families, while mobility hinders it. Families are produced more readily in new and denuded habitats, *i.e.*, in open communities than in closed ones, since in the latter individuals of various species have already become mingled with each other.

Aggregation usually modifies the composition and structure of existing communities. Its influence is especially important in communities destroyed by fire, cultivation, etc. In many instances, the change in soil conditions is slight and the course of succession is determined by the number of germules which survive. In forests, for example, if the number is large, the resulting sere is very short, consisting only of the stages (usually herbaceous and shrubby) which can develop while the trees are growing to the size which makes them dominant. But when the number of aggregated germules is small or none, the selective action of migration comes into play—the climax must await the arrival of the dominants—and the course of development is correspondingly long.

Mixed Aggregation.—Individuals are carried away from the family group by migration, and strange individuals are brought into it by the same means (Fig. 85). In the early growth of a family, due to the gradual spreading of the plants, neighboring families approach each other and finally mingle more or less completely. In both cases, the mixing of the two or more species to form a colony is due to migration. The conversion of a family into another community takes place usually through the invasion of mobile species. The change occurs when one or more individuals of a second species become established in the family group. The real nature of the community becomes more evident

Fig. 85.—A colony of sea blite (*Suaeda*) and salt bush (*Atriplex*) in a depression, showing mixed aggregation.

when several generations have brought about a considerable increase in numbers.

The appearance of each successive stage in succession is brought about by the interaction of migration and aggregation. Migration brings the species of each stage and aggregation, following ecesis, causes them to become characteristic or dominant. Migration marks the beginning of the initial, medial, and ultimate stages of a sere. It becomes relatively more marked with successive stages (*i.e.*, more kinds of plants are found in medial stages) and then falls off to a minimum. In dense, closed forests, it becomes extremely rare, and the ecesis of the migrants impossible. Aggregation, on the other hand, becomes more marked with successive stages, and a sere may end in what is essentially a family, *e.g.*, a pure stand of Douglas fir or Engelmann spruce with practically no undergrowth.

CHAPTER VII

COMPETITION AND INVASION

The coming together of plants in the processes of migration, ecesis, and aggregation results in competition. When a plant is carried into a group of other plants or is surrounded by its growing offspring, the struggle which results between the individuals is competition. This movement of a plant or a group of plants from one area into another and establishment in the new home is termed invasion. Since this process usually involves competition, it will be considered last.

COMPETITION

Properly speaking, the struggle for existence in the plant world is between each plant and its habitat, the latter being changed by competition in consequence of the demands made upon it by other plants. An exception to the rule is the case of host and parasite. Between host and parasite there is a struggle not very different from that between two animals. Competition always occurs where two or more plants make demands for light, nutrients, or water in excess of the supply. If there is enough of any one of these factors, such as water in a swamp, there is no competition for that factor. Competition is a universal characteristic of all plant communities and is absent only in the initial stages of succession where the pioneers are still far apart. It increases with the increase in population in successive stages and continues to exist when the vegetation is stabilized.

Competition is essentially a decrease in the amount of water, nutrients, or light available for each individual. It is consequently greatest between individuals or species which make similar demands upon the same supply at the same time, e.g., between a group of even-aged clover plants as compared with a mixture of clover and timothy. Conversely, among plants that are absorbing at different levels and receiving light at different heights, competition is greatly reduced. In a few instances only is there actually competition for room. Such may occur in thickly grown crops such as radishes, but it seems never to occur under natural conditions, although rarely one root may grow through another instead of around it. The crowding of the swelling roots is, however, only an incident in the competition for water. There is no experimental proof of mechanical competition between roots or rhizomes in the soil and no

148

evidence that their relation is due to anything other than competition for the usual soil factors—water, air, and nutrients. No matter how fully a soil seems occupied with underground parts, examination shows that there is usually room for more.

Competition and Dominance.—Properly speaking, competition exists only when plants meet each other on more or less equal terms. There is no competition between a host plant and the parasite upon it, but two or more parasites upon the same host may compete with each other. Parasite competes with parasite and host with host, though a rust, for example, may often be a decisive factor between two wheat plants. Neither does a dominant compete with a secondary herb of the forest floor, *e.g.*, an oak with jack-in-the-pulpit. The latter has adapted itself to the conditions made by the trees and is in no sense a competitor of the oak. Indeed, as in many shade plants, it may be a beneficiary and quite unable to grow in the area except for shade, humus, etc., afforded by the oaks. The case is different, however, when the seedlings of the tree find themselves alongside of the herbs drawing upon the same supply of water and light. They meet upon more or less equal terms, and the process is essentially similar to the competition between seedlings alone on the one hand or herbs on the other. The immediate outcome will be determined by the nature of their roots and shoots and not by the dominance of the species. Naturally, it is not at all rare that the seedling tree succumbs. When it persists, it gains an increasing advantage each succeeding year and the time comes when competition between tree and herb is replaced by dominance and subordination.

The sequence of competition followed by dominance is repeated in every bare area, *e.g.*, seedlings of one group—herbs, shrubs, trees—competing with those of another, and in each stage of the sere which develops upon it. The distinction between competition and dominance is well illustrated by the development of a secondary forest in a cut-over area or burn. All the individuals compete with each other at first, at least in so far as they occur in groups. With the growth of the shrubs they become dominant over the herbs and are, in turn, dominated by the trees. Herb still competes with herb and shrub with shrub, as well as with younger individuals of the next higher layer. Within the dominant tree layer, individuals compete with individuals and plants of one species with those of another. Thus, the rule, plants with similar demands compete when in the same area, while those with dissimilar demands show the relation of dominance and subordination. In a few cases, however, plants may be densely crowded and not compete with each other. This is illustrated by duckweeds (*Lemnaceae*) which often completely cover the surface of ponds and streams. The tiny fronds are on an equality with respect to light, and the water supply is far in excess of the demands.

Nature and Effects of Competition.—The importance of competition both in the development of natural vegetation and in crop production is so great that it has received careful study.[172] When groups of seedlings, especially of the same species, are closely spaced, competition begins almost immediately. In the sunflower, for example, the first leaves of adjacent plants unfold simultaneously. The plants may be so nearly of the same height that the difference is only a millimeter. Yet this may be decisive, since one leaf overlaps the other. It continues to receive light and make much food, while the shaded one makes less. A difference of 2 or 3 days with full or reduced photosynthetic activity is quickly shown in difference in growth. The second pair of leaves of the fully lighted plant develops earlier, the stem is thicker and can better transport food to the rapidly growing roots. These, because of their greater food supply, penetrate a little deeper, spread farther laterally, and have a few more branches than those of their competitor. The increase in leaf surface not only reduces the amount of light for the plant beneath it, but it also renders necessary the absorption of more water and nutrient salts and correspondingly decreases the amount available. New soil areas are drawn upon for water and nutrients, and the less vigorous competitor must absorb in the area already occupied. The result is that the successful individual prospers more and more and becomes dominant. The other loses ground in the same degree and it must get along with what is left. If this is too little to support life, it succumbs; in any case, its development is increasingly retarded.[761]

Effect of Competition upon the Growth and Functions of Plants.—Select 150 seeds of sunflower that are fairly uniform in size and soak them for 8 hours in tap water. Fill five containers of a capacity of at least 1 cubic foot with soil slightly drier than that in good tilth. Plant 4 seeds in one container, 16 in each of two others, and 50 in each of the two remaining containers. Soon after their appearance aboveground, thin the plants to 2, 8, and 32 per container, respectively, and in such a manner that all those in any container will be approximately equal distances apart. In the 2's and one series of 8's and 32's, keep the soil at a good water content so that competition will be for light only. In the second series, give the 8's and 32's only the same amount of water supplied to the 2's, regardless of the needs of the former, so that they will show competition for both light and water.

From week to week make careful observations on the growth of the plants. How soon does competition for light begin among the 8's? the 32's? By means of stakes and strings, prevent the plants from leaning far out. When the leaves greatly overlap, sketch, after noon on a sunny day, a leaf that is in part closely covered by another. Extract the chlorophyll and make a test for starch. When the 8's of the dry series are slightly flaccid and the 32's show wilting even in early morning, select after noonday a leaf of equal age (*i.e.*, fourth or fifth pair) from each of the three containers and make a test for starch. Also by direct observation in bright sunlight with the leaves still attached to the plants, determine the degree of opening of the stomata. By means of the cobalt-chloride method, determine likewise the relative rate of transpiration. Determine the light values under the plants of each of the 5 containers.

When the 2's have reached a height of 18 to 24 inches, cut the plants at the ground line, wrap in moist paper to prevent wilting, and secure the following data from each set, determining the average number in every case and arranging the results in the form of a table: height, diameter of stems above cotyledons, number of leaves, length and width of largest leaf, average leaf area of a few representative plants from each container, and dry weight. In a second table, using the 2's as 100 per cent, show the percentage reduction in leaf area and dry weight of the 8's and 32's under each of the two degrees of competition.

Competition within the Species.—The simplest case of competition is among plants belonging to the same species. At first, differences in height, leaf expanse, penetration, and spread of lateral roots are very slight. But as a result of competition, there is great variation in all

Fig. 86.—Representative sunflowers from the competition plots on July 2. The one on the right is from the 2-inch and that on the left from the 32-inch spacing.

of these characters as well as in the ability to produce fruits and seeds. This is particularly true of annuals and perennials belonging to the same generation. Unlike plants of different species and requirements, their needs are so similar that they cannot readily adjust themselves to the presence of others.

The course of competition among such plants is well illustrated by the following experiment: Cultivated sunflowers were grown in six large field plots under very uniform condition of soil, etc. The seeds were planted 2, 4, 8, 16, 32, and 64 inches apart, one rate of seeding in each plot. Competition among the 2-inch plants began soon after germination. Owing to elongation, these plants soon became tallest. Very soon, competition for light began among the 4's. Since each plant received more light and consequently could make more food than the 2's, they outstripped the latter but were, a little later, exceeded in height by the 8's. Thus, as the season progressed, each group in turn had for a time the tallest plants (Fig. 86). The 64's were so widely spaced that little or no competition occurred and they developed normally. The

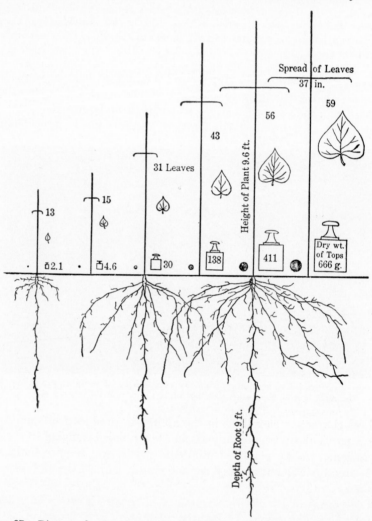

Fig. 87.—Diagram showing the relative development of mature sunflowers grown 2, 4, 8, 16, 32, and 64 inches apart, respectively, in field plots. The height varied from 3.3 to 10 feet, the diameter of stems from 5.7 to 47 millimeters. The relative leaf surface is shown in Fig. 88. The spread of leaves, *i.e.*, diameter of the plant, ranged from 5 to 37 inches.

average development of the mature plants in each plot is shown in Fig. 87. The correlation between growth of tops and roots is evident. The 2's, excluding suppressed plants which died, had an average height of 3.3 feet and a root depth of 5 feet; the 32's were 9.6 feet tall and 9 feet deep.

The small transpiring and food-making surface of the 2's (24 square inches) is in accord with the shallow penetration and slight spread of the lateral roots. The great leaf surface of the 32's (3,426 square inches) was supplied with water and nutrients by a network of roots that extended deeply and four times as widely (Fig. 88).

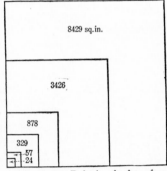

Repeated soil sampling showed that, in general, water content was lowest in the thicker plantings and more abundant in the thinner ones. Often, however, one of the vigorous, widely spaced plants was using as much water as the 16 or 256 smaller ones occupying a similar area. Each of the latter was not only deprived of sufficient water, having to share it with its competitors, but also its pale-yellowish, sickly color clearly indicated, what sampling confirmed, a lack of sufficient nitrogen. Competition for light was, moreover,

FIG. 88.—Relative leaf surface of sunflowers grown at distances of 2 to 64 inches apart in the field.

severe. In midsummer, for example, the light received by the lowest green leaves was 12, 24, 31, 33, 40, and 80 per cent of full sunlight, respectively, from thicker to thinner plantings. Hence, not only was photosynthetic activity greatly reduced in the denser plantings, but also dead leaves and completely suppressed plants were numerous.

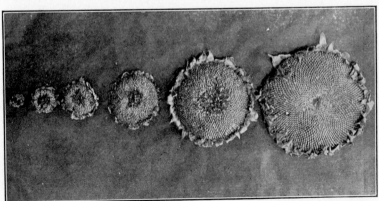

FIG. 89.—Heads of sunflowers grown at distances of 2 to 64 inches apart in the field. The largest is 8 inches in diameter.

The poor conditions for growth were clearly reflected in the production of heads (Fig. 89). Only a few of the dominant plants among the 2's bore seeds. These averaged only 15 per head as compared with 507 among the 16's and 1,803 among the 64's. The seeds, moreover, were very poor. In groups of 100, the relative weights were 0.9, 3.0, and 5.9

grams, respectively. Since repeated experiments on a wide range of annual plants have shown that heavy seeds give the greatest germination, most vigorous plants, and largest yields, the chances of reproduction by greatly suppressed plants are clearly decreased.[88]

Under natural conditions of field distribution, the development of plants is closely correlated with the degree of competition. This is illustrated in Table 3 where the number, height, and diameter of great ragweeds (*Ambrosia trifida*) were determined in a small, waste area on a flood plain.

TABLE 3.—DEVELOPMENT OF RAGWEEDS IN RELATION TO DEGREE OF COMPETITION

Number of plants per square meter	Average height, feet	Average diameter of stem, millimeters
12	11.3	19.0
20	10.6	13.0
33	9.3	9.9
64	8.4	7.4
73	7.8	7.2
84	6.8	6.2
154	5.0	3.4

Competition among monocotyledons is very similar, except that in grasses the number of stalks is increased by tillering.[682] Where Marquis spring wheat was grown at half the normal rate, normal, twice normal, and four times normal, differences were soon apparent. The thickly sown plants, because of competition for light, grew erect, while the thinly planted ones tillered and spread widely. The spindling, yellowish, nitrogen-starved, crowded plants contrasted strikingly with the deep green, shorter ones which were more widely spreading. The number of tillers decreased from four to one. The gradation in number and height of stems and number and size of leaves in older plants is shown in Fig. 90. The plants in the thinner plantings had more water, more nutrients, and a root system better developed for absorption. The larger plants, for example, had an average of 37 main roots, the smaller ones only 9. They also received more light, the range being 80, 58, 37, and 24 per cent of full sunlight, respectively, in the different plantings. The leaf area per plant ranged from 92.6 to only 6.9 square inches. At the time of harvest, the thickest planting averaged only 1 head per plant, there being 2 in the normal planting and 4 in the half normal. Moreover, as shown in Fig. 91, there was a marked difference in the size of heads. The yield from 1,000 heads under the several degrees of competition varied inversely with the severity of competition. The yield per acre was almost as great in the thinnest planting (19 bushels) as in the normal (21 bushels). Owing to the great increase in the number of plants, the yield was slightly

Fig. 90.—Representative plants of Marquis spring wheat from four plots with different rates of planting. The plant on the left is from the thinnest planting.

Fig. 91.—Heads of wheat of average size from plots with different rates of planting. The one on the right is from the thickest planting.

larger in the twice-normal planting (23.7 bushels) but fell to 21.6 bushels in the four normal.[172]

Much work has been done to determine the best spacing of cotton and other crop plants to obtain the highest yields.[522,615] In general, the results are similar to those obtained for wheat.[95] Among coniferous trees, crowding in forest stands reduces the quantity of seed produced in proportion to the density of the stand. Thinning promotes rapid growth.[563]

Competition between Different Species.—Competition is closer between species of like form, such as grass with grass, than between those that are dissimilar, such as grass with dicotyledon. Shrub competes sharply with shrub, and tree with tree, the outcome being a reduction in the number or size of the individuals or the total disappearance of one or more species. The characters of the root, stem, and leaf ordinarily determine the outcome. The greater the difference between species in one or all of these characters the less severe the competition. A deep taproot system such as that of the wild rose competes but slightly or not at all with a shallow-rooted grass. Neither does the taller rose receive light at the same level as the grass. Hence, the two may grow together with scarcely any competition except in the seedling stage.

In closed, stabilized communities in grassland, competition for water is so severe that the growth of all species is reduced. Often, they are unable to produce seed, especially during years of drought, and normally the inflorescence and number and size of seed are reduced. Water is the controlling factor, as may be shown by removing all the plants from a quadrat except the species under observation. The removal of competing plants results in an increase of water which causes a marked increase in growth. Figure 34 illustrates typical differences in growth during a single season. In the sunflower (*Helianthus rigidus*), growth in height increased 28 per cent and the diameter of the stem was doubled. The leaves were three times as broad, the heads twice as numerous and 35 per cent larger, and there were more and larger seeds. Where all but the central 10 square decimeters of vegetation were removed from other quadrats and the sod overturned, the yield in these central areas was increased two-thirds and, in some instances, almost doubled.

Light plays an important role in competition even in grassland, as has been fully demonstrated. Mixed cultures of various grasses and of grasses and dicotyledons have been studied in detail. Among the former, even in early summer of the first season's growth, the light intensity is reduced to 10 per cent or less. Hundreds of seedlings succumb and even the dominants may tiller only poorly. Seedling grasses, like seedling trees, often endure much shading. Figure 92 shows the development of a competition culture of tall panic grass (*Panicum virgatum*) and evening primrose (*Oenothera biennis*). *Oenothera*, being slightly taller and extending its roots deeper than those of the grass, soon gained the lead. The low light intensity, about 30 per cent, was shown by the attenuated grasses and the yellowish color of the lower leaves. In late summer, the light values were only 18 per cent at a height of 3 inches. By fall, 25 per cent of the grass had died and over half of the remainder was suppressed. Only a few of the grass leaves overtopped the competitor and received full sunlight. These were making photosynthate

Fig. 92.—*A*. Competition between tall panic grass and evening primrose. There are 264 grass seedlings and 48 of evening primrose in the central 100 square inches. *B*. The same culture 20 days later. The number of evening primroses is the same but there are 55 more grass seedlings.

almost twice as rapidly as the shaded leaves of the suppressed plants. By the end of the second season, the biennial *Oenothera* had completed flower-stalk production, seeded, and died. It failed to reproduce in the area the following spring. The few starved grasses that remained, in the absence of their competitor, made a renewed growth. They tillered abundantly and soon had complete and permanent possession of the area.

Prairie species show a great range in their ability to endure shading. The lower leaves of some, *e.g.*, prairie false boneset (*Kuhnia glutinosa*), will turn yellow and die when light is greatly reduced; others, like blazing star (*Liatris*), make a slow growth when the light values are only 5 to 10 per cent and may appear above the general grass level only after a period of several years. A dominant must have several characteristics. Among these are size—usually it has a stature as great as or greater than its competitors—abundance, and duration. It must occur in sufficient numbers so that it controls the area and be of long duration so that it can hold it against invaders.

Competition among Cultivated Crops.—Man's chief concern in growing plants is to secure the largest and best yields. One of his main problems, although usually not recognized as such, is to regulate the degree and kind of competition. Aside from the preparation of a good seedbed to promote rapid and uniform germination and establishment, and the maintenance of soil fertility, his chief efforts are directed toward tillage. Extensive experimental evidence shows that among both field and garden crops the chief value of tillage lies in weed control (*i.e.*, competition) and not in the preservation of a soil mulch.[137,913] Most cultivated plants have been so long aided by man that they no longer successfully compete with weeds.[508] If the latter are not controlled, the growth and yield of the crop are greatly reduced. In Illinois, for example, corn averaged 46 bushels per acre where weeds were kept down by scraping the soil surface but only 7 bushels where the weeds were allowed to grow.[622] Where the weeds have been eradicated or are insignificant, however, further cultivation is of little or no value, and if it is so deep as to cause root injury it may be distinctly harmful.

In well-kept fields, competition is between individuals of the particular crop. This increases with thickness of planting upon soils of equal fertility and water content. Since more widely spaced plants develop larger individuals and fruits, the reduction in yield is not proportional to the reduction in stand. It has already been seen that wheat sown at one-half the normal rate produces a yield nearly as great as that sown at the normal or even twice the normal rate. Where three grains of corn were planted per hill in hills 3.5 feet apart, and 7 per cent of the hills were missing, the yield was 86 bushels per acre. Where 13 per cent were missing, the yield increased to 88 bushels. A decrease of 17 per cent in the stand gave a yield of 84 bushels, and with a decrease of 57 per cent the yield was 57 bushels. In another experiment where three plants were grown per hill, the yield was 83 ears per 100 plants; two per hill yielded 96 ears; and one per hill, 168.[477] The yield of the two hills of potatoes adjacent to a space where the hill has been skipped may be 40 per cent more than that of two other competing hills.[536]

Frequently, greater yields are obtained by increasing the density of planting, but the size of both vegetative parts and fruits is reduced. This may be desirable, as in such crops as carrots, beets, etc. Onion sets of small size are obtained by very close planting, as is also the medium-sized head of cabbage or cauliflower. The total yield of potatoes may be increased by planting thickly, but the yield of the larger tubers is reduced.[104]

Variety and yield tests of corn and many other crops are usually made under the "ear-to-the-row" method of planting. The results of such tests have been shown to be often completely misleading because of the effects of competition. Where large and small varieties of corn, for example, were grown in alternating rows, the smaller variety yielded only 66 per cent as much as the larger one; and when planted in the same hill, only 47 per cent. The larger variety was 8 feet tall and had a leaf area more than twice as great as that of the smaller one which was less than 6 feet in height. Undoubtedly, the root system was proportionately more extensive. That the small variety was being robbed of light, water, and nutrients properly belonging to it was shown by yields where each crop was surrounded by its kind. In this test, the corn was grown in plots with five rows per plot, and only the three center rows were harvested. Thus, the so-called border effect, where the small variety was poorer and the larger one better, was eliminated. The yield of the small variety under these conditions was 85 per cent as great as that of the large one. Similarly, thin stands of wheat in rows alternating with thick ones yielded only 68 per cent as much as the thick. But the three middle rows in alternating five-row blocks of thin and thick stands yielded 90 per cent as much as the thick. Thus, it seems clear that any crop that is being tested should be surrounded by a crop of the same kind to eliminate the factor of unusual competition.[425,477]

In some periods in the development of a crop, competition may be distinctly beneficial. In most orchards, fertilizers evoke the greatest response when they are applied so that nitrogen is available early in spring. No cover crop should be competing with the trees for nitrogen at this time. A growth of sod often so reduces the supplies of water and nitrates that the size of fruit is greatly decreased and the yield much reduced. Oats sown in late summer, however, use a large amount of both water and nitrogen so that the growth of the trees is correspondingly checked. They ripen their wood and enter the winter properly prepared to withstand the cold. The mulch of oats, moreover, insulates against freezing of the soil and protects the tree roots which are more tender than the tops. It holds the fallen leaves about which the snow accumulates. The cover crop is plowed under in the spring and thus manure is added at a time when it is most needed.[77]

Evaluation of the Several Factors.—The effects of the several factors for which plants ordinarily compete, *viz.*, water, light, and nutrients, are almost always so integrated that they can be determined only under controlled conditions where all but one are eliminated.

In a series of experiments, large containers, 1 square foot in cross section, were filled with 2 cubic feet of fertile soil. Plants were grown in series, sunflowers and cockleburs (*Xanthium commune*) in different containers at the rate of 2, 4, 8, 16, and 32 per container, and wheat at the rate of 4, 8, 16, 32, and 64 plants. At the time of planting, the soil, which was of equal weight in each can, had an optimum water content.

Fig. 93.—Sunflowers competing for light and water. All are of the same age, but the 4's, 8's, 16's, and 32's received only as much water as the 2's.

Water loss from the surface was prevented by a thick gravel mulch (Fig. 93). Transpiration was determined by repeated weighings, and both water and a complete nutrient solution added as required in the control series. In the competition-for-water series, at every weighing each container received only the amount of water necessary to restore the original weight of the container with the smallest number of plants. Thus, competition for water became more and more severe as the number of plants per culture increased. Nutrients were maintained in some series by adding a nutrient solution in amounts proportional to the increasing density. In all but the thinnest cultures, there was also competition for light.

Where eight wheat plants were grown per container with both water and nutrients maintained, the dry weight per plant was 4.5 grams; where they competed for nutrients, only 4.4 grams, but where they competed for water, it was only 3.7 grams. Leaf areas in the same sequence were 35, 36, and 25 square inches. Denser cultures gave similar results

(Table 4). A progressive decrease in amount of growth also occurred even where competition was for light only. Similar results were obtained with cockleburs and sunflowers.

TABLE 4.—DEVELOPMENT OF MARQUIS SPRING WHEAT UNDER DIFFERENT CONDITIONS OF COMPETITION

(Average dry weight per plant in grams, leaf areas, in parentheses, in square inches)

Competition for	8's	16's	32's	64's
Water and light..................	3.7 (25.1)	2.0 (9.0)	1.2 (4.0)	0.7 (2.8)
Nutrients and light..............	4.4 (36.3)	2.2 (12.0)	1.8 (9.8)	1.0 (3.7)
Light only.....................	4.5 (34.6)	2.6 (11.6)	1.7 (7.8)	1.0 (3.1)

Competition between Root Systems of Crops and Weeds.—When a field is infested with weeds, competition with the crop plants often begins below ground soon after their root systems occupy the same portion of the soil. In fact, the total extent of roots of seedlings and mature plants is profoundly influenced by the presence or absence of competing species. For example, on the plains of central Canada the total length of the three seminal roots of wild oats reached 513 feet at the end of 80 days; the four or five of Marquis spring wheat 690 feet; but the six or seven of Hannchen barley 971 feet. The great importance of the early developed portion of the root system is shown in the fact that on land equally infested with wild oats, barley may produce a reasonably clean crop while wheat fails. But wild oats produces crown roots much earlier and in much greater numbers than any of the cereal crops. At maturity of the crop, the total length of the crown roots of Marquis wheat was 159 feet; wild oats 763 feet; and Hannchen barley 359 feet. Thus, unless wild oats is suppressed in its early stage of development by a cereal crop of uniform stand, there is little chance for this weed to be controlled, owing to its extensive crown-root system.[659]

Marquis wheat had a definite advantage over wild oats at 5 days after emergence, but had lost nearly all of this by the end of 22 days. After 40 days of growth, its root system was excelled by that of wild oats, which at the time of maturity was four times as long as that of Marquis wheat. Hannchen barley even at 5 days after emergence had a very great advantage over wild oats and steadily increased this predominance thereafter.[662]

These data are from plants grown in drill rows 6 inches apart. When grown without competition, these plants developed root systems and tops approximately ten times greater.[662] The total root length of Marquis spring wheat was 44 miles and that of wild oats 54 miles.[659] A single crown root of wild oats had a total length of 4.5 miles. In fact, practically all plants found in nature or in cultivated fields are greatly reduced in size because of competition with their own or other species.[662]

Crops of Marquis wheat and Hannchen barley were sown in the usual 6-inch drill rows and wild oats or wild mustard between the rows

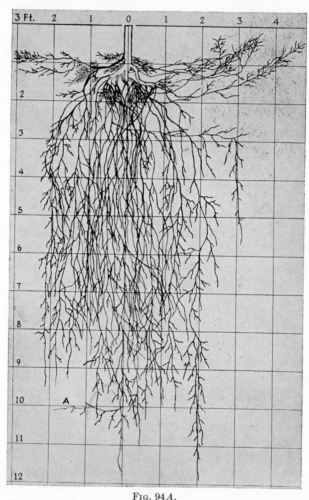

Fig. 94A.

Fig. 94.—Root systems of Delicious apple two years after transplanting: A, competition with maize planted in rows 3.5 feet on each side of the tree; B, without competition. On an average, competing trees extended deeper than the controls. (After W. W. Yocum.)

so as to simulate closely average field infestation by these weeds. Competition was very great between Marquis wheat and wild oats, where, 22 days after emergence of the shoot, the total root lengths were 184 and 119 feet, respectively. It was less in the case of Hannchen barley where the roots of the crop plant totaled 390 feet and those of the weed 80 feet.

The competitive ability of the root system is determined not only by the extent but also by the natural distribution of the roots. Those of barley were more concentrated near the surface than were those of wheat, which were more thinly and evenly distributed.[661] The wild oats

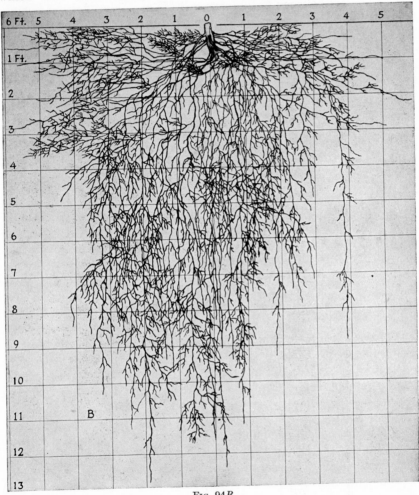

Fig. 94*B*.

scarcely produced seed in the plots of barley but were quite prominent in those sown to Marquis wheat. The roots of the wild mustard (*Sinapis-arvensis*) were about four times as extensive as those of the wild oats. At maturity the mustard was so well developed that it practically obscured the crop which was not worth harvesting.

In these experiments it was found that success in field competition depends mainly on prompt and uniform germination under adverse moisture conditions, the ability to develop a large, efficient, assimilating surface in the early seedling stage, and the possession of a root system with a large mass of fibers close to the surface, with the main roots penetrating deeply.

Competition between Fruit Trees and Maize.—The effects of competition on the roots of young apple trees, where the space between the rows is interplanted to corn, are marked. Where maize was grown 3.5 feet from the trees during two seasons, the average lateral spread of tree roots was 4.2 feet. Where the corn was grown 5 feet distant, the spread was 4.7 feet, and where 7 feet from the 2-year-old tree transplants, it was 5.1 feet. Trees without competition extended their roots 7.7 feet laterally. There was a marked tendency of the lateral roots to turn sharply downward as they approached the drier soil under the corn (Fig. 94). Where lateral spread was limited, depth of penetration increased. Thus, the average depth of tree-root penetration the second year was 11.3 feet where corn grew nearest the trees but only 9.8 feet where the annual competitor was 7 feet distant.[1026]

Role of Competition in Succession.—Competition exerts a controlling influence in succession. Among pioneers in a bare area, except in the hydrosere, it is usually restricted to the soil, where the roots compete with each other for water. As vegetation develops, competition for light plays an important part and the regular outcome, in many cases, is dominance. This is particularly true as the bare area becomes covered and success in ecesis comes to depend upon the ability to overshadow other plants. The taller plant gradually gains the upper hand, partly because it receives more light and makes more growth and partly because its demands are increased by greater transpiration. In order to meet this demand for a greater water supply, the root system develops more extensively and encroaches upon areas occupied by smaller plants. At the same time, the shorter plant receives less light, transpires less, and its needs for water diminish. This interplay of competition and reaction occurs in all communities with individuals of different height and extent, but in varying degrees. It is well illustrated in the different types of grassland. Short grasses, like buffalo and grama grasses, are not abundant in true prairie because of unsuccessful competition for light. In mixed prairie, there is enough water for the mid-grass cover and enough light for a fair understory of short grasses to thrive.

Where dicotyledonous herbs are abundant, competition for light is more severe. Thus, in grassland, as well as in forest, layers come to be developed although not with the same definiteness. *Antennaria*, certain species of *Astragalus*, and other prostrate plants form the lower or ground layer. The layer of grasses above is overtopped by one of dicotyledonous herbs such as goldenrods, asters, sunflowers, etc. The dominance of trees is only the outcome of a competition in which position means the control of light and, thus, of water. Where the water supply is in excess, as in submerged plants, competition of shoots alone may occur.

Competition, in affecting the supply of water and light, is most decisive during the development of the seedling and at the time of reproduction, particularly among perennials and woody plants. Accordingly, it plays a large part in determining the number of occupants and of invaders in an area in each stage of a sere and thus in helping to control the course of development.

The general effect of competition between one group of plants and the invaders in each stage of the sere has already been sketched under succession. Those invading species that show the greatest resemblance to the occupants in the form of leaf, stem, and root experience the greatest difficulty in establishing themselves. Invasion of shrubs by shrubs, *Phragmites* by *Typha*, etc., is very difficult. On the contrary, species of unlike life form enter either at a clear advantage or disadvantage, *e.g.*, shrubs into grassland or herbs into forest. A reaction sufficient to bring about the disappearance of one stage can be produced only by the entrance of invaders so different in form or nature that they change the impress of the community materially or entirely. Vegetation becomes stabilized when the entrance of such invaders is no longer possible. For example, while species of many vegetation forms may enter a forest, none of them is able to place the trees at a disadvantage. Hence, the final forest stage, though it may change in composition, cannot be displaced by another.

Competition in Relation to Conservation Projects.—Since cover in some form is the chief feature of conservation, the reduction or elimination of competition is a matter of primary concern. In sowing to restore pasture or range, it is essential to remove or break up the sod in order to give seedlings a fair chance for ecesis. Similar measures are necessary in the case of a nurse crop where temperatures are high and drought is frequent. The shelter thus afforded is often more than offset by root competition, and it is then desirable to restore the balance by utilizing an annual crop and sowing in the stubble. Among the alien or introduced species especially, very few are so well adapted to the plains as the native grasses. Hence, they require not merely the destruction of the latter by plowing, but also cultivation from time to time to prevent the return of the natives. In bringing about natural recovery on the range, especially in the mixed prairie, the first need is complete rest for a year or so, or at least a sharp reduction in the number of cattle, in order to restore the competitive balance. This permits the grasses again to reduce the forbs to their proper position of subordination and then to adjust the competition between themselves in such a way as to reestablish the mixed cover of mid and short grasses.

In regard to windbreaks and shelter belts of all sorts, a twofold competition is involved, to say nothing of that between the individuals and species employed. As has been shown so graphically by the timber claims planted a half century or more ago, it is imperative to cultivate to keep out weeds and grasses until the trees are large enough to accomplish this by shading. On the other hand, the roots of the trees often extend a considerable distance into the cultivated field and reduce or suppress the yield. This loss is the unavoidable cost of protection against the wind, and there is little recourse other than to leave a bare area of the proper width.

INVASION

Invasion is the movement of one or more plants from one area into another and their establishment in the latter. It is thus the complete

Fig. 95.—Coralberry (*Symphoricarpos*) invading grassland in eastern Nebraska.

and complex process of which migration, ecesis, and competition are the essential parts. It is going on at all times and in all directions. Invasions may occur in bare areas or in areas already occupied by plants. The former initiates succession; the latter continues the sere by producing successive stages until the climax is reached. But even then invasion does not necessarily cease. As a rule, however, invasion into a climax community is either ineffective or it results merely in the adoption of the invader into the dominant population. Practically all invasions of consequence either populate bare areas or produce new developmental stages.

Effective invasion is nearly always local. It is usually mass invasion such as shrubs into grassland or willows on to sand bars (Fig. 95). It operates between bare areas and adjacent communities which contain species capable of pioneering and between contiguous communities which offer somewhat similar habitat conditions or at least contain species of a wide range of adjustment. Invasion into remote areas rarely has any successional effect, as the invaders are too few to make headway against the plants in possession or against those much nearer a new area. The invasions resulting from the advance and retreat of the ice during glacial times were essentially local. They spread over large areas and moved long distances only as a consequence of the advance or withdrawal of the ice. The actual invasion at any one time was strictly local.

Invasion into a new area or plant community begins with migration and is followed by aggregation and competition, with increasing reaction. In an area already occupied by plants, ecesis is immediately followed by competition and reaction, e.g., decrease of light and water is quickly produced. Throughout the whole process of the development of vegetation, migrants are entering and leaving, and the interactions of the various processes come to be complex in the highest degree.

Kinds of Invasion.—Local invasion in force is essentially *continuous* or *recurrent*. Willows or cottonwoods, for example, may invade the new deposits made by a river only to be destroyed by unusual floods. But by invading the area each year or after each catastrophe, these deposits may finally be built up and covered with a willow-cottonwood forest. Likewise, trees might invade grassland only to be repeatedly burned with the grasses. By continuous or recurrent invasion, conditions may finally arise where the grasses disappear as the result of shading and prairie fires will cease. Between contiguous communities, invasion is *mutual*, *i.e.*, it takes place in both directions, unless the communities are too dissimilar. There is an annual movement from each community into the other, and often a forward movement through each, resulting from the invaders of the previous year. By far the greater amount of invasion into existing vegetation is of this sort. The result is a transitional area or ecotone between the two communities, e.g., shrub-herb area between woodland and grassland, water lily-bulrush area between floating plants and reed swamp. Such ecotones indicate the next stage in development. The movement into a bare area is likewise continuous, though not mutual, and, hence, there is no ecotone during the earlier stages. In continuous invasion, an outpost, such as trees or shrubs in grassland, may be continuously reenforced, permitting rapid aggregation and ecesis and the production of new centers from which the species may be extended over a wide area.

Intermittent invasion commonly arises through intermittent or periodic movements into distant regions. Such invasion is relatively infrequent but is often striking, owing to the fact that the invader often wanders far from the original home.   It is rarely of consequence in causing succession.   Invasion is *complete* when the movement of invaders into a community is so great that the original occupants are driven out.   This is characteristic of the major stages of succession where one life form replaces another.   Where the number of individuals is sufficiently small to be adopted into the community without changing it materially, invasion is said to be *partial*.   Partial invasion is more frequent though less conspicuous than complete invasion.   Between the two there are necessarily transitions.   *Permanent invasion* occurs when a species becomes permanently established in a more or less stable community.   The term is entirely relative.   Spike rush, for example, illustrates permanent invasion into a sedge meadow.   But in each sere, initial and medial stages are temporary in comparison with the climax.   Though the initial stages of a rock sere may last for centuries, they must finally pass in the course of development just as the climax stage will disappear should there occur a marked change in climate.[190]

Manner of Invasion.—Bare areas present very different conditions for invaders from those found in plant communities.   This is due to the absence of competition and often to the reactions the plants have exerted upon the habitat.   Conditions for germination are nearly always more favorable in plant communities, but the fate of the seedling and adult is then largely determined by competition.   Open communities are invaded readily; closed ones, with more difficulty if at all.   Open communities are those which have factors in excess of the demands of the existing populations; in closed ones, the plants are in close adjustment with the usual supply (Fig. 96).   A community is not necessarily open (desert, spruce forest) because a part of the surface is bare.   Secondary bare areas usually afford maximum opportunity for invasion.   This is partly due to lack of competition but especially to the fact that conditions are more or less optimum for the germination and growth of a wide range of species.   Primary areas (water, rock, sand) present only extremes of water content, and thus exclude all invaders except a few pioneers.

In all invasions, after the first or pioneer stage, the relative level of occupants and invaders is critical.   Invasion may occur at three different levels.   A community may be invaded at its level, *i.e.*, by species of the same general height as those in occupation, or below or above this level. When invasion is at the same height, *e.g.*, trees in forest, the level has no effect and the sequence of development is determined by other features such as ability of seedlings to endure shade.   If it is above the level of the occupants, such as mosses above crustose lichens, the newcomers become dominant as they stretch above their neighbors and soon give character to a new stage.   This is notably the case with shrubs and trees in which the close dependence of the sequence of stages upon life form is most evident. When invasion is below the existing level, it has no direct influence upon the dominant species unless the latter are handicapped as in overgrazed mixed prairie. Such invaders normally take a subordinate place as secondary components of the community. A unique exception is that of the peat moss, *Sphagnum*. In wet climates it may invade the forest floor where springs or seepage water occur. Holding the water like a sponge and annually increasing its territory, it may so waterlog the area that the forest disappears.

Fig. 96.—Invasion of salsify (*Tragopogon pratense*) into prairie at Lincoln, as a result of small bare areas due to drought.

To Determine the Water-retaining Power of Sphagnum.—Place loosely 100 grams of air-dry, commercial peat moss (*Sphagnum*) in a small sack of cheesecloth, and submerge it in water for an hour or longer. Reweigh and determine the percentage of water retained, based on the dry weight of the moss. Examine a living leaf under the microscope and make out the narrow, elongated, living cells containing chloroplasts and the intervening, larger, colorless dead cells. The latter are held open by spiral thickenings on the inner surface of the cell walls and air escapes through the pores as water enters the cell. Also, view the leaf in cross section.

Source of Seed.—It was long believed that seeds remained viable in the soil for a century or more and that this furnished the explanation of most successions, especially after fire or lumbering.[254] With the appearance of more exact methods, the consensus swung to the opposite extreme and has only recently begun to move to an intermediate position. While there are limits to the viability of seeds and of rootstocks, these are often wider than has been supposed, and the survival of some seeds in favorable conditions in the soil may be a matter of several decades and possibly a century in certain species.[93,222] Naturally, this depends in large measure upon the size and character of fruit or seed, those with hard coats usually living for a longer period.²⁸³   In general, viability is greater in forest and dense scrub and in early stages of the hydrosere and much less is grassland, though weeds are a frequent exception.

When the chaparral of southern California is burned, the area is covered the next season by a dense growth of forbs, chiefly annuals, and it is practically certain that the seeds of these have lain in the ground for 5 to 25 years or more.   In the Great Plains, grain fields abandoned after 3 to 16 years of shallow tillage are reclothed in 3 to 5 years with the climax grasses, *Agropyron smithii* in particular.   The hardy rhizomes

Fig. 97.—Western wheat grass (*Agropyron smithii*) re-covering silt-loam farm land abandoned 4 years, near Rosebud, S. D.   (*Photograph by W. L. Tolstead.*)

are broken up but not destroyed by plow and drill and develop rapidly after the competition of the grain has been removed (Fig. 97).   With better methods, both rootstocks and seeds are destroyed and the natural succession is much slower, requiring 20 to 40 years.   The weeds of the first few years are derived as a rule from seed in the soil, but the grasses invade almost wholly by virtue of fruits blown in from roadsides, hayfields, or other relict communities.   The first colonization is from such areas, and the pioneers continue to advance in the direction set by the prevailing wind.

Barriers.—Any feature of the topography or any physical or biological agency that restricts or prevents invasion is a barrier.   It may be a mountain range, a highly alkaline soil, or grazing animals.   Topographic features are usually permanent and produce permanent barriers.   Biological ones, *e.g.*, cultivation and burning, are often temporary and exist for a few years or even a single season. Temporary barriers are often recurrent, however. Barriers are complete or incomplete with respect to the thoroughness of their action. A water-filled depression permits certain plants to ecize, but a large lake is a complete barrier to most land plants, since they can neither migrate across it nor ecize in it. The chief effect of barriers upon invasion is exerted upon ecesis and not upon migration.

Physical Barriers.—Barriers are physical when due to some marked topographic feature such as an ocean, lake, river, mountain range, or desert. All of these affect invasion because of their dominant physical factors, *i.e.*, excess or deficiency of water, temperature, nutrients, etc. They prevent the ecesis of species coming from very different habitats, though they may, at the same time, serve as conductors of plants between similar habitats, as in the case of a river between two lakes. A body of water is a barrier to mesophytes and xerophytes; deserts set a limit to the invasion of mesic and hydric plants, while they favor xeric ones. By its reduction of temperature, a high mountain range restricts the extension of plants of lowlands and plains. It is also more of an obstacle to migration than most physical barriers, because of difficulty of movement up its slopes. Any bare area with extreme conditions is a barrier to the invasion of adjacent communities. It is not a barrier to the development of a sere upon it, since the proper pioneers are always able to invade.

Biological Barriers.—Biological barriers comprise plant communities, man and animals, and parasitic plants. Invasion is limited by a plant community in two ways. An association, *e.g.*, woodland, acts as a barrier to the ecesis of species invading it from associations of another type on account of the physical differences of the habitats. Whether such a barrier be complete or partial will depend upon the relative unlikeness of the two areas. Shade plants are unable to invade a prairie, though the species of open thickets or well lighted woodland may do so to a certain degree. A mature forest, on account of its diffuse light, is a barrier to sun-loving plants, while a swamp, because of its excess of water and poor aeration, sets a limit to the invasion of species of both woodland and grassland. Forests and thickets act as a mechanical obstacle especially to the migration of tumbleweeds and many other wind-distributed plants. Closed communities whether forest, grassland, or desert, exert a marked influence in decreasing invasion by reason of the intense and successful competition all invaders must meet. Closed associations usually act as complete barriers, while more open ones restrict invasion in direct proportion to the degree of occupation. Thus, the number of stages in succession is determined largely by the increasing difficulty of invasion as the area becomes stabilized.

Man and animals affect invasion by the destruction of disseminules. Both in bare areas and in seral stages, the action of rodents and birds is often decisive to the extent of altering the whole course of development. Man and animals act as barriers by flooding, draining, etc., or, when they turn the scale in competition, by cultivation, grazing, trampling, parasitism, or in other ways.

The absence of pollinating insects is sometimes a curious barrier to the complete ecesis of species far out of their usual habitat or range. When red clover was first introduced into New Zealand, it was unsuccessful as a crop, since it did not produce seed. With the introduction of the bumblebee, upon which the plant is usually dependent for pollination, the clover became a very successful invader.[914] Similarly, Smyrna figs when introduced into California grew well and blossomed but did not set fruit. Their ecesis was incomplete until the small wasp which effects pollination was also introduced. Parasitic fungi decrease migration in so far as they destroy seeds or reduce the number produced. They restrict or prevent ecesis either by the destruction of invaders or by placing them at a disadvantage with respect to the occupants.

Changes in Barriers.—A closed formation, such as a forest or meadow which acts as a decided barrier to invasion, may disappear completely as the result of a landslide, flood, or burn, or through the activity of man, and leave an area into which migrants crowd from every direction. A marsh or swamp ceases to be a barrier to prairie xerophytes during a period of unusually dry years, such as regularly occurs in semiarid regions. Conversely, during a series of wet years mesophytes may enter into the development of a sere at a stage where they are usually barred by deficient water content. The succession may be much shortened and one or more stages omitted. Many xeric habitats such as dunes, gravel slides, blowouts, prairies, etc., are barriers during summer and autumn but not during spring when the dry, hot surface becomes sufficiently moist to permit the germination and growth of invaders. The influence of distance as a barrier has been discussed under migration.

CHAPTER VIII

SOIL IN RELATION TO PLANT DEVELOPMENT

The soil is the unconsolidated outer layer of the earth's crust, ranging in thickness from a mere film to somewhat more than 10 feet, which through processes of weathering and the incorporation of organic matter has become adapted to the growth of plants. It is underlaid usually

Fig. 98.—An orchid (*Dendrobium*), showing aerial roots covered with white velamen. This is a modification of the epidermis consisting of layers of dead cells which readily absorb water during rains, etc. (*After Gager, General Botany, P. Blakiston's Son & Co.*)

by unconsolidated parent materials into which the deeper roots of plants frequently extend. The true soil or *solum* is generally made of the same parent materials which it covers. Nearly all higher plants except parasites and epiphytes are rooted in the soil (Fig. 98). The latter do not depend on the soil directly but secure nutrients or support from plants thus anchored. Even floating water plants secure the necessary soluble salts that have been dissolved from the soil. The soil often contains and acts upon a much more extensive portion of the plant body than does the atmosphere. Moreover, vegetation has played a remarkable role in the formation of this medium in which plants are anchored and from which they obtain their water and nutrients.

Nature and Origin of Soil.—The geological formations, through weathering, produce the parent materials of soil. These materials constitute the bulk of the soil and for a long time determine its physical character. Thus the chief component of most soils is derived from rocks. More than 90 per cent by weight of ordinary air-dried soil consists of rock fragments. The small, angular fragments have been derived from the rock and possibly later transported by wind or water (Fig. 99). During past centuries, rocks have disintegrated and they are still disintegrating by the action of such forces as alternate freezing and thawing, formation of ice in pores and crevices, erosion by wind and running water, and surface scouring by glaciers. The same physical

Fig. 99.—Disintegration of a granite boulder into gravel and sand and the further breaking down of these by the roots of herbaceous plants.

forces that have weathered the rock have, in most cases, moved the fragments to other places where the soil is formed. Accompanying this process of fragmentation is the exceedingly important process of chemical corrosion or decomposition, for plants cannot grow in rock fragments, no matter how small the particles, unless the nutrients locked in these particles as insoluble compounds are changed chemically to water-soluble substances. The latter alone can be absorbed by the roots. The fundamental reactions include hydrolysis, hydration, carbonation, and oxidation. They are common both to rock-weathering and to soil-forming processes.

The mineral matter derived from the rock material constitutes the matrix of the soil; it is very stable. The particles that have been exposed on or near the surface for centuries, even those of long-cultivated soils, scarcely differ from those of the deeper soil that have been protected and undisturbed.

The destructive physical and chemical activities of weathering must be followed or accompanied by constructive biological forces in order to build a soil. Following or accompanying the accumulation of parent material there is the introduction of living matter which is largely responsible for the constructional processes of soil development.[472] The residues of plants return more to the soil than the green plants have taken away. Throughout their lives plants have synthesized many organic substances such as sugars, starches, celluloses, fats, and proteins. Most of these materials return to the soil when the plant dies. The added organic matter produced by vegetation introduces a fundamental change. The substrate is no longer the former one of mineral matter alone, but now contains stored energy in the form of organic material. The soil soon becomes the abode of bacteria, fungi, and many other organisms. Throughout the whole process of soil development, plant and accompanying animal residues are converted, largely by the activities of microorganisms, into the dark-colored organic matter of the soil. Thus, the two functions of living matter in soil development are synthesis and decomposition. The total organic matter or humus of a mineral soil constitutes from less than 1 to more than 15 per cent of its dry weight. Sometimes soils are largely formed by the accumulations of organisms, as in peat or muck.

A true soil has five constituents: (1) the mineral particles of various sizes and in different stages of chemical decomposition; (2) organic matter in various stages of decomposition ranging from raw litter to well-decomposed humus; (3) the soil solution of various inorganic salts; (4) the soil atmosphere occupying interspaces not filled with soil solution; and (5) microorganisms, both plant and animal.

The chemical and physical characters of soils are determined, at least for a time, by the kinds of rocks from which they are derived. Soil derived from sandstone, for example, has much coarser particles and, consequently, a lower water-holding capacity and better aeration than the clay derived from limestone. The latter, moreover, may be rich in calcium carbonate; the former has little or none. Clearly, these factors have a profound effect upon the vegetation growing on the two types of soil.

Soil Texture.—Soils differ a great deal in the relative fineness or coarseness of the particles of which they are composed. These range from coarse gravel to dimensions below the visibility of the most powerful microscope. Texture is that property which has to do with the relative proportions of particles of different sizes. Of the three general groups of soil particles, the coarse ones are sand, those of medium size are silt, and the very fine particles are clay and colloids. The coarser particles of sand (0.2 millimeter in diameter or larger) have no colloidal properties and cannot absorb water or solutes. They do not cohere into crumbs or exhibit plasticity. Neither do they have any chemical action in the soil. They do have an important effect in counteracting certain unfavorable properties of clay.

The chief physical properties of clay are a high water-holding power, high plasticity or stickiness, a property of swelling when moist and of shrinking when dry, often accompanied by soil cracking. In fact, most of the colloidal properties of the soil are due to the clay fraction and decomposed organic matter. The inorganic soil colloids are complex aluminosilicates resulting largely from the partial weathering of feldspars and other primary minerals. The nature and amount of soil colloids determine more than any other constituent the character of the soil. They are so tremendously important as retainers of soil water and nutrients and in furnishing these to root hairs and roots that they have been designated the "protoplasm of the soil."

Base exchange is an important chemical reaction occurring in both the inorganic and organic colloids of soil. The colloidal nucleus or micelle is negatively charged and has the power to adsorb cations of calcium, magnesium, potassium, sodium, hydrogen, and other elements. Any cation can be replaced by another cation and thus go into solution and be made available for absorption by plant roots. Soil colloids are of three principal types which are designated as the hydrogen, the sodium, and the calcium colloids, which are more or less saturated with adsorbed positively charged hydrogen, sodium, or calcium ions, respectively. In the absence of calcium, magnesium, or other flocculating electrolytes, the hydrogen colloid is acid and easily dispersed into a colloidal suspension which may be readily leached from the surface soil. The sodium colloid is highly alkaline and is even more easily dispersed and likewise leached. But the calcium colloid is mildly alkaline and remains in a flocculated condition.[470] The colloids are never completely of one type in nature. Even the small absorbing power possessed by coarser soil particles may be due to a thin coating of colloidal materials. Coarser soil particles are cemented by clay into soil crumbs. Soil without clay would resemble a pile of sand. Chemically, clay is reactive in the presence of water. Fine sands and silts are intermediate in some of the properties described for coarse sands and clay.[749]

The actual diameters of the various particles are shown in Table 5. The relative amounts of these different grades of particles in a soil determine its texture. The coarse soil materials, consisting mainly of quartz or shattered rock fragments, represent the "skeleton" of the soil. Their function is largely that of anchoring the plant. Only the finer particles, the main products of weathering and decomposition, are very active in plant nutrition. The effect on the total surface of soil particles makes texture important as a soil property. The finer the particles the more surface is presented for the retention and solvent action of water and the greater is the absorbing area for plants. For example, coarse sand grains are 0.5 to 1 millimeter in diameter, but clay particles are so small that it requires approximately 65,000,000 of the largest of them to equal one grain of sand.[608] The clay particles are so finely divided that they exhibit the properties of matter in the colloidal state, one of which is an exceedingly great water-retaining capacity. The surface area presented by a single cubic inch of clay is 10 or more square feet, that of coarse sand only about 100 square inches.

With respect to texture, soils may be grouped into a number of classes such as sand, sandy loam, clay loam, and clay. Each is determined by the proportion of silt, clay, and sand that it contains. The class to which a soil belongs can be closely approximated by examination in the field and determined accurately by mechanical analysis. This consists of separating the soil into the grades of particles of which it is composed and determining the percentage of each. The coarser sands are separated by means of screens, the fine sand, silt, and clay, in water under the action of gravity after complete dispersion. This process of sedimentation is based on the principle that the larger particles sink more rapidly than the smaller ones. The texture of two very different soils is shown in Table 5.

TABLE 5.—DIAMETER AND PERCENTAGE OF VARIOUS SOIL PARTICLES AND THE TEXTURE OF A CLAY LOAM AND A FINE SAND

Source of soil	Fine gravel, 2 to 1 milli-meter	Coarse sand, 1 to 0.5 milli-meter	Medium sand, 0.5 to 0.25 milli-meter	Fine sand, 0.25 to 0.10 milli-meter	Very fine sand, 0.10 to 0.05 milli-meter	Silt, 0.05 to 0.005 milli-meter	Clay, less than 0.005 milli-meter*
Upland prairie, Lincoln, Neb...............	0.0	0.3	0.5	1.6	19.8	48.6	29.2
Forest nursery in sand hills, Halsey, Neb......	0.4	4.3	9.3	57.1	19.5	7.6	1.8

* The colloidal fraction of clay has diameters less than 0.002 millimeter.

The chief component of the first sample is silt, and because of its desirable proportions of sand and clay, the soil is designated as a clay loam. It has a good capacity for holding water—about 35 per cent of its dry weight when undisturbed in the field. The second is fine sand with a relatively low power of water retention, only about 15 per cent.

Many of the properties of a soil, such as content of air and water, depend upon the size of the soil particles rather than their composition. Soil texture not only exerts an important effect upon the water relations but also upon aeration, as well as the supply of nutrients. It profoundly affects the rapidity of the processes of decay of organic matter and its retention against leaching. The nitrogen content of a soil is closely related to its texture. A knowledge of soil texture is important in forestry,[1004] gardening, field-crop production, etc., and to an understanding of general plant distribution.

Soil Structure.—Structure is a term expressing the arrangement of the individual grains and aggregates that make up the soil mass. The irregularity in size and shape of the rock particles prevents tight packing and affords open, irregular spaces through which air and water circulate, while their weight and mutual pressure furnish the necessary resistance for firm root anchorage. The soil is not a mere physical mixture of its component parts. The particles are intimately commingled in crumbs or aggregates cemented with the soil colloids. Soils of single-grain structure like sand, where the particles function more or less separately, are fairly simple. They occur where there are insufficient cementing colloids to bind the particles together. Sandy soils tend to be dry, loose, and poor in soluble substances. A very complex structure is represented in clay where the soil granules or crumbs are composed of many particles bound together by colloidal or gluelike material originating from the finest clay and humus particles. Because of the excess of fine particles, the size of the interspaces or pores is so small that neither water nor air can move freely. Such soils readily become waterlogged. In drying they shrink and crack badly, often damaging plant roots. During drought the water moves very slowly through clay, and plants may not receive the necessary supply rapidly enough. A rich loam usually furnishes an example of a soil with an excellent structure. Some of the particles are large and function as individuals. Those of smaller size form a nucleus about which the still smaller particles aggregate into granules, a process termed *flocculation*. This aggregation of the smallest soil particles into groups or crumbs which act as individuals makes the soil much more porous. The larger interspaces permit the water to drain away as they become filled with air, while the smaller ones retain moisture.

The increase of smaller soil particles somewhat retards the movements of both water and air. Hence, loam soils are characterized by a higher and more uniform water content throughout than are sands. The fine crumbly soil structure known as *good tilth* is best suited for plants. Soil in good tilth must possess a water-stable crumb structure. When the crumbs are small enough to permit of good aeration but large enough to bind the soil together an ideal state is reached. Weathering is the effective agent in crumb formation, but its action is greatly facilitated by proper cultivation. Humus has a very important effect in lightening a heavy soil and binding a loose one, thus promoting a good soil structure (Fig. 100). Clay soils are usually improved in structure by the addition of lime which flocculates the particles into larger crumbs.

The structure of a soil largely determines its porosity. This, in turn, affects the absorption of water and, therefore, runoff and often the consequent erosion.[241] Structure has a marked effect upon the susceptibility of soil to wind and water erosion. During continued drought, soils without a cover of plants, even if they contain large amounts of clay, may be badly eroded by wind if the grains are grouped into fine crumbs

FIG. 100.—A field that has been listed and planted with corn. It has a fairly good soil structure. The corn grows slowly in the mineral soil at the bottom of the lister rows and receives more water than if surface planted. By repeated cultivation, the furrows are filled and the soil finally ridged up against the rows of corn.

or granules. Likewise the porosity of the underlying soil often determines the degree of erosion of bared soil on sloping lands. Where water penetrates too slowly, runoff and erosion are accelerated. Thus, soil structure affects the movement and storage of water in the soil and consequently soil aeration.[762] Water content and aeration, as well as compactness of soil, all profoundly influence root development.[241]

A good soil structure is maintained in nature by alternate wetting and drying, by freezing and thawing, by the action of organic matter and lime, and by the mechanical action of plants and burrowing animals. Poor structure is produced by the puddling action of rain on bare soil surfaces, poor drainage, alkali, etc.

The importance of roots in maintaining a good structure is often overlooked. As a result of the interlacing and clutching of earth particles by myriads of roots, the soil is compressed into granules whose identity, stability, and permanence are established by a surrounding colloidal film of humified root material.[744] Where the virgin prairie sod is first broken, it is mellow, moist, and rich. But after a few years of cultivation there occurs a great change in its physical condition. It becomes more compact, dries more quickly, bakes more readily, and often forms lumps and clods. But when grass is again grown for a few years, perfect tilth and freedom from clods are regained. The soil particles are wedged apart in places and crowded together in others. The small soil grains become aggregated together into larger ones. Each year many of the old roots die and are constantly replaced by new ones. The soil is filled with pores and old root channels; the humus from decaying vegetation helps cement soil particles into aggregates and thus lightens and enriches it.

The action of burrowing animals on soil structure is also important. Earthworms play a significant part. Their activities, in semiarid regions at least, are not confined to the surface layers. They sometimes penetrate to a depth of 10 feet. There are frequently thousands of them per acre. Burrowing everywhere, dragging down large vegetable fragments from above, they help to aerate the soil and keep it light. Rodents, ants, and various other animals mix and open up soil and subsoil and thus promote root penetration.[906] On the "hard lands" of the Great Plains, rodents have had an important effect upon soil structure, increasing water penetration and thus permitting the growth of certain deeply rooted species of plants. Insects, insect larvae, nematodes, and hosts of other organisms abound; all are instrumental in loosening the soil and thus affecting root development and plant growth.[342,442]

Humus and Microorganisms.—Humus comprises the more or less decayed organic portion of the soil. It consists of substances undergoing decay, of complex compounds resulting from decomposition, of constituents resistant to further decay, and of various substances synthesized by plant and animal microorganisms. It has no definite chemical composition since it is constantly changing as a result of the various processes of hydrolysis, oxidation, reduction, and condensation involved in decomposition. It has a high carbon content, usually about 55 per cent, and usually about 3 to 6 per cent nitrogen. In many soils, the elements carbon and nitrogen occur in the ratio of approximately 10 to 1. Humus comprises the total organic matter in soils.[950] It originates almost entirely from decay of plants and microorganisms and, with rare exception, only a small amount is derived from feces or the remains of animals. Humus is dark in color, light in weight, and more or less intimately mixed with the other soil components. It does not dissolve in water, but combines readily with various inorganic soil constituents. It exists in the soil in the colloidal state with water as the medium of dispersion, the water being adsorbed by the humus.[951] All soils that support vegetation contain humus. The amount may be very small in newly formed soils, such as wind-blown sand that bears only a sparse plant population, but it increases with the development of the sere.

To Determine the Amount of Organic Matter in a Soil by Loss on Ignition.—Select samples of soils from several habitats representing different stages of a sere, such as grassland, scrub, forest, etc. Samples should be taken to the same depth in duplicate and each sample very thoroughly mixed. Place about 5 grams of the dry soil in a crucible of known weight when oven dry. Heat in an oven at 110°C. for 3 hours or more, cool in a desiccator, and weigh very accurately. Ignite in a furnace or over a large burner at a low red heat until the organic matter is all oxidized. Cool again in a desiccator and reweigh. Calculate the percentage of humus based on the dry weight of the soil. This simple method, although widely used, is open to objection, since it sometimes gives results that are too high.

Based on dry weight, the organic matter of a mineral soil may constitute from less than 1 to more than 15 per cent of the soil. These low percentages are due to the fact that the mineral-soil matrix has a density about three times as great as that of the humus. Relative to volume, the humus may constitute 4 to 12 per cent and the mineral-soil components only 41 to 62 per cent, the remaining volume being pore space which is occupied by water and air.[747] The amount of humus varies with the climate. Arid soils contain less, partly because there is less vegetation from which it may form, and partly because of its too rapid oxidation. For example, fine-textured soils in Washington under 20 inches of rainfall have more than four times as much humus as soils of similar texture under 8 inches of precipitation.[851] Similarly, soils of the mixed prairie of western Nebraska under 16 inches of rainfall have only about 58 per cent as much organic matter as true prairie soils of the same texture under 30 inches of precipitation in the eastern part of the state.[745] Moreover, in humid regions most of the humus is concentrated in the upper portion of the soil, the deeper soil being poorly supplied. In soils of semiarid and arid regions the organic matter is distributed more or less uniformly from near the surface to a considerable depth. In soils that are very wet, decay is greatly retarded and plant remains may accumulate in such quantities as to constitute 85 per cent or more of the weight of the soil. This is the case in peat or muck.

Although much of the humus has its origin from aboveground plant parts, large amounts are formed from root decay and a smaller amount from the remains of soil organisms. The decay of the organic debris is brought about almost entirely by the activities of various groups of bacteria, fungi, protozoa, and other inhabitants of the soil.

The microscopic plants and animals of the soil are very diverse in food requirements, but they are alike in that all finally depend upon decomposable organic matter. They are the universal scavengers, the organic matter regulating and determining the nature of microbial populations as well as their activities. They are most numerous in the surface 4 inches of rich, well aerated soil, in which the soil flora and fauna seem very similar the world over as regards species.[218] During severe drought, the microorganisms live in the encysted form. Bacteria occur by the millions per gram of soil. They are most numerous in spring and fall, but their numbers vary from day to day and even from hour to hour.[218] They usually recombine 5 to 10 per cent of the carbon of the materials they have decomposed, but the amount varies widely. They thrive best in neutral soils and are mostly replaced by fungi in highly acid ones.

More than 250 species of soil-inhabiting fungi are known. Occurring in great abundance, they promote decomposition, often in soils that are too acid for bacteria to function effectively. Fungi transform into their own tissue 20 to 60 per cent of the carbon of the compounds they have decomposed.[750] By assimilating the ammonia and nitrates produced by decay, they save them from loss by leaching. *Actinomycetes* are a group of organisms, very abundant in soils, closely related to both bacteria and fungi. Many algae occur in the surface soils. Protozoa, including amoebae, ciliates, flagellates, etc., are of world-wide distribution. Certain species greatly decrease the bacterial populations by feeding upon them, but ultimately their remains are added to the humus of the soil. When all of the soil microorganisms are considered collectively, the amount of protoplasm in the surface 6 inches of a fertile soil is indeed great. It has been shown at the Rothamsted Experimental Station that amoebae alone may contribute 120 pounds per acre, flagellates about 75 pounds, bacteria from 1,500 to 7,500 pounds, and fungi an amount approaching that of the bacteria.[751] Thus, significant amounts of microorganic materials are added to the organic matter that these same organisms are so active in decomposing in their search for energy materials.

The first organic materials to disappear are the sugars, starches, pentosans, pectins, celluloses, and proteins. Their decomposition results in the synthesis of a proportional amount of microbial protoplasm.[949,954] In fact, the nitrogen and mineral residues, such as phosphates, potassium, and calcium, made available by the decomposition of plant remains, may again be largely utilized by the microorganisms and released gradually upon their death and decay. Only a small part may at once be made available to the growing plant. This is fortunate, since otherwise the rapidity with which organic matter is decomposed would result in the liberation of nutrients which would be either largely lost to the atmosphere or leached beyond the root horizon. Other organic materials such as lignins, fats, waxes, etc., are decomposed much more slowly by soil organisms.[949]   Thus, humus furnishes a small but continuous supply of nutrients for the growing plants.[952]

In the presence of air, oxygen is slowly but continuously absorbed during the process of decay and an almost equal volume of carbon dioxide evolved.   The organic materials are finally broken down into simpler compounds, the end products being carbon dioxide, water, ammonia, methane, and inorganic compounds of sulphur and phosphorus.   With the decay of the tissues, compounds of calcium, potassium, manganese, etc., are likewise returned to the soil.   The ammonia is immediately oxidized to nitrous and then to nitric compounds, which occur in the soil as nitrates.   The process of decay, however, is not one of immediate simplification.   Resynthesis of much material into microbial protoplasm occurs throughout.   Moreover, the various organic acids, etc., originating as intermediary products, react upon the minerals with which they are in contact, and these may thereby be made soluble and available to the plant.   During humus formation, the materials take on the characteristic dark color.[649]

Humus is being constantly formed and is continually being broken down.   Although essentially a transient soil constituent, in an undisturbed soil it is fairly constant both in amount and in composition. Various stages in its decomposition are always in progress.   It becomes an important source of nutrients for plants, and there is thus a close relation between the vegetation and the soil organisms.   The latter are dependent almost entirely upon growing plants to furnish materials upon which they live, while vegetation is equally dependent on the activities of the soil organisms for removing the residues of previous generations of plants and for the continued production in the soil of simple materials which are necessary to its growth.[747]   The enormous importance of this process in the economy of nature is evident, and the importance of the role of soil organisms can scarcely be overemphasized. Except for the work of the wrecking crews composed of myriads of microscopic organisms, which immediately attack the fallen vegetation and reduce it finally to water-soluble and, hence, usable compounds, plant residues would be distinctly detrimental to the soil.

Several factors profoundly influence the rate at which humus is formed and accumulates, as well as its chemical composition.   These include (1) the nature of the plant and animal residues, including those of microorganisms, from which it is formed; (2) the nature of the microorganisms active in the processes of decomposition; and (3) the temperature, moisture and nitrogen supply, aeration, and soil reaction under which they are decomposed.[953]

The decay of organic matter takes place most rapidly in warm, moist, well aerated soil, *i.e.*, under conditions most favorable to the development

of the organisms carrying on these processes.   In tropical climates there
is little or no accumulation, despite the luxuriant vegetation.   For each
decrease of 10°C. in mean annual temperature, an increase of two to
three times in humus content has been shown to occur.[449]   Raw humus is
an accumulation of litter in cold or dry soils or those with an acid or
alkaline reaction unfavorable to the growth of organisms causing decay.
Three distinct layers occur in the raw humus of forests.   *Litter* comprises
the upper portion of the forest floor, slightly or not at all decomposed.
The more or less decomposed organic matter just beneath the litter
constitutes a layer of *duff*.   A still deeper layer, in which the organic

Fig. 101.—Section of a peat deposit several feet in depth.

matter is so far decomposed that its original form is no longer distinguishable, is termed *leaf mold*.[17]   Certain coniferous forests and heaths
of cool climates have soils of this type where the disintegration of the
humus proceeds very slowly.   Conversely, accumulation of litter in the
deciduous forests of the United States, where it decomposes rapidly and
adds its fertility to the soil, is small—seldom exceeding 1 inch—compared
with the northern coniferous forests.[31]   Where organisms causing decay
are excluded because of poor aeration, the plant bodies accumulate as
peat.   The structures of the dead plants or parts of plants forming the
peat are often preserved (Fig. 101).

The effect of humus in improving the physical condition of the soil
is marked.   It acts as a weak cement to bind sand, lightens or opens
a clay soil by separating the particles, and thus increases percolation,
aeration, bacterial activity, and ease of root penetration.   Being very
absorbent, it helps to retain water so that in regions of moderate rainfall

vegetation growing in soils rich in humus is less likely to suffer from drought. In fact, its physical effects are so marked that when the organic matter present in a soil is very high the distinctions between sands, loams, and clays are practically obliterated. Soils that have lost humus are harder than formerly and in poorer tilth; they crack easily and expose great surfaces to evaporation.

The Soil Solution.—An analysis of water that has drained through a soil shows that it contains a great many substances which have been dissolved. Certain portions of the soil have gone into solution. The soil solution is very dilute, its concentration ranging from 0.05 to 0.2 per cent in ordinary cultivated soils. The salts are almost entirely dissociated into their component ions. The osmotic pressure of the solution is about 0.2 to 1 atmosphere, which is much less than the 5 to 20 atmospheres pressure commonly found in the cell sap of the roots of many plants. The clay yields calcium, potassium, iron, and magnesium. In addition to the mineral salts of plant ash, humus in the process of decay produces nitrates, sulphates, and phosphates. Other solutes are built by bacteria and other soil organisms, and still others are excreted by roots. All of the nitrate nitrogen, usually 50 to 300 parts per million of soil, much of the potassium, commonly 10 to 40 parts per million, but only a fraction of the phosphates (PO_4), 1 to 2 parts per million, is in the solution.[753] Oxygen and carbon dioxide are important dissolved gases. The soil solution is obtained for study by direct pressure, centrifugal force, or more conveniently by displacing it with other liquids. The moist soil must first be well packed into suitable cylinders with perforated bottoms and the solution displaced by the addition of water, ethyl alcohol, or paraffin oil added from above.

The soil solution is variable in its composition, partly because of the variability of the solvent power of the water, which, in turn, may depend upon its carbon dioxide content, and partly because of the nature and amount of soil colloids. They retain the solutes, except nitrates and chlorides, by adsorption.[912] Thus, the solid phase of clay and humus hydrogels contains ions in the imbibed water and the liquid or water phase also contains ions. The amount thus retained varies with the amount of water, partly adsorbed and in surrounding films. The more water present the more solutes go into solution. As the water increases, however, the concentration of the solution decreases. Root hairs with their gelatinous walls are in immediate contact with the soil particles. Owing to precipitation, absorption by the roots of plants, evaporation, and drainage, the water content is always changing. Vegetation, moreover, is constantly removing nutrients, and other amounts are lost by leaching. Cropping decreases the total concentration, and it is usually increased by fallow.[110] The activities of microorganisms continuously alter the amount of nitrates, and this, in turn, affects the amount of dissolved bases. The soil solution is constantly changing in both composition and concentration. It contains the reserve nutrients, and as these are absorbed by plants, new supplies (except nitrates and chlorides) are liberated from the colloidal soil complexes.[409,912] Plants grown experimentally in culture solutions of low concentration, continuously maintained, make almost as good a growth as in those of high concentration likewise maintained. Indeed, it is believed they would grow equally well if it were practicable continuously to maintain the concentrations of the weak solutions. In a study of the soil solution, the possibility must be kept in mind that substances may enter into a true solution and be absorbed by the plant before diffusing into the mass of the soil solution. This may result from the intimate relation between soil colloids and root hairs, a higher partial pressure of CO_2 and greater concentration of biologically produced acids existing at the surface of the absorbing tissue than exists in the soil water generally.[110]

Although over 30 elements have been found in the ash of plants, experiments with plant cultures have shown that only a few of these are essential to normal growth. This was determined long ago by adding various soluble salts to pure distilled water or water in clean quartz sand and observing the effect upon growth and yield. Such studies show that for normal growth plants need only the soluble salts of nitrogen, sulphur, phosphorus, potassium, calcium, magnesium, iron, and sometimes chlorine. It has been found that minute traces of other elements such as manganese and boron[91] are also essential for certain species,[89] the necessary amounts apparently having occurred as impurities in the chemicals used in the earlier experiments.[592,867,868]

Nearly all natural soils contain these elements in sufficient amounts to promote a good growth of vegetation. Only certain "sterile" sands, which consist almost wholly of silica, and a few other types of soil are really deficient in the necessary nutritive elements. Most unproductive sands are, moreover, unfavorable to vegetation, not because they are deficient in nutrients, but because they cannot retain a sufficient supply of water. Where land is continuously cropped, the addition of nutrients and especially nitrates as fertilizers greatly increases yields. The amount, however, must be in accord with the water supply. If the plants are stimulated to a luxuriant growth when water is abundant, they are greatly harmed by subsequent drought.

In native grasslands, nitrates are used as rapidly as they are formed. With rare exceptions, there is never an excess. When the soil is warm and moist and the plants are growing rapidly, nitrates are elaborated rapidly but not excessively, and the plants thrive. As the soil becomes dry and the plants begin to suffer, nitrification diminishes, and thus the plants are automatically saved from excessive nutrients in time of drought.[744] Different species of plants remove the various nutrients in different amounts. These differences are due both to the extent and to the degree of branching of the roots and to variations in their absorptive activity. Under natural conditions, the materials removed from the soil by growing vegetation are ultimately returned in plant remains or animal excretions. Those washed down into the deeper soil are often brought to the surface again through absorption by deeply penetrating roots. Certain soil constituents such as nitrogen compounds and calcium carbonate are easily leached out and large amounts lost annually in drainage water, but those of potassium and phosphorus are almost entirely retained in place by adsorption by the soil colloids. Thus, soils of arid and semiarid regions, occupied largely by grassland or desert vegetation, are potentially richer than well-leached soils in more humid regions.

DEVELOPMENT OF SOILS*

Soils undergo a process of development somewhat analogous to that of vegetation. Both are a product of their environment.[472] The controlling factors in the development of soil are climate and vegetation. Geologic materials including mantle-rock and bedrock are necessary, but are passive rather than active elements in soil formation. From them, the soils develop through constructional processes that involve the growth of vegetation, the accumulation and decomposition of organic substances, the formation of new chemical compounds, the progressive breaking down of the parent materials, the translocation of materials in the soil, and the formation of a more or less layered profile. Topography is important in so far as it affects the degree and kind of development through its influence on drainage and penetration and consequently on the water supply, salt content, amount of erosion, character and density of the vegetation, and other local conditions.

The development of soil and the production of vegetation are so intimately related that it is scarcely possible to study the one without some knowledge of the other. Functionally, the most important thing about a soil is its productivity for plants. Those characteristics which make a soil productive are themselves due to the operation of biological forces, particularly native vegetation. Perhaps the greatest influence of climate on soils is exerted indirectly through its partial determination of the kind of native vegetation under which the soil evolves.

* Papers by Charles E. Kellogg, principal Soil Scientist, Division of Soil Survey, Bureau of Chemistry and Soils, have been especially helpful in the preparation of this section.

The features assumed by the soil in its development from infancy through youth, maturity, and old age vary with the environment. Thus, all mature soils developed on undulating or gently sloping surfaces and for a long time undisturbed by injurious erosion, by deposit, or by the activities of man, owe their major characteristics not so much to the kind of rock from which they originated as to the nature of the climate in which they have developed.[900]   Hence, all stable, mature soils of a given climatic region belong to a climatic soil type.   They tend to show a similar sequence of horizontal layers, irrespective of the underlying rock, the latter causing only minor differences.   These layers occur in a definite sequence and differ from one another in one or more easily discernible features, such as color, lime content, texture, structure, and compaction. A vertical cut through these various horizons is termed a *soil profile*. The nature of the several layers has a profound effect upon the water, air, and nutrient relations of the soil and consequently upon root extent and distribution and nature of the plant cover.   The parallel development of soil and vegetation and the role of each in modifying the other are of great interest and importance (Fig. 102).

The constructional processes of soil development are due largely to the incorporation of plant parts among the mineral particles.   This may occur following the accumulation of the parent materials or along with it.   Vegetation introduces both directly and indirectly the biological factor into soil formation.[437]   Upon the fall of leaves and stems the organic matter of the plant, which has resulted from synthetic activity, is incorporated into the soil.   These residues supply food for visible and microscopic soil organisms; these soil organisms decompose the plant remains, which ultimately become incorporated into the soil as humus.

The two most important kinds of vegetation thus active in soil formation are forests and grasslands.   Differences of great significance occur among coniferous and deciduous trees and grasses as regards their rooting habits, the relative proportions and actual amounts of various elements they absorb, and the amounts they deposit in or on the soil surface with the fall of the leaves or the death of the tops.   Organic remains under a forest of conifers have a much lower content of bases, such as calcium, than those under a deciduous forest.   The ash (basic material) of a species varies within rather narrow limits, regardless of the nature of the soil on which it grows, but generally plants poor in bases and consequently producing an acid humus occur naturally only on acid soils.   Usually the best growth of deciduous trees is made in areas having a good supply of bases in the soil or underlying parent materials.   Under such conditions, the leaves are relatively high in bases, especially calcium.   Grasses absorb, in general, large amounts of calcium and likewise return large amounts of this element to the surface soil. Moreover, most grasses are only moderately deeply rooted and many species of arid climates are shallowly rooted. Where the bulk of absorption occurs in the surface layers, there is a tendency to reduce the

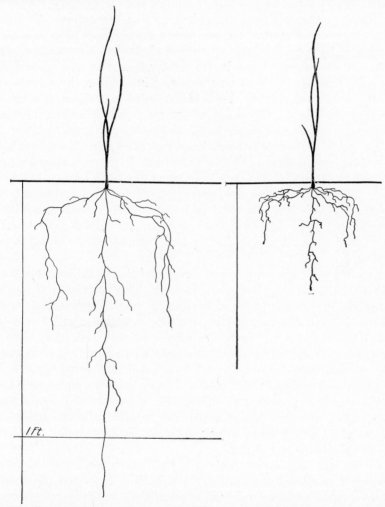

Fɪɢ. 102.—Onion seedlings of the same age. The one on the right was grown in compact soil, the left in loose soil. Both drawings are made to the same scale.

amount of leaching through the upper part of the soil. The converse is true with deeply rooted vegetation.

Soil Profile.—Most soils consist of particles of various sizes, chemical constitution, and degree of solubility. During long periods of time, calcium carbonate and other soluble materials are leached from the surface soils and carried down to lower layers or to ground water and consequently out of the soil. The finer, insoluble soil particles (colloidal clay, etc.) are also mechanically carried downward (under those types of soil formation in which they become dispersed) to variable depths which depend largely upon the amount of rainfall and the rapidity with which the water is absorbed and transpired by the vegetation. Thus, the surface layers of a mature soil are poorer in soluble salts as a result of leaching and are coarser grained because of eluviation or washing down of the colloidal clay. These layers constitute *A*, the *zone of extraction*. The soil immediately below this zone and into which the soluble salts and the finest soil particles have been carried is designated as *B*, the *zone of concentration*. Obviously, at greater depths there is a third zone *C*, where neither extraction nor accumulation has occurred.

The *A* and *B* zones or horizons constitute the solum (L. soil) produced by soil-building processes. The *C* horizon is the weathered parent material or unconsolidated rock from which (usually) the soil has developed. Each soil zone or horizon has a distinct color, texture, and structure. The soil is a natural body in dynamic equilibrium with its environment. The following example from an upland prairie soil in eastern Nebraska illustrates characteristics considered in describing soil profiles:

As a result of the processes of development, the mellow, surface 16 to 18 inches of soil has a *granular structure*. This layer has lost much of its colloidal clay. The forces of weathering, especially repeated freezing and thawing and alternate wetting and drying, together with the greater humus content and the favorable effects of root activities, have all combined to produce this excellent granular structure. It is distinctly different from that below (about 1.5 to 3 feet in depth), which has a higher clay content and which clearly shows a *prismatic structure*. Here, due to alternate wetting and drying, the tenacious clay, from which much of the lime has been leached, has formed irregular prisms, the surfaces of which are much more weathered, darker in color, and richer in nutrients, than the interior.

In the granular layer, roots penetrate easily and spread widely, thoroughly ramifying throughout the soil. This layer has the greatest supply of roots, certain dominant grasses and a few other species scarcely penetrating more deeply. Penetration is much more difficult and branching is less pronounced in the prismatic layer. Here the rootlets are found almost entirely appressed to the surfaces of the columns, where water penetrates most readily, air is most abundant, and nutrients apparently are more concentrated. Relatively few penetrate the interior of the prisms. When they enter the *massive* layer below, they assume a more normal branching habit and are much more easily excavated, since clay is less abundant and the lime occurs in such amounts as to give the soil a mellow structure. Since there is less clay, the soil expands and contracts less upon wetting and drying.

To Examine Soil Profiles.—Remove the exposed surface of weathered soil from a steep bank along a railway or road by means of spade or pick. Examine the several horizons of which the soil profile is composed. How deeply do the roots penetrate? Where are they most numerous? What is the depth of greatest compaction? Note and explain the changes in color from surface to subsoil. How do the different horizons vary in consistence? Place a small amount of soil on a watch glass and moisten with distilled water. Add a few drops of weak hydrochloric acid. Note the degree of effervescence. A very faint effervescence can be heard more easily than seen. If there is none, the soil is neutral or acid. Test each of the several

Fig. 103.—Soil profile on low, flat, forested silt loam soil. The prismatic form is typical of the *B* horizon of mature soils of southern Illinois developed under poor drainage. (*After Norton and Smith.*)

horizons and determine at what depth lime accumulation occurs. Compare this soil profile with one in lowland (Fig. 103).

Zonal Soil Groups.—Soils that are young, *i.e.*, recently derived from rock or built up by deposit due to wind or water, as well as badly eroded soils, do not show a profile similar to that of mature soils upon which climate and vegetation have acted and reacted for long periods of time. The character of the climate eventually alters the nature of the soil from nearly all kinds of rock to such an extent that the mature soil type is similar in its main features throughout a given climatic region.

The soils of the Great Plains, for example, consist of three great belts extending quite across the United States from Canada southward to Mexico.[567] These correspond, in general, to differences in degree of grassland climate and in the type of vegetative cover. All of the soils (from near the Rocky Mountains eastward to about the one hundredth meridian), when mature, are dark in color and underlaid by a zone of lime-carbonate accumulation, beyond which water usually does not penetrate. They differ, however, in degree of darkness of soil color and depth of the carbonate layer. Where precipitation is least, the soil is brown and the carbonates have accumulated at depths of only 12 to 18 inches. This delimits the area in which water and nutrients are absorbed by the native grasses. The effect of vegetation upon the profile is shown by its removal. Where land is broken, water penetrates quite beyond the carbonate layer. Had there been no vegetation to absorb the water, the layer of carbonate accumulation would probably never have developed.[811]

Where precipitation increases eastward, the carbonate layer is deeper, vegetation is more abundant and taller, and the soil is of a dark brown color. Still farther eastward the carbonate accumulations usually reach depths of 5 to 6 feet. The soil is black in color and continues dark to a greater depth (8 to 24 inches) than in any other part of this climatic region. The vegetation is of the deeply rooted, mostly mixed-prairie type.

Another zonal soil type is represented under a heavier rainfall eastward (prairie soils) where the soils are nearly black or dark brown in color and are leached of rock carbonates, which do not accumulate at a lower level. In this zonal type the soil is moist to a depth of many feet, in fact, often to the underlying water table. Roots of native plants penetrate very deeply (6 to 20 feet or more) and true prairie prevails.

Depending upon the nature of the climatic environment, there are three general processes of zonal soil development—calcification, podzolization, and laterization.[472]

Calcification.—The calcification process of soil development is most typically maintained under grasses or grasslike vegetation and climates with restricted precipitation. There may be considerable leaching, but not enough to remove the calcium and magnesium carbonates. Consequently these accumulate in the lower part of the solum. The plants absorb and transport bases from the lower soil horizons to the surface in relatively large amounts. The soil does not become acid, or if so only slightly acid, and the colloids, both organic and inorganic, in the presence of abundant calcium are not eluviated. The micropopulation is predominantly bacterial; the decomposed organic materials are relatively insoluble and remain in the upper part of the soil. There is little or no movement of clay or other colloidal material from the A to the B horizon. The kinds of grasses and their abundance determine largely the depth of color, content of organic matter, and thickness of the soil itself.

The calcification process is dominant in the genesis of several of the important zonal groups of soils including Prairie, Chernozem, Chestnut (or Dark Brown), Brown, Gray, and Desert soils (Fig. 104). The darkness of the soils is an expression of the density of the grass cover under which they developed. This in turn is the result of precipitation, the higher rainfall supporting the densest cover of vegetation, the lower the most sparse.

Prairie Soils.—These are grassland soils but were developed under a relatively high precipitation. They include the most humid upland grassland areas. They have been leached to the extent that they do not have a horizon of calcium carbonate as do all of the *Pedocals* (Gr. *pedon*, soil; *chalix*, lime) or calcium soils. Otherwise they are more closely related to them than to the other major soil group (*Pedalfers*), which also lack a

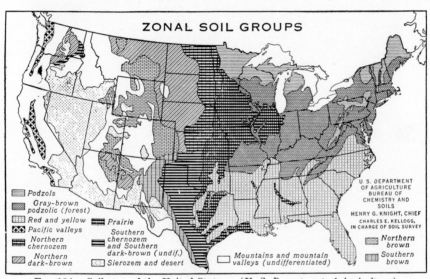

Fig. 104.—Soil map of the United States. (*U. S. Department of Agriculture.*)

"lime" layer. Prairie soils are very dark brown in color, rich in organic matter, especially in the upper portion, and are well supplied with the nutrients necessary for a luxuriant growth of grasses and forbs. The surface soils over most of the area are slightly acid. Their high fertility and the favorable climate make them among the most productive in the world for grain and grasses.[1013]

Chernozem Soils.—These are found in the most humid part of the drier regions having soils with a calcium carbonate horizon. This group of soils is one of the most important in the world. The black soils of the Russian and Siberian steppes, the plains of both North and South America, and extensive areas in India and Australia belong to this group. They develop under a continental climate usually with a small excess of evaporation over precipitation. The luxuriant growth of grasses has produced black soils, very high in content of organic matter and very fertile for cultivated cereals, especially wheat, as well as alfalfa, sorghums, etc. Calcium and magnesium are brought to the surface by the grasses. After their death and decay the elements are united with carbonic acid to form their respective carbonates, which are never leached beyond the depths of the roots of the grasses, *i.e.*, the general depth of water penetration. During the rainy season, the percolating water is highly charged with carbon dioxide liberated from the decomposing organic matter.

Fig. 105.—Three soil profiles. The Podzol (left) has a thick covering of forest duff, underlaid abruptly by a whitish A_2 horizon. A Chernozem is shown on the right and a Prairie soil in the middle. The scale in feet is approximately the same for all. (*Photographs, courtesy of C. E. Kellogg and (center) Nebraska Conservation and Survey Division.*)

This converts the calcium carbonate into the soluble and unstable bicarbonate, which is leached downward. Upon drying of the soil, it is deposited as calcium carbonate. This remains undissolved by any capillary water moving upward, since this water is not so highly charged with carbon dioxide. Thus the only upward movement is through the plants.

The deep distribution of humus through the profile is due in part to the action of earthworms, insects, etc., and the extensive burrowing of rodents. In addition, a large part of the humus is derived from the roots of the plants which decay where they grew throughout the soil profile. Thus, the luxuriant prairie grasses have exerted a powerful soil-building influence. Chernozems are somewhat less productive than Prairie soils, not because of lack of innate fertility, but owing to reduced precipitation (Fig. 105).

Other Pedocals.—With decreasing precipitation westward the vegetation becomes sparser, the soils become lighter in color, and the solum thinner. In progressively drier climates occur the *Chestnut* or *Dark Brown soils* and *Brown soils* of mixed prairie and its short-grass disclimax, the *Gray soils* of semideserts, and finally the *Desert soils*.[648] The vegetation of the Chestnut soils while not luxuriant is still well developed, especially the underground part. An abundance of roots, etc., grow and decay in the surface layer especially. The deeper layer, with less humus, is lighter brown and contains the calcium accumulations. The lime zone decreases in depth with decreased precipitation and the influence of vegetation on soil development becomes less and less.

The fertile Chestnut soils and the best Brown soils are used for wheat production, despite the hazardous climate. Grazing predominates over the more rolling Brown soils, as well as the Gray and Desert soils. Since the nutrients have not been leached, even the shallow Gray soils above the lime layer, though low in organic matter, are fertile.

Podzolization.—The process of podzolization is typically active in the formation of the *Podzol soils* of the northern, humid, cold temperate regions on heath lands and especially under coniferous forest. The conditions necessary for Podzol formation are a humid climate where precipitation exceeds evaporation, an acid soil, and an acid-humus producing flora. Podzols are also often well developed under hardwood and mixed hardwood and coniferous forest. There is sufficient moisture to remove the soluble salts completely from the soil. Trees, especially coniferous trees, absorb much less of the bases than does grassland vegetation. Conifers have a lower content of bases in their leaves and twigs, which are shed slowly, than do the broad leaves of deciduous trees, and there is relatively little shrubby or herbaceous undergrowth in coniferous forests. Not enough bases are returned to the surface soil to prevent it from becoming acid. Consequently the colloids become partly to almost wholly saturated with hydrogen. Thus, the occurrence of Podzol is intimately connected with the vegetation of a region.[1003] In pronounced Podzol soils, the soil type has been determined very largely by the plant cover. In fact, vegetation is the cause and podzolization is the effect.

Podzols.—The acidic *Podzol soils* are very unfavorable to insect life, earthworms, and bacteria. Low temperatures and poor aeration are contributing factors, and the tannins from coniferous trees are thought to have a toxic action, especially to bacteria. Bacteria are almost entirely replaced by the more acid-enduring fungi. These may grow in such abundance that their mycelia may be seen interwoven among the layers of raw humus. Such soils are low in organic matter. Decomposition of organic matter by fungi leads to the production of organic acids and relatively soluble substances, and to the reduction and solubility of iron. Both the soluble organic matter and the hydrogen-saturated organic colloids favor the mobility of the inorganic materials, especially iron-, aluminum-, and hydrogen-saturated clay colloids. In normal soil, under conditions of good drainage, the soluble iron moves downward, becomes oxidized, and accumulates in the *B* horizon. A large proportion of the colloids, both organic and inorganic, likewise become precipitated in this horizon.[472,437] Thus, the surface soil becomes impoverished of fine colloids and organic matter and of nutrients most essential for the growth of crops. As the reduced iron moves downward in true solution, it passes out of the influence of the soluble organic matter and is oxidized and precipitated in the lower horizons.[470] Hence, a concentration of iron, and frequently of aluminum, the solubility of which rises rapidly with increasing acidity, occurs in the *B* horizon (hence, Ped-Al-Fe-rs). Such a soil is acid throughout. These leached soils are not fertile from the standpoint of cultivated crops (Fig. 187) but, when cleared of the native forest, are responsive to intensive management and can support a successful agriculture of the subsistence type with emphasis on dairying.

The essential feature of a Podzol profile is its division into three main horizons, usually including several minor ones, more or less sharply differentiated from one another. A layer of organic matter (A_0), consisting of leaves of trees and other forest debris, covers the surface to a depth varying from 1 to 12 or more inches. The material is brown in color, acid in reaction, and only partly decayed. This raw humus layer may be sharply divided from the mineral soil below, but usually, in the United States, the upper portion of the mineral horizon contains more or less partly decomposed organic matter. The upper part of the mineral soil (A_1 horizon) is very thin and dark gray in color. The top varies from "salt-and-pepper" gray to nearly black, depending upon the amount of incorporated organic matter. The lower part (A_2 horizon) ranges in thickness from a mere film to a foot or more and is light gray in color. It has a friable or almost loose platy structure and has been thoroughly leached or eluviated.[568] Thus, the surface of the Podzol has been impoverished of bases, colloids, and nitrogen;[903] almost nothing but silica remains in this leached horizon (Fig. 105).

The *B* horizon has a more compact consistence. It is reddish, brown, or nearly black in color. The thickness varies from a mere film to several inches. The color becomes lighter with depth, shading off gradually into that of the underlying parent material. This horizon has been enriched by the addition of eluviated organic matter, compounds of iron and aluminum, etc. The enrichment at one place may not include all of these substances. In sandy Podzols the *B* horizon is cemented into a hardpan (ortstein) whereas in clayey Podzols the soil has an angular, small nutlike structure. The soil is acid in reaction.

The regional distribution of the coniferous forest in northern New England and in parts of Pennsylvania, New York, and the Lake States is approximately coincident with the distribution of the strongly leached or Podzol profile.[338] In parts of the New England states, for example, a surface layer of raw humus, often 4 to 5 inches deep, is underlaid with a few inches of a leached grayish soil, below which the thin, reddish-brown soil soon gives way to the parent rock. The absorbing roots of coniferous trees are often largely confined to the surface layer of raw humus.[621] A pronounced beneficial effect upon such a soil profile may be brought about by converting the coniferous forest into stands of hardwoods.[281,618] In fact, as a result of a change in the type of decomposition of organic matter, consequent of change in the nature of the vegetation, aeration, and reaction of the substratum, one soil may actually change into another.[281] A distinctly podzolized profile has altered in 20 years to a typical Gray-brown earth.[338]

Gray-brown Podzolic Soils.—These soils have developed under a deciduous forest, rich in undergrowth, with a moist temperate climate. In general, they have developed under a podzolization process but one less intense than that giving rise to the Podzol. The surface horizons contain more nutrient elements and more organic matter. Deciduous trees return bases to the surface of the soil more rapidly than do conifers. It has been estimated that a beechwood receives an annual dressing of 5 to 7 grams of calcium per square meter but a pine forest only 2 grams.[762] Most deciduous trees maintain a steady flow of bases from the soil layers into which their roots penetrate, to the surface, and it is a common silvicultural practice to include a proportion of them in a coniferous forest to reduce or prevent soil deterioration. The favorable influence of birch in the acid Podzols of the northern coniferous forests is pronounced.

Differences have been determined in the amount of lime, acidity, and nitrogen in the several stages of virgin forest succession on sandy soil in Minnesota. The litter, duff, and leaf mold of the A_0 horizon in the maple-basswood climax each contained about five times the percentage of lime and one and one-half to two times as much nitrogen as was found in the jack pine and Norway pine stages. More than a ton of lime per acre was found in the forest floor of the maple-basswood climax. The medial stage of white pine, interspersed with some hardwoods, exceeded the values obtained in the Norway pine forest. The acidity decreased from pH 4.5 in the duff of jack pine to 4.8 in white pine, and was 6.3 in the maple-basswood.[18,19,20]

The undisturbed profile of the Gray-brown Podzolic soils does not include a thick layer of raw humus. The accumulation of organic matter on the surface is rarely more than 1 or 2 inches in thickness. Although it is better decomposed than is the raw humus overlying well developed Podzols, yet it is not usually thoroughly decomposed into black, granular colloidal material. The A_1 horizon is a thin layer impregnated with organic matter. It is thicker than the corresponding horizon of Podzols and usually less acid in reaction. The A_2 horizon is darker in color than that of Podzols, being grayish brown or pale yellow. Neither is it usually so thoroughly eluviated. Like the B horizon it is strongly acid. Compounds of iron and aluminum but no organic materials have leached into the B horizon.[568]

Virgin Gray-brown soils are more fertile for agricultural crops than are those of the Podzol group, but less fertile than the Chernozems. The addition of lime and fertilizers greatly increases their medium natural fertility. The favorable climate under which deciduous forest develops permits the production of a wide variety of crops.

Red and Yellow Soils.—These soils of the southeastern United States have formed under the influence of both podzolization and laterization (*i.e.*, the leaching of silica).[472] The latter is more strictly a geological process than one of soil building. It seems to be the normal result of rock weathering under a hot climate with abundant rainfall. The color is an expression, in part, of high temperatures. Rate of humus decay, being a biochemical reaction, increases steadily with increase in temperature. Increased humidity reduces evaporation and results in greater percolation of water and hence greater leaching of bases and higher acidity.

The Yellow soils occupy the sandy regions of the Coastal Plains from North Carolina to eastern Texas. They occur predominantly on level lands where ground water occurs at a depth of a few feet, usually immediately beneath the solum, or has stood at that position until very recent geological time. Today they support a subclimax coniferous forest. The Red soils occupy the southeastern part of the United States north of the Yellow soils. They occur in regions of good drainage where the water table lies many feet below the surface and are forested mostly by deciduous trees.

The preceding groups of zonal soils develop under conditions of normal aeration and drainage. They derive their water entirely from precipitation. Hence their properties reflect closely both the climate and the vegetation. The close connection between soil and type of vegetation is clearly shown in the approximate correspondence of the important zonal groups of soils in the United States (and elsewhere) with the main types of vegetation. This is further indicated in the much used terms such as Chernozem steppe, Black Prairie soil, Brown Forest soil, etc.

Intrazonal Soils.—Saline soil (*Solonchak*), alkali soil (*Solonetz*), and degraded alkali soils (*Soloth*) are local, intrazonal soil groups and are not zonal soil types. They occur in regions that are receiving, or have received at some time, an excess of salts. They are areas of periodic excessive moistening and drying. Bog soils (organic soils) are those where peaty materials have accumulated under the influence of excessive moistening and deficient aeration. Various other types occur.

Tundra Soils.—Soils of the arctic region are closely associated with bog soils because of the poor drainage. They are also connected with a climate sufficiently cold to prevent the slight summer thaw from extending deeply.[437] They comprise the zonal group occurring in regions north of the Podzol. The vegetation of sedges, lichens, mosses, etc., tends to form a surface layer of very slightly decomposed peat. Biological and chemical action is reduced to a minimum, even weathering consisting almost entirely of rock fragmentation. Considerable mixing of the mineral soil and peaty surface layer results from the expansion and contraction of the water-laden soil in consequence of alternate freezing and thawing. As the surface materials freeze, pressure exerted on the viscous mass beneath forces it upward through the cracks. The characteristic blue-gray layer of slightly weathered clays, silts, and sands beneath the peat is indicative of poor aeration.

WATER CONTENT

Water content exerts a profound influence upon the form and structure of a plant (Figs. 106 and 107). Likewise, the most important differences between habitats are usually due, directly or indirectly, to differences of water content. Water is important to the plant in many ways. It is a component of protoplasm and, with carbon dioxide, is essential in building plant foods. It usually constitutes 70 to 90 per cent of the weight of herbaceous plants. All substances that enter plant cells must do so in solution. Water is the great solvent. It serves as a medium of transport of nutrients and foods from place to place, since their transport can take place, for the most part, only in solution. It keeps the cells turgid or stretched, a condition essential for their normal functioning. It also serves to prevent excessive heating of the plant, acting as a buffer in absorbing the heat generated by the multitudinous chemical reactions taking place in the plant. A large quantity of heat energy is utilized when liquid water is changed into the vapor form during transpiration. Shortage of water early in the life of the plant results in retarded growth, while later in its development it may induce premature ripening and seed of low viability. The greatest dangers which the plant has to meet are insufficient absorption and excessive transpiration.

Kinds of Soil Water.—After a heavy rain or irrigation, much of the water drains or sinks away. This is called *gravitational water*. But large

Fig. 106.—Sunflowers of the same age grown in fertile soil but receiving different amounts of water. That on the right was given just enough from a graduate each day to keep it alive, the next received twice this amount, the third four times, and the largest eight times as much.

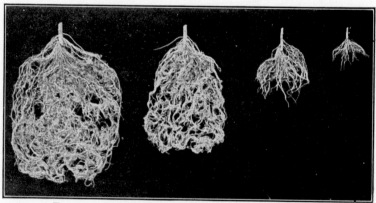

Fig. 107.—Root systems of sunflowers shown in Fig. 106.

amounts are retained in the minute spaces between the fine soil particles as thin films surrounding the particles and thicker ones where the particles touch each other, and a part is absorbed by the soil colloids. The downward pull of the "capillary" or film forces, augmented by the pull of gravity, reduces these films to a minimum thickness. The soil moisture is in such a state or condition that its movement as a liquid in any direction is so limited as to be practically negligible.[817]   Not all of this water is available to the plant.   Even air-dry soil contains appreciable amounts, as may be shown by heating dust in a closed container, when drops of water will be deposited on the lid.   The relatively small amount of moisture absorbed by dry soil from the atmosphere is termed the *hygroscopic water*.   It is held so tenaciously by the soil colloids that it is unavailable to plants.

The *hygroscopic coefficient* is a term used to designate the amount of water the soil can take up from an approximately saturated atmosphere at a constant temperature when exposed in a layer about 1 millimeter in thickness.[16,21]   This value has been used over a long period of years as an approximate measure of the nonavailable water held by soils.   A soil which contains no more water than the hygroscopic coefficient is regarded as incapable of yielding water to plants.   Since it is unavailable for plant growth, it may be subtracted from the actual water content of the soil to obtain the available water content.

The total amount of water that is held against the downward pull of capillarity and the force of gravity and does not drain through the soil is termed the *water-retaining capacity* or *field capacity*.   It is expressed in percentage of the dry weight of the soil.   It includes the hygroscopic water as well as the much larger quantity that the soil holds besides, commonly called *capillary water*.   The amount varies considerably in different soils; a coarse sand under field conditions may retain only 12 per cent of its dry weight of water, but a silt loam 35 per cent.   The smaller the particles of a soil the more film surface it will present for the retention of water.   Likewise, the greater the proportion of colloidal constituents, clay and humus, the more water there will be held.   The high absorptive power of soil colloids for water is due to the extremely large surface exposed by matter in the colloidal state.

Water-retaining Power.—The water-retaining power of the soil is determined by a number of factors.   Most important among these are soil texture or size of particles, soil structure, *i.e.*, the arrangement and compactness of the particles, and the amount of expansible organic matter and colloidal clay.   Since water is held as thin films upon the surface of the soil particles, and runs together forming drops and masses only in saturated soil, the amount necessarily increases with an increase in the water-holding surface.   The latter increases as the particles become finer and more numerous and thus produce a greater aggregate surface.   Dry sands absorb and retain about 0.5 inch of rainfall or irrigation water per foot of soil depth.   About 2 to 2.5 inches of water are required to wet a relatively dry clay loam to field capacity to a depth of 1 foot.   When the field capacity is attained, any additional water serves to increase the depth of penetration, but not the amount held at any given depth.

To Determine the Field Capacity of a Soil.—Secure two or more cylindrical liter graduates or similar glass containers. Fill with dry soil, packing it tightly. Add slowly only enough water to moisten about two-thirds of the soil to the field capacity. Keep the soil at a constant temperature for two days. If the soil column is wet to the bottom, repeat the experiment, using less water. If there is dry soil at the bottom of the container, discard the upper and lower 3 inches of moist soil and determine the water content of the remainder.

Organic matter affects water content directly by retaining water in large amounts on the extensive surfaces of its colloidal constituents and holding it like a sponge in its less decayed portions. It also has an indirect effect through soil structure. Sand particles are loosely cemented together by it; hence, percolation is decreased, and water-retaining capacity increased. Minute clay particles are enclosed in aggregates by the colloidal film of humus. This results in increased percolation and a decrease of the aggregate soil surface for retaining water by capillarity.

The Movement of Water.—The movement of water through a soil, except downward percolation when the soil is wet beyond field capacity, is extremely slow. Even in soils in contact with a water table, the upward movement by capillarity is not great. The distance to which water rises under these conditions is 35 centimeters in coarse sand, 70 centimeters in fine sand, and 80 centimeters in a heavy loam.[466] Lateral capillary movement of water is also confined to small distances. On level land, soil under cover remains dry even if surrounded by soil almost completely saturated.[733] Fine soil particles and colloidal matter greatly impede water movement in soils. When the surface foot of a loam soil is wetted to field capacity and no more rain falls, little or none of this water will penetrate deeper despite the downward pull of gravity and capillarity. Similarly when irrigation water is applied to a dry soil and equilibrium of soil moisture is reached, there is a fairly sharp transition from moist to dry soil. Moreover, if the soil is of uniform composition all of the moist soil shows approximately the same degree of wetness.[564] In heavy soils, however, adjustments take place slowly and for several days or even weeks water contents higher than the field carrying capacity may persist. Thus, for water contents below the field capacity, capillary movement of water is negligible.

Cases are on record in dry climates where a moist layer of soil due to excessive seasonal precipitation has remained moist for many years with layers of dry soil both above and below. In desert soils movement of water at low percentages is almost nil.[845] Russian investigators have shown that where water has percolated below 12 to 18 inches depth in clay, it never comes to the surface again except through absorption by roots. Even during seasons of extreme drought uncropped soils lose but little moisture from their lower depth except as it may diffuse upward or downward as water vapor resulting from high soil temperatures. The surface few inches may dry out, the depth varying with the type of soil, but capillary rise is impossible and continued loss of water from the surface cannot occur. This is in agreement with numerous experiments on mulching under a wide range of conditions which showed no appreciable conservation of water.[942] Thus, a mulched soil may contain no more moisture than an unmulched one kept free from all vegetation. High temperature and low humidity are the chief factors in promoting water loss by evaporation from surface soil. It is increased by wind, especially when humidities are low.

Available and Nonavailable Water.—If a rooted plant is allowed to wilt and die, an examination of the soil shows that some water still remains. The amount depends upon the kind of soil. It is small in coarse-grained sand, sometimes less than 1 per cent. In silt loam or clay, it may amount to 20 per cent or more. But all soils are alike in retaining some portion of the water content. This is due to the fact that the attraction for water of the colloidal soil particles increases as the films grow thinner, until, finally, they do not furnish water to the plant rapidly enough to keep it from wilting and subsequent death. Experiments indicate that the absorbing power of the plant, in terms of osmotic pressure, may be greater than the force with which the films of water are held about the soil particles. Unless the soil is quite moist and the water films relatively thick, capillary movement is very slow, and when the root hairs exhaust the water from the particles with which they are in contact, the plant wilts. This water relation is illustrated by the fact that seeds placed in a dry soil may swell slightly but not enough to germinate. But if they are moved about in the same soil or new soil particles continually brought in contact with them, germination takes place.[847]

The water retained in the soil at the time of permanent wilting is nonavailable for growth or the *echard* (to withhold). It is usually but a small part of the water commonly present, particularly in moist or saturated soil. Of the total water content or *holard* (whole amount), the larger portion can be absorbed by the plant and is consequently termed available water. The response of the plant is determined by the available water and not by the total amount present. Obviously, the available water or *chresard* (amount for use) differs for different soils. For example, a sandy soil may have a field moisture capacity of 12 per cent of which only 1 per cent is nonavailable. A clay loam with a field moisture capacity of 35 per cent may have 10 per cent nonavailable water.

The echard is not determined entirely by the type of soil, since some plants can absorb more water from a given soil than others, depending upon the nature and distribution of the root system. In spite of extensive experiments with a wide range of soils and plants, this phenomenon needs further study. Certain investigators have concluded that species differ only slightly in a given soil as regards the water content when permanent wilting occurs. The water left in the soil at this time has been termed the *wilting coefficient.* Taking 100 to represent the average wilting coefficient of the numerous species tested, an extreme range from 92 to 106 was found.[97] Among most of the plants, differences were even less and the conclusion was reached that they were so slight as to be without practical significance in the selection of crops for growth in semiarid regions.

The root hairs of any plant are in contact with only a portion of the soil particles and when the soil becomes dried below field moisture capacity, movement of water practically ceases.[943] The rate at which plant roots can develop in the soil and reach new supplies is extremely important. The water no longer comes to the roots; the roots must grow to the water. Hence, plants with extensively branched root systems, abundantly furnished with root hairs, and thus coming in contact with the largest possible soil surface, with conducting systems that rapidly transport the water, and with aerial parts morphologically and physiologically adapted to conserve water, would reduce the water content of the soil mass to a minimum before wilting. A high osmotic pressure would increase the pull on the water residues held by the soil colloids. Plants adapted to dry soils have much higher osmotic pressures than those of humid regions.

It would seem that plants with relatively scanty root development and tops poorly adapted for water conservation would leave a greater water residue at the time of wilting. Sorghum, for example, is much better adapted to semiarid regions than is corn. A study of the cause of this difference revealed the fact that both species possessed, at any period of growth, the same number of main fibrous roots and that the general extent of the roots in both a horizontal and a vertical direction was the same, *i.e.*, 3 to 4 feet on all sides of mature plants, and 6 feet deep. The length of the secondary roots was also found to be approximately the same. But both primary and secondary roots of the sorghums were more fibrous than those of corn and the secondary roots were twice as numerous. This root system, moreover, which, judging from the number of secondary roots, would be twice as efficient in the absorption of water, supplied a leaf area which was approximately only half as great as that of corn. Although sorghums also have other characteristics enabling them to endure drought, the thorough manner in which their roots ramify through the soil is of fundamental importance.[605]

The exact permanent wilting point is difficult to determine in many plants, and permanent wilting should not be confused with temporary wilting from which the plant recovers. A plant is permanently wilted only when it will not regain turgidity when exposed to a saturated atmosphere. It is most easily determined with large-leaved herbaceous species which readily show wilting. With rigid-leaved plants, as yucca, or leafless ones with succulent stems, like cacti, special methods (*e.g.*, balancing the plant) are necessary to determine the point when transpiration exceeds absorption. Several investigations point to the conclusion that the water content at the time of permanent wilting is not a constant but changes with the environmental conditions under which the plant is grown.[126]

Determining Nonavailable Water.—In order to determine the amount of water nonavailable for a plant in its own habitat, it is necessary to produce wilting by cutting off the water supply. This may be done by digging up a plant and transferring it to a container of large size. The soil must be protected both from the loss of water by evaporation and from the intake of moisture resulting from rain. Since the roots of most plants are very deep or spread widely, they are almost sure to be injured by such a procedure. It is much simpler to start the plant from seed or vegetatively under controlled conditions.

The soil mass should be very uniform throughout and not stratified or otherwise irregular in texture. It should be brought to a uniform water content before placing it in the container, otherwise it is very difficult to moisten it uniformly. Small volumes of soil might remain quite dry and thus introduce an error into the final moisture determination. The surface or sides of the soil mass should not be allowed to lose water except through root absorption, since they may become drier than the nonavailable point before the water in the central mass has been greatly reduced. Sudden fluctuations in temperature should also be avoided, otherwise water may distill from the soil and condense on the inner walls of the container as a result of differences in temperature. Thus, water may be made available for absorption which the roots otherwise might not be able to secure.[97]

To Determine the Amount of Water Nonavailable for Growth.—Mix thoroughly a quantity of screened potting soil, adding enough water from a sprinkler to bring it to an optimum water content. In the same way, prepare another lot consisting of one-third potting soil and two-thirds sand. Cover each lot and let it stand for 24 hours. Fill 4, glazed, gallon jars, 2 with each kind of soil, compacting the soil rather firmly. Plant seeds of corn, sunflower, or wheat, soaked for 4 hours, about an inch deep, and then cover the soil with an inch of dry sand to retard surface evaporation. Place the jars in much larger ones or in a large box and fill the interspaces with moist peat moss so as to maintain soil temperatures which fluctuate slowly and are as nearly uniform as possible. After a few weeks, when the plants have wilted so that they will not recover even when placed for 12 hours in a saturated atmosphere under a bell jar, remove the sand mulch and the surface inch of soil. Mix the remaining soil, which is thoroughly permeated by roots, and determine the water content of duplicate samples from each jar. If two kinds of plants are grown in one container, the relative time of wilting of each may be determined.

In field practice it has been found that the hygroscopic coefficient of the soil gives a fairly close approximation of the amount of water left in the soil at the time of wilting.[21] Since the root systems of plants in nature often occupy many cubic feet of soil and extend to great depths, the advantage of an indirect approximation of the nonavailable water at the different soil levels is obvious. Representative samples of soils are easily secured, air-dried, and the amount of water they will absorb from an approximately saturated atmosphere when exposed in thin layers at a constant temperature determined. This is the hygroscopic coefficient. It may be determined indirectly, where a moisture equivalent centrifuge is available, by dividing the moisture equivalent by 2.71. Moisture equivalent is the amount of water held by a soil after the wet soil has been subjected to a centrifugal force 1,000 times gravity for 30 minutes.

The *wilting coefficient* is considered by many investigators to be the approximate point at which water becomes nonavailable for growth. It is defined as the percentage of moisture remaining in the soil when a plant first undergoes permanent wilting. It is a higher percentage than the hygroscopic coefficient and may be derived by dividing the hygroscopic coefficient by 0.68. The wilting coefficient is also derived by dividing the *moisture equivalent* by 1.84, but this ratio does not seem to hold for all soils.[97,943a]

Determining Available Water.—Water content is one of the most important habitat factors, and an intimate knowledge of water relations is fundamental to the understanding of plant behavior and distribution of vegetation. In obtaining samples of soil for finding water content, a spade or trowel may be employed to secure shallow samples, but this method has the disadvantage of seriously disturbing the vegetation. In sampling, representative cores of soil should be obtained from the several depths to which the roots penetrate and in which they are absorbing. This is often to a depth of several feet, at least in dry climates. Sweet clover grown continuously for 2 years at Manhattan, Kansas, reduced the subsoil moisture to a depth of 13 feet.[632] Alfalfa in eastern Nebraska drew upon the subsoil moisture supply to a depth of 33 feet in a 6-year-old meadow and 25 feet in a 2-year-old field.[479] It depletes the subsoil of moisture, which may be only slowly restored during a long period of years.[478] Conversely, many deeply rooted prairie plants, such as *Rosa arkansana, Amorpha canescens,* and *Liatris punctata,* may live unharmed for many months when the first 3 to 4 feet of the root system are not permitted to come in contact with moist soil.[633]   In stony and gravelly soil, sampling for water content is difficult but elsewhere it is easily accomplished with practically no disturbance of the plant cover by use of a soil tube or geotome (earth cutter).   This has a sharp cutting edge on one end, contracted to a slightly smaller diameter than the bore of the tube, and a reinforcement on the other end, to allow forcing it into the soil (Fig. 108).   It removes the sample without compacting the soil.

The practice is to remove the vegetation from a square inch and sink the geotome to a depth of 4 to 6 inches.   The soil is then emptied, by

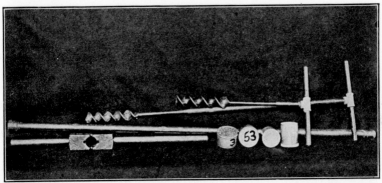

Fig. 108.—Soil tube and soil augers.   These are made in various lengths.   With the tube shown here, samples may be secured to a depth of 4 feet; with appropriate extensions to hold the soil tube, samples may be taken to the greatest depth of root penetration, 20 feet or more.

inverting the geotome, into a seamless metal can with a closely fitting friction or screw-cap lid.   A second sample is taken at a distance of a foot from the first, and a third, if necessary, to secure enough soil nearly to fill the container, which should hold at least 200 grams of moist soil.   Using the same holes, samples of the second 6- or 8-inch soil layer are secured. The cans are numbered in large figures on both side and lid.   If the first can is inverted after filling and the others placed in a row in sequence of depth, there is no possibility of confusion.   Samples below the first foot are secured in foot sections.   Only one of the holes need be used, since the soil core is sufficiently large for a sample.   Samples are always taken in duplicate, the second lot at a distance of a few feet from the first. This tends to equalize differences in soil texture, etc., and affords a reading even if one sample in the series is accidentally spilled.   When the sampling is completed, a record should be made of the containers in the manner indicated in Table 6, and water-content determinations made in the laboratory.

TABLE 6.—WATER CONTENT OF SOILS AT VARIOUS DEPTHS

Station and date

Depth of sample	Can number	Wet weight, grams	Dry weight, grams	Can weight, grams	Per cent water	Average per cent water
0 to 6 inches............	36	208.2	185.4	53.5	17.2 ⎫	
0 to 6 inches............	42	205.8	182.6	50.8	17.6 ⎭	17.4
6 to 12 inches...........	21	192.5	165.1	51.1	24.0 ⎫	
6 to 12 inches...........	13	209.1	178.1	50.2	24.2 ⎭	24.1
1 to 2 feet..............	4	229.5	193.1	51.6	25.7 ⎫	
1 to 2 feet..............	11	228.7	192.8	50.0	25.1 ⎭	25.4

The soil cans should be weighed to the nearest tenth-gram soon after the sample is taken, although, if necessary, they may be kept for several days without appreciable error. After determining the wet weight (including soil, can, and water), the lids are removed and placed with the cans in an oven kept at a temperature of 110°C. The dry weight (soil and can) is next determined, after one or several days, when the soil ceases to lose weight. Much more time is required to drive off the water from clays than from light-textured soils. Finally, the weight of the can and lid is determined. Since their weight remains fairly constant, this need be done only about twice each season. Water content is expressed in percentage of the dry weight of the soil. Thus, in making the calculation, the can weight is subtracted from the dry weight (dry soil and can) and the difference between the wet and dry weights (loss of water) divided by this number. From the percentages thus obtained, the nonavailable water, previously determined, should be subtracted.

Time and Place of Sampling.—Since the water content at depths greater than 2 feet usually changes rather slowly, it is not necessary to secure samples so frequently here as from the surface soil. In field practice it is usual to determine water content in the surface layers weekly, and during periods of stress at even more frequent intervals. The total amount of vegetation which can exist on a given area is often determined by the amount of moisture available at critical times. Differences in water content are invariably indicated by differences in the kind and development of vegetation. A series of stations on the crest, mid-slope, and base of a steep hill will show this correlation. The exact location of each station should be noted so that future readings may be made in the same place. Samples should not be taken, of course, in too close proximity to holes left in former samplings.

Various stages in the development of a sere should be studied in relation to their water content, and, if possible, weekly comparison made between the water content of such vegetational units as woodland, grassland, marsh, etc. Even small differences in slope, exposure, or topography frequently cause marked differences in water content. A slight depression, such as that worn by wheels in an old road, where water runs in, may have 5 to 10 per cent more moisture than the adjacent ridge from which runoff occurs. Minute differences in the structure of vegetation may often be explained by a determination of water content.

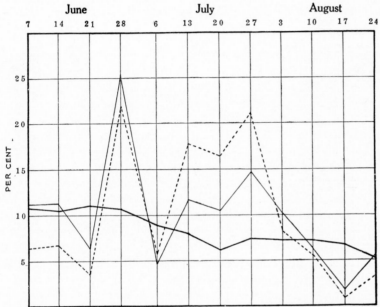

Fig. 109.—Available water content in prairie at Lincoln, Neb., during 1922; broken line at 0 to 6 inches depth; light solid line at 6 to 12 inches; and heavy solid line, where fluctuation is least, at 12 to 24 inches.

To Determine Water Content.—Select representative stations in two or more habitats and determine the water content each week. Show the results by means of graphs. The stations should also be used for the determination of other habitat factors. Also, determine the water content in different places in the same kind of vegetation, *e.g.*, forest, grassland, etc., and try to account for variations in kind and density of dominants. In a similar manner, study zones about ponds, etc. Give the reasons for the differences between the various stations. To what extent and in what ways are these reflected by the plants?

Interpretation of Data.—It cannot be too strongly emphasized that the measuring of the factors of the habitat is of little value unless the data thus secured are studied in relation to plant activities. The water available to the plant at the several depths at different times may readily be compared if the data are plotted in the form of a graph as shown in

Fig. 109. Graphs and charts are also useful in comparing the water relations of different communities (Fig. 110).

FACTORS MODIFYING WATER CONTENT

Water content of soil is directly or indirectly dependent upon precipitation. The indirect topographic factors, moreover, such as slope, surface, etc., largely determine the amount of runoff and thus greatly influence water content. Likewise, temperature and evaporation have a marked effect upon the rate of water loss from the soil surface. Each of

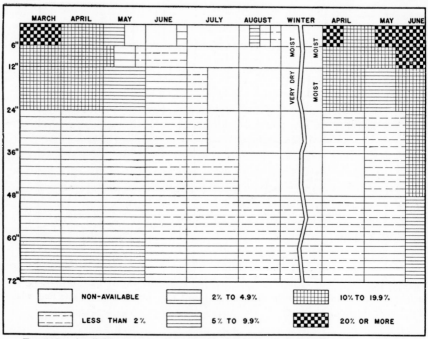

Fig. 110.—Available water content of upland prairie soil at Lincoln, Neb., at the several depths to 6 feet, during the great drought of 1934, until June, 1935. No samples were taken during winter but general soil moisture relations are indicated.

these factors will be considered in so far as it affects the water content of the soil.

Precipitation.—In all habitats except those where the supply of water is constant owing to the presence of springs, streams, ponds, or other bodies of water, the dependence of water content upon precipitation is absolute. Cover, kind and structure of soil, and slope determine how much of the water finds its way into the ground, but their action is secondary. Daily rains are able to keep practically any soil moist, regardless of its character or the slope.

Precipitation occurs in various forms, such as rain, hail, dew, frost, and snow. Of all these, rain is by far the most important. Except locally, hail is too infrequent to be taken into account. Frosts have, at best, only a slight and fleeting effect upon water content, especially in view of the fact that they usually occur outside the growing season.

Snowfall is often of great importance.[383] It not only acts as a cover to prevent evaporation but upon thawing it also enters the soil directly just as rain does. The rapid development of spring vegetation in climates where snow accumulation is great is largely determined by the water supply from the melting snow. Because of drifting, due to wind, protected hillsides, ravines, etc., are often better watered than exposed sites. The loss by runoff from slopes is much greater, owing to the frozen condition of the soil.

Dew is almost always too small in amount and too fleeting in temperate climates to add directly to the water content of the soil. By its own evaporation it increases humidity and thus decreases slightly the amount of water lost by evaporation from the soil and by bedewed plants. In certain tropical desert regions, such as those of North Africa, dew is of considerable importance. During the late winter and early spring, it provides most of the surface water upon which the ephemeral annuals live, rainfall being extremely light. It is deposited in large amounts owing to the greater moisture of the air at this time of year and the strong radiation of heat at night which cools the surface of the desert. In studying the water content of most habitats, however, a knowledge of rainfall will suffice.

Measurement of Rainfall.—Rainfall is measured by means of a rain gage, an instrument which collects in a narrow vessel the rain falling upon a large surface.[483] In the standard gage, the ratio of surface between receiver and tube is 10:1. A direct measure of the water in the tube must be divided by 10 to give the rainfall, or a standard measuring rod, upon which this compensation is already made, may be used. The purpose of the smaller, inner tube is to increase the depth of the water and permit of more accurate reading. Readings may be made to 0.01 inch. After a heavy rainfall, when the water from the inner tube has overflowed into the outer one, first the inner tube is read, emptied, and then the water from the outer one poured into it and the amount recorded.[565] Where rain gages are not available, it is fairly satisfactory to use the reports of rainfall obtained from a neighboring weather station when the latter is not more than a few miles distant, except in mountainous regions or others with very irregular topography. But even in level countries, marked differences in rainfall, caused by local showers, may occur. The effect of rainfall upon water content is best ascertained by taking soil samples in different habitats immediately after a rain and then determining the increase in water content.

Relation between Precipitation and Water Content.—Only a very general relation exists between the total amount of precipitation and the water content of soil. Many factors intervene to decrease the effectiveness of the rainfall in increasing water content about the roots of plants. Much of the water may be intercepted by the crowns of plants and evaporate again without reaching the soil surface. The rains may fall in such light showers as to have little influence upon wetting the soil. Conversely, it may be of such a torrential nature that only part of it can be absorbed and the rest is lost as runoff. Where temperatures are high and humidity is low, much water is lost directly from the soil by evaporation and the efficiency of the rainfall thereby greatly decreased. These losses are modified by slope, surface, and the cover of vegetation.

To Determine the Depth of Water Penetration.—After a heavy rain following a dry period, examine the soil in a plowed field, hard bare area, grassland, woodland, etc., and determine the depth of water penetration. What is the relation between this and the plant cover?

Rainfall Interception.—It is a matter of common observation that even isolated plants, especially trees and shrubs, intercept much rain. The soil surface below the plants may remain dry during light showers, while that not protected is rather thoroughly wet. Extended experiments have shown that much water is held as thin films on the upper surfaces of the leaves or as drops or blotches or retained in capillary depressions such as those adjacent to veins. Large quantities also accumulate on the surfaces and in the crevices of the bark of trunk and branches from which it evaporates.[418] The amount of water thus retained is reduced by the wind, but the rate of evaporation is increased.

The U. S. Forest Service has recorded rainfall at stations inside and outside of stands of timber in several forest types. In Maine, a good pulpwood stand of spruce and fir, including some paper birch, intercepted 26 per cent of the rainfall, and another forest of pure spruce and fir 37 per cent. An interception of 24 per cent was recorded under white pine and hemlock in Massachusetts, and 21 per cent under a virgin forest of white pine and hemlock in Idaho. In a 25-year-old pine forest, it was ascertained that 1 to 5 per cent of the precipitation reached the ground by running down the trunks of the trees.[630]

Rain gages placed in bur oak and linden forests in eastern Nebraska received 16 and 28 per cent less water, respectively, from a total precipitation of 14 inches during 3 summer months than a similar gage just outside the forest.[415] The mean interception loss under 11 different species of trees in New York was about 40 per cent of the total rainfall. The amount of water lost to the soil in this manner varied from 70 to 100 per cent in light showers and was about 25 per cent in heavy, long-continued rains. In these experiments, the water running down the trunks of the trees was caught and measured, and this was not included in the amount intercepted. Needle-leaved trees intercept more water than broad-leaved ones. In winter, interception by deciduous trees is 50 per cent of that of summer. Interception losses from fully grown crops of rye, red clover, etc., are only slightly less than those due to trees, but, of course, this effect is only of short duration.[418] Thus, it seems that wherever vegetation covers the earth, it intercepts a part of the precipitation and diminishes the water supply.[53] Exceptions occur in certain cases, especially where the moisture is precipitated as a fine mist. In South Africa, for example, a condensation gain of 80 to more than 1,000 per cent has been experimentally determined where large amounts of moisture are deposited upon the exposed crowns of forest trees and scrub.[569] The forests may be dripping wet, while the ground immediately beyond their margins is comparatively dry.[691] Interception of snow by the crowns of trees has also been determined. In a virgin stand of ponderosa pine with an understory of young trees, 27 per cent of the winter's snow had been intercepted up to the time of maximum storage.[630] Other investigators have reported smaller interception in other forest types. More study is needed in this important and interesting field.

To Measure Rainfall Interception.—Secure two or more of the small type of rain gages (diameter 3 inches) or substitute straight-walled vessels of equal cross-sectional area such as ½-gallon glazed jars. Place them under various types of vegetation such as forest, scrub, etc., or under isolated trees and bushes, maintaining a control in the open. After each rain or shower, measure the amount of water in each by pouring it into a graduate. Calculate the percentage intercepted.

Manner and Time of Precipitation.—The influence that a rain exerts in replenishing the soil water is not in proportion to its amount. Light rains falling on a warm, dry soil are totally converted into vapor within a few hours and have no effect upon the water content.[843a] Heavy rains are often of such short duration that runoff is very great and a relatively small amount of water enters the soil. Rainfall in deserts consists largely of these two types, and they are also very common in semiarid regions. Where a shower furnishes only 0.15 inch of rainfall, it is of no value in increasing water content.[836] Not infrequently, a monthly precipitation of 2 or 3 inches is distributed in so many light showers that it has little or no effect upon water content.

The seasonal distribution of rainfall also has a marked effect upon water content and, hence, upon the type of vegetation the latter will support. This is especially true in climates where there is a winter resting period. The great prairie and steppe regions of the temperate zones, for example, have their rainfall chiefly in early summer. Thus, the surface soil is kept moist and the grasses growing during their vegetative season. This is illustrated in varying degrees in the North American grasslands. Where rainfall is fairly abundant and occurs throughout the growing season, a mixture of both early- and late-blooming grasses, etc., is found. Where it is scanty and intermittent, the dominant grasses require only a few weeks to flower and seed. Over the greater portion of the Great Plains, the average annual precipitation is enough to insure the production of crops, but the uncertainty of the distribution of the rainfall makes crop production hazardous.[141] Precipitation during the growing season when temperatures are high is very beneficial in causing the soil organic matter to decay and thus make more nutrients available.

The amount of water lost in runoff depends primarily upon the manner of precipitation but also, in a large measure, upon the kind of cover, soil, and slope. Runoff is usually greatest where sudden heavy showers or rainstorms lasting for only a short time fall upon bare slopes or sparse or low-growing vegetation. The dry soil surface, poorly protected by a cover of plants, will not rapidly absorb water and especially if the soil is low in humus content and of fine, compact texture. Even on relatively level soils, such, for example, as those of the Great Plains, the water lost by surface runoff varies from 15 per cent in light showers to more than 50 per cent in torrential ones.[808] That runoff is great is shown by the large number of dry, sand-choked creeks and swales throughout the region. A continuous shower with gentle rainfall of long duration and with the necessarily high accompanying humidity would be many times as efficient. Where the soil is sandy, runoff is greatly reduced.

Runoff is small in forests. The force of the rain is broken by the trees, the undergrowth, and the forest litter, so that the water does not beat upon the soil. Some of the precipitation reaches the earth by running down the twigs and branches. The mat of duff and leaf mold, which in thrifty, unburned forest is often a few inches thick, absorbs several times its own weight of water like a huge sponge and when filled slowly passes it on to the mellow, mineral soil beneath. From here it seeps out gradually to springs and streams. Such streams furnish the best water supply for the most valuable irrigated lands. Even when the rain is so heavy that the soil is unable to absorb all of the water at once, the excess flows off with no erosion. Streams coming from virgin forests are seldom muddy and are subject to comparatively small variations in flow.[220]

Slope and Surface.—In addition to the amount and distribution of rainfall, the type of soil and plant cover, the steepness of slope, and the nature of the surface influence water content. The principal effect of slope is in controlling runoff and drainage and through them water content. Slope, also, has a less direct influence through its action upon heat and wind, both of which affect humidity, and this, in turn, the rapidity with which water is evaporated from the surface of the soil. The angle of the slope, moreover, largely determines the amount and type of soil accumulated. It is only on nearly level ground or gentle slopes that considerable depths of soil accumulate and undergo the characteristic development of mature soil. In general, rainfall lost by runoff increases with the angle of the slope, and the water absorbed correspondingly decreases. In two or more areas essentially similar in soil, cover, and rainfall, differences in water content are directly determined by differences in slope, although large water losses may occur on areas with very little slope.

The soil surface often shows irregularities which retard runoff and cause more or less of the rainfall to soak into the soil. The influence of these, though often not great, is always appreciable and, in many cases, of considerable importance. In dry regions, the increase or decrease in water content is clearly reflected in the development of the vegetation. The effects are usually measurable by means of soil samples, but it is impossible to express the character of the surface in definite terms.

SOIL AIR

Air and water fill the pore spaces of a soil. Soil has a very porous structure. The pore space increases with fineness of texture, degree of granulation, and abundance of organic matter. Thus, the total pore space of a sandy soil may be only 30 per cent of its volume, that of a loamy clay 45 per cent, but a heavy clay may have 50 per cent. Pore space is increased by the addition of organic matter; in grassland soils it is frequently as much as 60 per cent. Thus, only about one-half of the volume of the soil is solid matter (Fig. 111). Under cultivation, soils lose much of their organic matter and there is a considerable decrease in porosity. This is true also for cleared and cultivated forest land. Likewise, the trampling of grazing animals in forest and grassland pastures results in compacting the surface few inches of soil and reducing the pore space 10 to 20 per cent or more.[31] Many plants thrive best in a soil that contains approximately 40 to 50 per cent of its maximum water-retaining capacity. The rest of the interspace, about 20 per cent of the volume of a soil in good tilth, is filled with air. Dry soils contain much more air. Frequently, cultivated soils, during periods of drought, are too loose and dry for proper root development, and the plant is thus deprived of nutrients which the soil contains. Conversely, waterlogged soils have no air except that dissolved in the water, but certain plants grow well even under this condition. Soil in good tilth is filled with air spaces which are more or less continuous from the surface to the subsoil. Cracks, burrows, and spaces left by decayed roots, as well as the removal of water by absorption promote gaseous exchange among the different soil horizons. Thus the air can enter or leave a soil both by direct streaming and by diffusion.

Streaming of air into or out of the soil may be due to changes in temperature or variations in atmospheric pressure, causing expansion and

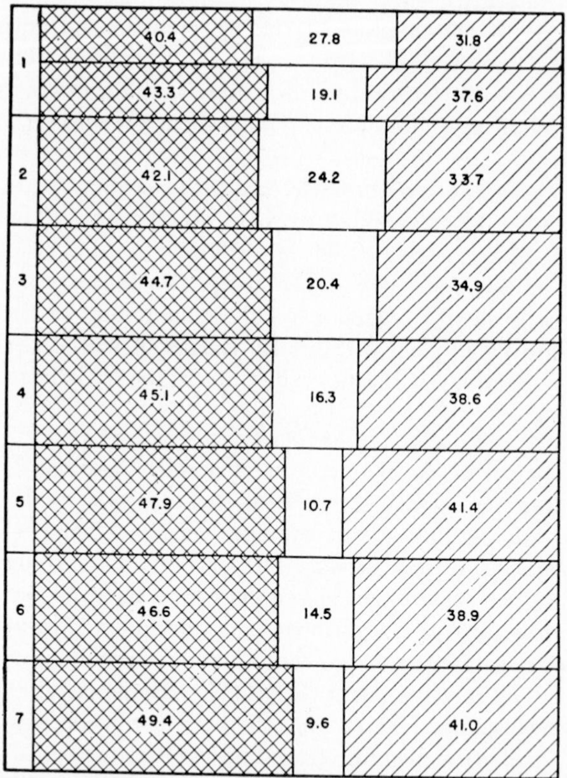

1	40.4	27.8	31.8
	43.3	19.1	37.6
2	42.1	24.2	33.7
3	44.7	20.4	34.9
4	45.1	16.3	38.6
5	47.9	10.7	41.4
6	46.6	14.5	38.9
7	49.4	9.6	41.0

Fig. 111.—Diagram showing percentage of solid matter (crosshatch) and total pore space in first 7 feet of a clay-loam soil covered with big bluestem. Portion of pore space occupied by water (single hatch) is based upon average water content during 1932. Unhatched areas represent air.[979a]

contraction of the soil air. Wind may force air into or suck it out of the soil; soil air is also displaced by the entrance of rain water. These agents combined account for only a small change in the soil atmosphere, which really occurs rather rapidly. Extensive experiments have shown that carbon dioxide is being formed within the soil at an approximate average rate of 7 liters per square meter per day.[737,738] If the soil air is to maintain its usual average composition, this would necessitate its complete removal every hour to a depth of 8 inches. Diffusion, which depends mainly on the cross-sectional area of the total pore space, is a constantly acting mechanism and is conceded to be the chief factor in soil air renewal.[467]

Composition of the Soil Atmosphere.—Because of its proximity to roots and microorganisms, both of which constantly give off carbon dioxide and absorb oxygen, soil air is somewhat different in composition from the ordinary atmosphere. In cultivated land, soil air contains slightly less oxygen, 20.3 per cent by volume, than the usual 21 per cent of the atmosphere. The amount of carbon dioxide is increased from the usual 0.03 to 0.15–0.65 per cent.[752] Under grassland or forest soil, air often contains much more carbon dioxide, 0.2 to 5 per cent or even more, and proportionately less oxygen, the amount increasing with depth, accumulation of organic matter, abundance of roots, etc. Eleven to 15 per cent has been determined in certain forest soils in summer. Below the dried mulch, soil air is always saturated with water vapor. The soil air is not static but, like the soil itself, constantly undergoing change.

Soil air is either in direct contact with roots and microorganisms or separated from them by only a thin film of water or colloidal matter. Within these films, the oxygen supply is very limited and the carbon dioxide content very high, as much as 99 per cent having been found.[755]

Oxygen is important in the process of breaking down insoluble minerals into a soluble form and the consequent enriching of the soil solution. This gas is no less important in the transforming of plant and animal remains into a condition where their nutrient materials become soluble and may be absorbed by plants. Biochemical oxidation proceeds rapidly, when conditions are favorable, and much oxygen is incorporated in the compounds produced.

Relation to Biological Activities and Production of Toxins.—Oxygen is also necessary for the germination of seeds, root growth, root-hair development, and absorption by roots. Without it, nitrification would stop, and earthworms and most other soil organisms would cease their activities. A few microorganisms could get their oxygen supply anaerobically by breaking down valuable compounds, such as nitrates, and would thus decrease the soil productivity.

Even roots can carry on respiration for a time without free oxygen, *i.e.*, anaerobically. Since the anaerobic respiration of plant roots, bacteria, molds, etc., gives rise to organic acids, alcohol, and other toxic substances, aeration is fundamentally connected with the production of soil toxins.[157]

There is little evidence of the presence of soluble toxins in normally aerated soils which are well supplied with nutrients and calcium carbonate.[754] These sometimes occur, however, in poorly aerated, sour soils deficient in calcium carbonate and in exhausted cultivated soil. They may consist of soluble aluminum, compounds of iron and manganese, and hydrogen ions as well as various organic substances. They may arise in the process of the decay of roots, from the decay of other organic matter worked into the soil, or as a result of acidity.[543a]

SOIL TEMPERATURE

The activities of plants are profoundly affected by temperature. Soil temperature is very important, since it affects the biological, the chemical, and the physical processes in soils. It influences the rate of absorption of water and solutes, the germination of seeds, and the rate of growth of

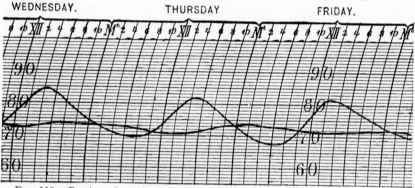

Fig. 112.—Portion of a soil thermograph record from the prairie at Lincoln, Neb., during the middle of June; curve with greatest amplitude indicates the temperature at a depth of 3 inches, the other one at 12 inches.

At what time of the day is the soil at 3 inches depth warmest? Coldest? Why is the soil warmest about midnight at 12 inches depth? The air temperature ranged from 45° to 80°F. In a forest, the temperature at 3 inches depth is no more variable than that at 12 inches in the prairie. Why?

roots and all underground (and, hence, aerial) plant parts as well as the activities of microorganisms. It is a great accelerator of all chemical reactions and affects many physical processes taking place in the soil.[75]

The soil receives its heat directly from the sun's rays, probably from warm rains, and from decaying organic matter. In summer, the surface layers are warmer, in winter the deeper ones. The temperatures of all layers in which roots exist have a primary significance. The daily range in temperature of the surface soil may be very great. Sometimes it reaches maximum temperatures of 120 to 150°F.[121] Such temperatures may cause destructive lesions on the stems of plants, e.g., flax, coniferous and other tree seedlings;[502] frequently, the plants droop and die.[358] Surface-soil temperatures above 130°F. often prove fatal to seedlings,[826] and soil temperature is thought to be one of the important factors controlling the distribution of forest types.[46,672] Lichens on the thin soils of dark-colored rock can endure even higher temperatures.

When the surface soil becomes warmer than the deeper layers, a heat wave is propagated downwards. It travels slowly, and at a depth of a few inches below the soil surface, temperatures are not so high or fluctuations so pronounced. In moist soil, the daily fluctuation is often only a few degrees at a depth of 1 foot and at 2 to 3 feet, depending upon cover, the daily fluctuations are imperceptible[282] (Fig. 112). Both maximum and minimum soil temperatures lag behind air temperatures except in the surface layer. At 3 inches depth in bare, nearly level, brown loam, this amounted to 2 hours, at 6 inches to 4 hours, at 1 foot to 8 hours, at 2 feet to 70 hours, and at 3 feet in depth to 80 hours.[857] Below about 3 feet, temperature changes are due to the average temperatures which constitute the seasonal wave of temperatures. The annual range in temperature decreases, moreover, with depth. In eastern Kansas, under a grass cover, where the annual variation of the air temperature was 92°F., it was 48°F. at a depth of 1 foot, 38°F. at 3 feet, and 28°F. at 6 feet in depth. During March there was a complete reversal in soil temperatures, the surface layers which were coldest during winter became warmest and the deeper ones progressively colder. In October the reverse condition occurred.[584] In general, the soil responds slowly to external air temperatures; roots have a much more uniform environment than shoots. The temperature of soils in the tropics may remain practically constant to great depths.

Factors Affecting Soil Temperature.—Among the factors that directly affect soil temperature are color, texture, structure, water content, amount of humus, and the slope of the soil surface with respect to the sun, as well as the presence or absence of a cover of vegetation. Of all these factors, water content is the most important for the reason that water has a specific heat about five times greater than that of the solid constituents of the soil.[130] This explains why wet soils are colder in spring than drier ones and why a heavy rain in summer lowers the temperature of the soil. Clay and peat soils are colder than sandy or loam soils, largely because of their greater water content. A dark-colored soil absorbs more heat and so warms more rapidly than one of lighter color which reflects the rays. This phenomenon is shown by the melting of snow under leaves or bits of wood and their consequent sinking below the general surface. In fact, the melting of snow may be greatly accelerated by sprinkling it with charcoal, a common practice in vineyards and orchards on mountain sides in southern Europe. Black paper mulches may raise the soil temperature 12 to 15°F. above that of bare soil by day and 4 to 5°F. by night.[886]

Soil Temperature.—The following four experiments should be performed on the same day, employing seven flats and eight accurate thermometers.

Effect of Slope upon Soil Temperature.—Fill three flats at least 4 inches deep with thoroughly mixed, black soil of good water content. Firm the soil compactly into the flats so that each has a level surface. Place the flats out of doors in an unshaded spot the day preceding the experiment so that the soil may take on the outside temperatures. Tilt one flat toward the south at an angle of 20 degrees, and the second toward the north at a similar angle, but place the third in a level position. On the morning of a clear, warm day, place one thermometer bulb in the center of each flat at a depth of ¾ inch. Cover the stem with the case and read every hour during the day. Express the results in the form of graphs. At noon, hold a cardboard 1 decimeter square at right angles to the sun's rays on each of the three flats and measure the length of the shadow cast on the surface of the soil. Multiply each number thus obtained by 10, the width of the shadow in centimeters, and thus determine the number of square centimeters over which a unit area of radiant energy (1 square decimeter) is dispersed.

Effect of Water Content on Soil Temperature.—Use two flats with fairly dry, black soil. Determine the surface area of one flat (*e.g.*, 14 by 14 inches) and slowly add enough water (at the temperature of the soil) from a sprinkler to equal ½ inch of rain (14 by 14 by 0.5 = 98 cubic inches, and 1 cubic inch = 16.4 cubic centimeters). Determine the temperature in each flat as before. Express the results in graphs.

Effect of Color on Soil Temperature.—Use a flat filled with light-colored sand. Over a 25-square-inch surface of the flat spread a pint of dry sand previously colored with 4 ounces of black ink. Determine the relative temperatures as above under the two conditions. Plot graphs.

Effect of Cover on Soil Temperature.- -Cover one flat, filled with loam as in the previous experiments, with a mulch of ½ inch of dead grass or leaf litter held in place by a fine woven wire of coarse mesh. Compare the hourly temperatures at a depth of ¾ inch with that of the control. Analyze the effect of the various factors in each and compare the four studies upon this basis.

Measurements of soil temperatures should also be made in different habitats and at various depths in the field. A sharp-pointed rod is useful in making a hole for the thermometer.

The degree of slope has a marked effect upon the amount of radiant energy received by the soil (Fig. 113). A slope of only 5 degrees may be equivalent to a latitudinal distance of 300 miles.[15] The soil warms more quickly, vegetation starts earlier, and crops like wheat may ripen several days earlier on south than on north exposures.[841] Delay in blossoming and consequent reduction of the danger of freezing of fruit trees is often brought about by planting orchards on north slopes. Slope is emphasized by latitude. In the far north, barley, for example, may be grown on south slopes, those facing north being covered until midsummer with snow.

Cover has considerable effect on soil temperature.[118] Soil is cooler in summer under a cover of vegetation such as grass which intercepts most of the radiant energy,[285] and especially under forest litter.[884] It is warmer in winter than similar bare soil, since the cover acts like a blanket of poor conductivity, thus reducing the rate of loss of heat.[534] Even a mulch of loose, dry soil, owing to its low conductivity of heat, reduces the extremes of temperature fluctuations in soil. Conversely, moist soil of compact structure is more uniform in temperature throughout. It is readily penetrated by frost to a considerable depth. There is usually no frost damage to roots where there is an insulating blanket of snow or of vegetation, living or dead.

The effect on depth of freezing is often marked, as it is also under a cover of snow. For example, under clean cultivation, the soil at Lincoln, Nebraska, froze to a depth of 19 inches but under a cover crop of millet to only 12 inches. After a snowstorm, accompanied by wind, less than an inch of snow was held on the otherwise bare soil which froze to a depth of 16 inches; 11 inches accumulated in the cover of millet and the soil was frozen to only 8 inches in depth.[266] Forest litter delays the freezing of the soil. It may keep it from freezing hard, and the depth of frost penetra-

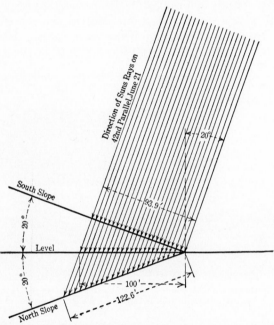

FIG. 113.—Diagram showing the distribution of a given amount of radiant energy on different slopes on June 21, at the 42d parallel North, *i.e.*, in the latitude of Chicago. (*From Lyon and Buckman. The Nature and Properties of Soils. Copyright 1922 by The Macmillan Company. Reprinted by permission.*)

tion is greatly diminished as compared with bare soil. The intergranular spaces are not filled so completely with ice; hence, the water from winter rains and melting snow or ice penetrates the soil under the litter, instead of running off as on the more compactly frozen bare soil.[562] It is significant that soil does not freeze until it is cooled several degrees below 32°F., and, indeed, some water remains in the liquid form at extremely low temperatures.[76]

Measurement of Soil Temperatures.—The daily range of temperature in the surface of the soil may be considerably greater than that of the air above, and for a study of surface conditions the thermograph is essential. This consists of a metal bulb an inch in diameter and 12 inches long, filled with a liquid which in expanding or contracting records the change upon a metal disk to which it is connected by a long, flexible tube. A pen, connected to the disk, records the temperature upon a chart which is marked off in degrees, hours, and days and is attached to an 8-day clock that causes the drum to make one complete revolution each week (Fig. 114).

In setting the instrument in the field, the tube is placed horizontally in a container filled with water. After 10 to 15 minutes, the temperature of the water is carefully determined by means of a thermometer which has been checked with a standardized one and the pen set accordingly, by means of the adjusting device, care being taken to turn the drum so that the correct hour is indicated. In placing the bulb in the soil, great care

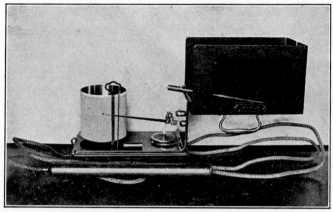

Fig. 114.—Soil thermograph with case opened and a thermometer with brass case placed in the top. The thermograph bulb is buried in the soil at any desired depth.

should be exercised to disturb the natural cover as little as possible, and after adjusting it horizontally at the desired level and burying the surplus tube-length at a similar depth, the natural cover, in so far as possible, should be restored. The exact position of the bulb should be marked. It should be placed at such distance from the instrument shelter that the soil will at no time be shaded by the latter. The shelter should be firmly held in place by means of stakes. Once properly adjusted the instrument needs little attention except to ink the pen, insert a new chart, and wind the clock once each week. The readings should be checked from week to week by inserting the thermometer in a small hole made by a sharp rod in the soil near the bulb. The best time is in the early morning when radiation and absorption of heat from the surface soil are about equal. Otherwise, the reading of the thermograph is apt to lag behind that of the thermometer.

The depth at which the bulb is buried varies with the purpose of the reading. Surface temperatures may be taken by covering the bulb with only a thin layer of soil. If temperatures for seed germination are desired, it should be placed shallower than that for the study of the root development of seedlings. If only one instrument is available a depth of 4 inches is the one usually employed. Other types of self-recording thermometers may be had.

Special soil thermometers possess a very long tube, the whole instrument being encased in a wooden jacket for protection. The soil thermometer is placed in the ground at the desired depth. The scale is then above the surface where it may be read directly. Since soil temperatures are relatively constant, especially at depths greater than 12 inches, frequent readings of them are consequently unnecessary. Ordinary thermometers, furnished with brass cases to avoid breakage in carriage. yield satisfactory results.

Relation to Activities of Higher Plants.—The rate of absorption, like all the physical and chemical processes taking place within the roots, is decreased by a lowering of the soil temperature. A low temperature permits only a slow rate of absorption. The effect of soil temperatures upon transpiration has been studied in connection with dwarfing in the alpine tundra of Pike's Peak. Temperatures between 55 and 100°F. exerted little influence, but transpiration fell rapidly below 55°F., being reduced to half at 38 and practically to zero at 34°F. The plants began to wilt at 40 and drooped badly at 34°F.[169] Even in the latitude of southern Arizona, the conditions of soil temperature for most favorable absorption do not prevail in winter, and the effect is a limitation of the development of both root and shoot of winter annuals.[128] This also explains the damage often done to trees, shrubs, winter wheat, and other plants in early spring by warm weather and high winds when the soil is still cold, if not frozen. Under these conditions, transpiration exceeds absorption. Winterkilling is, perhaps, more often due to drying than to freezing. It also results from smothering under impervious ice or snow and from soil heaving.

Favorable soil temperatures promote rapid seed germination and seedling establishment and are necessary for vigorous root growth. The warmer the soil in spring in temperate climates the more rapid are germination and growth. For example, the roots of the creosote bush (*Covillea*) elongated at the rate of 0.1 millimeter per hour at 59°F., 0.4 millimeter at 77°F., but 1.6 millimeters at the optimum temperature of 90°F.[132] Plants vary greatly in regard to temperature requirements for germination.[350] Wheat will germinate at a minimum temperature of 40°F., maize requires 49°F., but pumpkins require 52°F. Wheat germinates best at 84°F. but reaches its limit at 108°F.; but the optimum for maize and pumpkins is 93°F., and they continue to germinate until 115°F. is reached.[351] Soil temperature at the time of sowing profoundly affects the development of cereals. Germinating winter wheat must undergo a period of low temperature or it will fail to head.[579] Seeds buried in duff under a dense forest canopy often remain dormant because the temperature is not favorable to germination. Heavy thinning or cutting may admit sufficient heat to promote a good stand of seedlings.

A very important factor in the control of soil temperature is the maintenance of an optimum moisture supply. This can be promoted by drainage or irrigation, by proper methods of tillage to produce a good soil structure, and by maintaining sufficient organic matter in the soil.

Relation to Soil Organisms and Soil Reactions.—Many desirable biological and chemical soil reactions are retarded or stopped by unfavorable soil temperatures. Most soil bacteria do not become active until temperatures of 45 to 50°F. are attained. Temperatures of 65 to 70°F., which afford good root growth, also promote such changes as the decomposition of organic matter with the production of ammonia and the formation of nitrate nitrogen. Likewise, the fixation of atmospheric nitrogen depends upon similar favorable temperatures. In one experiment extending over a period of 3 weeks, the amounts of nitrates produced at 44, 94, and 111°F. were 4, 47, and 11 pounds per acre, respectively.[746] Surface-soil temperatures may become so high that bacterial activity is suspended and the organisms themselves may be destroyed.

The rapidity of rock weathering in the tropics illustrates the fact that chemical changes in the soil are greatly accelerated by high temperatures. The solvent action of water is greatly increased. Temperature also exerts a marked effect upon such physical changes as rate of percolation, evaporation, diffusion of gases, vapors, and salts in solution. The aspirating effect brought about by a small change in soil temperature is often so marked as to result in thorough renewal of the oxygen supply of the soil to a depth of several inches.

SALINE SOILS

In arid regions where drainage is very slight, as well as in marshes, etc., adjacent to seashores and other bodies of salt water, the soil salts may accumulate to such a degree, especially in lowlands, that they are distinctly harmful to most plants. The salts may have been present originally in the parent materials and not leached as they are under heavy rainfall. More commonly salts occur in poorly drained places or seepage areas where they accumulate upon the evaporation of the water that leaches them from adjoining land. These are areas of periodic excessive moistening and drying.[472] These accumulations of soluble salts are termed alkali.   Alkali in soils includes any soluble salt, regardless of its specific reaction, that occurs in sufficient concentration to injure crop plants.   It includes the chlorides, sulphates, carbonates, and nitrates of sodium, potassium, and magnesium and the chloride and nitrate of calcium.   Thus, even sodium nitrate, an important constituent of fertilizers, if in excess, produces a saline or alkali soil.   With the exception of the carbonates of sodium and potassium, all of the soil salts are neutral in reaction.   Hence, soils containing an excess of any of these neutral salts are more properly designated as salty or saline soils (*Solonchak*).

Fig. 115.—A saline area due to an excess of sodium chloride.   The dark-colored plant bordering the salt-encrusted area is sea blite (*Suaeda depressa*), and the lighter colored vegetation mostly saltbush (*Atriplex hastata*).   Salt grass (*Distichlis spicata*) occurs on the less salty soil in the background.

They are known collectively, however, as white alkali, from the white incrustation usually produced by them (Fig. 115).   The highly alkaline soils containing carbonates of sodium or potassium are called black alkali (*Solonetz*) because of the dark-colored incrustation which these salts produce by their solvent action on the organic matter of the soil.   In many places where vegetation is sparse, the color is brown or dark brown instead of black.   Desalinization, *i.e.*, removal of the excess salts as by drainage, and alkalinization (hydrolysis of sodium to sodium hydroxide and its reaction with carbon dioxide to form sodium carbonate) change a saline soil (Solonchak) to a deflocculated alkaline one (Solonetz).[472]   In many irrigated areas there are considerable tracts which have gone completely out of cultivation as a result of these processes.

White and Black Alkali.—Mix 200 grams of black potting soil with 4 grams of sodium chloride dissolved in 25 cubic centimeters of water and another lot with 4 grams of sodium carbonate.   Place each in a glass tumbler and add enough water to saturate.   Allow the tumblers to stand where the soil will dry out and note the crust formed in each case.   Incrustations of "black alkali" may be white if the soil is very low in organic matter, and the incrustations of "white alkali" may be black if the salts are calcium and magnesium chlorides and the organic matter high.

Saline areas are frequent from western Canada to the high plateaus of Mexico and in other arid parts of the world.   The salts have originated from the soils derived from the native rock.   In regions of greater rainfall, such as the eastern half of the United States, the excess salts have been leached out and finally accumulated in the ocean.   Plants of salt water, e.g., seaweeds, mangroves, etc., have certain adaptations such as high osmotic pressures or mucilaginous cell contents, etc., characteristic of halophytes.[957]

In about 16 of the western states, soil alkali furnishes one of the chief problems in agriculture.   Approximately 13 per cent of the irrigated land of the United States contains enough alkali to be harmful to crops, and over extensive areas the soil is so filled with salts, that only a scanty vegetation can exist.[376]

Why Salinity is Harmful.—Saline soil is harmful to plants in a number of ways.   A concentrated soil solution, due to excess of salts and to loss of water by surface evaporation, may delay seed germination either temporarily or indefinitely by hindering water absorption.   The seeds of most halophytes probably germinate only when the soil solution is diluted by rains.   If germination is successful, a later concentration of salts may cause the movement of water from the root hairs to the soil.   This gives rise to a condition of plasmolysis; absorption is inhibited and wilting and death may result.   Even if the plants can grow, their nutrition is deranged, unless they have become adapted to the excess supply of ions into which the salts are dissociated.

Wheat plants can make a good growth in the presence of a quantity of salts that will not permit the formation of well filled heads of plump grain.   Various kinds of fruit trees can endure a concentration that seriously injures the texture, sweetness, flavor, and keeping quality of the fruit.   The burning quality of tobacco, the length and fineness of cotton fiber, and the purity coefficient of sugar cane and sugar beets may be impaired by a quantity of salts too small to interfere seriously with the growth of the plants.[464]

Injury due to excess salts is often shown by chlorosis.   The bark of plants may be corroded at the soil surface by salts, especially by the carbonates, concentrating in the surface soils during drought.   In this way, the bark on plants in orchards and vineyards may be so thoroughly destroyed that the passage of food from the leaves to the roots is prevented. Alkali carbonates may, moreover, affect soil structure detrimentally, at least to most plants, by dissolving out the humus and deflocculating the clay and by producing impervious colloids through chemical reaction. Many saline soils are underlaid by a hardpan, produced in this manner, which is impervious to both water and roots.

The limit of tolerance to salt is determined, in part, by the species, a phenomenon clearly revealed in zonation about saline depressions. Soil samples to a depth of 4 inches from zones of saltwort (*Salicornia rubra*), sea blite (*Suaeda depressa*), and *Atriplex*, at Lincoln, Nebraska, where the salt is sodium chloride, reveal a concentration of 2.3, 1.8, and 1 per cent, respectively, of the dry weight of the soil. About Great Salt

Fig. 116.—Showing method of determining the effects of different concentrations of salt on the germination of wheat. The sand is half saturated with water and contains no Na₂CO₃ (two tumblers on left). The others contain 1,000, 1,500, and 2,000 parts per million of this salt, respectively, based on the dry weight of the soil.

Lake, where there is great desiccation of the soil in summer, *Salicornia* grows in soil with a salt content ranging from 0.5 to 6.5 per cent. Even salt grass (*Distichlis*) may endure a salinity of 2 per cent. In extreme cases saline soils are devoid of vascular plants, as on the strands of this lake, although various algae occur in the lake where the salinity varies from 14 to 27 per cent.[286]

Since the concentration of the salts in any soil varies with the water content, soil moisture should be determined as well as the percentage of salts in the oven-dry soil. Furthermore, tolerance depends upon the kind of salt. Although sodium carbonate is about as toxic to plants in water or sand cultures as sodium chloride, under natural conditions it is the worst of the alkali salts. This is because of its harmful effect upon the soil also, which intensifies the injury to the plant. The time of concentration of the salt in the surface soil is also of great importance. Winter wheat, for example, which usually tolerates less than 0.4 per cent, planted in the fall might fail upon an area which would successfully grow spring-sown clover, although the latter is less tolerant of salt (Fig. 116). Finally some plants, such as sugar beets and alfalfa, which are very sensitive to salt injury in their seedling stage, are quite resistant later in life. Because of complicating factors such as variation in water content (and hence dilution of salts), organic matter, antagonism of the salts, adsorption, etc., the degree of tolerance varies within limits. Only a very few useful plants can grow where more than 1.5 per cent of the dry weight of the soil within the root zone consists of soluble salts.[464]

To Determine the Effect of Different Kinds and Concentrations of Salt on the Germination of Wheat.—Weigh out 1,000 grams of fairly coarse, dry sand. Place it in a jar and add enough water from a liter graduate to saturate it, noting the amount needed. Measure out enough dry sand to fill three large tumblers, and weigh. Weigh out four more similar lots. To the first lot add 50 cubic centimeters of water containing 1,000 parts per million of sodium chloride based on the dry weight of the soil. Then add enough water to half saturate the sand. After mixing very thoroughly, fill each of the three glass tumblers. Plant 25 selected seeds of wheat about 1 inch deep in each. To prevent evaporation from the surface and consequent increase in salt concentration, invert a second tumbler over the first and keep it in place by means of four large, gummed labels. Label the glasses and place them in rows in the greenhouse in strong, diffuse light.

Proceeding in the same manner, use a concentration of 1,200, 1,500, and 2,000 parts per million, respectively, and also soil without salt, as a control. In another series, sodium carbonate may be used at the same rates.

At the end of a week, count the seedlings that have appeared above ground in each case and tabulate. Repeat at the end of the second week. At the end of 3 weeks, also count the number of seeds that have germinated but from which seedlings failed to appear. Also, note the nature of the roots and tops of the plants grown under the several conditions. When these results have been obtained, the experiment may be repeated with other concentrations if desired. Explain the effects of an excess of salts upon germination and growth.

In field practice, the degree of salinity is usually determined by the electrical-resistance method. This consists in passing a current through a mixture of 20 grams of soil and 50 grams of distilled water. Resistance varies inversely as the total salt content. This method is not reliable when much organic matter is present. The percentage of the different kinds of salts present can be ascertained only by chemical analyses.[232]

Various methods of reclaiming saline and alkali lands are employed.[464] Among these are scraping the salts from the surface when they have accumulated there; plowing them under; leaching them from the furrow bottoms into the subsoil and preventing their accumulating at the surface by efficient mulches, etc. The most satisfactory and permanent method is to add sufficient water to leach and drain out the excess salts and thus entirely to free the soil of them. This process often requires a period of several years. Where sodium carbonate is present, additions of gypsum ($CaSO_4$) with subsequent flooding may be effectively employed[1020] or sulphur may be added to the soil. The latter slowly forms sulphuric acid which neutralizes the sodium carbonate. Moreover, calcium is brought into solution as calcium sulphate which exerts a further beneficial effect.[469]

To Determine Chlorides by Volumetric Precipitation from a Chloride Mixture.— Many saline soils are due almost entirely to sodium chloride. Place 200 grams of oven-dry soil in a liter of water and shake thoroughly from time to time during the following 24 to 48 hours. Allow to settle. Filter twice, taking out all possible cloudiness. Titrate a 50-cubic centimeter aliquot against standard silver-nitrate solution, using potassium chromate as the indicator, *i.e.*, put a few drops of the indicator (10 grams of K_2CrO_4 dissolved in 100 cubic centimeters of water) into the soil extract and add $AgNO_3$ from the burette until the solution turns pink. The silver from 1 cubic centimeter of standard $AgNO_3$ solution (4.792 grams $AgNO_3$ per liter of distilled water) unites with 1 milligram of chlorine. Hence, multiply by 20 the number of cubic centimeters of silver nitrate used to neutralize the 50 cubic centimeters of aliquot to find the total amount of chlorine in the 1,000 cubic centimeters of soil extract. Multiply this by the factor 1.6486 to obtain grams of NaCl extracted from the 200 grams of soil. What percentage of salt does the soil contain?

ACID SOILS

In humid regions, the soil is frequently acid. The causes of soil acidity are complex. It is due primarily to the leaching of soluble basic salts, especially calcium carbonate. In soils of organic origin, calcium carbonate originally occurred only in small amounts. When basic salts are present in only very small proportions, the soil develops more or less marked acidity, most generally as the result of the accumulations of humus under conditions of poor aeration but sometimes by the setting free of acid from the mineral constituents of the soil, as explained below. Either mineral or organic acids may occur. Nitric acid may be produced by nitrifying bacteria; sulphuric acid by the oxidation of sulphur-bearing compounds; hydrochloric acid by the interaction of salt water and soils in the vicinity of saline areas; and carbonic acid is continually produced in large amounts and is universally present in soils. Numerous organic acids, *e.g.*, oxalic, lactic, and acetic, are formed by the decomposition of celluloses and other organic compounds, and certain organic acids are actually secreted by roots in poorly aerated soils. Amino acids are also formed by decay of materials of organic origin. It is believed that both the inorganic and organic colloids of the soil adsorb various substances. Probably, by a combination of physical and chemical processes, the molecules, atoms, or ions are adsorbed on the surfaces of the colloidal particles. H ions are among the substances adsorbed. A neutral salt in the soil, *e.g.*, calcium chloride, may replace some of the adsorbed H ions, and the latter, going into the soil solution, increase acidity. Moreover, acidity may result from the double decomposition of certain salts already in the soil.[990]

In general, acidity is due to the absence of sufficient calcium and magnesium bases to counteract the acids of whatever origin. The decrease in the amount of bases is brought about by the continual leaching of these soluble compounds. These carbonates, in the presence of acidulated water, form the soluble bicarbonates and are carried downward in the soil. When the soil becomes drier, as a result of absorption by roots, they are deposited as the insoluble carbonate, *i.e.*, the movement is gradually downward.

Surface soils are generally more acid than subsoils. In humid regions, hilltops, ridges, and uplands of rolling topography may be acidic as a result of the gradual leaching of the bases to lower slopes and level lands where the soil may be neutral in reaction.[758] Inwash of soil from uplands which are acid may reverse this condition along smaller streams. Soils of high altitudes are generally more acidic than those of lower ones.[123]

Hydrogen-ion Concentration.—The strength of an acid solution is not dependent upon the total quantity of acid present in it but rather upon the number of hydrogen ions in a certain volume of the solution, *i.e.*, upon the hydrogen-ion concentration. According to the modern ionic theory, many compounds when in solution undergo electrolytic dissociation into positively and negatively charged particles known as *ions*. In dilute solutions of hydrochloric acid, for example, only a small portion of it is in actual solution as molecules of HCl. The greater portion is almost completely dissociated into positively charged H ions and negatively charged Cl ions. The characteristic properties of sourness and reddening of blue litmus are due entirely to the presence in the solution of the H ions. In weak acids, *i.e.*, where the acidic properties are only slight, as in vinegar (acetic acid), the molecules are dissociated to only a small extent. There are only a few H ions present in their solutions.

Normal solutions of acetic and hydrochloric acids each contain 1 gram of hydrogen per liter; the total quantity of acidic hydrogen is the same in each. If each solution is greatly but equally diluted (*e.g.*, 0.001 N), the hydrochloric acid is 97 per cent ionized, since it is a strong acid; but the weak acetic acid is only 13.6 per cent ionized.[348] The former contains many times more H ions than does the latter. That the *total* acidity of the two acids is the same is shown by the fact that it takes the same amount of an alkali to neutralize each. But since it is the ionized hydrogen only that is responsible for the acidity of a solution at any given moment, it should be clear that the hydrogen-ion concentration of a solution, such, for example, as the soil solution, is, for biochemical purposes, a much more valuable criterion than is the potential alkali-neutralizing power.[602]

Even pure distilled water is ionized to a slight degree. But since there are as many OH (hydroxyl) as H (acidic) ions, the solution is neutral. For convenience of expression the actual hydrogen-ion concentration, *i.e.*, the number of free hydrogen ions present per liter of solution, is not used; instead a number indicating the logarithm of the reciprocal of the hydrogen-ion concentration, termed the pH value, is employed. For water this is pH 7. Since for pH 7 there is exact equality between H and OH ions, it follows that on either side of this value one or the other will be in excess. Thus, values of pH below 7 indicate acid solutions— the smaller the value the greater the acidity—and values above 7, alkalinity. For each unit decrease in pH the hydrogen-ion concentration becomes 10 times each preceding concentration.[991] The hydrogen-ion exponent is a measure of the intensity factor of acidity and not of the acid or acidic substances present. Hydrogen-ion concentration in a soil varies considerably, sometimes 1 pH unit, with rainfall and season and is also modified by the growing vegetation.[865] Strongly acid soils have pH values of 4.5 to 5.0. Extreme values of pH 2.8 have been determined in the subalpine ericaceous heath balds of Tennessee[123] and 9.7 in saline soils of California.[816]

Methods of Determining Acidity.—Methods for the determination of the pH value are electrometric and colorimetric.[145] Much new and very satisfactory equipment has been devised. The colorimetric method is simple, relatively inexpensive, and the apparatus easily portable. It is usually accurate to within 0.1 pH unit and is thus satisfactory for all ordinary soil investigations. The method is based upon the fact that a series of indicators have been found whose colors depend upon the prevailing pH and which are sensitive to changes in pH within certain well defined limits. For example, bromthymol blue is yellow for values of pH below 6.5; between 6.5 and 7 it changes through various shades of green, until for higher values it becomes blue. Thus, by the use of several indicators, some of which have a lower range of values and others a higher range than bromthymol blue, the degree of acidity or alkalinity of the soil or other solution may be determined.[62,757]

To Determine Soil Acidity.—Measurements of soil acidity are made by determining the hydrogen-ion concentration of a suspension of soil in (neutral) distilled water, hydrogen-ion concentration being a measure of the degree of acidity. Air-dried soils offer a more comparable basis than fresh soil samples, and they are generally used for the determination of pH value. A soil-water ratio of 1:2 is well adapted to both colorimetric and electrometric determinations of hydrogen-ion concentrations of most air-dried soils.[865] Use some standard colorimetric method, such as the Hellige, LaMotte, or LaMotte-Morgan soil-testing sets, etc., directions for which accompany the apparatus. Test a number of soils from different habitats and the several layers of the same soil. Do you find a definite relation between acidity and the kind and composition of the plant community?[510,758]

Effects upon Plants.—An acid soil solution with accompanying low temperatures, etc., may affect plant growth by checking the work of nitrifying bacteria and all forms of nitrogen-fixing bacteria. Earthworms are sensitive to soil acidity. An acid grassplot at the Rothamsted Experimental Station in England contained no earthworms, although they were abundant in an adjoining nearly neutral one.[24] The absence of earthworms and general decrease in soil organisms prevent the normal decay of humus and promote the accumulation of carbon dioxide and resulting toxic organic substances. Acidity also has a marked effect upon the availability of soil salts. The solubility of phosphate, calcium, magnesium, iron, aluminum, and manganese is markedly influenced.[385] The harmful effects of acidity may be due to an increased concentration of aluminum[1017] or manganese.[74,493] In acid soil, the crumb or flocculated structure of clay may be destroyed and the soil put in poor physical condition. As a consequence, the water content is increased and aeration diminished. Furthermore, plants need lime, which occurs in too small amounts in acid soils, since it is a necessary nutrient and also acts as a neutralizing and precipitating agent within the cell sap.

Among cultivated plants, certain varieties grow fairly well even in soils that are acid.[198,199] Timothy, flax, redtop, and rye belong to this group. These plants have a low lime content, make a relatively slow growth, but possess extensive root systems which thoroughly permeate large volumes of soil. Most leguminous plants grow poorly on acid soils. In general, they are plants of high lime content, make a rapid growth, and, because of their coarse taproot systems, have a relatively medium or low absorbing power for lime. They have difficulty in securing enough lime for their needs.[934] Onions, peanuts, and tobacco are examples of crops injured by acid soils; buckwheat, cowpeas, and potatoes tolerate strong acidity. Acidity in soils may be corrected and such soils made more productive to most crops by the addition of some form of lime. The "lime requirement" of a soil depends not only upon its pH but also upon the extent to which it is buffered by humus content, clay, and phosphates. Buffer action is the resistance offered by a solution to variation in its pH value as a result of the addition or loss of acid or alkali.[464]

Soils more acid than pH 3.7 normally are not forested but clothed with heaths of low shrubs, lichens, etc., or with bog thickets. In eastern North America, soils with pH of 3.7 to 4.5 frequently support stands of tamarack, black spruce, and hemlock, or aspen and birch. Within a range of 4.5 to 5.5 the majority of coniferous trees and many northern deciduous trees are found. Moderately or slightly acid soils (pH 5 5 to 6.9), characterized by relatively great activity of microorganisms, high availability of mineral nutrients, good structure and aeration, are very favorable to tree growth. On such soils occurs the bulk of the great deciduous forest.[1004]   Nearly neutral to alkaline soils are characteristic of the great grassland areas.

Certain species such as blueberries (*Vaccinium*); mountain laurel (*Kalmia*), and azaleas (*Rhododendron*) grow only in acid soils.   This is, perhaps, an adaptation following long periods of adjustment resulting from the sorting out of plants by the process of competition.[992]   These acid-requiring plants are, moreover, all endotrophic mycorrhizal species and it seems probable that it is the mycorrhizal fungi rather than the flowering plants themselves that require the acid condition.

Certain species of plants have been grouped into lime-loving (*calciphilous*) and lime-fearing (*calciphobous*) species according to whether they grow on limestone or siliceous soils.   Experiments have shown, however, that the calciphobous species, such as the common brake (*Pteris aquilina*), also flourish in a soil rich in lime, provided other soluble salts are not in excess.   Similar results have been obtained with the sorrel (*Rumex acetosella*), which has adapted itself to soils so acid as to be unfavorable to most field crops.[994]   When lime is added, its yield is increased, but the sorrel is then largely replaced by clover or other plants that can compete successfully in the limed soil.[695]   Conversely, many calciphilous plants will grow in limeless soil if man prevents competition from better adapted species.   Communities developed on soils with an approximately neutral reaction are usually composed of the largest number of species.   The subject is complicated, however, by the fact that the reaction of the soil is often stratified.[756,757]   The surface layer may be quite acid, the deeper ones rich in lime, thus presenting two partial habitats.   Unless acidity is quite marked, its effects are usually overshadowed by the water and air relations.   In bogs, aeration is the dominant factor and acidity is concomitant.   A definite correlation between acidity and the presence of sphagnum has been established.[511]

In nature it is difficult to find marked changes in acidity without at the same time discovering great physical, chemical, and other differences in the environment.[432]   Habitats with the same pH but differing in other factors show corresponding differences in vegetation.   The difficulties involved in measuring these other factors and integrating their effects have often caused their potency to be minimized and the cause of difference assigned to the readily measurable differences in acidity.[512]

CHAPTER IX

REACTION AND STABILIZATION

A plant or a community produces various effects upon the habitat. All such effects are termed reactions. These are not to be confused with the impress which the habitat makes upon the plant. A habitat offers a certain amount of the factors—water, light, nutrients, etc.—to growing plants and the vegetation adjusts and adapts itself to this supply. If water is not abundant, it takes on a xeric impress; if in excess, a hydric one. But in any case the plants react upon the habitat, changing one or more of its factors to a decisive or appreciable degree. Such changes, however, cannot go on indefinitely. After many generations of plants have grown on an area and it has been occupied successively by the various stages of a sere, there finally appears a community of plants which is in dynamic adjustment with the habitat thus modified under the control of the particular climate, *i.e.*, essential stabilization is attained. Stabilization in turn is the very essence of conservation, both natural and man made, as shown in a later section.

GENERAL REACTIONS

The effects of habitat on plant and of plant on habitat are mutually complementary and often very complex. As a rule, there is a primary reaction accompanied by several or many secondary ones. Trees decrease light and by so doing they also modify temperature, humidity, and evaporation. Sometimes two or more factors are affected directly and critically, *e.g.*, marsh grass greatly reduces both water content and light. Thus, vegetation exerts its reactions entirely on the physical factors.

The reaction of a community is usually more than the sum of the reactions of the component species and individuals. Although it is the individual plant that produces the reaction, the latter usually becomes recognizable through the reaction of the group. A community of trees casts less shade than the same number of isolated individuals, but the shade is constant and continuous and, hence, controlling. The leaf litter that forms the duff and leaf mold is only the total of the fallen leaves of all the individuals, but its formation is completely dependent upon the community. About isolated trees, it is blown away or dries in the sun and it rarely accumulates except where the trees are in groups.

234

Widely scattered plants can scarcely accumulate wind-blown sand and hold it in dunes, nor can scattered floating ones cause much sediment to settle from silt-laden water.

Some reactions are the direct consequence of a functional response on the part of a plant. This is exemplified by the decrease of water by absorption, the increase of humidity as a consequence of transpiration, and the weathering of rock by the excretion of carbonic acid. Others are the immediate outcome of the form or habit of the plant body. For example, the successful reaction of pioneers in gravel slides is produced

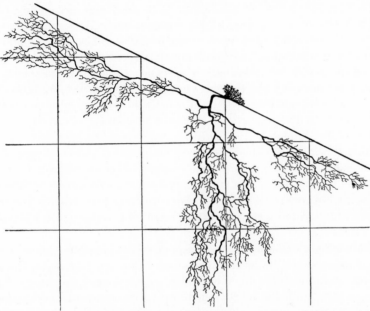

Fig. 117.—A gravel-slide plant (*Paronychia jamesii*). Because of the extensive root system, the gravelly soil within a radius of two or more feet of the plant is held more or less firmly in place. Compare Fig. 45.

almost wholly by mat, rosette, or bunch forms with extensive or deep-seated roots (Fig. 117). In a primary area, the reaction is exerted by each pioneer alone and is then augmented by the family or colony. It extends as the communities increase in size and comes to cover the whole area as vegetation becomes closed. Reactions are often felt for a considerable area around the individual or group, especially where exerted against the eroding action of wind or water or the slipping consequent upon gravity. In most secondary areas or seral stages, the reaction is the combined effect of the total population. But the preponderant role is played by successful competitors and particularly by the dominants. These determine the major or primary reactions, in which the part of the secondary species is slight or negligible.

Role in Succession.—In the development of a primary sere, reactions begin only after the ecesis of the first pioneers and are narrowly localized about them and the resulting families and colonies. They are largely mechanical at first and consist in binding sand or gravel, producing finely weathered material, or building soil in water areas, etc. In secondary seres, extensive colonization often occurs during the first year and reaction may at once be set up throughout the entire area. The reactions of the pioneer stage may be unfavorable to the pioneers themselves, or they may merely produce conditions favorable to new invaders, which succeed gradually in the course of competition or become dominant and produce a new reaction unfavorable to the pioneers. Naturally, both causes may and do operate at the same time The general procedure is essentially the same for each successive stage. Ultimately, however, the time comes when reactions are more favorable to occupants than to invaders, and the existing community becomes more or less permanent, constituting a climax or subclimax. In short, a climax vegetation is completely dominant, its reactions being such as to exclude all other species. In one sense, succession is only a series of progressive reactions by which communities are selected out in such a way that only that one survives which is in entire harmony with the climate. Reaction is thus the keynote to all succession, for it furnishes the explanation of the orderly progression by stages and the increasing stabilization which produces a climax.

Stabilization and Climate.—The progressive invasion typical of succession everywhere produces stabilization. The habitat has been occupied for longer or shorter periods by the populations of the several stages in the sere. From the beginning, there has been a steady or recurrent stream of invaders, and the development of the formation, like the growth of any organism, has been continuous or renewed. Where the dominating newcomers were of a different life form from the previous occupants, the change stood out clearly, as when floating plant consocies were replaced by those of reed swamp. The particular stage persisted just as long as the new life form was able to produce a reaction sufficient to control the community. Owing to reactions, the habitat is constantly brought nearer medium or mesic conditions. The vast majority of species are not pioneers, *i.e.*, xerophytes or hydrophytes, but mesophytes with comparatively high but balanced requirements for ecesis. The final outcome in every sere is the culmination in a population most completely fitted for the mesic conditions brought about by the reactions of past plant generations. Such a climax is permanent because of its close harmony with the essentially stable habitat. It will persist just as long as the climate remains unchanged, always provided that migration does not bring in a new dominant from another region, an exceedingly rare event.

In many cases, dominance is primarily due to the control of water content as in grassland, or of light as in reed swamp, or of both as in scrub. Thus, the essential cause of the temporary stabilization with each change of life form is dominance. But until the final stage of development is reached, the populations are held in a certain stage only until the reactions become distinctly unfavorable to them or until the invasion in force of a superior life form. Thus, reaction is not only the cause of

FIG. 118.—Climax forest of tamarack (*Larix*), white fir (*Abies*), and western red cedar (*Thuja*) Idaho.

dominance but also of the loss of it. It makes clear why one community develops and dominates for a time, only to be replaced by another, and why a stage able to maintain itself as a climax finally appears.

Stabilization is increase of dominance. Every complete sere ends in a climax, *i.e.*, a point is reached where the occupation and reaction of a dominant are such as to exclude the invasion of another dominant. The climax is thus a product of reaction operating within the limits of the climatic factors of the region concerned. The climate determines the dominants that can be present in the region and what life form will constitute the final stage of development of the formation. Thus, climate is a stabilizing cause of succession. Reaction determines the relative sequence of stages and causes the selection of one or more of the final dominants. The climax is the mature or adult stage of vegetation. The climax formation is the fully developed community, of which all initial and medial communities are but stages of development. The causes that retard the complete maturing of the organism by handicapping or destroying some stage have been pointed out in discussing the subclimax.

Although the climax marks the close of the general development, its recognition is possible only by a careful study of the whole process. Duration is in no wise a guide, since even pioneer stages may persist for long periods, and subfinal stages often appear to be climax. Development should be traced in all parts of the climatic region where dominants occur which are similar to the one supposed to be climax. Once attained, the climax will persist, except for catastrophes such as fire, flood, landslides, etc., until there is a fundamental change in climate, or until an essentially new flora develops as the outcome of long-continued evolution (Fig. 118). This is an event that has occurred but once in the last 100 million years or so, with the rise of angiosperms.

Reaction and Coaction.—Reaction denotes the collective effect of organisms upon the habitat, while coaction refers to the influence of two or more species or individuals upon each other. Reaction may comprise the total effect of the biotic community upon physical factors, though it is exerted chiefly by plants on land and by animals in large bodies of water, or the term may be applied to the specific operation of a particular grouping, layer, or species. Among animals, reactions may be individual and of little importance, like that of the badger, or they may be by social groups as with earthworms, ants, or prairie dogs, and correspondingly significant. For animals likewise, reactions may be variously combined with coactions, a process illustrated by such burrowers as gopher and mole and by harvesting ants or rodents, to say nothing of man.

Kinds of Reactions.—These may be grouped in various ways, from the standpoint of cause or effect, agency or matrix, etc. The soil as a fixed substratum is much more affected, largely by virtue of accumulation, and its reactions are consequently more numerous than those in air, with water-bodies occupying an intermediate position. Soil reactions may be conveniently arranged with respect to the factor directly concerned, under (1) soil formation and structure, (2) water content, (3) air content, and (4) solutes. On the same basis, air reactions may be considered under (1) wind, (2) temperature, humidity, and rainfall, and (3) light. However, since these factors are discussed in relation to plant response in the respective chapters, it is desirable here to treat the reactions upon them from the standpoint of conservation. Naturally, these constitute but part of the picture and coactions must also be taken fully into account.

In fact, it is coaction that regularly sets in motion the destructive processes due to man and domesticated animals, which reaction must be invoked to control. Taken together, they make up the sum total of conservation, and they are first considered separately only for greater convenience in analysis.

Plant Cover.—At the outset it is desirable to pass in review the features or qualities of vegetation that render it so valuable under natural conditions and its removal such a menace under utilization. This is largely

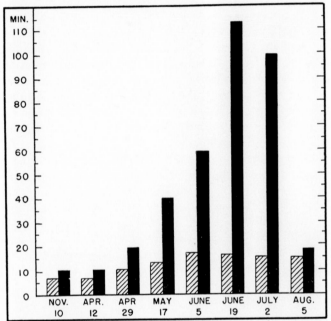

Fig. 119.—Relative efficiency of underground parts of lowland winter wheat without tops (hatched) and with tops (black) in preventing erosion.

a consequence of cooperation by virtue of which dominant species live together on fairly equal terms, as subdominants do likewise. Their respective needs, though similar, are not identical, and the usual result is the production of a continuous or closed cover, the essential character of which is given by the dominants. Such exceptions as occur in the form of a partial or open cover are found in the early stages of priseres or in such xeric climaxes as sagebrush and desert scrub. In practically all other instances, open cover in itself is an indicator of disturbance.

In terms of both production and protection, the chief quality of cover is its density or closeness of canopy. Closely associated with this are height of stem and depth and spread of root, and all three are to a large degree properties of the life form, such as forb, grass, shrub, or tree, or of the subform, tall, mid or short grass, sod or bunch grass. Duration is likewise an important matter, as expressed in annual or biennial by contrast with perennials, and the latter differ further, inasmuch as the shoot is underground or aerial. The persistence of dead stems and leaves may play a significant part, and this is usually augmented when they accumulate on the ground as litter. Even when all living parts have disappeared above ground, litter may act as a fairly adequate substitute.

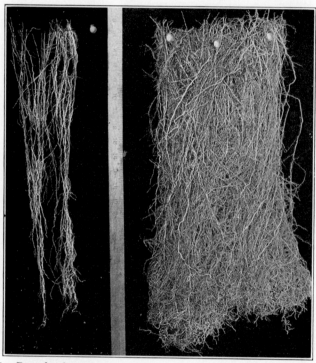

Fig. 120.—Root development from similar blocks of sod of *Panicum virgatum*, 25 square inches in area and 5 inches thick. The roots are about 2 feet long. Tops from the sod on the right were unclipped; those on the left were clipped six times during the summer. Roots of clipped plants weighed only 2.6 per cent that of the unclipped.

This is particularly true when it is renewed year after year, a fact that renders fire a peculiarly undesirable type of disturbance. Root systems reflect their respective life forms to a greater or less degree, and the number, branching, spread, depth, and duration of roots are all features to be taken into account.

The relative efficiency of roots and tops of plants acting together, and underground parts alone, in protecting the soil from erosion has been determined. Numerous paired samples of field and pasture crops as well as of various weeds and true-prairie vegetation were employed.[505]

The samples consisted of 0.5 meter quadrats secured intact to a depth of 1 decimeter from which the tops of the plants from one sample were removed by clipping. Water was applied at a constant rate and force, after the samples were inclined at an angle of 10 degrees, and the time was recorded for the complete washing away of the soil. Results with a cover of wheat are shown in Fig. 119. A dense cover of alfalfa was less efficient than that of fully grown wheat; the roots alone were slightly more effective than those of wheat. The erosion ratio of roots alone to roots and tops of brome grass was about 1:7. Even a cover of dead crab grass (*Digitaria sanguinalis*) placed on bare soil increased the period for complete erosion 15 times. The most formidable line of defense by the grasses against erosion is above ground, although the soil is also held in a remarkable manner by roots and rhizomes. Native bluestem prairies have 3 to 4 tons per acre (dry weight) of underground parts in the surface 4 inches of soil.[977] With continued close grazing of tops this is reduced to one-half or less and in old pastures underground parts may be less than 1 ton per acre (Fig. 120). Roots continue to be useful after they are dead and even after they have decayed, since they leave soil channels down which water may move.

SOIL REACTIONS

Reactions of the Plant Cover.—With few exceptions, the cover of vegetation reacts favorably upon soil, not only protecting it from wastage but under natural conditions also improving its fertility and texture. A striking exception is afforded by streamside communities, which usually transpire large amounts of water and reduce local water supplies in consequence.[72] This is naturally a reaction of all vegetation, but sometimes it is offset by the moisture contributed as a source of local rainfall. The reduction of soil nutrients by crops rarely finds a counterpart in nature, even native hayfields maintaining their yields over long periods.

The primary effect of cover is to retard the movement of water or wind over the surface of the soil by means of stems and leaves and to filter water into the soil along the roots or old root channels, a process in which litter and leaf mold also play leading roles.[664] This slackening has a direct effect upon the rate and amount of runoff, with immediate consequences in reducing the frequency and magnitude of floods, and the amount of erosion with its twin evils of removal and deposit. At the same time, absorption and infiltration with consequent percolation are increased proportionally, thus renewing the water content of the soil, regulating the flow of streams, and providing water of the proper quality for reservoirs and especially for urban use (Fig. 121). Practically all other reactions upon the soil are contributory to these primary ones, but among them the effects of organic materials and minerals seem to be of

Fig. 121.—Detail of plant cover in runoff plots in (top) native prairie, (center) over-grazed prairie, and (bottom) prairie killed by overgrazing and trampling. The plots were only a few meters apart on similar soil and slope (10 degrees). Runoff from a 3-inch rain in 1.5 hours was 11.3, 50.5, and 71.6 per cent, respectively, and erosion 0, 355 pounds, and 4.7 tons of soil per acre.

the first importance, especially under cultivation. Humus appears to render loose soils less erosive, while the nutrients stimulate growth and increase density of cover, and contribute to the litter when in organic form. Practically all these properties are found in the so-called "green manures" or cover crops, which in addition serve to protect the soil from erosion during the rainy season, as in orchards in California, or during the period in which seedlings are becoming established, as in artificial regeneration. The values are often secured in largest measure by nodule-bearing legumes, which occupy a unique position among the plant reactors to be utilized for erosion control.

Reaction of Plant Cover in Protecting Soil against Erosion.—Construct three boxes, of boards 1 inch thick, each 1 meter long and ½ meter wide inside. Bore four 1-inch holes in one end of each, two of the holes being near the bottom of the box. Fill each box with well screened soil of good water content. If the soil contains much clay, thoroughly intermix it with one-third sand. The holes should be closed with corks. Plant two boxes to Sudan grass, millet, or oats, broadcasting the seed at a rate of about 1 per square inch. It is best to fill the boxes to within ½ inch of the top; sow the seed, and add another ½ inch of soil. Keep the surface soil moist to insure good germination. The third box is unplanted, but water regularly to compact the soil, and keep all weeds removed.

After 30 days, or when the plants are 6 to 12 inches tall, tilt the box with the bare soil at an angle of 10 degrees, remove the corks, and apply water from a hose with nozzle adjusted so as to simulate a moderate rainfall. This is best done by attaching a shower-bath nozzle to the hose and adjusting so that the water descends *vertically* and in drops as it reaches the soil. A temporary frame of 12-inch boards may be built about the box with soil to prevent splashing of the muddy water. Note the time required to wash away the entire contents of the box. If one or two dead leaves of elm or other deciduous tree are moistened and placed over the bare soil before applying water, an interesting phenomenon may be observed. *Without readjustment* of the rate of application of water, determine the time required to wash away the soil from the second box, tilted at the same angle after the tops of the plants have been clipped to the soil surface and removed so that the soil is held by the roots only. Finally, determine the time for complete erosion when both tops and roots protect the soil. Record your observations and discuss the application of the principles concerned to grazing and crop production.

Erosion and Plant Cover.—Decrease in water content and soil fertility and change in soil structure are all closely related to erosion caused by runoff. The latter is greatly influenced by plant cover. Upon areas from which vegetation has been partially or completely removed, the raindrops beat upon the bare soil like millions of little hammers. The soil is compacted and its absorbing capacity is reduced. Reduced absorption results largely from the fact that dashing rains churn the bared soil into muddy suspensions. As the water percolates into the earth, the suspended soil particles filter out, partially close the pore spaces, and finally seal the soil to such a degree that it absorbs but little.[549] The excess water accumulates on the surface and in running off removes with it the surface-soil particles, the humus, and the dissolved salts. Whether there is a more or less uniform washing away of the soil over the entire area, as in sheet erosion, or whether it is by the formation of gullies, landslides, or erosion along river bottoms, the results are the same. The remaining plant cover is destroyed, the richest portion of the soil is removed, leaving exposed a hard, compact, poor absorbing surface. Water content is often further affected by a lowering of the water table, which results in a constant tendency of the water in the upper layers

Fig. 122.—Fighting a forest fire. During a recent 5-year period, fire destroyed 56,000,-000 acres of forest in the United States, and in many cases exposed the soil to erosion. (*U. S. Forest Service.*)

to sink to a lower level. Soil removed from the uplands causes great destruction in silting over vegetation of adjoining lowlands and in impeding navigation.[56,191a,853]

The mantle of soil that clothes the mountains and protects the headwaters of streams acts as a great natural reservoir. It is largely from this source that water for irrigation is obtained. The effectiveness of this natural reservoir is decreased in proportion as the soil is removed or its absorptive capacity lessened by erosion. The gradual release of water through spring-fed streams is replaced by destructive floods. Nearly half the United States—the hilly half—is being seriously impaired by water erosion. This has been brought about largely by the removal of the natural plant cover, as in the process of clearing forests from nonagricultural land, through destructive lumbering, fires, and overgrazing (Figs. 122 and 123).[55,721a]

Forests, chaparral, grassland, and all kinds of plant cover, living or dead, protect the soil from erosion.[50a,291] This effect is due partly to protection afforded by aboveground parts, in part to the results of humus accumulation, and in no small degree to the binding action of roots and rhizomes. Soil is warmer in winter and cooler in summer under a plant cover and especially in forests and scrub. Hence, snow begins to melt earlier than on exposed ground. Melting proceeds more gradually,

Fig. 123.—View of a mountain slope in North Carolina, after the removal of the forest. In cutting such a forest enough young trees should be left to hold the soil and insure a new timber crop. (*U. S. Forest Service.*)

however, where it is retarded by the forest cover after warm weather begins. Thus, the water from the gradually melted snow is more apt to be absorbed, especially since the soil in forests freezes less deeply. Only the removal of the cover of vegetation and subsequent erosion reveal its beneficial effects.[1034]

The cutting of the forest cover on a small watershed in Colorado, although in a region of coarse, permeable soil, increased the volume of silt discharge 8.5 times. Within 3 years after the brush cover on a canyon drainage in southern California was destroyed by fire, the soil lost 45 per cent of its water-holding capacity. In Utah, the runoff after rainstorms on overgrazed land was seven times as great as on adjacent areas that were moderately and conservatively grazed.[775] Most of the worn-out lands of the world are in their present condition because much of the surface soil has washed away and not because they have been worn out by cropping.[252] Under cultivation, the rate of erosion is often appalling. Certain Piedmont areas have entirely lost the 8 or 10 inches of topsoil within a period of only 30 years. Measurements in Missouri have shown that on a slope of less than 4 per cent, when plowed annually and cropped with corn, the surface soil to a depth of 7 inches is entirely removed in a period of 50 years.[610] The removal of the same thickness of soil in grassland would require thousands of years. Left to herself, nature brings about an adjustment between erosion losses, soil-forming processes, and the development of vegetation. It is only when man interferes that erosion becomes a seriously destructive force.

Measurement of Runoff and Erosion.—It is manifest that all methods and installations for promoting conservation must be based upon the actual conditions at the outset and that this demands definite quantitative information of the processes concerned. Since cover is the major control, and hence the chief tool, experimental measures are essential to determining the kind and amount of reaction for each community or often for a particular species. But conditions also vary greatly between different sites or terrains. The soil may range from rock or gumbo at one extreme to sand or gravel at the other; the terrain may be level and smooth or it may be rough and slope at almost any angle, and disturbances of all kinds and degree may be superimposed upon soil or slope, tillage being the most important.

Experimental plots are usually narrow rectangles in form, but they vary much in size in accordance with conditions and objectives. They may be as small as 3 by 33.3 feet and as large as ¼ acre; the three sizes at the erosion experiment stations are 6 feet wide and 36.3, 72.6, and 145.2 feet long, giving 0.005, 0.01, and 0.02 acre, respectively.[548,981] They are naturally placed lengthwise of slopes and enclosed by a frame of boards, or galvanized iron, sunken edgewise in the soil, or by cement walls. The area of cover selected should be as uniform as possible and sufficient in extent to permit duplication of each plot at the least, though triplicates are better when man-power permits. Slope and soil should be essentially uniform and especially so when row crops or fallow are to be studied. The composition and density of the cover are determined by means of permanent quadrats to be charted or photographed and supplemented by clip quadrats in pasture or range. The reaction of different covers is measured and compared from the first year of installation, but in many cases the plots are to be specially treated, and this renders it essential to make a preliminary run for 2 to 3 years before the several treatments are applied. In addition to the norm thus obtained, it is necessary to include control plots for comparison throughout the period of measurement. The equipment for measuring runoff and eroded material ranges from simple receptacles of galvanized iron placed below the plots to complete installations of intensity gages and concrete tanks.

The rate and depth of penetration, as well as the increase in water content, can be determined with fair accuracy by means of soil samples taken immediately after a rain and at definite intervals. The usual method, however, is by means of lysimeter cans or larger wooden or concrete tanks, which measure both the runoff and the percolation water or "runout." These are supplemented by phytometers with controls that permit the determination of transpiration and evaporation from the soil. The chief purpose of such an installation is to afford comparisons of the reaction effectiveness of different covers, but it is also employed in connection with differences in soils, litter, rainfall intensity, etc.

Reactions of Animals.—For the present purpose, it is sufficient to consider the reactions of animals in land communities, which are due primarily to disturbance. The accumulation of bodies and excreta may play a large part in ponds and bogs, and doubtless is not without significance in soils, but the effect is usually merged in the much greater one produced by plants. Disturbance regularly involves more or less coaction, often as the initial process, and hence reaction as a major feature is largely confined to burrowing animals, using this term in a wide sense.

Burrowing forms are found in many groups, such as worms, Crustacea, spiders, insects, and several orders of land mammals. The habit is almost completely lacking in birds, the burrow owl regularly being a tenant and not a builder. Moreover, burrowing becomes an important reaction only by virtue of numbers or social habit, as illustrated by earthworms, ants, and certain familiar rodents. In this country, the most important burrowing reactors comprise the prairie dog, pocket gopher, ground squirrel, and kangaroo rat, all of them especially characteristic of grassland. In the aggregate, earthworms move enormous amounts of soil, at the same time improving the humus content and increasing the porosity, but the value is lessened by the general abundance of cover and litter in their haunts. By contrast, the influence of ants is more or less unfavorable to penetration, especially for those that build large hills in a considerable clearing.

With respect to rodent burrowers, there is some difference of opinion concerning their reactions.[341] It is evident that they serve as cultivators, moving or mixing the soil of different layers, working in plant materials and adding excreta, and improving the air and water relations in general. The doubt is raised in connection with the mounds of loose material and the underground tunnels in relation to runoff and erosion. It is natural to assume that the loose soil is added to the material swept from the surface and that the holes and tunnels initiate gullies. However, instances of the latter appear to be exceptionally rare and hence negligible, while the effect of the mounds is rather to increase penetration and reduce runoff. When they occur in abundance on steep slopes, such mounds often form a fairly definite pattern of terraces, with a corresponding retarding effect upon runoff and erosion. However, in such concentrations it is probable that the benefit is more than counterbalanced by the forage consumed.

Man as a Reactor.—Practically all kinds of disturbances wrought by man comprise both reaction and coaction. However, in the case of fire or lumbering, coaction is direct and purposeful, while reaction may follow

Fig. 124.—Dust cloud rolling over a west-central Kansas town, 1935. (*Photograph by Potter.*)

as the primary objective or it may be merely incidental. In the breaking of prairie for crops, reaction is the immediate process and coaction in terms of destruction, though simultaneous, is only an incident. This is largely true also of the building of roads and railways, but the preponderance of reaction is seen particularly in major engineering structures, such as canals, reservoirs, levees, etc. Draining and impounding involve a double reaction, first through construction and then by changing the water relations, which leads to the destruction of the existing vegetation. Grazing resembles fire and logging in being a coaction, and like them also, it may lead to reaction in some form and degree.

Whatever the process and the respective roles of coaction and reaction, the final result of man's activities has been to bare the surface of the soil more or less completely and thus provide opportunity for restoring the cover through the agency of succession. But this gets under way slowly, while destructive processes do not wait. Moreover, cultivation is repeated from year to year, overgrazing becomes cumulative, and fire recurs frequently, with the consequence that succession cannot start or is soon halted and destruction becomes more or less continuous or recurrent (Fig. 124). The damage once done, it can only be repaired by man turning to the use of coaction and reaction for constructive rather than destructive effects. Often this involves no more than a minor change in practice, such as plowing on the contour, leaving the stubble on the ground, or the application of an old method to a new situation, such as terracing in fields or furrowing in pasture.

AIR REACTIONS

The cover of vegetation reacts in some fashion upon all the physical factors present in the air, exerting its greatest quantitative effect upon light and the least upon composition. While there is considerable difference in the amount of oxygen and carbon dioxide in soils, both movement and diffusion in the air are such that the variation is slight, with occasional exceptions near the ground in dense cover. By contrast, the reduction brought about in light intensity may reach a thousand-fold, but this is primarily concerned with plant response and hence is discussed in the appropriate chapter. For the present purpose, the factors of chief importance are wind in relation to erosion and deposit, and the combination of humidity and temperature in connection with transpiration and evaporation, in tilled fields especially. The immediate reaction is upon wind and the water relations are then modified in consequence.

Reaction upon Wind.—It is a well known fact that vegetation acts as an obstacle to the movement of air, retarding or deflecting it and hence modifying its effects. Such a reaction is most evident within forest or thicket, or in the lee of trees or tall shrubs, but it is found also in grassland to a high degree and even in the short-grass disclimax there is comparative calm at the surface of the ground. Simultaneous readings of anemometers in the mixed prairie gave the following velocities for a pure stand of western wheat grass (*Agropyron smithii*) 2.5 feet tall: at 3 inches (anemometer on ground), 0; at 1 foot, 225 feet per minute; at 5 feet, 1,500 feet per minute. For blue grama (*Bouteloua gracilis*) 8 inches tall, the readings were 60 feet per minute on the ground; for grama-buffalo grass, 5 inches high, 75 feet per minute at the surface; and for scarlet mallow (*Malvastrum coccineum*) 6 inches tall, 180 feet per minute. The mid grass, owing largely to the dense stand of its sod form, eliminated movement at the surface of the soil in a wind of approximately 18 miles per hour. The short grasses reduced it to approximately one twenty-fifth, and even the perennial forb to about one-eighth, indicating that the annual weeds of the subsere have great value in holding the surface of the soil against the force of the wind. In none of the areas could any movement of soil particles be detected.

The reaction that cover exercises upon wind in slowing its speed so that it is unable to pick up dust or roll sand along is equally effective in causing it to drop the load it carries.[79,471] In consequence, every collection area where the wind is actively eroding is matched in the direction of movement by one of deposit in which cover, and sometimes other

Fig. 125.—Dune ½ mile long blown from field sown to a row crop; the collection area is disked to prevent further blowing; "Dust Bowl", Dalhart, Tex. (*Photograph by C. J. Whitfield, courtesy of U. S. Soil Conservation Service.*)

obstacles, catches the load and begins to build dunes of sand or topsoil. Once started, such dunes will continue to grow through wind action alone to considerable and sometimes great heights, wherever there is a continuous supply of material from a bare area, especially during drought periods (Fig. 125). In fallow or abandoned fields, the characteristic process is one of drifting, in which fence rows and roadsides often take such an active part as to become more or less buried. Unlike most forbs, tumbleweeds and Russian thistle in particular break off and roll away to turn fences into barriers that are then overwhelmed by sand. Snowbreaks along railways and highways often encounter a like fate, and low windbreaks are not infrequently submerged in silt (Fig. 126).

The most important features of cover in producing an effective reaction upon wind are density, height, and life forms, a much-branched shoot often compensating for density in terms of stems. Roots are in general

less effective than in erosion by water, but the ability of crowns and rootstocks to send up shoots when buried is of much importance. Perennial
or woody stems are most efficient by virtue of persisting throughout the
year and of these, evergreens or conifers take the first rank.   However, in
grassland, dead cover is nearly as effective in reaction as the living, and
this is measurably true of dense stands of weeds, apart from Russian
thistle.   It is obvious that the height and density of grasses and forbs
will vary greatly from wet to dry seasons and that a reaction sufficient
during the one will become inadequate in times of serious drought.   However, this is true only of the earlier stages of the subsere in abandoned
fields, since a grass cover is rarely if ever overgrazed to the point of per-

Fig. 126.—Fence buried by drifting top soil, Burlington, Colo.

mitting material erosion by the wind.   Even in sand hills, serious blowing
is usually confined to small areas of concentration about windmills,
corrals, feeding grounds, etc.

Reaction by Windbreaks.—Groves, woodlots, hedges, and windbreaks
are all essentially artificial communities of trees or shrubs, and a shelter
belt is little more than a planned series of windbreaks.   The reactions
produced are the same in quality for all, and they differ in quantity in
accordance with height, width, density, and composition.   The influence
upon air factors within the community is practically identical with that
of a forest in so far as the canopy is closed.   Light, temperature, and
humidity are much modified in the well known manner, and such communities provide shelter against heat in summer and cold in winter, just
as native woodland does.   However, their most important reaction is to

break the force of the wind, *i.e.*, reduce its velocity to the point where it no longer endangers crops through excessive transpiration and evaporation. Windbreaks may also exert a beneficial reaction in connection with the drifting of soil or of snow, but for such purposes care must be taken to locate them at the proper distance, in order to prevent blowing or harmful deposit.

The distance at which windbreaks produce some helpful action upon velocity and hence upon crops differs widely with the observer, ranging from about 5 to 40 times the height of the trees.[43,236] This discrepancy appears to be due partly to the kind of measure used, whether physical factors or crop yields, the latter being much less dependable, and partly to the end point. The best studies indicate that a tangible reaction rarely extends to 20 times the height of the windbreak and adequate effects are usually restricted to 5 to 10 and less frequently to 15 times its height. At the maximum effect, evaporation may be reduced as much as 70 per cent at a distance of 1 to 2 times the height of the windbreak, but with a wind of 15 miles per hour, it averages 15 to 20 per cent reduction. With respect to temperature, the daily range is about 9 per cent greater in the protected zone, but it is doubtful whether this is more often beneficial than otherwise. Humidity seems to be little affected in the leeward belt, and the major ultimate effect of a windbreak is the conservation of soil-water content in the protected area beyond the tree roots. The undesirable effects consist in the reduction of soil water by the roots in this zone and the decrease in light intensity in the shadow cast by the trees. Species differ much in relative extent of roots and consequent sapping action; the distance for cottonwood has been found to be little more than the tree height, while for osage orange it was half greater, and for mulberry twice as great. The amount of light lost to crops was about twice as great on the north side for osage orange and honey locust as for cottonwood, as it was also for the north side in comparison with the south. The damage to corn in the different situations ranged from 51 to 103* per cent, with an average of 70 per cent; for wheat the range was 121 to 146, and the average, 134.[43]

Grain crops in Russia were larger under protection of windbreaks during extreme seasons, but were sometimes reduced in average ones. During years of drought, wheat yields in the steppe were increased approximately 2 to 8 bushels per acre by protection, oats 12 to 29 and rye 4 to 12 bushels.[742] In California, fully protected orange groves produced 13,200 pounds per acre in contrast to 10,640 pounds for partly protected ones, and the value of the fruit per acre was, respectively, $507 and $271.[601]

* Where the percentage of damage exceeds 100, it means that the loss of crop was greater than the yield of a strip whose width is equal to the height of the trees.

Finally, the major reaction of windbreaks in reducing velocity brings about a better distribution of snow and correspondingly improves the water content. In addition to their effect in causing the deposition of loads of dust is the more important one of preventing blowing and consequent drifting within the zone of reaction to the leeward. Moreover, evaporation from reservoirs is materially reduced, a benefit that may figure largely in future conservation in the Great Plains especially.

Reaction and Rainfall.—Transpiration returns a stupendous amount of water vapor to the atmosphere during the growing season.[1034] The magnitude of this reaction depends directly upon the kind of vegetation and indirectly upon climatic conditions, especially rainfall and evaporation. Forest naturally makes the largest contribution, amounting in some cases to nearly twice the loss from a free water surface, but true prairie and many field crops approach it in this respect.

Forests transpire enormous amounts of water. An acre of mature oak trees absorbs 2,000 to 2,600 gallons per day. The large amounts of water transpired by forests contribute somewhat toward increasing the moisture content of the atmosphere above. Hence, the air over forests contains a much larger amount of moisture and is consequently cooler than that over a bare area or one covered with herbaceous vegetation. If all the moisture given off by the forest could be made visible as a fog, heavily forested areas would appear enveloped by a damp mist, more dense over coniferous than over broadleaf forests. The condensation of vapor on the surface of leaves as dew or hoarfrost is much less than an inch per year in northern latitudes but increases in southern latitudes and especially in tropical forests. In damp, tropical forests, so much moisture is condensed that during clear, still nights drops of dew fall continuously from the leaves as in rain. A similar phenomenon occurs in the redwood belt on the Pacific Coast.

From the above it is fairly probable that forest transpiration furnishes some part of the moisture for regional or local rainfall, and that grassland and cropland play a similar if somewhat smaller role.[163] From this assumption have followed two interesting conclusions. One is to the effect that the planting of forests increases precipitation, and the other that breaking the prairie and sowing crops has a like influence.[430,496] The latter is now known to be a mistake, as proved not only by rainfall records but especially by the fact that the transpiration from crops is little if any greater than from the undisturbed prairie. With respect to reforestation, the inference is logical and there is some evidence to support the idea of a rainfall increase. However, in regard to forest planting in a grassland climax and climate, it is highly improbable, owing not only to climatic limitations, but especially also to the fact that such areas are necessarily small and local. This is particularly true of groves and windbreaks, and hence of shelter belts, which at the most cover but 1 to 2 per cent of the surface and consequently exercise no material effect over the region as a whole. In fact, it has been supposed that the removal of eucalyptus forest in Australia and its replacement by grass and crops has increased the rainfall.[712]

A Study of Reactions.—Make a study of an area where forest or scrub has replaced grassland or where the reverse change has occurred, as a result of cutting or fire. Make a detailed list of the various kinds of reactions that have occurred as a result of the change in plant populations. A similar study of grassland and cultivated fields of maize or wheat may also be made.[265]

CHAPTER X

COACTION AND CONSERVATION

General Relations.—The primary relation between plants and animals is that of the food supply. This arises from the fact that plants manufacture practically all the food used by the world of organisms and in so doing provide most of the materials and shelter utilized by animals. A direct outcome of this is the necessary association of animals with plants in the same community, out of which springs a multitude of interactions.[686] Plants constitute the permanent basis of the biotic community on land, not merely because they are stationary, but especially because of their direct relation to the environment or habitat. They are subjected to the immediate action of the latter, and, in turn, they exert a marked effect or reaction upon the habitat. By contrast, animals are more dependent upon food supply and cover than upon physical factors, and hence their most striking relations are with plants. These are termed *coactions* and together with the action of the habitat upon organisms and the reaction of the plants upon the habitat make up the three major processes of every community.

While the number of concrete coactions in any community is limited only by the number of species and individuals in it, these fall into but a few categories. From the standpoint of the organisms concerned, coactions may exist between plants, between plants and animals, and between animals, man, of course, to be included. In the present instance, the concern is chiefly with those between plants and animals, where the universal relation is that of the food supply. Growing out of this is the coaction of shelter and of materials and a more general one of contact or disturbance, such as is seen in the trampling of herds or the carriage of fruits by attachment. Coactions may be mutually helpful, as in pollination or in the carriage of fleshy fruits, or they may be antagonistic or injurious to one of the organisms, as exemplified by grazing animals, parasitic insects, or bacteria.

Utilization and Conservation.—The activities of primitive man were much like those of other omnivorous animals, and it was not until he began to graze cattle and till the soil that distinctive coactions appeared. With the appearance of the nomadic stage, however, the utilization and consequent destruction of plants and animals have gradually spread over the globe and have become so wasteful as to force him to a new and constructive set of activities known as *conservation*.[302] In short, he has reached the point where destruction must be halted or at least counter-balanced by changed practices, or where some degree of restoration of original conditions must be brought about. It has been shown in the previous chapter that destruction often involves reaction as well as coaction, and it is likewise true that conservation must combine both of these processes in the proper degree.

In nature especially, the numerous coactions of the plants and animals of a community form an intricate network of processes, most of them still awaiting detailed study. In consequence, it proves desirable to select for treatment a few outstanding examples as representative of the various types. Such are pollen, seed, and other food coactions on the one hand, and on the other the disturbances caused by man directly or indirectly, as seen in clearing, lumbering, overgrazing, cultivation and construction, or in changed populations of animals, such as game, predators, rodents, fish, or insects.

POLLINATION

One of the universal coactions of plants and animals is that exhibited in pollination, *i.e.*, the transfer of pollen from the anther to the stigma.[627]

Significance and Methods.—The retention of the macrospore on the sporophyte, an advance characteristic of the flowering plants in contrast to the existing ferns and fernworts, made imperative some method of transferring the pollen grain or microspore. The open pistils of pines lent themselves to the transport of pollen by the wind, but the closed pistils of true flowers seem to have been dependent upon insect pollination from the first, since nearly all simple flowers exhibit this method. In fact, this coaction is so fundamental and so completely reciprocal as to have had a large share in the evolution of both flowers and insects. Its importance, however, does not rest so much upon the structure of flowers as upon the nature of fertilization itself.

Since nearly all flowers with corolla possess both stamens and pistil, it would be expected that the pollen would fall directly from the anthers upon the stigma to produce pollination. This is so simple and yet so rare that it can be explained only by some fact of the first importance. The explanation was long ago supplied by Darwin,[225] who demonstrated by experiment that the best seeds and most vigorous offspring resulted from the transfer of pollen from one flower to another or, better still, from one plant to another. It is obvious that pollination takes place only by this method in all monoecious and dioecious plants, while in perfect flowers the same result is secured by having the anthers and stigmas mature at different times.

Arrangement of Stamens and Pistils.—Since the transfer of pollen from anther to stigma is imperative if fertilization is to ensue, the relative position and development of stamens and pistils become matters of great import. They not only affect the method of transfer but also determine the kind of fertilization that results. In the great majority of cases, stamens and pistils occur in the same flower, which is then said to be perfect (*monoclinic* plants). With wind pollination especially, the stamens and pistils are in different flowers (*diclinic*), and these may be borne on the same plant (*monoecious*) or on separate plants (*dioecious*). In perfect flowers, the overwhelming rule is for anthers and stigmas to mature at different times (*dichogamy*), with the result that self-pollination becomes difficult or impossible. The anthers may shed their pollen before the stigma becomes receptive (*protandrous*), or the stigma may ripen first (*protogynous*). Flowers regularly open before or upon the maturing of anthers or stigma, but sometimes they remain partly or completely closed as in certain violets (*cleistogamous*) and must then be self-pollinated.[494]

Production of Pollen and Nectar.—The total amount of pollen produced by a species is determined by the number of flowers and stamens, and by the size of anther and pollen grain, as well as by the number of plants in a particular community. As a general rule, the amount of pollen produced increases with the danger of loss. Pollen grains are exposed to the double risk of injury by weather and loss in transit, especially in transfer by wind.[1012] Furthermore, they are often used for food by insect pollinators, and the number of grains actually transported may then be very small. Quantity production of pollen is attained in simple open flowers, such as those of the buttercup, anemone, and strawberry, by means of a large number of stamens, and this compensates the heavy loss arising from the visits of pollen-seeking insects. Among the wind-pollinated plants the greatest loss occurs in the dioecious trees, such as cottonwood and ash, and such monoecious conifers as the firs, in which the pistillate cones are above the staminate ones. The need of compensation for loss under such conditions is very great and the amount of pollen required is enormous. In many trees, this waste of pollen is offset by the production of a vast number of small flowers, and especially of reduced ones in which the stamens have been emphasized at the expense of sepals, petals, and pistils. This process is still in operation in the various species of maples, which range from perfect flowers with all four parts to the greatly reduced ones of the dioecious box elder.[164]

Among the insect-pollinated flowers, the number of stamens and, hence, the amount of pollen produced decrease as the method of pollination becomes more and more perfected, and also the number of flowers is often much reduced. Simple or primitive flowers may have several hundred stamens, but with increasing specialization of the flower for pollination the number drops to ten, five, and even one. In a large number of irregular or zygomorphic flowers, the stamens are but four or two and in the majority of the orchids but a single one (Fig. 127).

The production of nectar varies from species to species within limits almost as wide as those for pollen. While, however, the amount of pollen is fixed for each flower and, hence, to a large degree for the species concerned, the nectar flow fluctuates from season to season, day to day, and even hour to hour in some plants. It is directly influenced by the growing conditions for the season and often exhibits a distinct daily rhythm. This is so marked in such plants as the buckwheat that they are visited by bees only during the hours of the so-called *flow*. In many species, nectar is produced more or less constantly as long as it is removed. It accumulates when visitors are few or absent, but to very different

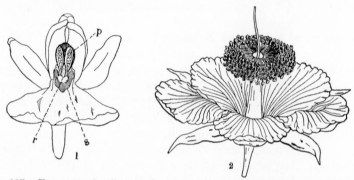

Fig. 127.—Extremes of pollen production. 1, an orchid (*Orchis*); *p*, pollen mass in anther cell; *r*, retinaculum; *s*, stigma. 2, a baobab flower (*Adansonia*) with a column of stamens. (1, *after LeMaout and Decaisne; 2, after Baillon*.)

degrees, depending upon the activity of the nectar glands, the size of the flower, and the nature of the plant. In some instances, the nectar is only a layer or droplet on a tiny nectar pad, while in others the nectary may consist of a long tube or spur with several cubic centimeters of nectar in it.

Protection of Pollen and Nectar.—The modifications that protect the pollen serve likewise for the nectar, though the latter may also be guarded by a special device of its own. In many instances, the protection afforded is secondary, the feature concerned having been developed primarily for other reasons, but the most striking devices serve directly for protection. The latter is exerted chiefly against the danger of wetting the pollen by rain or dew and the dilution of the nectar, though the nectar may also be guarded against marauders. Pollen is rarely if ever protected against loss or waste by visitors, since its free exposure promotes pollination and is offset by the large amount available.

The damage due to wetting is chiefly seen in the loading and transport of the pollen, though this may sometimes be injured by premature germination. Wind-pollinated species usually escape both handicaps, since the small flowers dry readily, as a rule, and the anthers are, for the most part, hung out for shedding during favorable weather. The extent to which bees are discouraged by dilute nectar is uncertain; at any rate, they return promptly as soon as the flowers are sufficiently dry to be profitably visited.

The devices that serve to protect pollen and nectar are of three kinds: (1) morphological, (2) mechanical, and (3) seasonal. The first

Fig. 128.—Protection of pollen by the form and position of the flower in the bearberry (*Arctostaphylos uva-ursi*).

and third seem to accomplish protection incidentally, while devices of the second type probably owe their existence to the necessity for protection. Morphological contrivances are purely structural or positional; to the first belong all those in which protection results from the structure or shape of the flower or its parts, or the flower cluster. Protection in consequence of the position of the flower or cluster occurs in a large number of species in which the face is turned downward or the tubular corolla is horizontal or drooping (Fig. 128). Mechanical devices comprise movements of the flower or its parts, or of the inflorescence. In most cases, protection results from the closing of the corolla, more rarely from that of other flower parts or in composites from the movement of the ray flowers and bracts (Fig. 129). It may also be secured by the bending or drooping of the flower stalk or the stalk of the entire cluster. Movement is most rapid and conspicuous in day bloomers and night bloomers, while its value for protection is greatest in ephemeral flowers, which usually wilt and close a few hours after opening. Day blooming and night blooming bring about the effective protection of pollen

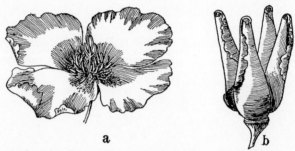

a   b

Fig. 129.—Protection of pollen in the California poppy (*Eschscholtzia californica*) by (*b*) the rolling of the petals in wet weather. (*After Kerner.*)

during the time when it is not being removed and may be injured, though the habit probably bears a more important relation to insect visits.

The Life History of a Flower.—All of the flowers of a plant exhibit the same behavior, which is characteristic of each species or often of the entire genus. This is made up of a round of changes that begin with the bud and continue their orderly progress until the fruit ripens or the seeds

Fig. 130.—The pollination story of the timothy (*Phleum*). (*Drawn by Edith S. Clements.*)

are freed. Practically all of these are concerned with the details of the task of promoting cross-pollination or of securing self-pollination when needed and of protecting pollen and nectar. Such a round of life may consist of little more than opening the flower, shedding the pollen, and ripening the stigma, or it may embrace a score of changes and movements in which all the flower parts take a share. It stands in the most intimate relation to the actual work of pollination by insects and largely determines the number and effectiveness of the latter as coactors.

The life history of a wind-pollinated flower is simpler than that of those pollinated by insects, though it often comprises a number of stages, as is shown by timothy (Fig. 130). In the geranium (Fig. 131), it is

Fig. 131.—The life history of a geranium flower (*Geranium*). (*Drawn by Edith S. Clements.*)

more complicated, while the fireweed probably exhibits a maximum number of stages (Fig. 132). In addition to the movement of the bud

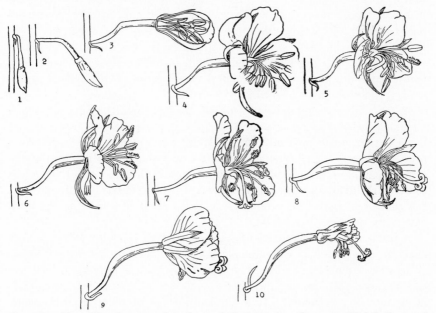

Fig. 132.—The pollination story of the fireweed (*Epilobium*). (*Drawn by Edith S. Clements.*)

into the horizontal position and those of the maturing fruit, the group of stamens and the style uniformly pass through a regular sequence of changes. The minor details of the behavior may be modified by water and heat relations, rain and cold delaying the process or warm weather hastening it, with a corresponding effect upon the rate of development.[164]

The Round of Life of a Flower.—Label five well developed buds of one plant by means of small tags and follow their development as far as the young fruit, recording the changes in growth and position and the behavior of the four parts at some time between 6 to 8 a.m., 12 to 2 p.m., and 5 to 7 p.m. This is usually best carried out by a cooperative group of students.

Kinds of Pollination.—When pollen is deposited on the stigma of the same flower, the latter is said to be self-pollinated, and the process is termed *autogamy*. If the transfer is from one flower to another, cross-pollination or *allogamy* takes place. Most species of perfect flowers are modified in such a way as to give a decisive preference to cross-pollination, but many of them may be self-pollinated when necessary. It is obvious that diclinic species, in which stamens and pistils are found in different flowers, are susceptible of cross-pollination alone. When anther and stigma are present in the same flower but ripen at different times, as in dichogamy, cross-pollination is an all but universal result and self-pollination is a rare occurrence. The latter is frequent, however, if not regular in homogamous flowers in which anthers and stigma mature simultaneously and can alone take place in all closed or cleistogamous ones. Self-pollination is the invariable rule in a relatively small number of plants which are apparently well adapted to the transfer of pollen, and such cases throw some doubt upon the accepted view that cross-pollination necessarily produces better offspring.

Many devices have been thought to insure self-pollination when allogamy fails for any reason, and careful observation shows that these do bring anther and stigma into contact in most instances. Their effectiveness, however, is usually small and often lacking, in consequence of the earlier removal of all the pollen or the drying of the stigma. Even when flowers are covered to prevent these consequences, it has been found that the setting of pods and production of good seeds are more or less difficult, in native species at least.

Cross-pollination has been distinguished as *geitonogamy* when it concerns two flowers of the same plant and as *xenogamy* when the transfer is between different plants. The latter has been supposed to be more advantageous in the production of vigorous offspring, but this view needs further experimental test. It is a logical inference from the work of Darwin, which showed that cross-pollination yielded better results, and is likewise supported by the remarkable vigor of many hybrids. Hybridization itself results from the cross-pollination of two varieties or species and has yielded a myriad of new species and forms in field and garden. A special investigation to determine its role in nature indicates that it is rare, but this is an assumption to be tested in many different floras.

Agents of Pollination.—Pollen is transported by animals, by wind, and by water. The last is unimportant, since it concerns but a few submerged aquatics,[1021] the great majority of hydrophytes being pollinated by the wind. In temperate and boreal climates especially, wind is the agent utilized by the large majority of trees and shrubs, by practically all grasses and sedges, and by many other herbaceous species with inconspicuous flowers. Wind-pollinated species regularly produce enormous amounts of pollen and possess some device for sifting this out on the wind, such as the hanging catkins of poplars and birches or the slender filaments of plantains and grasses. Styles and stigmas have been correspondingly modified for catching wind-borne pollen and have increased the receptive surface to the maximum, usually taking a bushy form but sometimes becoming long threads, like the "silk" of corn. This emphasis upon filament and stigma has been accompanied by the dwindling of the corolla, and, in consequence, most wind-pollinated flowers are small and inconspicuous.

Among animals, insects are the chief pollinators, though a similar role is assumed by hummingbirds, and, in the case of cultivated plants especially, man plays a significant part. Any insect that works in or among flowers may become a pollinator, but as a regular activity, pollination is carried on by a few groups. The bees and their relatives are by far the most important,[546] followed by the butterflies and bee flies and at a much greater distance by the beetles. Bumblebees and honeybees are the most numerous and efficient, the honeybee outranking all other species in industry and intelligence.[400,658] For sheer efficiency the hummingbird is probably without a peer among pollinators, but it is excelled by the bees in number and especially in the range of flowers visited. Orioles and other birds are known to visit flowers occasionally; some tropical flowers are pollinated by bats, and a few of the arums by snails (Fig. 133).

Attraction of Insects by Flowers.—It has long been recognized that insects are attracted to flowers by color, form, and odor as well as by nectar and pollen, but there has been much diversity of opinion as to the relative importance of the first three factors. It is difficult to discriminate between them by observation alone, when all three are present in the same flower, and consequently it becomes necessary to resort to experiment, by which each can be employed separately. A large number of experimental studies have been made during the past 50 years, and these have recently been compared and summarized in the light of a comprehensive investigation dealing with many species of flowers and insects in nature.[167] The conclusion has been reached that in the honeybee the

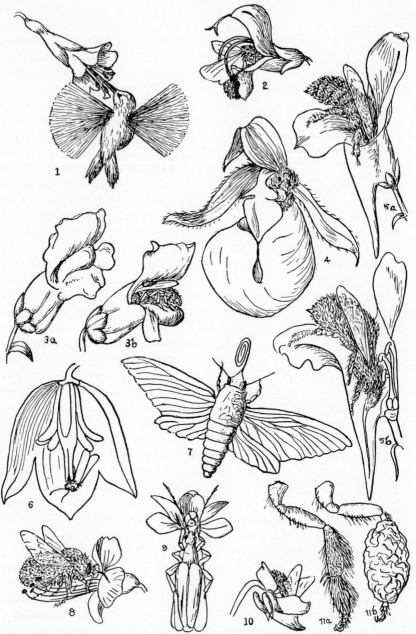

Fig. 133.—Flowers and their visitors.   (1) Ruby-throated hummingbird and humming-bird trumpet; (2) blue sage pollinated by bee; (3) snapdragon; (4) bee escaping from pouch of lady's-slipper and rubbing against an anther; (5) butter-and-eggs; (6) yucca flower being pollinated by pronuba moth; (7) sphinx moth with long sucking tube; (8) bee on flower of horse chestnut; (9) beetle on tway blade; (10) honeybee in violet; (11) leg of bee with pollen basket: *a*, empty; *b*, loaded with pollen.   (*Adapted by Edith S. Clements.*)

attraction exerted by color and form is about four times greater than that of odor, nectar, and pollen combined. It is possible that the influence of odor is somewhat greater in those flowers with a marked perfume.

In general, it seems to be well demonstrated that odor is the attractive feature for distances of more than 10 meters, color in mass for intermediate ones, and color and form in detail within 2 meters or so, depending greatly upon the size and color of the flower or cluster. For the majority of flowers without a marked fragrance, odor can be effective only near at hand. In the midst of a group of plants or of flowers, odor can exercise little influence. It is not only general in such instances, but it is also most powerful at the flower or cluster on which the insect is working. Such conditions do not permit it to go straightway and without hesitation to the next flower or head, and guidance by color and form alone can explain the assured and rapid flight of bees in the midst of flowers.[256]

Since the senses of sight and smell differ greatly in the various groups of insects, the relative importance of the three attractive factors will be modified accordingly. On the basis of their behavior, bees have the best vision, followed in order by bee flies, butterflies, moths, and beetles. Because of the very different structure of the eye, hummingbirds evidently discern flowers at a distance of 100 yards or more and masses of bloom at much greater distances. On the other hand, it appears probable that fields of buckwheat, alfalfa, or mustard can be located by pollinators a mile or more away by the odor alone.

Experimental Pollination.—In the experimental study of the relation between flowers and insects, it is necessary to observe in detail the round of life of each flower and the behavior of the important pollinators that visit it. With this as a background, it is possible to fashion a variety of experiments to determine the effect of color, form, and odor, the competition between insects for flowers and between flowers for visitors, the efficiency of different species, their learning capacity, power of memory, and intelligence. Among the effective devices employed are the mutilation of flowers by reducing or removing parts, the addition of parts, artificial flowers, painting natural flowers in various colors, adding odor or nectar, masking odor or parts, and direct experiments with color, form, or odors. The efficiency of flowers in dusting bees with pollen, of the bees in transporting loads, and of flowers again in securing effective deposit on the stigma have all been studied experimentally.

Changes in the position of flower present new problems in landing to the visiting insect, especially in the case of inversion, but these are solved with more or less readiness, the time required depending chiefly upon the shape of the flower and the kind of visitor. The consequences of increasing the attractive surface of the corolla or of reducing it by mutilation are much more striking. Splitting the hood of monkshood

(*Aconitum*) and turning the sepals back rendered such flowers more than four times as attractive as the normal ones. On the other hand, cutting away half of the corolla reduced its effectiveness to one-half or even to one-tenth in practically all cases and demonstrated the paramount importance of the corolla for attraction. When both lips were removed in the wild bergamot (*Monarda*), the number of visits was a twentieth of that for flowers with the upper lip removed and a tenth of that for those with the lower lip cut off. The removal of the petals in the geranium usually reduced the visits to zero, while cutting them to half their length diminished visitors in proportion.

Natural flowers painted with water colors have been found to be about five times as attractive as artificial flowers made of paper. The latter were visited about a fifth as often as the normal flowers, though much depends upon the closeness of the resemblance, some investigators obtaining abundant visits to them. In general, honeybees are more discriminating than bumblebees, though individual differences are considerable in both. As to colors, blue was regularly preferred to all others, red being the least attractive.[167]

Attraction and Guidance of Visitors.—In the case of regular flowers such as the geranium, remove the petals from several, cut them to half the normal length in an equal number, and employ the same number of unmutilated blossoms. Record the number of visits during a unit period to each and estimate the value of the corolla. Cut off one or both lips of an irregular flower and note the effect upon the visiting insects. Place flowers in inverted or other unusual positions and note the behavior of the visitors.

Competition for Visitors.—Many suggestions as to the relative effectiveness of different species in terms of attraction can be obtained by observing the behavior of visitors to a mixed group, but experiment is indispensable to definite results. These cannot be secured by placing the flowers of two or more species side by side, since bees, in particular, pay little attention to artificial groupings. In consequence, it is necessary to fasten an equal number of competing flowers on another plant and desirable, also, to make a similar reciprocal installation on the other species. This is due to the fact that the most intelligent species of pollinators have learned that they work most rapidly and effectively by devoting themselves exclusively or nearly so to the species with the greatest honey flow at the particular time. Young bees and very old ones are much less methodical than workers in their prime, and butterflies are even more easily turned aside in their quest. While installations for conclusive results require time and care, however, much information as to the habits of insect visitors and the attractiveness of different flowers may be obtained by placing bouquets of one species in the midst of the plants of another.

Competition for Insect Visitors.—Select a plant that is being abundantly visited and place among the flowers an equal number from a plant that differs conspicuously in the color, size, or structure of its flowers. Record the number of visits made to each species by the various kinds of visitors during a period of 10 to 30 minutes.

The degree of constancy shown by each pollinator can be determined by the composition of the pollen loads carried by bees, the pollen grains of the various flowers being readily recognized under the microscope. During the maximum period of flowering of the raspberry (*Rubus deliciosus*), the loads of 22 honeybees contained the pollen of this species alone; after this time the loads were obtained from six different species, though in all but one instance it was 99 per cent pure. Among bumblebees the constancy was less, but even here it was not lower than 90 per cent as a rule.

SEED PRODUCTION AND DISTRIBUTION

In the production and distribution of seeds, animals usually play an important and often a controlling part. Hence, this is a coaction of primary importance in a study of vegetation.

Seed Production.—Under the usual conditions, the number of seeds produced by an insect-pollinated species depends chiefly upon the success attained in pollination. The abundance of each species, as well as its survival, is determined primarily by the number of seeds that germinate and seedlings that become established. At each step in this fundamental process of ecesis, animals enter the situation and their coactions largely or wholly determine the number of seeds available, their dissemination, and the final fate of seedling or adult plant. Insect parasites destroy large numbers of seeds and fruits before they mature, and a similar effect is exerted by some birds, such as the nutcrackers and jays. In general, much greater destruction is wrought at the time the seeds are ripening or after seed or fruit has left the parent plant; birds, rodents, and man each having an especially decisive share in this.[961]

It has been found that in some regions practically all the seeds of the limber pine are eaten out of the cones when still green, while in forests of lodgepole pine the toll of cones and seeds taken by birds and rodents is so complete that reproduction rarely occurs until a fire has driven the animal population out. A single kangaroo rat may store as much as a bushel of grass fruits in its burrow, and harvester ants may gather all the fruits of desert grasses over considerable areas. So great is the consumption of seeds in many species, and trees especially, that adequate reproduction is possible only during years in which climatic and growth conditions cooperate to produce a crop much beyond the needs of the animal members of the community. Such seed production is a consequence of the climatic cycle and marks a maximum phase of the food cycle, which, in its turn, is reflected in a population maximum.

Seed Distribution.—The dissemination of seeds by animals and man may result from each of the four major coactions, *viz.*, food, material, shelter, and contact, but it centers about the first, with the last second, perhaps, in importance. Among those seeds or fruits utilized as food, successful distribution depends almost wholly upon protection against digestion. The disseminules of most herbs lack such protection more or less completely and are regularly destroyed in the digestive tract of birds but to a somewhat lesser degree in that of mammals. A considerable number of trees and shrubs have been specialized for such distribution by devoting a portion of the fruit to the attraction and reward of the disseminator and by protecting the seed against digestion by means of a stony cover, developed usually by the fruit. Such fleshy fruits are among the most successful migrants, though their distribution is usually local, as fence rows filled with red cedar, sumac, and similar shrubs testify. Nut fruits and cones are collected by rodents in vast numbers, but they are carried little if at all beyond the forest edge, and it is only by chance that a seed here and there escapes consumption.[152,500]

Most effective of all is dissemination by contact and attachment, since the dry fruits chiefly concerned are not used for food by the animals that transport them. The movement of "sticktights" and "tickseeds" is, for the most part, local or at least within woodland, where they abound, but the various burs, such as cockleburs and sandburs, were often carried over considerable distances by migrating buffalo. Carriage by man has been the outstanding process during the historical period, not merely because of his world-wide migration, but especially also on account of the fact that he produces innumerable disturbed areas in which ecesis is possible. Roadways and trackways have served as universal pathways of migration, in which disturbance is the characteristic feature. In a large number of species, the carriage has been incidental to the transport of foodstuffs or materials and, hence, wholly unintentional, but in the aggregate it has been far in excess of all other methods of long-distance migration. In addition to actual transport by railroads is the unique action of vortex winds due to passing trains, which have been the main factor in the distribution of ruderal and native species for many hundred miles. No other migration agent is in the least comparable with man in the effectiveness and extent of its action. Water is similar in acting over long distances, but only a relatively small number of seeds and fruits can withstand immersion for more than a few days at most.

COACTIONS OF THE PLANT BODY

Food coactions are concerned where the plant body is employed for food by animals or man. The outstanding coaction of this group is grazing, under which may also be included browsing when trees and shrubs are concerned rather than herbs. The number of instances in which the plant body is utilized for food is incalculable, but these may all be arranged in a few major groups. The latter comprise the coactions between aquatic animals, chiefly invertebrates, and plankton; between insects and leafy shoots; rodents, grazing animals and herbs; browsing animals and foliage; and between a heterogeneous group and wood in various forms. Birds are usually not concerned, since even when they attack seedlings, it is usually for the sake of the seed itself. In this general category belong also the interactions of bacteria, fungi, and other plant parasites with animals, and with other plants as well, but these are not considered in the present account. Man ranges over almost the entire field of coactions, but only the most important ones can be discussed here.

Grazing Coactions.—The primary relation is that of food supply, with the natural assumption that the coaction is wholly beneficial to the animal and injurious to the plant. In the first case, the chief exception is constituted by poisonous plants, such as *Astragalus, Delphinium, Lupinus, Oxytropis,* and *Zygadenus,* while minor exceptions are furnished by plants with spines or harmful awns, such as cacti, needle grasses, etc. The damage done the plant by grazing or browsing depends largely upon the life form. The annual is often destroyed and the perennial herb injured in various ways and to different degrees; low shrubs may be kept in a dwarf, leafless condition, while tall ones and trees are little affected. On the other hand, grasses, sedges, and similar forms with basal meristem in the leaves and shoot buds near the ground suffer slight damage from the removal of their foliage if this is not too frequent. Every species is injured by overgrazing, but grasses withstand this better than all others and are actually benefited by moderate cropping. This not only removes the dead litter which is undesirable for several reasons but also seems to promote the growth of leaves and buds; at least, it has been found that the growth of grasses under complete protection is distinctly less than with properly regulated grazing.

Grassland resists trampling more successfully than any other type of community, though as with grazing the amount of damage is determined by the severity of the process. Trampling, when not too severe, is beneficial in scattering and planting seeds and fruits and, to some degree, offsets the harm done by grazing while fruits are being formed. When animals are crowded as about wells, in corrals, or in bedding grounds, trampling is extreme and usually results in the complete destruction of the vegetation and the initiation of secondary seres.[771] Such areas are marked by colonies of weeds, which serve as indicators of disturbance and persist until the cause is removed. When the disturbance ceases, such seral communities gradually yield to the competition of the returning grasses and the climax grassland is more or less completely restored. A fairly permanent effect of overgrazing and trampling is registered in the short-grass subclimax of the Great Plains, where the taller species are kept down in consequence of their life forms being more susceptible to injury. The composition of grassland may also be much modified because earlier or more palatable species bear the brunt of the grazing coaction, even to the point of disappearance.[177]   The most striking change of this type, however, is to be encountered in grass associations containing scattered shrubs, such as sagebrush or mesquite. The latter are eaten much less than the grasses and, as a result, increase correspondingly in number, until they appear to dominate the entire community. Experimental exclosures have demonstrated that the shrubs gradually disappear under the competition of the grasses when the latter are protected from grazing and indicate that much of the large area covered by sagebrush, creosote bush, mesquite, and other shrubs is actually climax grassland.[155]

Rodent Coactions.—In all essential respects, these are similar to the relations that exist in the case of grazing or browsing by the larger mammals.[907]   The main differences lie in the fact that the effect exerted by each individual is much smaller and more localized, and that control, for either practical or research purposes, is much more difficult. Apart from the influence upon the seed crop already mentioned, the major damage done by rodents is inflicted upon the leafy shoot, though pocket gophers, moles, and other tunneling forms do great injury to roots and underground stems, both directly and indirectly. The coactions differ from genus to genus and family to family and depend almost wholly upon habits and life history. The wandering jack rabbit behaves much as do cattle but on a smaller scale (Fig. 35); the social prairie dog works great changes in the plant covering of his towns, and the provident cony cuts and stacks hay for his long winter above timber line. Although more intelligent as to poisonous plants and apparently less susceptible also, rodents do fall victims to the most poisonous species. Spines and thorns likewise exercise an influence, though some species, such as the woodrat or pack rat, actually turn these to good purpose in the construction of nests.

Although the effect produced by a single rodent is small, the total influence of a vast population of many species is great and often decisive. When they are more or less restricted in their movements, as prairie dogs or kangaroo rats, the final effect may be as striking as in an extreme case of overgrazing and trampling by cattle (Fig. 134). The original grasses of a prairie-dog town are often completely replaced by annual weeds, the area about a kangaroo-rat mound may be wholly bare, and the runways of jack rabbits may be almost as well worn as cow paths.[946]

Rodents exert little or no effect in planting seeds, largely because of the heavy toll they usually take, though burrowing forms and pack rats have more value in this connection.

Coactions upon woody plants are less frequent, but they are not without importance. Perhaps the most outstanding examples are furnished by the beaver, which employs aspen and birch in particular for construction materials as well as food.[33] Because of their choice of trees, much more damage is done by porcupines, rabbits, and other bark-eating rodents, which may kill a large tree in consequence of consuming only a portion of the bark. Similar consequences of a relatively small coaction are to be found in the damage to trees wrought by sapsuckers, nut-storing woodpeckers, and bud-eating grouse among birds.[581]

Fig. 134.—General denudation by kangaroo rats in desert scrub in Arizona.

Human Coactions.—It is evident that man stands alone with respect to the number and variety of his coactions with plants. Like the animals, he derives, directly or indirectly, his entire food supply from plants and he has produced far-reaching changes by learning to control this supply. He is likewise susceptible to many coactions from the plant and one of his chief tasks has been to understand and control these, not merely in the case of foods, poisons, and drugs, but especially also in that of parasitic bacteria. The most striking coactions have had to do with mass effects upon vegetation, as represented by fire, cutting, and clearing. All of these processes bring about the destruction of one community in whole or in part and its replacement by another, either as a result of planting or in consequence of succession. These have been discussed briefly in preceding chapters and it merely needs to be further emphasized that all man's uses of plants, both native and cultivated, rest upon the basis of coactions. While they differ in details, cultivated fields and natural communities bear the same general relation to physical factors, exhibit the same basic processes of competition and reaction, and are subject to similar coactions on the part of man and animals.[899]

In his role as a coactor, man exerts a number of primary effects upon vegetation, which may be conveniently grouped as follows: (1) removal of cover wholly or in part, as in clearing, breaking, lumbering, or fire; (2) production of crops, in the widest sense; and (3) natural regeneration or artificial restoration of cover. The first is necessarily and universally destructive of native vegetation, the last is reconstructive, and the second may be harmful or helpful in its relation to conservation, in accordance with the type of cover formed. In agriculture where removal is followed by tillage, coaction passes immediately into reaction, which provides the necessary opportunity for erosion, both by water and by wind. To remedy this, it then becomes necessary to reverse both sets of processes and turn them into agents for stabilization and control.

Man is likewise the greatest coactor with other animals, both directly and indirectly, and the principle just expressed applies equally well in the field of wild life. Destructive coactions must be replaced by constructive ones, and natural or artificial propagation must be invoked to restore a dynamic balance within species as well as communities, just as in the plant cover itself.

Sequence of Coactions.—In many instances, the influence of plants and animals upon each other does not stop with the immediate or primary coaction. The development of a new relation or the concrete working out of an old one sets in motion a train of mediate or secondary consequences in which an entire series of species or communities may be involved. The introduction by man of a new fruit or crop for food or materials often means the bringing in of fungi or insects parasitic upon it and ultimately of the parasites upon these. With the seed of grains come those of weeds; the latter not only demand the further attention of man, but they also produce new interactions with native species and their plant and animal associates, the waves of influence extending far beyond our present knowledge. One of the final effects is to be found in the establishment of quarantine regulations, both national and state, to prevent or control such coactions.

The best known of coaction sequences have followed upon the introduction by man of the English sparrow and starling into the United States, of the thistle into Australia, and of the bumblebee into New Zealand, but the same process has been exemplified in the case of every cultivated species brought from abroad and every stowaway, whether weed, fungus, or insect. The clearing or breaking of ground for cultivation, the cutting of trees for timber, and the burning of forests have all set up sequences of far-reaching significance, the understanding of which is indispensable to scientific agriculture and forestry and to conservation especially. One of the most illuminating examples of these complex sequences is found in the effect of man upon predatory animals. The complete destruction of the latter appears to be a simple and beneficial primary coaction, until it is found to be accompanied by an increase in the rodent population with a corresponding decrease in the yield of grazing range or cultivated field. In short, it tends to defeat in some measure the very purpose it was designed to promote—the greater production of cattle and sheep. The protection of game animals—in itself an exceedingly desirable objective—similarly leads to far-reaching sequences of coactions, as in the case of deer, elk, and bison in national parks or forests.[2]

CONSERVATION OF SOIL AND WATER

As already stated, conservation is primarily a matter of substituting helpful coactions for harmful ones or of compensating for the latter in whatever fashion proves necessary. This applies with equal force to reactions, especially upon wind, water, and soil, since these follow coactions immediately or occur simultaneously. As a reactor, man far surpasses all others, the mantle of vegetation being everywhere subject to use and abuse by him. In consequence, conservation is chiefly the application of cover coactions to situations produced by destruction, together with direct reactions upon the soil or indirect ones upon wind and water.[161] Though all areas modified by man have much in common as to the effects produced and their human significance, they fall most conveniently into groups on the basis of the community, the nature and degree of disturbance, and the corrective measures demanded. Cultivated field, grass, and forest all present more or less typical differences in cover, kind of disturbance, and control processes, as well as in the physical factors of climate and soil. In all three, however, the basic principle of protection by cover is foremost, though it is often to be reenforced by the addition of engineering works, such as reservoirs, dams, terraces, etc.

Cultivated Fields.—In the case of all field crops as distinct from those of pasture or woodland, the protection afforded by the native cover is completely lost and the upper portion of the soil much loosened and modified. The extent to which a crop compensates for the lost cover is determined by its nature, as well as the associated tillage and the type of precipitation and soil. In fallow, such compensation is lacking entirely; in row crops such as corn and grain sorghums it is regularly low, while in those sown broadcast it approaches that of pasture, for the period from early growth to the removal of stubble. The effectiveness of a crop cover is also related to the degree of reaction upon the soil by cultivation, both in the preparation of the field and in later treatments. For this reason especially, plowing a field on the contour is indispensable to good farm practice (Fig. 135).

While the amount of surface covered is the first consideration in protection, slope, soil, rainfall intensity, and drought are all matters of major importance. Each of these may appear as the ruling factor or they may be variously combined, though high rainfall and frequent drought are for the most part mutually exclusive. The steeper the slope the greater must be the protection afforded by the cover, as well as by supplementary devices, such as terraces, that involve reaction. Penetration and runoff are related but opposite processes, and the soils

Fig. 135.—Contour listing of corn in a terraced field in eastern Nebraska to prevent erosion. (*Photograph, courtesy of Soil Conservation Service.*)

that promote the one reduce the other, gravel and sand being at one extreme and silts and clays at the other. A gentle rain may be largely absorbed by most soils and even on considerable slopes, while torrential ones produce runoff, erosion, and flooding not only in proportion to their intensity but also to sparseness of cover, degree of slope, and hardness of soil. Drought belongs in a different category, since it operates primarily on cover and hence acts chiefly through its reduction or removal. It also affects the texture of the soil, but even in wind erosion, this is negligible unless the cover is greatly reduced or lacking.

Perennial crops, such as alfalfa, clover, and other legumes, provide almost complete protection for the entire surface of a field; broadcast annuals come next, with rowed annuals last. For a practical cropping system, in which there must be a working compromise between protection and profit, it is indispensable to combine the respective crops in space or in time, to resort to engineering structures, or to utilize both as needed. Combination in space is illustrated by strip cropping in which a complete cover, preferably of perennials, alternates across a field with rowed or broadcast annuals[1028] (Fig. 136). Less advantageous but of especial value with respect to the conservation of fertility is rotation, in which row crops of high nutrient requirements are grown in a 3 to 5 year rotation with small grains and with grasses or legumes which produce much more

Fig. 136.—Strip cropping in South Carolina. Soil and water conserving strips of wheat alternate with strips sown to cotton. (*Photograph, courtesy of Soil Conservation Service.*)

favorable cover and nutrient reaction.[609] A longer rotation with pasture or woodland, or with game coverts, yields even greater values in some respects in the case of large farms.

Terraces are the chief structures for the control of erosion in tilled or abandoned fields, and they are usually combined with some other feature, such as spillways, check dams, floodways, reservoirs, etc.[526,1028] (Figs. 137 and 138). They are of value on any field with a perceptible slope and the need for them rises with the angle until this becomes about 15 degrees, when strip cropping is to be preferred. The height, width, and number of terraces are determined with reference to slope, soil, and crop, and they are located along contour lines. They should be constructed in such a way as to interfere as little as possible with cultivation and to reduce the tendency to ponding with attendant silting and waterlogging when the interval is too great. This disadvantage can be largely overcome by spacing them more closely and lowering the height, or still better by means of one or more subterraces. Terraces of proper design should obviate overflowing or breaking through and should deliver runoff to the spillway without ponding or gullying.

Pasture and Range.—In all important respects these are essentially identical, pastures merely being smaller and formed for the most part

Fig. 137.—Terraces have been made in this eastern Nebraska field so that there will be a minimum of soil erosion and a maximum of water retained in the soil. (*Photograph, courtesy of Soil Conservation Service.*)

with cultivated or introduced species, such as timothy or bluegrass. A grazing cover is nearly always made up of perennial dominants, the chief exceptions being where overgrazing has produced a disclimax of annual grasses or seral stages composed of weeds. Where undisturbed, a grass cover is more or less complete, but its density and hence its protective value will be largely determined by the life form, whether sod or bunch grass, or tall, mid, or short grass. They will also depend to some extent upon climate and soil, a fact well illustrated by the decrease in density from true to mixed prairie and to desert plains, in accordance with diminishing rainfall. However, under the prevailing utilization, over-grazing plays the decisive role, often reducing some or all of the native species to a minor position or leading to their complete disappearance through competition. Even more serious from the standpoint of erosion and flood control is the effect of keeping the grass cover eaten down and thinned out to a point where its protective role is largely gone.[144]

In spite of all this, the recuperative power of native grasses is surprising, and under normal conditions, they respond quickly to any material reduction in grazing pressure. A decrease in the number of stock per acre during the period of regeneration is a satisfactory measure, but this is often impossible. Excellent results may be obtained by an interval of complete rest, and especially through rotating the herd by season or year. Natural recovery by such means is probably the most certain and rapid and much the most inexpensive of all methods. However,

FIG. 138.—Check dam near the head of a ravine. Navajo Reservation, N. M.

when overgrazing has weakened the grasses beyond the point of fairly prompt recuperation, it becomes necessary to sow or plant in order to restore an adequate cover.[305] To render either of these steps successful over most of the open range, it is necessary to break up the sod and stir the soil to some degree. Scattering seed broadcast over the undisturbed surface is a waste of time, as has been frequently demonstrated through the west.[292,1007] As a rule, sowing can be done most successfully by furrowing or disking the sod, or by combining this with pasture terraces wherever the slope demands it. In drier regions or during dry seasons, it is usually desirable to employ a mulch of hay or to utilize a nurse crop, preferably in the stubble form. In some species, such as wheat grass and buffalo grass, chopped rootstocks or stolons may be used, especially with buffalo grass which is usually a poor producer of seed.

In sowing introduced species, greater care must be taken as a rule; thus, for crested wheat grass the ground is plowed and harrowed and the seed drilled in.[721]   Transplants are readily set in rows or furrows, or each individual placed in a small basin to reduce competition and increase the penetration of rain.   Grasses that form sods, such as buffalo, wheat or Bermuda grass, make the most satisfactory transplants, since they can be handled mechanically in strips, much as bluegrass is for sodding lawns[781] (Fig. 139).   The strips are placed several yards apart and are planted in a shallow trench of the proper width in order to take root rapidly.

Fig. 139.—Collecting buffalo-grass sods for artificial revegetation, Hays, Kan.   (*Photograph by D. A. Savage; courtesy of U. S. Bureau of Plant Industry.*)

As stated in the chapter on reaction, even an open cover of short grass is sufficient to prevent the blowing of soil, but greater density is required to stop rapid runoff and erosion.   Hence, over the heavily grazed western ranges, especially where there is some slope, it is desirable to employ pasture terraces in addition.   These are run along the contours as in cultivated fields, but they are much smaller and simpler, consisting usually of a ditch a foot or so deep with a ridge or berm of soil above it. With a wide interval of 30 feet or more, water often accumulates in harmful amounts in the ditch.   Consequently, it is preferable to reduce the runoff between terraces by means of furrows a few inches deep and 2 to 3 feet apart.   Such a treatment of the sod also promotes natural seeding and rootstock propagation and affords a favorable condition for sowing or transplanting, as well as the penetration of water.

Forest and Chaparral.—In general, a cover of woody vegetation usually excels grass and far surpasses field crops in protection against erosion and flooding, though in the case of climax forest this may be offset by a higher rainfall.[48] The effectiveness depends largely upon life form and litter, though crown density is an important feature likewise. Coniferous forest possesses an advantage in the evergreen canopy and perhaps also in the slower decomposition of its needles. When stands are open as in parkland and savanna, the favorable reaction upon water and soil is much diminished, in correspondence with the distance between trees. Most scrub communities are of this type, but the chaparral of the west is a unique form of dwarf forest, which attains its best expression in southern California. Its value for the control of erosion and floods approaches that of forest and perhaps no forest equals it in the value of the water supply derived from it.

Though the reduced protection due to logging may be considerable, the chief damage occurs when clean cutting is followed by burning the slash. The effect is much the same as when a severe fire runs through forest or chaparral, removing cover and litter completely and giving full opportunity for runoff and erosion. In deciduous woods and chaparral, fires usually lead to abundant root sprouting, and an effective cover may again be formed in the course of a relatively few years. Though conifers rarely produce root sprouts, many species of pine spring up readily from seed after a fire and develop a protective cover that may persist until the hardwood climax replaces it.

In all these areas, the greatest danger occurs during the period between the burning of the cover and its renewal, in which the soil may remain exposed and unprotected for a number of years. This period can often be shortened by planting to the species of tree that yields an efficient cover most quickly. With chaparral, however, the interval of maximum risk before the cover is renewed by root sprouts is usually but 2 to 3 years, and it has proved a successful measure to bridge this gap by sowing a vigorous annual such as mustard (Fig. 140). This makes a dense stand the first year and is then gradually replaced through the competition of the sprouts of the original dominants. It is evident that areas bared by other causes may be protected by planting or sowing and that similar results may be secured in subclimax or climax grassland under conditions favorable to the growth of trees or shrubs.

Windbreak and Shelter Belt.—These differ only to the extent that the shelter belt is a more or less orderly arrangement of separate windbreaks.[43,941] In methods, materials, reactions, and purposes, they are identical. Windbreaks proper are composed of trees or shrubs, or of both, though tall grasses or forbs may have something of the same value in strip cropping. The simplest form is a single row of individuals of one species, such as osage orange or cottonwood in the middle west or eucalyptus or cypress in California, but a grove or woodlot is perhaps more frequent. The most effective type comprises several kinds of trees and shrubs arranged with the lower growing species placed outside to give better shelter and greater wind deflection. These qualities are found in larger measure in coniferous windbreaks than in those composed of deciduous trees, but the choice of species is smaller and establishment is often more difficult. The need for windbreaks increases as the climate becomes less favorable, and their success will often depend upon com-

Fig. 140.—A burned watershed protected by a crop of mustard sown from airplane. Juncal Reservoir, Santa Barbara, Calif. (*U. S. Forest Service.*)

pensation given by soil or topography. When located on looser soils with low nonavailable water, they can be planted under much lower rainfall, and this is naturally true also of valleys with their higher water content.

The chief reactions of a windbreak have been described; hence it will suffice here to discuss the coactions concerned in their planting and maintenance. Since windbreaks are most valuable in climax grassland, it is clear that some compensation must be offered for the climate, which is drier than that of forest. As an initial step, this demands not only the destruction of the original grass cover, but also precautions against its return, owing to the fact that the grasses as climax dominants have a constant advantage in the competition with the trees, especially when these are in the seedling stage. The tillage that keeps the area free of grasses and weeds also increases the porosity of the surface soil. Grazing and browsing must be prevented until the trees are sufficiently tall not to be easily damaged. Rodents must likewise be excluded by fencing or killed by poisoning when the plants are young, and rabbits may do harm for a long time by girdling trunks at the base. Grasshoppers are less frequently a serious menace, but they must be reckoned with during outbreaks, when they may eat young twigs in addition to all the foliage.

In regions with severe winters, windbreaks are valuable in providing shelter for cattle, as well as in reducing the rigors of blizzards for man. Throughout the year, they may provide cover for the successful management of quail and pheasants and under proper conditions for rabbits also. At proper distances, they may have much value as snowbreaks or dust screens for highways.

Highways and Erosion Control.—In the course of widening and straightening highways and reducing grades, the cover has often been removed over the entire right of way. More serious still is the deepening of cuts and the raising of fills to the point where erosion of the steep slopes becomes a matter of the first concern in costs of maintenance and safety of travel. Because of the loose soil, the slopes of a fill suffer the most serious damage, especially in mountainous regions, where they may extend downward for several hundred yards and threaten road sections below. Natural succession operates too slowly to protect these, and it becomes imperative to treat them the first season after construction. This is best done by building terraces strengthened by stakes and wattles, reenforcing these by planting cuttings of such rapidly growing species as willow or baccharis, and then sowing to a catch crop of grain or other annuals for immediate protection of the surface[504] (Fig. 141). Cut slopes are somewhat simpler, since the exposed surface is much firmer as a rule, and when not too long, they may best be handled by reducing the slope and rounding back the upper portion. In deep cuts, however, such slopes also require the use of terraces to permit the rapid and complete restoration of a cover, particularly in sandy soils.

After slopes have become stabilized, it is usually desirable to replace the temporary control by means of species of greater permanence and of higher ornamental value.[161] This is most satisfactorily done by using those native species found in or near the area concerned. These are not only the most likely to succeed and to require the least watering and other care, but they also have the great advantage of blending the highway into the local landscape. They not only remedy the destructive coactions and reactions unavoidable in road making, but they may also be utilized to increase the attractiveness of the landscape. Furthermore, the use of native species in something of their community relations lends itself most effectively to the conservation of the natural vegetation by restoration and in situations where it can be most easily seen and appreciated.

Control of Floods.—Few regions are free from occasional or recurrent disaster by floods, but these are most frequent and destructive at the bases of mountain ranges and in the middle and lower reaches of great river systems[630,853] (Fig. 142). In general, serious floods are caused by destructive coactions upon the plant cover, fire, grazing, and clearing being most important, but floods of serious nature locally may also arise from high-

FIG. 141.—Overcast slopes of mountain highway held by wattled and planted terraces. U. S. Forest Service, San Dimas Experimental Forest, Calif.

way construction in mountain areas. Removal of the forest cover together with hill cultivation is the major cause in the wooded regions of the east; overgrazing is the process chiefly responsible in the west; and fire is the cause in the chaparral of southern California.

As is true likewise of erosion, flooding must be prevented at the source. This is in the uplands and hills, where it is best controlled by means of cover where runoff can be prevented from accumulating to the proportions of a flood. In a forest climate, this demands not merely the adequate protection of existing woodland, but also the reforestation of cut-over lands and of abandoned farms. Hand in hand with this must go the best possible control of runoff and erosion on cultivated lands and the use of engineering structures to delay the movement of water into the larger streams of the uplands. These are chiefly check dams, diversion ditches, and small basins, supplemented farther down by debris basins, reservoirs, and floodways. In the lower course of such a river as the Mississippi, where the bed is being built up by deposit, levees and spillways are indispensable and may continue to be so under extreme conditions. But with the proper control by cover and reservoirs in the upper tributary systems, it seems evident that they will become less and less important.

Fig. 142.—Effects of the La Crescenta-Montrose flood of January, 1934, caused by fire on the mountains behind. California.

In regard to grassland, cover is perhaps even more effective in the control of floods, probably because of lower rainfall, and the first need is to restore its density to the point where it can serve this purpose. This requires the substitution of a regulated system of grazing for the current practice of overgrazing in order to secure a working balance between use as forage and as protection. With furrow control as an adjunct, other measures may not prove necessary under moderate conditions of overgrazing. For more severe conditions, seeding or planting is essential and then, as wherever restoration is a slow process, terraces and other structures must also be employed until the cover becomes fully adequate. On watersheds protected by chaparral and with a long dry season, a complete system of fire protection is the first need. As indicated in the previous chapter, the period of greatest danger comprises the years between burning and the general restoration of the cover through root sprouts. The risk is by far the highest for the first and second year when the ground is still bare, and it is during this time that sowing to produce a rapidly growing temporary cover, such as mustard, provides almost complete insurance against disastrous flooding.

CONSERVATION OF WILD LIFE

In the strict sense of the term, wild life includes native vegetation as well as the animals that dwell in it, especially since it is impossible to consider these adequately without the plants. It is now generally recognized that plants and animals are constantly interacting to form a biotic community, usually best exhibited in the climax. As has been seen, this may be completely destroyed or variously modified in composition by the coactions of man, or the animal members may suffer reduction or eradication without corresponding influence upon the plant matrix. Conversely, the animals themselves may consume or trample vegetation to such an extent as to threaten their own existence and thus bring about a movement to other fields. In the current and special sense, wild life refers to the larger animals and birds that are regarded as game and to their predators. The group has vague and shifting limits, even including introduced species of partridges and pheasants, and is best defined as comprising all the animals concerned in the various processes of conservation.

Numbers of Animals.—It was formerly supposed that the numbers of animals in nature exhibited a fairly definite balance, the populations being maintained at a level by competition and by predators.[170] This assumption has now been replaced by one of dynamic or fluctuating balance in accordance with which it is recognized that numbers shift within the widest limits, usually producing a cycle of maximum and minimum abundance. Under the disturbances caused by man, however, there is often a progressive decrease in numbers of game animals and birds, of predators, or of rodent pests, which is brought about by hunting or by poisoning. This may have far-reaching effects upon other species and the populations concerned may become too small to show the presence of cycles. Since conservation is at bottom a matter of maintaining or restoring numbers, it is primarily a task of aiding favorable coactions and of hindering or removing unfavorable ones. The favorable coactions have to do with food and cover and the harmful ones with man, predators, and disease. Any one of these may set a limit to numbers, and in many cases all of them have cooperated to produce the present condition. Back of all these, moreover, is that of the basic control exercised by climate and weather, which seem to set in action the processes that produce cycles or at least a tendency to fluctuating numbers.

Climate.—This may operate directly upon animals, affecting vigor, survival, and reproduction, or it may act indirectly through one or more of the major coactions just mentioned. Though wind, flood, blizzard, and drought may each take a high toll, especially of young, such occurrences are relatively rare and play but a small part in decreased numbers. Even the losses due to drought and to extreme cold are more a consequence of the lack of food and cover than of the excessive temperatures. Hence, the indirect influence of local climate or weather during the year is a much more decisive matter as it operates upon the amount of food and cover produced. Since rainfall is the factor that fluctuates most widely from year to year, the supply of water, as the most critical of physical factors during the growing season, largely determines the growth and density of vegetation, and this in turn the amount of food and cover.

Rainfall is known to vary in a more or less definite cycle, the effects of which are most felt in grassland and desert with relatively low precipitation. There is increasing evidence that such cycles are related to those of sunspots and that the 11-year cycle of the latter is thus reflected in the production of food and cover, and hence in that of animal populations. At least, most of the cycles found in animal numbers have a length approximating that of the 11-year cycle of sunspots or its divisions.

Food and Cover.—Since these are both features of vegetation, it is clear that they will increase or decrease in general relation to the latter and hence in conformity with the seasonal conditions. They also vary much with the kind and amount of local disturbance, weed and brush being especially adapted to quail and rabbits, while draining and flooding often are decisive as to the persistence of waterfowl, muskrats, and other water animals. The amount of food is usually more significant than its quality, since it often determines activity and survival under extreme conditions in winter. Even more important in connection with abundance is the fact that the number of eggs in a brood or young in a litter and the number of broods or litters in a season rise rapidly with the food supply. This is especially true of such prolific animals as rabbits and lemmings, the latter producing four litters with as many as 8 to 11 young each during a year of maximum.

Like food, cover of the proper kind is also a compensation or protection against great cold, as well as deep snow, since both help to maintain the body temperature. This is true of many of the large mammals, but the significance is probably greatest among rabbits, quail, grouse, etc. For these, cover may be even more important in terms of concealment from predators than as shelter. Thus, for quail recent studies of cover in Wisconsin indicate that this is the most important factor in the number of birds that a locality can maintain.[270] In consequence, the carrying capacity of a particular area is determined by the cover in terms of food, shelter, and concealment, though at a particular time any one of these may become the decisive factor.

Predators.—In scientific usage, the term predator is applied to the carnivorous mammals, such as the wolves, large cats, and badgers; the insectivorous ones, such as moles and shrews; the raptorial birds, like hawks and owls; most reptiles; and the predaceous insects, such as tiger beetles, ladybirds, and water boatmen. In this sense, many of our common birds are predatory, from crows and blue jays at one extreme to flycatchers and warblers at the other. In the popular opinion, however, predators are chiefly those animals and birds that prey upon big game, game birds, and domesticated animals.

All predators are characterized by a destructive coaction, but their role in conservation is based upon a number of relations. Perhaps the most important of these is the nature of their prey. When this consists largely of harmful rodents or insects, the predatory habit is beneficial from the human point of view, and this is true also when such game as deer becomes too abundant under protection. Likewise, many of the owls and hawks, such as the marsh hawk and barred owl, are assets to the farmer, while others like Cooper's and sharp-shinned hawks are the fiercest enemies of wild birds and poultry. The practice of individuals as well as of official agencies has been to destroy all predators without much question as to the balance between good and evil effects and with little if any accurate knowledge as to their place in the general plan of conservation. The usual result has been to set up new and often less desirable series of coactions.

Both predators and their prey are concerned in the fluctuations and movements of population that characterize the animal world under more or less natural conditions. This has been long known for the lemming migration at the time of maximum abundance, when their enemies congregate and follow them in great numbers.[170] It has even been suggested that some of these are able to reproduce only when the lemming maximum provides an excess of food over that of ordinary years. Still more striking and definite is the change in the numbers of lynxes, foxes, and martens in correspondence with maxima and minima of the snowshoe rabbit in the boreal region of North America, as determined by the records of the fur trade.[807] No such great shifts in numbers are known for settled regions, but studies of quail and grouse in the United States leave no question of a more or less constant heavy toll taken by hawks in particular.

The plant and animal parasites that produce fatal diseases in wild life are probably a universal factor in cycles of abundance. Their virulence seems to rise with the increase in numbers and to be greatest at the maximum. A sudden drop at this time has been referred to as the "crash," and it is assumed to be due to a particular disease becoming epidemic under crowded conditions that entail severe competition for food.

Man and the Conservation of Wild Life.—Man is the greatest of all predatory animals, a role somewhat obscured by the fact that he has learned to conserve the supply of many species by means of domestication. The fate of the bison and the passenger pigeon shows how rapid destruction can be with the aid of firearms, while the widespread reduction in waterfowl foretells a similar outcome. Moreover, the direct destruction caused by overhunting and overfishing has often been obscured by indirect consequences brought about by draining, flooding, fire, dams, stream pollution, and so forth. Clearing and cultivation have everywhere forced game animals back into less accessible regions, especially mountains, and overgrazing by domestic cattle has further restricted their feeding grounds.

Over against the enormous wastage of wild life by man are to be placed such constructive measures as bag limits, closed seasons, game refuges, and a few bison and other reserves. All of these have been quite inadequate to the task, however, and it has become finally clear that game in particular and wild life in general can be properly conserved only by management as a half-wild crop. This demands the conservation and multiplication of all existing stocks until a proper annual surplus warrants the renewal of shooting and fishing under more effective regulation. Small game, such as quail, turkey, grouse, and rabbits, may become a farm or estate crop, somewhat as in England today, while big game will be a product of national forests and of game reserves for breeding and hunting purposes. To save the large carnivores from extinction, wilderness areas are imperative, and these offer the only possibility of restoring biotic communities to something like their original condition.

CHAPTER XI

RELATION OF UNDERGROUND PLANT PARTS TO ENVIRONMENT

Half of a plant and often much more is frequently hidden from view; rhizomes, corms, etc., are buried in the earth and roots extend far into the soil. Many kinds of bacteria, algae, and fungi live entirely in this substratum. Because the soil hides the roots from view, they are the least understood and least appreciated part of the plant. All who deal with plants and vegetation, nevertheless, should have a vivid mental picture of the plant as a whole. It is just as much of a biological unit as an animal, and clear conceptions of the behavior of plants and communities cannot be had by a study of the aboveground parts alone. It is important to know not only the usual or normal development and activities of roots but also how these are modified by changes in the soil environment.[391,555a,736]

Extent of Roots.—Although the roots of some plants are sparse and superficial, in the majority of both native and cultivated species the root systems are, in proportion to tops, deeply penetrating and very extensive[660] (Fig. 143). Those of sweet corn, for example, extend laterally more than half as far as the stalk extends upward, and the root depth is equal to the height of the stalk.[973] The roots of field corn extend 4 feet laterally, and the depth is often 8 feet.[969] The lateral spread of pecan roots is about twice that of the branches above ground.[683,1016] Apple trees planted in deep, porous loess soil in eastern Nebraska, penetrated, by the end of three years, to a depth of 14 to 16 feet and spread laterally 7 to 10 feet.[1026] At the age of 17 years, all the soil between rows 33 feet apart had been occupied and a depth of 30 to 35 feet had been attained.[1001]

Rate of Root Growth.—The rapidity of root growth is quite as remarkable as root extent and, like it, is closely correlated with the environment.[936] In many common grasses, the rate of root elongation is over ½ inch per day. Roots of the primary system of winter wheat have been found to grow at a similar average rate over a period of 70 days. When the main vertical roots of corn begin to develop, they sometimes penetrate downward, under exceptionally favorable conditions, at the remarkable rate of 2 to 2.5 inches per day during a period of 3 to 4 weeks.[968] The roots of the squash, which spread laterally in the surface foot of soil, sometimes to distances of 20 feet or more, have a similar rate of growth and rapidly

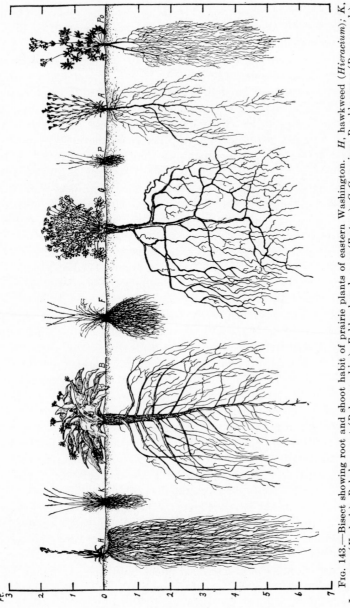

FIG. 143.—Bisect showing root and shoot habit of prairie plants of eastern Washington. *H*, hawkweed (*Hieracium*); *K*, June grass (*Koeleria*); *B*, balsamroot (*Balsamorrhiza*); *F*, blue bunch grass (*Festuca*); *G*, Geranium; *P*, a bluegrass (*Poa secunda*); *A*. a composite (*Hoorebekia*); *Po*, cinquefoil (*Potentilla*).

produce a network of branches.   A seedling tree of honey locust, although only 13 weeks old and 9 inches tall, produced a widely spreading root system that extended well into the fourth foot of soil.   Other native species often develop with equal rapidity when the soil environment is most favorable to root growth.

Activities of Roots in Subsoil.—The great extent of the root systems of most plants and their usual thorough occupancy of the subsoil have led to investigations concerning their activities at these depths.[208]   Experiments have shown that the roots are active in the absorption of both water and nutrients to the maximum depth of penetration.   In one experiment, barley was grown in the field in large cylindrical containers 18 inches in diameter and 3.5 feet deep.   The containers were filled in such a manner that each 6-inch layer occupied the same depth in the container that it had formerly occupied in the field.   Each layer of soil, of known optimum water content, was separated from the one above and below by a thin wax seal.   The seals effectually prevented any movement of the water from one soil layer to another but permitted the roots to develop in a normal manner.   When the crop was ripe, it was found that the water had been absorbed from the several levels in the following amounts, beginning at the surface: 20, 19, 16, 16, 14, 12, and 11 per cent, respectively, based on the dry weight of the soil.   It was, moreover, further ascertained from barley grown in other containers and examined at various intervals, that during the period of heading and ripening of the grain, the bulk of absorption was carried on by the younger portions of the roots in the deeper soil.   Similar results were obtained with various other plants.

In other experiments, measured amounts of nitrates (400 parts per million of soil) were placed in the soil at various levels.   Corn, for example, removed 203, 140, and 118 parts per million, respectively, from the third, fourth, and fifth foot of soil.   Thus, the materials necessary for food manufacture were taken from the deeper soil in considerable quantities, although to a lesser extent than from the soil nearer the surface, which the roots occupy first and where they absorb for the longest time, at least in annuals.   The deeper portions of the root systems are often particularly active as the crop approaches maturity.   Nutrients absorbed by them may produce a pronounced effect both upon the quantity and upon the quality of the yield.   Many native species must absorb their nutrients from the subsoil, *i.e.*, below a depth of 2 to 3 feet, as is clearly indicated by the root habit.   Little or no branching occurs in the surface layers, and structural changes, such as the production of an abundance of cork, preclude absorption by the main root.[633]   Thus, the student of environment must consider not only the conditions in the surface soil but also the whole substratum to the depth of root penetration.

Value of a Knowledge of Root Relations.—A knowledge of root development and distribution and of root competition under different natural and cultural conditions is not only of much practical value, but also it readily finds numerous scientific applications. The phenomena of plant succession, whether ecesis, competition, reaction, or stabilization, are controlled so largely by edaphic conditions and particularly by water content that they can be properly interpreted and their true significance understood only by a thorough knowledge of root relations. It is an aid to the forester in selecting sites for reforestation and afforestation.[1025] Ponderosa pine, for example, because of its prompt germination and immediate deep rooting, can grow on dry, warm slopes. Likewise, Douglas fir germinates quickly and produces roots 6 to 8 inches deep during the early part of the season. It thus becomes established where the slower growing and more shallow-rooting spruce, hemlock, and cedar fail[413] (Fig. 144).

A knowledge of root relations leads to the intelligent solution of problems of range management and improvement and, indeed, of all problems where natural vegetation is concerned. For example, land is classified upon the basis of the kind and development of the natural vegetation, into that fit for agriculture, that which will grow forests, and that of value for grazing only. Obviously, the root habits are of great importance in indicating the water and other soil relations. When they are taken into account, the natural vegetation may indicate not only the possibilities of crop production but also the kind of crop that can be most profitably grown.[808]

It is an interesting fact that in both field and garden the part of the plant environment beneath the surface of the soil is more under the control of the plant grower than is the part which lies above. He can do relatively little toward changing the composition, temperature, or humidity of the air or the amount of light. But much may be done by proper cultivating, fertilizing, irrigating, draining, etc., to influence the structure, fertility, aeration, and temperature of the soil. Thus, a thorough understanding of the roots of plants and of the ways in which they are affected by the properties of the soil in which they grow is of the utmost practical importance. Something must be known of the character and activities of the roots that absorb water and nutrients for the plant and the position that they occupy in the soil before other than an empirical solution can be had for the following problems: What are the best methods of preparing the land for any crop, the type of cultivation to be employed, the best time or method of applying fertilizers, the application and amount of irrigation water, kind of crop rotations, etc.? A complete scientific understanding of the relation between soil and crop cannot be obtained until the mechanism is understood by which the soil

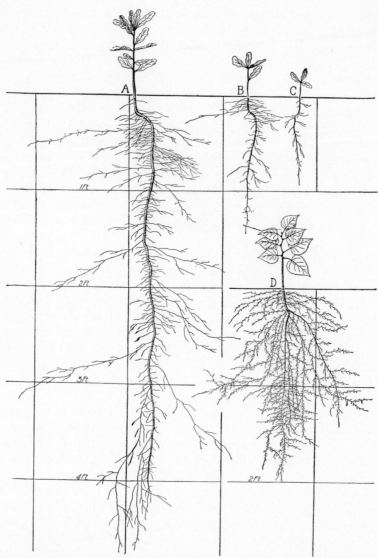

Fig. 144.—One season's growth of bur oak (*Quercus macrocarpa*): *A*, in a clearing; *B*, in a bur-oak forest; and *C*, in a linden forest. The soil in all three habitats was moderately moist but the light in the oak forest was 5 to 20 per cent and in the linden forest only 1 to 8 per cent of that in the clearing. *D*, linden (*Tilia americana*) grown in a clearing, at the end of the first summer. Its roots are not so well adapted to upland soils as are those of the bur oak. (*After A. E. Holch.*)

and the plant are brought into favorable relationships, *i.e.*, the root system.

RESPONSE OF ROOTS TO ENVIRONMENTAL FACTORS

Roots, like aboveground parts, are profoundly affected in activity, external form, and structure by change in environment.   The habits of roots, moreover, like those of shoots, are more or less characteristic for every kind of plant.

Heredity.—The primary form of the root is governed, first of all, by the hereditary growth characters of the species or variety (Fig. 145). Some species have taproots that develop rapidly and penetrate deeply;

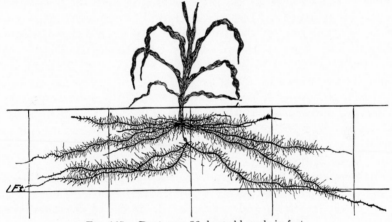

Fig. 145.—Dent corn 36 days old, scale in feet.

others branch near the soil surface, and the taproot soon loses its dominance; still others are characterized by fibrous roots which may spread widely or penetrate nearly vertically downward.   Great variation occurs within a genus and sometimes within the species or variety.[480]   One blazing star (*Liatris punctata*) has a strong, much branched taproot reaching depths of 13 feet, another (*L. scariosa*) possesses a large number of fibrous roots originating from the base of a corm.   Field corn typically has three roots in its primary root system; in sweet corn there usually is only one.[985]   Certain varieties of cane have been found to have inherent differences as to rate and depth of root penetration, total root production, and suitability of roots to soil type.[944]

Inbred strains of corn differ greatly in the character and extent of their root systems.   Certain strains have such a limited and inefficient root system that they are unable to function normally during the hot days of late summer when the water content is low.   Among 50 types of Indian chillies there are known to be five different heritable types of root systems.[614]   It has been shown that the form of the fleshy portion of the roots of mangels and sugar beets is a heritable character.   Where a dwarf variety of peas having a shallow root system was crossed with a tall variety having a deep one, it was found that the root characters are hereditary and segregate out in the second generation according to the Mendelian ratios.[443]

There is evidence that after long periods of time, during which the soil conditions have had time to impress themselves upon the variety of plants, by a process of natural selection a condition of equilibrium between the type of plant and the soil may be attained.   The roots of flax, for example, grown for centuries on the black soils of the peninsula of India, are deep, somewhat sparse, and well adapted to ripen the plant quickly with the minimum of moisture.   Varieties on the well watered but poorly aerated alluvial soil have well developed but superficial root systems. When the flax from the black soils is grown on alluvium, the deep, sparse root system is developed, although it is fatal to the well-being of the crop.   When the experiment is reversed and the type which suits the alluvium is grown on black soils, there is, again, little or no adaptation to fit the new conditions.   The root systems of the varieties are just as characteristic and just as fixed as the differences in seed and other above-ground characters of these plants.[421]   Heredity in root habits deserves further investigation.

Environment.—Within the species or variety, root modifications are usually brought about by the operation of such factors as water content, aeration, soil structure, and nutrients.   In fact, the character of the root system is usually an indicator of soil conditions.[896]   By more or less profound modifications of their root systems, many plants become adapted to different soil environments; others are much less susceptible to change.   Among forest trees, for example, the initial or juvenile root system of each species follows a fixed course of development and maintains a characteristic form for a rather definite period of time following germination.   The tendency to change when subjected to different external conditions becomes more pronounced as the seedlings become older.   But some species exhibit much earlier tendencies to change than others, and widely different degrees of flexibility are also shown. Hence, certain species, such as red maple (*Acer rubrum*), are able to survive, at least for a time, in various situations from swamps to dry uplands.   The roots of others, such as bald cypress (*Taxodium distichum*), are so inflexible that they can grow only under certain favorable conditions and their distribution is thus greatly limited.[923]   Great variability also occurs in the rooting habits of cultivated trees.   For example, it is well known that the California walnut is widely adaptable to so many soils that it is most generally used as stock for the English walnut in that state.   Many fruit trees show much less plasticity, certain varieties failing unless grafted on other stock, the roots of which adapt themselves to soils underlaid with alkali or containing excessive moisture or to dry situations.

Of 28 native grasses and other herbs studied in two or more widely separated habitats, 25 showed very striking changes in their root habits as to depth of penetration and position and number of branches; one

Fig. 146.—Plants of false Solomon's-seal (*Smilacina stellata*): *a*, from a gravel slide; *b*, from a spruce forest.   Scale in feet.

exhibited only moderate differences, and two showed practically no change (Fig. 146).   The roots of many cultivated crops of field and garden are very plastic, responding readily to environmental change. Sometimes the root variation is so great and the growth habit so profoundly changed that the roots are scarcely recognizable as belonging to the same species.

Response to Low Water Content.—A relatively low water content, provided there is enough to insure good growth, stimulates the roots to greater development, resulting in a greatly increased absorbing surface. Corn grown for 5 weeks in a moist, rich, loess soil (available water content 19 per cent) had a total root area which was 1.2 times greater than that of the transpiring surface of stems and leaves. Corn, with similar hereditary characters, grown in like soil, with an available water content of only 9 per cent, had a root area 2.1 times greater than that of the tops. The total length of the main roots in the two cases was about the same as was also their diameter. In neither case did the main roots make up more than 11 per cent of the total absorbing area. In the drier soil, 75 per cent of the area was furnished by the primary laterals and the remaining 14 per cent by branches from these, but in the moister soil the primary branches furnished only 38 per cent of the root area. It seems as though the plant had blocked out a root system quite inadequate to meet the heavy demands for absorption made by the vigorous tops, and as the soil became drier the remaining 51 per cent of the area was furnished by an excellent development of secondary and tertiary branches.

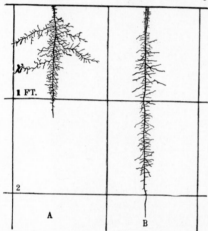

Fig. 147.—Sugar beets about 2 months old: *A*, dry land with practically no water available in the second foot; *B*, irrigated soil.

Maize in loess soil with only 2 to 3 per cent of water in excess of the hygroscopic coefficient had about one-third more laterals than in a similar soil of medium water content, in proportion to the length of the main roots. The absorbing area, moreover, in comparison to tops was greater. Similar results were obtained with 2-month-old alfalfa, although here the area of the taproot system was exceeded by that of the tops. Thus, a low water content, within certain limits, stimulates increased root development.

Figure 147 shows the difference in the root habit of seedling sugar beets due to water content, and Fig. 148 the effect upon root development of corn. In the latter case, the corn grown in irrigated soil had about 12 branches per inch of main root as compared with 27 in dry land. Branches in the drier soil were, moreover, twice as long and had approximately twice as many sublaterals. Such a root system, of course, is much better fitted to withstand drought, and its wide distribution throughout the soil mass brings it in contact with a greater supply of nutrients. It should be clear, however, that the ideal root system is not necessarily one with the most extensive branching but one that fully occupies the soil to an adequate depth and throughout a radius sufficient to secure at all times enough water and nutrients. Where the soil is very dry, root development is greatly retarded or even ceases, and the aboveground parts are consequently dwarfed. For example, on the short-grass plains, roots of alfalfa and wheat, which normally penetrate several feet deep, although more profusely branched, are almost entirely

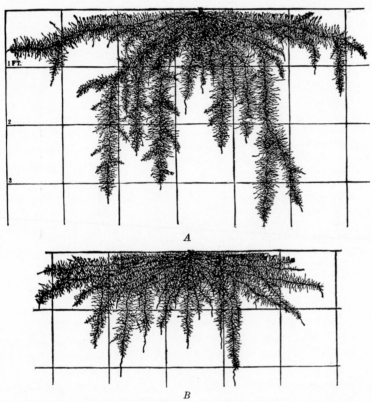

FIG. 148.—Roots of dent corn 8 weeks old: *A*, grown without irrigation, only 2 to 4 per cent of water available at any depth; *B*, fully irrigated in fertilized soil. The heights of the stalks were 2 and 3 feet, respectively.

confined to the surface 2 feet of soil because of lack of sufficient water in the subsoil to promote growth (Fig. 149).

To Determine the Effect of an Excess or Deficiency of Water on Plant Growth.— Fill three large pails, at least one of which is of galvanized iron and will hold water, with air-dry potting soil to within 2.5 inches of the top. Add 2 inches of soil of good water content. Plant seeds of sunflower and cover the soil with a mulch of coarse sand or fine gravel ½ inch deep. Water sparingly if needed. When the cotyledons are unfolded, thin the plants to about five well spaced individuals per container. To the metal container (hydric series) add enough water each day so that water stands an inch above the surface; to the mesic one give enough to moisten thoroughly the soil throughout; but to the xeric one add only enough water (daily, if need be) to keep the plants from badly wilting.

When the mesic plants have reached a height of 8 to 12 inches and have produced several pairs of leaves, cut the plants in all the containers at the ground line. Wrap each lot separately in moist paper to preserve for further study. By means of a trowel and ice pick, make an examination of the root extent under each condition of growth. Secure a root system as complete as possible from each container. Wash away the soil and float the roots out in shallow black trays. From this study and that of the tops, complete the following table:

Character	Xeric	Mesic	Hydric
Depth of penetration, centimeters..............			
Approximate lateral spread, centimeters........			
Number of secondary laterals per centimeter...			
Number of tertiary laterals per centimeter.....			
Relative abundance of root hairs.............			
Average height, centimeters..................			
Average diameter of stem, millimeters.........			
Average number of leaves....................			
Average leaf area, square centimeters.........			
Average dry weight, grams..................			
Other characters, *e.g.*, color, pubescence, evidence of disease, etc...........................			

Response to High Water Content.—Where the surface soil is wet and the water table is at no great depth, plants root shallowly.[66] This is a response to lack of aeration. An extreme case is found in bogs. Here the roots and rhizomes form a mat only a few inches thick above the water level. The roots are superficially placed because the parts assume the horizontal position above the water level, or the taproot dies and is replaced by horizontal laterals, or, where the roots are all vertical, they die at the water surface.[263] A number of species have only shallow roots where the water table is high but deeper ones in moist peat or mineral soils.[410] Trees growing in bogs are likewise shallowly rooted.[724] The larch or tamarack (*Larix laricina*) has no taproot. All the roots are horizontal and above the water level. They are so shallowly rooted that trees are sometimes overturned by the wind and the entire root system exposed. Cedars, spruce, ash, pin oak, etc., when growing in wet soil with a high water table have shallow but widely spreading roots. The same is true of cottonwoods and willows of sand bars and low beaches.

Certain species characteristic of swamps and bogs have roots or rhizomes that grow under water[979] (Fig. 150). Among these are the cattail (*Typha*), great bulrush (*Scirpus validus*), reed (*Phragmites*), arrowhead (*Sagittaria*), cotton grass (*Eriophorum*), birch (*Betula pumila*), and water willow (*Decodon*). In certain palms, mangroves, etc., some of the roots grow directly upward. Erect projections from horizontal roots of the bald cypress (*Taxodium*), known as *knees*, develop where the tree grows in swamps.[1011] These supposedly are organs for aeration.[513] In most cases, an oxygen supply is afforded the underground parts of swamp plants by gas exchange through large internal air spaces;[792] in some, *e.g.*, *Salix nigra*, it has been shown that the roots will grow for a time even in

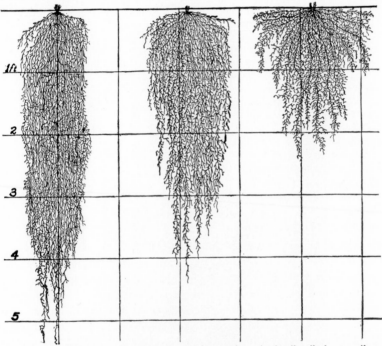

Fig. 149.—Average root development of winter wheat in fertile silt loam soils under a precipitation of 26 to 32 inches (left), 21 to 24 inches (center), and 16 to 19 inches (right). Average from studies made in 20 fields.

the absence of atmospheric oxygen. Roots of pitch pine may grow in water.[596]

Root Habits Modified by Irrigation and Drainage.—Keeping the surface soil too moist during the early life of the plant may promote a more shallow rooting habit, and the crop may later suffer from drought, unless watered very frequently. One of the most difficult problems of irrigation is to apply the water in such a way that plants are not made surface feeders. Otherwise, the natural advantages of the roots widely penetrating the subsoil for nutrients are lost. Conversely, delay in time or amount of water used may tend to promote a deeper rooting habit.

The proportion of roots to tops may be definitely increased by decreasing the soil moisture.

Roots respond in both amount and direction of growth to differences in water content and aeration.[402] By varying these factors through the application of more or less water, not only the root system but also the aboveground plant parts and yield may be varied, since a close correlation exists between the growth of roots and tops.

Raising the water table even temporarily by irrigation causes the death of the deeper roots in many plants and usually results in a decreased

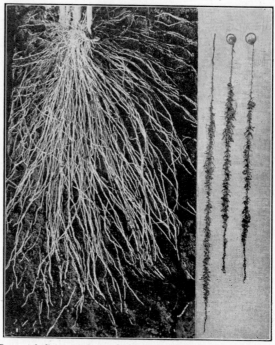

Fig. 150.—Roots of the great bulrush (*Scirpus validus*) about 2 feet long, grown in a saturated soil (left), and a few roots from very dry soil. Note the almost complete absence of branching in the first lot and the marked development of laterals in the second one.

yield. The roots of some species succumb more readily than others. Among many plants, top development depends upon a sufficient root supply, as was clearly illustrated in the case of the cotton plant. The amount of shedding of leaves and bolls was directly proportional to the extent of the root system that was submerged and died as a result of a rising water table. But when the water table was again lowered, a new growth of tops took place simultaneously with a new growth of roots into the area thus provided for root extension.[39]

The general shape of the root system of trees and other plants may be controlled more or less by regulating, under irrigation, the depth of the water table. If the subsoil is waterlogged and thus unaerated, deeper roots will not develop or, if already grown, will soon die as the water table rises. In either case, there is a marked tendency toward the production of an abundance of roots so superficially placed that cultivation results in more or less serious root pruning. Under such conditions, moreover, plants are more sensitive to drought, temperature changes, etc.[824] They require heavier irrigation and greater amounts of fertilizers than those more deeply rooted.

The proper drainage of swamps and bog lands for cultivated crops should be determined with reference to root relations. Extensive experiments have shown that the water table, if at a shallow depth, determines the limit of root penetration and thus, to a large extent, controls the yield of many common meadow grasses, such as timothy, meadow fescue, and bluegrass.[652] Even when the water table is high, only rarely does a root penetrate into the saturated soil, although in well drained soils these grasses are quite deeply rooted. In pasture mixtures, this water relation may be an important factor in determining which species will thrive and become dominant and which will disappear. Many coarse marsh grasses and grasslike plants can thrive in wet situations, since the anatomical structure of their roots permits of rapid gaseous exchange. But most cultivated plants require well aerated soil. For example, corn in well drained soil frequently penetrates 6 feet or more, but in peat marshes where a system of underdrainage kept the water table almost stationary at about 2.5 feet, the roots, upon reaching a level 18 inches above the water table, where the peat soil was very wet and poorly aerated, turned aside and failed to penetrate more deeply. This inhibition to deep root penetration is clearly reflected in the dwarfed stature and reduced yields of the aboveground parts[261] (Fig. 30).

The maximum depth to which the water table should be lowered depends largely upon the nature of the soil as well as upon the root habits of the crops to be grown. If the soil is coarse and capillary action consequently low, too great lowering of the water table may result in a soil too dry to afford maximum yields. Sugar beets, alfalfa, and other plants with taproots 5 to 20 feet deep require a deeper and better drained soil than melons or other cucurbits where the main portion of the roots occupies the surface foot on all sides of the plant to a distance of 15 to 20 feet. For the latter, sandy loams with a clay subsoil are ideal, since they warm quickly and promote rapid root growth but still retain moisture sufficiently well for the shallow root system.

Response to Nutrients.—The response of native plants to nutrients except where they occur in excess (*e.g.*, alkali) has received little study, but that of cultivated plants is fairly well known.[948] Crops grown in rich soil have roots that are shorter, more branched, and more compact than those grown in similar but poorer soil. Fruit trees with tops of equal size may have twice as much root material by weight on poor soil as in loam. Roots are also shorter in more concentrated nutrient solutions.[735] Plants grown in soils with alternate layers enriched with nutrient solution branch much more profusely in these layers. Plants so arranged that one-half of the root system grew in soil rich in nitrates and the other half in poor soil gave similar results. Of course, enriched soil promotes better shoot development, which, in turn, furnishes a greater food supply for further root growth.

To Determine the Effects of Nitrates on Root Development.—Roll pieces of light galvanized iron 12 by 18 inches into the shape of cylinders 1 foot high. Let the edges overlap so that each fits snugly into a ½-gallon, glazed jar. Thoroughly mix a quantity of dry potting soil with half its volume of dry sand. To one lot add 400 parts per million by weight of sodium nitrate dissolved in water. Bring both lots of soil to an optimum water content. Fill one cylinder with one kind of soil and the second with the other, slightly compacted by jolting, and close all crevices or seams with plasticene or modeling clay. Plant a dozen soaked seeds of barley 1 inch deep in each and then cover ½ inch deep with dry sand. When the third leaf has fully developed, unroll the cylinders and compare the root systems in regard to length and branching. This is best done by floating them in water in black trays.

When roots enter a soil area enriched by the decay of former roots, the greater degree of branching is often very marked. They frequently follow the paths of their predecessors to considerable distances, branching in great profusion. Similar branching, which may be due partly to better aeration, frequently occurs in earthworm burrows. Marked contrasts in the degree of branching of roots as they penetrate different soil strata are often to be attributed to differences in richness of soil. Frequently, root stratification is due to water content, but the factors of water and nutrients often operate together (Fig. 151).

It has been shown experimentally that in every case where roots came in contact with a soil layer rich in nitrates, they not only developed much more abundantly and branched more profusely but also failed to penetrate as far into the deeper soil. On the other hand, it has been shown that wheat and barley seedlings grown in both soil and culture solutions low in nitrates produce remarkably extensive root systems, although the shoots are small. Fertilizing the surface layers of soil with nitrates and thus stimulating surface root production in regions where these layers have very little or no available water during periods of drought appears to be distinctly detrimental to normal crop production. Nitrogen leaches readily, and that produced by bacterial action in summer fallow (*i.e.*, where the land is cultivated without a crop) may mostly occur at depths of 3 or more feet by the next spring.[851]

The effect of phosphates in promoting root growth in length and number of branches has long been recognized. They are beneficial wherever drought is likely to set in, because they induce the young roots to penetrate rapidly into the moister layers of the soil below the surface. Wheat, on land treated with phosphates, was found at the end of 3.5 months to be rooted almost twice as deeply as in similar soil to which no phosphates had been applied.[524,962] Nutrients may also affect the size and shape of the fleshy portion of root systems. Potash fertilizers, for example, may result in sweet potatoes being considerably shorter and thicker, while nitrogen in excessive quantities tends to produce long potatoes.[793]

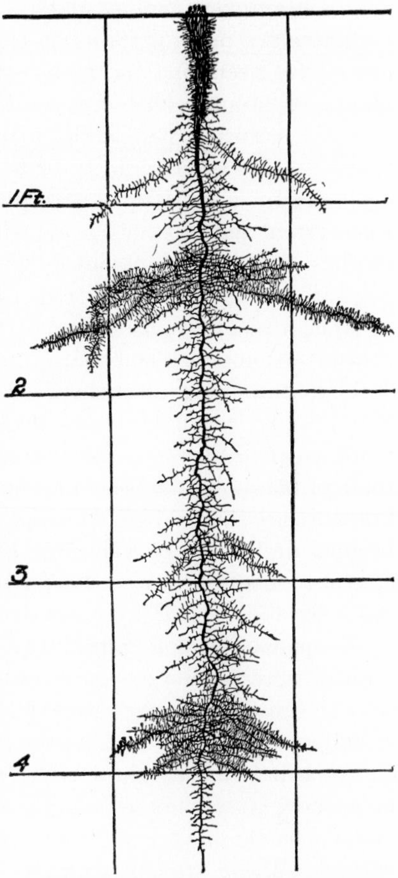

Relation to Salinity and Acidity.— Studies of root systems in soils impregnated with salt point out clearly that the adaptation of plant to habitat is often largely one of root distribution above or below the layers of greatest salt concentration. Shallow-rooted native species which cannot endure salt may grow upon land which contains it at depths below those of root penetration. Orchards and vineyards are sometimes planted in soils of rather high salt content, and the root systems may become thoroughly established in a nontoxic lower layer of soil which is less saline than the surface layers.

Deeply rooted plants, such as alfalfa and trees, may penetrate the salty stratum after getting a start in the surface soil when, because of rain or irrigation, the salts have been leached deeply. Later, as the salt, because of evaporation of water, becomes more concentrated in the surface, the roots penetrate deeply.

Fig. 151.—Root of sugar beet grown in fine sandy loam soil, showing root stratification in the second foot and fourth foot where layers of clay were encountered.

In this way, some plants not exceptionally tolerant may withstand what seem to be excessive quantities when the whole absorbing zone is not considered.[376] Alfalfa, sugar beets, and cotton, all of which have seedlings sensitive to salt, may get a good start due to heavy rains or irrigation which dilute the harmful salts so much that the seedling stage may be safely passed. But if they encounter a strongly saline stratum a foot or two below the surface, these plants may prove less resistant than the fibrous-rooted cereals which may absorb in the upper less saline soil. In California it has been found that the roots of lemon are unusually susceptible to alkali injury, while experiments in Australia indicate that the sour orange is the best stock for orange and lemon in sections where the irrigation water may contain considerable alkali.

Extensive investigations on the effect of soil acidity on root development have been made on moor soils in Europe. The roots of cultivated plants were found to penetrate into the soil only as deeply as the addition of basic materials had sufficiently freed the soil of free acids. Certain native species were found to be less sensitive, their roots occurring in the deeper soil. Experiments with potted soils showed that the length of the root system agreed very closely with the depth of the acid-freed root bed. Studies of root development in the field, where the deeper soil layers were freed from acid by the addition of lime, confirmed the pot experiments.

Wheat seedlings grown in nutrient solutions with a high hydrogen-ion concentration developed root systems that were abnormal in being short, stubby, and much branched. The protoplasm of the root hairs was found to be coagulated and flocculated, and the hairs were probably rendered ineffective as absorbing organs. Excessive acidity affects the roots of plants by partially or wholly retarding growth in length.[960] The branches are short and end abruptly.[901] The roots often thicken and soon become dull white or yellowish brown in color.[7] Sometimes, as in the case of root rot of conifers, injury to the roots resulting from acidity of the soil leads to infection by fungi which cause root decay.

Response to Soil Structure.—Where other factors are the same, roots penetrate more deeply and spread more widely in soils of loose than in those of compact structure.[241] Layers of compact soil often play an important part in shaping the root system. Ponderosa pine seedlings transplanted in clay-loam soils with their roots against one side of a hole show a marked tendency to grow a one-sided root system, the growth being away from the side of the hole and into the looser soil within. When transplanted by the usual "trencher" method, the roots invariably develop only in the plane corresponding to the longitudinal axis of the trench.[935] In plowing for cultivated crops on heavy soils, the depth should be varied from year to year so that a too firm "plow sole" will not develop at a certain level and tend to confine root development to the plowed layer.[450, 471]

To Determine the Effect of Soil Compaction upon Root Habits.—Screen about 250 pounds of a fertile, loam soil and bring it to a good, uniform water content. Secure two strong boxes made of durable wood an inch in thickness and well painted, or lined with galvanized iron. The boxes should be about 10 by 10 inches in inside dimensions and 24 inches deep, one side being held in place by iron bands. Weigh one box, and then fill it with soil, compacting the soil only by jolting the box repeatedly on the floor during filling. Weigh out 30 per cent more soil than that contained in the first box and fill the second one by tamping firmly with a large wooden tamper each shovel of soil placed in the second box, using the entire amount. Plant seeds of sunflower, wheat, or other plants in a little noncompacted surface soil in each container. It is best to use a single species in each box and to thin the plants to about eight well spaced individuals. Cover each container with a thin mulch of fine gravel. Water sparingly. When the plants are 3 to 4 weeks old, tilt the boxes at an angle of 45 degrees, take off the sides, and remove the soil about the roots with an ice pick. Determine the depth of penetration, approximate number and spread of lateral roots, whether the taproot is straight or crooked, and any other points of interest. Make a drawing to scale of a typical root system from each environment, and suggest the reasons for the differences obtained.

In heavy clay soil, the fleshy roots of beets, carrots, parsnips, etc., are often irregular and misshapen, as are also those of the sweet potato. Difficulty of root penetration of both main roots and branches is indicated by a tortuous course. The fleshy, cylindrical roots of native plants are sometimes flattened into bands in penetrating rock crevices.

Response to Aeration.—The dependence of root development of most plants upon aeration is clearly shown by waterlogging the soil.[57,724] In a few days, the usual cultivated plants turn yellow, show wilting, and may ultimately die. But they may survive submergence for weeks, provided the water is kept well aerated. Even cranberries and blueberries, which will stand submergence for months when inactive, are harmed by waterlogging the soil only 3 or 4 days in summer.[58] Rice, too, at least in pot cultures, grows better when the soil is frequently irrigated and drained. The regular presence of air passages or aerenchyma in amphibious and floating hydrophytes, as well as the often constantly open stomata, indicates the importance of a supply of oxygen.

In nutrient solutions, plants grow best where constant and thorough aeration is given. The superiority of roots grown in aerated cultures is shown not only by their greater weight but also by their greater extent and degree of branching[229] (Fig. 152).

Exclusion of oxygen from the roots of most plants interferes with the respiration of the protoplasm of the root cells, resulting in its death and the consequent failure of the roots to function as absorbers for the plant. The cessation of water intake is soon followed by the progressively decreasing turgor of the shoot and leaves and, finally, by wilting and death.[539] Roots respond somewhat differently to variations in the composition of the soil atmosphere.[490,543] Roots of the mesquite (*Prosopis*) continue growth for a considerable period of time in a soil atmosphere containing less than 3 per cent oxygen, while those of a cactus (*Opuntia*) promptly cease growing. An increased air supply to the roots of certain species favors root branching and accelerates root growth[427] (Fig. 153).

Plants growing naturally in well drained soils are much more sensitive to the composition of the soil atmosphere than are those in poorly drained and poorly aerated habitats.[136] Certain deeply rooted species

Fig. 152.—Roots of corn grown in water cultures, all about 6 weeks old. Those on the left were constantly aerated, those on the right not at all. The nonaerated plants had only 58 per cent as great a leaf surface and 55 per cent as great a dry weight as the aerated ones.

like alfalfa are able to grow for a time in an atmosphere containing only 2 per cent oxygen. It seems probable that one of the beneficial effects of good rains, especially in heavy soils, is the increased oxygen. Although

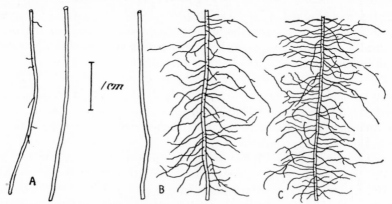

Fig. 153.—Relative branching of roots of cattail: A, in saturated soil; B, in wet but drained soil; and C, in relatively dry soil.

displacing the soil gases, rain water is a solution highly charged with oxygen and has a markedly stimulating effect upon growth.

Orchard trees have been known to die from "puddling" of the soil and the resulting deficient aeration. Also, trees are sometimes killed by cattle trampling and packing the ground above them to such a degree that the air supply in the soil is deficient. In heavy soils, such large quantities of carbon dioxide may be produced by a sod of grass roots growing under fruit trees that the trees and fruits do not develop normally.[422] It has been experimentally demonstrated that many plants respond to an increased carbon-dioxide content of soil by developing roots which are much shallower and more widely spreading in the surface soil. Carbon-dioxide content of garden soils may sometimes be so high as to be detrimental to the root development of some common species.

A deep, well prepared seedbed is essential to good aeration, especially in humid regions. It not only promotes plant growth directly by lightening and warming the soil and conserving moisture but also indirectly by promoting various biological activities, especially ammonification and nitrification. The preparation of a good seedbed as against none resulted in an increase in the yield of corn of 14.5 bushels per acre in Illinois.[622] Underdrainage has a very beneficial effect, since large quantities of air move into the interspaces formerly occupied by water.

To Study the Effects of Aeration on the Growth of Roots and Root Hairs.—Secure rhizomes of *Typha* in early spring before growth has begun or in the fall after the soil has been thoroughly frozen. Select eight rhizomes 3 or 4 inches long with good growing points and remove all of the roots. Secure two containers 2 feet deep and 8 to 12 inches in diameter. Place 2 inches of gravel in the bottom of each, after having perforated the bottom of one to afford good drainage. Fill both with screened potting soil. Plant the rhizomes about 3 inches deep, four in each container. Fill one container with water and by stirring somewhat, so that the air may escape, thoroughly saturate the soil and throughout the experiment maintain the water at a level 2 inches above the soil surface. Keep the second lot of soil wet at all times by flooding the surface on alternate days. Catch the water as it drains through in order to use it again.

At the end of 3 or 4 weeks remove the sides of the containers, wash out the root systems, and compare them in regard to differentiation into water and soil roots, length, degree of branching, development of root hairs, etc. A third container with 18 inches of dry soil overlaid with a 6-inch layer of moist soil gives excellent comparative results. Explain the results secured. Which is controlling, water or air?

Response to Temperature.—If other conditions are favorable, roots of various plants will grow at soil temperatures below 40 and as high as 120°F. Little is known of the most favorable temperature for root growth, but for many temperate crop plants it probably lies between 60 and 80°F.[272,647] It seems probable that species with extensive roots in the surface layers of soil, *e.g.*, cucurbits, cacti, etc., grow better at higher temperatures than those with deep roots. Certain cacti make their best root growth at a temperature of 93°F., although the rate of growth is also correlated with the length the root has already attained. It has been found in growing peas in water cultures that, if insolation is not excessive, the amount of daily fluctuation of root temperature between 44 and 84°F. affected growth but little.

Root growth occurs in certain native species at temperatures so low as to be distinctly unfavorable for others, as has been fully demonstrated. The shallow root habit of certain desert plants is thought to result from subsoil temperatures too low to promote root growth. The general distribution of many cacti seems closely related to the response of the roots to the temperature of the soil, although the effect of aeration is also a contributing factor.[130,131]

Root systems superficially placed are subject to temperature changes quite unlike those experienced by more deeply seated ones. That soil temperatures have an influence on general plant growth is shown by the practice of florists of using bottom heat for certain plants. Cuttings often require definite soil temperatures for rooting. In some plants, considerable vegetative growth can be produced, despite unfavorable atmospheric conditions, by maintaining a soil temperature favorable to root development.

In regions where plants grow in soil underlaid with a frozen substratum, the decrease in temperature with depth must exert a profound effect upon root activities. Alternate freezing and thawing of a soil tears the roots and sometimes causes losses of 25 to 50 per cent among forest seedlings.[349] Shallow-rooted plants may be heaved entirely out of the ground. Experiments have shown that there is a direct relation between resistance to winterkilling and the extensibility of roots of certain plants. The roots of certain perennial vegetable crops such as onions and beets were killed at winter soil temperatures of 34°F. and a new root system grown the following spring. Those of carrots partly died, but the root system of parsnips was unharmed.[973]

Aeration and Soil Temperature.—Some fundamental relations exist among rate of root growth, aeration, and soil temperature.[134] Under normal conditions of aeration, the rate of root growth is known to be influenced by soil temperatures in such a manner that there are three well defined temperatures for growth. These are the maximum or highest temperature at which root growth is possible; the optimum, at which temperature growth is most rapid; and the minimum, below which it ceases. But under a diminished oxygen supply, these cardinal temperatures seem to be greatly modified. As the oxygen supply in the soil air is decreased, rate of growth diminishes in a soil with a high temperature. For example, corn roots, in a soil atmosphere of 96.4 per cent nitrogen and only 3.6 per cent oxygen, at a temperature of 30°C., grow about one-third as rapidly as at the same temperature under normal conditions of aeration. But at 18°C., growth is increased to about two-thirds the normal rate at that temperature (*i.e.*, 18°C.) when the soil is well aerated.   Similar results have been secured for cotton and other plants, which to attain a fair rate of growth at high soil temperatures must be in a well aerated soil; otherwise, the rate of growth is considerably reduced.[133]

Response to the Aerial Environment.—The environmental factors that affect the root are not only those of the soil immediately about it but also those affecting the shoot.   Through the shoot the root system is influenced by the aerial environment.   The amount of light or the degree of humidity, temperature, etc., affects root development, by its effect upon food manufacture, water loss, and other activities of the shoot. Plants adapted to shade or diffuse light, when grown in full sunshine, develop better root systems and thus meet the greater transpiration demands.   The effect of light on the growth of roots has been further demonstrated in the case of white-pine seedlings.   Darkness induces the growth of tall seedlings with poorly developed roots; diffuse light, the growth of shorter plants and longer roots; and full light produces short, stocky plants with long, branching roots.   For example, seedlings of similar age grown in a Vermont nursery under full shade had unbranched taproots 3.5 centimeters long.   Those grown in half shade were 4.5 centimeters long and had the beginnings of laterals.   Seedlings grown in full light had taproots 5.2 centimeters long and a lateral development of roots nearly seven times as great as those in half shade.   Among 50 seedlings excavated about 3 weeks later, the lengths of the root systems were 4.5, 8.2, and 13.8 centimeters and the total number of lateral branches 5, 143, and 468, respectively.[114a]

RELATION OF ROOTS TO CULTURAL PRACTICES

Root distribution and development are greatly modified by various cultural practices, but our knowledge is very incomplete and a great deal more experimental work should be done in this field.

Transplanting.—Transplanting consists of lifting the plant from the medium in which its roots are established and replanting it in a different location.   It is a violent operation, because the younger roots with their root hairs are, as a rule, torn away in the process of lifting.   This is just the part of the root system that is most active in absorption.   Taking up plants for transplanting results not only in breaking many of the roots but also especially in injury to the taproot.   As a consequence, many new roots are formed.   These do not grow so long as the original ones but form a more compact root mass about the base of the plant.   Hence, the root system is less disturbed when the plant is finally transplanted into the field.   Thus, although the root system of a transplanted plant may be less extensive than that of an undisturbed one, upon removal to the field the transplanted plant carries more roots with it and, consequently, more readily reestablishes itself (Figs. 154 and 155).

Nurserymen transplant trees and shrubs two or three times in order to force root development near the stem and thus to insure the pres-

Fig. 154.—Cabbage seedlings not transplanted (left), and transplanted once and twice respectively. Note the greater amounts of soil held by the roots of those that were transplanted.

ervation of more young roots when the plants are lifted for shipment. Hence, they have a better chance for recovery when again set out. This explains why nursery-grown trees and shrubs usually survive transplanting so much better than those secured from places where the roots

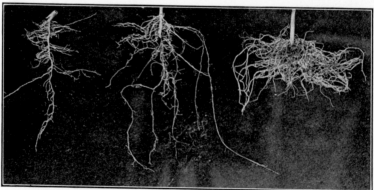

Fig. 155.—Roots of plants shown in Fig. 154.

have made their natural growth. Likewise, market gardeners find that transplanting young plants of cabbage, tomatoes, etc., while growing in cold frames, is a great advantage in assisting them to endure the final removal to open ground.

Effects of Transplanting.—Sow two flats of cabbage, tomatoes, peppers, or other easily transplanted crop. After 2 or 3 weeks, when the seedlings have the first pair of leaves well developed, transplant those from one flat to two similar ones, spacing the plants 2 inches apart. At the same time, thin those in the remaining flat so that they will be similarly spaced. Two weeks later, transplant the plants from one flat a second time, increasing the distance to 4 inches. After 2 weeks, determine (1) the effect of transplanting upon size of tops; (2) the amount of moist earth held by the roots when the plants are lifted with a trowel; and (3) the root development as shown by carefully washing away the soil and floating the roots out in water in black trays. To what are to be ascribed the differences obtained?

Transplanting is not beneficial in itself but only an expedient to grow plants out of their normal season or to give seedlings special care in cultivation, watering, protection from insects, etc. Experiments have clearly shown that the general effect of transplanting is to retard growth, delay fruiting, and reduce yield. The degree of retardation varies with the kind of plant, its age, and the conditions of transplanting.

Certain species, *e.g.*, cabbage, tomatoes, and beets, easily survive transplanting, others, such as peppers, onions, and carrots, are transplanted with more difficulty, and a third group consisting of corn, beans, melons, etc., are very difficult to transplant successfully even at an early age. Plants of the first group retain a relatively large proportion of their root system when transplanted, a fact due, in part, to their network of fine branches; the retained roots are much less suberized and, consequently, more efficient absorbers; and the rate of new root formation is much greater.[545] Obviously, the soil into which plants are transplanted should be in excellent tilth and brought into firm contact with the well distributed roots.

In the transplanting of trees, both depth and spacing should be given careful attention. If the roots are placed either too deep or too shallow, the plant is at a decided disadvantage. Proper spacing in forest planting is necessary to obtain well balanced and wind-firm root systems.[5] Orchard and shade trees as well as trees planted for windbreaks are not infrequently so closely spaced that insufficient room for proper root development results in a marked decrease or actual cessation of growth. The time of transplanting and of early spring cultivation should also be considered in relation to root development.

Correlation between Root and Shoot Development.—The maintenance of a proper balance between root and shoot is of very great importance. If either is too limited or too great in extent, the other will not thrive. The root must be sufficiently wide spread to absorb enough water and nutrients for the stem and leaves, which, in turn, must manufacture sufficient food for the maintenance of the root system.[207] It is a well established fact that grasses develop a better root system when they are undisturbed or mowed only once or twice a year than when they are closely and frequently grazed. In fact, one of the most important objects in the various systems of range and pasture management is to permit the seedling grasses to become well rooted before the tops are removed by grazing. Constant grazing starves the roots as does also too early and too frequent cutting of crops like alfalfa.[527,635] The absorbing area of the roots of winter wheat, exclusive of root hairs, increases rather uniformly with the transpiring area of the shoot and is constantly 10 to 35 per cent greater.[983]

FIG. 156.—A properly pruned lilac (*Syringa*) about 6 weeks after transplanting. The stem is about 2 feet high.

In transplanting crops of various kinds, many of the roots of the young plants are necessarily destroyed. Hence, the top must be pruned back or the plant protected from excessive water loss until the balance between the absorbing and the transpiring systems is reestablished (Fig. 156).

Pruning the tops retards root growth. Experiments with 3-year-old almond trees showed that the development of both the top and root system was inversely proportional to the severity of the pruning of tops. The spread of the roots was over a third greater where pruning was light than where it was severe.[30] Pruning back the vines of sweet potatoes greatly reduces the yield. The tops of large, transplanted blocks of prairie-grass sod were clipped fortnightly during summer. Total dry weight of roots was usually reduced to about 10 per cent or less than that of unclipped controls.[67] Clipping seedling grasses invariably retards root penetration, the extent of root injury depending upon the species and the frequency of clipping[380,657,732] (Fig. 120).

Root Habits and Tillage.—Differences in growth and distribution of roots in the soil are responses to differences in physical and chemical conditions of the substratum in which they live. Tillage methods are a means of bringing about these changes. The depth of intertillage exerts a marked effect upon root habit and often upon yield. For the highest yields, cultivation should never be deep enough to injure the roots seriously. They should be allowed to occupy the richest portion of the soil, which is usually the furrow slice. The proper type of cultivation is

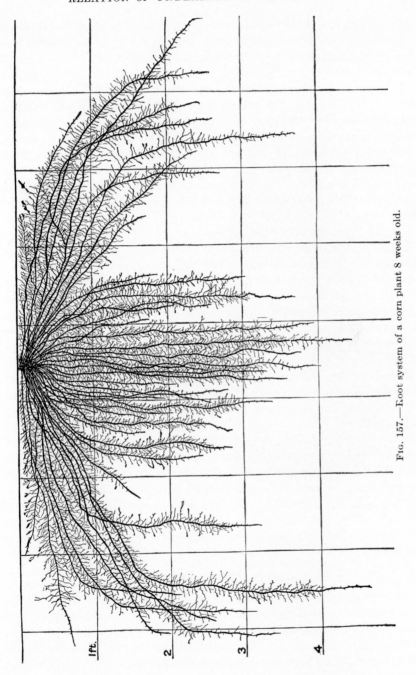

Fig. 157.—Root system of a corn plant 8 weeks old.

deep enough to kill the weeds but shallow enough to reduce root injury to a minimum. A decrease of 2 to 8 bushels per acre in the yield of corn was brought about by deep cultivation in Illinois[1006] and a decrease of 13 bushels in Missouri[399] (Fig. 157).

Extensive experiments with corn, cotton, and various garden crops have shown that the chief benefit of cultivation is derived from keeping down weeds which compete with the crop. Where weeds are few or absent, tillage is of little or no benefit. The roots of nearly all crops so thoroughly permeate the surface soil that little water is lost by direct evaporation. Cultivation, if at all deep, will destroy many of the roots and the plant will be unable to utilize the nutrients in this the richest portion of the substratum. When the roots are cut they usually branch more profusely.

It has been repeatedly demonstrated that mulching the soil and lack of tillage result in a marked growth of fibrous roots in the surface layers. Roots of fruit trees and other plants are often very superficial under a straw mulch.[1026] Irrigated trees under clean, shallow cultivation formed a thick mat of fibrous roots immediately below the soil mulch. Where they competed with grasses the roots were uniformly distributed to a depth of 2.5 feet.

Depth of rooting can be controlled to a considerable extent by the use of cover crops or by intercropping. If the surface soil is depleted of its moisture by absorption, roots of both crops penetrate more deeply. The effect that one kind of plant may have upon the root habit of another by modifying soil conditions is well illustrated in the case of chaparral and Monterey pine at Carmel, Calif. The trees growing in an open stand among the shrubs died when the latter were cleared away. A new growth of pine, however, flourished on the same area. The chaparral had shaded the soil and lessened evaporation from its surface, and the dense layers of rootlets and accumulated humus held the moisture in the surface soil. Consequently, the trees were shallowly rooted and died of drought when the protecting cover was removed and the soil became desiccated. Seedling trees in the changed habitat evidently rooted more deeply.[129]

ROOT HABITS WITHIN THE COMMUNITY

Since each plant association has its own particular climate of which the water relation is usually the controlling factor, it is not surprising that these vegetational units often reveal marked differences in the general or community root habit of at least the dominant species. These are most fully known in certain grassland associations and in the southwestern deserts, although valuable information is also available in otner communities including seral stages in the Rocky Mountains.

The native plants of the true prairie of eastern Kansas, Nebraska, and Iowa have developed very efficient, widely spreading, and deeply penetrating root systems. The bluestems (*Andropogon*), tall marsh grass (*Spartina*), and wheat grasses (*Agropyron*) all have root systems which reach depths of 5 to 8 feet (Fig. 158). Those of June grass (*Koeleria*), wild rye (*Elymus*), and needle grass (*Stipa*) are less extensive, *i.e.*, 1.5 to 5 feet. Many-flowered psoralea (*Psoralea*), wild licorice (*Glycyrrhiza*),

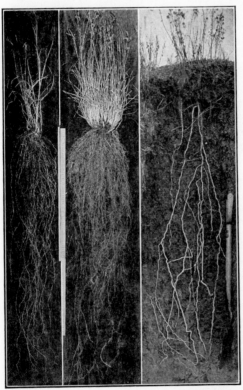

Fig. 158.—Big bluestem (*Andropogon furcatus*) and little bluestem (*A. scoparius*). The white lines are meter sticks, and the other plant is false prairie boneset (*Kuhnia glutinosa*), with roots often extending to a depth of 15 feet or more.

ground plum (*Astragalus*), lead plant (*Amorpha*), and numerous sunflowers, goldenrods, asters, mints, roses, etc., are all deeply rooted. Frequently, the taproot and its major branches reach depths of 8 to 12 feet and depend little or not at all on the surface soil for moisture.

Of 43 species selected as typically representative of the true prairie flora, only 14 per cent absorb almost entirely in the surface 2 feet of soil; 21 per cent have roots extending well below 2 feet but seldom beyond 5 feet; but 65 per cent have roots that reach depths quite below 5 feet, a penetration of 8 to 12 feet being common and a maximum depth of over 20 feet sometimes being attained.[966] In this association there is sufficient rainfall to wet the soil very deeply, but it is not too wet for good aeration, while aerial conditions promote high transpiration. Root depth of many species is less in the prairies of Illinois.[872]

The roots of prairie species are grouped into about three more or less definite absorbing layers, many of the more deeply rooted species having few or no absorbing roots in the first foot or two of soil. The layering of

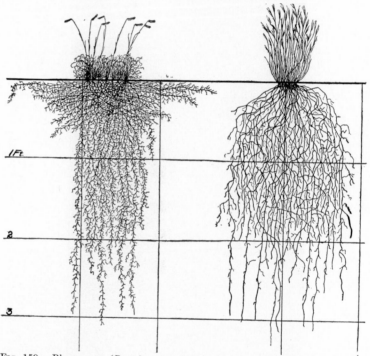

FIG. 159.—Blue grama (*Bouteloua gracilis*) and wire grass (*Aristida purpurea*).

the roots reduces competition and permits the growth of a larger number of species. Little relation between layering and seasonal activity is apparent, however. The periods of most active growth and flower production of plants rooted at various levels occur synchronously.

On hard-loam soils of the short-grass disclimax of western Nebraska and Kansas and eastern Colorado, a distinctly different type of community root habit occurs. Because of the low precipitation and high runoff, only the surface 18 to 24 inches of soil is regularly moist. Absorption by the minutely and profusely branched fibrous roots of the dominant short grasses, *i.e.*, blue grama (*Bouteloua gracilis*), buffalo grass (*Buchloe*),

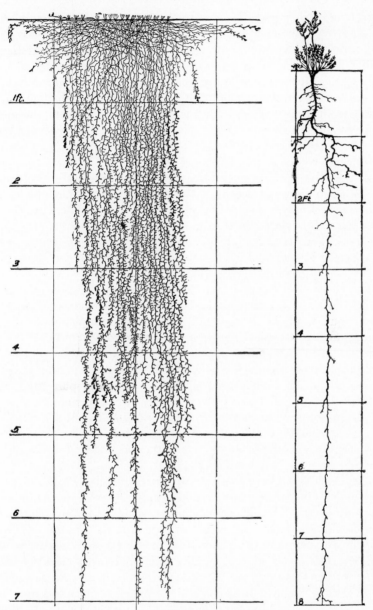

Fig. 160.—Buffalo grass (*Buchloe dactyloides*) and loco weed (*Oxytropis lamberti*) in mixed prairie.

Muhlenberg's ring grass (*Muhlenbergia torreyi*), and hairy grama (*Bouteloua hirsuta*), is confined usually to the surface 1.5 to 2 feet of soil (Fig. 159). This is true, also, for numerous annuals, and the cacti are notably shallow-rooted, spreading many feet just beneath the surface of the soil (Fig. 222). All these species are well fitted to absorb vigorously following light showers, because of the widely spreading shallow roots, a character little in evidence in the true prairie. Where, because of run-in, rodent burrows, or sandier soil, water penetration is deeper, ground plum, loco weed (*Oxytropis lamberti*), *Psoralea tenuiflora*, and a few other more deeply rooted species sparingly occur.

In the mixed-prairie association, where conditions are intermediate, dry soil often occurs at depths of 4 to 5 feet, and the short grasses penetrate more deeply. The roots of species common also to the true prairie are abbreviated in depth. This is usually correlated with the development of a more or less extensive surface-absorbing system. Thus, the root habits are intermediate between those of true prairie and the short-grass disclimax[9] (Fig. 160).

The effect of soil type in relation to water penetration may greatly modify the kind of vegetation and depth of root penetration within an area of equal rainfall. In eastern Colorado, for example, under 17 inches rainfall, conditions typical of short-grass disclimax occur on hard loam soils. But where the soil becomes more sandy, water penetration is greater and more deeply rooted grasses, *e.g.*, wire grass (*Aristida*) and other species, become dominant. Where the substratum is nearly pure sand, runoff is practically nil, and water penetration reaches a maximum. Here the very deeply rooted bunch grasses, *Andropogon hallii*, *A. scoparius*, sand reed (*Calamovilfa*), etc., dominate. Many other very deeply rooted herbs also occur, both vegetation and root habit being markedly different from that on sandy loam soil (Fig. 161).

The Palouse (*Agropyron-Festuca*) prairie of the Pacific northwest grows under a moderate winter and low summer precipitation of about 23 inches annually. The silt loam soils are usually deep and have a high water-retaining power. In early summer, the surface-soil layers lose all of their available water, a fact indicated by the early maturing of the dominant, *Festuca ovina*, and certain other shallow-rooted grasses (Fig. 143). As the season advances, drought occurs in the deeper soil, the subsoil usually being quite thoroughly depleted of its moisture. Bluebunch wheat grass (*Agropyron spicatum*), another dominant, matures early, dries out in July, but renews growth upon the advent of the autumn rains. Little provision is made for absorption in the surface soil, the root system penetrating to about 4 feet. Many of the other species absorb in the first 4 to 6 feet of soil; a few penetrate more deeply. Nearly all mature by midsummer, late blooming grasses being noticeably absent.

Under the same Great Basin type of rainfall but where it is only 16 inches or less in amount and falls upon a deep, pervious soil, conditions

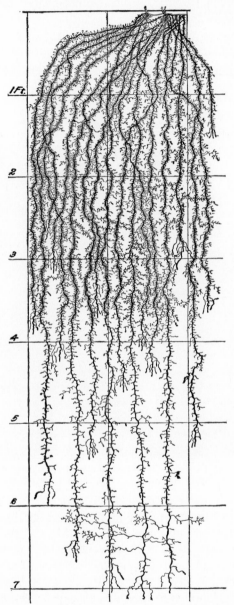

FIG. 161.—Root system of sand hill bluestem (*Andropogon hallii*).

are less favorable to the growth of grasses. Here the vegetation constitutes the *Artemisia-Atriplex* or Basin sagebrush association. The sagebrush (*Artemisia tridentata*) has a taproot system which branches widely and penetrates to a depth of 5 to 11 feet. It also has a highly developed system of laterals for absorption in the shallower soil (Fig. 162). Shad scale (*Atriplex confertifolia*) is likewise well provided with a root system excellently adapted to absorb both in the shallow and in the deep soil. These dominants are illustrative of many other shrubby, half shrubby, and perennial, herbaceous species of the Great Basin.

Fig. 162.—Sagebrush (*Artemisia tridentata*) showing generalized type of root system with deep taproot and widely spreading laterals, many of which are in the surface soil. (*After Kearney, et al.*)

Root systems of annual plants in the desert scrub association, *e.g.*, about Tucson, Ariz., are all quite shallow. Most of them do not penetrate to depths greater than 8 inches. Here the precipitation is only about 11 inches annually and there are two rainy seasons, one in summer, another in winter. Winter annuals are, in general, characterized by a prominently developed taproot and a meager development of laterals. Roots of summer annuals penetrate to about the same depth, but the lateral branches are much more prominent and the total absorbing surface greater. This is apparently correlated with the more rapid growth and greater transpiring surface of the latter.   The perennials have three types of root systems: (1) the generalized type, where both taproot and laterals are well developed (*e.g.*, creosote bush, *Covillea*, and mesquite, *Prosopis*); a specialized type (2), with strong development of taproot and few branches, such as *Ephedra*, or (3), with laterals very highly developed, as in most cacti.   On the upland the roots do not penetrate, as a rule, deeper than 12 inches, the depth of available soil.   Those on the flood plains reach depths of 6 to 16 feet or more.   Perennials with the generalized type of root system have the widest local distribution, and those with the pronounced development of the taproot have the most limited.   In general, there is a tendency to form three layers of roots in the soil, the uppermost of annuals, followed closely by the root layer of cacti and a much broader, deeper-seated layer composed of taproot systems with or without prominent laterals.   The wide spread of laterals in many of the dominants explains the characteristic open spacing of the desert scrub and the bushlike habit.[128]

Little is known of the root extent of mature trees in forests.[711,882,980] It seems very probable, however, that under the relatively high rainfall necessary for the development of deciduous forests, for example, the subsoil is often quite too moist and consequently too poorly aerated for deep root penetration.[84]   Both the shade from the forest cover and the surface mulch of litter, moreover, tend to prevent evaporation and promote the thorough occupancy of the surface soil by roots.   It seems probable that the bulk of the roots of the plants of the deciduous forest may occur in the surface 1 to 3 feet, but where the trees grow on well drained uplands much greater depths are attained.[66,253,929b]

A Study of the Root Habits of Plants.—A thorough study of the entire root system of even a single plant is usually a laborious, time-consuming process,[566] but many facts of ecological interest and importance may be learned in the course of the regular field work.   A spade and hand pick, one end of which is drawn out to a sharp point, and an ice pick should be a part of the field equipment.   Examine and compare the relative coarseness or fineness of the roots of grasses which are adapted to low, moist soil and dry, upland soil, respectively.   Follow the rhizomes of various sod-forming grasses and ascertain the distribution of the roots upon them.   Examine the underground parts in the surface soil of various herbaceous species that form dense societies.   Study the nature of the shallower roots of various legumes, composites, etc.   Do all absorb in the surface soil?   The roots of seedlings should also be examined, especially those of trees.   Do they show any adaptations to thrive in moist or dry soil?   Examination of the roots of beech, oaks, etc., will reveal an intimate fungus-root relation known as mycorrhiza (p. 329).   In freshly cut banks along roadways, railway cuts, eroding streams, etc., it is usually possible to examine root penetration and distribution to great depths.   Are the native plants of your region deeply rooted? Can you discover to what depths various field and garden crops penetrate and how widely the roots spread?[277,973]   What factors are concerned in the behavior in different habitats?

ROOT HAIRS AND FACTORS AFFECTING THEIR DEVELOPMENT

The formation of root hairs in plants possessing them is apparently not a morphological necessity, as are other organs or tissues, but seems to be related to the direct influence of some factors of the environment, especially water content and oxygen supply.[135] Some aquatic angiosperms and several gymnosperms such as the firs (*Abies*), redwood (*Sequoia*), and Scotch pine (*Pinus sylvestris*) produce no root hairs. On the other hand, certain plants that grow in very dry places (*e.g.*, piñon pine) produce root hairs that have thick, lignified walls, that persist for several months or even years.[993] Others such as redbud (*Cercis canadensis*), honey locust (*Gleditsia triacanthos*), Kentucky coffee tree (*Gymnocladus dioica*), as well as a rather large number of composites, have root hairs of several years' duration.[587] It seems probable that in all of these cases the habit of producing thick-walled root hairs was formed at a time when these species grew only in very dry situations.

In roots that are permanently hairy, the root-hair zone may be general or limited to either the distal or proximal region of the root. Where root hairs persist in either herbs or trees, there is little or no secondary thickening of the root. In most plants, the initiation of a layer of periderm or cork marks the end of absorption, but this begins to form only after the root hairs cease to function. In the roots of most grasses, both the epidermis and fleshy cortex may slough off, except the innermost layer or endodermis. It becomes cutinized or suberized and the roots appear dead. The deeper portions, however, are clothed with root hairs that are absorbing vigorously, although the older portion of the root system is serving merely for anchorage and conduction.

The absorbing area of the root is greatly increased by the growth of root hairs.[243a] For example, in the corn plant it has been calculated that the area is 5.5 times that of a hairless root of similar size; in garden peas, 12.4 times, and in certain other plants, as much as 18 times.[798] It is not surprising, therefore, that the amount of water and air in the soil has a marked effect upon the development of root hairs.[1009] The root-hair zone, though often only a few millimeters long, may extend through distances of many centimeters, especially on rapidly growing plants in moist soil. The length of life of an ordinary root hair is, in part, moreover, dependent upon the environment. In dry soil it is shorter; in well aerated, moist soil, of longer duration; and the root-hair zone may be 2 or more feet in length. Both air roots and water roots are commonly without hairs, although root hairs on some plants are readily produced either in a saturated atmosphere or in an aqueous medium provided that calcium is present in the latter.[193,276] Hairs are more abundant, even in the same species, in soil beneath flowing water than where the water is standing. This is in accord with the fact that oxygen is necessary for the development of root hairs, and their usual absence or weak development in ponds or swamps is due, in part, to low oxygen content. In moderately moist soils, the roots of many plants are almost woolly with root hairs, there are fewer in wet soil, and usually none in water. Of course, if soils become very dry, both root hairs and young rootlets die. Root-hair development may also be retarded by a very concentrated soil solution such as occurs in saline soils. Extremes of temperature are also inimical to their growth. They develop in the light and dark about equally well, provided there is ample moisture.[446,863]

The intimate contact of root hairs with the water and solutes that form a film around the soil particles is due to the presence of mucilaginous materials in the outer lamella of the wall, which in some plants has been shown to be pectin mucilage.[423,729] Hence, the high efficiency of root hairs as absorbing organs. The osmotic concentration within the root hairs varies with the medium in which they grow. It is least where water is abundant, often only 3 to 4 atmospheres. This, however, is much greater than the osmotic pressure of the soil solution which is only 0.2 to 1 atmosphere in ordinary agricultural soils. Osmotic pressure within the root hairs increases as the soil becomes drier or in plants adapted to dry and especially saline habitats to many times that amount.[407] The osmotic pressure may, moreover, be increased by increasing the rate of transpiration.[433]

Fig. 163.—Propagation by stolons, buffalo grass (*Buchloe*).

UNDERGROUND STEMS AND ROOT OFFSHOOTS

Aside from absorption and anchorage, other activities of underground plant parts are storage and propagation.[519] Vegetative reproduction is very largely by stems of which the commonest and most efficient type is the rhizome, although tubers, bulbs, corms, and root offshoots also play an important part (Figs. 163 and 164). These same organs are frequently enlarged and serve for food accumulation, especially in perennial herbs, where the aboveground parts die at the end of the growing season. These underground parts are not confined to plants of a particular habitat but occur widely in swamps, woodlands, grasslands, and sandy wastes. Usually, however, they are larger and thicker, especially rhizomes, in species inhabiting swamps or moist soil and finer and often shorter in harder or drier soil.[761]

Some rhizomes may compose the entire stem system, *e.g.*, various violets and most ferns, in which case they give rise to aerial leaves, but usually they bear only scale leaves. They may be simple or only slightly branched, as in Solomon's-seal (*Polygonatum*) and certain rushes (*e.g.*, *Juncus balticus*). Each season the younger portions extend a few inches forward, the older parts frequently decaying. This gives rise to *linear migration* by which the plant invades new areas. Where several shoots develop each year, the line of migration is clearly evident (Fig. 78). More commonly, rhizomes are greatly branched and grow in all directions from the parent area. The result of this *radial migration* is to form more or less symmetrical communities, the central portions of

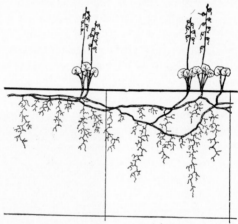

Fig. 164.—Propagation by underground stems, wintergreen (*Pyrola chlorantha*).

which may be unoccupied by the particular species. The decay of the older portions in branched rhizomes results in the multiplication of individuals. This, however, is not so important as the advance into new territory.[253]

By means of rhizomes and root offshoots, plants may invade closed communities, such as grassland, where propagation by seeds or stolons would be difficult or impossible. It is in this effective manner that many shrubs and half-shrubs extend their area of occupation, *e.g.*, coralberry (*Symphoricarpos*), hazelnut (*Corylus*), rose (*Rosa*), and ninebark (*Opulaster*) (Fig. 73). The rhizomes of sumac (*Rhus glabra*) are often 25 feet long. Various species of willows, poplars, plums, and the osage orange spread widely by means of root offshoots.

Many of the longest and best developed rhizomes are found among plants growing in loose, sandy soil. Here the elongated, sharp-pointed buds penetrate the substratum with ease. In general, rhizomes grow parallel to the soil surface at a depth of a few inches, varying with the species.   Where they are covered with shifting sand, the rhizomes ascend, sometimes vertically, producing roots abundantly.   When soil is removed, they descend to the proper level.   Thus, the surface 1 to 2 feet of sand hills or dunes may contain a tangled mat of rhizomes and roots of sand-binding species, especially grasses.   In *Redfieldia* the much branched stems are frequently 20 to 40 feet long and sometimes buried 4 feet deep (Fig. 165).

Sod-forming grasses, carices, and rushes, *e.g.*, bluegrass, sedges, and spike rush have the rhizome habit well developed.   But in bunch grasses

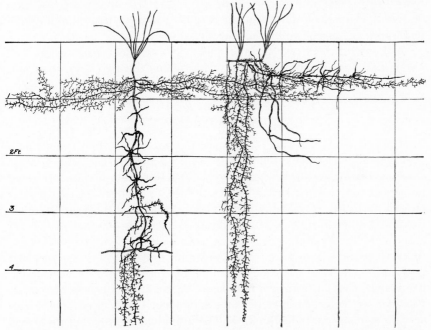

Fig. 165.—Rhizomes and roots of *Redfieldia flexuosa;* the plant on the left has been buried to a depth of nearly 4 feet.

like orchard grass, certain wheat grasses, etc., the stem grows up parallel with the parent culm until it emerges from the axillary sheath.   Some species, such as little bluestem, form a sod under favorable conditions of water content but resort to the bunch habit where the soil is dry.   Many goldenrods, sunflowers, yuccas, asters, mints, and sages migrate by means of rhizomes.

In bogs, because of little mechanical resistance, the underground parts are remarkably straight, and in both bogs and swamps the depth of penetration is often limited by the water level.   The thick, coarse rhizomes of cattails, arrowheads, swamp reed, great bulrush, etc., however, grow at depths of 3 to 12 inches, often below the water table.[263]

Such rhizomes, like roots which grow below water, are very rich in aerenchyma. Stems of certain woody species, such as water willow (*Decodon*), produce aerenchyma upon coming in contact with water, but most woody species such as willows, birches, and alders have little or none.

The hollow rhizomes of *Phragmites* occur from near the soil surface often to a depth of 18 inches. Those of *Typha*, *Sagittaria*, and *Polygonum* occupy the soil at various levels. Differences in the depth of rhizomes in swamps and the degree to which they occupy the soil have led to classification into competitive and complementary communities. Since there is still much unoccupied space, and no competition for water or dissolved nutrients (although air may be deficient), light and not room underground appears to be the controlling factor.

Although tubers, corms, and bulbs are excellent organs for food accumulation and protection of growing points during cold or drought, they are much inferior to rhizomes as organs of propagation. This is because of their slight elongation and consequent lack of migration.

SOIL ORGANISMS

The soil is not a mass of inert inorganic material. It is the home of countless billions of microorganisms—bacteria, fungi, algae, and protozoa—which throng its dark passageways. Earthworms, insects, etc., and numerous burrowing animals find in it food or shelter. A single gram of loam from the surface soil may contain 14,000,000 to 58,000,000 bacteria, and in some soils even at a depth of 3 feet, as many as 37,000 per gram have been found.[106,218] The mycelia of fungi permeate soils, especially those rich in humus. The toadstools and puffballs of forest and grassland are most conspicuous, but hundreds of species of smaller, mold-like forms occur in countless numbers. Algae are frequently abundant. Protozoa are common in most soils, and sometimes a gram of soil may contain as many as 10,000 to 2,000,000 individuals. Many of these feed chiefly upon soil bacteria.[747]

The Relation to Nitrogen.—Among this vast assemblage of dwellers in the soil, certain groups deserve especial mention, since they are concerned very directly with the supply of nitrogen, a constituent of the protoplasm and a substance most indispensable to plants. The ammonia liberated in the breaking down of proteins, a process called *ammonification*, is oxidized to nitrites by certain kinds of bacteria (*Nitrosomonas* and *Nitrosococcus*). The nitrites are further oxidized by other bacteria (*Nitrobacter*) to nitrates, which is the form of nitrogen most favorable to green plants. The process of nitrification is exceedingly important since plants cannot use nitrogen from the abundant supply in the air but must rely entirely upon compounds absorbed in solution through the roots. Hence, the presence of mineral salts containing combined nitrogen is a factor of great importance in soil productiveness. Since the supply of nitrates is constantly diminished by leaching and absorption by plants, its renewal is imperative.

Several species of soil bacteria functioning independently of higher plants possess the power of taking the free nitrogen from the air and incorporating it into organic compounds. In this way, much nitrogen is added to the soil. A gain of from 25 to 40 pounds per acre per year has been determined by different investigators. Both nitrifying and nitrogen-fixing bacteria thrive in the humus, and it is largely due to their activities that soils containing much humus are so productive.

Nitrifying and nitrogen-fixing bacteria, like all other soil organisms, are profoundly affected in their activities by the environment. Acidity of the soil has an important effect upon bacterial processes. It may increase to such a point that the decomposition of plant tissues is hindered, a layer of peat being formed similar to that developed under poor aeration. The degree of acidity that is toxic varies greatly with different species, nitrifying and nitrogen-fixing bacteria being very intolerant of acidity. Extreme alkalinity is also detrimental. The water content of soil and the temperature likewise exert a profound effect. Most soil bacteria do not become active until temperatures of 45 to 50°F. are attained. In one experiment, the amount of nitric nitrogen produced per acre in a period of 3 weeks was 3.6 pounds at 44°F., 17.8 pounds at 78°F., 46.6 pounds at 94°F., but only 10.8 pounds at 111°F. Under favorable temperature, only 2.8 pounds were formed in dry soil and 8.2 pounds in one of medium water content, but 29.6 pounds per acre during a similar 3-week period where the water content was very favorable.[746] Much larger quantities are, moreover, produced in rich than in poor, eroded soils.

Among certain plants, notably the legumes, which are very rich in nitrogenous compounds, a close relationship exists between other species of nitrogen-fixing bacteria and the roots. Here, the bacteria are found in the root nodules as on clovers and alfalfa.[915] From 40 to over 250 pounds of nitrogen per acre may thus be added to the soil in a single season through the activities of these bacteria. This explains why the practice of growing leguminous crops and plowing them under as green manure has such a stimulating effect upon the growth of succeeding crops. The occurrence of legumes and other nodule-bearing plants among native vegetation is undoubtedly of great significance in maintaining soil fertility. Nodules reach their best development in neutral or nearly neutral soils which are not too rich in nitrates.[324]

Experiments with the development of nodules on legumes have shown that they become much larger when soil temperatures are most favorable. In the soybean, a consistent increase in dry weight of nodules occurred as the soil temperature increased from 15 to 24°C. At higher temperatures, a progressive decrease occurred. Alfalfa, red clover, and field peas likewise gave a maximum nodule production at a soil temperature of about 24°C.[459]

Relation to Disease.—The soil factors exercise a strong influence upon the development and expression of disease.[90,458] Many diseases, such as chlorosis of tobacco, pineapple, coniferous seedlings, etc., are due to the deficiency or unavailability of sufficient magnesium or iron. Yellow berry of wheat is caused by a low available supply of nitrogen.[456] Potash hunger of potatoes results in discoloration of the foliage, wilting, etc. Disease may be caused by an excess supply of nitrates, calcium, or magnesium salts or a disturbed water or air relation. Blossom-end rot of tomatoes, for example, is due to drought,[727] and straight head of rice probably to poor aeration. Soil temperature is an extremely important environmental factor since it has a marked effect upon disease-producing organisms.

Frequently, the influence of environmental factors on the host seems to be the fundamental cause of susceptibility to disease. Proper soil and other conditions for a vigorous development of root and shoot are desirable. Corn and wheat seedlings, for example, are sheathed at the outset with protective coverings, chiefly of pectic substances, through which invasions of soil organisms may rather easily take place. But in normally balanced seedling development, the cell membranes of the protective coverings pass quickly to a condition of maturity where celluloses and even lignin or suberin predominate. Thus, because of chemical changes in the cell walls, the tissues which were subject to invasion change rapidly so that they become relatively resistant. The soil and air temperatures that promote this normal balanced seedling development vary with the crop. In wheat, for example, they are low, but in corn, much higher.[239,240]

It has been clearly demonstrated that many soil-borne diseases are conditioned in their occurrence by the factor of soil temperature. Cabbage yellows,[461] flax wilt,[923] tomato wilt,[148] and tobacco root rot[453] are examples of diseases caused by soil-inhabiting fungi gaining entrance to the host plant through the root system. In each case, the disease has been experimentally developed in destructiveness ranging consistently from 0 to 100 per cent of the crop by changing the single factor of soil temperature.[458] The temperature ranges employed were well within those reasonably congenial to the respective hosts (Fig. 166). For example, flax wilt, which, like the wilt of cabbage and tomato, is favored by a high temperature, gives extreme development of disease at 24 to 28°C. but none above 38 or below 14°C.[460] Conversely, tobacco root-rot development is favored by lower soil temperatures, the most favorable range being between 17 and 23°C.[453]

The regional distribution of a plant disease is sometimes determined by temperature. The presence of onion smut, for example, is dependent upon the soil temperature during the seedling stage of the growth of the host. Infection and development of smut are favored by relatively low temperatures and inhibited by high ones, with 29°C. as approximately the critical point. Hence, though common in the north, it is almost unknown in the south, although annually introduced with northern grown bulbs.[955] In the Pacific northwest, soil temperatures of 0 to 5°C. are decidedly unfavorable to successful infection of wheat by stinking smut. This holds, also, for temperatures higher than 22°C., while 15 to 22°C. are optimum for its development.[457]

The soil reaction often exerts a controlling effect upon disease-producing organisms. The slime mold (*Plasmodiophora brassicae*), which pro-

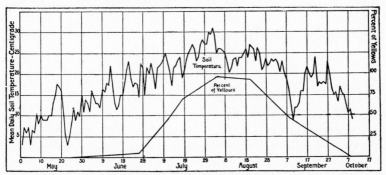

Fig. 166.—Graphs showing the relation of temperature to the development of cabbage yellows. (*After Jones, et al.*)

duces clubroot of cabbage and other crucifers, is most injurious in acid soils. By the addition of lime, the soil becomes a more favorable habitat for the roots of the host but much less so for the parasite. The fungus (*Gibberella saubinetti*) producing wheat scab does little or no harm at pH 5.5. A potato-scab fungus (*Oospora*) is less tolerant of acid soil than is its host. Consequently, potatoes can be grown well in certain soils and remain entirely free from attack. Some of the most important problems of plant pathology deal with the relation of environmental factors to the occurrence and severity of disease.[420]

Mycorrhiza.—In many plants such as the pines, oaks, orchids, and many ericads, fungi are habitually associated with the roots.[586,588] A mycorrhiza (*i.e.*, fungus root) is a structure composed of root and fungus. If the fungal mycelium occurs on the outside of the root and between its cells, as on many oaks, hickories, pines, beech, etc., the mycorrhiza is ectotrophic (*i.e.*, nourished outside). In an endotrophic mycorrhiza (*i.e.*, nourished within), as in red maple (*Acer rubrum*), orchids, many

Ericaceae, etc., the fungus occurs inside the root where certain cortical cells usually contain closely interwoven clumps of hyphae which often enfold the nucleus. The root hairs, which are usually sparse, may also be filled with hyphae[717,718] (Fig. 167).

Ectotrophic mycorrhizas are caused by many kinds of fungi, those on forest trees apparently always by Basidiomycetes, many having been synthesized experimentally.[580,599] The hyphae of the mushroom penetrate the outer cell walls of the rootlet and often split them by dissolving the middle lamella. They then continue to grow until they develop a fungus mantle which completely envelops the rootlet. Simultaneously, branches of the mycelium penetrate between the outer cortical cells of the rootlets, causing the walls to split and the cells to be pushed apart. Since further elongation of the rootlet is inhibited by the fungus mantle, excessive branching is induced. The branches also are soon infected and

Fig. 167.—Cross section of ectotrophic mycorrhiza on red spruce (*Picea rubra*), and an endotrophic mycorrhiza on red maple (*Acer rubrum*). (*After McDougall*.)

covered by the fungus, and, consequently, most plants showing a good development of mycorrhiza have roots that are short and thick and present a coral-like appearance (Fig. 168).

They vary in color, depending upon the kind of fungus, from white to bright yellow, brick red, or dark brown. They usually occur only in the upper layer of humus-filled soil on the smallest rootlets, the hyphae composing the fungal root mantle connecting with the mycelia that permeate the humus. A single tree may show three or four kinds of mycorrhizas differing in form, size, color, and texture, but each is due to a different fungus. More usually, only a certain species of fungus appears always to be associated with a particular tree species. Only a small portion of the root system may bear mycorrhiza, but here root hairs are few or wanting, or, at the other extreme, as in the Indian pipe (*Monotropa uniflora*), the entire root system is compacted into a clump of fungus mycelium and does not come in contact with the soil at all.

Endotrophic mycorrhizas are best known in the *Orchidaceae*, *Ericaceae*, and *Gentianaceae*.[714] The rootlets containing the fungus are sometimes transformed into beadlike galls. In most cases, the fungi concerned are apparently not Basidiomycetes but microscopic molds, for the most part not well known. Apparently, they are specialized forms rather than ordinary soil fungi. Many orchids are entirely dependent upon mycorrhizal fungi. Under natural conditions, the seeds of some orchids do not germinate unless infected by mycorrhizal fungi, although germination may be brought about artificially by the addition of appropriate culture media, *e.g.*, those containing fructose. In other species, the seeds germinate but do not develop beyond the seedling stage unless they become infected with the proper kind of fungus. Orchid roots are characteristically fleshy and tuberlike. They differ much more from ordinary roots than those

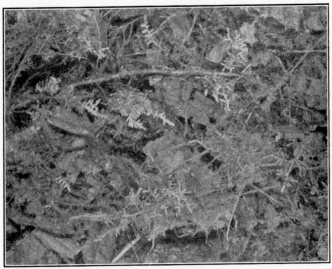

Fɪɢ. 168.—Ectotrophic mycorrhiza on the hornbeam (*Carpinus*) in leaf mold. (*Photograph by W. B. McDougall.*)

associated with ectotrophic fungi. Some plants, as *Corallorrhiza* and *Epipogon*, have no roots, the underground parts consisting entirely of branched, fungus-infested rhizomes. Endotrophic mycorrhizas are common also among the *Ericaceae*, certain genera such as *Vaccinium, Calluna*, and *Rhododendron* being more or less dependent upon mycorrhizal fungi. Since the fungi can grow only in an acid substratum, these higher plants can flourish only in an acid soil.

Distribution and Significance.—Mycorrhizas are of extremely wide distribution and of common occurrence.[111] Mycorrhizal fungi have been recorded for every group of chlorophyll-bearing plants except the algae. Even the cultivated cereals have been added to the constantly growing list. An extended survey of natural forest environments in North America and Northern Europe has shown that about 95 per cent of all tree roots are normally mycorrhizal.[390a,390b] Mycorrhizas are associated abundantly with plants rooted in forest mold. They are rare in water and wet soil, except in bogs where organic matter is abundant. They are especially common on bulbous and tuberous plants.

Many investigators consider the relation of the fungus to higher plants one of parasitism,[111] a relationship which seems clearly evident in some species, such as certain orchids. On the other hand, some higher plants, e.g., the colorless *Monotropa uniflora*, appear to be parasitic upon the fungus. Much experimental evidence, however, points to the conclusion that among many species and particularly coniferous forest trees, mycorrhizas exhibit a symbiotic relationship.[599,719] Experimental evidence supports the belief that the fungus appropriates carbon compounds from the green plant and may also be benefited by certain other substances. On the other hand, it is well known that forest humus is low in nitrates, particularly if the reaction is acid. In such acid soils, where the nitrogen supplies exist in the form of organic compounds of relatively complex type, coniferous mycorrhizas abound. Experiments show that on such soils tree growth with mycorrhiza is much greater than without, the fungi making the nitrogen readily available for the trees. The fungi, moreover, apparently absorb certain salts more readily than do root hairs. If either nitrogen, potassium, phosphorus, or calcium is available in less than optimum quantities, as is usual in forest soils, mycorrhizas become very abundant. Thus, it seems that mycorrhizas possess a vital significance for trees and other plants.[390] Widespread failures of tree seedlings in nurseries as well as pure culture experiments involving the use of mycorrhizal fungi for inoculating soils clearly indicate that trees are often incapable of existing in the absence of mycorrhiza.[390,611a,929a]

CHAPTER XII

HUMIDITY, WIND, AND EVAPORATION

The habitat, *i.e.*, the kind of place in which plants grow, is marked by development similar to that of the formation. When, moreover, the plants within a community are examined as individuals, it soon becomes apparent that life conditions within the common habitat of the community are much diversified. Plants growing side by side (*e.g.*, bluegrass and goldenrod or bur reed and water plantain) are not subject to exactly the same conditions. The immediate environment of the two may differ more or less as to water content, nutrients, light, temperature, humidity, wind, and other factors. Furthermore, if the environment of a single species is critically examined, it will usually be found to be far from uniform. During the early stages of development, seedlings, especially of trees and other tall-growing plants, and rosette forms, as those of evening primrose, occupy a very different habitat from that of the mature plants of these species. This is true both above and below ground, for soils are usually very different with increasing depth as regards water content, nutrients, aeration, etc., and the developing root, like the shoot, lives in several layers.[1024] Thus, the term habitat has come to have both a general and a more limited and specific meaning.

Factors of the Habitat.—Every part of the environment that exerts directly or otherwise a specific influence upon the life of the plant is a factor of the habitat. The habitat is a complex in which a factor acts upon other factors and is, in turn, acted upon by them. Plants show the effects of an increase or a decrease in factors by functional responses (*e.g.*, decreased photosynthetic activity in shade), by differences in growth, and by changes in structure. Species vary widely in the nature and degree of response. Only certain factors are the direct causes of plant response, while others affect the plant only through these. Water, humidity, light, temperature, solutes, and soil air are direct factors of first importance because of their variation from habitat to habitat. Temperature may also act indirectly. Other direct factors, such as carbon dioxide, oxygen, and gravity, are negligible because of their constancy.

Habitat factors fall naturally into three groups: (1) those that affect the activities of the plants directly; (2) those that exert an indirect effect; and (3) those whose effect is only remote and is exerted usually through an indirect factor. This grouping does not include the so-called biotic

factors which are of such diverse nature that they are considered separately under coactions.

DIRECT FACTORS	INDIRECT FACTORS	REMOTE FACTORS
Water content	Precipitation	Altitude
Humidity	Soil composition	Slope
Light	Wind	Exposure
Temperature	Pressure	Surface
Solutes		
Soil air		

Absorption is primarily dependent upon water content, transpiration
upon humidity and temperature, and photosynthesis upon light. Solutes
directly affect plant nutrition, and soil air is essential for respiration of
most roots. Precipitation and soil composition indirectly affect absorption by modifying water content. Atmospheric pressure and wind
indirectly affect transpiration, wind through its influence upon humidity.
The physiographic factors are all remotely related to vegetation. Slope
and surface modify water content through their effect upon precipitation
and runoff. Altitude, acting through temperature and precipitation,
modifies humidity. Light is reduced in cloudy regions, a condition frequently resulting from the effect of altitude and slope on temperature and
wind. Numerous other interrelations occur. Although the environmental factors are closely interwoven, those directly affecting the plant are few.

The chief factors of the aerial environment of plants are humidity,
light, temperature, and wind. All are much more subject to rapid fluctuations than are the factors of the soil. As in the soil, an extremely
important environmental relation is that of water. The amount of water
vapor in the air is one of the chief factors influencing vegetation.

HUMIDITY

The moisture of the air which is in the form of vapor is termed
humidity. It is one of the most important factors since it directly
affects the rate of transpiration. The amount of water that a plant
loses frequently determines whether it can or cannot grow in a given
habitat. Owing to the nature of the medium in which it occurs, water
vapor, which comports itself in some ways as though oxygen, nitrogen,
and carbon dioxide were not present, is much more uniformly distributed
than is the water in the soil, but it also fluctuates to a much greater
degree.

The actual amount of water present in the air is called the *absolute
humidity*. It is expressed as grains per cubic foot or grams per cubic
meter of air. The amount of water vapor in the atmosphere taken by
itself does not determine the dryness or wetness of a climate.[483] Climates
recognized as dry are not necessarily deficient in actual moisture, since

even in desert regions the amount of moisture in a given unit of space may equal or even exceed that in other districts commonly considered as moist. For example, a cubic meter of space over the dry desert of the southwest is known to contain as much moisture in summer as a space of similar volume along the moist shores of the Great Lakes. Because of the higher temperatures in the desert, the relative humidity is very low and water exposed quickly evaporates. Conversely, in the lake region the amount of vapor that can remain in the air is lessened by the lower temperatures and the air is more nearly saturated.[227]

The *relative humidity* is the ratio, expressed as a percentage, of the water vapor actually present in the air (unit of space) at a certain temperature to the amount necessary to saturate the same unit of space under similar conditions. For example, 50 per cent relative humidity means that the space contains one-half the amount of water vapor necessary to saturate it (100 per cent). The lower the relative humidity at a given temperature the more rapidly the air will take up water from the transpiring leaf or from a moist soil surface.

Modifying Influence of Temperature and Wind.—Humidity is affected by temperature, wind, altitude, exposure, cover, and water content of soil. High temperatures increase the capacity of the air for moisture and consequently lower the relative humidity. At low temperatures, the air will hold less moisture and consequently its relative humidity is increased. This accounts for the increased precipitation with altitude on the windward sides of mountain ranges of moderate elevation where the ascending air currents are cooled. For example, in the alpine meadows at the summit of Pike's Peak, 14,100 feet altitude, the annual precipitation is 30 inches. In the subalpine forest at 10,200 feet, it is 25 inches, but decreases to 22 inches in the montane forest at 3,500 feet and to only 15 inches on the treeless plains at the foot of the mountain.

The air in a room 20 by 20 by 10 feet, if completely saturated at 80°F., contains approximately 3 liters of liquid water in the form of vapor. But at 60°F. it could hold only half this amount, and at 0°F. only 0.15 liter. Hence, of two regions, or two habitats with the same rainfall, the warmer is the drier. During the day, the relative humidity falls as the temperature increases and rises in the evening as the air grows cooler. Each change of 1°F. in temperature usually produces a corresponding variation, but in the opposite direction, of 1.5 to over 2 per cent humidity, depending upon the locality.[483] The air may become saturated with water and moisture may be precipitated out as dew even during dry weather if the night temperatures are sufficiently low. With a given amount of water vapor in the air, transpiration from plants and evaporation from the soil are increased with a rise of plant and air temperatures.

Temperature of leaves has a pronounced effect upon rate of water loss.[217,217a]

Wind has a powerful effect upon humidity in that dry winds lower the amount of air moisture by removing the moist air about plants and mixing it with dry air. This has the effect of keeping the immediate humidity low and promoting transpiration.[612]

Since the velocity of the wind increases with the height above the soil surface, trees especially suffer from the drying effects. Low-growing vegetation such as rosette and mat forms are much less affected. Transpiration is often so greatly increased and growth so much retarded on the windward side of trees, that the larger part of the exposed crown is on the

Fig. 169.—Limber pine (*Pinus flexilis*) at timber line on Long's Peak, Colo. Under ordinary conditions this tree grows to a height of 50 feet and has a diameter of 1 to 2 feet (*Photograph by Pool.*)

leeward side. In prairie-planted groves, for example, the drying effect of southwest winds results in the dwarfing or death of the trees on the exposed sides of the grove, the protected trees attaining a much greater height.

The height to which many plants can attain is limited by their ability to absorb and transport water upward rapidly enough to replace that lost through transpiration. On wind-swept coasts and on high mountains, excessive water loss results in a stunted and gnarled growth.[902] This is, however, partly due to the mechanical effect of the wind. The gnarled, sprawling, much-branched, elfin timber grows through the short summer of high altitudes in cold soil from which absorption is difficult and under the drying effect of high winds (Fig. 169). So adverse are the conditions of the environment that trees several hundred years old may be only a few inches in diameter and attain a height of only a few inches or, at most, a few feet. Similarly, in arctic regions, because of winterkilling due to drought, willows, alders, and other woody species, instead of growing erect, develop the sprawling or espalier shape, parts not covered with snow in winter being regularly killed back. Practically all, moreover, of the herbaceous species are long lived and have their resting buds protected near the surface soil. Herbs, too, may form a one-sided growth or take on a prostrate habit, form cushionlike clumps, and, in extreme cases, may be confined to depressions.

The drying effect of winter winds, particularly in late winter when the air is warm but the soil still frozen, often results in winterkilling of

Fig. 170.—Buds of shellbark hickory (*Carya ovata*) in different stages of opening. Note the telescopic expansion of the bud scales which finally drop off.

many trees, shrubs, winter wheat, etc. The chief value of protective coverings to tender growing points, such as the scales of buds, is to keep them from drying out. That freezing does them no harm is evident from the appearance of ice crystals on very cold days. The bud scales are cutinized, suberized, or covered with hairs or resin. In addition to furnishing mechanical protection, they also inhibit rapid freezing and thawing, which are most harmful to plants.[999] Because of telescopic expansion, buds may greatly elongate in spring and thus protect the delicate leaves or flowers within (Fig. 170). Hot, dry winds frequently do much damage to vegetation, especially growing crops, by promoting excessive water loss. Wheat and other crops may ripen prematurely and the yield be greatly reduced. At such times, the temperature is high and the humidity very low. Long-continued, warm, dry winds injure blossoms by evaporating the secretion of the stigmas. In the arid southwest, enormous numbers of cones of evergreen trees die during their first season due to hot, dry winds.

Moist winds exert an opposite influence. Winds that blow across large bodies of water are damp. If constant or frequent, as in certain parts of California, they may permit the growth of mesophytes in an area which would otherwise have a desert vegetation. The distribution of the redwood forests of California is largely controlled by the wind-blown, ocean fogs.[185]

Influence of Pressure and Physiographic Factors.—The view is not uncommon even among meteorologists that pressure influences relative humidity by changing the density of the air and hence its power to hold

Fig. 171.—A sharp ecotone between prairie and forest on a wind-swept slope in eastern Washington. Balsamroot (*Balsamorrhiza*) and xeric grasses are characteristic of the southwest exposures.

moisture. This is erroneous, since the amount of water vapor required to saturate a given space is entirely independent of the pressure of the other gases present and is determined solely by the temperature of the vapor itself. However, low air pressure does increase the rates of evaporation and transpiration through a reduction in the density of the air. But in nature reduced air pressures with altitude are accompanied by low temperatures, which more than offset the effect of reduced pressure on evaporation and transpiration.

Exposure, *i.e.*, the position of a slope with respect to the sun, affects humidity through the action of sun and wind. Slopes longest exposed to the sun's rays receive the most heat; consequently, slopes with a southern exposure regularly show somewhat lower humidities than those with northern exposures. The effect of wind is most pronounced upon those slopes exposed to prevailingly dry winds. As a rule, these are southern or southwestern, and for reasons of both temperature and wind, they are usually the driest slopes of hills and mountains (Fig. 171).

Cover increases humidity by reducing the influence of both temperature and wind. In addition, a living cover supplies moisture to the air in consequence of transpiration from the plants that compose it. Since vegetation is giving off water in large amounts, the relative humidity among and just above the plants is greater than that above bare, dry soil. This increase in relative humidity is one of the community effects of vegetation upon the habitat which permits various species to grow because of the decreased transpiration. Differences are often so marked that they have an effect upon the layering of communities as in reed swamps, permitting species to grow near the soil that could not withstand the drier air above.[1022] The leaves produced by a single species are, moreover, often more xeric in the upper strata. In fact, this is found in most tall-growing plants, for example, cereal crops.[495]

To Determine the Effect of the Surrounding Vegetation upon Humidity and Transpiration.—Secure a cylindrical metal container 5 inches in diameter and 11 inches deep that fits loosely into a slightly larger one with perforated bottom. Place the larger container in the center and on a level with the top of a still larger one that should have an area of at least 1 square foot and a depth of 12 inches (Fig. 172). Fill the latter with potting soil compacted to within an inch of the top. Plant thickly seeds of oats, wheat, or Sudan grass, cover with soil to a suitable depth, and, finally, add a thin mulch of coarse sand or fine gravel. The small, insert container should be filled and seeds planted in a similar manner, after which it should be placed in position in the center of the larger one. Water as necessary but thoroughly the night before the weighings.

On a bright day, when the crop has made a good growth and is at least 6 to 8 inches tall, remove the insert container by the use of two pairs of long-handled pliers and with a minimum of disturbance to the surrounding plants. Weigh it to the nearest half gram and also at the end of each hour throughout the day. During the first hour, place the insert container in a position similar to that which it formerly occupied but away from surrounding plants. During the second hour, place it in the center of the grass community, thus alternating its position hour by hour. Compare the results with those of another student who left his phytometer in the community the first hour.

Plot the hourly losses and consult the hygrothermograph record for temperature and humidity (p. 343) during the experimental period before drawing your conclusions. What is the paramount factor concerned? How is this affected by the two places of exposure? What other physical factors play a part?

Evaporation from the surface of moist soils increases humidity. This is particularly noticeable in forests and thickets where the air is sheltered from the sun and wind. In general, the air near the soil surface is more moist than that near the top of a cover of vegetation.

Effect of Climate and Habitat.—The general humidity of a habitat depends upon climate and location with respect to bodies of water. Forested regions generally have high humidities, while the humidity of deserts is low.   Under the canopy of a tropical rain-forest the humidity may remain between 80 and 100 per cent for weeks;[595] in dry grassland or desert it may regularly fall to 15 per cent or less almost every afternoon.[171] Coastal regions are moist, provided the wind does not blow continuously offshore; inland regions are relatively dry; lowlands are more humid; and tablelands and mountains usually less humid.

In a particular habitat the relative humidity approaches or reaches saturation during a rain or fog and then often gradually diminishes to a minimum just before the next rainstorm.   There is also a daily maximum and minimum.   The highest relative humidity, except when disturbed by

Fig. 172.—Insert phytometers (plant measure) of beans and oats.   The latter has been removed from its case in the center of the larger container.   The surrounding community has a great influence upon the rate of water loss and photosynthesis.   Transpiration is often reduced 30 to over 50 per cent.

cloudy or rainy weather, usually occurs near the time of sunrise, and the minimum from 2 to 4 hours after noon, or the reverse of the hours of the occurrence of the maximum and minimum temperatures.   Variations within the habitat chiefly arise through differences in protection from sun and wind.

Measurement of Humidity.—Humidity is measured by means of a psychrometer (chill measure).   There are three types of psychrometers, the sling, cog, and stationary (Fig. 173).   All consist of a wet-bulb and a dry-bulb thermometer set in a case.   The dry-bulb thermometer is an ordinary thermometer, but the wet bulb is one covered with a clean linen cloth which is moistened with distilled water.   In using the sling or cog psychrometer, the thermometers are whirled about in the air.   The dry-bulb thermometer indicates the normal temperature of the air, the wet-bulb instrument gives the reduced temperature resulting from chilling due to evaporation.

If the air is moist, there is little evaporation; if it is dry, evaporation is rapid and the result is a marked "depression of the wet bulb." Evaporation produces a decrease in temperature depending upon the amount of moisture in the air. Tables have been prepared for almost all possible combinations of air temperatures and wet-bulb depressions, showing the corresponding relative humidities.

For field work, the cog psychrometer is the most convenient and satisfactory. Since the instrument must be moved about in order to

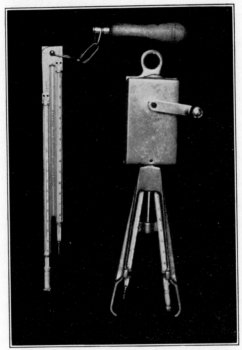

Fig. 173.—Sling and cog psychrometers. The latter is about 14 inches long.

prevent the accumulation of moisture about the wet bulb, the stationary psychrometer is of little value. The sling psychrometer is liable to be broken in using unless there is a space free from vegetation for a distance of 2 yards. The cog psychrometer is smaller, more compact, and the danger of breaking in use or in carriage is extremely small. It has the further advantage of making it possible to take readings among plants and in layers of air only a few centimeters in thickness and in any position. To secure the necessary temperature range, centigrade thermometers are often used and the readings thus obtained converted into Fahrenheit temperatures (by multiplying by 1.8 and adding 32) before the humidity can be determined from the tables.

Making a Reading.—Considerable practice is needed in making an accurate reading.[343] In general, readings should be taken facing the wind and preferably in the shade of the body, although they may be made in full sunshine with but slight error. It is also a wise precaution to shift the position of the instrument a foot or more during the reading, except when the humidity of a definite layer is desired. The cloth of the wet bulb is first moistened with clean water. Distilled water is preferable but tap water and the water from streams may be used without appreciable error if the cloth about the wet bulb is changed occasionally to prevent the accumulation of dissolved material. The water is poured slowly upon the cloth of the bulb until it is completely saturated, the excess shaken off, and care taken not to wet the dry bulb. As the cloth, when perfectly dry, absorbs water slowly, a pipette or a brush is usually a valuable aid in quickly wetting it.

The temperature of the water is of slight consequence, though readings can be made more quickly when the temperature is not too far from that of the air. The psychrometer is held so that the bulbs are in the layer of air to be studied and rotated at an even, moderate rate. As the reading must be made when the mercury of the wet bulb reaches the lowest point, the instrument is usually stopped after 100 revolutions, and the position of the column is noted. The lowest point is often indicated by the tendency of the mercury to remain stationary. As a rule, the lowest point can be known with certainty only when the next glance shows a rise in the column. Check readings of this nature must be made at the end of every 25 to 50 revolutions in order to make sure that the mercury has not reached the minimum and then begun to rise while the instrument is in motion. In noting the final reading, care must be taken to secure it before the mercury begins to rise in consequence of stopping the movement. For this reason, it is desirable to shade the psychrometer with the body when looking at it in the sunshine and to take pains not to breathe upon the bulbs or to bring them too near the body. At the moment when the wet bulb registers the lowest point, the dry bulb should also be read and the results recorded.

Use of Humidity Tables.—To ascertain the humidity, the difference between the wet- and dry-bulb readings is obtained. This difference together with the dry-bulb temperature (in degrees Fahrenheit) is referred to the tables. A variation in temperature has less effect than a variation in difference. In consequence, the dry-bulb reading is expressed in the nearest unit, and the difference is reckoned to the nearest half degree. Measurement of humidity is affected by pressure; it is necessary to use the table computed for the normal barometric pressure of the place under consideration. Humidity tables are usually computed for pressures of 30, 29, 27, 25, and 23 inches. For mountainous regions over

7,000 feet high, additional tables are desirable, but the table of 23 inches will meet all ordinary requirements, since the effect of pressure is small within the usual range of growing-period temperatures.

The Hygrograph.—A continuous record of humidity may be obtained by means of the hygrograph. This consists essentially of strands of human hair about 8 inches long, clamped at both ends. In moist air the hairs become longer, in dry air, shorter. They are attached to a lever in such a manner that a pen which writes on a rotary drum is raised with an increase in humidity and lowered in dry air.

Experience has shown that the hygrograph gives fairly reliable humidity records in dry climates but must be frequently checked in

Fig. 174.—Hygrothermograph and shelter. The hairs regulating the humidity pen are on the left under the protecting shelf; the silvered thermometric bar regulating the temperature pen is on the right. The door of the shelter has been removed.

moist ones where it is exposed to high humidities. This is done by means of a cog psychrometer, and the pen is then adjusted on the drum to show the proper percentage of humidity. The initial adjustment, of course, is made in the same way, the hairs being stretched tighter or loosened by turning the screw supporting the frame upon which they are held.

It is convenient for comparison to record both humidity and air temperature upon the same record sheet. The temperature pen is regulated by means of the expansion and contraction of a silvered thermometric bar exposed to the air. Such an instrument is called a *hygrothermograph* (Fig. 174). The temperature records are thoroughly reliable and the instrument need be checked only once or twice a week. At the end of the week the clock is wound, a new record sheet placed on the drum, and the pens inked. The humidity pen should be filled with the green ink, the one recording temperature with the purple ink. Upon removal of the record, the station and date are recorded. Care should be exercised to see that the pens are set on the line indicating the proper time of day and that they do not interfere in passing each other near the middle of the record sheet. It is best to adjust the instrument at a time when the humidity is not changing too rapidly, *i.e.*, between 10 a.m. and 4 p.m. The pens must be released at the end of the week or they will buckle against the vertical bar which holds the record on the drum.

The hygrothermograph should be properly housed in a well ventilated, waterproof, wooden shelter painted a light green. This should be lined

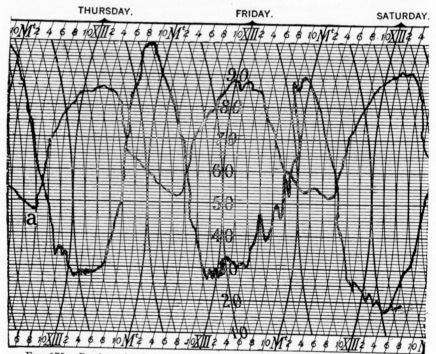

Fig. 175.—Portion of a hygrothermograph record showing the temperature (line *a*) and humidity in the short-grass plains from June 30 to July 2, 1921. At what time was the maximum air temperature reached? Does the lowest humidity occur at about the same time? Why?

with a small-meshed wire screen to prevent the entrance of large insects and furnished with a removable door. The shelter should be of sufficient size to permit the opening of the instrument without its removal and to store the necessary equipment for adjusting the recording devices, *viz.*, psychrometer, small bottle of distilled water, humidity table, camel's-hair brush for dusting the hairs, glycerin inks, and a standardized Fahrenheit thermometer. The shelter, with the floor level, should be fastened firmly in place by means of strong stakes. The door should open to the north, so that the sun cannot shine upon the instrument, and be furnished with a good lock. A double roof with space between is desirable.

Interpreting the Records.—It should be observed that the hygrothermograph records are ruled in two arcs corresponding with those described by the temperature and humidity pens, respectively. The time of day for the temperature pen (XII indicating noon and M midnight) in 2-hour intervals is indicated at the top of the record sheet, that for humidity at the bottom. The numbers on the horizontal lines ranging from 10 to 100 indicate both percentage of humidity and degrees Fahrenheit. Thus, in Fig. 175, the humidity at 4 p.m., June 30, was 28 per cent and the temperature 85°F. The next morning at 4 a.m. when the temperature had fallen to 53°F., the humidity was 100 per cent.

Constructing Graphs.—Where it is desired to obtain the average daily humidity (or temperature) by weeks, this may be done as follows: Add the humidity at the 2-hour intervals for the entire week and divide by the total number of intervals. If it is desired to ascertain the average day humidity, which is of most importance to vegetation, add all of the 2-hour readings beginning at 6 or 8 a.m. (according to the season) to 6 p.m. inclusive, continuing for the 7 days, and divide by the tota¹ number of readings. From these data, graphs similar to those in Fig. 179 may be constructed, and the humidity (or temperature) of different communities compared.

Periods of low relative humidity are very trying for vegetation, since they almost invariably occur at times when water content is also low. The weekly record should be given careful study since such periods are usually more important than the averages. During times of protracted low water content and low humidities, some types of vegetation remain dormant. These are also periods of great forest inflammability.[343]

To Measure Relative Humidity.—With the cooperation of two or more other students, make simultaneous readings every half hour of the relative humidity in several adjacent stations such as thicket, woodland, prairie, or swamp. Plot the results in the form of graphs. Also, make readings at the same station at different levels. Operate a hygrothermograph on a lawn, in a grove, or in other vegetation where the instrument may be observed and frequently checked. If possible, secure two instruments and compare the humidity and temperature in two different habitats.

Vapor Pressure Deficit.—The pressure exerted by a gas or vapor is determined by its amount in a unit volume of space and by the temperature. Vapor pressure deficit is the difference between the pressure exerted by the water vapor actually present in the atmosphere at a given time and a given temperature and the pressure that would be exerted if the space were saturated with water vapor at the same temperature. The difference in pressure is expressed in millimeters or inches of mercury. A relative humidity of 100 per cent at 20°C. corresponds to a vapor pressure of 17.55 millimeters of mercury. This multiplied by 0.60 (the humidity expressed as a percentage) gives a vapor pressure of 10.53 millimeters. The vapor pressure deficit is the difference between 17.55 (the maximum vapor pressure at 20°C.) and 10.53 millimeters (the actual vapor pressure) or 7.02 millimeters. Tables of pressure of saturated aqueous vapor may be found in the Smithsonian Physical Tables.[293]

The vapor pressure deficit may also be defined as the difference between the saturation vapor pressure for the current temperature (dry bulb) and the saturation pressure for the temperature of the current dew point, *i.e.*, temperature necessary to induce condensation of water vapor. Hence, the tables of vapor pressure and dew point of the psychrometric tables may be used for its calculation. Here the pressure is expressed in inches of mercury. For example, if the depression of the wet bulb at 70°F. is 5°, the dew point is at 62°F., *i.e.*, the air must be cooled to 62°F. before it becomes saturated. Saturation pressure at 70°F. is 0.732 inch, but at 62°F. it is only 0.555 inch. Hence the vapor pressure deficit or the difference between these two figures is 0.177 inch.

In spite of current views, vapor pressure deficit or saturation deficit does not bear a direct causal relation to evaporation or transpiration. This is actually determined by the difference or gradient between the vapor pressure of the evaporating surface and that of the air above it. The frequent correspondence between saturation deficit and evaporation is due in part to the relation between the gradient at the evaporating surface and the deficit in the surrounding atmosphere. Under normal conditions, the temperature of water or leaf surface may differ little or but briefly from that of the air, and the saturation deficit then becomes a fair index of evaporation opportunity.

WIND

The effect of wind in modifying humidity has been discussed; its mechanical and erosive effects will now be considered.[280,572] Because of the friction of the soil surface and masses of vegetation, the velocity and, hence, the pressure exerted by the wind rapidly increase with height. This explains the greater velocity attained on exposed seacoasts and at higher altitudes that are free from or above the obstructions created by masses of vegetation. By its strength, wind may destroy large areas of timber and do much damage by blowing down crops. Often, only branches or twigs are broken or leaves (*e.g.*, wheat, corn, etc.) torn by wind whipping. The actual pressure exerted by the wind depends upon the character and dimensions of the surface as well as the density of the air. At sea level, a wind with a velocity of 10 miles per hour exerts a pressure of approximately ⅓ pound per square foot; at 30 miles, this is increased to about 2.5 pounds; but over 9 pounds pressure per square foot is exerted at a velocity of 60 miles.[860] Even higher velocities and pressures occur, especially on mountain tops. By its persistence, it causes permanent curvatures and malformations of plants upon which it impinges.

Wind-driven dust, snow, and hail exercise a marked abrasive effect upon vegetation, sometimes to the extent of wearing away the bark of trees or shrubs in wind-swept areas. The blowing of soil is an ever present menace during the spring months in the Great Plains and many other regions. The surface of whole fields is blown away and the soil deposited on others. In both the process of erosion and of deposit, the crop may be destroyed.[141,417] Even clay soil may be loosened and transported. In muck land, damage is often great, the light, organic materials being readily removed unless the soil is kept damp or protected from the wind.[372] Blowing of soil often reaches its maximum in sand where destructive "blowouts" occur, and valuable forests are sometimes covered by dunes.[509,777]

The wind may do much harm in blowing fruits or blossoms from trees or other plants and by preventing insects from working among the flowers. It is an important agent in the distribution of weeds and spores of many disease-producing fungi, such as rusts and chestnut blight. By means of whirlwinds, heat waves, and convection currents, spores are carried high into the air and over long distances. Viable spores have been caught at heights of more than 11,000 feet.[597,877] Warm winds may hasten the melting of snow, particularly in open fields, resulting in accelerated runoff, especially if the soil is frozen, and consequent floods. Conversely, the wind has a beneficial effect in drying the soil in spring and in equalizing temperature on the leeward sides of large bodies of water. By mixing the cold and warm air, wind sometimes prevents frost damage on cold, clear nights. The warm, dry, chinook winds of mountainous regions, particularly marked in Montana and Wyoming, cause the snow to evaporate very rapidly and leave the ranges available for winter grazing.

Effect upon Transpiration.—Although the depressing effect of wind upon plants has long been recognized, very few measurements of a quantitative nature have been made.[71,280] Recent studies have shown the effect of continuous wind velocities of 5, 10, and 15 miles per hour on the transpiration of sunflowers where an optimum water content of the soil was constantly maintained.[572] The rate of transpiration, after the first week, increased with increasing wind velocity. At the end of 6 to 7 weeks the three lots of plants were using water at rates about 20, 35, and 50 per cent, respectively, higher per unit area of leaf surface than control plants grown in still air. There was a decrease in leaf area and in height and diameter of stem with increasing wind velocity. The dry weight was reduced one-half to two-thirds under a velocity of 15 miles per hour. The water requirement increased, the maximum increment observed being about 50 per cent under the highest wind velocity. Plants grown under high wind velocities showed the gnarled and twisted appearance characteristic of trees growing in windy habitats. Even a wind velocity of 2 miles per hour, when occurring intermittently at intervals of several hours, increased the transpiration rate 20 to 30 per cent. Higher velocities resulted in greater initial losses, often an increase of 78 to 138 per cent, but these high losses were not maintained. Wind had the same relative effect at night as during the day, causing approximately the same percentage increase in the transpiration rate.

Modifying Wind Movement.—The force of the wind may be modified in a number of ways, *viz.*, by windbreaks, by sowing grain in furrows,

Fig. 176.—A cottonwood grove forming a windbreak. Corn within a few rods north of the windbreak is badly damaged by shade and reduced water content. (*After Bates.*)

and especially by "strip planting," etc.[471] Strip planting consists of growing various crops, *e.g.*, corn, wheat, sorghum, or native hay, in alternate, long, narrow strips at right angles to the prevailing wind.[417] This reduces the wind effect, since at all times a part of the soil in the field is protected by a cover of vegetation.[808] In dry lands the method of seeding the grain in furrows somewhat deeper and farther apart than those made by the ordinary wheat drill has many advantages. Not only does it promote better and more certain germination when the surface soil is dry, but the furrows also retain the snow, which otherwise might be blown from the field, and give better protection to the grain during times of low temperatures and high winds. There is, moreover, less injury from the heaving of the soil as a result of alternate thawing and freezing in spring and less injury from soil blowing and from drought.[765]

A difficulty, however, is the occasional filling of the furrows with drifting soil. The modifying action of windbreaks and shelter belts on wind has already been discussed (p. 252)[79] (Fig. 176).

The way in which man may modify the local environment, even of a desert, is well illustrated in certain irrigated orchards in California, which have been planted to alfalfa and shielded by an efficient windbreak. Factor measurements made in such orchards and in the desert to windward show that the climatic complex is greatly ameliorated. The

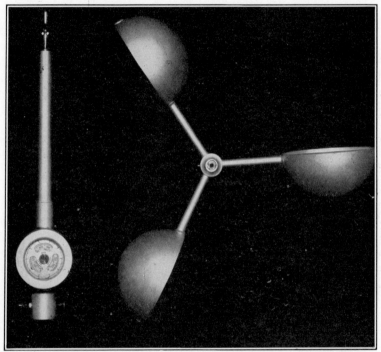

FIG. 177.—Weather-Bureau type of anemometer. The cups have been detached from the top of the stem by loosening the setscrew.

alfalfa transpires at a tremendous rate and literally bathes the trees in a moist atmosphere. The windbreak retards the movement of the relatively moist air away from the vicinity. The evaporation of the water from the soil and plants tends to lower the temperature of the air. As the soil is largely shaded, the high soil temperatures are also reduced.

Measuring Wind Movement.—Wind movement is measured by a rotating anemometer (wind measure), as shown in Fig. 177. The standard Weather-Bureau anemometer is the most practical for field work, although the simple form of hand anemometer is useful in ascertaining the effects of cover. The latter records wind movement in feet per minute. The standard anemometer is practically a self-recording instrument, the wind movement being registered up to 990 miles, but as the dials run on without any indication of the total number of revolutions, it should be visited and read each day. Directions for reading the dials (to 0.1 mile) accompany the instrument.

The anemometer is securely fastened by means of a thumbscrew to a stake driven vertically into the ground. Readings are ordinarily taken with the revolving cups at the general level of the vegetation. Care should be exercised that their movement is not retarded by contact with the growing plants. It is sometimes necessary to dig a pit for the stem of the anemometer in order that the cups may be at the same height as that of low-growing vegetation. For comparative readings, two or more instruments should be operated at different heights and long-time readings of wind movement obtained from different plant communities. The data are recorded as miles of wind movement per hour.[447]

To Measure Wind Movement.—Secure two anemometers of the Weather-Bureau type. Operate them at different levels in various plant communities during a period of 1 or more days (*e.g.*, in prairie just at the height of the vegetation and 3 feet above). Also, compare the wind movement at the same level in different plant communities. By means of hand anemometers make simultaneous readings of wind movement in a field of grain, clover, meadow, etc., below the level of the vegetation and just above it.

EVAPORATION

A knowledge of the humidity, wind movement, air temperature, and sunshine of a habitat throws much light upon the environment in which plants grow and vegetation develops. The desiccating power or "evaporation stress" of the atmosphere as affected by all of these factors is of great importance to plants. Much emphasis has been laid upon the water content of soil as directly determining the character of vegetation and its rate of development. Of almost equal importance is the loss through transpiration of moisture that is absorbed. The evaporation rate, when measured directly, gives the integrated effect of humidity, radiant energy (*i.e.*, temperature and light), and wind. While there is no instrument that integrates the effect of these different stimuli to water loss in a manner similar to that of plants, yet this objective has been attained to some extent. Indeed, different plants, because of differences in stomatal movement, density of cell sap, colloidal content of cells, incipient drying, etc., respond differently. Nevertheless, the process of evaporation from a suitable evaporating surface (*e.g.*, porous clay cup) is closely similar to that from a plant body. The readings of the loss of water from atmometers (vapor measure) placed at the general level of the transpiring vegetation in different habitats give one of the most useful records of the evaporation stress of the air as it affects the surrounding vegetation.

Measurement of Evaporation.—Evaporation is measured in a number of ways. At many state and federal experiment stations the rate of water loss in inches is determined for the 6 summer months (April to September) from large open tanks.[96] These circular tanks of galvanized iron are 8 feet in diameter and 2 feet deep. They are set 20 inches deep in the soil and filled with water to within 4 inches of the top. The amount of water evaporated is determined by means of a gage, corrections being

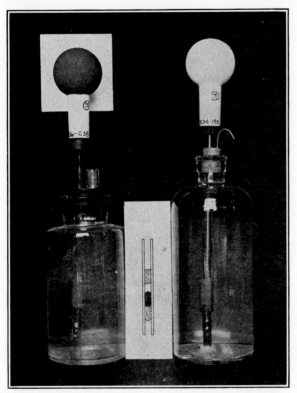

Fig. 178.—Porous-cup atmometers. The nonabsorbing device with wool plugs and mercury trap is shown in the center.

made for precipitation during the interval between readings. The rate of evaporation from water in a tank is about the same as from a wet soil surface, although it is greater from the latter where the soil is dark in color. Many valuable data have thus been obtained for broad climatological studies, but obviously such a method is quite impracticable for measuring evaporation in different plant communities.

The evaporimeters most widely used are the porous, clay-cup atmometers devised by Livingston. These are either cylindrical or spherical in shape and white or black in color (Fig. 178). The cups are made of a very fine grade of clay. The lower part is waterproofed with varnish or shellac and the evaporating surface thus reduced to a definite area. The porous surface should never be handled, since the pores will become clogged with oil or dirt.

In operating, the cup is first filled with distilled water and allowed to stand for a short time until the clay walls have become saturated. It is then again filled and stoppered tightly with a rubber cork through which a glass tube extends. The excess water is forced into the tube. The apparatus is quickly inverted and the second cork on the tube (which must be full of water) inserted into the supply bottle, air bubbles being excluded. The latter should contain about a liter of distilled water. As the water evaporates from the outer surface of the cup, it is supplied by the rise of fresh water from the bottle, so that the cup is always full. A curved brass tube with a capillary bore through the bottle stopper permits the equalization of the air pressure without permitting the exit or entry of water. The bottle is filled to a file scratch on the neck, and the loss of water is determined by the number of cubic centimeters used in refilling it.

Spherical cups have the advantage of always exposing half of their surface directly to the sun regardless of its altitude. The black cups absorb more radiant energy than the white ones and consequently give higher evaporation losses during the day. In fact, the differences in the losses from the white and black cups exposed in the same place have been used as a measure of radiant energy (light).[116] The losses from one kind of cup or other evaporating system cannot be directly compared with those from another.[538] Spherical cups are widely used.

Obviously, if the atmometer cup permits of evaporation, it will also absorb water during rain. To prevent its doing the latter, numerous nonabsorbing devices have been made (Fig. 178). These consist of mercury traps so arranged that while water may be drawn into the cup, its movement in the reverse direction is prevented. Nonabsorbing mountings, although absolutely necessary for reliable field readings, somewhat complicate the apparatus. In the simplest form, a twisted wool plug is inserted into one end of the tube, about a centimeter of mercury placed above it, and a second plug put in place at the opposite end. Water is sucked into the tube and the plugs well soaked. The rubber stopper, through which the tube extends, is then forced into the inverted, water-filled atmometer in the usual manner. The valve may be built in a separate glass tube and attached to the supply tube.

Owing to the variations in the clay in the cups, different atmometers give different evaporation losses per unit of surface. But every cup is standardized by comparison with a standard cup whose rate of evaporation under certain uniform conditions is known. Each cup bears a number and a coefficient. By multiplying the actual loss from the cup during a given period by its coefficient, the loss from the standard cup, had it been used, is obtained. For example, cup 947, coefficient 0.70, evaporated 140 cubic centimeters. The corrected loss is 98 cubic centimeters. Thus, evaporation rates from widely different habitats or countries may be directly compared.[300,963]

To prevent the pores of the cup from becoming filled with impurities, especially lime, only distilled water should be used. Rinsing occasionally with weak corrosive sublimate prevents the growth of algae, bacteria, and fungi. The cups may also be cleaned from time to time with a stiff toothbrush and distilled water. If these precautions are taken, the rate of water loss from the cup under identical conditions varies but little. After a few weeks' use, however, they should be restandardized.[538]

Making Readings.—For hourly readings or those for shorter intervals, the cups may be mounted on small graduates, corrections being made for the space occupied by the glass tube.[784] In field practice, readings are made daily or weekly. Evaporation rates are measured for the purpose of determining how great an evaporation stress the plant or vegetation has to withstand and can withstand without injury. Critical periods are sometimes brought about by high evaporation stress when water content is abundant, but usually they occur and are most harmful when it is very low. Careful attention should be given evaporation readings during such periods; they may be obscured in the average weekly record. Evaporation records are of less significance, moreover, at a time when vegetation is dormant, whether as a result of drought or of cold.[540] For example, evaporation losses are usually highest in the short-grass disclimax at a time when the dominant grasses (*Buchloe, Bouteloua*, etc.) have dried and cured on the ground.

Position in the Field.—The exact position of the atmometer in the field is determined by the object in view. If this is to ascertain the evaporation losses about seedlings on the forest floor, the cups should be placed at the same height as the transpiring seedlings. Fully grown undershrubs are transpiring at a different level, and the tops of the crowns of trees are subject to a much greater evaporation stress. In swamps, for example, the evaporation rate rapidly increases with height. It may vary from 100 per cent at the level of the highest vegetation to 30 per cent at half this height and fall to only 7 per cent near the wet soil surface. Thus, evaporation gives a direct clue to layering of vegetation.[321,1022]

Many plants as well as soft-bodied insects are confined to the lower layer, although the latter frequently move to higher levels at night or on cloudy days when the evaporation stress is decreased. Consequently, the atmometer should be placed at the level where the evaporation rate is to be determined. In grassland, it is the rule to place the cups at the general level of the mass of vegetation, none of which is allowed to touch the cups. Usually, it is necessary to excavate a hole in the soil to receive the bottle. This should be done with a minimum of disturbance to the vegetation, and to prevent caving, it should be lined with a cylinder of light, galvanized iron sunk flush with the soil.

Comparison of Data.—Readings at the several stations should be made as nearly at the same time of day as practicable and in the same sequence. The corrected readings from the various habitats or partial habitats may then be directly compared. If they are taken at regular

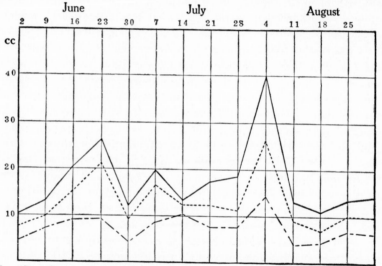

Fig. 179.—Graphs showing the average daily evaporation by weeks in prairie (upper line), hazelnut thicket (middle), and linden forest, in southeastern Nebraska during 1917.

intervals over a considerable period of time, comparison is best made by means of a series of graphs, as shown in Fig. 179.

To Measure Evaporation.—Equip atmometers with nonabsorbing devices and measure the evaporation losses at the same level in two or more plant communities. Also, compare the relative rates of evaporation in the same community, and preferably in one that shows well marked layers, at different heights above the soil surface. What is the order of importance of the several factors that influence evaporation? Give reasons for this.

Evaporation and Plant Distribution.—The rate of evaporation has a marked influence not only on the amount of the water lost from plants through transpiration but also in reducing the water content of the soil. The latter is an important feature, especially in dry regions. Evaporation determines the efficiency of rainfall in a great measure, especially where the rainfall is less than 30 inches annually.

In Montana, where evaporation is low, 14 inches of precipitation are sufficient to support a good growth of short grasses; 17 inches are required in Colorado; and 21 inches in Texas. Evaporation from the large, open tank in Montana during the 6 summer months is 33 inches, but it is 54 inches in northwestern Texas. The extra 7 inches of precipitation are needed to counteract the higher evaporation rate in Texas. Similarly, the rate of evaporation increases from about 30 inches in North Dakota to 60 inches in southwestern Kansas. Since it requires nearly 10 inches of rainfall to offset the extra 30 inches of evaporation, it is apparent why under 20 inches of rainfall in North Dakota the true prairie is well developed and excellent crops of spring wheat are grown, while under a similar rainfall in western Kansas mixed-prairie vegetation thrives and only the most drought-enduring crops such as kaffir and milo are cultivated. Thus, the lines of equivalent rainfall, because of the factor of evaporation, extend much farther eastward than do those of actual rainfall.[96] During a single year, evaporation may lower a reservoir of water only 15 inches in Ontario, but 8 feet in California, and even 12 feet in Egypt.[288]

The effect of the rate of evaporation upon transpiration alone is marked. It requires only 518 tons of water to produce a ton of alfalfa near the Canadian line at Williston, N. D.; 853 tons at Akron in eastern Colorado; but 1,005 tons are required at Dalhart in the Panhandle of Texas.[101] During the years 1911 and 1913, the average water requirement (*i.e.*, the pounds of water used to produce a pound of dry matter) of 25 varieties of crops grown at Akron, Colo., was approximately 21 per cent greater than during 1912. This was due almost entirely to a decrease of 25 per cent in the evaporation rate in 1912, resulting from decreased solar radiation caused by fine volcanic dust in the upper air from Mt. Katmai, Alaska.[98,243]

The ratio of precipitation to evaporation gives the nearest approach that is yet possible toward an ideal index of the external moisture relations of plants.[541] The rainfall-evaporation ratio at Lincoln, Neb., is approximately 60 per cent. The line with this ratio extends northwestward across the Dakotas and nearly straight southward into Texas. In general, the drier types of grassland lie between lines with ratios of 60 and 20 per cent. The desert has a lower ratio. Between 60 and 80 to 85 per cent, the true prairie abounds; eastward where the ratio is greater than 100, *i.e.*, where rainfall exceeds evaporation, continuous forests occur.[933] Unfortunately, evaporation data over North America as a whole are very meager, and the preceding data apply only to the conditions during a single year. Were evaporation data available in quantity similar to that of precipitation, a much clearer picture of the water relations in connection with plant distribution would be possible.

CHAPTER XIII

TEMPERATURE

Temperature is like water in its action upon plants in that it has more or less to do with nearly every function, but as a working condition and not as a material. All the chemical processes of metabolism and also many physical processes such as diffusion, precipitation, and coagulation as in cell-wall formation, etc., are dependent upon temperature and accelerated by its increase up to an optimum.[646] With a decrease in temperature to a certain minimum, growth in size is retarded; at lower temperatures, cell division and photosynthesis are also checked; and, at a still lower minimum, respiration ceases and death ensues. Thus, temperature is not only necessary for life processes but also furnishes the energy for some of them. Radiant energy, for example, is absorbed in photosynthesis and set free in respiration.

The responses to the stimulus of temperature are not localized in a particular organ but occur everywhere in the protoplasm throughout the living tissues. Temperature has no direct formative effect on the structure of the plant, except in so far as it affects the rate of growth. It does, however, have a profound influence in altering not only the rate but also the products of metabolism. At low temperatures, for example, many plants elaborate an abundance of polysaccharides.

The habitat plays an important part in determining the influence of temperature upon each species. A particular species has been accustomed for countless generations to certain extremes of heat and cold as well as to certain seasonal sums of temperature. Temperatures beyond these extremes check the plant's activity and this is usually true of the total heat available during the growing period.[671] These temperature adjustments become so deeply impressed in the protoplasm of a species that there results a more or less fixed habit as regards temperature. Thus, in temperate regions, for example in deciduous forests, low temperatures of winter become a necessary experience to the trees. It is a phase of the environment to be endured and, also, a necessary means of stimulating developmental vigor. Winter is not a recurrent catastrophe to vegetation but a stimulus to renewed growth. The effect of habitat is well shown by many seeds, bulbs, corms, tubers, buds, etc., which are merely plantlets or growing points securely protected against drought. They have accommodated themselves to a long period of cold, in consequence of which it is often impossible to cause them to grow without either naturally or artificially subjecting them to cold[200,233,235] (Fig. 180).

In connection with germination, temperature has a marked influence upon ecesis;[375] it greatly modifies growth; and in the opening and closing of flowers and flower heads it has a direct effect upon reproduction.[806] Consequently, it not only has an effect upon the individual but also upon the development of vegetation as well.

Measurement of Temperature.— With the aid of a thermometer, the measurement of temperature is an easy task. In determining the temperature of the air, direct or reflected sunlight must be excluded from the thermometer as fully as possible. The thermometers should be standardized instruments, reading accurately at least to 1 degree, since the errors in cheap thermometers are not uncommonly as great as the differences between two conditions that are being studied. As these are both delicate and expensive, they must be used with great care, particularly in the field. To prevent breakage, they should be carried in felt-lined, individual brass cases. In making readings of air temperature, precautions are necessary to expose the bulb to the full effect of the wind, if any, and to keep it away from the hand or body. The instrument must be left in position until the mercury becomes stationary. In some cases, as when the wind blows fitfully, the mercury

Fig. 180.—Two branches from a Persian lilac (left) that wintered out of doors except the ends of the branches which were admitted through an opening into a greenhouse. On the right are two branches from a lilac wintering in a greenhouse, except the ends of the branches which extended outside. Photograph made on March 1, 3 weeks after all parts of both plants were placed in the greenhouse. Note that only rarely has a bud opened except on the parts of the stems that have been chilled.

constantly rises and falls. The mean of the fluctuation is taken as the proper reading. Temperature readings in the surface of the soil are made with the bulb just covered with soil; these should be supplemented by a reading on the surface.[121]

Since temperature is an extremely variable factor, isolated readings are of little value, and it is best to use automatic thermometers or thermographs. Maximum and minimum thermometers may be used to record the extreme temperatures during day and night.[672,931] The maximum is a mercurial thermometer with a constriction in the tube just above the bulb; this allows the mercury to pass out as it expands but prevents it from running back, thus registering the maximum temperature. The minimum thermometer contains alcohol. The column carries a tiny dumbbell-shaped marker which moves down with it but will not rise as the liquid expands. This is due to the fact that the liquid expands too slowly to carry the marker upward, while the surface tension causes it to be drawn downward as the alcohol contracts. The thermometers are mounted in an oblique position. The mercury of the maximum thermometer is driven back into the bulb by rapid whirling and the thermometer then placed with the bulb slightly elevated. The minimum thermometer is set for registering by raising the free (lower) end so that the marker runs to the end of the column and is then placed in a level position.

These thermometers should be exposed in an appropriate shelter which must not absorb radiant energy sufficiently to become heated within. This danger is largely overcome by the use of a double roof, a partly open floor, and walls made of slats which sufficiently overlap to exclude overhead light but not enough to retard the free circulation of air.[343]

To Determine Maximum and Minimum Temperatures.—Place properly sheltered maximum and minimum thermometers in each of two communities, preferably in early spring or late fall. Obtain and compare the highest and lowest temperatures during a period of several days. Also, determine the minimum temperatures in valleys or depressions and on adjacent hilltops or benchlands (p. 366). Explain the differences obtained in the two sites.

Obviously, the most valuable record of temperature is a continuous one, such as is obtained by means of a thermograph. This should be set up and appropriately housed in the field, preferably two or more being simultaneously operated in different habitats. For a comprehensive study of a layered plant community, such as a forest, more than one will be required, for temperatures and temperature variations of different layers may be widely different. A study of the thermograph records will reveal many things not shown by the maximum and minimum readings. It will show not only when the high and low temperatures occur but also how long they persist. The time relation is an extremely important one. In open thickets or woodland, for example, the sun may shine directly upon the shade plants and so increase their temperature and promote transpiration as to cause them to droop. Because of little air movement, a high temperature is attained. But soon the plants are again in the shade and absorption overtakes water loss. Were the high temperatures and consequently decreased humidity maintained, these mesophytes might succumb.

The greater number of species and of individuals pass through their entire life cycle without being exposed to extreme heat or cold. Extremes of temperature have little significance for them. Low-temperature effects are confined to plants that appear very early in the growing period and those that linger toward the close. Notwithstanding the fundamental relation of temperature to plant metabolism and its general controlling influence on growth, in developmental communities at least, the measurement of temperatures is not of primary importance. The water content of soil, humidity, and light are usually the decisive factors in determining the relation of a community to neighboring ones. Each community usually exists well within the temperature limits that might be critical for it, and the indirect effect of temperature on humidity and evaporation is nearly always of greatest importance.

Temperature Records.—Mean annual temperatures are of practically no value in a study of vegetation, because they take no account of season. The mean annual temperature in certain parts of Siberia is $-15°C$. This is very much below the minimum at which any vegetation could grow, yet here is a forested region. The summer is short but hot. Not only are the forest trees able to grow and mature seed but also a luxuriant herbaceous vegetation abounds.

Monthly means are much more significant in conveying an idea of the temperature relations, and the monthly mean maxima and minima are the most useful temperature data published by meteorological stations. Maximum and minimum temperatures are very important factors in the development of vegetation, since plants and particularly cultivated crops may be damaged by a few hours of excessive heat or killed by a brief period of low (usually freezing) temperatures. Weekly means are more valuable than monthly means in studying the relation between temperature and plant growth. Most valuable of all, however, are the daily temperature records. This is true particularly of the occurrence and duration of high or low temperatures during the early and late portions of the growing season, as well as at times of extremes throughout the whole growing period. Together with a record of humidity, they are of the highest value in the study of environment. They can be had only by securing a continuous record during the successive days by means of a hygrothermograph.

The mean temperature for the day is approximated, where minimum and maximum thermometers only are used, by averaging the two readings. Where a thermograph is employed, a nearer approach to the true mean may be obtained from the sum of the hourly temperatures divided by 24. It is sufficiently accurate to average the readings of the even hours. The average day and night temperatures for weekly periods may also be determined. These may be plotted in the usual way for comparing the temperatures in different habitats or in different strata of the same habitat. The daily maximum and daily minimum for weekly periods may be similarly compared. Mean maximum and mean minimum temperatures are often more important to vegetation than the mean daily temperatures because they represent more clearly the actual range of temperatures that plants experience.[904]

Plant Temperatures.—The temperature of the plant tends to follow closely that of its environment.[541] Unlike warm-blooded animals, plants do not possess temperatures that are independent of the surrounding medium. In general, stems or leaves are rarely very much warmer or cooler than the air that surrounds them and roots can seldom possess a temperature very different from that of the soil.[607] Certain plant activities, notably respiration, bring about an evolution of heat. But, since respiration is vigorous only at relatively high temperatures and the rate decreases with a lowering of temperature, the amount of heat produced is little when an increase in temperature may be most needed. Even when vital processes are most vigorous, a marked rise in temperature is prevented by outward conduction and radiation.[105, 217] Similarly, any considerable decrease in the temperature of the tissue is automatically adjusted by intake of heat from without.[51]

There are exceptions to the rule, however, that are worthy of mention.[485] Temperature of the plant, especially that of stems and leaves, may be 10 to 15°C. higher than that of the air.[175, 858] In case of a sudden change in temperature, the plant responds more slowly than the air, and its temperature is for a time higher or lower. This is due to the abundance of water and its high specific heat. The plant lags in the change in proportion to its mass and surface. This is well illustrated in certain cacti where they are unharmed by a few hours of freezing temperatures but are killed by a longer exposure, for example, 19 hours in the giant cactus (*Carnegiea gigantea*).[333]

In winter, under direct sunshine, differences as great as 25°C. occur on the south and north sides of tree trunks just beneath the bark. Every cloud obscuring the sun for a few minutes will cause the bark to freeze if the air temperature is sufficiently low. With the passing of the cloud, the cambium may warm up above its freezing point within a few minutes. Changes of 10°C. sometimes occur within a period of 3 minutes. The high temperature, accompanied by rapid evaporation during the day, falls rapidly after sunset. The pronounced change may cause the death of the tissue next to the wood and the subsequent peeling of the bark. These internal temperature fluctuations are important on account of their relation to sunscald, crotch injury, frost cracks, etc., found among trees of northern climates. They result in openings that afford entrance to wood-rotting fungi. In spring, the higher temperatures of the sunny side may result in a decrease in hardiness of the tissue exposed to the sun, with a break in dormancy and attendant injury upon sudden freezing. Temperature changes under light-colored bark such as that of birch, poplar, etc., are much less marked than under dark-colored bark, and whitewashing fruit trees is a common method of reducing or preventing sunscald.[387]

The internal temperature of pine needles in sunshine and in still air during winter has been found to be as much as 18°F. higher than that of the surrounding air.[258] Many buds and densely hairy leaves are examples of aerial parts that exhibit considerable influence in retarding the transmission of heat because of the nature and condition of their surfaces. Rough surfaces absorb and radiate a greater proportion of energy rays than do smooth ones. The color is highly important, red leaves, for example, absorbing more heat than green ones and the white portions of variegated leaves least of all.

The heating effect of direct sunshine upon green leaves is limited not only by the loss of heat by conduction and radiation but also by the cooling effect of transpiration. Even in intense sunshine the temperature of turgid, rapidly transpiring leaves may be as low as that of the surrounding air.[175,607] The cooling effect of transpiration may be shown by comparing the temperatures of vigorously transpiring leaves with those of dead ones. This lowering of temperature commonly amounts to 3.5 to 9°F.[217]

In taking the internal temperatures of plants, such as thick stems, roots, large buds, or other bulky parts, a thermometer with a small, flat bulb is useful. A small slit is cut or a hole made with a small cork borer and the bulb sunk into the tissues. Temperature readings are less easily obtained in the case of ordinary leaves. Approximate differences in temperature between air and leaf may be made by rolling the leaf while in position tightly about the thermometer bulb. But for exact readings, thermoelectric methods for the determination of leaf temperatures must be used.[606] Further study of plant temperatures is needed.

To Compare the Temperature of Plants with That of the Surrounding Air.—Bore a small hole in the stem of a cactus, leaf of agave, bud of horse-chestnut, potato tuber, or other bulky plant part. Insert a small thermometer with flattened bulb that is only about 2 millimeters wide and 1 millimeter thick. Determine the temperature of the plant part and that of the surrounding air. Remove the plant (or part) to a very much colder or warmer place and ascertain how long a period of time is required for the living organ to take on the temperature of the air. Do fleshy roots have the same temperature as the surrounding soil? What are the causes for the difference between plant and air or soil temperatures?

Bore a hole, just large enough to receive the bulb of the thermometer, tangentially under the bark of a tree on both the sunny and the shady side. Carefully insert the thermometers and seal them in place with modeling clay. What differences do you find in temperature? Why? Compare that of trees with light- and dark-colored bark of about the same thickness, *e.g.*, birch and cherry.

Variations in Temperature.—As in the case of light, there is a daily and an annual fluctuation in temperature. The amount of heat received depends upon the angle of the sun's rays and their consequent absorption. The actual temperatures at the surface of the earth are greatly modified by radiation, conduction, and convection. In consequence, the maximum daily temperature does not occur at noon "sun time," as in the case of light, but somewhat later, often about 2 to 3 p.m. The minimum is not reached at nightfall, but just before sunrise upon the following morning. The maximum temperatures for the year do not occur at the June solstice, but a month or two later. Similarly, the minimum falls a month or more after the December solstice.

Variation of temperature occurs with changes in latitude and altitude. High latitudes receive the sun's rays at a greater angle than equatorial ones, and the absorption of heat by the atmosphere is correspondingly greater, thus leaving less for the soil surface. In so far as absorption is concerned, high mountains receive more heat than lowlands. The loss by radiation, however, is so much greater that mountainous regions are uniformly colder than plains or lowlands lying on the same parallel. This is due to the rarity of the air, which allows heat to pass through it readily. Although the air on mountain tops is colder than that of the plains, the surface temperature of the soil is often considerably higher. On Pike's Peak the surface of the soil may show a temperature of 140°F. while the air 5 feet above is 70°F. and the soil 10 inches below the surface 55°F. This difference, however, is far overbalanced by the rapid radiation at night.

Temperature also varies with the slope. This is due to the fact that a square decimeter of sunshine covers this amount of surface only when the rays strike at right angles. As the angle diminishes, the rays are spread over more and more surface until at an angle of 10° a square decimeter receives but 17 per cent as much heat as at 90°. This has more effect upon soil temperature, humidity, etc., than on the plants directly, owing to the fact that stems and leaves have the same position upon a slope that they do upon the level. Furthermore, temperature differs at various levels in the air and the soil. Air and soil temperatures naturally affect each other. The highest temperatures are usually found between the two, *i.e.*, at the surface of the soil. In summer, the temperature rapidly decreases in both directions. In the air, this is due to the fact that radiation becomes imperceptible a short distance above the ground, while the influence of the wind becomes more and more noticeable. Heat penetrates the soil slowly, either on account of poor conductivity or because of the great capacity of the water for latent heat. The air is ordinarily warmer in the daytime than the soil, especially on sunny days. It loses heat more rapidly, however, and after a sudden decrease in temperature or at night the soil is usually for a time warmer than the air.

Influence of Other Factors.—Many factors exert a marked influence upon temperature, among which clouds and wind are, perhaps, most important. During the day, clouds reflect a considerable portion of the insolation from their upper surface, and, consequently, the temperature at the surface of the earth is decreased. At night clouds intercept heat radiated from the earth and, in consequence, the temperature of the surface soil and the air in contact with it is lowered but little. Hence, in

Fig. 181.—Orchard heaters in operation in a California citrus grove. (*Photograph by U. S. Department of Agriculture.*)

spring and autumn, frosts are not likely to occur during cloudy weather. Fogs, high humidity, a cover of scrub or forest growth, and, in fact, anything that retards direct insolation by day and solar radiation by night, have a similar effect in making the temperature of the habitat more uniform. Cover, whether dead or alive, reduces day temperatures by screening out the sun's rays and increases night temperatures by retarding radiation.[448] It is for this reason that forests and scrub are cooler in summer and warmer in winter than other areas that are similar except for cover.[140]

Winds cause the temperature to rise when they blow from a warmer region and to fall when they come from a cooler one. On clear, still nights in early spring in temperate regions, frosts are likely to occur which destroy the early vigorous growth, especially that of cultivated plants. The end of the growing season may be similarly shortened, especially for annuals, by early frosts in autumn. But on windy nights where the heavy, cold air is prevented from settling to the ground and constantly mixed by winds with the warmer air, freezing is much less frequent. Since the surface of the land warms up in sunshine about four times as rapidly as that of water and cools much more rapidly at night, the stabilizing effect of large bodies of water, *e.g.*, the Great Lakes, on temperature of adjacent land is obvious. Such areas are often well adapted to fruit growing, since spring opens late, after danger of frost has largely passed, and early frosts in fall are uncommon.

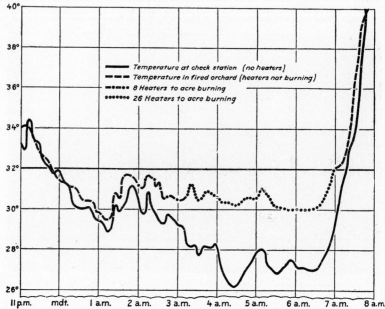

Fɪɢ. 182.—The rise of temperature as affected by heaters and fires placed in orchards. (*After Corbett, et al., U. S. Department of Agriculture.*)

Valuable orchards are often protected from damage when frost is imminent by building numerous smudge fires which surround the trees with artificial clouds of smoke, or, more usually, by the use of charcoal or oil burners (Fig. 181). These not only add heat to the atmosphere but also especially cause convection currents that keep the entire mass of air more or less thoroughly mixed. Such procedure is especially effective on still nights (Fig. 182). Truck crops are often protected in a similar manner or by preventing radiation by a suitable covering of paper, cloth, etc.[192]

Soil temperature, which modifies the air above the surface, is greatly affected by the water content and also by the color of the soil. Wet soils, because of the high specific heat of water, warm slowly, and especially if they are light in color.   Thus, a wet soil, such as a marsh, lowers the air temperature, partly by increasing humidity which, in turn, decreases insolation.   In such low areas, frosts are especially frequent and severe.

The effect of exposure is closely connected with slope.   Slopes that face south and west receive the most sunshine and are regularly warmer than north and east slopes.   Hence, in mountainous regions, forest communities, whose upward extension is directly or indirectly limited by temperature, may occur much higher on warmer slopes.[45,667]   Lodgepole pine (*Pinus contorta murrayana*), for example, is generally found in Colorado

Fig. 183.—Timber line on the east side of Pike's Peak at about 11,000 feet altitude. The forest consists of Engelmann spruce (*Picea engelmanni*) and limber pine (*Pinus flexilis*). (*Photograph by Pool.*)

between altitudes of 8,000 and 10,000 feet.   But on warm, south slopes it may extend as high as 11,000 feet and as low as 7,500 feet on cold north ones.[728]   Timber line, *i.e.*, the uppermost extension of forest growth, is often 1,000 feet higher on south than on north slopes[838] (Fig. 183).   In general, the larger the mountain mass and the higher the mountains the greater the altitude to which the tree limit attains (Fig. 184).   Ponderosa pine (*Pinus ponderosa*) may extend far upward into the Engelmann spruce (*Picea engelmanni*) zone on dry, well insolated slopes, while the spruce follows the deep canyons almost down to the plains where the canyons are watered by cold streams and subject to cold-air drainage.

In growing fruit trees and other crops in regions of rough topography, careful account should be taken of the slope and temperature relations. Strawberries may be brought to bearing many days earlier if planted on a south-facing slope where both soil and air are warmer.   North slopes may be selected for orchards to retard blossoming and consequent damage by late frosts.[15]

Temperature Inversions and Cold-air Drainage.—In hilly and other rough lands, a well marked, local temperature effect is often noted in valleys or depressions into which the denser, cold air sinks at night during the summer. On benchlands and the upper slopes of tablelands, the average temperature may be 6 to 10°F. or more above that of the valley bottoms below, which during the day are warmest.[42] Such temperature inversions are particularly effective on cold, calm nights and in arid or semiarid regions where there is little cover to prevent rapid radiation. Sometimes the line of temperature variation between the layer of cold air below and warmer air above may be so marked that blossoms on the lower part of a tree will be frozen while those above escape freezing and

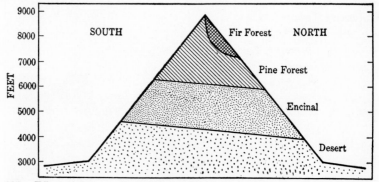

Fig. 184.—Effect of slope on distribution of desert vegetation, oak woodland, yellow pine, and Douglas fir forest in the Santa Catalina Mountains in Arizona. (*After Shreve.*)

form fruit abundantly. This settling of the colder air is termed *cold-air drainage*. It often creates distinct air currents as it pours down mountain canyons by night. Sometimes, certain species or communities of plants are limited in their upward distribution to the warmer exposed ridges but do not occur in the area subject to cold-air drainage. Timber line on mountains is profoundly modified by the effects of cold-air drainage, as a result of topography.

Temperatures Favorable and Unfavorable to Plants.—Plants are adapted to a wide range of temperature. Some species are able to grow in extremely low or extremely high temperatures as long as water is available in the liquid form. In fact, some of the lower forms of plant life such as algae may grow and fruit in arctic waters at temperatures below zero, the salt of the ocean lowering several degrees the temperature at which the water congeals. Conversely, numerous algae and bacteria thrive in hot springs at temperatures as high as 77°C. and a few fungi can endure temperatures of 89°C. In general, the temperatures of the plants' own habitat are most favorable to their development. For tropical plants, air temperatures above 90°F. are most favorable. Most temperate plants make their best development between 60 and 90°F., while arctic and alpine species may grow at temperatures only slightly above the freezing point.

Plants are subjected to a considerable range of temperature during their period of growth. They grow only when the temperature remains within certain limits, and mature and die or become dormant when it falls too low or becomes too high. Thus, low temperatures enforce a resting period upon plants of temperate and boreal regions just as there is a resting period for vegetation in climates where there is at certain periods an insufficient water supply to meet the demands of transpiration. In both cases the response is the same. The plant reduces water loss by shedding its leaves or in other ways, and life activities are maintained at a low rate.

Optimum Temperatures.—The temperature at which a plant functions best is called the optimum. Optimum temperatures for the various physiological processes, *e.g.*, photosynthesis, respiration, and reproduction, are themselves difficult to delimit because each depends upon a group of physical and chemical factors any one of which may limit a particular process. In general, the various optima for the different physiological processes do not coincide, that for respiration, for example, being much higher than the optimum for food manufacture. Hence, it seems clear that the ecological optimum or temperature at which the plant as a whole develops best is never a mere point but a range of several degrees at least. As the chemical and physical processes within the plant are quickened by a favorable temperature, demands for water and nutrients are also increased. Only when these are abundant do there occur optimum conditions for metabolism and growth. For germination and seedling development, these are much lower than those for the fruiting plant.

Maximum Temperatures.—The maximum temperature that can be tolerated without injurious effects in the plant, often resulting in death, varies greatly with the species. It seems to be an inherent quality of the protoplasm, fixed as a result of the impress of certain temperature relations throughout untold generations. Such temperatures are very closely connected in nature with alterations in the water relations, *i.e.*, available water supply to the roots and the cooling effect of water loss from leaves and shoot, and these become almost hopelessly confused with the temperature effects. At high temperatures, because of water or other relations, the growth rate rapidly falls and soon a point is reached beyond which the plant dies. At about 40°C., changes begin to occur in the protoplasm that are inimical to the life of the plant, and most plants succumb at temperatures between 45 and 55°C.

Like minimum temperatures, maximum ones vary widely with different species. Some tropical plants carry on their life processes at temperatures so high that most plants if subjected to them would die in a very short time. Furthermore, a plant withstands extremes of heat and cold much better in some stages than in others. It is least resistant in the active condition when the tissues are filled with water and most resistant in the resting state typical of spores, seeds, corms, etc. When dry, seeds can endure temperatures above 100°C. although they are readily killed at 70°C. if water-soaked. Certain species of yeasts have been shown to be capable of enduring a temperature of 114°C. when dormant, and bacteria in the spore condition are able to withstand temperatures of 120 to 130°C.

Minimum Temperatures and Freezing.—The minimum temperature at which any plant can continue activity is approximately the freezing point of water. Some arctic and alpine plants (*e.g.*, marsh marigold, *Caltha;* dog's-tooth violet, *Erythronium*) may produce their flowers after coming up through banks of snow and may continue to flourish, although the temperature falls below freezing every night. The activities of marine algae at temperatures below zero have been mentioned. On the other hand, many tropical plants are retarded in growth at 20°C. and are frequently killed at 10°C. The minimum temperature, moreover, varies greatly at different times of the year and with different conditions of the plant as well as with its previous experience with low temperatures.[881,1019] The chief difference lies in the amount of water the plant contains. The watery leaves and herbaceous stems of plants of temperate climates, for example, are usually killed by an exposure to 0°C. and frequently at temperatures 2 to 4°C. above freezing.[805] The drier seeds and inactive underground parts resist the long continued effect of temperatures of −30 to −40°C., dry seeds being uninjured by −193 to −250°C.[535] Death by winterkilling or cold at any time is usually a matter of desiccation and its attendant results brought on by low temperatures.

Since the cell sap always contains solutes that depress its freezing point, only temperatures lower than 0°C. cause the water to congeal. Plant tissues can be undercooled several degrees below the freezing point[999] and warmed up again without injury provided no ice formation occurs.[787,1018] A plant or its growing parts (buds, cambium, etc.) are not necessarily killed, even though they are solidly frozen. Arctic explorers on the coast of Siberia report plants, such as certain mustards (*Cochlearia*), being overtaken by winter and exposed to extremely low temperatures (−46°C.) while still in the flowering stage. In spite of this, they began again to blossom quite unharmed upon the recurrence of warm weather.

To Observe the Appearance of Ice Crystals in Buds.—On a cold day in winter when the temperature is 15°F. or lower, cut sections of buds of white birch (*Betula alba*), red elm (*Ulmus fulva*), or lilac (*Syringa*). This must be done in a place where the temperature is well below freezing and the sections mounted in cedar-wood oil so that the water from the melting ice cannot evaporate. Immediately examine them under a microscope that has been thoroughly cooled. Note the crystals of ice between the bud scales which they have more or less pushed apart. Observe closely the changes as the ice slowly melts and the spaces in which the ice is collected shrink as the water is reabsorbed by the cells.

Nature of Freezing Injury.—When plant tissues freeze, water is withdrawn from the cells much as it is when they wilt, and crystals of ice form in the intercellular spaces. This explains the flaccid condition often observed in frozen plants. The film of pure or nearly pure water on the outer surface of the cell wall freezes first. Water is then withdrawn from within the cell wall, next from the protoplasm, and finally from the cavities or vacuole to replace this film. It is the force of crystallization that causes the water to move outward. After equilibrium is established between this force and the water-retaining power of the cell at any temperature, no more water freezes unless the temperature becomes lower.[999] It seems almost certain that death is not due to cold but to the results attending this process of desiccation.[435] Whether the cells are killed directly by loss of water on freezing or by changes taking place as a result of this water loss, the rate of thawing has no effect, since they are already dead. But among plants capable of standing some ice formation in their tissues, slow thawing is least harmful, since it enables them to reabsorb much of the water that has been withdrawn into the intercellular spaces that might be lost if thawing were rapid.[138,139,739] Plant tissues may perish while thawing as well as while freezing.[434]

The result of withdrawal of water from the cell is a greater concentration of the salts within. This may be accompanied by an increased hydrogen-ion concentration. Certain proteins are precipitated in strong salt solutions, and it is generally believed that the chief cause of injury or death by freezing is the precipitating of proteins from the desiccated protoplasm, though some regard the injury as mechanical, due either to the pressure of ice or to stress set up by the displacement of water.[529] For example, it has been shown that approximately one-third of the proteins in frozen plants of cereals are precipitated. In the tender begonia, protein precipitation occurs at −3°C.; in winter rye, at −15°C.; and in pine needles, not until a temperature of −40°C. is reached.[329a]

Resistance to Freezing.—Water-imbibing substances and osmotic pressure decrease the outward movement of water from the plant cell.[235] In general, it has been found that plants and tissues with the greatest water-retaining power are also the most resistant to both freezing and drought. Hence, it is rarely the youngest tissues or parts that are injured by freezing. In winter wheat, for example, injury progresses in a given plant from the older to the younger leaves, and the crown containing the dense protoplasm characteristic of meristematic tissues is the most hardy.[573] In northern latitudes, most evergreen trees, shrubs, and herbs, as the temperatures become lower, convert their reserve supply of starch into fats and oils. This also occurs in certain deciduous trees like the birch. It is well known that water in the presence of fatty oil in the form of an emulsoid may be much undercooled before ice formation takes place. Moreover, in many cases, an abundance of sugar occurs in the cell sap.

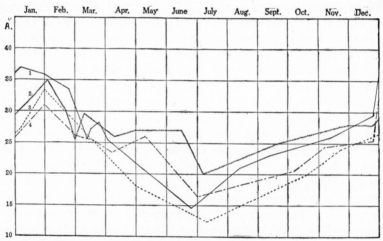

Fig. 185.—Increase in atmospheres of osmotic pressure of cell sap in leaves of evergreen plants in Idaho during fall and winter and decrease during spring and summer: 1, white fir (*Abies grandis*); 2, Douglas fir (*Pseudotsuga taxifolia*); 3, a shrub, *Pachistima myrsinites*; and 4, ponderosa pine (*Pinus ponderosa*). (*After Gail.*)

A consistent increase in the osmotic pressure of the cell sap of evergreen trees and shrubs with decrease in temperature during fall and winter has been demonstrated[308,532] (Fig. 185). This further decreases the freezing point of the water, and the danger arising from the salting out of the proteins is further minimized. During freezing or as a result of freezing, sucrose may be changed to the reducing sugars and the osmotic efficiency consequently greatly increased.[576] The presence, moreover, in the cell of these nonelectrolytes decreases the tendency to precipitate proteins.[636,638]

Pentosans, mucilages, and pectic bodies, which have a high water-retaining power, are abundant in many plants and further decrease the danger from desiccation and consequent death.[638] In the living leaves of *Pyrola*, a typical evergreen herb of boreal forests, ice formation does not begin until a temperature of −31°C. is attained.[434,938]

Thus, as a result of various modifications of metabolism and proto-plasmic content resulting from long experience with periodically low temperatures, plants have become adapted to freezing by their ability successfully to resist desiccation. In fruit trees, such as plums, for example, it has been demonstrated that while the hardy varieties may not have a higher water content than the nonhardy ones, the buds are able to retain a nearly uniform water supply under conditions of extreme cold (drought), while the nonresistant varieties become desiccated and die. In the "hardening" of plants, similar changes are produced.[894] The mechanism of frost resistance is not yet fully understood; cell permeability seems closely correlated with hardening against frost.[529] The seat of the major resistance may be the living protoplasm.

Hardening.—Hardening is the practice of rendering plants less susceptible to drought and frost injury. Seedling vegetables grown in a greenhouse or hotbed are very susceptible to drought and freezing. If they are placed in a cold frame for a few days at a temperature several degrees above freezing and watered sparingly before setting into the field, they increase in hardiness to a point where some varieties will withstand frost. In fact, certain varieties, such as cabbage, may be frozen stiff without injury. Cells which are sensitive to a few degrees of frost may become capable, in extreme cases, of enduring $-40°C$. or even lower temperatures without injury.[528] The hardening process in plants is accompanied by a marked increase in the water-retaining power of the cells that enables them upon freezing to retain a large proportion of their water content in the unfrozen state. This is associated with a decrease in total water content; an increase in the amount of hydrophilous colloids, such as pentosans, together with an increase in their power to hold water; and an increase in the amount of osmotically active substances such as sugars. Other important changes also occur. The proteins of the proto-plasm are changed to forms that are soluble in water and less easily precipitated.[681,739] For example, by subjecting the expressed sap of non-hardened and hardened cabbage to a temperature of $-4°C$., a tempera-ture that would kill the nonhardened cabbage but not the hardened plants, it was found that 31 to 44 per cent of the proteins in the former were precipitated but only 9 to 11 per cent of the latter.[386]

The first three changes mentioned above may take place in a rela-tively short period of time when the activity of the plant is limited by cold or drought; the last is important only in plants hardened by prolonged exposure to cold. Hardy species and varieties of plants possess the ability to initiate these changes to a greater or lesser degree; while non-hardy ones possess it only to a slight degree or not at all.[739] Winter wheat, for example, hardens readily, and certain varieties can withstand drought and extremely low temperatures, but oats seem to lack this ability and are resistant neither to drought nor to low temperatures.[766]

Some plants may be hardened by subjecting them to drought before the advent of freezing. It is a common practice among foresters thus to harden seedlings in nurseries, and similar results may be obtained by withholding water in orchards, if under irrigation, or otherwise by the use of appropriate, late-sown cover crops. The changes in the cell are similar to those brought about by hardening due to low temperatures. Perennial plants, in general, are much less likely to be winterkilled if they undergo a period of moderate drought than if they are kept wet and green up to the time of severe freezing. The hardiness of some plants, e.g., certain varieties of peaches, is due to the slowness with which they absorb water in spring. The sap in the buds remains at such a high concentration that they are not readily injured by freezing.[388, 455, 604]

In recent years mechanical refrigeration has been extensively used in selecting cold-resistant varieties of wheat, alfalfa, and other crop plants.[681, 766]

The Sum of Temperatures.—The activity and growth of any plant depend upon its receiving the requisite amount of heat during the growing period. The influence of temperature on the size of the plant is very great because of its control over growth. The sum of the temperatures that act upon a plant is of the first importance in determining its general appearance. The effect may be produced either by temperatures that are more or less constantly too low or by shortness of season, which is equally effective in reducing the total amount of heat available for the use of the plant[672] (Fig. 186).

Since temperature is one of the most influential of all climatic factors affecting plant growth, it has received much attention in connection with crop production. In spite of much study, very little is known about the relationship between air temperature and the development of any crop. Could the heat requirement of various crops be stated in terms of temperature and time, it would be of immense advantage to agriculture.[803]

For many years, an effort has been made to determine the total of the effective heat units necessary to grow various crops to maturity. Since all temperatures below the minimum are ineffective in promoting growth, it was first necessary to select a plant zero, i.e., a temperature above which growth begins. Since this varies for different crops and, to some extent, with other conditions such as latitude and altitude, length of day, etc., different plant-zero points have been suggested, such as the mean daily temperature of the average date of planting.[482, 484] The latter is about 37°F. for spring wheat, 55°F. for corn, and 62°F. for cotton. It varies but little, regardless of where the crop is grown.[52] The plant zeros most used, however, have been 43 and 40°F., and three summation processes have been employed to determine the effect on plant growth of temperature sums above this point.[541]

Remainder Indices.—By the process of remainder indices of temperature efficiency for plant growth, which has been used most frequently, all mean daily temperatures above the plant zero during the life of the crop have been added together. This would be 10° for a day with a mean temperature of 53°F.; 15° for one with 58°F.; etc. Obviously, a degree of heat at 60°F. is of much more value in promoting growth than one at 50°F. Hence, it is not surprising that the total units for a given crop in a particular region vary so widely that they have little significance.

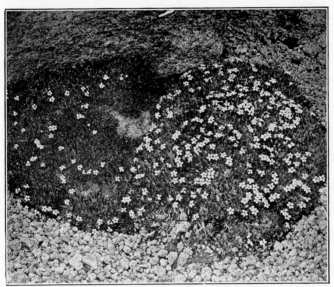

Fig. 186.—Alpine mats of moss campion (*Silene acaulis*) growing on the north side of a rock. The effect of different temperature sums is shown by the number of flowers.

The heat units for corn in Ohio during a period of 27 years varied from 1,232 to 1,919 from sprouting to flowering, and from 897 to 1,607 from flowering to ripening.[803]

Merriam's division of the United States into life zones and crop zones is based upon the sums of heat thus determined, together with the mean temperature for the 6 hottest consecutive weeks. The sums thus obtained at various stations were plotted and connected by isothermal lines. The United States was thus divided into various life zones. The transition zone, for example, has for its northern boundary lines connecting stations with heat sums of 10,000°F. (northern parts of Minnesota, Wisconsin, and New York), while its southern boundary is along a line with 71.6°F. for the 6 hottest weeks (northern parts of Iowa, Illinois, and

Maryland). From the standpoint of natural vegetation, this classifica-tion is necessarily unsatisfactory, since temperature is far less critical than water to native species. For example, it places such diverse vegetational units as climatic grassland, ponderosa-pine forest, and sage-brush desert in the same subdivision of a zone, *i.e.*, arid transition. The conclusions reached by this author have been largely adopted by many of the earlier students of plant and animal geography, despite the exceed-ingly tentative nature of the data on which they are based.[473] The zonal terminology has, moreover, been so widely used that the student will do well to familiarize himself with it.[600]

Exponential Indices.—Exponential indices of temperature efficiency for plant growth are based on the fact that the physiological processes of plant metabolism are chemical and physical and follow the principle of van't Hoff and Arrhenius. This principle states that the chemical-reaction velocity approximately doubles for each rise in temperature of 18°F. On this basis, indices of temperature efficiency have been cal-culated, assuming that general plant activity occurs at unity rate when the daily mean temperature is 40°F. and that this rate is doubled with each rise of 18°F. in the daily mean. Thus, with a daily mean of 58°F. the rate becomes 2, with a mean of 76°F. it becomes 4, etc. Hence, the index of efficiency I may be found for any temperature t by substituting in the formula $I = 2^{\frac{t-40}{18}}$ (*e.g.*, that of 94° would be $2^3 = 8$).[541] Increasing temperature is not accompanied by increased growth throughout the range of the growth rate from the minimum to the maximum. Instead of the growth of wheat, for example, doubling at 100°F. that which occurred at 82°F., it actually decreases. An optimum temperature can always be found above which the previously increasing growth rate begins to decrease.

Physiological Indices.—Physiological indices of temperature efficiency for plant growth take into account the optimum temperature. The method is of such a nature that both low and high temperature values give efficiency indices of zero, and intermediate temperature values give indices whose graph shows a well defined maximum. Variations in the growth rate of corn seedlings were experimentally determined at different constant temperatures of long duration.[525] From these, the efficiency index for each degree of temperature between 36 and 118°F. was calculated. For example, the value at 36°F. is 0.1; 40°F. is 1.0; and 58°F. is 16.1. At 89°F. it reaches a maximum of 122.3 and falls again to 0.1 at 118°F. This method is more promising than any of the preceding and as a laboratory experiment and a basis for ecological investigation the information obtained is of great value.[537] In nature, however, any one temperature is not long maintained. Care should be taken in applying the results to plants in the field, and maps of temperature efficiency and provinces constructed on these bases, as their authors realized, may be considered scarcely more than suggestive. Finally, it must be remembered that temperature is only one of a series of a complex of environmental factors that affect plant growth.

Influence of Temperature on Vegetation.—There are probably few places on the surface of the earth that are either too hot or too cold for some plants to grow. Even in boreal regions, the temperature in summer is always well above the limits at which growth is possible, although this period may extend over only a few weeks. Consequently, many species, especially annuals, are excluded. Plants of alpine and high arctic regions are almost exclusively low-growing perennials in which rapid growth is due to utilization of food accumulated the previous season. Similarly, plants of the hottest deserts, where continuous growth is limited by extreme heat, have living parts buried deeply in the soil. Upon the advent of a moist or rainy season, when the temperatures are reduced and water becomes available, they draw upon their reserve food supplies and rapidly develop.

Temperature has no effect upon plant distribution in local migration, but it has a profound influence upon ecesis of the migrants.[930] Considering temperature alone, ecesis is more certain if the migration is east or west than if it is northward or southward. Generally, also, the chances for ecesis are greater equatorward than they are poleward. Migration to the east or west does not essentially change the relation of the plant to temperature. Migration equatorward means that the plant must accustom itself to higher temperatures as well as to greater annual sums. Maximum temperatures may be directly operative in preventing the extension of plant ranges, the temperature of the soil surface and of the air just above being especially important. While adjustment to higher temperatures is taking place, the plant may be at a disadvantage in competition with others already well established.[759]

Plants that migrate northward, in addition to a corresponding adjustment to lower temperatures and a lower sum, run an increasing risk of encountering a fatal minimum.[841] This risk is greatly increased by the fact that southern plants require a longer period for their life cycle than northern ones and in a northern latitude are often unable to reach maturity before the regular appearance of killing frosts. The evergreen habit is clearly advantageous where the growing season is very short, none of the very restricted period during which temperature is high enough for photosynthesis being squandered in the production of a new canopy of foliage.[677] Such species occur regularly in cold climates and at high altitudes. It frequently happens that the limiting condition preventing the occurrence of certain species in an area is the nature of the surroundings during a dormant period. In fact, it may be found that the length of the dormant period during which growth cannot occur is as important in plant distribution as is the duration of the growing period itself.[337] Even dormant plant protoplasm may be destroyed at extremely low temperatures.

The same fundamental rule of distribution applies to mountains, the increasing cold upward makes ecesis more uncertain than it is downward. The grouping of species, which is a process in the formation of vegetation, is in accordance with these facts. In consequence, vegetation exhibits zones extending east and west upon continents. The isothermal lines are usually deflected southward with increase in altitude. This occurs on either side of the three main mountain systems of North America. They bend northward near the Atlantic and Pacific oceans. Along mountain ranges the zones are, in general, lengthwise of the range, although many minor factors such as the extent of the mountain masses, slope exposure, air currents, and proximity to bodies of water interrupt a regular distribution.[362]

While temperature is the most important factor in determining the general distribution of vegetation, its effect is much greater upon the flora than upon the kind of vegetation. Grassland, forest, and desert all occur in each of the great temperature zones of the earth, but the component species of forest, for example, in each zone are very different.[672] Temperature also is the most important factor in determining the distribution of crop plants. The northern limit of the successful commercial production of cotton is determined almost entirely by temperature conditions.[484] The isotherm of 10°F. for the daily minimum temperatures of January and February, for example, coincides, in general, with the northern boundary of winter-wheat culture in the United States, if this boundary is taken as the line beyond which spring wheat is grown more commonly than winter wheat.[764] Potatoes, on the other hand, give the highest yields in regions with lower summer temperatures, since tuber growth is retarded by high temperatures. Temperatures of the growing season alone limit the growth of certain crops such as corn, while others, e.g., grapes, are limited by the temperature of the nongrowing season as well. East of the Rocky Mountains, the agricultural areas have more or less distinct boundaries that correspond, in general, with the east and west trend of isothermal lines. The more important ones from south to north are the humid subtropical crop belt, the cotton belt, the hard winter-wheat region, the corn and winter-wheat belt, the corn belt, the spring-wheat region, and the hay and dairy region (Fig. 187).

Relation of Air Environment to Disease.—The close relationship that exists between temperature, humidity, and other conditions of the weather and plant disease has long been recognized.[420]   So obvious is this relation to the relative damage to grain by rust or mildew that the grower often believes that unfavorable rainfall or temperature is the direct and only reason for this trouble.[462,909]

Some diseases are due directly to unfavorable environmental factors, for instance, tipburn or sunscald to high temperatures, and russeting of apples and pears to high humidity.   The latter, for example, results from a cracking and weathering away of the epidermis of the fruits and an increased development of corky parenchyma beneath.   It occurs especially in humid climates or during rainy seasons and is due entirely to high

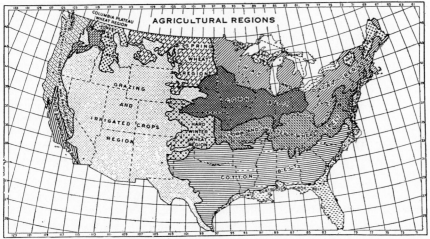

Fig. 187.—Agricultural regions of the United States.   (*Courtesy of U. S. Department of Agriculture.*)

humidity.   In dry climates, under irrigation, the fruit is smooth skinned since russeting does not occur.[309]   The great majority of plant diseases, however, are due to bacteria or fungi.

Excessive shade, whether due to clouds or to foliage, and high temperatures accompanied by wind, high humidity, and heavy dews are ideal conditions for the rapid dissemination and development of a variety of bacterial diseases.   Under such conditions, fire blight of pear, caused by *Bacillus amylovorus*, often breaks out like a conflagration, spreading over whole orchards.   Other bacterial diseases such as the black spot and canker of the plum, bean blight, and angular leaf spot of cucumber spread rapidly and become most destructive under conditions of cloudy weather and heavy dews.   Black rot of cabbage likewise develops rapidly under similar conditions.   During moist, warm autumns, bacterial diseases of the potato may destroy almost the entire crop over extensive districts.

Weather conditions, to a large extent, also determine the spread and severity of fungus diseases of plants, since favorable moisture and temperature relations are necessary for spore germination and consequent infection of the host. Humid days in midsummer are absolutely necessary for bad epidemics of the late blight of potato caused by *Phytophthora infestans*. The control of carnation and chrysanthemum rusts in the greenhouse, if the spores are present, depends upon keeping the leaves free from moisture and maintaining a low humidity. The amount of rust on asparagus in California is directly proportional to the occurrence of dew. Cereal rusts are most destructive when the weather is damp and cool.

Relation of Infection of Cereal Rusts to Humidity.—Fill six 2.5-inch flowerpots with potting soil in good tilth. Plant 15 kernels of some susceptible wheat, such as Little Club or Marquis spring wheat in each. At the end of a week, or when the first leaf is nearly full grown, thin to 10 per pot by pulling out the other plants. Inoculate each plant with viable rust spores of *Puccinia graminis tritici*, by moistening the leaf and rubbing it lightly between thumb and finger and then transferring the spores to the wet leaf surface with a flattened needle.

Place two pots under a large, closed bell jar together with a glass of water, and two others under an open bell jar raised a centimeter from the greenhouse bench and containing also a glass of water. Put the remaining pots on the bench without cover. The plants should be transferred to their respective places immediately after inoculation and before the leaves dry. In case of bright sunshine, shade the containers and plants to prevent high temperatures.

Determine the humidity under each set of conditions at least twice during the 48-hour period of inoculation. This may be done by cutting a circular hole 5 millimeters in diameter in the center of a thick felt paper large enough to cover the bottom of the bell jar. Make a slit from the hole to the edge of the paper and insert a cog psychrometer just above the whirling device. A similar paper inserted from the opposite side reenforces the first, and when the two are held against the bottom of the bell jar they close the latter while the humidity is being determined.

After 48 hours, place all the plants, properly labeled, in a group on the greenhouse bench. At the end of 10 to 14 days cut away all but the original leaf and determine the percentage of rusted plants in each lot.

(Rust spores may readily be obtained in summer and an abundant supply maintained at all times by inoculating new host plants every 3 or 4 weeks.)

Brown rots of stone fruits are intimately associated with abundant precipitation and a humid atmosphere. A week or more of damp weather during the period of ripening of peaches, plums, or cherries may result in such abundance of the fungus that the entire crop over an extensive area may be ruined. Likewise, the fungus causing black rot of grapes is most destructive under similar conditions.

The destructiveness of the dry rot of potatoes caused by species of *Fusarium* gradually increases as the relative humidity is increased. With a high humidity at a given temperature, the rotting is always greater than at 5 to 10°C. higher with a low humidity.[330,521] Moisture and tem.

perature play a leading part in determining the severity of apple scab, the disease being most severe where the climate is humid and cool in spring and early summer.

Environmental conditions may affect the various diseases quite differently. During a cool summer in southern Wisconsin, tobacco grown on "tobacco-sick" soil was practically a failure as a result of the excessive development of the root-rot fungus. But during a hot summer on the same soil, a good crop of fairly healthy plants developed. Conversely, the cabbage crop on old "cabbage-sick" soil during the cool summer was relatively free from "yellows," another parasitic disease caused by a soil-inhabiting fungus, while during the hot summer following, the disease practically ruined the whole crop.[462]

Explanation of the occurrence and severity of a parasitic disease requires not only identification of the causal organism but also the defining of the environmental factors favorable or unfavorable to its development. Because of the complexity of the environment and the continually changing combinations of factors, the latter is often the more difficult.[287,1008] Development of technique for determining the specific effects upon the metabolism of host and parasite of individual environmental factors is relatively recent, but much progress has been made and the outlook is promising.

CHAPTER XIV

LIGHT

Light is one of the most important factors determining the growth of plants and the development of vegetation. The sun is the source of energy for plants. Light is that part of the radiant energy which is visible to the eye. It is from this radiant energy that chlorophyll absorbs certain wave lengths (from about 0.75 to 0.4 micron or μ) which enable the chloroplasts to manufacture food. The word sunlight is commonly used to mean solar radiation in a general sense, thus including ultraviolet and infrared wave lengths. Sunlight comes to the surface of the earth

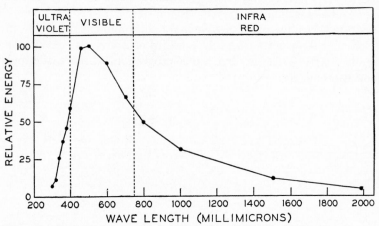

FIG. 188.—Distribution of energy in the ultraviolet, visible, and infrared regions of the solar spectrum at the earth's surface. (*Drawn by P. R. Burkholder from data by Fowle.*)

in electromagnetic waves, which are measured in thousandths of millimeters (microns) or millionths of millimeters (millimicrons). The wave lengths and distribution of energy in the visible region of the solar spectrum, the ultraviolet, and infrared are shown in Fig. 188. The value of solar radiation at sea level is approximately 1.5 gram calories per square centimeter per minute. In terms of illumination this corresponds to 10,000 foot-candles.[481] Only about 39 per cent of the total radiation reaching the earth from the sun is visible light. About 60 per cent is infrared, and 1 per cent is ultraviolet.

A very small amount of the radiant energy striking the leaf is used in the photosynthetic process. In the case of *Polygonum, Tropaeolum,* and

Helianthus, it was found to be only 0.42 to 1.66 per cent of the radiant energy available for photosynthesis.[105] Much of the radiant energy, including especially wave lengths longer than those visible, is absorbed and changed into heat energy. Of the total radiant energy incident upon a leaf, about 50 per cent is thus transformed and used in the vaporization of water; 19 per cent is lost by reradiation; and 30 per cent reflected from the surface of the leaf or transmitted through it.[874] Thus, the study of the effect of light upon plants and vegetation in general is greatly complicated because of the accompanying heating effect. The process of photosynthesis is conditional on temperature, the rate increasing, at the usual temperatures to which the plant is accustomed, according to van't Hoff's law, provided no other factor becomes limiting. The rate approximately doubles with a rise in temperature of 18°F.

EFFECTS OF LIGHT ON PLANTS

Light affects plants in many ways. Through its action chlorophyll and other pigments, growth substances or hormones, as well as carbohydrates are synthesized. Light influences the number and position of the chloroplasts, the opening and closing of stomata, and has a profound effect upon transpiration. It is the photic stimulus that results in tropic responses, as the turning of stems and leaves. Through the action of light in the formation of specific chemical substances, profound influences are brought to bear on processes of growth and those concerned in the differentiation of specialized cells and organs, as is illustrated in development of palisade in leaves, the growth of storage organs, and roots. Light influences the whole course of development of the plant, exerting a profound effect upon its characteristic form and structure.[112]

Production of Chlorophyll.—Light is necessary for the formation of plant pigments. A primary response of the plant to light is the production of chlorophyll. This response does not occur in plants such as bacteria, fungi, and broom rape (*Thalesia*), in which the power to make chlorophyll has never been attained or has been lost in consequence of parasitic or saprophytic habits. Certain plants, moreover, such as seedlings of most conifers, young fern fronds, some mosses and one-celled algae, become green in the absence of light.[654] With these exceptions, plants with plastids produce chlorophyll only in light, and the chlorophyll practically always disappears in continued darkness. Although sometimes formed in darkness, chlorophyll cannot function in synthesis of carbohydrates without light.

The occurrence of chlorophyll beneath the outer bark in trees, however, indicates that only a small amount of light is required. The necessary light intensity varies in different species. In some, such as Norway maple (*Acer platanoides*) and peppergrass (*Lepidium sativum*), it forms in shaded habitats at less than 0.3 per cent.[1035] At least over 1 per cent is required in temperate climates, however, for the species most tolerant to shade to carry on sufficient photosynthesis for growth. There is probably no place even in dense forests where plants could not form chlorophyll, but there are many places where even very tolerant plants cannot carry on photosynthesis, at least rapidly enough to live.

Chlorophyll content varies in the same species or plant from year to year, with increasing age of the plant, with environmental conditions, and even from day to night.[401] It has been found for a variety of plants, that the concentration of chlorophyll per unit area or weight of leaf increased with decreasing light intensities until the intensity was so low it hazarded survival.[821]

Shade leaves of the more plastic species have a higher chlorophyll content compared with corresponding sun leaves or sun species. The relative chlorophyll content also varies widely among different plants and the rate of photosynthesis has recently been found to vary with the concentration of chlorophyll.[265,284]

Influence upon Number and Position of Chloroplasts.—The clue to the internal structure of the leaf is found largely in the light relation. It has been seen that only a small amount of the radiant energy absorbed by the chloroplasts is used in photosynthesis and that a large amount is converted into heat, which produces vaporization of water. This process results in maintaining a lower temperature in the leaf. The effect is not so pronounced in the shade, owing to less insolation. In the upper part of the leaf which receives full sunshine, and where chloroplasts are much more abundant, they are arranged in line with the direction of light and thus screen each other from the full effect of the radiant energy. This reduces the amount of water loss. It has been shown that a single layer of chloroplasts absorbs about 30 per cent of the light falling upon it. Absorption in the second layer is reduced to 21 per cent, in the third to 15 per cent, and in the fourth to 10 per cent, but deeper layers of chloroplasts absorb very little light.[875] Light was found to pass through only 5 layers of chloroplasts in a bean (*Phaseolus multiflorus*) but through 9 in the castor bean (*Ricinus communis*).[875] Since the chloroplast may undergo a change of position under different light intensities and also contain variable amounts of photosynthate, the absorption of light by a leaf is variable.[709]

In the shade, the danger of excessive water loss is slight, while the need of obtaining all the light possible is imperative. Accordingly, the plastids, which are fewer in number, are arranged at right angles to the light rays, thus increasing the surface for absorption. This arrangement of the plastids is not only found in sun and shade leaves, but it is also typical of nearly all horizontal leaves (Fig. 189). The lower portion of the horizontal leaf is just as truly shaded as a leaf growing in a forest, and the chloroplasts are arranged in such fashion as to receive as much light as possible. This arrangement is usual but it is not absolute, owing to local modifications due to the position of air passages and the necessity of the diffusion of water and solutes from cell to cell.

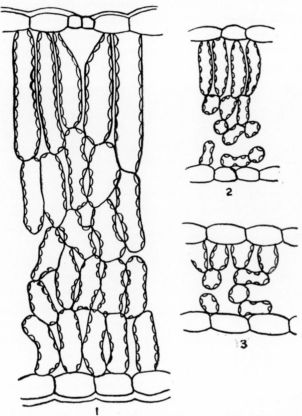

Fig. 189.—Position of chloroplasts in (1) sun leaf of narrow-leaved four-o'clock (*Allionia linearis*), (2) in a leaf of the shade form, and (3) in one found in very deep shade. (*Drawn by Edith S. Clements.*)

Changes in Leaf Structure.—The leaf undergoes the greatest modification as a response to light (radiant energy) of any organ of the plant.[149] Stems may be modified to some extent when they contain chloroplasts. Roots, not being exposed to the light, show only indirect effects such as result from differences in growth due to an increased or decreased supply of photosynthate and the response to a well lighted (hence, usually dry) or a moist, shady habitat.[382]

Differences in the thickness of leaves grown in the sun and shade are usually marked. Leaves from the interior of a lilac bush or the crown of a linden or hard maple tree are so much thinner than those exposed to full sunshine that they may readily be distinguished by the feel alone. Shade results in thin leaves often with a single layer of palisade cells and loosely arranged chlorenchyma. A variety of plants grown under 1 to 20 per cent light developed only one layer of palisade tissue; those under 70 per cent had two distinct layers. Thickness of the leaf increased with increasing light intensity.[333,821] The sponge cells, which elongate more or less parallel to the surface, are due to the action of diffuse light or shade upon the chloroplasts. The development of sponge tissue increases the light-absorbing surface. It is found in nearly all leaves where the

Fig. 190.—Prickly lettuce (*Lactuca scariola*) grown under full greenhouse light (left), 25 per cent of this (center), and 10 per cent (right).

light is diffuse; leaves of shrubs and herbs that grow regularly in the deep shade of forest consist largely or entirely of sponge tissue. Cells that normally form palisade in the sun develop into sponge cells in the shade. Conversely, sponge cells under strong illumination develop into palisade.[150]

The amount of palisade developed in the upper portion of leaves receiving sunlight from above varies not only with the intensity of the illumination but also with available water content of soil. Palisade is much better developed in dry than in wet soil even under equal illumination. Moreover, where absorption is difficult because of poor root development due to low soil temperatures, palisade development is promoted. This is well illustrated by many alpine plants. Owing to low atmospheric pressure occurring at high altitudes coupled with intense illumination in the habitat, water loss tends to be excessive compared with absorption.

Similarly, in plants growing under conditions of deficient aeration, excess of acids or alkalies, palisade development is promoted.[932]   It reaches its maximum development in very dry, exposed situations such as deserts. Here, because of dry soil, absorption is relatively difficult, while high vapor pressure deficit and high illumination promote excessive water loss.

Where the under surface of the leaf is also highly illuminated, for example by the reflection of light from white sand, palisade also develops

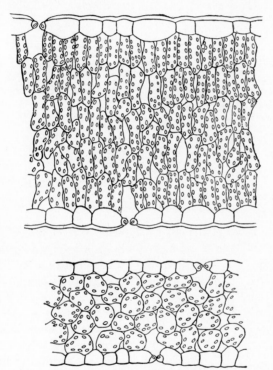

FIG. 191.—Cross sections of leaves of plants shown in Fig. 190 grown in 100 per cent (upper) and 10 per cent greenhouse light.

in the lower part.   Some plants have their leaves "edge on" to the noonday sun.   In these so-called *compass plants*, such as prickly lettuce (*Lactuca scariola*), and rosinweed (*Silphium laciniatum*), two sides of the leaf are equally illuminated and palisade develops more or less equally on both (Figs. 190 and 191).   Conversely, in plants like the mullein (*Verbascum*) where the chlorenchyma is screened from intense light by a dense growth of hairs, palisade tissue is poorly developed.   In deep shade there is little or no difference in the intensity of the light received by the two surfaces, at least it is too weak to develop palisade, and shade leaves are often composed of a uniform chlorenchyma of sponge throughout.

The amount of palisade development in the same plant may vary greatly. The leaves of a tree that are fully exposed to the sun are very

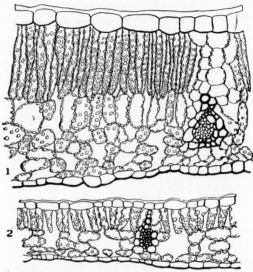

Fig. 192.—Leaves from (1) the south periphery and (2) center of the crown of an isolated sugar maple (*Acer saccharum*). (*After Hanson.*)

different from those of the shaded interior of the crown[366] (Figs. 192 and 193). Great differences exist in the internal exposed surfaces of foliage

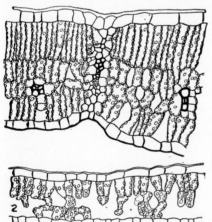

leaves not only in different species but also in sun and shade leaves of the same species. The ratio of the internal to the external exposed surface is low for shade leaves, the former often being 7 to 10 times as great; it is intermediate for leaves of mesomorphic type, 12 to 20 times as large; and high for xeromorphic sun leaves, ranging between 17 to 31 times the external surface. The palisade type of mesophyll exposes 1.6 to 3.5 times as much surface, per unit volume, as the sponge type.[937]

Fig. 193.—Leaves from (1) the south periphery of an isolated basswood (*Tilia americana*), and (2) from the base of a tree of the same species growing in a forest. (*After Hanson.*)

In many plants, the transpiration rate from equal external surfaces of the sun leaf and shade leaf is in the ratio of about 10:1. Palisade tissue may be correlated with development of chloroplasts as is indicated by the absence of palisading in albescent leaves. In many plants, it is

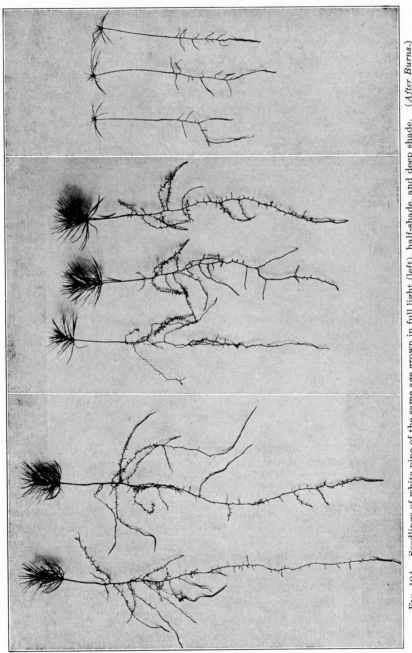

FIG 194 — Seedlings of white pine of the same age grown in full light (left), half-shade, and deep shade.   (*After Burns.*)

discontinued sharply with failure of chlorophyll development. Finally, there are many instances, especially among monocotyledons, where palisade is never developed, and in some dicotyledons it seems to form without regard to external factors.

Changes in Form of Leaves.—The form of the leaf is largely determined by the action of light upon the chloroplasts and the consequent change in the form of the cells that contain them. Owing to the direction in which they elongate, sponge cells tend to produce an extension of the leaf at right angles to the incident light, while palisade cells extend the leaf in line with it. Hence, leaves that contain an excess of sponge tissue are relatively broader, while those in which the palisade is preponderant are relatively thicker. Leaves of the peach averaged about 65 per cent greater in area and those of the apple 224 per cent greater when grown under 15 per cent light intensity than those developed in full sunshine.[332,333] Similar results were obtained with a number of common herbaceous plants. In general, sun leaves, which are produced in a relatively xeric habitat, are smaller and thicker than shade leaves grown in a mesic environment. This holds true not only for sun and shade forms of the same species but also for sun and shade plants generally. Similar differentiations occur in leaves of the same tree, shrub, or herb with a dense crown of leaves. Change in thickness may, moreover, be brought about by modifying the water content of soil without change in the intensity of light.[332,891,932]

The outline of shade leaves is more nearly entire than that of similar leaves grown in strong insolation. Although this is not absolute, it may usually be shown by comparing the sun and shade forms of a species with lobed or divided leaves. There appears to be a clear correlation between lobing of leaves and rate of water supply and loss from the plant, but more experimental work is needed to fully establish this relationship.

The stems of plants grown in moderate shade are regularly taller and often more branched than corresponding sun forms as a result of the forces that promote elongation (Fig. 194). It is clear that upon a stem with elongated internodes the leaves interfere less with the illumination of those below them. This is also true of the branches, which serve further to carry the leaves away from the stem and from each other in such a way that the plant obtains the greatest possible exposure of its leaf surface. Thus, the very efficient photosynthetic organ required for low light intensities is provided by the large, thin leaves of shade plants. They are rich in chlorophyll and widely spaced on the stem.

Relation to Stomatal Movement.—Light is the most important environmental factor modifying stomatal movement. In nearly all plants, stomatal opening is correlated with the presence of light when other conditions for opening are favorable (Fig. 195). When they become unfavorable, however, the influence of light is modified by the action of other factors and finally nullified. When the water supply becomes low, stomata may close even in the light. In a few plants, light seems to have little or no part in producing stomatal opening.[544,788]

The amount of water in the leaves and the acidity of the guard cells are the two internal conditions directly concerned with stomatal move-

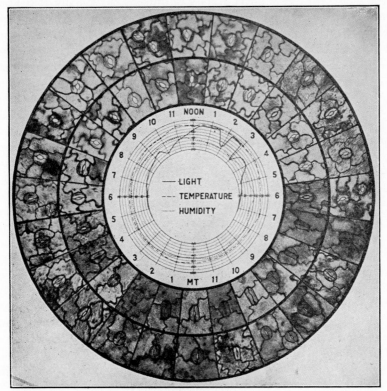

Fig. 195.—Stomata from the upper (outer circle) and lower epidermis of heavily irrigated alfalfa, and environmental factors during a 24-hour day. The figure consists of 48 separate microphotographs. (*After Loftfield.*)

ment.[783] Under normal conditions, the sap of the guard cells is more acid when the stomata are closed. The cause of the increased acidity is not certainly known. It may be due to the accumulation of organic acids in darkness which are oxidized to carbon dioxide and water in the presence of light or it may be caused by the accumulation of carbon dioxide resulting from respiration. This accumulation does not occur in light, since the carbon dioxide is used in photosynthesis, and hence, light decreases the acidity of the guard cells.[785] This makes conditions more favorable for greater hydration of the hydrophilous colloids of these cells as well as for the hydrolytic action of diastase. The increased intake of water by the guard cells results in greater turgidity and tends toward stomatal opening.[433,1002] At the same time that the starch is changed to sugar, osmotic pressure is greatly increased, and the stomata open. A reversal of the process, *i.e.*, increased acidity, appearance of starch, and decrease in turgor, occurs when the stomata close. The starch content of the guard cells may never wholly disappear, but usually it is lowest about 10 a.m. It rapidly increases during closure (Fig. 196). The rapid initial response of increased turgidity when light acts upon the guard cells is probably to be ascribed to colloidal hydration, while hydrolysis of carbohydrates seems to be a slower but probably more powerful reenforcement.[785,786]

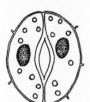 

Fig. 196.—Stomata from lower epidermis of a cocklebur (*Xanthium commune*). Note the absence of starch in the chloroplasts in the open (day) condition and its abundance at night when the stoma is closed.

Other Effects of Light.—The excess energy received from both the visible and infrared radiation is largely eliminated by the evaporation of water. Intensity of radiation is of great importance in controlling the rate of transpiration and hence, indirectly, the rate of water absorption. Intense light is nearly always associated with dry habitats and high transpiration. A linear relation between water loss and light intensity has been determined under a rather wide range of conditions in *Helianthus*.[571] Daily records of radiation over a period of two growing seasons in Colorado were correlated with daily rates of transpiration.[100] The mean correlation coefficient of transpiration with radiation of a wide variety of leguminous crops was 0.48, and for a similar lot of cereals 0.65. Among certain varieties of maize the ratios were as high as 0.80. At night, water loss by transpiration amounted to only 3 to 5 per cent of that lost during the daylight hours.[99]

Phototropic response is believed to be due to growth accelerating substances (hormones), light having an influence on both the formation and the transport of these growth regulators. Light has a profound influence on hardening of plants against cold.[237,939] It favors the germination of a large number of seeds and fruits, but it inhibits or interferes with others. It modifies the permeability of protoplasm, the absorption and use of solutes,[408] and affects the physiological processes of growth and differentiation in various ways.[112,827]

EXPOSURE OF LEAVES TO LIGHT

Through long periods of evolution plants have become so molded in form and in structure as to bring the photosynthetic organs into advantageous relation with the controlling factor, light. The latter occurs rather equally distributed in all directions; hence, the aerial plant parts are usually radially symmetrical. Since light is of such a nature that it cannot be transmitted far into the plant, the latter has become adapted by profuse and slender branching and ultimately by flattening and expanding the termini into the structures called leaves. In proportion to the amount of structural material involved, coniferous trees with a broad base and progressively shorter branches upward, diverging from

Fig. 197.—Blue spruce (*Picea pungens*); note the arrangement of the branches in layers.

the excurrent trunk, approach the ideal for maximum illumination. Leaf arrangement resulting from such branching has been likened to a series of meadows, one superimposed upon the other without the interference of shading (Fig. 197). Upon the periphery of this framework the photosynthetic organs are displayed (Fig. 198). The almost hemispheric crown of the deliquescent trunk of an isolated elm or maple is similarly advantageous as regards leaf exposure to light.

Many species have developed special methods of securing the display of their foliage in the light without the expenditure of sufficient materials to hold them erect.[197] Among such climbers are those which ascend merely by leaning against other plants (*e.g.*, a nightshade, *Solanum dul-*

camara); those which climb by hooks and thorns (*e.g.*, the bedstraw, *Galium*, and various brambles); root and tendril climbers such as Virginia creeper and English ivy; as well as the more specialized group of twining plants. Since climbers are most abundant in forests, and especially in dense tropical ones, but few in open grassland or desert, it seems that this habit must have resulted from the struggle for light.

The exposure to light has been obtained with little expenditure of materials for stems.[1015] A grapevine, for example, with a diameter of

FIG. 198.   FIG. 199.

FIG. 198.—Branch of blue spruce showing typical loss of leaves near center of crown due to decreased light. This occurs although water content of soil is optimum.

FIG. 199.—Virginia creeper or woodbine (*Parthenocissus quinquefolia*) about 7 feet long. The total transpiring surface of 23 square feet was supplied with water through six small stems, averaging only 3.5 millimeters in diameter.

stem of only a few centimeters may have a foliage area quite as great as that of the tree which upholds it, although the latter has a trunk several inches thick. The structure of the stem is so modified as to be given over largely to conduction, as may be easily demonstrated (Fig. 199).

To Compare the Rate of Water Conduction in Climbing and Nonclimbing Plants. Select stems of some woody vine such as grape (*Vitis*) or Virginia creeper (*Parthenocissus*) 6 to 10 millimeters thick, and cut a section 8 to 10 centimeters long. Select and cut branches of maple or oak or other tree of the same diameter and length, avoiding the nodes if possible. The sections should be cut under water or immediately placed in water. Procure rubber tubing that will fit closely over the stems. Fill a long piece of the tubing with water, siphoning it from a 2-liter container placed 10 feet above the worktable. While the tubing is filled with water, fasten it securely over one end of the stem and collect in a graduate the water that is conducted by the stem. Connect the second stem to another tube in a similar manner and determine the relative conducting power of the tree and climber for a period of 10 to 30 minutes. Examine the stems closely and suggest an explanation of the differences noted.

Foliage display in grasses and many other monocotyledons (*e.g.*, sedges, rushes, iris, cattails) is of a distinctly different but scarcely less efficient type. Here the leaves develop in such positions that they cast relatively little shade, and light is permitted to penetrate nearly or quite to their bases. At some time of the day, except in extremely dense growths, all of the leaves receive direct sunlight, and the total surface can be utilized in the manufacture of food. The advantage afforded by such an arrangement, together with the rhizome habit and basal growth, goes far toward accounting for the dominance of grasses and grasslike plants in the treeless portions of the world.

Many intermediate forms abound. The foliage of many plants is arranged in a mosaic, *i.e.*, the leaves are fitted together like the stones in a mosaic and in such a manner that each leaf is exposed to the most possible light. Plants such as dandelion, mullein, plantain, and evening primrose form rosettes near the soil. In these, each leaf is arranged so that it fills a space in the circle, and overlapping is reduced to a minimum. Where one leaf does overlap another, photosynthetic activity in the shaded portion of the latter is greatly reduced, in the case of the dandelion often 50 per cent. The positions of leaves in response to light are very diverse, as may be seen almost anywhere. Epiphytes have solved the light problem by perching high upon other plants.[684] Sometimes, they are so abundant as to cause considerable injury by shading the plant affording the support. In the same way, epiphylls, such as various species of lichens, characteristic of the moist tropics, are very injurious to the leaves on which they occur. In coniferous forests, the needles of the trees are sometimes shaded and even killed by the pendant growths of various lichens such as *Usnea* and *Alectoria*.

RECEPTION AND ABSORPTION OF LIGHT

Plants possess no special structures for the reception of light. The radiant energy impinges upon all of the aerial parts, the characteristic form of the leaf being chiefly to increase the surface for absorption of both light and carbon dioxide. The general effect of the epidermis is to reduce the amount of light that enters the leaf, owing partly to reflection and partly to absorption. The amount of light reflected depends upon the quality or wave length and angle of incidence of the light and the texture and pigmentation of the leaf.

Dark green leaves like those of the lilac reflect less light than paler green ones such as the white poplar. A green leaf of geranium reflected

16 per cent of diffuse daylight but a white one 38 per cent. Reflection from the white, hairy under surface of the leaves of white poplar is sometimes 50 per cent of the incident light.[848] In general, smoothness or hairiness of the cuticle does not necessarily result in high reflection. A thick cuticle or one coated with wax or a dense coating of hairs absorbs much light and that reaching the green tissue is diffuse. In deserts and alpine regions where such structures are pronounced, only 15 to 25 per cent may be transmitted to the chlorenchyma.[791]

The light that enters the leaf must pass through the colorless epidermis and is then absorbed by the chlorenchyma. In submerged hydrophytes, epidermal chlorophyll usually occurs in abundance, but among terrestrial plants, chloroplasts in the epidermis are rare even in those species growing in dense shade, with the exception of ferns. Some light passes entirely through the leaf, but ordinarily this is slight. Thick or fleshy leaves absorb practically all the light that enters them. Thin leaves placed in sunshine transmit considerable light, but plants with such leaves are usually confined to shady habitats, where the light is very diffuse and the absorption relatively complete. From 0 to 10 per cent transmission has been determined for various leaves. Brown and Escombe in their classical investigations found that the various leaves with which they experimented absorbed 65 to 77 per cent of the incident radiant energy.[105] This is in close agreement with more recent researches.[875]

To Determine the Relative Amount of Light Absorbed by Various Leaves.— Select representative sun and shade leaves of a tree or shrub and of herbs grown in full light and dense shade. Variegated leaves of geranium, ribbon grass (*Phalaris*), or *Abutilon*, and others with prominent veining such as kidney bean (*Phaseolus vulgaris*), etc., should also be used. Place one leaf of each on the glass of an 8- by 10-inch printing frame, cover with a sheet of printing-out paper such as "solio," and fasten the back of the frame in place. Expose to the sunlight for 10 to 30 minutes until the paper about the leaves is thoroughly blackened and the network of veins shows very plainly. Remove the leaves and compare the relative darkening of the paper (*i.e.*, penetration of rays chemically active on the sensitized paper) under the different leaves. Hold the leaf to the light and explain why the veins are printed so clearly. Make a list of the leaves in order of their absorption of light rays. The leaf prints may be kept permanently by "fixing" them for 5 minutes in a bath containing 150 grams of sodium hyposulphite dissolved in 500 cubic centimeters of water. The prints should be washed in water before drying.

NATURE OF THE LIGHT FACTOR

Differences in latitude, altitude, and climate cause variations in light which modify the rate of photosynthesis and growth in plants. Differences in light during the growing season in tropical and temperate climates are not great enough, however, to modify the rate at which photosynthesis proceeds.[392] Plants of arctic regions have been shown to make carbohydrates continuously during the 24-hour day, and produce an amount almost as great as would be formed during the shorter day in a temperate climate. Many species of evergreens are known to make photosynthate in winter in sufficiently large amounts to balance that oxidized in respiration. This may occur at temperatures near freezing.[825]

The effect of light is exerted upon plants by change in its quality, direction, intensity, or duration. In nature, the *quality of light* on clear days is apparently very little if any different in various habitats. Exceptions occur in species of plants which grow in the forest. Change in the quality of the light is due to differential absorption and reflection by leaves. Under canopies of needle-leaved trees, the change is slight but beneath broad-leaved canopies a higher percentage of green light occurs.[492] This phenomenon has been verified by many investigators.[403,848] Even though the light in forests is changed somewhat in quality, it still contains a sufficient percentage of the various wave lengths to produce approximately normal plant growth, *i.e.*, differences encountered in the forest are too small to be of much practical importance. Modification of the quality of light has only a secondary influence upon the growth of the plants of the forest floor and is far less important than the decrease in intensity. Light reaches the forest floor by filtering through or between the crowns of trees or by reflection from the leaves and twigs. The amount of light passing unabsorbed through leaves is small, 0.03 to 0.6 per cent for sun leaves and 0.3 to 2 per cent for shade leaves.[115] A simple experiment shows that the thickness of one leaf is often enough to screen the light so completely that photosynthesis in the leaf just below is entirely inhibited.

The quality of the light is modified by clouds, fogs, etc. Water vapor in the air absorbs a great deal of the long wave lengths, particularly infrared. During the winter, a higher percentage of red light and a lower one of blue light reach the earth than in summer. In general, the red end of the spectrum permits excessive tissue and cell elongation; the blue-violet light exerts a retarding effect upon growth by keeping the cells smaller. It seems possible that the difference of vegetative growth at low and high altitudes and in clear and foggy climates is partly due to differences in the quality of the light.

Infrared radiation is of no value to plants except as it increases temperature.[25] It is not known to be injurious to them, although it may sometimes cause sunscald in fruits or other massive organs not cooled by rapid transpiration.

Ultraviolet radiation of shorter wave lengths than those found in sunlight has a pronounced injurious effect upon plants.[704,705] The development of red pigmentation in apples is brought about by the blue-violet and ultraviolet of sunlight. This results from its influence upon the living cells.[25] The presence of flavone and anthocyanin in alpine plants has been ascribed to the action of intense light, particularly the shorter wave lengths. Full sunlight, although it varies in quality, is far more satisfactory for the growth of plants than any part thereof, or than any artificial source that has been discovered.

The *direction of the light* is of little importance except where the illumination is strongly one-sided. The radially symmetrical development of a tree or other isolated plant shows clearly that strong diffuse (north) light is sufficient for normal development. Only plants on the edges of forests, thickets, etc., are often bent toward the source of light. Within the mass of vegetation such movements are lacking except in a few plants such as the mallow (*Malva rotundifolia*), cotton (*Gossypium*), and sunflower (*Helianthus*). These species have leaves that are so sensitive to light that the leaf blades are turned at right angles to the sun's rays in the morning, and by a gradual shift in position they follow the sun through its course, facing westward in the evening. By an orientation of the flower stalk, the sunflower head often behaves similarly.

The *change in light intensity* necessary to produce a response varies for different species, and it is also influenced by the intensity in which the species normally grows. The normal extremes are full sunshine, represented by 1, and a diffuseness of 0.002, *i.e.*, light only one five-hundredth that of sunlight. Photosynthesis is so completely dependent upon light that it is affected by very slight differences of intensity. On the contrary, such responses as the movement of chloroplasts and changes in leaf structure are produced only by much greater differences.

The *duration of light, i.e.*, length of day, exerts such profound effects upon the rate of development, flowering, and fruiting and upon the distribution of plants that it will be separately considered (p. 410).

MEASUREMENT OF LIGHT INTENSITY

The measurement of light intensity is not a simple process and it becomes increasingly difficult where it must be made in the field and often in a small space among plants. No photometer that is entirely satisfactory has yet been devised.[489] Ideally, both quality and intensity of the light should be determined for different hours of the day and for different days of the growing season in various habitats. Illuminometers are best suited for measuring visible radiation.[822] The Weston Sun-lightmeter has been found useful in both field and greenhouse. It consists of a special photoelectric cell with a sensitive ammeter calibrated directly in foot-candles (Fig. 200). The range covered by this instrument is approximately the visible spectrum, which is the most important, ecologically and physiologically. It is only necessary to turn the searching unit to the light, and then read the light values in foot-candles on the instrument scale. The readings may be made instantly and directly, the apparatus is rugged and compact and hence suitable for field use. The practicability of almost simultaneous measurements of light both inside and outside of a woodland, a cover of grassland, etc., is of great importance, owing to the necessarily variable character of natural illumination. Moreover, a large number of readings can be obtained in a comparatively short time and average values thus determined.[763] It is most convenient to express the habitat illuminations as percentages of the light in the open.

A very useful instrument for measuring approximate differences in intensity in different habitats is the simple photometer.[78] It has been very extensively employed. In principle, it is based upon the fact that the darkening of sensitized photographic paper is proportional to the product of the light

Fig. 200.—Weston Sunlightmeter.

intensity and the time of exposure. By this method, only the rays chemically active on the sensitized paper (*i.e.*, the blue end of the spectrum) are measured, and it is assumed that the intensities of the others vary in proportion.

The instrument consists of a tight metal box containing a central disk upon which a strip of photographic paper is fastened in a groove (Fig. 201). The disk is revolved past an opening 6 millimeters square, which is closed by means of a spring that operates

Fig. 201.—Simple photometers. The one on the right has a stop watch attached.

a slide working between two flanges. It is graduated into 25 parts that are numbered. A line just beneath the opening coincides with the successive lines on the disk and indicates the number of the exposure. The proper movement of the wheel for each successive exposure is indicated by a click. The metal case is made of two parts which fit together in such a manner that the bottom can readily be removed and the paper placed in position. The paper used is a slow printing-out paper such as solio. Strips 6 milli-meters wide are cut lengthwise on a straightedge from 8- by 10-inch sheets with the emulsion side up. The paper is placed in the groove on the disk with the ends inserted downward through the small opening. It is best to crease the ends of the paper so that it will fit tightly before inserting the cork plug, which holds it in position. Great care should be exercised not to touch the emulsion side of the paper which is turned outward on the disk. When the paper is securely fastened in position, the cover is inserted and held in place by the thumbscrew on the side. The cover should be revolved until the 6-millimeter opening in it is just opposite the number 1 on the disk. A recent model of the stop-watch photometer is of vest-pocket size and all the operations are automatically made by pressing a plunger.

Making a Standard.—The photometer is held in one hand with the slit directed toward the noonday sun. A watch with a large second hand is held with it, thus leaving the other hand free to operate the shutter. An exposure is made by quickly withdrawing the slide in such a way as to uncover the entire opening, at the same time keeping the eyes fixed on the watch. The closure is made automatically simply by releasing the shutter. After a little practice, it is easy to expose the paper for the exact time desired. After each exposure the dial should be immediately turned to the next number.

The standard is obtained by making successive exposures 1, 2, 3, etc., to 8 seconds in length in full sunshine at noon on a clear day. Great care should be exercised to make the time of exposure exact. It is desirable to make a second series to serve as a check upon the first. The standard is then removed in a dark room and placed in a light-tight box, such as is used for photographic films or plates. It should be used only in weak, electric light. When kept in a cool place and handled carefully, the standard and solio strips may be kept several weeks without appreciable change. It is best, however, to make a new standard from time to time during the growing season to serve as a check upon the original.

Making Readings.—The best practice in making readings is to secure a decided tint that falls between the extremes of the standard. It is practically impossible to obtain a sunshine equivalent for very faint tints and equally difficult to match the very deep ones obtained by long exposure. Consequently, the most satisfactory method is to expose until a good tint is secured but one that is not deeper than the 5-second tint of the standard. In deep shade, this often requires several minutes, and in such places it is usually more satisfactory to stop the exposure with the lighter tint, approximating the 1- or 2-second exposure of the standard. The stop-watch photometer, which differs in having a stop watch which automatically indicates the time of the exposure, is somewhat more convenient and increases the accuracy of the reading. In taking readings, the date, time of day, place of reading, number of instrument and of exposure, and the time of the exposure in seconds must be carefully recorded. As a rule, readings are made only on clear days, except where the light values of cloudy days are desired for special purposes. After a strip has been completely exposed, it is removed in the dark, and a new one is put in place. In removing the strip, the number of each exposure should be marked on the reverse side of the paper.

Comparison with the Standard.—The light intensity denoted by each exposure is ascertained by comparing it with the standard. It is best to cut off the part of the strip on which the first reading was made and hold it with tweezers while comparing with the standard until the tint that matches is secured. With a little practice, this may be readily done. Skill and certainty in making the tints match are obtained by comparing the exposed strip with the standard a second time. If this is done without reference to the first results, the two comparisons serve as a valuable check upon each other. Proceeding in this manner, all of the readings are matched with the standard. Interpolations between colors may be made, if desirable, when the proper match is secured for a particular exposure. The comparative light intensity is found by dividing the duration of exposure in seconds by the duration for the standard tint. Thus, if an exposure in shade for 100 seconds matches a 2-second standard, the light is fifty times more diffuse or weaker than the sunlight. The latter is taken as unity, and the light intensity in the shade is $2 \div 100 = 0.02$, *i.e.*, 2 per cent.

Measuring Light Intensity.—Make a series of light readings in the several habitats where other factors are being measured. It is best to make three readings, using different lengths of time of exposure in each place, and average the results. In forest, scrub, etc., where the light is not uniform, move the photometer slowly back and forth during the exposure, keeping the opening directed toward the sun, in order to secure an average of the light intensities. Are the light values the same at different levels in grassland, scrub, and forest? Give reasons for your conclusions. Compare that of the interior of the crown of a tree with the light received by the leaves on the north and south periphery. Also determine light intensities in the greenhouse and on cloudy days. The photometer may likewise be used to determine the amount of light that penetrates through various leaves by holding the leaf closely over the slot during the exposure. Similar measurements should be made with the Sunlightmeter.

CAUSES OF VARIATION IN LIGHT INTENSITY

Among the most important factors causing variations in the light are the humidity of the atmosphere and the amount of cloudy weather. Even very fleecy clouds in front of the sun result in appreciable reduction of light, but the light may be increased by reflection from white clouds. It is greatly reduced by heavy clouds and fogs. The total radiation received on a cloudy day may be as low as 4 per cent of that during the same season and station during a day of full sunshine.[822] In certain oceanic climates, heavy fogs are so prevalent and the light is reduced so regularly that it may become a limiting factor to photosynthesis and growth. In northern latitudes, such as Alaska, where rainfall is abundant but the temperature too low for the best development of vegetation, the amount of sunshine becomes an exceedingly important climatic factor. Arid regions have higher hourly light values and higher yearly totals than humid regions in the same latitude.

Both intensity and quality of light are markedly reduced by a layer of water, and submerged plants grow under an illumination quite different from that of terrestrial ones. The fact that bodies of water are blue or greenish blue indicates that the long waves of light are absorbed to a much greater extent, and that the short wave lengths only are reflected, or transmitted to any considerable depth. When the surface of the water is smooth, 20 to 25 per cent of the light may be reflected, and in rough water this may be increased to 50 or even 70 per cent. The optimum depth for photosynthesis of certain submerged aquatics in the clear lakes of northern Wisconsin has been shown to be about 5 meters on clear days and the maximum depth about 15 meters.[796] In the ocean, even light of short wave lengths may be reduced under the most favorable conditions to approximately 10 per cent at a depth of 10 meters.[307] The red pigment, phycoerythrin, of the red algae (*Rhodophyceae*) is complementary to the blue light rays and because of this the plants of the deep water are able to absorb the latter much more advantageously.[889] Many recent studies have been made on light intensity and the distribution and growth of plants of inland waters.[987]

The light of the forest floor may be reduced to 1 to 10 per cent, but due to the movement of the foliage and the variation of the position of the sun, it is constantly changing. The light intensity may rapidly change from 2 to 5 per cent to 40 or more in a sunfleck. Above an understory of young trees and shrubs growing in a forest with a closed canopy, the light is often about 20 per cent, but below the understory only about 1 to 5.[825]

The intensity of the light varies throughout the day and the year. Except where plants are considerably shaded, it is only for a short time near sunrise and sunset that light is a limiting factor to photosynthesis when the sky is clear. The daily maximum occurs at noon "sun time," a point which itself moves back and forth through the year. The greatest light intensity occurs when the sun is at its highest altitude, i.e., when the angle that it makes with the surface of the earth is greatest, and lowest when this angle is least. The effect of angle upon light intensity is due to the absorption of the light waves by the atmosphere. This absorption is greatest near the horizon, where the pathway of the waves is longest, and it is least at the zenith.

Altitude affects the amount of light by decreasing the distance that the waves must travel through the atmosphere, thus decreasing absorption. The highest values of solar radiation ever measured at the surface of the earth (on high mountains) are about 1.75 gram calories per square centimeter per minute or approximately 12,000 foot-candles.[481] It is estimated that 20 per cent of a light ray is absorbed by the earth's atmosphere before it reaches sea level. At the top of Pike's Peak (altitude 14,100 feet), the absorption is 11 per cent. In the one instance, the light is 80 per cent of that which enters the atmosphere; in the other, 89 per cent. The difference in intensity is altogether too small to have any important effect on photosynthesis.

The amount of light received by a south-facing slope is greater than that received by a level area, and that striking a north-facing slope is least. Except that the duration of light on the south slope is longest, the difference is of little significance. Leaf position as regards incident light is the same in all cases. The vegetation on north-facing slopes of steep mountains and valleys in north temperate regions may receive little or no direct sunlight. The sharp difference in the type of vegetation as compared with fully insolated slopes is due to differences in temperature and water relations of soil and air. There is abundant light for photosynthesis, although it is diffuse light in the former community.

INFLUENCE OF DECREASED LIGHT INTENSITY

All green plants require light, although bacteria and fungi may flourish even in dark caverns and in the depths of the ocean. In fact, many species of saprophytic plants are killed by exposure to light, a fact clearly recognized in sanitation. Many saprophytic and parasitic fungi that can grow vegetatively in the dark require light for reproduction.

The total absence of light results in greatly attenuated, weak stems with tissues weakly differentiated and little mechanical tissue. There are few or no branches and the leaves fail to expand, often being reduced to mere scales that usually lack palisade tissue. The root system is poorly developed. The plant is pale yellowish or whitish in color, due to lack of chlorophyll and is said to be etiolated. This characteristic elongation of stems in darkness appears to be the result chiefly of a considerable increase in the length of the component cells.[720] Etiolated plants illuminated only 2 to 10 minutes daily showed profound changes in their form and structure.[708]

In the weak light of deep shade the internodes are less elongated, the thin leaves unfold and develop chlorophyll, the weak stems are succulent, and roots are poorly developed. Under light intensities of about 20 to 50 per cent of full sunshine, maximum vegetative expansion is usually attained. The leaves reach their greatest area and the plant its maximum height. The root system is of moderate size.

Extensive experimental work has been done with sunflowers where both the amount of available water and the degree of insolation were controlled. The results indicate that water assumes the major role in stem elongation, and light the larger part in the production of dry matter, the two necessarily being integrated in the adaptation characteristic of shady habitats.[168] Intensities higher than 50 per cent sometimes cause a decrease in growth, especially in plants which normally grow in shade. It has been found in Germany that several weeds made their best growth in about two-thirds full light while the cultivated crops produced a maximum dry weight under full light, showing a marked decrease when shaded.[1030] In full sunshine there is usually a considerable decrease in length of internodes, height of plant, and area of leaves. For best development most plants require full sunshine, providing other factors are not limiting. Rate of growth usually increases with increased light intensity up to 50 or even 100 per cent. This seems to be true even of forest plants.[825]

Effect of Light Intensity on Form and Structure of Plants.—Construct in the greenhouse a series of two or three shade tents 1 meter square and high. The framework of wooden strips, $\frac{1}{4}$ by 1 inch, may be nailed to a table or greenhouse bench and the cloth fastened to it by means of thumbtacks. Light intensities of approximately 10, 5, and 1 per cent may be obtained by using coverings of white cheesecloth, muslin, and double thickness of black cambric, respectively. The tent should be so constructed that the lower half of one side may be easily opened. Ordinarily, the humidity may be controlled by the amount of watering, but if it becomes too high, a hood for ventilation should be arranged at the top or sides.

Practically all flowering plants will show some adaptation to the different light intensities, although some are much more plastic than others. Start seedlings of various species in ordinary greenhouse light, *e.g.*, sunflower, four-o'clock (*Allionia*), dandelion, shepherd's-purse (*Bursa*), bedstraw (*Galium*), evening primrose (*Oenothera*), etc. Then place two of each species in each tent and keep two for controls. Water as necessary; the weaker plants in deep shade will require but little.

During the growth of the plants, make occasional readings of the light intensity and humidity in the several tents and that of the greenhouse outside. Also, make one determination of the starch content of a representative leaf of each species for each habitat. Follow from week to week the effect of shade upon leaf size and outline and form of the rosette in dandelion; note the stretching of the petioles and internodes in *Bursa* and *Oenothera*, and observe other differences in growth and behavior. When the plants are well grown, make an outline drawing or photograph of one series of four plants, all to the same scale. Select a representative leaf from each form, and make a leaf print for the four forms of each species. Cut cross sections of the leaves of one series and make out the differences in total thickness, development of palisade, sponge, thickness of cuticle, etc. Prepare a concise account of the adaptation of one of the species concerned to different light intensities, explaining, in so far as possible, the changes observed.

Partial shade increases succulence and delicacy of structure. Many vegetables such as asparagus, cauliflower, celery, and lettuce do best under such conditions. Half-shade is employed in forcing rhubarb, and in pineapple culture, especially in Florida. Tea is grown in the shade of taller trees often planted in alternate rows, since under these conditions the leaves attain their best quality and yield. Coffee is likewise produced most profitably in subtropical regions when partially shaded by forest trees. Ginseng, which normally grows in woodland shade, is protected from full sunshine when grown commercially by frames made of slats. Partial shade produces large, broad, thin leaves with poorly developed veins and relatively large air spaces and an abundance of sponge parenchyma, as is shown by the growth of tobacco for cigar wrappers under conditions of half-shade.[998,389] It must be constantly kept in mind, however, that reducing the light also has a marked effect upon other factors, especially soil moisture, humidity, and temperature. In forest nurseries and elsewhere, lath shelters are widely used to maintain the proper conditions for seedbeds of many kinds of trees.

While diffuse light promotes the development of vegetative structures, intense light favors the development of flowers, fruits, and seeds. The great profusion of flowers in grassland throughout the growing season is largely due to the strong light. In deciduous forests, flowers are abundant only before the new leaves of the forest canopy are developed; in dense coniferous forests, flowers are never abundant. The greatest profusion of brightly colored flowers is found in alpine meadows where the light is very intense. Under extremely high light intensities, transpiration becomes excessive. Structural changes occur which protect the plant from excessive heating and desiccation. The vegetation is often characterized by plants with low stature and small leaves of considerable thickness. Rapid transpiration is promoted by an increase in water-conducting tissue.

Many crops grown for their vegetative parts, such as potatoes, carrots, turnips, and garden beets, yield best where there is a high percentage of cloudy days. Conversely, the greatest grain-producing areas are in regions where there is a high percentage of bright, sunny days. Such are the grasslands of the central United States and of eastern Washington. Fruit is likewise produced in great quantities where the light intensity is but slightly reduced by clouds or atmospheric moisture during the entire growing season and often under irrigation, especially in California, Washington, and Colorado. The yield of cotton fiber and seed is greatly reduced throughout the cotton belt during unusually cloudy, wet years, although the plants make an excessive vegetative growth.

TOLERANCE

Tolerance is the ability of a tree or other plant to survive, grow, and develop in shade. Formerly it was believed to be entirely a response to decreased light, but it is now known that soil moisture, temperature, and other factors may play a large part. Seedlings of hard maple, beech. linden, spruce, and hemlock are all very tolerant of shade. Those of light-demanding trees such as willow, cottonwood, jack pine, and lodge-pole pine are intolerant. Similarly, many shrubs and herbs such as sumac, bluestem grasses, and sunflowers are light demanding, while the spicebush and bloodroot grow in deep shade. Tolerance in trees is an inherent characteristic, which is better developed in some species than in others.

The light relation beneath a forest composed of intolerant trees is very different from that of one of tolerant species. In general, the crowns of intolerant trees are open and the foliage thin, and much light penetrates through the canopy and reaches the forest floor. Seedlings of such trees, however, have difficulty in becoming established even in this moderate shade. Those that succeed grow rapidly in height. The dense forest canopy furnished by tolerant species has many layers of leaves, since leaves grow also on the inside of the crowns. The seedlings tolerate the deep shade, growing slowly perhaps for many years until, upon the death of older trees, they are finally released from the shade. Beech and hemlock, for example, are able to stand suppression and make slow growth with no apparent lessening of vigor, and after 100 or more years they are still able to make a rapid development if released from near-by competitors.[419]

It is because of the adjustment of certain types of vegetation to decreased light intensity that layering occurs. Layers may be seen in various plant communities such as reed swamp, grassland, and scrub, but they are most pronounced in forests.

The number of layers is controlled mainly by the density of the forest canopy, although other factors such as water content often play an important part. In an open woodland, where much light filters through between the leaves and branches and where there is an adequate supply of water, layers of shrubs, tall herbs, low herbs, and a ground layer of mosses, lichens, liverworts, and fungi are usually more or less developed. But where the crowns of the trees grow closely, as in medial or climax stages of deciduous forests, because of decreased light, some of the layers and frequently all but the low herb and ground layers disappear. The herbs show their most vigorous development during spring and early summer before the leafing out of the trees still further reduces the light. In such habitats, intolerant plants cannot ecize. The real shade plant is one which not only can grow under low light intensities but also exists for a long period under conditions unfavorable for photosynthesis. A tree to become established in a closed forest must function and grow as a seedling and sapling in very subdued light, although later in life it may take its place in the forest canopy and receive full sunshine. Hence, only those that are tolerant can ecize.

A knowledge of tolerance is especially important in forest management.[45] In fact, technical forestry or silviculture is, or at least was, largely based on the concept that the different species of the forest vary in their demands for light, i.e., their tolerance of shade.[47,50] The outcome of mixed plantations depends upon the difference in tolerance between species. Intolerant species will disappear, since they cannot reproduce themselves in shade. Tolerance likewise determines the outcome of plantations made under the canopies of old trees that do not reproduce themselves. The methods of cutting or thinning are similarly determined, less valuable but tolerant species, such as hard maple, often being removed to promote the growth of less tolerant but more valuable ones, such as white pine.[281] In the natural development of forests through the various successional stages, light is usually a controlling factor.

Trees may be grouped according to their ability to carry on photosynthesis and grow in decreased light intensities, i.e., according to their tolerance. The following sequence, however, is not absolute, the most tolerant being placed first:[1035]

Broadleaf Trees	Coniferous Trees
Very tolerant:	Very tolerant:
Sugar maple (*Acer saccharum*)	Yew (*Taxus*)
Beech (*Fagus*)	Spruce (*Picea*)
Linden (*Tilia*)	Hemlock (*Tsuga*)
	Firs (*Abies*)
	Cedars (*Thuja*)

Broadleaf Trees	Coniferous Trees
Tolerant:	Tolerant:
Elms (*Ulmus*)	White pine (*Pinus strobus*)
White oak (*Quercus alba*)	Douglas fir (*Pseudotsuga*)
Red oak (*Q. borealis*)	
Ash (*Fraxinus*)	
Black oak (*Q. velutina*)	
Intolerant:	Intolerant:
Soft maple (*Acer saccharinum*)	Ponderosa pine (*Pinus ponderosa*)
Bur oak (*Q. macrocarpa*)	Larch (*Larix*)
Birches (*Betula*)	Lodgepole pine (*Pinus contorta murrayana*)
Poplars (*Populus*)	
Willows (*Salix*)	

It may be noted, for example in the development of deciduous forest, that the species characteristic of climax stages of succession are more or less tolerant. Extensive lists of tolerance of trees of both eastern and western North America may be found in texts on silviculture.[35,926]

Methods of Determining Tolerance.—There are several methods of determining the relative tolerance of forest trees.[1035] Empirical scales of tolerance may be prepared by studying such characters as density of crown, self-pruning, relative height growth, and the growth of the young stand under the old. An examination of the interior of the crown of intolerant trees, *e.g.*, soft maple or ponderosa pine, will show that nearly all of the leaves occur on a peripheral hollow shell where they are well illuminated. The crown is not dense. In the pine, the lower whorl of branches, clothed with needles only on their termini, extends outward in such a manner that the branches are only slightly shaded by those just above and these, in turn, only moderately so by those still higher. The leaves of intolerant trees cannot make food in weak, diffuse light. Conversely, the density of the crowns of hard maple and linden, for example, is much greater and the interior fairly well clothed with shade leaves.

In the forest, the lower leaves and branches of intolerant trees die and fall to the ground. The more intolerant the species the more rapidly self-pruning occurs. In fact, intolerant trees clear themselves of many branches even when they grow as isolated individuals. Hence, in the forest the tree grows slender and straight, its height being very great in relation to its diameter. Tolerant species, such as *Thuja*, retain their branches, and the stem is thick in proportion to its height. The Indians found that certain spindling, close-growing, intolerant trees, upon the removal of the bushy tops, made a very desirable framework for their tepees, hence the name *lodgepole* pine (Fig. 202). Finally, a study of the growth of young trees under the parent trees throws much light upon their ability to endure shade. In mixed forests with a closed canopy, saplings of oak and hickory may succumb under light intensities where those of elm, beech, and sugar maple will thrive.

The most direct way of determining the tolerance of forest trees is to measure the light intensity under various forest canopies where the seedlings are growing or fail to grow. In doing so the great variation in intensity from hour to hour and day to day throughout the season must be considered. Even in the dense, tropical rain-forest of Brazil where the light averages less than 1 per cent, sunny spots at times received as much as 16 times the shade illumination.[474,595] The minimum light for sustained growth of ponderosa-pine seedlings is about 25 per cent, for Douglas fir 5 per cent, but that for Engelmann spruce is only 2 per cent.[44]

Fig. 202.—A young forest of closely growing Douglas fir, tamarack, and white fir. Note the absence of branches due to low light intensity.

The minimum light at which photosynthesis occurs in ponderosa pine has been found to be 17 per cent, but only 1.9 per cent is required for the very tolerant sugar maple.[117] In a virgin stand of Norway pine studied in relation to light and to other vegetation, approximately 35 per cent light, or a crown density of about two-thirds, seemed to offer satisfactory conditions for the establishment of Norway pine seedlings. An understory of shrubs which reduced the light to less than 5 per cent, quite effectively excluded seedlings of coniferous trees.[823]

Seedlings of ponderosa pine were grown in a nursery in Arizona under uniformly favorable conditions except for reduction in insolation. All of the plants with 10 per cent light died the first winter and those with only

20 per cent succumbed within 5 years. Plants in half-shade made slightly less height growth and only about half the growth in diameter of those in full sunlight.[674] Douglas fir and Engelmann spruce seedlings in the nursery attained their best development in half-shade but became too spindling when light was reduced to 25 per cent.[499] Other investigators have also found the best development of coniferous trees in light intensities approaching full sunlight.[415]

A climax deciduous forest is a dark forest. Even when the sun shines brightly, a condition resembling twilight prevails at noonday in the beech-maple climax. The dominant beech and maple alone may reproduce satisfactorily, shrubs are few, and only the most tolerant herbs prevail. The relative light intensities during midsummer in a mixed forest of black and bur oak and one of linden in Nebraska, where each species was reproducing its kind, respectively, were as follows:

	6 a.m.	8 a.m.	10 a.m.	12 M.	2 p.m.	4 p.m.	6 p.m.
Oak forest.....................	5.3	5.5	20.0	20.0	20.0	11.6	10.0
Linden forest..................	1.8	2.0	6.6	10.0	4.6	4.3	2.5

In the oak forest, layering was pronounced; in the linden community, all but the ground layer had disappeared and no tree seedlings except those of the very tolerant linden were able to survive.[415] If a tree is to maintain itself, it must make in addition to food for respiration a sufficient amount for growth. Food reserves must be accumulated to withstand unfavorable seasons and also for reproduction of the species.

A Study of Tolerance.—From your field observations supplemented by use of the various methods of determining tolerance, make a list of the more important forest or shade trees of your region. Use one list for deciduous and one for evergreen species and subdivide each into very tolerant, tolerant, and intolerant species.

A study of leaf structure gives much information about the tolerance of a species. Leaves that adapt themselves most completely to a variety of light conditions are naturally those which will survive best if placed under severe conditions as regards reduced light. This method, however, can give only relative comparisons, since the structure of leaves is variable even under the same conditions of light. It is difficult to classify intermediate species on the basis of structure.[516] As already pointed out, leaf structure is also profoundly affected by the water relation.

Factors Affecting Tolerance.—In using these criteria of tolerance, it must be kept in mind that soil moisture may also play an important and often a controlling part. When photosynthetic activity is low, development of roots is decreased more than that of the aboveground parts. Consequently, a seedling with insufficient light is subjected to much greater danger from drought or lack of soil nutrients. A classical example is that of Fricke's experiment in Europe where isolated groups of 10-year-old Scotch pines were found growing among their 70- to 100-year-old parents. The younger generation was growing poorly, apparently because of deficient light due to the crowded condition. A trench 10 inches deep was dug around a group in the spring, whereupon the new needles increased their growth to twice that of their neighbors and also that of the preceding year. An herbaceous flora, moreover, appeared beneath the pines, quite in contrast to that of adjacent, similar areas. In digging the trench, the widely spreading, superficial roots of the parent

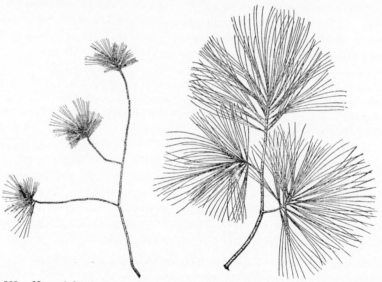

Fig. 203.—Normal development of needles of white pine (*Pinus strobus*) (right), and their poor growth in the dense shade of tolerant deciduous trees.

trees, which extended into the territory occupied by the younger generation, had been cut. The vigorous growth was thus a response to increased water content and perhaps nutrients but not to increased light[295] (Fig. 203).

Trenching experiments with white pine in New Hampshire gave similar results.[206,927,929] In Africa the experiment was modified by using well watered, potted plants of forest-tree seedlings and determining their growth in different degrees of shade under a forest canopy in comparison with the natural reproduction. The conclusion was again reached that water was more important than light.[692] Much evidence has been brought forth in Finland which shows that it is root competition rather than competition for light which determines the space relations of trees in forest on poorer soil types.[1] By growing tree seedlings on plots in forest with and without surrounding trenches, the importance of root competition between parent trees and their offspring has been further demonstrated in Germany.[275] From these and similar experiments, it has been concluded by certain workers that root competition is the dominant factor in determining the composition and growth of the understory.[925]

Researches in the ponderosa pine forests of Arizona, where soil moisture is a critical factor, do not support the conclusion of assigning to soil moisture the major portion of the influence formerly attributed to light. Here the seedlings grow in open grassy situations and do not become established under groups of trees. In these forests, on the Colorado Plateau, heat obtained from the radiant energy appears to be scarcely less important than moisture.[669] Seedlings benefited but little from trenching.[670]

Bur oak, red oak, hickory, linden, and walnut were grown in southeastern Nebraska in prairie, oak forest, and linden forest. The light values varied from full sunlight in the plowed prairie, to an average of 10.4 per cent in the oak, and 3.5 per cent in the linden forest. The development of both roots and shoots was the greatest for all species in the prairie and least in the linden forest, where most of the seedlings died before the end of the third season. Photosynthesis was very rapid in all species in the prairie; it was weak at the oak station, and very weak in the linden forest. Soil moisture was adequate for good growth in all three sites. Survival, photosynthesis, and growth were directly correlated with light intensity and inversely correlated with water content of soil. During severe drought, the ameliorating effects of shade provided by a forest canopy sometimes enables plants to survive better in forest than in the open.[324]

It is thus apparent that both light intensity and root competition are important factors in the growth of plants in forest. Undoubtedly the development of the undergrowth of shrubs, herbs, mosses, etc., on the forest floor is often greatly affected not only by the amount of light received but also by competition for water and nutrients. Which of these factors is the more important in a given area depends upon which one the more nearly limits plant growth. In the dense, dark forest on well watered, rich alluvial soil, it may be light; in a well lighted upland opening stocked with even aged saplings, it may be soil moisture. Improved growth may be brought about either by increasing the amount of light or by eliminating root competition. In thinning a stand by partial cuttings, both factors are reduced and, perhaps, often in about equivalent degrees.

Tolerance also varies with soil fertility and such climatic factors as temperature. Plants in warm regions require less insolation than the same species when grown farther north or at higher altitudes. White pine, for example, can stand less shading in Maine than in the mountains of North Carolina. Norway maple can live under 2 per cent light in Vienna, but 20 per cent is required in northern Norway. Since by far the greater part of the radiant energy is transformed into heat, the reason for these facts seems clear.[1035] In fact, in a study of tolerance, emphasis must be placed upon the physical effects of radiant energy. Many intolerant trees, such as ponderosa pine, rarely form close, dense stands. Hence, much of the thermal effect of the radiant energy is lost because of wind movement. Among tolerant trees of dense stands, such as spruce, there is little air movement, and consequently the total heating effect even of low illumination is high.[44]

DURATION OF LIGHT

The duration of the light period in nature varies from 12 hours at the equator to continuous sunlight throughout the 24 hours during a part of the year at very high latitudes. Thus, tropical plants are exposed to intense light during half of each day while arctic plants grow in weaker light continuously or nearly so throughout the summer. The long summer days of high latitudes enable plants to develop rapidly and mature quickly. Photosynthesis is continuous under such conditions although lowest at midnight. Species transplanted from lower latitudes and grown under the continuous sunlight of northern Scandinavia for 2 months had the vegetative period considerably shortened.[797] Timothy grown at a set of six stations from Savannah, Ga., to Fairbanks, Alaska, had its vegetative period progressively shortened from south to north. The season of blooming progressed at a constantly accelerated rate due to the gradually increasing length of day.[271] It is largely due to the longer day, although, in part, to the protection afforded by the surrounding mountains from cool night winds, that oranges ripen earlier in the northern end of the Central Valley of California than 400 miles farther south.[655] Likewise, the continuous or long daily periods of sunshine during summer make it possible to produce bountiful crops of hay, potatoes, and other vegetables along the coast of Alaska. The potato, which is a cool-climate crop, gives enormous yields, and grains and various garden plants grow rapidly, owing to the long period of illumination, along the Mackenzie River at the Arctic Circle.[10,11,224]

Numerous experiments have shown that continuous light produces maximum growth in some plants under the intensities and qualities of radiation that have been employed.[312] Many plants produce at their maximum under a 17- to 19-hour day.[26] Continuous illumination produces definite injury in certain species; still others, while showing no injury, are unable to benefit from it.[27]

Effect of Length of Day.*—There is a marked tendency for plants of temperate climates to flower and fruit at only certain periods of the year. The yellow bell, redbud, crocus, violet, etc., blossom early in spring. As summer approaches, the iris, rhododendron, and poppy begin to bloom, while asters, dahlias, and chrysanthemums are characteristic of fall. These differences in time of reproduction are not related to temperature but to the daily duration of light and darkness. Even though appropriate temperatures are provided out of the regular flowering and fruiting season, often the flowers and fruits fail to appear.

FIG. 204.—Long-day and short-day plants of red clover and evening primrose. One lot of the seedling clover and one rosette of *Oenothera* were grown six weeks under the short days of winter, and the others (center) were, in addition, illuminated until midnight.

Violets kept in the light daily for a period corresponding to the daylight hours of spring, bloom at all seasons of the year. Similarly, chrysanthemums blossom in midsummer, provided they are given daily illumination of a duration equal to that of the late autumn days. If the short winter day is extended by means of electric illumination until midnight, iris will blossom in December, provided, of course, that the temperature, water, and nutrient relations are suitable. Ordinary 40-watt, incandescent lights placed a few feet above the plants may be used. But even an average light intensity of about 5 foot-candles at the surface of the soil is sufficient for bringing many plants into bloom, although, in some cases, higher illumination is more efficient[468] (Fig. 204).

* Materials for this section, exclusive of illustrations, have been secured mainly from the publications of Garner and Allard.

The striking effect of length of day upon reproduction was discovered by Garner and Allard at Washington, D. C., while experimenting with a newly developed variety of tobacco. It grew only vegetatively during the summer but flowered and fruited abundantly when grown in the greenhouse in winter. By shortening the midsummer daily exposure to sunlight, flowering and fruiting were easily induced. Experiments were then extended to include many other species, and numerous investigators have studied various phases of the problem.

A large number of species are more or less responsive to the daily

FIG. 205.—Cosmos about 60 days old. Those in blossom received light from 9 a.m. till 4 p.m. daily; the others throughout the long summer days of June at Lincoln, Neb. They were placed in the small jars for photographing.

light period.[3] In many species, the action of the light period under ordinary circumstances is dominant, the response of the plant being prompt and certain under a rather wide range of environmental conditions. Some species and varieties respond to long days by flowering and fruiting, others to short ones. While, as a whole, there are sharp contrasts between the two groups, there are many species which apparently form an indeterminate or neutral group.

Long-day and Short-day Plants.— Some plants require long days for successful flowering and fruiting, although they make a vigorous vegetative growth during short ones.[922] Typical examples are the radish, iris, red clover, the smaller cereals, evening primrose, and spinach. These flower regularly during the long days of late spring and early summer. All may be brought into blossom and fruitage in midwinter, however, if artificial light is used to prolong the daily illumination period to 15 or 16 hours.

Short-day plants such as beggar-ticks (*Bidens*), tobacco, dahlia, ragweed, and cosmos continue to develop only vegetatively under a long-day illumination. They come into blossom normally only when short days occur. This is true of a large group of plants including most late-blooming summer annuals.[312] Experimentally, they may be caused to flower in midsummer by excluding the early morning or late afternoon light for a few hours each day (Fig. 205). If, however, these plants are darkened for the same number of hours (even 4 or 5) during the middle of the day, the vegetative period is not materially shortened. Cosmos under a short day, although dwarfed in stature, blossoms within 60 days after the germination of the seed, while under long-day illumination it continues growth and may attain a height of 15 feet.

Indeterminate or Neutral Group.—Certain species of plants belong to a neutral group which is less sensitive to daily light duration. They apparently have no critical length of day for reproduction and under suitable conditions for growth they tend to flower at all latitudes and at all seasons of the year.[311] The cultivated sunflower, for example, is not materially influenced in time of flowering by the length of day, at least in medium-high latitudes, although the stature attained is greatly affected. Buckwheat also belongs to this group. When it flowers under a very short day (5 to 7 hours), however, it makes only limited vegetative growth and soon completes its life cycle. Under a day of 11 to 18 hours, the plants make a better vegetative development, and flowering and maturing of seeds continue for a much longer period. Chickweed, dandelion, and groundsel also belong to this group.

To determine to which group a species belongs, it is only necessary to grow it under daily light exposures of 10 and 18 hours, respectively, and observe under which, if either, daily light period flowering is accelerated.

When exposed to a day length in excess of the critical, there is in the short-day type pronounced, long continued elongation of the stem without flowering; while exposure to a day length shorter than the critical quickly initiates reproductive activity. On the other hand, in the long-day plant, exposure to a length of day in excess of the critical results in elongation of the axis, which is promptly followed by flowering; while exposure to a length of day below the critical tends to limit development to a leaf-rosette stage.[311]

A study of the interrelation of day length and temperature has been made with both long-day plants (beets and *Rudbeckia*) and short-day plants (soybeans). The critical light period for flowering may be altered to a certain degree by temperature, and conversely the favorable temperature range for flowering may be shifted by the action of day length.[880]

The number of species belonging to this indeterminate group appears to be far greater than that of the other two groups. Alpine plants transplanted from Pike's Peak to the plains at the base, or to the coast at Santa Barbara, Calif., bloom in response to the temperature and not length of day.[174] Most of the species taken from the deciduous forest and the prairie flower several months earlier in California, and in general, the displacement of seasonal aspects by long winters or late springs is a well known phenomenon. With experimental day lengths of 5, 10, and 15 hours, practically all the species tested have blossomed in the reverse order, the long-day plants first. Recently, it has been found that species with a definite response to the photoperiod may change this completely under a different temperature.[730]

Everbloomers.—In temperate regions most plants have a comparatively short period of flowering and fruiting each year, the length of time varying with the species. In some, however, reproductive activity continues through several months. These are known as everbloomers or everbearers.

Near the equator, where the days are always 12 hours long, many plants have developed the everblooming or everbearing habit. Under natural conditions, the seasonal change in length of day in the United States is such that only a few plants show a pronounced type of everblooming. A number of common weeds such as chickweed (*Stellaria*) and dead nettle (*Lamium*) are of this class. These plants continue to grow and to flower in the field more or less persistently not only throughout the summer but also in the winter, if removed to the greenhouse. They are conspicuously different in their behavior from the majority of nontropical plants which have their definite floral season.

Several species of plants, when exposed to a length of day distinctly favorable to both growth and sexual reproduction, show a tendency to exhibit the "everblooming" or "everbearing" habit, *i.e.*, the ability to continue both vegetative and reproductive activities more or less successfully together. Apparently such plants may normally belong to any of the preceding groups. Conversely, by subjecting plants to daily light exposures unfavorable for reproduction, many species have been kept for a very long time in apparent vigor. Red clover was thus maintained for a period of 4 years under a 10-hour day,[922] and live-forever (*Sedum spectabile*) for 9 years under a 12-hour daily light period.[317] When exposed to a long day such plants promptly blossom.

Many annual plants such as soybeans and ragweeds, when subjected to a particular length of day, complete two annual cycles as regards vegetative growth, flowering and fruiting within a period of about 4 months. The perennial aster behaves in a similar manner. Conversely, under certain light exposures, the vegetative development of annuals may be lengthened almost indefinitely, the plants behaving like nonflowering perennials. Thus, it appears that the cycle of alternating vegetative and reproductive activities as an annual event is due to the yearly periodicity in the length of day. Lengthening the day in autumn resulted in prompt renewal of active growth and abundant development of new leaves in the tulip tree.[315] The usual rapid leaf fall of certain other woody species was replaced by a continuous dropping of the leaves.[506] It has been found possible to reverse the sex in hemp, maize, and other species by modifying the length of day.[789,790]

To Study the Development of Long- and Short-day Plants.—During the short days of late fall or winter, arrange a black curtain and overhead lighting in such a manner that one bench in the greenhouse may be artificially illuminated until midnight, while the rest of the greenhouse is in darkness. The curtain should be drawn aside by day so that temperature, humidity, and all other factors except length of the period of illumination are the same. Transplant into large pots, rosettes of evening primrose (*Oenothera biennis*), and rhizomes of iris that have been subjected to freezing temperatures. Also, grow seedlings of red clover, cosmos, Biloxi soybean, ragweed (*Ambrosia*), or other long- and short-day plants, 2 or 3 weeks before beginning the experiment. Select six of the best plants of each species, place three under long-day illumination, and leave the other three under that of the short day. Examine and compare the development of each species once each week. The experiment should be continued at least 6 weeks or until the plants blossom.

Effect on Food Accumulation.—Plants also differ in the light period best suited to the production of reserve food supplies such as occur in tubers, bulbs, corms, and thickened roots. Such light periods do not usually correspond with those that promote maximum shoot growth, although shoot growth is adequate. Many plants produce tubers or fleshy roots only under the influence of a comparatively short day. Such are the Irish potato, Jerusalem artichoke (*Helianthus tuberosus*), and yam. In all cases studied, typical tuber formation takes place as a result of decrease of the daily light period below the optimum for stem elongation. Thus, tuberization is greatly favored by the shortening of the day in fall following the long summer days of high latitudes. In Puerto Rico, increase in yields as great as seven-fold was produced by certain varieties of potatoes under a 10-hour day as compared with one of 15 hours.[582] The length of day determines the type of root system in *Dahlia;* fibrous roots were correlated with a long day and storage roots with a short one.[1032] A close correlation has been found between the transpiring and absorbing surfaces of representative long-day, short-day, and indeterminate types of plants.[978] Conversely, bulb formation, as illustrated by the onion, takes place as a result of increase in the daily light period above the optimum for stem growth.

Cause of Behavior.—In addition to influencing the fundamental process of photosynthesis, the duration of the daily light period may definitely control other parallel processes of fundamental importance in plant growth and development. It may determine not only the quantity of carbohydrate produced but also the utilization of this material. It is not possible, however, to explain the effect upon this basis alone. Although many investigators have studied the method of action of the light period in influencing the characteristic photoperiodic responses, yet little progress has been made in determining the mechanism involved.

The same is true of the closely related process known as *vernalization,* *i.e.,* bringing to the spring state.[436,579] It consists in accelerating the occurrence of the flowering stage in plants, such as winter wheat, so that they will bear fruit although planted in spring, and in causing late-flowering plants to become early bloomers. This is accomplished by partially soaking the grain or seed and then subjecting it to a process of chilling at temperatures above freezing for a period of several days. Since the temperature is low and the grain not fully swollen, the embryo makes but slight development but undergoes a pronounced physiological change. The effect of the chilling is to hasten the occurrence of flowering, since the length of the vegetative cycle of the plant is greatly shortened. Thus, either chilling of the soaked seed, or alternation of light and darkness may endow a plant with a potentiality for earlier flowering. In thermophilic plants, such as millet, maize, sorghum, soybeans, and cotton, the partly soaked seeds are not subjected to low temperatures but to high ones, 20 to 25°C. or higher, and kept in complete darkness. This removes the need for short-day illumination for flowering, such as the plants are accustomed to in subtropical and warm temperate climates.[69]

The light response can be definitely localized in the plant.[313] Flowering may be confined not only to a certain branch or stem but also to a particular region of the stem.[316,491] Capping the stem tip of *Helianthus tuberosus* has the same effect on development of underground stems and on tuberization as covering the whole plant to provide a short day. The controlling influence is therefore centered in the growing tip.[1033] It may be found that the action of light on the differentiating tissue is direct and of a photocatalytic nature.[27,313] It is of extreme interest that an exposure of 10 successive short days was necessary to obtain flowering in short-day plants when they were afterward exposed to long days. A longer pre-exposure was necessary to obtain abundant flowering, and one of 21 days was prerequisite to successful fruiting.[312]

Effect on Distribution.—Plants that require a long day to flower and fruit obviously cannot maintain themselves in the tropical zone even though increase in altitude may afford favorable temperatures. The existence of the more extreme types of short-day plants is likewise impossible. Passing from the equatorial regions into higher latitudes, temperatures promoting active vegetative growth are restricted to a summer period which, other conditions being equal, becomes progressively shorter as the polar regions are approached. The summers are characterized by lengthening periods of daylight and the winters by decreased length of day. Should plants like the ragweed, which requires about a 15-hour day to blossom, migrate northward, flowering would be progressively delayed later and later in the year until the days become sufficiently short. The seeds might freeze before maturing. If the plants were carried still farther north, they might not be able to blossom at all because of a too great length of day during the growing season.[14] Hence, they could not ecize. Frost resistance, for example, is one of the chief factors determining the northward range of woody plants. To endure frost, trees and shrubs must terminate their vegetative growth before the advent of freezing weather.[323,507] The ability to do this has been shown for certain species to depend to a considerable extent upon the length of day.[613] However, for native species temperature remains the major control in north and south distribution, as shown by the occurrence of a hundred or more dominants and subdominants of the prairie over a stretch of 20 degrees of latitude from Saskatchewan to Texas. Thus, any comprehensive study of the factors affecting the distribution of plants should take account of length of day along with the usual ones of temperature, water content, and light intensity.

Practical Significance.—Among field and garden crops, some plants are grown for their vegetative parts alone, others for their fruit or seed, and in still others maximum yields of both vegetative and reproductive parts are desired. A difference of 2 or more weeks in time of planting may definitely determine whether the plant activities will be directed toward the purely vegetative or the reproductive form of development. These facts strongly emphasize the importance of accurately knowing the correct time for planting each crop in order to secure the highest returns. Even different varieties and strains of the same species differ markedly as to the particular length of day most favorable for flowering or for vegetative development.[272] Failure of acclimatization of many species believed due to unfavorable temperature may actually have resulted from an unsuitable length of day. Radishes, for example, do not blossom in the tropics and the biennial beets of temperate regions become annuals in Alaska.

Knowledge of *photoperiodism*, as these responses to length of day are called, should aid the plant breeder to secure for any particular region earlier or later varieties, more fruitful or larger growing forms, and improved everbloomers and everbearers. The problem of extending the northern or southern range of crop plants is also more clearly defined. Judgment as to the adaptability of species in a new region is, moreover, placed on a more adequate basis. Plant breeding should be greatly simplified and hastened through artificial control of light duration. Plants may be made to blossom at will at any time of the year, and crosses between parental types heretofore impossible, because of their flowering at different times of the year, accomplished.[520] With proper knowledge of the specific requirements of each kind of plant, florists should be able to force flowering at any desired time during the year. The methods involved are simple and the results decisive.

CHAPTER XV

PLANT RESPONSE AS A MEASURE OF ENVIRONMENT

Any attempt to determine exactly the causes which are producing modifications in the individual plant, and consequently in vegetation, must include careful measurements of all the factors of the habitat. These must be made with instruments of precision in order to ascertain the exact amount of each factor that is present. Measurement forms a basis for determining the ratio between the stimulus and the amount of functional and structural adjustment that results. A fundamental and apparently inevitable objection to all instruments, however, is their failure to express factor differences in terms of plant activities. While, moreover, instruments record the individual factors, most of them fail to integrate the various factors concerned. This is a serious drawback, since measurements of functions are regularly obtained as sums. Even with a complete set of measurements of habitat factors, the interpretation is difficult, for the amount or intensity of any factor necessary to produce a functional or structural response can be determined only by observing the response of the plant. Thus, while factor intensities must be measured by instruments, the effects that produce changes in vegetation must be determined by the living organism, the plant.

The *phytometer* (plant measure) is designed to express the physical factors of the habitat in terms of physiological activities.[165,690] It consists of plants grown, at least for a time, in the several habitats that are to be compared. Several plants are employed in each habitat so that variability of the individual is checked out.

Control Phytometers.—Phytometers are of many kinds, one of the simplest consisting of plants in sealed containers (Fig. 206). Since the factors of the soil may be varied at will, these are termed control phytometers. The containers are filled with fertile soil of good water content, in which the seeds are planted, and covered with a sand mulch until the seedlings have appeared. An optimum water content is maintained by watering from time to time in amounts just sufficient to bring the container back to its original weight. For long-time experiments, provision is also made for aeration by means of a tube (automobile-tire stem) with threaded end, soldered to the bottom of the container and to which an exhaust pump may be attached. When the seedlings are well established, the pots are sealed. This is done by first making a paper pattern and determining just where the hole to receive the stem is to be bored in the cork. The cork is partly cut and then broken in halves and fitted about the stem. A little modeling clay may also be placed about the stem. This affords a waterproof seal and the plants may now be placed in groups in the several habitats. It is best to place the containers in the ground nearly level with the surface of the soil and if the weather is hot the metal tops should also be insulated with soil, dead leaves, or other materials. By reweighing at intervals of a few days, the relative transpiration in the several habitats may be determined. If the original leaf area and dry weight of a few of the seedlings in other containers are

Fig. 206.—Sunflower phytometers used for measuring rate of transpiration, increase in dry weight, etc., in a field of sunflowers. All were seedlings when placed in the field; the two in the middle at the level of the surrounding plants, the two on the right below, and the two on the left above this level.

determined at the time the experiment is begun, growth at the end of the period may be measured in terms of leaf area and dry weight.

Table 7 gives the results obtained from 12 phytometers of green-ash (*Fraxinus*) seedlings placed in a sumac thicket, in the adjoining prairie, and in the tension zone between the two, respectively, during a period of 8 days in midsummer.

Table 8 shows the average responses of sunflower phytometers in the same habitats during another period of 6-day duration.

By the use of similar phytometers of bur oak and other tree seedlings, it was found that transpiration in an oak forest in Minnesota was less than half of that in a hazelnut thicket, and the water loss in the latter less than a third of that in the prairie.

Since phytometers are often placed in habitats that make extreme demands upon the plants, it is best to use species that are as hardy and vigorous as possible. If the leaf area is to be measured, species with simple, entire leaves or large leaflets are to be preferred. Sunflowers, beans, the smaller cereals, various tree seedlings, or similar native species have been found most satisfactory. Sometimes the plants are attacked and ruined by grasshoppers or June beetles or in other ways.

TABLE 7.—WATER LOSS FROM PHYTOMETERS OF TREE SEEDLINGS

Number of phytometer	Water loss, grams	Leaf area, square inches	Water loss, grams per square inch	Average loss, grams per square inch
Sumac thicket				
1	28.5	13.05	2.2	
4	24.0	9.15	2.6	
7	10.5	4.85	2.2	2.50
10	34.0	11.20	3.0	
Tension zone				
2	14.5	4.65	3.1	
5	17.5	4.80	3.6	
8	22.5	7.60	3.0	3.25
11	30.5	9.30	3.3	
Prairie				
3	37.5	6.40	5.8	
6	45.5	6.65	6.8	
9	65.5	12.30	5.3	5.72
12	62.0	12.35	5.0	

TABLE 8.—TRANSPIRATION AND GROWTH OF SUNFLOWERS IN THREE HABITATS

Responses	Sumac thicket	Tension zone	Prairie
Water loss, grams....................	133	611	802
Increase in leaf area, square inches......	56	66	74
Increase in dry weight, grams..........	0.76	1.89	2.44

Sod-core Phytometers.—Water loss from various types of grassland has been measured by means of fitting metal cylinders, 1 square foot in cross section and 3 feet long, tightly over undisturbed cores of sod and sealing the bottoms in place. The phytometers were then placed in holes just large enough to contain them, which were surrounded by undisturbed vegetation. The short-grass plains disclimax lost water at an

Fig. 207.—Phytometers, 82 square inches in cross-sectional area and 2.5 feet deep, in which the native sod has been placed. They fit into metal-lined holes just deep enough so that the soil surface within is on a level with the surrounding surface. The cans extend 2 inches above the soil surface, hence there is no runoff or run-in during rains. Provision is made to prevent waterlogging. Planks temporarily placed on permanent frames 18 inches high permit weighing without disturbance of surrounding vegetation.

Fig. 208.—Bundles of barley from representative square meters from field plots. All are from the same lot of seed planted at the same time in fertile soil: left, in eastern Colorado; center, north central Kansas; and right, eastern Nebraska.

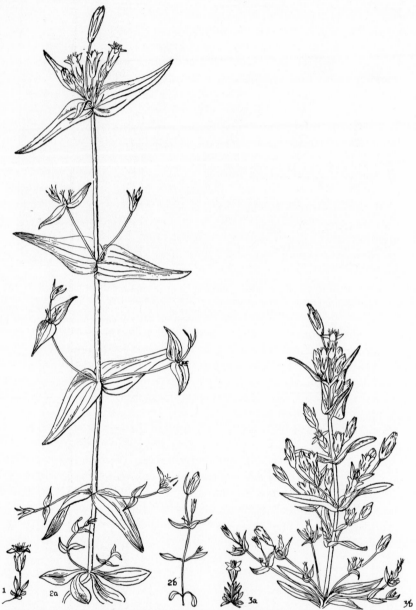

Fig. 209.—Adaptation forms of the rose gentian (*Gentiana amarella*).   (1) alpine dwarf;
(2a) normal shade; (2b) dry shade; (3a) drought; (3b) normal sun.   (*Drawn by Edith S.
Clements.*)

average rate of approximately 1 pound per square foot per day. In mixed prairie, where the vegetation is much more luxuriant, the loss was 1.3 pounds, and in true prairie, where conditions are much less xeric, about 0.85 pound per square foot[974] (Fig. 207).

Free Phytometers.—Phytometers are not confined to plants sealed in containers, but may also consist of transplants or plants grown from seeds, etc. These are subject to the complete factor complex of the habitat and are thus unlike sealed phytometers where the factors of the soil are under control. Some degree of control may be secured, however, if desired, by watering, shading, thinning, etc. Planting in different situations to determine the comparative behavior of seedlings has been practiced chiefly by foresters. Douglas fir in Arizona, for example, succeeds better under a cover of aspen than in the open, probably because of decreased transpiration, as indicated by the fact that evaporation was 50 to 90 per cent less. Difficulty of establishment of true-prairie species in the short-grass disclimax and forest trees in prairie has been fully demonstrated by seedling phytometers.[171] In these studies, transplant phytometers consisting of large blocks of sod were also widely employed. The behavior of upland species in swamps or bogs and species of wet soil in well drained areas can best be studied by means of reciprocal transplants. The responses of plants to different amounts of salt or to acid soils may be similarly determined. In some cases (community phytometers), square meters of soil to a depth of 8 inches have been moved from one habitat into another and the effects upon the vegetation studied. In such experiments, the control community, after being excavated, is again planted in its own habitat.[171]

Phytometers have been extensively used in measuring climatic conditions[769] (Fig. 208). The clip quadrat is a type of phytometer, and the phytometer method is being employed in all experiments where plant production is used as a measure of environment.[967] Extensive studies of the adaptations shown by alpine plants when transplanted at lower elevations and lowland plants in various mountain habitats are throwing much light upon the whole problem of the origin and differentiation of species[73,166] (Fig. 209).

CHAPTER XVI

ADAPTATION TO WATER

In nature, there are many types of habitats as regards water content. But no plants can ecize in both very wet and extremely dry situations. Each species flourishes only in those habitats where it finds a suitable water relation.

Types Produced by Adaptation to Water.—In the course of evolution, many species have become adapted in both structural and physiological features to habitats with an excessive water supply. Plants that live wholly or partly submerged in water or in very wet places are known as *hydrophytes* (Gr. *hudor*, water; *phyton*, plant). Plants of ponds, streams, and other bodies of water both fresh and salt, as well as those of swamps and wet meadows, belong to this group.

By far the greatest number of plants live in an environment that is characterized by a medium water supply, such as is found in the important agricultural districts of the temperate zone as well as in moderate altitudes in parts of the tropics. The plants of forests, meadows, and prairies usually belong to this group. Plants of habitats that usually show neither an excess nor a deficiency of water are known as *mesophytes* (Gr. *mesos*, middle; *phyton*, plant). In general, definite structures for increasing water supply or decreasing water loss are either slightly developed or completely absent.

Plants that grow habitually where the evaporation stress is high and the water supply low show characteristic adaptations to a decrease in water content. They are termed *xerophytes* (Gr. *xeros*, dry; *phyton*, plant). Certain species of deserts, alpine peaks, sand hills, plains, and high prairies belong to this group. As among hydrophytes, plants of this group include species from many families entirely unrelated phylogenetically, although some, as a result of the impress of the environment, have come to resemble each other more or less closely in vegetative characters, such as various cacti in arid portions of America and certain spurges in African deserts. Likewise, the vegetation of the arctic region resembles that of the antarctic in its general physiognomy, although the two areas have practically no species in common.[643]

Hydrophytes, xerophytes, and mesophytes are readily distinguishable as groups, since each has a more or less definite habitat and characteristic appearance. Between hydrophytes and mesophytes on the one hand,

and extreme xerophytes and mesophytes on the other, there are
found all gradations of form and all
degrees of structural adaptations
due to intermediate or partial
habitats. Partly on account of the
influence of humidity and partly
because many habitats pass very
gradually into each other, it is
impossible to establish an absolute
correspondence between each group
and the water content.

HYDROPHYTES

Typical hydrophytes grow in
water, in soil covered with water,
or in soil that is usually saturated.
With respect to their relation to
water and air, they may be arranged
into three fairly natural groups, *viz.*,
submerged, floating, and amphibious plants. Since the aquatic
environment everywhere shows
great uniformity, hydrophytes, and
particularly the submerged and
floating forms, show fewer adaptations than plants living under the
more variable habitat characteristic
of xerophytes. The structural
adaptations are chiefly in response
to excessive water content, which,
of course, implies a decreased
oxygen supply.[289] They consist of
a decrease of tissues protecting
from water loss and mechanical
injury, a reduction in supporting
and conducting tissues, and a
marked increase in aeration of the
tissues with a corresponding
decrease in palisade (Figs. 210 and
211).

Submerged Plants.—Plants
growing entirely submerged show

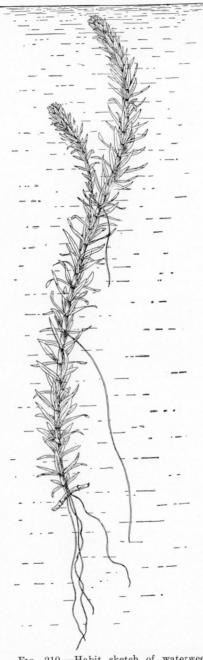

Fig. 210.—Habit sketch of waterweed
(*Elodea canadensis*). Both leaves and stem
are green and the roots also contain chlorophyll if they receive sufficient light.

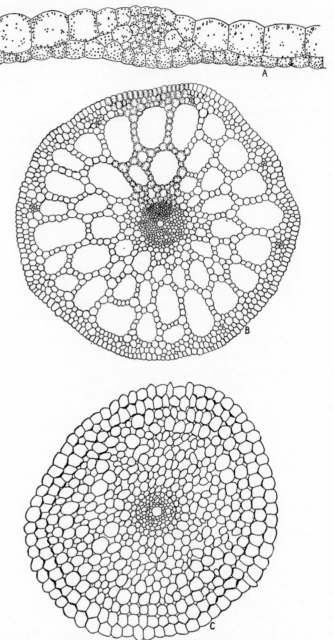

Fig. 211.—Detail of *Elodea*. *A*, cross section of a leaf showing the much reduced fibrovascular bundle. *B*, cross section of stem. Note the chloroplasts in the epidermis and the abundance of aerenchyma throughout the relatively large cortex. The stele consists entirely of thin-walled cells which are not differentiated into xylem and phloem. An intercellular passage occupies the center of the stele. *C*, a cross section of the root showing the much reduced stele and large air passages in the cortex.

the greatest variations from the usual form and structure typical of mesophytes.

Ecological Anatomy of Submerged Plants.—A thorough understanding of the profound changes brought about by the water environment can be had only by a study of representative specimens.

STEMS

Cut transverse sections of the stem of a submerged species of pondweed (*Potamogeton*) or other submerged hydrophyte and compare it with a typical mesophyte, such as a sunflower, in the following respects:

Epidermis.—Is there any cuticle or are all parts readily permeable to water? Compare the rapidity of wilting of portions of stems of the two plants when exposed for a time to the air. Do the epidermal cells contain chloroplasts?

Cortex.—Explain the relative proportion of the stem occupied by cortex and stele in the two species upon an environmental basis. Compare, also, the relative amounts of intercellular space and depth to which chlorophyll extends. Is there any collenchyma in the submerged plant? Stain with iodine and note where starch is most abundant and give reasons for this.

Central Cylinder.—Are there any fibrovascular bundles or any tracheary or fibrous tissue? The air space in the center of the stem marks the normal position of the xylem (Fig. 211). Explain these modifications on an environmental basis. Make a drawing about 4 inches long of one-fourth of the cross section, showing all its parts. Examine sections of the stems of the hornwort (*Ceratophyllum*) or of *Najas, Zannichellia*, etc.

The structure of the stem of water milfoil (*Myriophyllum*), a part of which grows in the air above water, should also be examined and compared with the preceding plants in regard to each of the preceding characters. The relatively undifferentiated vascular strand should be noted.

LEAVES

Examine and compare the leaves of *Potamogeton* in detail with those of a mesophyte in regard to epidermal characters, vascular bundles, and mesophyll. Draw a cross section, filling in the chloroplasts. Also, cut sections of the leaves of any of the other submerged species. How do these compare with leaves of mesophytes?

ROOTS

Examine the roots of *Potamogeton*, or other submerged species which possess them, and compare them in regard to size, branching, root hairs, and internal structure with those of typical mesophytes. Compare those growing in water with those growing in soil.

The roots, stems, and leaves of higher plants of this ecological group are greatly modified. The epidermis of all of these organs is noncuticularized and is thus able to absorb gases and nutrients directly from the water. The roots are greatly reduced in size, poorly or not at all branched, and destitute of root hairs except where they grow in the mud. In some species (*e.g., Ceratophyllum*), they have entirely disappeared. The older portions do not become impermeable with age, *i.e.,* suberized or cutinized, as in land forms, but absorb throughout their entire life.

Even in wholly submerged plants that are rooted, at least part of the water and nutrient materials are often obtained from the soil.[120] Plants growing in the same body of water make a better development when rooted in a rich, humus-filled soil than where they grow in sand.[924] Experiments have shown that many species cannot secure enough of certain nutrients to make the usual vigorous and continued growth unless they are rooted in the substratum, where some produce root hairs.[107,194,700]

The greater density of the water as compared with air renders support less necessary, and the stems are usually long and slender with a poorly developed vascular region. The mechanical need for developing the vascular bundles near the periphery of the stem, as in mesophytes, so as to secure maximum rigidity, no longer exists. Consequently, the cortex occupies a much larger area in proportion to stele, an arrangement that greatly increases its photosynthetic activity. In many species such as *Elodea, Zannichellia,* and *Najas,* the fused xylem strands are reduced to a central intercellular passage which is surrounded by phloem.[353]

The leaves are greatly reduced in size and thickness.[195] Although water is much richer in carbon dioxide than is the air, diffusion is relatively slow. The absorbing surface is consequently greatly increased and the tissues brought into close contact with the source of supply by finely dissected or thin, linear, or ribbonlike leaves, often only two or three cells thick.[114] This adaptation may have resulted, in part, also from mechanical stress due to moving water. Although sclerenchyma strands occasionally occur, especially along the margins of the leaves where they give tensile strength, the general absence of supporting tissue is shown by the collapse of the plant when it is removed from the water. The thin leaves present an increased surface in proportion to tissue involved, for the reception of the diffuse light. The plastids are usually large and motile. Stomata are absent, except where vestigial, and these are functionless.

The chlorenchyma of both leaves and stems is of the shade or sponge type. In the few cases where both palisade and sponge are present, they are, doubtless, relics of a former structure. The epidermal layers, unlike those of land plants, are best supplied with carbon dioxide and frequently contain the chloroplasts most abundantly. Air chambers and passages filled with gas are common in all the vegetative organs, *i.e.,* the aerenchyma is abundant.[354] They consist of regular spaces extending through the leaf and often long distances through the stem. These spaces are usually separated by partitions of chlorophyll-bearing tissue only one or two cells in thickness. The air spaces not only afford buoyancy but also retain some of the oxygen resulting from photosynthesis to be used in respiration. Likewise, a part of the carbon dioxide that accumulates in these reservoirs at night may be used when the plant is illuminated.

Vegetative reproduction is highly developed and flowers and seeds are less abundant than in most habitats, a response found in most types of aquatic plants.[626] *Elodea*, for example, reproduces rapidly by fragmentation; *Eichhornia* by runners; and duckweeds (*Lemna*, *Spirodela*, etc.) form new thalli so rapidly that under conditions favorable to growth they may soon cover the surface of a pond (Fig. 212). When sexual reproduction in submerged plants does occur, the flowers are usually fertilized at or above the surface of the water.[1021]

FIG. 212.—Water hyacinth (*Eichhornia*) propagating by runners. The bladderlike floats are the enlarged air-filled petioles.

Aquatic flowering plants are those that have exchanged terrestrial for aquatic life.[23] Most of them are restricted to shallow waters and to the vicinity of shores. In the bodily organization of most of them there is much that indicates ancestral adaptation to land. The well developed epidermal system, for example, often retains stomata, although they cannot function under water. Only in a few species is the pollination aquatic, water and not air being the medium through which the pollen is dispersed.

Floating Plants.—Plants of this group have undergone striking modifications in form and structure; even the aerial parts show their close association with the water habitat.

Ecological Anatomy of Floating Plants.—Examine various free-floating forms such as duckweeds (*Lemna*, *Spirodela*, or *Wolffia*), water hyacinth (*Eichhornia*), and water fern (*Salvinia*). Why do they not become wetted when plunged under water? Note the method of vegetative propagation in the duckweeds where each thallus or frond represents an individual plant. How does *Eichhornia* propagate vegetatively? Cut sections of the thallus of a duckweed, the swollen petioles, and leaves and stems of water hyacinth and explain why each kind of plant floats. In cold water in late autumn duckweeds form winter buds which have more compact tissues than the thalli produced earlier in the season. Being heavier than water they sink to the bottom of the pond where they remain alive until spring, while those that remain afloat freeze.

Examine the roots with regard to branching habit, root hairs, and the conspicuous root pockets that fit over the ends of the roots. Are these of any advantage to the plant?

Examine the floating leaves of one or more species of water lilies (*Nymphaea*, *Castalia*), or water shield (*Brasenia*). Examine and draw cross sections of the leaves showing the stomata, air spaces (aerenchyma), and sclereids. Of what are sclereids composed and what is their function? Why is it essential that the leaves of floating plants be not easily wetted? How is this protection accomplished in the water lily? Does the petiole give the leaf mechanical support? The stems consist usually of thickened rhizomes rooted in the mud. Would you expect the petiole to have some vascular elements for the conduction of water, nutrients, and food? Examine sections under the microscope.

Many species of this group are free-floating forms, others are rooted in the mud and only the leaves and flowers float on the surface of the water. In the *Lemnaceae*, where the leaf and stem are represented by a tiny thallus, the roots are in the process of disappearing. *Spirodela* has several, *Lemna* but one, and *Wolffia* none. Such typical water roots are hairless. In addition to having the characters described for those of attached, submerged plants, they possess root pockets. The function of these enlarged rootcap-like structures is not so apparent as is the rootcap of terrestrial plants.

Most attached species (water lilies, pondweeds, etc.) develop long, horizontal stems, rootstocks, or tubers. By means of these, they migrate rapidly through the water or mud and, as a consequence, the plants usually form conspicuous communities. The root systems are poorly developed, probably as a result of an excess of water and the reciprocal diminution of air. The petioles are much elongated. The aerating system is greatly emphasized, and supporting tissues, such as fibro-vascular bundles, are reduced. The leaves that have developed under water are like those of submerged plants, but in both form and structure of the upper portion, floating leaves are essentially similar to those of amphibious plants. They are usually coated with wax which prevents the wetting of the upper surface and the clogging of the stomata by water. Stomata are found only on the upper surface, with the exception of a few cases where they persist with loss of function upon the lower side (Fig. 213). The palisade tissue of the leaf is often well developed, but is usually exceeded by the sponge tissue which is filled with large air chambers (Fig. 214).

Amphibious or Emersed Plants.—Plants of this group are adapted to live partly in water and partly in air. The two partial habitats are very different and usually the response of the plant is marked.

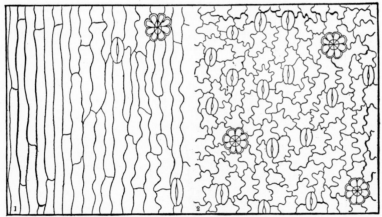

Fig. 213.—Upper epidermis of (1) a submerged leaf and (2) of an aerial leaf of northern water starwort (*Callitriche bifida*), showing the decrease in the number of stomata. (*Drawn by Edith S. Clements.*)

Ecological Anatomy of Amphibious or Emersed Plants.—The cattail (*Typha latifolia*) is a good representative of this group (Figs. 215 and 216). Cut sections of the thick rhizome and examine for relative proportion occupied by cortex and stele.

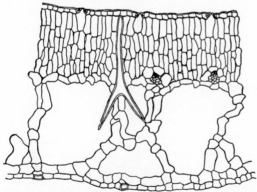

Fig. 214.—Cross section of the leaf of a water lily (*Nymphaea advena*). Note the stomata in the upper epidermis and the slime glands in the lower one, also the large Y-shaped, thick-walled sclereid which probably furnishes mechanical support. Photosynthetic activity is confined to the upper half of the leaf, the large, air-filled lacunae in the lower part affording buoyancy.

In the cortex, note the thickened endodermis, columns of bast fibers, and occasional bundles, together with the well developed aerenchyma, and hypodermis of thin-walled parenchyma.

Examine cross sections of roots. What effect has decreased water content and increased aeration upon root branching and root-hair development (p. 322)?

FIG. 215.—Habit sketch of cattail (*Typha latifolia*).

Examine sections of freshly cut leaves and, later, prepared slides of the same. Make out clearly, by cutting the leaves lengthwise, the nature and position of the I beams and diaphragms separating the large air spaces. To what portion of the leaf is photosynthetic activity confined? Examine the structure of one of the I beams in detail.

Draw an aerial and a submerged leaf of some heterophyllous species such as yellow water crowfoot (*Ranunculus delphinifolius*), mermaid weed (*Proserpinaca palustris*), or water cress (*Roripa americana*). Examine the changes in size and structure of aerial and submerged leaves of species of water starwort (*Callitriche*) or mare's-tail (*Hippuris*).

Most species of amphibious plants have extensive underground or creeping stems which are rooted in the mud and spread rapidly. Thus, while the roots and portions of the stem as well as frequently part of the leaves are under water, at least a portion and often most of the shoot is aerial. Plants of tidewater marshes and other places subject to periodic inundations belong to this group. In addition to numerous vascular plants, many algae are also included here. In fact, some of the latter cannot live if they are constantly under water.

The vascular species of this group are closely related to mesophytes and are the least specialized of water plants. Owing to their frequent occurrence at the water's edge, many amphibious plants have a wide range of adjustment and may grow for a time as mesophytes or partially submerged.

The roots exhibit the usual characters of plants growing in water-logged soil. Their extent, degree of branching, and root-hair development vary directly in proportion to decrease in water content and increase in aeration (Fig. 153). Owing to variation in the water content of marsh habitats, the rhizome structure may show both hydric and xeric adaptations. In *Typha*, for example, the prominence of mechanical and conductive tissue indicates mesophytic tendencies; the abundance of storage parenchyma and aerenchyma, hydrophytic ones.[393,1023] The thickened endodermal layer affords a means of protection against water loss during drought. Since both mechanical and conductive tissues are well developed, the plants are able to grow erect without being supported by the water. Perhaps the most distinctive feature of the stems of amphibious plants is the large internal air chambers crossed by frequent diaphragms that are pervious to air.[864] These are important in affording aeration to the submerged parts,[179] as may be shown by an experiment in which all the rootstocks are cut at the water's edge and the aerial shoots below the water level. In most cases, the plants will not recover.

The leaves of amphibious plants show the greatest variation in both form and structure when the plant is subjected alternately to the air and water environment. The lower leaves of some species are covered, either normally or by a rise in water level. When they develop under

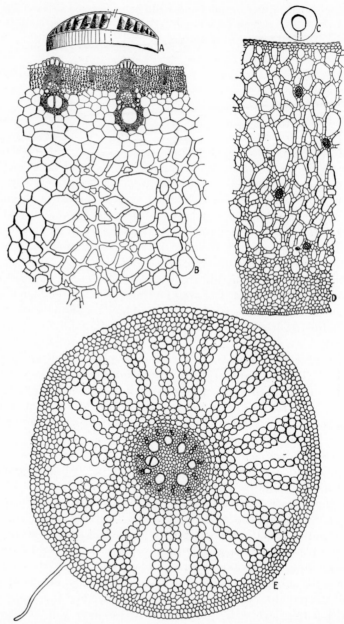

Fig. 216.—Detail of structure of *Typha latifolia*. *A*, section of leaf showing I beams, air chambers, and diaphragms. The parallel lines indicate the position of the portion greatly enlarged in *B*. *C*, outline of a cross section of a rhizome showing relative proportion of cortex and stele and the part shown in detail in *D*. *D*, the epidermis, consisting of a single layer of cells; exodermis consisting of many small cells; aerenchyma and columns of bast fibers; and thick-walled endodermis. *E*, cross section of a root showing abundance of aerenchyma.

water, they take the form and structure of submerged leaves. The aerial leaves are usually large and entire, showing a marked tendency to increase the exposed surface (Fig. 217). This is clearly shown by experiments with *Ranunculus sceleratus* grown under varying conditions of water content. Floating leaves and those of plants grown in saturated soil are larger than those on plants grown in drier soils, but they change little or not at all in thickness. The lake cress (*Radicula aquatica*), water crowfoot (*Ranunculus aquatilis*), and mermaid weed (*Proserpinaca palustris*) are representative. Changes in size and structure without dissection of the leaves are shown in some species of pondweed (*Pota-*

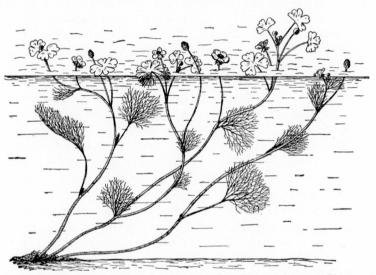

Fig. 217.—Habit sketch of a water crowfoot (*Ranunculus aquatilis*).

mogeton), water starwort (*Callitriche autumnalis*), and others. Many species are less plastic.

The change in the form and structure of the submerged leaf seems clearly related to the absorption of carbon dioxide from the water, there being no danger of drying. As soon as the leaves begin to develop above the water surface, the danger of desiccation is nullified by the production of a cuticle, with its necessary accompanying stomata. In a plant such as *Ranunculus aquatilis*, these changes may be brought about at will by growing portions of the plant in air or in water. Where stomata are present, they have only slightly cutinized walls and in most hydrophytes are almost always open, many species such as *Typha* and *Scirpus validus* having lost the power to close them even in extreme wilting.[544] Compared with mesophytes, the cuticle is usually thin and destitute of hairs.

The stomata are numerous and usually more abundant on the upper than on the lower surface. The palisade tissue is represented by one or more well developed rows, but this portion of the leaf is regularly thinner than the sponge parenchyma. The sponge tissue contains large air spaces or numerous large air chambers, usually provided with thin plates or diaphragms of cells. The palisade is reduced as the air spaces and sponge tissue increase. Hence, the chloroplasts are exposed more completely to the sunlight, and water loss is augmented. The fibrovascular system is more efficient than in other types of hydrophytes.

An explanation has recently been proposed which satisfactorily accounts for the origin of a cuticle in land plants and in parts of hydrophytes exposed to the air. It also reveals why a cuticle is poorly developed or absent in absorbing roots and in all submerged parts of hydrophytes. Meristematic tissues always contain fatty substances, such as fatty acids, fats, and lipins, which migrate to the plasmatic interfaces during the processes of vacuolation and differentiation. Subsequently, they migrate into and along the walls separating the protoplasts until they reach the surface of the root or shoot. Sodium, potassium, and magnesium soaps of fatty acids move quite readily along cellulose walls saturated with water, but calcium soaps are immobile. Many of these fatty substances contain unsaturated fatty acids which are liable to undergo rapid change in the presence of oxygen, oxidizing and condensing into varnishlike substances insoluble in water. Thus, the cutin of the cuticle is formed. Cutin is merely a name for an aggregate of substances varying in specific composition but having the same general characters, most important of which is their low permeability to water. In submerged plants the fatty substances largely pass on into the surrounding water (unless it is predominantly calcareous, when insoluble calcium soaps may accumulate) and are never oxidized, *i.e.*, little or no cuticle is formed. The thinness or absence of a cuticle on absorbing water roots or soil roots is similarly explained. Conversely, where large intercellular spaces occur, as in hydrophytes or in the cortex of the roots of many plants, the endodermis may be quite waterproofed, except for passage cells, by oxidized fatty acids forming cutin or suberin.[523] The production of cuticle in water roots with chlorophyll and nonproduction of it when chlorophyll is absent is explainable on the ground that the oxygen produced by photosynthesis is necessary for the oxidation of the fats.[194]

MESOPHYTES

Mesophytes grow in habitats that are neither extremely dry nor wet. The oxygen supply about the roots is moderate, the solutes are neither extremely dilute nor too concentrated. Because of variation in light however, mesophytes are differentiated into sun and shade forms. A mesophyte possesses a form or structure that is more or less characteristic by reason of the absence of distinct modifications. Notwithstanding its apparent lack of a distinctive impress, a mesophyte is as much a product of its habitat as the well-marked hydrophyte or xerophyte.[590]

Mesophytes stand midway between hydrophytes and xerophytes. For this reason, they pass, on the one hand, into dry-land plants and, on

Fig. 218.—A corn plant (*Zea mays indentata*) with leaves rolling as a result of drought.

the other, into amphibious plants. Various xerophytes and hydrophytes have, moreover, often found themselves in conditions that changed them into mesophytes. Many of them have, in consequence, retained characters of leaf, stem, or root that are to be regarded as ancestral rather than as the result of adaptation to the present habitat.

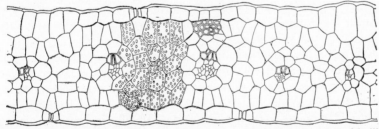

Fig. 219.—Cross section of a leaf of corn showing two groups of the enlarged bulliform (bubblelike) cells in the upper epidermis. These constitute the rolling device. Upon loss of turgidity in these cells the leaf rolls inward.

The roots of mesophytes, such as common field and garden crops, plants of meadows, and species of deciduous and moist evergreen forests, are usually extensive and much branched. Root length, except perhaps in the case of trees, usually equals or exceeds the height of tops, and the volume occupied by roots likewise usually equals and often greatly exceeds that occupied by the aboveground parts. Root hairs are nearly always abundant.   Conditions for humus accumulations are favorable, bacteria and fungi are plentiful and often intimately associated with the roots in nodules or as mycorrhizas.

The foliage of mesophytes shows a maximum development.   The leaves are large and of moderate thickness (Figs. 218 and 219).   Owing to the thin, transparent epidermis, which is moderately cutinized, and an abundant development of chlorophyll, they are of a deep-green color. This is quite in contrast to many xeric species.   The stomata are abundant and, except in woody plants, usually distributed on both surfaces. They are relatively uniform in structure, and the guard cells show a maximum capacity for movement.

Number of Stomata.—Where a species is subjected to increased drought, whether climatic or brought about by competition, the result is often a dwarfing of the plant and an increase in the number of stomata per

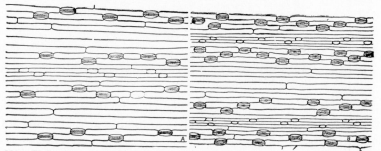

Fig. 220.—Unit areas of the epidermis of oats equally magnified.   That with the fewer stomata and larger cells was grown under less xeric conditions.

unit area.   The stomata develop early, and if there is not enough water to cause the normal cell hydration and growth, all of the leaf cells are dwarfed[109,1023,1027] (Fig. 220).

Extensive investigations in England have shown that in general smaller leaves at any level on the plant have greater stomatal frequency than larger ones.   There is a frequency gradient from the base to the apex of the plant, the higher leaves, regardless of size, having a greater number of stomata per unit area than the lower ones.   A study of numerous grasses and forbs in true prairie showed a similar relationship (Table 9).

The rate of transpiration was highest from the leaf areas with the greatest number of stomata, where insolation, wind movement, and evaporation were also greatest.   This distribution of stomata is greatly influenced by the water relation as is shown by the fact that no such gradation develops in plants grown in a very humid atmosphere.   The frequency of stomata, moreover, is not constant over the entire area of even a single leaf, but certain well-marked tendencies of distribution are evident. In dicotyledons, there is a frequency gradient from the base to the apex of the individual leaf and from the midrib to the periphery. This seems clearly related to distance from the water supply, cells at the base and near the midrib having the largest supply and attaining the greatest growth. The stomata are consequently fewest per unit area in these portions of the leaves.[760]

TABLE 9.—AVERAGE NUMBER OF STOMATA PER SQUARE MILLIMETER FOR SPECIES OF TRUE PRAIRIE

Species	Prairie habitat	Lowest living leaf	Middle leaf	Highest leaf
Andropogon furcatus	Low	198	224	311
Elymus canadensis	High	76	103	127
Andropogon scoparius	High	319	369	418
Erigeron ramosus	Low	180	298	367
Erigeron ramosus	High	265	319	383

A study of the woodland flora showed that the shrub layer had a greater stomatal frequency than the more mesic herbaceous one and that the tree layer, which is exposed to greatest desiccation, had the largest number per unit area of all. Likewise, the flora at the margin of the forest showed a greater stomatal frequency than the protected one beneath the forest canopy.

Similar relations have been found for the smaller cereals as a consequence of climatic drought; the number of stomata in barley, for example, increased progressively from 65 to 91 per square millimeter. Where drought was due to competition, a progressive increase in the number of stomata has been found in sunflowers planted in various densities in the same field. The plants ranged from 64 to 4 inches apart. The increase in the number of stomata per unit area is directly correlated with a decrease in their size.

TABLE 10.—STOMATAL CHARACTERS IN RELATION TO DENSITY OF PLANTING

Distance between plants, inches	64	32	16	8	4
Average number of stomata per square millimeter	295	411	411	427	455
Average length of guard cells, microns	27	26	24	19	18
Average width of guard cells, microns	16	16	15	14	13
Average number of chloroplasts per stoma	23	21	20	19	15

Stomata of sun leaves are smaller than those of shade leaves and those of plants growing in dry habitats are smaller than those of plants growing in moist ones. Stomatal frequency cannot be regarded merely as a means of adaptational adjustment with respect to transpiration, since the number of stomata per unit area increases as conditions for water loss become more severe.

In general, stomata are usually more numerous on the less exposed or lower surface of the leaf. In nearly all trees and in many shrubs, they are confined to the lower side. Exceptions occur in many shade plants, where the exposure on the two surfaces is equal, and in aquatic plants. The change in the number of stomata is well illustrated by a buttercup (*Ranunculus sceleratus*). When grown in water with the leaves floating, no stomata developed on the lower surface but in only moderately moist soil 40 per cent occurred on the lower surface.

XEROPHYTES

Xerophytes have originated from mesophytes. They have gradually undergone changes under the impress of increasing drought until they have become well fitted to endure extremely xeric conditions. The great desert areas of the world bear evidence that life characteristic of them has developed along several independent lines. Different families and different genera show in every case their closest relationships to those of adjacent regions of greater moisture. Deserts occupy one-fourth or more of the land surface. They have been the scene of a vast development originating in remote geological times and involving a large number of species.[844] Xerophytes are much greater in number of species and more diversified in form, structure, and physiological adaptations than are hydrophytes.

The structural changes found in the foliar organs or modified foliar organs of xerophytic plants were regarded according to the classic view as modifications of the mesophytic leaf. At the same time it was considered that these modifications reduced the amount of transpiration in the xeric plant. Modern experimental work has shown that this conception of xerophytes is a generalization often based on insufficient data. Many species of plants with xeromorphic structure are by no means xerophytes.[1014] Numerous investigations have shown that although succulent desert plants have a low intensity of transpiration, other types of xerophytes may transpire as much or more than mesophytes under high tension of the environmental factors, notwithstanding their form and structure. Of course, this high rate of water loss is not long maintained in deserts, since favorable water content is exceptional.

Types of Xeric Environments.—Xerophytes are the characteristic plants of deserts, but they are by no means confined to them. Neither are all desert plants xeric. Xerophytes may occur in any habitat in which low water content is accompanied by atmospheric conditions which promote rapid water loss. Structural and physiological modifications common to xerophytes have been evolved under many different degrees and kinds of xeric environments. In fact, several types of deserts are readily distinguishable. First are those with very low rainfall and a hot, dry, windy climate such as is characteristic of the thorn-scrub deserts of the southwest. In contrast is the less xeric *Artemisia-Atriplex* type of the west. More extreme than either, and almost if not quite excluding all types of plant growth, are the saline deserts in which aridity is supplemented by a soil with such an excess of salts that absorption from it is extremely difficult or impossible.

Other types of xeric habitats such as plains and tablelands are xeric because of low rainfall, often coupled with high runoff and great evaporation. Rock ledges and cliffs afford local xeric areas, even in climates suited to mesophytes. Similarly, sand hills, dunes, and shingle beaches may be, for a time at least, populated with plants of xeric habit. This is because of rapid percolation and shifting of the surface soil and, especially, the intense insolation at the soil surface.

Classification of Xerophytes.—Plants of xeric habitats have been classified as (1) drought escaping, (2) drought evading, (3) drought enduring, and (4) drought resisting.[812] Annuals adapted to such a short growing season (4 to 6 weeks) that they can complete their life cycle from germination to maturing seed during a brief period of water supply escape drought. The second group of plants evade drought by conserving the scanty moisture supply as a result of small size, restricted growth, growing far apart, or by low water requirement. They thereby evade early desiccation.

Drought-enduring plants are largely desert shrubs such as creosote bush (*Covillea glutinosa*). Like drought-evading plants, they make very little growth in a single season and are usually small and widely spaced. When soil moisture is reduced below that available for growth, the leaves wilt or dry in place or may drop off entirely. The plants continue alive, however, enduring the drought and making no new growth until water is again available to the roots. Most of the plants can endure long, dry, hot periods. For months they may be without any water available for growth and then rapidly start growth in the event of rainfall. The characteristic vegetation of semideserts and deserts of North America is of the drought-enduring type.

The fourth group resists drought by accumulating a supply of water that is used when none can be secured from the soil. By means of this stored water, they may continue to grow for long periods, often flowering and ripening seed. Here belong the succulents such as cacti and *Agave* and other species with fleshy stems or leaves or roots. They are able to extend their root area even in dry soil and are thus better fitted to secure water when the soil is moistened[812] (**Figs. 221** and **222**). To this type also belong many epiphytes. Other drought-resistant species are non-succulent plants with large reservoirs for water in their stems or underground organs. Such are many trees of African grasslands, which, following the long drought and grass fires, spring into bloom before the rains.

More recently xerophytes have been divided on the basis of drought resistance into two types, succulents and true xerophytes, the succulents being considered as atypical, highly specialized, and relatively restricted forms.[577] Because of their great storage and slow expenditure of water, they are immune from the potent influence of an internal water deficit, nor do such typical representatives as the cacti, *Agave*, etc., yield high osmotic pressures, a common characteristic feature of xerophily.

Fig. 221.—A drought-resisting plant. This cactus (*Opuntia camanchica*) has blossomed and the fruits, which appear as small branches, are ripening. The fleshy green stems, in addition to storing water, perform the work of leaves.

Characters of Xerophytes.—Xerophytes are distinguished by the capacity to survive long periods of drought and dehydration of their tissues without injury or with only slight injury. Thus, a chief characteristic of xerophytes seems to be an extensive resistance to wilting. While mesophytes wilt with a small reduction of water content of their tissues (even 1 to 2 per cent), xerophytes may lose 8 to 25 per cent or more of their water before they wilt.[743]

True xerophytes are characterized by certain anatomical and physiological features. These include (1) a decrease in the size of all cells including the guard cells, (2) a distinct thickening of cell walls, (3) a strongly developed palisade in the mesophyll, (4) a denser network of veins than in mesophytes, and (5) an increase in the number of stomata per unit area.[1023,1027] Physiologically (6) the intensity of the rate of transpiration is increased when water is plentiful, (7) there is a rise in

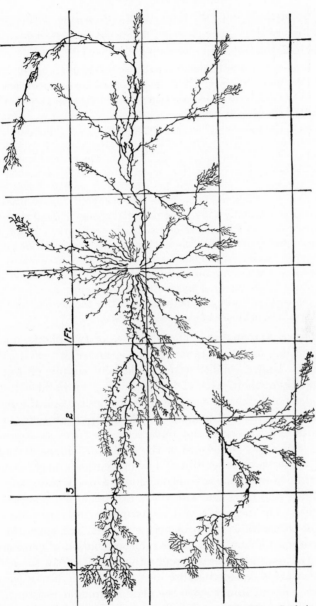

Fig. 222.—Top view of surface roots of cactus shown in Fig. 221. Scale in feet. Aside from three to five vertical roots which reach depths of 2 to 3 feet, the entire absorbing system occurs in the surface 1 to 4 inches of soil.

the osmotic pressure, and (8) the capacity to endure permanent wilting is greatly increased.[577] The Russian physiologist and ecologist, Maximov, maintains that the last is the most important, as has long been believed.

Of the essential factors inducing a xeromorphic structure must be mentioned solar radiation, and a water deficit in the leaves leading to the deflexion of water from the embryonic tissues. This shortage of water does not permit of the normal development of the cells during the so-called "stretching growth," or period of cell enlargement. The cell walls, therefore, cease to expand comparatively early, and proceed to become thicker. The result is the production of smaller cells with thicker walls. This decrease in cell size leads to other structural peculiarities, e.g., a denser network of veins (for the number of cells occupying the spaces between the veins . . . is more or less constant), smaller leaves, and so on. Intense radiation induces the cells of the chlorenchyma to grow perpendicularly to the leaf surface, thereby converting potential spongy mesophyll into palisade tissue. This results in an increase of assimilative capacity. At the same time, the increased number of stomata allows of more rapid transpiration per unit area. Finally, intense insolation combined with deficiency of water leads to higher osmotic pressures, which in turn are apparently related in some way to an increased power of resistance of the protoplasm to injury during wilting. Such may be accepted as a working hypothesis regarding the xerophytism induced in plants by the direct influence of external conditions.*

Behavior of Xerophytes.—The responses of two plants, one of mesomorphic and one of xeromorphic structure, under two environments are instructive.† Under conditions of a plentiful supply of water and a moist atmosphere their rates of transpiration may be identical. When placed under conditions of increasing aerial desiccation the mesophytic plant will show a marked increase in rate of transpiration. Very soon the absorption of water will not replace the loss from transpiration and the deficit will result in closure of the stomata. Transpiration at this stage will decrease considerably and photosynthesis may almost cease. Because of the high cuticular transpiration the loss of water will continue at a rapid rate and the plant will wilt. If drought continues, it will dry out and die. The behavior of the xerophyte will be quite different. The rate of transpiration also increases at first, and since the stomata remain open for a longer time under the combination of external factors, the plant will lose more water through the stomata than the mesophyte. This is not a great danger because its tissues can endure a considerable dehydration without injury since the plant is drought resistant. Photosynthesis will also continue much longer than it did in the mesophyte, an important advantage possessed by the xerophyte. Plants cannot stop their water loss without also decreasing the rate of photosynthesis.

---

* Copied by permission, from "The Plant in Relation to Water."[577]

† This paragraph is rewritten from Maximov, "The Physiological Significance of the Xeromorphic Structure of Plants."[578]

Sooner or later, however, the stomata in the xeric plant will also close. Then only cuticular transpiration will occur. As the cuticle of the xerophyte is almost impermeable, especially when dry, the amount of water loss will be quickly reduced to a minimum and the plant, although in a state of permanent wilting, will remain alive for a long time. The tissues will lose only small quantities of water.

While cuticular transpiration in mesophytes has been found to be 10 or more per cent that of stomatal transpiration, that of xerophytes is much less. In some cases it is reduced to practically nil. When conditions more favorable to growth again occur, the xerophytic plant will recover and start its activities anew. Thus, it is a capacity to reduce water loss to a minimum in time of water scarcity that characterizes the water utilization of xerophytes.

Xeromorphic structures such as thick cuticle, waxy covering, or abundant development of hairs have little value in directly reducing the rate of transpiration of xerophytes so long as the stomata are open. But when the plant is wilting and the stomata are closed so that the loss of water takes place only through the cuticle, then all of these anatomical modifications manifest their protecting properties.

Climatic conditions of deserts are characterized by extreme variations. Great fluctuations in temperature and humidity may occur not only annually but also daily. Deserts are at times cool and humid. The life of most desert plants depends upon their ability to become active during relatively short but comparatively favorable periods. This is chiefly during rainy periods and during the short periods following when water is available for plant growth. Their activity occurs chiefly in the morning when the plants are sufficiently saturated with water that has accumulated in the tissues during the night when the stomata were closed.

Xerophytes are drought-resistant plants rather than plants which are benefited by dry conditions. Their growth and yield are increased by watering. Their capacity to endure permanent wilting is the test of drought resistance. Since physiological activities cannot be determined from anatomical data alone, experimental tests for xerophytes must be employed. Many species which anatomically appear to be drought resistant are not actually so. The easily observable structural peculiarities appear to be of less importance than the capacity to endure without injury a great loss of water. The capacity of the protoplasm to undergo considerable variations in its degree of hydration without loss of vital activity or irreversible coagulation seems of paramount importance. The key to drought resistance may be found in the physico-chemical properties of the living protoplasm rather than its structural products.[639] The functional approach to the phenomenon of xerophytism should supplement or replace the anatomical one. It should include primarily the water relations but also those of nutrition and other physiological activities as well.

Adaptations to a Decreased Water Supply.—The effect of a deficiency in the supply of water must be met by changes that decrease the demand arising from water loss, by modifications that increase the supply by adding to the absorbing or storage capacity of the plant, or by the capacity of the protoplasm to bind water so effectively that it may long remain dormant but quickly revive when water becomes available. These changes affect cell metabolism and result in modifying the form

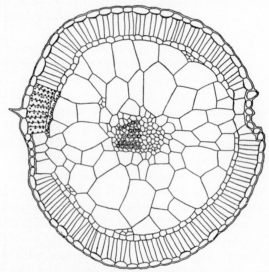

FIG. 223.—Section of leaf of the Russian thistle (*Salsola pestifer*) showing the large amount of water-storage tissue.

and size of various organs as well as their structure. Plants have become adapted to drier habitats both physiologically and structurally.[576] In fact, there is increasing evidence that the products of the changed metabolism induced by drought directly account for certain structural changes.

Succulence.—This is one type of adaptation common to many species of deserts and is illustrated by *Cactaceae*, species of *Euphorbia, Stapelia,* and others. The parenchymatous elements show an exaggerated development in relation to the more rigid tissues, these masses of thin-walled cells remaining distended and turgid. Succulence may originate as a direct result of aridity, but all succulent plants are not necessarily xeric. The reduction of the water content of a cell below a certain point results in the conversion of polysaccharides, with a low imbibition capacity, into pentosans.   The latter, especially when mixed with nitrogenous substances under the organization of the living plant, have a high hydration capacity, the action having the force of regulatory adjustment.   Since the change is irreversible, the pentosans result in permanent succulence.[561,873]

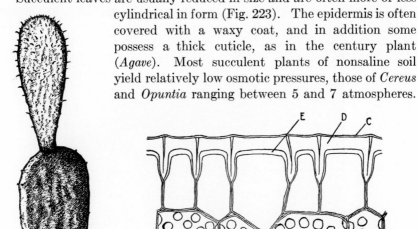

Succulent leaves are usually reduced in size and are often more or less cylindrical in form (Fig. 223).   The epidermis is often covered with a waxy coat, and in addition some possess a thick cuticle, as in the century plant (*Agave*).   Most succulent plants of nonsaline soil yield relatively low osmotic pressures, those of *Cereus* and *Opuntia* ranging between 5 and 7 atmospheres.

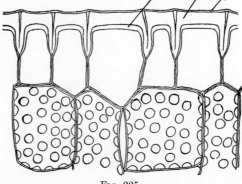

FIG. 224.   FIG. 225.

FIG. 224.—A cactus (*Opuntia*) showing deciduous, scalelike leaves on the young shoot. Although the shoot is only 4 weeks old, the leaves are beginning to fall.

FIG. 225.—Section from a leaf of *Aloe*: *C*, showing the cuticle; *D*, cutinized portion of the epidermal wall; and *E*, layer of cellulose.   The first row of chlorenchyma is also shown.

A Study of Succulent Leaves.—Examine the leaves of Russian thistle (*Salsola pestifer*) and century plant (*Agave*).   Draw a thin segment of one type.   In *Salsola*, note the sharp differentiation between chlorenchyma and water-storage tissue.   In fresh leaves of the century plant, make out the peculiar epidermal characters consisting of wax grains, cuticle, cuticular layer, and cellulose layer of the epidermal walls. Note the extent of palisade and depth to which chloroplasts occur.   Compare the rate of wilting of excised shoots of Russian thistle with that of sunflower, bean, or other mesophyte.

Little or no water is absorbed by desert succulents during severe drought, the plants drawing upon the water reserves in their tissues. When the stomata are closed, transpiration is so greatly reduced that these reserves are sufficient to tide the plant over for many months or even several years without rain.   Since succulents can endure relatively severe drying, they are able to use their stored water almost completely.

Desert succulents such as *Euphorbia, Stapelia,* and the *Cactaceae* have decreased water loss by the extreme reduction or loss of leaves and by reducing the stem surface. In the cactus, for example, leaves are wanting except during the early stages of growth, and then they occur only as small scales at the nodes (Figs. 224 and 225). The stems may remain smooth and round or become fluted by the presence of vertical green ribs or become flattened in various degrees, but they are always

Fig. 226.—Papago Indian, near Torres, Mexico, drinking the water which he has squeezed from the tissue of a cactus (*Echinocactus*) into the cavity formerly occupied by the tissue. (*After Coville and MacDougal.*)

thick and fleshy. Fluted stems, such as those of the giant cactus (*Carnegiea gigantea*), undergo accordion-like expansion and contraction during moist and dry periods, respectively.[559] The flattened types present a small amount of surface in proportion to the mass of contained tissue; the surface is further reduced in the thick, cylindrical type and reaches a minimum in the spherical form. Growth is slow because of the small surface exposed to light, although the chlorophyll extends much deeper than in most stems and leaves, but some species attain the proportion of trees and may have a reserve supply of many tons of water stored in the pulpy interior[559] (Fig. 226). Their xeromorphic characters usually include a highly developed cuticle and sunken stomata, hence the plants lose water very slowly when the stomata are closed.

Thickened Walls.—Another form of xerophytism is expressed in thickened cell walls and protective coverings. These result from the accelerated conversion of the polysaccharides into their anhydrides or wall materials (celluloses, etc.). This metabolic change is also induced by a depleted or lessened water supply in the cells.[560] The result is that the plant structures take on the indurated qualities so characteristic of many desert species. Desiccation promotes the development of cork.[710] Even in mesophytes the advent of winter or extreme summer drought usually results in the closure of the lenticels by the growth of a layer of cork. The thickness of bark varies with the habitat, usually being least in moist places and greatest in deserts, alpine regions, etc., where factors promoting desiccation are greatest. In plants of xeric habitats, the conducting tracts are also well developed. Not only are the vessels more numerous, larger, and longer, but also the walls are much thicker than in mesophytes. Lignification begins earlier and is pronounced, and the rings of growth, whether one or more a year, well developed. Bast fibers and sclerenchyma reach their highest development. Because of thicker epidermal coverings or deeper-seated chlorophyll, or because the chloroplasts are paler or fewer (as in cases of excess of salt), desert plants usually have a dull grayish color quite in contrast to the bright green of mesophytes and hydrophytes. This use, moreover, of carbohydrates in making wall materials, etc., is accompanied by a limited growth, particularly in stems and leaves where the effects of aridity are greatest. Hence, dwarfness is common among plants of xeric habitats. Frequently, it results in spinescence, which is also promoted by intense light and extreme desiccation. The two types of transformation of carbohydrates, *viz.*, the formation of increased cell-wall materials and hydrophilous colloids resulting in succulence, may take place in different parts of the same plant. In fact, wall materials are abundant in the peripheral cells of cacti, for example, and pentosan and mucilage accumulation in the interior.

Cuticular transpiration is greatly decreased or completely prevented by heavy cuticularization and extreme cutinization of the epidermis. In extreme cases the cuticle is sometimes thicker than the diameter of the epidermal cells. Heavily cutinized leaves are usually leathery in texture. The cells of the epidermis are sometimes protected against water loss by the secretion of a coating of wax, resin, or other material, or by the development of hairs.

Internally, leaves of xerophytes (except succulents) contain much mechanical tissue. This is believed to be connected with the necessity of giving rigidity to these organs which must remain for long periods in a

wilted condition.   The thickened epidermal coverings give rigidity as
do also the mechanical fibers which accompany the bundles and form I
and T beams.   Hypodermal cells consisting of layers or masses of greatly
lignified fibers or merely cutinized cells similar to the epidermis often
occur immediately beneath the epidermis.   Thus, wilted stems and
leaves of xerophytes do not droop like those of mesophytes which have
lost their turgor.   They are not readily bent by the wind, a process which
accelerates loss of water, nor are the water-conducting tracts sharply
bent or constricted.

   Leaves of xeric grasses which fold or roll into a tube illustrate one
function of such mechanical tissues.   In fact, often more than half of the

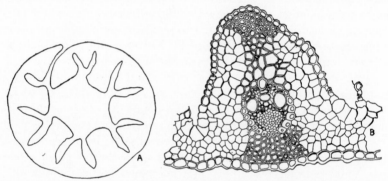

Fig. 227.—A. Outline of a rolled leaf of wheat grass (*Agropyron smithii*).   B. Detail
of one of the segments of the leaf showing bulliform cells of the rolling device on either side
and the I beam, which consists of bundle and woody fibers and gives rigidity to the flaccid
leaf.

leaf is given over to mechanical tissue and nongreen cells containing water
(Fig. 227).   The stomata usually occur most abundantly or entirely on
the upper surface.   Hence, when the leaves roll upward and inward, due
to decreased turgidity on the upper surface, or fold so that the edges
touch, water loss is greatly decreased, since the lower surface of the leaf
is usually heavily cutinized.   Experiments have shown that the transpiration rate of certain xeric prairie grasses is reduced to only 5 to 10 per
cent normal when the leaves roll during drought.

   To Determine the Rate of Transpiration of Open and Rolled or Folded Leaves.
Determine the average loss by transpiration of a well established xeric grass in a sealed
container from 8 a.m. till 5 p.m.   Repeat the weighings after so much available water
has been transpired that the leaves have rolled or folded.   Calculate the percentage
of loss during drought compared with that during an equal preceding period.

   A grass leaf consists essentially of a series of parallel bundles, varying
chiefly in size and amount of mechanical and conducting tissue, between
which chlorenchyma is supported (Fig. 228).   Immediately surrounding

the bundle is a sheath of cells often with much thickened, lignified walls. Commonly there occurs a second layer of thin-walled parenchyma cells, either with or without chlorophyll. Strands of sclerenchyma tissue ordinarily accompany the bundles and frequently form with the larger ones I or T beams of mechanical tissue extending across the leaf. The epidermis, especially the lower or dorsal one, is highly cutinized. Over the vascular bundles the epidermal cells are often smaller and thick walled, while bulliform (motor) cells, usually greatly enlarged, occur on the upper surface between the larger veins. Frequently, they lie at the bottom of well-defined grooves or occupy the entire thickness of the leaf. They are thin walled, and when they lose their turgidity through desiccation, the leaf rolls upward and inward. Thus, the stomata, which usually occur in rows and nearly always only in the depressions of the

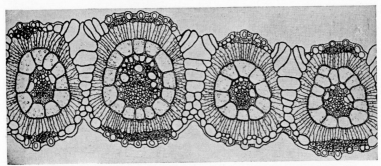

Fig. 228.—Cross section of leaf of blue grama grass (*Bouteloua gracilis*).

ventral surface in the most xeric species, are well protected from water loss. Mechanical tissue is very effective in preventing the collapse of the leaf and permitting it to roll. The remainder of the leaf is given over to chlorenchyma, except in cases of extreme xerophytes where water-storage tissue occurs. The tissue is compactly arranged, the chlorenchyma cells being either nearly isodiametric or somewhat elongated.

To Observe the Rolling and Folding of Leaves.—Detach leaves from various xeric grasses and watch them fold or roll as they dry. This may be hastened by cutting cross sections only a millimeter or two in length. Examine with a binocular microscope the upper and lower surfaces of wheat grass (*Agropyron*) or needle grass (*Stipa*). Detach a leaf and follow the process of rolling as it dries. Examine freshly cut sections of the above and also of *Bouteloua* or *Buchloe* to determine the mechanism of rolling. Note especially the amount of tissue not concerned in photosynthesis.

Osmotic Pressure.—The concentration of the sap of a species is not constant. It may be influenced by any of the environmental conditions affecting transpiration, by the products of photosynthesis, or by the supply of available water. The sap density of any species usually shows variations corresponding to the degree of aridity of the habitat, the highest osmotic pressures, except in succulents, usually being found in more drought-resistant species. Extended experiments over a wide range of materials show that the highest osmotic pressures are found in xerophytes and the lowest in hydrophytes, mesic species occupying an intermediate position[378] (Table 11).

TABLE 11.—OSMOTIC PRESSURES IN ATMOSPHERES OF THE CELL SAP OF VARIOUS PLANT GROUPS

Ecological type	Osmotic pressure		Ecological type	Osmotic pressure
	Herbs	Woody plants		
Xerophytes:				
Jamaican coastal deserts..	....	30.0	Salt flats (*Salicornia, Allenrolfea*).................	34.6
Arizona desert..........	15.2	25.0	Greasewood-shad scale (*Sarcobatus vermiculatus, Atriplex confertifolia*).............	32.0
Mesophytes, Long Island....	10.4	14.4	Shad scale (*Atriplex confertifolia*).................	22.4
Hydrophytes:				
Jamaican rain-forest......	8.8	11.4	Sagebrush (*Artemisia tridentata*)....................	22.0

High osmotic pressure causes considerable tension of the cell walls through increased turgor and thus prevents visible wilting for a long time, even though the water deficit continues to increase. Thus while delicate shade plants, such as the balsam (*Impatiens*), may wilt with a loss of only 1 or 2 per cent of their water content, strongly xerophytic plants may not show signs of wilting until the water content is reduced 30 per cent or more. This delayed loss of turgor enables the plant to continue photosynthesis longer. The chief importance of high osmotic pressures in desert plants is believed to be during the period of wilting when there is a real danger of excessive water loss.

Among mesophytes, the osmotic pressure within the root hairs increases somewhat as the soil water becomes less and the solutes more concentrated. Likewise, the cell sap of the leaves, when the plants are grown in dry places, often shows an osmotic pressure greater by several atmospheres than that of similar plants in moist situations.[378,433]

During the great drought of 1934, as the water content of soil in true prairie gradually decreased (p. 210), the osmotic pressure of all prairie plants studied increased. This increase was frequently 30 or more atmospheres among moderately deeply rooted upland plants, but among deeply rooted upland plants and plants growing in low, moist habitats, the increase was usually only 2 to 10 atmospheres. Watering increased the water content of tissues and lowered osmotic pressures.[893]

Among xerophytes generally, especially woody species and plants of saline areas, high osmotic pressures usually prevail.[407] This is combined in the plants of the latter group with the ability to resist the toxic action of concentrated salts within the cell, which would undoubtedly be injurious to many other species.

A correlation between plant succession and osmotic pressure has been shown in Utah, where one plant community gradually replaces another more tolerant to salt as the soil becomes less saline.[379] In the saline deserts about Great Salt Lake the succession in the sequence indicated in Table 11 is from the vegetation of the salt flats to sagebrush.[809] The osmotic pressure decreases gradually in each of the several stages from the initial one to the climax. The osmotic pressures are the averages for several woody species in each community.[498]

Other Changes.—In proportion to their tops, the roots of xerophytes are frequently greatly elongated, much branched, and densely clothed with root hairs. In many species the leaves are greatly reduced or wanting, and in others the stem is so reduced that the leaves seem to spring directly from the top of the enlarged root. In such short-stemmed forms, the internodes are little or not at all developed and the rosette of leaves either lies flat on the soil surface or forms a hemispherical group of radiating and often more or less fleshy or bayonet-like leaves, as in certain species of *Agave* and *Yucca*.

A few desert shrubs lose their leaves during long periods of drought but may regain them after a few days following even moderate precipitation, a phenomenon that may be repeated several times during the course of a year.[426] Loss of leaves also occurs in all deciduous trees and shrubs growing in climates which are periodically dry, as a temporary adaptation to drought. The latter may result either from an actual deficiency of water, as in certain semitropical and tropical climates, or from its low availability due to frozen soil.

CHAPTER XVII

PLANTS AND PLANT COMMUNITIES AS INDICATORS

Every plant is a product of the conditions under which it grows and is, therefore, a measure of environment. It indicates in general, and often also in a specific manner, what other species would do if grown in the same place. The dominant species are the most important indicators, since they receive the full impact of the habitat usually year after year. Furthermore, plant communities are more reliable indicators than individual plants. It has been seen that in the development of vegetation species are not indiscriminately mixed without regard to their fitness to be companions but that the members of the community are adapted to each other and to their common surroundings. A community of hard maple, buffalo grass, spike rush, creosote bush, and sea blite would be an absurdity. Each species thrives in a habitat quite different from that of the others. One immediately associates beech, linden, spicebush, and various other trees, shrubs, and herbs of similar habitat requirements with hard maple. In the same way, desert species such as cacti, yucca, etc., are associated with the creosote bush. Each plant and community, moreover, bring to mind a more or less definite soil or climate.

A plant or community may indicate a deficiency or an excess of water and often accompanying secondary or concomitant factors. Cacti, yucca, sagebrush, and xerophytes in general are associated with habitats of low water content as well as usually with high temperatures and low humidity. Cattails and bulrushes, as well as other hydrophytes, indicate in a general way an excessive water supply and consequent poor aeration. Greasewood, saltwort, and other halophytes denote an excess of soil solutes just as definitely as such woodland forms as wild ginger and ginseng indicate, with other woodland species, habitats with low light intensities. A seral community, e.g., reed swamp, not only indicates the present condition of the habitat but also what the previous conditions were and what future conditions will be.

Plants are indicators of *conditions, processes,* and *uses* (Fig. 229). Many species such as salt grass (*Distichlis*) and reed (*Phragmites*) indicate a water table at or near the surface soil; others such as Washington palm (*Washingtonia*) and greasewood (*Sarcobatus*) indicate ground water at a greater depth, while the mesquite (*Prosopis*) is an indicator of a deep water table, the roots sometimes extending to a depth of 30 to 50 feet

Fig. 229.—Mohave River valley, showing zones of vegetation due to different depths of ground water. Desert scrub in the foreground, salt grass in the lowland back of the desert scrub, and flood-plain forest of poplar, willow, and mesquite along the river. (*U. S. Geological Survey, Photograph by D. G. Thompson.*)

Fig. 230.—Cut bank of Santa Cruz River near Tucson, Ariz.. showing the depth of roots of the mesquite (*Prosopis*). (*Photograph by V. M. Spalding, Carnegie Inst. Wash., Pub., 113.*)

(Fig. 230). Certain species are confined almost completely to areas with specific water-table depths.[598] Various species indicate such processes as erosion, lumbering, trampling, fire, etc. Others are of great value in indicating the uses for which lands may best be employed, *viz.*, agriculture, grazing, forestation, etc.,[155,680] and still others denote past climates.[160]

INDICATORS OF AGRICULTURE

The most reliable natural indicators of the agricultural possibilities of a region are to be found in its native vegetation.[808] For many centuries, the natural vegetation has been sorted out by climate as well as by the soil in its process of development, until usually only species well

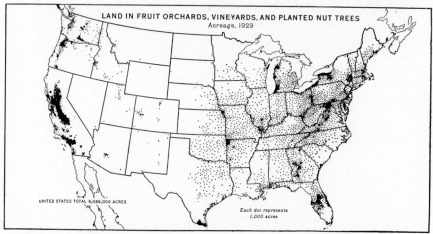

Fig. 231.—Distribution of fruit orchards, vineyards, and planted nut trees in 1929. Each dot represents 1,000 acres. The greatest areas of production of tree fruits and nuts such as apples, peaches, pears, chestnuts, pecans, etc., and such bush fruits as blackberries, currants, and raspberries (aside from irrigated districts) are in those portions of the United States formerly occupied by forest trees and shrubs. (*U. S. Department of Agriculture.*)

adapted to a given environment now occur in abundance. The growth of the plant cover is a measure of the effects of all the conditions favorable or unfavorable to plant development. The natural plant cover, if properly interpreted, indicates the crop-producing capabilities of land better than any series of meteorological observations or soil analyses (Figs. 231 and 232). This does not minimize the importance of the study of environmental factors, since the significance of the various types of vegetation can be interpreted only by an understanding of the conditions under which the plants grow, especially where agriculture is not already well established.

Forests as Indicators.—Since the earliest settlements in America, agriculturists have been accustomed to judge the quality of land by the forest trees growing upon it. The pioneers in the Ohio Valley who settled on lands covered with sugar maple and beech were more prosperous than those on oak and pine lands.   Forests should be examined not only as to the species but also as to the form and size assumed by the trees growing in arable soils.   For example, post oak (*Quercus stellata*) and blackjack oak (*Q. marilandica*) are very different in their habit of growth on upland and lowland or on sterile sandy soil.   When thus considered, forests form a safe criterion for evaluating the potential productivity of the land.   This is especially true where tree growth is correlated with the development of the shrubs and perennial herbs of the forest floor. Not only the market value of the land but also the tax rate has been

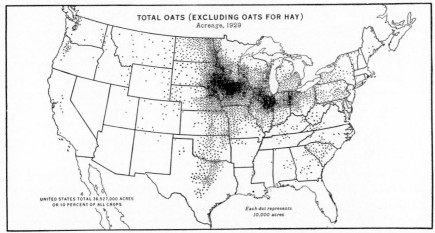

Fig. 232.—Distribution of oats in 1929. Each dot represents 10,000 acres. The cereal crops, *viz.*, corn, spring and winter wheat, oats, barley, sorghum, and millet, all of which are grasses, have their center of greatest production in that portion of the United States originally covered by grassland. (*U. S. Department of Agriculture.*)

frequently determined by the type of vegetation.   The accuracy with which experienced farmers were able to evaluate the productivity of timberlands by their forest growth excited the wonder even of agricultural investigators.   Thus, "black oak and hickory uplands," "gum bottoms," "hackberry hummocks," "post-oak prairie," "red-cedar prairie," etc., each had certain cultural values or peculiarities of soil well understood by the farmer.[404]

Many years ago, it was noted that

... in the long-leaf pine uplands of the cotton states, the scattered settlements have fully demonstrated that after 2 or 3 years' cropping with corn, ranging as much as 25 bushels per acre the first year to 10 and less the third, fertilization is absolutely necessary to further paying cultivation.   Should the short-leaved pine mingle with the long-leaved, production may hold out for 5 to 7 years.   If oaks and hickories are superadded, as many as 12 years of good production without fertilization may be looked for by the farmer; and should the long-leaved pine disappear altogether, the mingled growth of oaks and short-leaved pine will encourage him to hope for from 12 to 15 years of fair production without fertilization. [405]

Grasslands as Indicators.—The relation between the native vegetation and possibilities of the land for crop production is well illustrated by the various types of grassland in central North America. The great grassland area extending across the Mississippi Valley from the forests of the east to the foothills of the Rockies is not characterized by a uniform vegetation throughout. The true prairie of the eastern portion is distinctly different from the desert plains of the west and southwest, and between these two regions is a broad belt of mixed grassland where mid and short grasses intermingle. The chief causes of these differences in grassland vegetation are the differences in the quantities of soil moisture supplied by the rainfall and the length of time during which soil moisture is available. Decreased relative humidity southwestward is also an important factor. Differences in soil structure, resulting from differences in climate and vegetation during its development, are also pronounced. These factors, which have so largely determined the type of grassland, exert striking influences on the development of both root and shoot and, hence, influence crop growth and yield.

True Prairie.—Mid grasses constitute by far the greater portion of the grasslands of Minnesota, Iowa, Illinois, and Missouri, as well as of the eastern third or more of the Dakotas, Nebraska, Kansas, and Oklahoma. Originally, they covered the climax areas to the exclusion of other species, and the tall grasses were confined to meadows, ravines, and the bases of slopes. During the period of settlement, however, they suffered much from overgrazing, clearing and burning, with the result that their tall-grass competitors, notably *Andropogon*, gradually moved up the slopes and today appear to be essential members of the prairie relicts. The two types have been referred to as high and low prairie, but the tall grasses actually formed postclimax meadows, and they make a disclimax when they replace the mid grasses more or less completely as a result of human disturbance.

For the most part, the mid grasses range from 2 to 4 feet tall, while the tall grasses reach 5 to 6 feet or even more. Apart from stature, they have much in common and hence may be considered together as indicators, in spite of the fact that the tall grasses are not actual climax dominants. The latter comprise big bluestem (*Andropogon furcatus*), goldstem (*Sorghastrum nutans*), tall panic grass (*Panicum virgatum*), tall marsh grass (*Spartina pectinata*), and wild rye (*Elymus canadensis*). The chief mid grasses are needle grass (*Stipa spartea*), dropseed (*Sporobolus asper* and *S. heterolepis*), little bluestem (*Andropogon scoparius*), side-oats grama (*Bouteloua curtipendula*), and June grass (*Koeleria cristata*) (Fig. 233). The indications of the grasses are reenforced by a host of societies composed largely of legumes, composites, mints, and roses.[971]

The mid grasses of the true prairie assume the bunch form for the most part but with a tendency to develop short rhizomes and thus produce a more or less uniform dense cover. They are usually rooted to a depth greater than their height in the fertile dark soil, and some of them are able to continue growth into the autumn. This is possible because of the presence of abundant soil moisture. Even in the drier portions, the soil is usually moist to a depth of several feet, and moisture is continuous

Fig. 233.—Upland true prairie in eastern Nebraska. Needle grass (*Stipa spartea*) is the most conspicuous species.

to the water table in eastern areas with higher rainfall. The surface soil may dry out each year and drought may occur in late summer and fall, but the subsoil, into which the deeper roots penetrate, is permanently moist as a rule. Such conditions favor the development of deeply rooted species in large number and in fact the true prairie is characterized by this type of root habit.[965,966] Most of the features indicated are more or less emphasized in the so-called *low prairies*, characterized by the tall grasses of the postclimax.

Conditions Indicated for Crop Growth.—The relationship, origin, and life form of the dominants of the true prairie furnish general indications of much value as to the preferred crops. The andropogons are not only distant relatives of corn, but they are likewise subtropical in origin, as is *Sporobolus* also. On the other hand, *Agropyron* is closely akin to wheat and like the needle grass (*Stipa spartea*) characterizes a temperate climate.

The invasion of the disturbed uplands by the tall *Andropogon furcatus* and *Sorghastrum nutans* is suggestive of the conquest of much of the region by corn.[38]

Mixed Prairie.—This community lies west of the true prairie from southern Canada to northwestern Texas, whence it extends through northern New Mexico and Arizona. The name is derived from its two-layered nature, mid grasses forming the upper story and short grasses the lower. The latter have suffered much less from overgrazing and have consequently replaced the mid grasses over most of the area. Before this relation was understood, the nearly universal presence of a short-

Fig. 234.—Short-grass disclimax in eastern Colorado. The dominant grasses are blue grama (*Bouteloua gracilis*) and buffalo grass (*Buchloe dactyloides*).

grass cover led to the assumption that this was the climax of the Great Plains. It is now generally recognized that short grass is a grazing dis-climax and that its climatic indications are those of the original mixed prairie to which it belongs. Consequently, a short-grass sod indicates overgrazing alone, and the degree of this may be read off by the extent to which the mid grasses have vanished and the sod itself has been further modified by competition among the short grasses (Fig. 234).

The mid grasses of the Great Plains are in part those of the true prairie, as in the case of wheat grass (*Agropyron smithii*) and June grass (*Koeleria cristata*), or they are closely related species, such as needle grass (*Stipa comata*) and sand dropseed (*Sporobolus cryptandrus*) (Fig. 235). The most important dominants of the short-grass type are blue grama (*Bouteloua gracilis*), buffalo grass (*Buchloe dactyloides*), and the sedges,

Carex stenophylla and *C. filifolia.* Societies play a much smaller part, both in number and in extent, than they do in the true prairie, as a consequence of reduced rainfall.

Mid grasses, and *Agropyron* in particular, are still generally present in the mixed prairie but usually in reduced forms, which rarely flower under continual grazing. There are also considerable stretches where the original relation obtains, in which the short grasses are entirely subordinate to their taller associates. For the most part, however, grazing keeps all the grasses in the condition of a low sod, in which grama, buffalo

FIG. 235.—Mixed prairie of wheat grass (*Agropyron smithii*) and needle grass (*Stipa comata*) with short grasses beneath; Scotts Bluff, Neb.

grass, or the short sedges are dominant. The rainfall ranges from 10 to 15 inches less than in the true prairie and the penetration into the soil is correspondingly restricted, though it necessarily varies between rainy and dry periods. Penetration of water determines the depth to which roots may grow, and these in turn fix the limit at which leached salts accumulate to form a more or less definite carbonate layer. The latter generally occurs at a depth of 16 to 30 inches and may be from 8 to 20 inches in thickness, while below it the subsoil is dry.

When the natural vegetation is destroyed by cultivation, the depth of penetration is increased, even if the land is continuously cropped, and with alternate years of cropping and summer fallow, this depth is even greater. In the former case, water seldom penetrates below 2 to 3 feet and under the latter practice only now and then beyond 5 to 6 feet. Consequently, the deeper subsoil is constantly dry, owing to a precipitation usually less than 23 inches, great evaporation, and considerable runoff.

Conditions Indicated for Crop Growth.—The major difference between cropping systems in the true and mixed prairie is indicated by the change in dominants. Taller and more mesic species are replaced by those of lower stature and greater ability to resist drought. Thus, *Stipa spartea* gives way to *S. comata*, and *Sporobolus asper* and *S. heterolepis* yield to *S. cryptandrus*. *Andropogon scoparius* disappears except as a postclimax relict, and *Bouteloua curtipendula* and *Koeleria cristata* decrease greatly in abundance at the lower elevations. *Agropyron* alone maintains and improves its position, to become the indicator of wheat as the leading crop. In spite of the general impression during the recent period of drought, wheat at the many dry-land stations in the Great Plains has produced an average of 17 to 31 bushels per acre for the last 10 years. The presence of short grasses is in accord with the general reduction in rainfall, but in the original mixed prairie, they were regularly subordinate to the mid grasses.

INDICATORS OF SOIL TYPE

Extensive studies in the Great Plains have shown that under the same precipitation and other climatic conditions the native vegetation may vary greatly and, in fact, different communities may occur within a radius of only a few miles.[808] These differences are due to the type of soil. The hard, compact, very fine sandy- and silt-loam soils, which are by far the most extensive, are occupied by the short-grass disclimax, with more or less mid grass. Where the soil contains an admixture of sand, runoff is greatly reduced and the water penetrates to greater depths, often to 3 or 4 feet. This sandy-loam type of soil is clearly indicated by the abundance of certain characteristic species which are taller and more deeply rooted than are the short grasses on the "hard lands." Chief among these are wire grass and *Psoralea* which form an open growth in the grama-grass sod (buffalo grass being rarely found) since moisture in the deeper soil is often insufficient to produce a continuous growth of the taller, deeply rooted plants.

Where the soil becomes so sandy that all of the rainfall is absorbed and there is no runoff, the bunch-grass (*Andropogon scoparius*) type of vegetation prevails. This deeply rooted mid grass is accompanied by the tall sand-hills' bluestem (*Andropogon hallii*) and sand reed (*Calamovilfa*), by sand sage (*Artemisia filifolia*), bush morning glory (*Ipomoea leptophylla*), etc., which constitute a tall-grass postclimax to the mixed prairie (Figs. 236 and 237).

The short-grass disclimax indicates much runoff, limited water penetration, and a growing season shortened by a limited water supply.   Such land is not well adapted to late-developing, deeply rooted crops such as

Fig. 236.—Bush morning glory (*Ipomoea leptophylla*), an indicator of sandy soil.   The plant is perennial from an enormous root which serves for storage of water and food.

Fig. 237.—Sand-hill sage (*Artemisia filifolia*), an indicator of sandy soil.

corn, although early-maturing crops, such as winter wheat, often give a good yield.   Owing to the high fertility, crops make a rank growth when water is plentiful early in the season and are thus poorly fitted to withstand drought.

Wire grass indicates soil into which almost all of the rainfall penetrates and where surface evaporation is greatly reduced. The moisture is distributed to a considerable depth and when drought threatens, plants are able to draw on the reserves found in the deeper layers of soil. The native vegetation indicates this longer growing season. Fertility is still sufficiently high so that crops grown on wire-grass land, even during favorable years, are almost as good as on short-grass land, and during dry years much better crops are produced. Wire grass is frequently a subclimax stage in the secondary succession in abandoned fields and then denotes disturbance rather than type of soil (Fig. 238).

Fig. 238.—Wire-grass community established as a result of breaking short-grass land, Yuma, Colo. (*After Shantz.*)

Bunch grass indicates soil of a texture that insures the penetration of practically all of the water that falls. Little water is lost directly by evaporation from the sandy soil. Crop growth is much less luxuriant on this land owing to decreased fertility; the retardation in growth itself aids in conserving the water supply. The native plants indicate a long season for growth, and, like them, the roots of crops spread widely and deeply and plants rarely wilt because of drought. Lands of the bunch-grass and wire-grass type are locally known as "corn land."

Crop failures occur most often on short-grass land and least often on bunch-grass land. During favorable years, yields are highest on the former and least on the latter. Wire-grass land represents a safe intermediate condition; during favorable years crops are almost as good as on short-grass land, and during dry years a fair crop can often be produced. Many of the older settlers in eastern Colorado have moved from short-grass land on to wire-grass land, where there is much less likelihood of crop failure. The newcomer in the region, however, almost invariably chooses the hard or short-grass land because it is darker in color and looks like the soil he has been accustomed to farm successfully in the east.[808]

Why a Knowledge of Plant Succession Is Necessary.—From the preceding it may be seen that in eastern Colorado short-grass vegetation indicates a loam soil, wire grass a sandy loam (or an old field), and bunch grass a sandy soil. These correlations do not hold eastward under a higher rainfall, where the subsoil of even compact loam may become quite moist and favorable to the growth of bunch grass. Careful studies must be made of various plant communities in relation to their physical environment before their indicator significance becomes clear. A knowledge of successional sequence is also imperative. When mixed-prairie vegetation is plowed under and the area subsequently abandoned for a time, runoff is decreased, water penetration increased, and loss by absorption greatly reduced. Upon such areas of loam soil, there often develops a thriving community of wire grass, the wind having brought in the propagules from plants perhaps many miles away (Fig. 238). This community persists for a long time but after a period of 20 to 30 years the area returns to the mixed-prairie climax. Similarly, when wire-grass land is broken, bunch-grass vegetation may temporarily gain possession of the area. If wire grass is repeatedly burned, there is a tendency toward the development of a pure short-grass cover.[808]

INDICATORS OF SALINITY

In large portions of the western half of the United States, rainfall is so light that the excess salts of the soil have not been leached away and carried to the ocean but have accumulated, especially in lowlands, forming saline spots often of great extent. Such areas are characterized by plant communities especially adapted to secure water from strong soil solutions. Some species are able to tolerate more salt than others; some will not endure it but make a fair growth in dry, nonsaline soil. Could the prospective settler foretell what types of vegetation indicate the presence or absence of salts in quantities likely to be injurious to cultivated crops and what types indicate conditions favorable or unfavorable to dry farming, it would be distinctly advantageous.

Accordingly, several investigators in the United States Department of Agriculture set to work to determine the indicator significance of the various plant communities.[465] An extensive area near Great Salt Lake in Utah was selected for this study, since it was representative of Great Basin conditions. Some of the soils contained an excess of salts; much of the land was still covered with the original plant communities; but enough had been tilled either by methods of dry-land or irrigation farm-

Fig. 239.—A close stand of sagebrush (*Artemisia tridentata*) indicating a deep, porous soil.

ing to serve as a check. Saline areas are characterized by relatively few species which form a very open cover of vegetation. Boundaries between the different communities are, moreover, often very abrupt and distinct.

Fig. 240.—Shad scale (*Atriplex confertifolia*), indicating saline soil.

Sagebrush, which is the most important type of vegetation in the Great Basin, makes an excellent growth on the nonalkaline, light-textured, deep, well drained soils of the uplands (Fig. 239).   White sage, a low-growing grayish half-shrub, occupies the finer-grained, easily puddled soils, where the subsoil is saline.   The large, woody, somewhat spiny and bushy-topped shad scale occurs on more gravelly soil with a saline subsoil (Fig. 240).   In certain areas it is accompanied by greasewood, a spiny, woody shrub 2 to 5 feet tall and tolerant of considerable salt.   On lower ground, extensive salt-grass flats give way to even more saline areas characterized by saltwort and species of similar tolerance of salt.

After a thorough study of the water content of the soils in each community together with analyses of their salt content (90 per cent of which is NaCl), and an investigation of root distribution, the following indicator significance was determined for each (Table 12):

TABLE 12.—SOIL CONDITIONS AND INDICATOR SIGNIFICANCE OF PLANT COMMUNITIES

| Community | Soil, water content, roots, etc. | Salt content | | Capable of crop production | |
		First foot	Deeper	Without irrigation	With irrigation
Sagebrush (*Artemisia tridentata*)	Light-textured soil, low runoff. Plants very deeply rooted	Nonsaline, usually dry in summer	Nonsaline, usually dry in late summer	Yes	Yes
White sage (*Kochia vestita*)	Finer soil, easily puddled, limits penetration of water. Plants rooted in surface 1.5 to 2 feet	Nonsaline, usually dry in summer	Saline, usually dry in late summer	Precariously in wet years	Yes, if alkali can be removed
Shad scale (*Atriplex confertifolia*)	More gravelly soil, roots 2 to 3 feet deep	Nonsaline, usually dry in summer	Saline, usually dry in late summer	Precariously, more favorable than *Kochia* land	Yes, after alkali is removed
Greasewood-shad scale (*Sarcobatus vermiculatus* and *Atriplex confertifolia*)	Fair water content in surface foot, well drained in summer. Moist below 2 feet. Roots of greasewood 6 to 7 feet deep	Saline or nonsaline, usually dry in summer	Saline, moist	No	Yes, after alkali is removed
Grass flats (*Distichlis spicata*, *Sporobolus airoides*)	High water content, good even in summer. Roots shallow	Moderately saline, moist	Moderately saline, moist	Probably not	Possibly with drainage
Salt flats (*Salicornia utahensis*, *S. rubra*, *Allenrolfea occidentalis*)	Moist to very wet. Plants mostly shallow-rooted	Much salt, moist to wet	Saline, moist to wet	No	No

The salt content in the soils of the several communities decreased from 2.5 per cent in the salt flats to 0.8 per cent in the greasewood, while the sagebrush soil had only 0.04 per cent. Thus, it may be seen that each plant community indicates not only a certain concentration of salt or freedom from salinity but also other edaphic conditions upon which the success or failure of crop production directly depends. For example, a good stand and growth of sagebrush indicate land that is well adapted to both dry and irrigation farming; but where the stand is thin and the growth poor, the depth of good soil is usually too limited for profitable crop production, at least without irrigation. Conversely, greasewood indicates land unsuitable for dry farming, but it may be made to produce good crops when the excess salt is removed by irrigation and drainage. These general principles probably apply, in the main, throughout much of the Great Basin.

INDICATORS OF GRAZING

In grazing practice, four classes of stock must be considered, *viz.*, cattle, horses, sheep, and goats.[155] Each has more or less definite prefer-

Fig. 241.—Aspen forest with *Erigeron, Geranium*, etc., indicating the weed type of grazing.

ences as to the type of vegetation grazed and each affects the pasture or range in a markedly different manner. Cattle and horses prefer grass, sheep prefer other herbs and weeds, and goats prefer shrubs or "browse" (Fig. 241). Thus, a uniform community of grass indicates grazing for cattle and horses; one of nongrassy herbs, grazing for sheep; while browse indicates pasture land for goats. Ecotones between chaparral and grassland or desert scrub and grassland indicate mixed grazing where various types of stock may profitably be handled together. In fact, this is often true of various grassland areas, most of which have an abundance of nongrassy herbs.   Montane savanna of ponderosa pine and various woodland communities of the same type are also indicators of grazing. So, too, are the meadows, parks, and areas of aspen in subalpine forest. Many potential grazing lands give a greater economic return when used for crop production.   Such are the true prairie and much of the mixed prairie with its short-grass disclimax, and often only the poorer areas with a scantier growth of vegetation are left for grazing.

INDICATORS OF OVERGRAZING

The highest grazing efficiency consists in producing the largest amount of forage from a pasture or range each year.   Experiments have shown that the removal of the herbage several times each growing season, especially if the first harvest is made a short time after the beginning of growth in spring, seriously weakens the plants and immediately decreases their forage production.   Vigorous plants that have not been weakened by overgrazing produce a large yield of forage and a viable seed crop which matures fairly early.   Plants seriously weakened by overgrazing produce but little forage and usually fail to develop any seed.[768]   Grazing a pasture to its maximum capacity year after year invariably results in a sharp decline in its carrying capacity, i.e., the number of stock it can support. Until a study of indicators of overgrazing was made, judgment as to the condition of the pasture was based on general observations, such as the abundance and luxuriance of the plant cover as a whole and the condition of the grazing animals.   Unfortunately, until the plant cover had been greatly disturbed or a large proportion of the more valuable species actually killed, deterioration was not recognized.   When this stage of depletion has been reached, many seasons of proper management are required to reestablish the original forage cover.

Overgrazing results in definite modifications of grassland, as has been clearly recognized.   Before the ranges were overgrazed, the grasses of the red prairies of Texas were largely bluestems (*Andropogon*), often as high as a horse's back.   After pasturing and subsequent to the trampling and hardening of the soil, the wire grasses (*Aristida*) spread over the whole country.   After further overstocking and trampling, the wire grasses were driven out and mesquite grass (*Hilaria*) and buffalo grass (*Buchloe*) became the most prominent species.   The occurrence of any one of these as the dominant is, to some extent, an index of the state of the land and of the stage of overstocking and deterioration that has been reached.[859]

When the enormous herds of buffaloes roamed the prairies of eastern Kansas and Nebraska, tall and mid grasses were closely eaten and much trampled.   The prairies, moreover, were repeatedly burned.   Burning and trampling were distinctly more favorable to the short buffalo and grama grasses than to their taller competitors. The westward movement of the buffalo and their decrease in numbers coincided with the incoming of the settlers and the decrease in prairie fires. This resulted in renewed growth of the taller grasses and the gradual shading out of the buffalo and grama grasses. It explains the belief of the pioneers that the bluestems (*Andropogon*) followed in the wake of the settlers and drove out the buffalo grass.

Degree of Overgrazing.—The degree of overgrazing is shown by two types of indicators—those due primarily to the fact that they are not eaten, and those that invade because of disturbance. The more palatable species are eaten down, thus rendering the uneaten ones more conspicuous. This quickly throws the advantage in competition to the side of the latter. Because of more water and light, their growth is greatly increased. They are enabled to store more food in their propagative organs as well as to produce more seed. The grazed species are correspondingly handicapped in all these respects by the increase of less palatable species and the grasses are further weakened by trampling as stock wanders about in search of food. Soon bare spots appear that are colonized by weeds or weedlike species. The weeds reproduce vigorously and sooner or later come to occupy most of the space between the fragments of the original vegetation. Before this condition is reached, usually the stock are forced to eat the less palatable species, and these begin to yield to the competition of annuals. If grazing is sufficiently severe, these, too, may disappear unless they are woody, wholly unpalatable, or protected by spines.

Signs of Overgrazing.—There are several conspicuous signs of overgrazing, some or all of which may be observed in many pastures, for overgrazing or trampling for a period will produce indicators that may readily be recognized. Obviously, these indicators are not the same in all parts of the United States, but once the underlying principles of overgrazing are comprehended, a little study will reveal them anywhere (Fig. 242).

The predominance of annual weeds and short-lived, unpalatable perennials indicates severe overgrazing and characterizes pastures in advanced stages of depletion. Prominent among these are knotgrass (*Polygonum*), lamb's-quarters (*Chenopodium*), tansy mustard (*Sophia*), annual brome grasses (*Bromus tectorum, B. hordeaceus*), peppergrass (*Lepidium*), squirreltail (*Hordeum jubatum*), etc. Characteristic species representing a less pronounced degree of overgrazing are gumweed (*Grindelia*), yarrow (*Achillea*), ironweed (*Vernonia*), vervain (*Verbena*), thistle (*Carduus*), goldenrod (*Solidago*), abundance of cactus (*Opuntia*), etc. (Fig. 243). Early indicators of range deterioration are a decrease in abundance of the more valuable species of grasses, such as needle grasses

(*Stipa*) and wheat grasses (*Agropyron*) in prairie; an increase in the less valuable ones, *e.g.*, wire grass (*Aristida*), accompanied by an increase in the short grasses (*Bouteloua, Buchloe*) where they are associated with the

Fig. 242.—Overgrazed range in western Nebraska indicated by the abundance of cactus (*Opuntia*).

Fig. 243.—Gumweed (*Grindelia*) and ironweed (*Vernonia*) in an overgrazed pasture.

taller ones. This is followed or accompanied by a marked increase in vigor and abundance of societies, such as sages (*Artemisia*), goldenrods (*Solidago*), asters, etc.

Thus, the species that are increasing on an area reveal one of two things. If they represent stages earlier in the successional development than that of the predominating vegetation when the range is at its highest efficiency, the area is being misused and its carrying capacity is decreasing. If, on the contrary, the species that are increasing are those of the climax stage or at least higher than the original vegetation as a whole, the plan of grazing is satisfactory. In the former case, proper remedial measures such as reducing the number of stock, deferring grazing until the more important species have produced flower stalks and seeded, etc., will initiate a succession that will again culminate in the climax vegetation. In humid climates, especially, this may often be hastened by artificial seeding.

Other signs of overgrazing, especially in forest and scrub, consist of damage to tree reproduction, *e.g.*, ponderosa pine, aspen, etc.; remnants of dead shoots of palatable woody plants such as coralberry (*Symphoricarpos*), serviceberry (*Amelanchier*), willow (*Salix*), etc.; and, everywhere in general, erosion, roots of vegetation exposed by trampling, bare soil, and deeply cut trails where formerly the cover of vegetation was intact.

To Study the Degree of Overgrazing.—Visit a number of pastures and make a careful examination for indicators of overgrazing. Compare the vegetation about gates, watering troughs, or shade trees where the animals collect and trample the grasses with that of the pasture generally. Try to determine the past history of the pasture and, if possible, the original type of vegetation. Do the different pastures show the same degree of overgrazing? What are the most important indicators of disturbance? Are the indicators different in pastures for cattle or horses and sheep or hogs? Which shows the greatest disturbance and why? What remedial measures would you suggest?

INDICATORS OF FOREST

Forest indicators are of three chief types, *viz.*, those that have to do with existing forests, those that indicate former forests, and those that indicate the possibility of establishing new forests. Obviously, every forest climax indicates a forest climate although of different quality. The deciduous forest indicates one with long, hot summers and moderately cold winters with an abundance of both summer and winter precipitation. The three Rocky Mountain climaxes, *viz.*, woodland (*Pinus-Juniperus*), montane (*Pinus-Pseudotsuga*), and subalpine forest (*Picea-Abies*) indicate climates with a progressive increase in rainfall and corresponding decrease in temperature and length of growing season. The forest formation that is the climax for a region indicates the type of forest that will naturally develop or redevelop in all bare or cleared areas. The various groupings of species and the differences in density and growth of dominants and subdominants serve to denote differences in edaphic conditions and minor changes in the factor complex.[620] Seral communities likewise indicate differences in edaphic conditions or habitats. They often indicate the nature of the original area (whether wet or dry) or the nature of the disturbance (such as fire, wind throw, lumbering, etc.) and the particular stage in the development of the succession.

Indicators of Former Forests.—Such indicators are either actual relicts of the forest itself or seral communities that mark particular stages of succession toward reforestation. Brush or scrub are characteristic indicators of fire in forest regions. Aspen (*Populus tremuloides*) and birch (*Betula*) are typical indicators of fire in forest communities throughout boreal North America as well as in many mountainous regions. This is due to their ability to form root sprouts, and the trees often occur in

Fig. 244.—Reproduction of linden or basswood (*Tilia americana*) by sprouts after cutting.

groups as a consequence (Fig. 244). Among certain species of pines, the cones remain closed upon the branches for many years but open readily after fire, thus furnishing a large number of seeds for immediate germination. Three important species of this type occur in western North America, *viz.*, lodgepole pine (*Pinus contorta murrayana*), jack pine (*P. banksiana*), and knobcone pine (*P. tuberculata*). These are all typical indicators of burns and form subclimaxes of great extent and duration in areas frequently swept by fire.

After the forest cover has disappeared because of fire, lumbering, lack of reproduction due to overgrazing, or other factors, the area is freed from the competition of climax species and conditions made favorable to the growth of many subdominants. As a result of excessive seed production, the ability to produce root sprouts, or the opening of cones by fire, these rapidly and often completely occupy the ground. Fires of recent occurrence are indicated by an abundant growth of liverworts and mosses such as *Marchantia, Funaria,* and *Bryum,* which frequently cover the soil, and by characteristic annuals and perennials as hair grass (*Agrostis hiemalis*), fireweed (*Epilobium angustifolium*), everlasting (*Anaphalis margaritacea*), thistles (*Carduus*), milfoil (*Achillea*), bracken (*Pteris aquilina*), and other species with wind-blown propagules. Burns of greater age are characterized by various shrubs that have developed from root sprouts. Raspberry (*Rubus strigosus*), hazelnut (*Corylus americana*), and huckleberry (*Vaccinium macrophyllum*) are characteristic species. The number and distinctness of these seral communities and their duration depend chiefly upon the severity of the burn. In the western forests, the shrubs are normally replaced by aspen, birch, or alder, which later give way to subclimax or climax forest. In the cedar-hemlock forests of the Pacific northwest, Douglas fir, the most valuable of lumber trees, forms a remarkably permanent subclimax over an enormous extent due to repeated burns.

Such seral communities not only indicate the possibility of reforestation, but they also make it clear that artificial means, such as periodic removal of the forest, must be resorted to where it is desirable to maintain the subclimax as a relatively permanent type.

Planting Indicators.—Indicators of sites for planting are of two kinds, *viz.*, those that indicate the former presence of a forest, and those that suggest the possibility of developing forest in grassland or scrub areas. These are indicators of reforestation and afforestation, respectively.[36,497]

The obvious indicators of reforestation are relict survivors, or trunks and stumps. Charred fragments of wood or pieces of charcoal in the soil are less obvious but equally conclusive. Where there is no direct evidence of the original forests, indirect evidence is often furnished by indicator communities which bear a direct relation to forest. Such are seral and subclimax communities that show a successional relation to the forest climax and societies of shrubs or herbs which formed layers in them. Thus, areas of coralberry (*Symphoricarpos*) or prickly ash (*Zanthoxylum*) with societies of Solomon's-seal (*Polygonatum*), bloodroot (*Sanguinaria*), and similar mesophytic herbs indicate former forest lands.

Indicators of afforestation are either savanna, *i.e.*, isolated trees or clumps of trees in grassland, chaparral, or tall-grass prairie in which the water requirements are very near those of trees.

The indicators of sites for planting or sowing serve also to indicate the preferred species. In reforestation, for example, the general rule is to employ the species of climax trees that were in possession, unless reasons of management may make it desirable to employ a subclimax dominant. Species somewhere in contact with grassland or scrub give the clue to the selection of those best adapted for afforestation.   Thus, ponderosa pine from the foothills has been successfully grown in the grass-covered sand hills of Nebraska and is also one of the best species for planting in loam soils.

Where the virgin timber has nearly or altogether disappeared, as a result both of severe burns and of grazing, and has been replaced by shrubs, herbaceous vegetation, and wide stretches of aspen extending over an area originally occupied by several forest types, the question of deciding what species to plant on a given site becomes very difficult. But even in such cases a study of the existing vegetation furnishes the most valuable guide, as has been repeatedly demonstrated in forest practice.

Thus far, practical afforestation has been confined chiefly to the sand hills of Nebraska and Kansas, although conditions for afforestation have been carefully studied in the Great Basin.[36,49]   In Nebraska, where afforestation has been successful, four indicators of its possibility are present.[861]   These consist of valley and canyon relicts of woodland (both deciduous and evergreen); a savanna-like growth in contiguous uplands (principally of ponderosa pine); shrubs that show a close approach to the water requirement of trees (*viz.*, sand cherry, willow, hackberry, wild plum); and tall grasses, (*Andropogon*, etc.) indicating similar water relations.   In Kansas, where afforestation failed, these indicators were largely lacking.

LAND CLASSIFICATION

The classification of land is an endeavor to forecast the type of utilization that will yield adequate or maximum returns.[814]   The natural plant cover is a result of all the growing conditions where it is produced.   It is an index or measure of the factors influencing its growth and serves as an indicator of the possibilities of producing other plants on the land. Consequently, it is invaluable in classifying lands in regard to their suitability for agriculture, grazing, or forestry.   If agriculture is possible, indicators may be used to denote the greater feasibility of humid, dry, or irrigation farming or the importance of combining grazing with dry farming.   Where grazing is concerned, the type of vegetation determines whether cattle, sheep, or goats are preferable or a combination of two or three.   Similarly, the vegetation may be employed to determine the possibility of afforestation or reforestation as well as the most promising dominants for any particular region.

During the last 30 or 40 years, a large number of the homesteads taken have proved failures, and the percentage of failures will steadily increase as still less promising regions are entered, unless adequate knowledge of the potentialities of the lands is to be had.   Consequently, all the principal types of vegetation occurring on the unreserved public lands and the patented homestead lands west of the one hundredth meridian have been classified with special reference to their suitability for grain farming, forage production, or grazing. The relative carrying capacity of the different types of grazing lands has, moreover, been determined. A total of 102 types of vegetation are used as illustrated by the following:[13]

Sagebrush (*Artemisia tridentata*).—The sagebrush type consists of a miniature forest or scattered brushland of sagebrush. Plants vary in height from 1 to 7 feet. This is the most common shrub throughout the Great Basin, growing in well drained loamy soils. The height and abundance of plants are governed by the depth, quality, and moisture content of the soil. A dense stand of tall sagebrush is indicative of very

Fig. 245.—Mesquite (*Prosopis*), a leguminous tree growing in Arizona and the arid southwest.

favorable possibilities for the production of small grains without irrigation. It represents the best type of land in the Great Basin for farming, either arid or by irrigation. This type is grazed by stock, mainly sheep, during fall and winter when little or no herbaceous feed is available.

Mesquite (*Prosopis*).—Areas supporting little or no vegetative growth other than mesquite are classified in this type (Fig. 245). This shrub varies in size from only a few feet to trees 30 feet high. It occupies a large acreage in southern New Mexico and Arizona and has considerable economic value for the stock feed supplied from the leaves and beans. The roots and the thicker stems also supply considerable fuel. It is very common in deep fertile soil along drainage channels where subirrigation is usually received. The better types of this land are capable of producing forage crops such as sorghums, corn, and millet, during very favorable years. It has a carrying capacity of 5 to 15 head of cattle per section.

Creosote Bush (*Larrea*) **and Cacti** (*Opuntia* spp.).—This type grows in rather broken or rocky areas in southern New Mexico and the desert regions of Arizona, southern Nevada, and southeastern California. It is made up of a scattered growth of creosote bush and an abundance of cacti, especially the barrel cactus which varies in diameter from 1 to 1.5 feet, and in height from 2 to 4 feet, and the round-stemmed opuntias, especially the dense spiny *Opuntia spinosior*.   It is nonagricultural unless irrigated and of little or no value for grazing except over the large areas where it has invaded desert plains grassland.[13]

Similar classifications, perhaps refined by quantitative methods and increasing experience, must sooner or later be used in all new regions of the world where maximum economic returns are desired.

CHAPTER XVIII

CLIMAX FORMATIONS OF NORTH AMERICA

Nature of Climaxes.—An airplane view of the continent of North America would reveal the fact that it is covered with three great types of vegetation, *viz.*, forest, scrub, and grassland. A closer scrutiny would disclose that these are themselves composed of strikingly different communities, such as evergreen and deciduous forest, which are found in climates equally different. These units, of vast extent and great permanence, are termed climaxes or formations; they are the product of climate and, hence, are controlled by it. Each formation is the highest type of vegetation possible under its particular climate, and this relation makes the term *climax* especially significant, as it is derived from the same root as *climate*. The formation and climax are identical, and, hence, the same great community may be termed a formation, a climax or, for the sake of emphasis, a climax formation.

Each climax owes its characteristic appearance to the species or dominants that control it. These dominants exhibit the same vegetation or life form—tree, shrub, or grass, as the case may be—and thus serve to give to the climax the imprint of its climate. The dominants all belong to the highest type of life form possible under the prevailing climate; in forest they are all trees of the same type, in grassland all grasses or sedges, and so forth. It is necessary, however, to distinguish plants that are merely conspicuous or abundant from those that are actually dominant. This is particularly true of the various savanna communities, in which the trees and shrubs are much more conspicuous than the grasses, but the latter are in actual control of the habitat. In the true and mixed prairies, the dominant grasses are often more or less concealed during the growing season by tall forbs, such as *Erigeron*, *Psoralea*, and *Solidago*. These are termed *subdominants* and constitute seasonal societies subject, in large measure, to the control of the grasses.

Animals also play an important part in the climax and are intrinsic members of the community along with the plants. They are not dominants, since they are not directly responsive to the climate in the way that plants are and they exert little or no controlling reaction upon the habitat. Their presence and abundance are determined, in the first instance, by the plant dominants, and, like the forbs, animals could be regarded as subdominants. For a number of reasons, it is more convenient to employ a distinct term and call them *influents* in reference to their abundance and corresponding importance. Their significance and role in the climax are likewise determined by the life form, which finds its primary expression in the food relations or coactions.

Before the advent of civilized man, nearly the whole area of each climax was occupied by the dominant species. The exceptions were the numerous but relatively small and scattered portions in which succession was taking place in primary areas of water, dune sand, or rock. With the opening of the historical period came a great increase in the destruction of natural communities by fire, lumbering, and clearing for cultivation. Such effects stand in the closest relation to the period of settlement and the intensity of human coactions, and they have led to the all but complete disappearance of the climax in regions long cultivated. Nevertheless, all areas within the sweep of climate and climax, whether bare or denuded by man, are marked by a more or less evident successional movement of communities and, hence, belong to the climax in terms of its development. In consequence, each climax consists not merely of the stable portions that represent its original mass but also of all successional areas, regardless of the kind or stage of development.

Tests of a Climax.—Each climax is the direct expression of its climate; the climate is the cause, the climax the effect, which, in its turn, reacts upon the climate. So intimate is this relation that the climax must be regarded as the final test of a climate rather than human response or physical measurements. Climates are to be recognized and delimited by means of their climaxes and not the reverse, not merely on account of the cause-and-effect relation but also by virtue of the fact that the effect is much more visible and less variable than the cause. No matter how complete his equipment of meteorological instruments, the ecologist must subordinate such measures of climate to the judgment of the plant community, if his results are to be both accurate and usable. The paramount importance of formations and associations in indicating climates makes their objective recognition of the first importance, and for this purpose a number of guiding principles have been established.

The first criterion is that all the climax dominants must belong to the same major life form, since this indicates a similar response to climate and, hence, a long association with each other. Neither forbs nor woody plants are to be considered as dominants in grassland, nor are evergreen trees proper dominants of deciduous forest. The second principle is that one or more of the dominant species must range well throughout the formation or occur in the various associations to some degree. This is exemplified in the prairie climax by *Stipa comata, Bouteloua gracilis,* and *Agropyron smithii* and in the deciduous forest by *Quercus borealis* and *Q. macrocarpa.* The third criterion is that a large number and usually the majority of the dominant genera extend throughout the formation, though represented by different species. This is true of *Stipa, Bouteloua, Andropogon, Agropyron, Poa,* and *Sporobolus* in the grassland, and of *Quercus, Carya, Acer, Tilia,* and *Betula* in the deciduous forest and of *Pinus, Picea,* and *Abies* in the coniferous forests.

A fourth principle is derived from the degree of equivalence exhibited by the dominants of two contiguous associations where they meet in the ecotone between the two. The existence of such a transition area over a wide stretch indicates that the dominants are sufficiently alike to belong in the same formation but dissimilar enough to characterize different associations. A fifth deals with the relation of the various associations to proclimaxes or proclimax species.* Thus, in the grassland climax, the several species of *Andropogon* are postclimax to four of the associations, and occasional relicts suggest that they were formerly in the case of the other two. *Ulmus, Fraxinus,* and *Juglans* bear a similar relation to the three associations of the deciduous forest. This principle applies likewise to relict areas of adjacent formations, such as the preclimaxes and postclimaxes discussed in an earlier chapter. The sixth criterion arises out of the evolution and relationship of formations and the phylogenetic comparison of similar formations in the two hemispheres. As in the case of genera and species, formations have arisen from the modification of earlier ones, just as associations have been produced by the differentiation of formations under the compulsion of climatic changes. In fact, it is most probable that the modifying action of climatic cycles has been exerted simultaneously upon both community and species.

Classification.—The formations of a continent may be grouped in several ways in accordance with the emphasis placed upon the various criteria. Perhaps the simplest classification is that based upon geographic position, which necessarily reflects climatic relations to some degree. The most definite is probably the grouping, upon the basis of life form, into forest, scrub, and grassland. The causal relation is best shown when climate is fully taken into account, but this leads to the difficulty found in the fact that the climaxes are themselves the best indicators of climate. The most fundamental and, hence, the most natural classification is grounded upon evolution and relationship, as in the case of species and genera. This, furthermore, possesses the great advantage of including the other criteria to the extent that they are important and thus leads to a natural system that is both comprehensive and objective. It is evident that such a classification depends upon thoroughgoing investigation in the field, of both the intensive and exten-

---

* *Proclimax* is a general term which includes all the communities that simulate the climax to some extent in terms of stability or permanence, but lack the proper sanction of the existing climate. It thus includes subclimax, preclimax, and postclimax, as well as disclimax (p. 82).[162]

sive kind, and that it must ultimately deal with more than one continent. The following grouping makes use of life form and climate for the primary divisions, but the arrangement of climaxes within these is as natural as the consideration of a single continent permits.

LIST OF FORMATIONS AND ASSOCIATIONS

Scrub Climaxes:

TUNDRA CLIMAX

THE TUNDRA

Extent and Nature.—The tundra stretches from the Atlantic to the Pacific Ocean, occupying the broad zone between the tree limit and the region of perpetual snow about the north pole. The main body reaches farthest south as narrow belts along cold bodies of water such as Hudson Bay and the Labrador Current, but as alpine tundra this climax occurs on high mountains southward into Mexico and reappears with its composition much modified on the Andes of South America. Throughout this vast range it is characterized by the grass life form, together with a host of perennial forbs belonging largely to the same genera of northern origin. In consequence of low temperatures, short seasons, and drying winds, the plants are typically dwarfed, the dense sward often rising but a few inches above the level of the soil. The season is short, often lasting but 2 months, and frost or freezing may occur at any time during the growing period, especially at night. The precipitation varies greatly, being highest in coastal regions, but evaporation and wind movement are marked, and the water content correspondingly decisive. The light relations are unique, both in the arctic where day and night divide the year, and on alpine summits where the blue and ultraviolet rays are stronger than at low altitudes.

Practically throughout the Northern Hemisphere, the tundra lies in contact with a boreal or subalpine forest of fir, spruce, and their associates. The component species naturally differ from Europe and Asia to Arctic America and to the Cordilleras of the United States and Mexico, much as they do in the tundra climax itself. The latter, however, lives under uniform and rigorous conditions, and, in consequence, an exceptionally large number of species occur more or less throughout it. The tundra of northern Europe and Siberia is remarkably like that of North America and it is only between arctic and alpine tundra that considerable differences are found. In the present knowledge of this vegetation, two formations can be distinguished, one Eurasian, the other American, and both of these can be further divided into arctic and alpine associations.

The alpine areas represent relict communities that were left behind as the main mass of the tundra retreated in the wake of melting glaciers. The three great mountain systems of the continent furnished a haven for arctic species to a degree determined chiefly by elevation and extent. In the east, they persisted only on a few isolated peaks such as Mount Washington and Mount Katahdin, which lie only a few hundred miles south of the present limits of arctic tundra. In the Sierra Nevada, alpine tundra occurs a thousand miles southward of the arctic, while in the main Cordilleras it reaches 2,000 miles into the Sierra Madre of Mexico. As a consequence, it has been found desirable to recognize three associations, *viz.*: (1) Arctic tundra, which may well include the alpine communities of New England; (2) Petran tundra, found in the Rocky Mountains; and (3) Sierran tundra, confined to the Sierra Nevada and Cascade Mountains.

Arctic Tundra.—As already indicated, this constitutes the great mass of the tundra climax and, with the exception of the small rear guards in New England, is confined chiefly to the arctic regions. It follows the coast as a solid and usually broad band from the Alaskan peninsula to Newfoundland, covering the islands of the Arctic archipelago but only the coastal fringe of Greenland. It occupies the mountain ranges and elevated plateaus of the interior, where it is much interrupted by the boreal forest[699] (Frontispiece).

The tundra climax consists chiefly of four communities, the successional relations of which are little understood as yet. It seems probable that the climax proper is represented by an association of sedges, grasses, and forbs, much interrupted by proclimaxes and forming various mixtures with them (Fig. 246). The cotton-grass bogs are to be regarded as the subclimax of the hydrosere, the heath moors probably as postclimax, and the lichen-moss tundra as the subclimax of the xerosere or as a preclimax. The dominants of the climax association are various species of *Carex*, such as *rigida, rupestris, incurva*, etc., *Luzula spicata* and *L. nivalis*, and a large number of grasses, *viz.*, *Agrostis, Aira, Alopecurus, Arctagrostis, Calamagrostis, Danthonia, Festuca, Phleum, Poa*, and *Trisetum*. The moister or more open climax areas, as well as the subclimax ones, are brightened by a host of perennial forbs, which are much reduced in number where the competition of the sedges and grasses is severe. These subdominants occur mostly in mixed societies, which characterize two aspects, one early in July and the other in late July and August. The genera of chief importance are the following: *Anemone, Caltha, Ranunculus, Dryas, Geum, Potentilla, Astragalus, Lupinus, Saxifraga,*

Papaver, Draba, Cerastium, Lychnis, Silene, Androsace, Dodecatheon, Primula, Oxyria, Gentiana, Polemonium, Myosotis, Castilleja, Pedicularis, Achillea, Arnica, Artemisia, Senecio, and *Lloydia*. All of these appear also as subdominants in the alpine tundra, though the number of species in some genera is reduced.

The submerged stage of the hydrosere is represented chiefly by *Hippuris vulgaris, Ranunculus purshii,* and *Sphagnum fuscum,* and the amphibious one by *Caltha palustris radicans, Ranunculus pallasi, Cardamine pratensis, Eriophorum scheuchzeri, Equisetum variegatum,* and many species of *Carex.* The drier swamps contain *Senecio palustris, Pedicularis sudetica, Polygonum bistorta, Potentilla palustris, Saxifraga hirculus,* etc., together with other species of *Carex* and *Eriophorum.* The pioneers on

Fig. 246.—Arctic tundra near the Arctic Circle, altitude 2,800 ft., north of Fairbanks, Alaska. (*Photograph by R. W. Chaney.*)

sand dunes are *Elymus arenarius, Artemisia comata, Epilobium latifolium, Helianthus peploides,* etc., while *Mertensia maritima, Cerastium alpinum, Polemonium boreale, Alopecurus alpinus,* and others grow on the more stable beach. The transition to the tundra is effected by *Festuca ovina, Luzula nivalis, Oxyria digyna, Papaver nudicaule, Draba, Senecio, Dryas, Primula,* and many species of *Saxifraga.*

The postclimax of heaths and of willows and birches, often much mixed, occurs on rich, moist soils or on protected slopes and in valleys; the heath moor, in particular, often represents a late stage of the *Sphagnum* bog. The dominants are *Cassiope tetragone, Empetrum nigrum, Andromeda polifolia, Arctostaphylos alpina, Ledum palustre, Rhododendron lapponicum, Rubus chamaemorus, Loiseleuria procumbens, Alnus sinuata,* several species of *Vaccinium* and *Betula,* and many of *Salix.* The preclimax of mosses and lichens consists principally of species of

Sphagnum, *Dicranum*, and *Polytrichum* and of *Stereocaulon*, *Alectoria*, *Cetraria*, and *Cladonia*. The latter exhibits by far the greatest number of species, the largest life forms, and greatest abundance, the dominant species of the first importance being *Cladonia silvatica* and *C. rangiferina*. The lichen carpet attains an average height of 4 to 5 and a maximum of 10 inches and under such conditions simulates a climax more or less closely.[451,656]

Petran Tundra.—The alpine tundra of the Rocky Mountains finds its best expression between 11,000 and 14,000 feet, though it is progressively lower to the northward and is also depressed by streamways and lake basins. The northern limit is in west-central Alberta, where it comes in contact with Sierran tundra, and the southern on the high peaks of New Mexico and northern Arizona. The general western limit is in Utah and Idaho, though relicts of this community are also to be found in the mountain ranges of Nevada. Much the largest part of the association is found in the extensive alpine zone of Colorado, but considerable areas occur in New Mexico, Utah, and Wyoming. At its lower edge the alpine tundra lies in contact with the subalpine forest, while above it reaches to the summit of the highest peaks (14,500 feet), though greatly reduced in species and dominance.[155,205]

The number of dominants in this association is very large, though the leading role is assumed by a relatively small group. The typically climax condition is constituted by the sod-forming or densely bunched sedges, especially *Elyna bellardi*, *Carex rupestris*, *C. filifolia*, *C. pyrenaica*, *C. nigricans*, *C. nardina*, etc. The grasses are of less importance, though they play a considerable part but more particularly in the subclimax communities. *Poa* exceeds all others in the number of species, but *Agrostis*, *Aira*, *Danthonia*, *Festuca*, *Phleum*, *Trisetum*, and the grasslike *Luzula* are represented by one or more species of distinct significance. All of the genera and many of the species are likewise present in the arctic tundra (Fig. 247).

The number of subdominant forbs is very large, and, for the most part, they constitute mixed societies of several species. These mark three more or less well defined aspects, *viz.*, early, middle, and late summer. A large number of the species are endemic, while of a total of about 90, a third occur in the Sierran tundra also, another third in the arctic, and the same number in Eurasia. This uniformity in distribution is largely a coincidence, for the species are not the same throughout. The genera are, however, practically identical for the circumpolar region and the two mountain systems, the endemic species of the latter, as a rule, being recent and direct descendants of those of wide distribution.

In accordance with the rule, alpine societies are best developed in subclimax or disturbed areas, in which the control of the dominant sedges and grasses is not yet complete.   In the ultimate consociation of *Elyna bellardi*, for example, the dominance of this sedge is so complete as practically to exclude all but a few individuals of the forbs that thrive in the more open communities of *Carex rupestris* and the grasses.   The vernal aspect rules through late June and early July and consists chiefly of *Primula angustifolia, Androsace chamaejasme, Eritrichium argenteum,* and *Caltha leptosepala,* often with several species of *Ranunculus, Draba, Trifolium, Thalictrum alpinum,* and *Besseya alpina.*   The summer aspect

Fig. 247.—*Polygonum, Geum,* and *Polemonium* in alpine tundra, altitude 12,000 feet, Rocky Mountain Park, Colo.

prevails during most of July and early August and is characterized by a larger number of species of somewhat taller stature.   Chief among these are *Geum turbinatum, Actinella grandiflora, Mertensia alpina, Polygonum bistorta* and *P. viviparum, Artemisia scopulorum, Polemonium confertum, Erigeron uniflorus, E. grandiflorus, E. compositus, Antennaria alpina, Allium acuminatum, Potentilla rubricaulis,* and *Carduus hookerianus.*   The major dominants of the late summer are *Campanula rotundifolia alpina, Gentiana frigida, Castilleja pallida occidentalis, Solidago virgaurea nana, Haplopappus pygmaeus, Pentstemon hallii, Senecio taraxacoides,* and *S. fremontii*[182] (Fig. 186).

Sierran Tundra.—The alpine peaks of the Sierran climax are slightly higher than those of the Rocky Mountains, but the tundra is often depressed by permanent snowcaps of great size. In the northern ranges its best expression occurs at 8,000 to 11,000 feet, though in the mountains of the upper Columbia Basin it may descend as low as 6,000 feet. In the Sierra Nevada the alpine climax is best developed between 10,500 and 13,000 feet. In general, the oceanic climate raises the timber line and lowers the snow line, with the consequence that the Sierran tundra is usually much less massive than the Petran. At its northern edge this association passes over into the arctic tundra, while in the mountains of Montana and Alberta it merges with the Petran climax. It reaches its southern limit on San Jacinto Mountain, where it is represented by only a half-dozen relict species.

As in the other two associations, sedges constitute the chief dominants of the Sierran tundra, with *Poa*, *Agrostis*, and *Calamagrostis* next in importance, followed by *Trisetum*, *Festuca*, and *Luzula*. While the sub-dominants are much the same as in the Rocky Mountains, the most important ones belong to different species, though these, in turn, vary much from north to south. The much higher precipitation promotes growth, and the forbs, in particular, are often much less dwarfed than in the Petran tundra, resembling the meadows of the latter. On such peaks as Mount Rainier, the spring aspect consists chiefly of *Erythronium montanum* and *E. parviflorum*, which appear as rapidly as the snow melts and even push through the snow banks themselves. The midsummer aspect comprises species of *Lupinus*, *Castilleja*, and *Erigeron*, together with *Potentilla*, *Polygonum*, *Valeriana*, etc.

FOREST CLIMAXES

The Boreal Forest

Extent and Nature.—Together with the tundra, the boreal forest possesses the distinction of stretching across the continent as a broad band, interrupted only by the tundra-covered mountains of the Yukon and Alaska. The climax dominants are conifers and chiefly evergreen, but they are more or less mixed with the subclimax aspens and birches throughout or replaced by them over considerable stretches. The northern boundary runs from the Mackenzie delta to the east of Great Bear and Great Slave lakes to Fort Churchill on Hudson Bay; it then swings around the bay to the northeast but reaches the coast only near Newfoundland, owing to the influence of the cold Labrador current. From Cook Inlet in Alaska the southern boundary trends southeastward to the aspen savannas of Saskatchewan, eastward to Lake Winnipeg, and thence to northern New Brunswick (Frontispiece).

Although the climate is less severe than that of the tundra, it is still very rigorous, and through the northern third or more the trees are much reduced in stature and diameter. Over much of the vast region the trees do not leaf out before the first of June and the leaves fall early in September. The precipitation ranges from more than 40 inches in the east to less than 15 in the Yukon and is generally below 20 inches in the interior. The winters are long and severe; the snowfall is not excessive and the air is relatively dry. The ground is snow covered or frozen for nearly three-fourths of the year, and the subsoil is more or less permanently filled with frost. In general, the drainage is poor and the soils shallow and immature.[818]

As already noted, the boreal forest lies in contact with the arctic tundra along its entire northern border, reaching the polar sea only at the Mackenzie delta. It passes gradually into the Barren Grounds through a transition belt in which the timber steadily diminishes in stature and the species are reduced to two or three. Along the rivers this reduced forest may extend as much as 200 miles into the tundra, finally breaking up into isolated outposts. On the other hand, the tundra extends even farther southward into the forest along the low mountain ranges and on the plateaus, especially in Alaska and the Yukon. To the southwest, this climax mixes with the subalpine forest in the Yukon and British Columbia and even with the northward extension of the coast forest in Alaska. One of its subclimax dominants extends well southward into the prairies of Alberta and Saskatchewan to form a characteristic belt of savanna.[533,623] From the region of the Great Lakes eastward the boreal forest has long been in contact with the pine forest and the deciduous forest. The repeated shiftings of the glacial period, together with the striking influence of lakes and rivers, have led to widespread alternation and mixing of the three climaxes, further complicated by fire and lumbering.

The boreal forest of North America has itself been differentiated from an earlier circumpolar mass and, hence, stands in close relationship to the coniferous forests of northern Europe and Siberia. It is even more closely related to the subalpine forests of the Rocky Mountains and the Sierran-Cascade system, which are to be regarded as more recent climatic modifications of it. The elevation of the Appalachians has been too slight to produce such a result, though the presence of *Picea mariana* and *Abies fraseri* in the southern ranges is evidence of such a tendency, which is further confirmed by the zone of boreal forest on the high peaks of New England.

Because of the general uniformity of conditions and their very gradual change to the north and west, this climax is not so distinctly marked off into associations. The disappearance of balsam fir and jack pine, however, the increased importance of aspen and birch, and the entrance of alpine fir and lodgepole pine make the recognition of two associations necessary, though it must be admitted that the ecotone between them is a very broad one. The subclimax associes plays a much larger part than usual in most climaxes, owing to the fact that the subclimax dominants outnumber the climatic ones. Moreover, they not only take possession of fire-swept or lumbered areas but also assume a regular role in the succession found in the innumerable bogs and muskegs and on sandy or rocky plains.[381]

The Spruce-Larch Forest.—This association reaches from Labrador, Newfoundland, and New Brunswick on the east to the Rocky Mountains

Fig. 248.—Mature tamarack (*Larix laricina*) in almost a pure stand and a few small black spruce (*Picea mariana*). (*Photograph, courtesy of U. S. Forest Service.*)

of northern British Columbia and the Yukon and in its extent across the continent is exceeded only by the arctic tundra.[363] In its strictest sense, its climax dominants are restricted to two species, the white spruce, *Picea glauca* and the balsam fir, *Abies balsamea*, but the several subclimax trees may assume climax roles as well. This is primarily an outcome of the climatic relations as the tree limit is approached, in either latitude or altitude. Increasingly rigorous conditions cause the climax species to dwindle in importance or drop out, while the less exacting ones persist. Thus, the larch or tamarack, *Larix laricina*, which is typical of bogs or muskegs through the heart of the forest, becomes essentially a climax tree along the northern border (Fig. 248). This is likewise true of the paper birch, *Betula alba papyrifera*, which is elsewhere characteristic of burns or of immature soils. The black spruce, *Picea mariana*, grows commonly with larch in or about bogs, but it becomes climax on rocky plateaus or on high mountain slopes, and the aspen, *Populus tremuloides*, often exhibits the same tendency (Fig. 249). The jack pine, *Pinus banksiana*, appears to assume subclimax or climax roles with equal readiness, but its definitely subclimax nature in the more temperate lake forest indicates that it is usually climax in the boreal one. The large-toothed aspen, *Populus grandidentata*, belongs in lowland or fire subclimaxes

Fig. 249.—Forest of black spruce (*Picea mariana*) in a muskeg covered with sphagnum. (*Photograph, courtesy of U. S. Forest Service.*)

and is rarely if ever a climax species. Two other trees are frequent in the eastern portion of this association, *viz.*, arborvitae, *Thuja occidentalis*, and red maple, *Acer rubrum*. Both are more or less subclimax in nature, but they also persist well into the climax community. The former, however, is regarded as belonging properly to the lake forest and the latter probably to the deciduous one.

The characteristic undergrowth of the spruce-larch forest is supplied by the heath stage of the bog succession. The most important species are *Kalmia glauca*, *K. angustifolia*, *Ledum palustre*, *L. groenlandicum*, *Chamaedaphne calyculata*, *Rhododendron canadense*, *Empetrum nigrum*. *Rubus chamaemorus*, *Andromeda polifolia*, and several species of *Vaccinium: pennsylvanicum*, *caespitosum*, *uliginosum*, *vitis-idaea*, *oxy-*

coccus, etc. Most of these grow taller and more open as the larch and spruce close in on the moor, and the least tolerant species drop out as the canopy thickens with the entrance of balsam and white spruce. The margins of the moor are occupied by taller species, such as *Alnus incana* or *A. crispa*, *Viburnum cassinoides*, *V. pauciflorum*, *Corylus rostrata*, *Cornus stolonifera*, *Pyrus arbutifolia*, *Myrica gale*, *Betula pumila*, *Spiraea salicifolia*, etc., and of these *Alnus*, *Corylus*, and *Spiraea* persist well into the shade. The most successful shade plants are the dwarf or creeping shrubs, such as *Gaultheria procumbens*, *Vaccinium oxycoccus*, *Cornus canadensis*, *Mitchella repens*, and *Epigaea repens*, with which are associated *Coptis trifolia*, *Clintonia borealis*, *Pyrola elliptica*, *Chiogenes hispidula*, *Aralia nudicaulis*, etc. The various species of *Sphagnum* usually disappear before the subclimax is reached, but *Polytrichum* and *Cladonia* sometimes persist into the climax.

The Spruce-Pine Forest.—This association covers northern British Columbia, the Yukon, and Alaska up to the limits of the tundra in the north and to an altitude of 1,000 to 2,000 feet in the mountains. It possesses the white spruce in common with the eastern association, but the balsam fir and jack pine have disappeared, the larch is rare in Alaska, and the black spruce much less frequent. The three deciduous species, especially the paper birch, play a much larger part, and two new dominants enter from the subalpine forest of the Rocky Mountains, *viz.*, lodgepole pine, *Pinus contorta murrayana*, and alpine fir, *Abies lasiocarpa*. In the north, even the white spruce becomes subordinated to the poplars and birches, though it persists in the south to Cook Inlet and beyond, where it is mixed with *Picea sitchensis*, *Thuja plicata*, and *Tsuga heterophylla* of the coast forest. Owing to the fact that the peninsula of Alaska is largely surrounded by cold waters, and as well to the number of mountain ranges, its climate is arctic and tundra is the prevailing climax. It is chiefly along the Yukon River and its tributaries, and the Pacific Ocean, that forest climaxes are possible.

The bogs of black spruce and occasional larch exhibit many of the heaths and other shrubs of the eastern association, and the undergrowth of the climax areas is likewise much the same, until the influence of the Pacific Ocean is felt. In such regions, *Alnus*, *Cornus*, *Ledum*, *Ribes*, *Vaccinium*, and *Viburnum* are joined by *Gaultheria shallon*, *Menziesia*, *Echinopanax*, etc., from the coast forest, and this undergrowth becomes controlling in mixtures of the two climaxes.

The Birch-Aspen Associes.—This is the characteristic fire subclimax throughout both associations. It is composed chiefly of the paper birch and aspen, though the balsam poplar and jack pine take some part in it. The first two may appear as pure or nearly pure consocies, or they may be mixed in various degrees, often with a sprinkling of balsam poplar.

The latter is rarely pure, except occasionally on flood plains, but the jack pine usually constitutes a consocies, owing to the relation between its closed cones and seeding.   Birch and aspen occur more or less abundantly as relicts in the climax forest, and particularly at the margins, where fire and clearing have been at work.[623]   They are, however, at an increasing disadvantage in competition with the climax dominants as the latter grow taller, and they gradually drop out and finally disappear in the mature forest.   The undergrowth is better developed than in the climax as a result of the more open canopy.   It is often dominated by *Pteris aquilina*, which finally yields to the original forbs of the climax.*

The Subalpine Forest

Extent and Nature.—As has been indicated earlier, the three great mountain systems of the continent have served as pathways for the southward extension of the boreal forest during cold-wet phases of the climatic cycle and as refuges for it with the return of warm-dry phases. Because of its lower elevation, the Appalachian system has been less effective in this respect; but one or two new species have been evolved and the subalpine community is poorly developed and little differentiated from the boreal.   It has been quite otherwise on the much higher ranges of the Rocky Mountains and the Sierra-Cascade system.   Not only are all the conifers different in species from those of the boreal forest proper, but they also differ decisively in the two associations of the subalpine forest.   The deciduous trees have, moreover, decreased in both number and abundance, the three major species now being represented only by the aspen, except for the northern portions of the Rocky Mountains.

As the name suggests, the subalpine forest occupies the upper slopes of the high ranges, usually forming a belt 2,000 to 3,000 feet in breadth between the alpine tundra above and the montane climax below.   It stretches from southern Alaska and adjacent British Columbia to Mexico and Lower California, wherever the altitude is sufficiently great.   It is found on all the higher ranges of the Great Basin but in reduced form and reaches its eastern limit on the Front Ranges of the Rockies from New Mexico northward.

The subalpine climax bears a relationship to three different formations, namely, the boreal, the coast, and the montane forest.   The direct

* The student may well consult the following general sources of information on plant communities of North America for further details:
    Clements, "Climax Formations of Western North America," in *Plant Indicators*.
    Shantz and Zon, "Natural Vegetation."
    Shelford, *et al.*, "Naturalist's Guide to the Americas."
    Harshberger, "Phytogeographic Survey of North America."

relationship is with the first, since the chief dominants of both belong to the two genera *Picea* and *Abies*, the species of which are also related. The general connection with the coast forest is shown by the presence of *Abies*, *Larix*, and *Tsuga* in both, though represented by different species. *Picea engelmanni*, moreover, is fairly common and *Abies lasiocarpa* not infrequent in the transition association. The relationship to the montane forest is indicated by the presence in each of closely related species of *Picea* and *Abies*, though these two genera play a less important role in the lower zone. *Pinus contorta* and *Populus tremuloides* are common to both, though much more abundant in the subalpine region (Fig. 61).

In spite of its occurrence on many separate ranges, the subalpine forest possesses a high degree of unity. Its two chief dominants, *Picea engelmanni* and *Abies lasiocarpa*, occur practically throughout, except for California. *Pinus contorta* extends from the mountains of Yukon to the San Pedro Martir of Lower California and the Front Ranges of Colorado. *Pinus flexilis* and *P. aristata* are found through the larger part of the two associations, though represented by distinct varieties. Two other important dominants are *Tsuga mertensiana* and *Larix lyallii*, which, though essentially coastal in character, occur in the transition area of northern Idaho and Montana, *Larix* even reaching the Rockies in southern Alberta. The other important dominant, *Abies magnifica*, though found only in California and southern Oregon, may well be regarded as the ecological representative of *A. lasiocarpa*.

The ecological unity of the subalpine formation is emphasized by its constant relation to the montane forest below and the alpine tundra above it. Its geographic and topographic relations serve to explain the uniformly boreal climate in which it flourishes. This is characterized by a short growing season, relatively high precipitation, largely in the form of snow, and wide diurnal and seasonal range of temperatures. The long winter is marked by high winds and excessive transpiration in relation to the holard, and these have a controlling influence in determining the holard.

The two associations reflect the wide separation of the two Cordilleras, except in the north, and the resulting differentiation of two subclimates. The warrant for distinguishing them is found in the fact that *Picea engelmanni* and *Abies lasiocarpa* are the two major dominants in the Rocky Mountains but are lacking in California; that *Tsuga mertensiana* and *Abies magnifica* are confined to the western association; and that the two pines, though closely related, are represented by different varieties or nascent species. *Pinus contorta*, moreover, assumes the role of a climax dominant in the Sierran community, while its variety *murrayana* is a subclimax one in the Petran.

Petran Subalpine Forest.—This association extends from the mountains of northern British Columbia and Alberta to northern New Mexico and Arizona. It also occurs on the Blue Mountains of Washington and Oregon and in reduced form is found on the higher ranges of the Great Basin and southward along the Sierra Madre into Mexico. In altitude, it ranges from 3,000 to 7,000 feet in the north and from 8,000 to 12,000 feet in Colorado and New Mexico.

The precipitation in the central part of the area varies from 22 to 40 inches a year, and the snowfall from 8 to 14 feet. On the interior ranges the rainfall may be somewhat less. The evaporation is lower than in the

Fig. 250.—Petran subalpine climax of Engelmann spruce (*Picea engelmanni*) and subalpine fir (*Abies lasiocarpa*), in Colorado.

montane zone, the reduction ranging from 25 to 50 per cent. At the lower limit, the growing season is nearly 4 months long; at the upper, between 2 and 3 months. The mean temperatures are 5 to 10 degrees Fahrenheit less than in the montane forest, and near timber line frost occurs frequently during the summer.

The mass of the association is constituted by *Picea engelmanni* and *Abies lasiocarpa*, much fragmented in the north by the burn communities of *Pinus contorta murrayana*[152] (Fig. 250). *Pinus flexilis* and its variety *albicaulis* are more abundant northward and even *Larix lyallii* enters the community in southern Alberta. In northern Colorado, the usual grouping is *Picea*, *Abies*, *Pinus murrayana*, and *P. flexilis*, while southward the lodgepole pine drops out and *P. aristata* appears. On the desert ranges of the interior, *P. flexilis* and *P. aristata* alone remain to represent this climax. The characteristic fire subclimax is formed by the lodgepole pine, *Pinus murrayana*, which covers great areas with a pure stand from central Colorado northward. It is often accompanied by aspen, which finally yields to it, while beyond the range of the pine, the former constitutes similar subclimaxes. Mixed societies of grasses and forbs usually attain a striking development in the aspen community, but they are much reduced under the denser canopy of the pine or of the spruce-fir climax. The most important genera are *Aquilegia*, *Arnica*, *Campanula*, *Castilleja*, *Erigeron*, *Fragaria*, *Polemonium*, *Solidago*, and *Thalictrum*, many of them represented by the same or related species in the montane forest.[45,667]

Sierran Subalpine Forest.—Certain dominants of this association reach their northern limit in Alaska, but in its more typical expression this forest stretches southward from British Columbia along the upper slopes of the ranges. Its eastern limits are found where it comes in contact with the Petran association in Alberta and Montana or on the eastern slopes of the Sierra Nevada. It is much reduced in the cross ranges of southern California and its last outposts disappear in Lower California. The altitude of this zone rises steadily from Alaska southward, from 2,000 to 4,000 feet at the north, 5,000 to 8,000 feet in the central portion, to 7,000 to 10,000 feet in the Sierra Nevada. The climatic relations are much the same as in the Petran association, with the important exception that the precipitation is much higher, ranging in the Sierras from 50 to 75 inches. A half to nearly all of this may fall as snow, the total snowfall sometimes exceeding 50 feet in depth.

The characteristic dominants of this forest are six, *viz.*, *Tsuga mertensiana*, *Pinus contorta*, *P. albicaulis*, *P. balfouriana*, *Larix lyallii*, and *Abies magnifica*. Three other dominants, *Picea engelmanni*, *Abies lasiocarpa*, and *Pinus flexilis*, are more typical of the Petran forest, while *Abies amabilis*, *A. nobilis*, *Pinus monticola*, and *Chamaecyparis* are more important in the coast forest. The two dominants of the greatest extension are *Tsuga* and *Pinus contorta*, ranging from Alaska to the southern Sierras, while *P. albicaulis* occurs from British Columbia to the thirty-sixth parallel. *Larix* is more restricted, while *Abies magnifica* is confined to California and Oregon, and *Pinus balfouriana* grows only in California (Fig. 251).

The large number of dominants and the extensive range make the groupings exceedingly varied. There is a marked tendency toward pure consociations near timber line, while in the lower part of the zone two or more dominants usually occur in mixture. In the ranges of the upper Columbia Basin, *Abies lasiocarpa* and *Picea engelmanni* are regularly present and are usually associated with one or more of the following: *Pinus contorta*, *P. albicaulis*, *Larix*, and *Tsuga*. *Tsuga* and *Abies* grow together in Alaska, while farther south *Picea, Larix, Pinus albicaulis,* and *Abies amabilis* are commonly associated with them. In the Sierra Nevada, *Tsuga* occurs with *Abies magnifica, Pinus contorta,* and *P. monticola* through most of the width of the zone and with *P. albicaulis* in the upper portion. *Pinus balfouriana* is associated with the first group in the lower portion of the forest, with *P. monticola* higher up, and with *P. albicaulis* at timber line.

<small>Fig. 251.—Sierran subalpine climax of subalpine fir (*Abies lasiocarpa*) and lodgepole pine (*Pinus contorta*), in Oregon. (*Photograph by G. E. Nichols.*)</small>

The Sierran subalpine forest is not rich in societies and most of those present have been derived from the alpine tundra or the montane forest, the shrubs, in particular, coming from the latter.

The Lake Forest

Extent and Nature.—As the name implies, this is preeminently a lake formation, being centered on the Great Lakes and recurring to the eastward in New York and New England where the larger lakes and rivers produced similar conditions. Since sandy soils likewise furnish favorable water and temperature relations, the pines, in particular, are to be found on sandy plains through much of this region. The most extensive stands of white pine, *Pinus strobus,* were originally found in central and northern Michigan and in eastern central and northern Minnesota. Farther east, the forest was more fragmentary, consisting chiefly of relict communities of varying size, found about bodies of water, on sand plains, or on the slopes of the Allegheny Mountains in Pennsylvania and to the southward. The climax dominants, white and red pine and hemlock, occur over a much wider area, smaller relicts, as a rule, persisting through southern Ontario and Quebec, much of New Brunswick and central Maine.

The climate of this forest has a wide geographic as well as annual range. The annual precipitation varies from a mean of 25 inches in Minnesota to one of nearly 45 inches in the mountains of the east. The temperature extremes during the year may range from −50 to 105°F., and in the northern portion frost may occur in any month of the summer. The growing season averages 4 months, though white pine and hemlock persist under favorable local conditions in regions where it is much longer.

The Pine-Hemlock Forest.—The lake forest consists of a single association, in which *Pinus strobus*, *P. resinosa*, and *Tsuga canadensis* are the climax dominants. It has been so long cut off from the related montane and coast forests of the west that they cannot be grouped in the same climax, though their phylogenetic relationship seems evident. In fact, the climax nature of the lake forest itself may be easily questioned today, because of the great vicissitudes it has experienced. No other association has suffered so severely from lumbering and consequent fire, partly because of the quality of its timber, but chiefly because of its proximity to long-settled and well-populated districts. In southern Ontario where white pine with considerable red pine constituted formerly 60 per cent of the forest, logging and fire have reduced this to scattered relicts, about which effective reproduction is still further handicapped by the coactions of man. It is such universal disturbance that is primarily responsible for the doubts as to the actual existence of a pine-hemlock climax, but earlier historical and physical factors have had a large share as well.[103,554,645]

During the repeated mass migrations of the glacial-interglacial cycles, this entire climax suffered not only the most severe buffeting but also the most intense competition from the boreal forest along one border and the deciduous forest on the other. Its migration before the ice front or in the wake of its retreat was, moreover, peculiarly handicapped by the solidarity of the great mass of the hardwood forest and, during the recent period, by that of the boreal forest as well, to say nothing of the barriers constituted by the Great Lakes. In a region with such marked extremes of climate, each phase of every major climatic cycle has increased its disadvantage. The cold-dry phases have permitted the encroachment of the boreal climax, the warm-wet ones that of deciduous forest, not over a uniform terrain but one fragmented by lakes, rivers, and mountain ranges to the extreme. One striking consequence has been the inclusion of many small, relict areas of pine, hemlock, or both well within the mass of deciduous or boreal forest. When all the evidence is assembled and weighed in the light of these various processes, there seems little doubt that the pine-hemlock forest represents a genuine climax, now sadly depleted and fragmented, especially by the hand of man.*

The climax dominants of this association are red or Norway pine, *Pinus resinosa*, white pine, *P. strobus*, and hemlock, *Tsuga canadensis*. A frequent associate of the pines is the jack pine, *P. banksiana*, but this belongs properly to the subclimax. On mountain slopes the red spruce, *Picea rubra*, is associated with white pine especially but is, perhaps, even more frequent in montane communities of white spruce and balsam fir. Southward, *Pinus rigida* also enters this community and serves to connect it with the subclimax pine forest of the southeast. The arborvitae, *Thuja occidentalis*, often plays a role of considerable importance, but it, too, is to be regarded as a subclimax species. The white cedar, *Chamaecyparis thyoides*, likewise exhibits affinities with this group but is rarely of much importance even in the subclimax (Fig. 252).

The difference in the ecological requirements of the three climax dominants is such that they are not frequent in mixture, but this has undoubtedly been, in part, an outcome of lumbering. The two pines occur together throughout most of the western portion, but the greater tolerance of the white pine for shade originally produced extensive pure stands.[59,184] Over the eastern part of the area, the relict areas appear frequently to be either pure pine or hemlock, but in the original forest the two consociations grew side by side as well as in mixture.[86,640] The view that hemlock is properly a member of the deciduous forest runs counter to the rule as to the identity of life forms and has not taken sufficient account of the nature of relicts. Since its tolerance of shade and its water requirements are greater than those of the white pine, the hemlock approaches beech, maple, and chestnut closely in its demands. Its proper climax position is disclosed, however, by the relict communities in the maple-beech association, where it is found all but invariably on the cool northerly slopes.[996]

The number of genera common to the pine-hemlock association and the coast and montane forest of the west is so great as to indicate that they were originally derived from the same coniferous climax. The transition association of the coast climax, in particular, has a species corresponding to practically every one of the lake forest. *Pinus strobus*

* The most conclusive testimony has been furnished by Sargent, who saw this forest in much its original condition and set it apart as a distinct community.[778]

is represented by another white pine, *P. monticola;* the red pine by the ponderosa pine, *P. ponderosa;* and the jack pine by another species of the same character, *P. contorta. Tsuga canadensis* has a reciprocal species in *T. heterophylla, Thuja occidentalis* in *T. plicata,* and *Larix laricina* in *L. occidentalis.* The presence of *Chamaecyparis* on both coasts is a further point of resemblance. The montane forest is more nearly related to the coast climax, but it also contains the three types of pine as well as

Fig. 252.—Pine-hemlock forest (*Pinus strobus* and *Tsuga canadensis*) in Pennsylvania. (*Photograph, courtesy of U. S. Forest Service.*)

a group of more recently evolved southern pines corresponding, in some measure, to the numerous species of the pine subclimax of the southeast.

The characteristic subclimax of the pine-hemlock forest is formed by the consocies of jack pine, *Pinus banksiana.* As in practically all species of this group, the cones not only remain on the trees for a number of years, but also they open tardily and sometimes only as a result of fire. This species is, in consequence, especially fitted to take possession of burned areas as pure stands; its preference for sandy plains is likewise to be explained by its lower requirements, though in such situations it may be the subfinal stage of the normal prisere. Birch and aspen also occur in a fire subclimax in this forest, though largely as a result of mixture with the boreal formation.[488] *Thuja occidentalis* is regarded as the typical subclimax of the hydrosere, usually forming a fairly distinct and nearly pure zone about the drier margins of bogs. At its inner edge it is frequently associated with *Picea mariana* and *Larix laricina;* though the latter belong properly to the boreal climax, the frequent occurrence of relict bogs in the northern portions especially of the pine-hemlock climax gives these two species more or less subclimax importance in the latter.

The undergrowth of this forest is rather poorly developed, owing to the dense canopy, particularly in the hemlock consociation. Moreover, from its position, the species of shrubs and herbs are common to boreal or deciduous forest for the most part. They are necessarily shade plants of a more or less extreme type, largely ferns and fernworts, *Asplenium, Polystichum, Lycopodium;* orchids, *Calypso, Goodyera;* saprophytes, *Corallorrhiza, Monotropa, Hypopitys;* and such undershrubs and forbs of the ground cover as *Mitchella, Chimaphila, Gaultheria, Pyrola, Circaea, Viola,* etc.

THE COAST FOREST

Extent and Nature.—This climax has its greatest development along the Pacific Coast, as its name implies. The main body stretches from southern British Columbia to northern California, but several of the major dominants extend much farther northward as well as southward. *Picea sitchensis* finds its northernmost limit at Cook Inlet in Alaska, while *Tsuga heterophylla* and *Chamaecyparis nootkatensis* reach nearly as far. *Thuja plicata* occurs in southern Alaska, and *Abies amabilis* is found at the extreme southern end. *Sequoia sempervirens* ranges farthest to the south, its last outposts lingering in the Santa Cruz and Santa Lucia Mountains of California. While the best expression of this climax is along the coast, it extends to the Cascades and covers their western slopes. Eastward it passes into a broad transition forest that reaches to the western ranges of the Rocky Mountains in northern Montana and adjacent British Columbia. In altitude, the coast forest extends from sea level to 3,000 to 5,000 feet in the coast ranges and the Cascades.

Geographically, this forest belongs to the coast and the Columbia Basin. At the higher levels, the latter resembles the former in being a region of relatively high rainfall and low evaporation. The exceptional extension along the coast is partly a matter of high rainfall but is due chiefly to the remarkable oceanic compensation between Alaska and California. The temperatures as well as the rainfall are less uniform from east to west, but this is reflected in the mixing of two climaxes and the differentiation of a transition community.

The closest relationship of the coast forest is with the montane climax, due, in some degree, to their direct contact at present. This is naturally best exemplified in the transition association, while the generic composition of the coast association is more like that of the pine-hemlock forest of the northeast, as already indicated. Both the former show an affinity with the boreal forest in the presence of *Abies* and *Picea*, though this may really be through the subalpine forest. The most important dominant in common is the Douglas fir, *Pseudotsuga taxifolia*, which reflects the climatic relations in being climax in the montane formation and subclimax in the higher rainfall of the northwest. The chief contact of the coast forest is with the montane, until this yields in the north to the subalpine and the latter to the western association of the boreal climax. About Cook Inlet the grouping may include a single dominant of each of the last three.

The Cedar-Hemlock Forest.—This is much the more massive and continuous of the two associations. The dominants are fewer and the composition less varied, though the northern and southern extremes show striking differences from the central portion. The trees are taller, the canopy denser, and the shrubby layer often developed to form almost impenetrable thickets. The most typical expression is found in western Washington and British Columbia, whence the forest decreases in width and number of dominants in both directions, *Picea* and *Tsuga* forming the northern and *Sequoia* the southern outposts.[628,696]

The essential character of the coast forest is given by *Tsuga heterophylla, Thuja plicata, Picea sitchensis*, and *Sequoia sempervirens*, though the typical grouping comprises the first two together with *Pseudotsuga taxifolia*. *Picea* is confined to the vicinity of the seacoast and *Sequoia*, though more southern, restricted chiefly to the fog belt; the several species of *Abies* and *Chamaecyparis* range well into the adjacent communities.[111] With respect to abundance and extent, *Pseudotsuga* is much the most important dominant. It is the typical species of burned areas and, hence, properly constitutes a subclimax, a conclusion further supported by its relatively low tolerance.[414] Much of the area formerly covered with *Tsuga, Thuja*, and various associates is now a pure stand of Douglas fir, in which the hemlock and cedar persist in deep canyons or other protected places. This species is likewise a major dominant of the montane forest as well as of the transition association and, in consequence, passes readily from the role of subclimax to climax dominant.

This association constitutes a coniferous forest of unrivaled magnificence, in which the mature trees reach heights of 200 to 300 feet and diameters of 15 to 20 feet.[629] This is a direct outcome of the moderate temperatures and excessive rainfall with frequent or constant fog. Over much of the area the annual rainfall is in excess of 80 inches, the range being 50 to 120 inches. In the United States, all but 10 to 30 per cent of this falls during the 6 winter months, and much the same conditions obtain to Sitka and beyond. The absolute minimum as far north as Sitka is but −4°F. (Fig. 253).

In a region of such excessive precipitation, the water relations of the dominants are less clear or at least are much modified by temperature. The general relation to the factor complex is indicated by the altitudinal range, though this is not in full accord with that of latitude. The typical fog-belt trees are *Picea sitchensis*, *Sequoia sempervirens*, and *Chamaecyparis lawsoniana*, which indicate maximum conditions as to water

Fig. 253.—Climax forest of western hemlock (*Tsuga heterophylla*), red cedar (*Thuja plicata*), and Douglas fir (*Pseudotsuga taxifolia*), Mount Rainier, Washington. (*Photograph by G. E. Nichols.*)

content and humidity. These are followed by *Thuja plicata* and this by *Tsuga heterophylla* and *Abies grandis*. The ability of *Abies amabilis*, *A. nobilis*, and *Chamaecyparis nootkatensis* to endure more xeric conditions is shown by the fact that they occur also in the subalpine zone, where the first is frequent at timber line. *Pseudotsuga* is the most xeric of all the dominants, a fact in complete accord with its subclimax nature and its importance in the montane forest.

Shrubby societies are characteristic of this forest and those of forbs are correspondingly reduced. *Gaultheria shallon* and *Echinopanax horridum* are two of the most typical subdominants, while *Acer*, *Berberis*, *Ribes*, *Rubus*, *Rhododendron*, *Sambucus*, and *Vaccinium* are the genera represented by two or more species. Among the ferns, *Blechnum spicant*, *Polystichum munitum*, and *Pteris aquilina* are widespread, while the ground cover is composed chiefly of *Oxalis oregana, Asarum caudatum, Fragaria vesca, Trientalis latifolia, Trillium ovatum, Disporum smithii, Streptopus roseus,* etc.

The Larch-Pine Forest.—This association occupies the eastern slopes of the Cascades below the subalpine zone. It stretches across the mountains of northern Washington into Idaho and northwestern Montana, reaching its limit on the western slopes of the Continental Divide. It is found on the Gold and Selkirk ranges of British Columbia, the southern

Fig. 254.—Forest of western white pine (*Pinus monticola*) *A,* western red cedar (*Thuja plicata*) *B,* and western hemlock (*Tsuga heterophylla*) *C,* on bottomland in northern Idaho. (*Photograph, courtesy of J. A. Larsen.*)

Bitterroot Mountains of Idaho, and the Blue and Wallowa ranges to the west.[424,518]

This is primarily a transition forest between the coast and the montane climaxes, but it occupies such a large area that it cannot well be regarded merely as an ecotone. Over most of the region the dominants of the coast forest are characteristic, and for this reason it is assigned to this climax. The trees, however, are reduced in size and the association is less dense and exclusive, owing to increasing remoteness from the coast. Of the four major dominants of the coast association, *Picea sitchensis* has disappeared, *Tsuga* and *Thuja* diminish in importance and then disappear, and *Pseudotsuga* shares the control with several other important species. Over most of this forest the rainfall is only 20 to 35 inches, and

30 to 60 per cent of this falls between the first of April and the end of
September, a proportion twice as great as in the cedar-hemlock forest.
The mean temperature is about 7°F. lower and the minimum ranges from
−25 to −49°F. (Figs. 118 and 254).

The chief contact of the transition forest is with the montane climax,
and, in consequence, its dominants are almost equally divided between
the two formations. Five are derived from the coastal association and
three from the montane forest, while *Pseudotsuga* belongs to all three but
is here more of the montane type. *Pinus monticola* and *Larix occidentalis*
reach their optimum development in northern Idaho and the adjacent
regions and may well be regarded as the two most typical dominants of
this forest. Likewise, while *Abies grandis* ranges from the coast to northwestern Wyoming, it is more characteristic of the transition region.
Toward the east the major dominants of the coast association are the
first to drop out, followed by those of the transition community, while
Pseudotsuga, Pinus ponderosa, P. contorta, and *Picea engelmanni* continue
into the Rocky Mountains as chief dominants. The undergrowth varies
in harmony with the behavior of the dominants; it is essentially the same
as in the cedar-hemlock forest in the western portion, becomes a mixture
in the central, and finally passes over more or less completely into that of
the montane forest in the east.

THE MONTANE FOREST

Extent and Nature.—This is the most extensive and, perhaps, the most
important of all the western forest climaxes. It extends from the foothills of western Nebraska and South Dakota and the mountains of western
Texas to the Pacific Coast and reaches from the mountains of central
British Columbia to those of Mexico and Lower California. It occurs
throughout the ranges of the Great Basin and on those of the southwestern deserts where the altitude permits. Geographically, this
formation is typical of the great Cordilleran system, from which it extends
out upon the many plateaus to the eastward as well as in the interior.
Its climatic range rivals that of the grassland in so far as latitude is concerned, both extending several degrees northward into Canada and even
farther southward into Mexico. The vertical range of this climax is
often more than 6,000 feet in the Rocky Mountains and it may be somewhat more in the Sierras and Cascades. The corresponding range in
rainfall and temperature is vast. The pine consociation of this forest
frequently occurs in a rainfall of 20 inches or less from Colorado to Arizona and in one of 50 to 60 inches on the Pacific Coast. As to distribution, 50 per cent or more falls in summer along the Rockies, while along
the Sierras and Cascades 70 to 90 per cent falls during the winter. For
temperature, there is a difference of more than 20°F. in the mean for

northern Montana and southern California and of 60°F. in the lowest recorded minimum. In spite of this, the regular association of the three major dominants throughout the area indicates that the climate is essentially a unit from the standpoint of vegetation.

In structure, the montane forest is most closely related to the coast climax, as is shown by the broad transition between the two and by the importance of *Pseudotsuga* in both. Its widest contact is with the subalpine formation, the two touching and mingling for thousands of miles along the ranges of the Rocky Mountains and the Sierra-Cascade system. These two forests are similar in appearance, but they differ fundamentally in composition, origin, and climatic and successional relations. Along the lower margin, the montane forest makes the most varied contacts, touching woodland in the south, grassland along the eastern front, chaparral in California especially, and this or sagebrush in the ranges of the Great Basin.

The unity of this vast formation is demonstrated by the occurrence of the three major dominants, *Pinus ponderosa*, *Pseudotsuga taxifolia*, and *Abies concolor*, from Colorado to California and from Montana to Mexico. It is further emphasized by the more or less constant presence of *Pinus contorta*, *P. flexilis*, and *P. albicaulis* in both associations. There is also marked agreement as to the genera of the societies, more than three-fourths of these being common to both.

The Petran Montane Forest.—This is the characteristic forest of all the ranges between the Great Plains and the Sierra-Cascade axis and is by far the most extensive of all the forest associations of the continent. At the north its area is relatively narrow where it yields to the coast forest in Montana and British Columbia, and it is broadest in the center, where it stretches from western Nebraska to the eastern slopes of the Sierras in Nevada. The range in altitude naturally varies with the latitude; in general, it is from 4,000 to 7,000 feet in the north to 6,000 to 9,000 feet in the south, but the consociation of *Pinus ponderosa* in the form of savanna often extends much lower.[394,593]

By virtue of their abundance and wide occurrence, *Pinus ponderosa*, *Pseudotsuga taxifolia*, and *Abies concolor* take rank as the major dominants of this association.[668] The lodgepole pine, *Pinus contorta murrayana*, comes next; it is typically the subclimax dominant of the burn subsere but is so exclusive and permanent owing to repeated fires that it is conveniently considered along with the climax. *Pinus flexilis* and its variety *albicaulis* are of wide range both in altitude and in geographical area but generally of secondary abundance. Several other pines are of local importance in Arizona, New Mexico, and Mexico, but these are all of restricted distribution, as is also the one spruce, *Picea pungens*, in the central Rockies. In general, *Pinus ponderosa*, *Pseudotsuga*, and *Abies* occur together throughout the mass of the association. To the northwest, *Abies* becomes secondary or is absent, while in the Wasatch Mountains of Utah the pine is usually lacking, and in the desert ranges the Douglas fir. The lodgepole pine covers large areas in the central and northern Rockies but disappears to the southward, where its subclimax role in burns is taken by the aspen[997] (Fig. 255).

The most xeric of the major dominants is *Pinus ponderosa*, followed by *Pseudotsuga* and *Abies;* the most mesophytic is *Picea pungens.* *Pinus contorta murrayana* is nearly as xeric as the ponderosa pine, but has a

Fig. 255.—Ponderosa pine consociation of the montane forest. (*Photograph by G. E. Nichols.*)

wider range of adaptation. Much the same is true for *P. flexilis* and *P. albicaulis*, while the three southern pines resemble *P. ponderosa* in this respect. The rainfall limits for the montane forest are approximately 18 to 20 inches for the lower margin and 22 to 23 inches for the upper, though ponderosa pine persists in savanna with a precipitation of 15 inches and lodgepole outposts may be found at even lower limits (Fig. 55).

The shrubby layers of the montane forest are fairly well developed, the genera, for the most part, being much the same as in the deciduous and pine forests of the east. The lower layer consists of *Opulaster, Rosa, Viburnum, Ribes, Jamesia,* etc., and the more open upper one of *Acer glabrum, Betula occidentalis, Prunus pennsylvanica, Cornus stolonifera,* etc., together with scattered aspens and willows. The herbaceous societies are also grouped in two layers and exhibit two well-marked aspects, spring and summer, with the autumn one brief and less distinct. The characteristic genera of the upper layer are *Mertensia, Thalictrum, Geranium, Actaea, Castilleja, Erigeron, Solidago, Aquilegia,* and *Haplopappus,* while the ground carpet is composed of *Fragaria, Viola, Pyrola, Atragene, Saxifraga, Goodyera,* etc.

The Sierran Montane Forest.—This forest extends to central Oregon along the Cascades but little beyond the border in the Coast and Siskiyou ranges. In its typical expression it is practically confined to California, where it is replaced by the coast forest in the northwest and by the Petran along the eastern slope of the Sierra Nevada. It is fragmentary in the southern Coast Ranges but is the characteristic forest of the cross ranges, reaching its southern limit in reduced form in the mountains of Lower California. The range in altitude is exceptionally great; in the north it occurs at 1,000 to 3,000 feet in the Coast Ranges and at 2,000 to 6,000 feet in the Cascades. In the central Sierras the limits are much the same, but the upper limit rises to 7,000 to 8,000 feet in southern California and even to 8,000 to 10,000 in Lower California.

The major dominants of the association are *Pinus lambertiana, P. ponderosa, Pseudotsuga taxifolia, Abies concolor,* and *Libocedrus decurrens.* All of these occur from the northern limit in Oregon to the San Pedro Martir Mountains of Lower California, though the Douglas fir is represented in the south by the variety *macrocarpa,* as ponderosa pine is at the upper limits by its variety *jeffreyi.* The remaining species are all of secondary importance, three of the pines, *Pinus attenuata, P. muricata,* and *P. radiata,* taking the role of a fire subclimax in the various areas, after the model of the lodgepole pine in the related association. Of frequent occurrence are three species of broadleaf trees, *viz., Quercus californica, Q. garryana,* and *Arbutus menziesii,* the last an evergreen suggestive of the role of *Magnolia* in the east. These are considered to be relicts of former more extensive forests of similar type and now play a subclimax part, especially in the fire succession (Fig. 256).

This association grows under a rainfall of 80 inches in the coast ranges of northern California, but this amount decreases rapidly toward the south until it reaches 20 inches in the San Jacinto and San Pedro Martir Mountains. In spite of this, the great mass of the association is constituted by the five major dominants, though in the most variable proportions. While mixed forest is the rule, ponderosa pine and Douglas fir often occur in extensive pure stands, or they may be mixed more or less equally. *Abies concolor* may occur pure, but to a lesser degree, while *Pinus lambertiana* and *Libocedrus* are practically always found in mixture, of which they rarely make more than 15 per cent. *Sequoia gigantea,* which is localized in the central Sierras, is occasionally found in pure communities but is usually associated with *Pinus lambertiana* and *Abies.*

The most important subclimax tree is *Pinus attenuata*, which ranges throughout the Sierras as a dominant in burns. In general, however, fire-swept areas are covered for a long time by a subclimax chaparral very like that of the foothills in ecological behavior but composed, for the most part, of different species of the same genera, *Ceanothus, Arctostaphylos, Quercus, Prunus, Rhamnus*, etc. With the return of the forest, these persist in decreasing number and abundance as a shrubby layer until the dense canopy of the climax precludes the great majority of them. As the shrubs decrease, the herbaceous layers become more

Fig. 256.—Sierran montane forest of ponderosa pine, sugar pine (*Pinus lambertiana*), and white fir (*Abies concolor*), Yosemite, Calif.   (*Photograph by G. E. Nichols.*)

important and remain characteristic of all but the densest climax portions. The genera are largely the same as in the Petran association, a small number such as *Adenocaulon, Microseris, Monardella*, and *Lotus* being restricted wholly or chiefly to the Sierran region.

THE DECIDUOUS FOREST

Extent and Nature.—This is unique in being the only formation of the deciduous life form on the North American continent, though there are relicts of related communities on the Pacific Coast and in Mexico. It is directly related to the similar forest of central Europe and Asia, the generic dominants being practically the same but the species almost wholly different. It is essentially a temperate forest, in contrast with the coniferous forests of the boreal and mountain regions, on one hand, and the evergreen tropical forest, on the other. Together with the grassland it forms the great vegetational mass of the continent, and their broad contact and reciprocal movement render it desirable to treat them in sequence, in spite of the difference in life form. The striking feature of this relation is the great wedge that has been driven into the forest by climatic changes, the apex of which lies in northwestern Indiana, while outposts of the movement are still to be found in Ohio and Michigan.

The general northern limit of the deciduous forest runs from central Minnesota along the southern shore of Lake Superior eastward to southwestern Quebec. Throughout much of Nova Scotia and New Brunswick, except the colder coastal regions, it alternates or mixes with the boreal forest, and it bears a somewhat similar relation to this and the pine-hemlock forest along the northern shores of Lake Huron and Lake Superior to its northwestern edge in Manitoba. From southern Maine it stretches south to central Georgia, southern Louisiana, and eastern Texas. Relicts of it occur throughout the coastal plain and as far south as the Everglades and indicate that the pine forests of this region are to be regarded as subclimax. On the west, a fairly continuous body of hardwoods extended from northeastern Texas and adjacent Oklahoma through the southern half of Missouri and lower Illinois to Indiana and thence northwest through southern Wisconsin to southeastern Minnesota. Long tongues of the oak-hickory association persist along all streams of the true prairie and in reduced form along the rivers of most of the mixed prairie. Two large bodies of xeric species of oak occur in Texas and Oklahoma, where they are known as Cross-Timbers and constitute relicts of a former much wider extension of this formation.[221,298,487,910]

As already suggested, the deciduous forest has no phylogenetic relationship with any other existing climax of North America, its nearest relatives being the similar forests of Eurasia, from which it has long been separated. The evidence from paleoecology, however, shows that many of its dominants once stretched much farther west and indicates that the oak communities of the Pacific slope are remnants of such early forests. The longest and most significant contact of the hardwood forest is with the prairie, the two alternating over a large portion of the middle west. On the north, the interruption caused by the Great Lakes has served to obscure the contacts with the coniferous climaxes and the three climaxes mix and alternate with each other to almost every conceivable degree. The climatic limit on the south and east is probably the Gulf of Mexico and the Atlantic Ocean, but the actual contact is with a broad belt of pines mixed with hardwoods, with which the relation is that of climax and subclimax.

As in other vast formations, the climatic relations exhibit a wide range, the rainfall from east to west and the temperature from north to south.   The maximum precipitation occurs in the south and east, where it reaches 50 to 60 inches; the minimum is found in the northwest with less than 30 inches, owing to the compensating action of decreased evaporation.   For the same reason, the western margin of the hardwood climate runs from somewhat more than 35 inches in Texas to about 25 inches in Minnesota.   The growing season in the northern portion is about 5 months with an average temperature of about 60°F., while for the southern part it is 2 or 3 months longer and the average about 65°F.

The unity of the climax is shown by the large number of major dominants that occur through the major portion of the area.   This is true not only of many species of *Quercus* and *Carya* but also of the ultimate dominants with the highest requirements, such as *Tilia*, *Acer*, and *Fagus*. Practically all three of the latter attain the northern and southern limits or approach them, while *Fagus* is found all along the main body of the forest, *Acer* reaches the true prairie along the Missouri, and *Tilia* has persisted still farther west.   Such subclimax genera as *Betula*, *Fraxinus*, *Juglans*, and *Ulmus*, moreover, are widespread, maintaining the same general relation in all the associations.   Finally, there is also great unity in the shrubby and herbaceous undergrowth, many species occurring from the Atlantic Coast to the Missouri, well beyond the limits of the climax climate.

The threefold differentiation of the formation has been chiefly a consequence of the climatic influence of the Appalachian system in the east and of the steady decrease in rainfall toward the west.[866]   The one has produced a grouping of dominants of relatively restricted range, such as *Castanea*, *Liriodendron*, *Quercus montana* and its relatives, while the other has transferred the dominance to *Quercus* and *Carya*, which make somewhat smaller demands.   In accordance with these facts, it is necessary to recognize three related associations, *viz.:* (1) maple-beech, (2) oak-chestnut, and (3) oak-hickory.   A further reason of great significance is that the deciduous climax has been the scene of a remarkable evolution of arboreal species and this has played an inevitable part in the structure of the associations.   Recent intensive studies of deciduous forest in the Appalachians reveal a mixed association comparable to the mixed prairie and thus more or less representative of the original undifferentiated complex.[81,82]

The Maple-Beech Forest.—This is regarded as the typical association of the climax, because of the greater requirements of the dominants and their smaller number and of its greater similarity to the old-world forest. It characterizes the more humid and cooler northern and eastern portions of the climax area, and the two major dominants, *Acer saccharum* and *Fagus grandifolia*, are the most tolerant of shade.   Although beech is theoretically the ultimate dominant, the requirements of the two are so nearly the same that they are regularly associated on more or less equal terms.   Other important dominants are *Betula lutea, Tilia americana, Quercus borealis, Q. alba, Q. bicolor, Liquidambar styraciflua, Castanea dentata,* and *Liriodendron tulipifera.*   All but the first two are more important in their respective associations, and their abundance increases in the corresponding ecotone.   A frequent constituent is the hemlock, *Tsuga canadensis,* which has much the same requirements as the maple and beech and is often found associated with both but the latter especially.[201,202,325]   It is, however, regarded as a relict of a former southward

Fig. 257.—Climax of beech (*Fagus grandifolia*) and maple (*Acer saccharum*) in northern Indiana.

extension of the pine-hemlock forest, owing to its preference for cool north slopes or deep valleys, and not as a member of the climax proper (Fig. 257).   Ash, elm, red maple, walnut, and other species of birch likewise occur with beech and maple, but they are considered as members of a subclimax stage belonging to the hydrosere.[641]

The general effect of fire in the maple-beech association is to develop or maintain a subclimax of oak-hickory.   This is essentially a preclimax, since the oaks and hickories are more xeric and are found throughout the association on hills, drier slopes, and on lighter soils as the subclimax stage of the xerosere.   To the north and east, however, where pines occur in abundance, the rule obtains and a burn subclimax of one or more species of jack pine or similar scrub pines develops.   Along the contact with the pine-hemlock forest, this is regularly the jack pine proper, *Pinus banksiana*, where it is present, but much the most significant communities of this type are found from the New Jersey pine barrens south and westward along the coast to Texas. A number of species are concerned, ranging from *P. rigida, P. echinata,* and *P. virginiana* in the north to *P. echinata, P. taeda,* and *P. palustris* along the south Atlantic and Gulf coasts, to eastern Texas. The extent of this great pine belt has naturally led to the assumption that it is climax in nature, but its ecological character, as well as actual successional studies at widely separated points, leaves little or no doubt that it is essentially a fire subclimax.[555,575,685,988]

Probably no other forest climax in North America exhibits such a wealth of societies as the deciduous forest. A large number of these range throughout from east to west, though their extension from north to south is not so great. There are a considerable number of small trees such as *Carpinus, Ostrya, Prunus, Cornus florida, Acer, Sassafras, Crataegus,* and *Alnus,* while shrubby species of the upper and middle layers are usually much more abundant. The chief members of the upper shrub layer, which is often merged with *Ostrya, Cornus,* etc., are *Hamamelis, Zanthoxylum, Amelanchier, Pyrus, Rhus, Ilex,* and *Viburnum.* Lower species of the last two are frequently associated with *Cornus, Corylus, Rubus, Rhus toxicodendron, Symphoricarpos,* etc.[80,1005] In mountain regions, members of the heath family, *Oxydendron, Vaccinium, Kalmia,* and *Rhododendron,* often become important or characteristic.

The herbaceous societies constitute three or four aspects, of which the vernal and autumnal are the most striking. The vernal societies make most of their growth while the canopy of leaves is still somewhat open, and contain many species with well developed underground parts that promote early flowering. Among the most important of these are *Erythronium, Sanguinaria, Claytonia, Dicentra, Uvularia, Trillium, Arisaema, Anemone, Anemonella, Isopyrum, Viola, Aquilegia, Smilacina, Polygonatum, Geranium,* and *Phlox,* together with *Orchis, Cypripedium,* and other orchids. The summer aspect is usually characterized by such shade plants as *Impatiens, Laportea, Urtica, Sanicula, Osmorhiza,* etc., while the autumn is marked by a host of composites, especially *Aster, Solidago,* and *Eupatorium.* These attain their best expression in more open woods, especially of the oak type, where the first two genera may each be represented by a half-dozen species. A striking feature of the woodland societies is the relative abundance of genera with spiny or hooked fruits, such as *Agrimonia, Desmodium, Phryma, Lappula,* etc.

The Oak-Chestnut Forest.—The characteristic dominants of this association are the chestnut, *Castanea dentata,* the chestnut-oak, *Quercus montana,* scarlet oak, *Q. coccinea,* and tulip tree, *Liriodendron tulipifera.* The red oak, *Quercus borealis,* and white oak, *Q. alba,* are frequent

associates, as well as *Liquidambar* and *Carya ovata*. It is in this association that the number of species of trees reaches a maximum, with a
corresponding variety in the composition of the community. Like the
other two associations, it has been much modified by fire and cutting
where it has not been cleared for cultivation, but it has been further
changed in the last three decades by the ravages of the chestnut blight,
which has killed this dominant over most of its range.

Fig. 258.—Longleaf pine (*Pinus palustris*), in Alabama. (*Photograph, courtesy of U. S.
Forest Service.*)

This association lies in contact with the maple-beech on the north,
and a more or less broken tongue of the latter extends southward along
the Appalachian axis. On the west it is bordered by the oak-hickory
forest, though in the Mississippi Valley the two are more or less separated
by a broad belt of swamp forest.[921] In the Piedmont region of the
southeast this community passes into one composed of oak-hickory and
pines that stretches to the coast, the subclimax pines often appearing
to be a true climax where fire has more or less completely removed the
oaks. Through the region of the oak-chestnut forest, the oak-hickory
community also represents a preclimax characteristic of drier sites or
thinner soils. In its most xeric form it is composed of the post oak,
Quercus stellata, and blackjack, *Q. marilandica*, and recurs through the

major part of the entire formation. The pine subclimax is sometimes a preclimax, in which one species is regularly dominant; this may be loblolly pine, *Pinus taeda*, shortleaf pine, *P. echinata*, pitch pine, *P. rigida*, or longleaf pine, *P. palustris*, with more or less *P. virginiana*, *P. serotina*, or *P. caribaea*, according to the region (Fig. 258).

Coastal and fluvial swamps from Virginia to Texas exhibit a typical forest community that seems postclimax in nature, though it is actually a stage in the hydrosere. Its most striking dominant is the swamp cypress, *Taxodium distichum*, or the sour gum, *Nyssa aquatica*, though these frequently occur as codominants. The transition to the climax is marked by the water oak, *Quercus nigra*, sweet gum, *Liquidambar*, swamp oak, *Quercus prinus*, or live oak, *Q. virginiana*. Farther north these dominants mix with the sycamore, *Platanus occidentalis*, ash, elm, silver maple, etc., which constitute a subclimax of the maple-beech and oak-hickory associations.

The Oak-Hickory Forest.—The major dominants of this association are red oak, *Quercus borealis*, black oak, *Q. velutina*, white oak, *Q. alba*, and bur oak, *Q. macrocarpa*, shellbark hickory, *Carya ovata*, and mockernut, *C. alba*, with pecan, *C. pecan*, in the southern portion (Figs. 56 and 57). A number of other species play an equally important part in more restricted regions or are found more or less scattered throughout. Such are scarlet oak, *Quercus coccinea*, willow oak, *Q. phellos*, laurel oak, *Q. imbricaria*, *Q. muhlenbergii*, *Q. rubra*, *Q. texana*, pignut, *Carya glabra*, and bitternut, *C. cordiformis*. Two other oaks, *Quercus stellata* and *Q. marilandica*, are frequent associates, but they belong largely to the subclimax. Dominants from the other associations are abundant in the respective ecotones and some occur more or less widely through it, particularly *Acer saccharum* and *Tilia americana*. In addition, this climax regularly forms mixtures with the subclimax dominants of lowlands, such as the swamp oaks, red gum, *Liquidambar*, ash, elm, walnut, etc.[83] (Fig. 259).

The oak-hickory forest is much more interrupted than the two related associations, owing to the intrusion of the prairie through its entire length from Canada to the Gulf of Mexico. On the west, it stretches from southeastern Minnesota to central Indiana and thence southwestward through southern Illinois and Missouri to eastern Oklahoma and Texas. It is abundant in southern Michigan, but it regularly alternates there with the maple-beech forest, which occupies the better soils. This same preclimax relation obtains through much of Indiana and Ohio and recurs practically throughout the entire deciduous formation where soil or slope exposure delays the development of the climax or fire destroys the latter. It reaches far out into the prairie climax, though with the dominants steadily dropping out; in southeastern Nebraska, most of the major dominants are present, but the majority disappear in the first hundred miles and only one, *Quercus macrocarpa,* persists into northeastern Wyoming.[8,226] In the southeast, the oak-hickory climax lies between the oak-chestnut association and the coast, but it has been replaced over much of this region by the fire subclimax of pines. The relict areas of beech in this region suggest that the oak-hickory community was once subclimax to an original maple-beech association.[988,989]

Extensive areas of oaks, the Cross-Timbers, occur as two massive belts through central Texas and extend more or less broken into Oklahoma.[910]

Fig. 259.—Mixed forest of white oak, shagbark and pignut hickory, etc., in winter, in northern Indiana. (*Photograph, courtesy of U. S. Forest Service.*)

These have usually been regarded as portions of the oak-hickory forest, but this is hardly true in the climax sense. They are composed almost wholly of post oak and blackjack, *Quercus stellata* and *Q. marilandica,* which are usually not true climax dominants. On careful examination, the Cross-Timbers have proved to be chiefly oak savanna, in which the grasses are climax dominants. The soil is typically light and sandy, and the oaks are relicts from a former moist phase of the climatic cycle that have been able to maintain themselves against the competition of the grasses by virtue of the favorable chresard of the sandy soil. In this prairie climate, the oaks constitute a postclimax, since the climax forest would return in the event of a shift to a wetter climate. Conversely, the post oak and blackjack constitute a subclimax in the succession within the mass of either of the three climax associations and, hence, a preclimax that would become dominant in the case of a swing to a drier climate.

The relation of the oak-hickory association to the subclimaxes in swamps and in burned areas is much the same as that indicated for the oak-chestnut forest. The dominants of the cypress swamp are essentially identical and the development into the climax takes place through the agency of practically the same species. This is also true, in a large measure, for the pine subclimax, though the northerly species have disappeared, leaving the widely distributed *Pinus echinata*, *P. taeda*, *P. palustris*, and the more southern *P. caribaea*. Through the northern part of the association, the associes of river bottoms consists of ash, elm, silver maple, walnut, and sycamore or cottonwood, as in the case of the other two associations (Fig. 60).

THE GRASSLAND CLIMAX

THE PRAIRIE

Extent and Nature.—The grassland or prairie formation is the most extensive and the most varied of all the climaxes of the North American continent. It ranges from southwestern Manitoba, southern Saskatchewan, Alberta, and British Columbia to the highlands of central Mexico and from western and southern Minnesota to northwestern Indiana, southern Illinois, central Missouri, and eastern Texas to the coast of California and Lower California. Some of the dominants persist in the tall-grass postclimax, which occurs as outposts in Ohio and Michigan. The eastern half is massive and is broken only by the fringing forests of river valleys, but the western is greatly interrupted by the many mountain ranges and its continuity much reduced in consequence. In altitude the prairie ranges from the seacoast in Texas and California to the grassy parks of the Rocky Mountains at 7,000 to 9,000 feet, though the upper limit here rarely exceeds 6,000 feet and elsewhere it is usually much lower.

The prairie owes its character to the dominant grasses, most of which assume the life form known as *bunch grass*. In general correspondence with the rainfall, these fall into three well defined groups based upon stature and known as *tall grasses*, *mid grasses*, and *short grasses*, which are more or less characteristic of the various associations. With the grasses are associated a much larger number of subdominant forbs, which often give the prairie a distinctive tone and fall into mixed societies in accordance with the season or aspect. Woody plants are few in species and generally unimportant because of their low stature, except where disturbance, and especially grazing, has given them an advantage. Over large areas of climatic grassland, sagebrush, mesquite, or similar shrubs are abundant and often appear to be controlling, but these are almost invariably responses to overgrazing (Fig. 237). Similar savannas of mixed trees and grasses are frequent around the margin of the formation, as well as where it lies in contact with montane or deciduous forest, or with woodland, but these are primarily postclimax areas left in consequence of climatic changes.

Like the deciduous forest, the prairie finds its nearest relative in Eurasia, the steppes of Russia and adjacent Asia being prairies in all essential respects. They are to be regarded as descendants of one original grassland, identical in their basic climatic and ecological relations but differing considerably in the component genera and much more in the species. There is also a certain degree of phylogenetic relationship with the pampas of South America and at least a significant interchange of species between the grassland and the tundra, alpine as well as arctic.

The grassland climax lies in contact with more formations than any other on the continent. The sole complete exception is the tundra, though the contact with the subalpine and the lake forest is slight. The outstanding relations are with the deciduous and montane forests, with the woodland climax, and with the three scrub climaxes—sagebrush, chaparral, and desert scrub. The main body of the prairie touches the deciduous forest throughout the entire length of its greatly indented western border and comes in contact with the montane forest along the front ranges of the Rocky Mountains. In New Mexico and Arizona, it usually confronts the woodland climax above, as also in the southern portion of the Great Basin, while below it alternates and mingles with the desert scrub and sagebrush. In California it is bordered by the coastal sagebrush and chaparral above, and in the northwest it lies in contact with the montane or transition forest.

In general, the climax prairie lies west of a rainfall of 25 to 30 inches in the north and of 35 to 40 inches from eastern Illinois to central Missouri, eastern Oklahoma, and Texas. There is a general correspondence between the main body of the formation in the middle west and the region in which 70 per cent of the annual precipitation comes between April 1 and September 30, but this is less significant than it seems. As a consequence of its peculiar life form, grassland occupies wide limits between climax forest and xeric scrub or woodland. In terms of rainfall, this means a range of 35 to 10 inches or less, with great differences in distribution likewise. From a summer precipitation of 70 to 80 per cent of the annual amount in the middle west, the percentage drops to 40 to 50 in Arizona and to 10 to 20 along the Pacific Coast, the rainfall changing from the summer to summer-winter and then to the winter type. The primary correlation is with rainfall sufficient in amount and frequence at a time of favorable temperatures to permit the growth and reproduction of the grass domi-

nants.   The closeness of this correspondence is exemplified by winters of
two rainfall maxima in California, during which the grasses bloom in
December and again in the spring.   The wide range of temperature for
the grassland is shown by the fact that it meets winter extremes of $-50°F$.
or lower in Canada and summer ones of $120°F$. in the south; the season in
the north is but 3 to 4 months; while in the south and along the Pacific
Coast frost may occur but rarely if at all.   Throughout this vast area,
however, the grasses pass a long period in the resting stage, in relation to
low temperatures in the north and low rainfall in the south and west.

The unity of the grassland climax is evidenced, in the first place, by
the large number of genera that occur as dominants more or less throughout, such as *Stipa, Agropyron, Koeleria, Poa, Sporobolus, Elymus,* and
Bouteloua.   Even more significant is the occurrence of such species as
*Stipa comata, Koeleria cristata, Agropyron smithii, Poa scabrella, Elymus
sitanion, Aristida purpurea,* and *Bouteloua gracilis* in all or nearly all the
associations.   Other dominants, like *Andropogon scoparius, A. furcatus,
A. saccharoides, Elymus canadensis, Sporobolus cryptandrus,* and *Bouteloua
curtipendula,* are found in three cr four of the six climax associations.
Genera of the subdominants are also largely the same through the entire
formation, though it is only exceptionally that the same species grows in
the different associations.   The unity of the climax is further indicated by
the mixed prairie with its short grasses and mid grasses, which serves to
connect the true prairie with the bunch-grass prairies and the desert
plains.   Even the Pacific prairie of California, which is today completely
shut off by desert and mountain from its related associations, has practically all the dominant genera and some of its species in common with
them.

The True Prairie.—The dominants of this association are mid grasses
of both the sod and the bunch life form.   The major dominants are
*Stipa spartea, Sporobolus asper, S. heterolepis, Andropogon scoparius,
Koeleria cristata, Agropyron smithii,* and *Bouteloua curtipendula,* often
with *Andropogon furcatus* and *Sorghastrum nutans* from the postclimax
and *Stipa comata* from the mixed prairie.   Such short grasses as *Bouteloua
gracilis, B. hirsuta,* and *Buchloe dactyloides* are not infrequent, but they
constitute relict areas of little extent, except where favored by overgrazing.   *Agropyron* is a sod former, *Andropogon scoparius* and *Bouteloua
curtipendula* are intermediate in habit in this community, while other
major dominants are bunch grasses.   *Stipa spartea, Sporobolus asper,* and
S. heterolepis are the three most characteristic dominants, since they do
not occur as such in any other association[707] (Fig. 233).

Cultivation has almost completely removed the true prairie over most
of its area and its original limits have been pieced together only during
the past decade from the numerous relatively small and scattered

fragments. It occupies a fairly distinct belt between the tall-grass and mixed prairies, reaching from Manitoba into southern Oklahoma. To it belong southern Manitoba, western and southern Minnesota, southern Wisconsin, northwestern Indiana, most of Illinois, northern and western Missouri, and the eastern half of Oklahoma; the western limit runs from Oklahoma through central Kansas and Nebraska northeasterly through the Dakotas. Because of the gradual change of climate from the postclimax to the mixed prairie, the influence of topographic features, and the all but complete removal of the original cover over large

Fig. 260.—True prairie in eastern Nebraska showing dominance of June grass (*Koeleria cristata*) following the great drought.

areas, the exact limits of the several prairies can never be set, and the boundary lines drawn on any map can be only general approximations (Fig. 260).

This association is most closely related to the mixed prairie and somewhat less closely to the postclimax prairie with both of which it is in contact, as well as being nearly enclosed by them. It forms a broad ecotone with the first on the west and with the second on the east, in which the respective dominants meet on nearly equal terms. Several of its dominants are more abundant in the mixed prairie, and this is strikingly the case with the relict short grasses. The ecotone on the east has been broadened by the much greater destruction of the bunch grasses during the period of settlement and the consequent encroachment of the coarse bluestems, *Andropogon furcatus* and *Sorghastrum nutans*, which have spread well into the climax itself.

The true prairie contains a larger number of striking societies than any other association of the grassland. The postclimax prairie receives more rain, but this advantage is offset by the larger demands of the tall grasses and their overshading action, while the number in the mixed prairie and other associations is restricted by the lower rainfall. The dominant grasses and the subdominant forbs are in active competition for water and, to a smaller extent, for light and nutrients, but, as a rule, the grasses have a decisive advantage and societies can flourish only where there is enough water for both. Competition between societies is avoided in a considerable degree by their flowering at different seasons, as a result of which three characteristic aspects develop. The number of subdominants in each is usually large, and hence the societies are mixed, consisting of several fairly abundant species. The spring aspect is marked especially by *Astragalus crassicarpus, Baptisia leucophaea, Callirrhoe alcaeoides, Phlox pilosa, Sisyrinchium angustifolium,* species of *Lithospermum, Viola pedata* and *V. pedatifida, Anemone caroliniana, Tradescantia virginiana,* etc. The summer aspect exhibits mixed societies of two or more of the following, together with a host of less important ones: *Psoralea tenuiflora, P. argophylla, Erigeron ramosus, Amorpha canescens, Petalostemon candidus, P. purpureus, Glycyrrhiza lepidota, Echinacea pallida, E. angustifolia,* and *Helianthus rigidus.* The societies of late summer and autumn are composed chiefly of composites, largely species of *Solidago, Aster,* and *Liatris,* together with *Coreopsis, Bidens, Kuhnia, Artemisia, Carduus, Helianthus,* and *Vernonia* (Figs. 4 and 8).

The Tall-grass Prairie.—This consists of tall grasses, often 6 to 8 feet high and belonging mainly to the sod-forming type.[776] Over most of the area the major dominants are *Andropogon furcatus, Sorghastrum nutans,* and a tall form of *Andropogon scoparius.* With these occur more or less abundantly *Elymus canadensis* and *Panicum virgatum,* and, less frequently, two mid-grass dominants of the true prairie, *viz., Stipa spartea* and *Sporobolus asper.*[820] In the south, there are, in addition to the three major dominants, a large number of regional dominants, such as *Andropogon glomeratus, A. ternarius, Erianthus, Elyonurus, Heteropogon, Trachypogon,* and *Paspalum.*

Tall-grass prairie occurs in three forms characterized by the same general dominants but of different ecological import. The most familiar lies within the deciduous forest or forms a narrow, interrupted belt along its margin (Fig. 261). It is preclimax to the forest and may also serve as a subclimax in its development; at the same time it is a postclimax to the true prairie. In this latter relation it is found generally in sandy plains, sand hills, and other dune areas in the grassland, the most notable being the sand-hill complex of central Nebraska. In these the tall grasses already mentioned are supplemented by others, such as *Calamovilfa longifolia, Andropogon hallii, Eragrostis trichodes,* and *Triodia flava.* Even more widely distributed but often misinterpreted is the community derived by the movement of the andropogons from valley and lowland into the true prairie as a result of disturbance. This constitutes a disclimax that has often been mistaken for a true climax in the eastern part of the true prairie especially.

The societies of the postclimax prairie are essentially those of the true prairie, reenforced by additions from the deciduous forest and the mead-

Fig. 261.—Tall-grass postclimax of *Andropogon furcatus* and *Sorghastrum nutans* near Lake Village, northwestern Indiana.

ows included in it. The number of species of composites is considerably larger, especially of *Aster, Solidago, Silphium,* and *Helianthus.*

The Coastal Prairie.—From its general location near the Gulf of Mexico, this association has the highest rainfall of any, though this is partly offset by a longer season and greater evaporation. The mid grasses tend to approach the tall grasses in stature, and the number of dominants is likewise increased (Fig. 262). A significant feature over much of its area is the presence of short grasses of the genera *Bouteloua, Buchloe,* and *Hilaria,* producing a resemblance to mixed prairie. The latter differs, however, inasmuch as the short grasses are climatic dominants, while in the coastal prairie their presence is due primarily to overgrazing. They are more abundant in the west and are moving eastward in the wake of grazing, the eastern portion consisting of the original taller grasses alone. A similar result has taken place in the true prairie of eastern Kansas and Nebraska, where *Buchloe* in particular has spread far eastward and frequently forms a pure stand in pastures.

The major dominants of the coastal prairie are *Andropogon saccharoides* and *Stipa leucotricha;* the latter, in particular, serves to distinguish it from the true prairie to the north and the mixed prairie on the northwest. Even more than *Stipa spartea*, it finds its limits within the association to which it gives character. In addition to the two andropogons and goldstem from the postclimax prairie, there is a large number of regional dominants in the southeastern portion especially,

Fig. 262.—Coastal prairie of *Stipa leucotricha*, Travis County, Tex. (*Photograph by B. C. Tharp.*)

notably *Elyonurus, Trachypogon, Erianthus, Paspalum, Sporobolus,* and *Heteropogon.* The short grasses are *Buchloe dactyloides, Hilaria cenchroides, Bouteloua trifida, B. texana,* and *B. hirsuta,* together with the slightly taller *Cenchrus tribuloides* and *Panicum obtusum.* In the number of dominants and the wealth of genera and species of grasses, this association excels all others of the grassland formation.[910]

The closest relationship of this community is with the true prairie, though the line of contact with this is narrower than with either the mixed prairie or the desert plains. Its major dominants belong to the same genera, and it bears a similar relation to the postclimax associes, into which it passes on the east. It possesses *Stipa, Bouteloua, Buchloe,* and *Aristida* in common with the mixed prairie, but the first alone as a climax dominant. The short grasses *Hilaria, Bouteloua trifida,* and *B. texana* are derived from the desert plains, but these two associations have no climax dominant in common owing to the marked difference in rainfall. The societies belong to much the same genera as those of postclimax and true prairie, but there are naturally more species of southern origin.

The Mixed Prairie.—This community owes its name to the fact that the climax comprises both mid grasses and short grasses, on more or less equal terms. The major dominants of the widest distribution are *Stipa comata, Sporobolus cryptandrus, Agropyron smithii,* and *Koeleria cristata* of the mid grasses, and *Bouteloua gracilis* and *Buchloe dactyloides* among

Fig. 263.—Mixed prairie of *Stipa, Calamovilfa, Bouteloua,* and *Carex,* near Agate, Neb.

the short grasses. Intermediate in stature are *Hilaria jamesii, Elymus sitanion, Bouteloua curtipendula,* and *Aristida purpurea.* Additional short grasses and sedges of importance are *Bouteloua hirsuta, Carex filifolia, C. stenophylla,* and *Muhlenbergia gracillima,* while *Stipa viridula* is abundant in the north and *S. pennata* in the south (Figs. 235 and 263).

The mixed prairie covers by far the largest area of any of the grassland associations, stretching from northern Alberta and Saskatchewan through the Staked Plains of Texas and from central North Dakota and Oklahoma on the east to western Wyoming and eastern Utah and southwestward through northern New Mexico and Arizona to the Colorado Valley.[9,146,147,693,779] While it is not uniform through this vast extent, the presence of the major dominants over nearly all of it leaves no doubt of its unity. The chief modification is a result of overgrazing, in consequence of which the mid grasses are often little in evidence and the short-grass plains thus produced appear to be climax in nature.[808]   The next most important variation is due to the distribution of the many dominants, by which the composition changes from north to south particularly.   While the four major mid grasses, together with *Bouteloua gracilis* and *Aristida purpurea*, are found practically throughout, they vary much in importance and with the regional dominants form various combinations within the association. *Stipa viridula*, *Carex filifolia*, and *C. stenophylla* are largely restricted to the northern portion, *Buchloe* and *Aristida* are most abundant in the middle region, and *Hilaria*, *Stipa pennata*, *Elymus sitanion*, and *Muhlenbergia torreyi* are wholly or largely southern.   The closest relationships of this association are with the true prairie; with the desert plains and coastal prairie next, though it possesses several dominants in common with the Pacific prairie, in spite of the isolation of the latter.

The transition from the true to the mixed prairie is very gradual and the corresponding ecotone unusually broad.   The best limit is set by the disappearance of *Stipa spartea* and *Sporobolus asper*, which are replaced in the mixed prairie by very closely related species, *S. comata* and *S. cryptandrus*.   In Nebraska the relation is further disturbed by the extensive sand-hill region, in which the high chresard favors a postclimax of tall grasses far beyond their proper climate.   The societies of the mixed prairie are largely derived from the true prairie, in the central portion, at least, and the decrease in the number and abundance of these also serves to mark the change from one association to the other.   With the decrease in rainfall of 10 inches, the more mesic forbs disappear or are much reduced in stature or abundance, with the result that societies play a much less important part, especially in a rainfall of 15 inches or less. *Psoralea tenuiflora*, *Petalostemon*, *Tradescantia*, *Helianthus rigidus*, *Solidago missouriensis*, *Liatris punctata*, etc., persist over much of the area, especially in sandy soils or on broken hills with more available water, but more xeric subdominants from the west are now more important. Among these are *Oxytropis lambertii*, *Sophora sericea*, *Malvastrum coccineum*, *Artemisia frigida*, *Gutierrezia sarothrae*, several species of *Astragalus*, *Pentstemon*, and *Opuntia*.

The Short-grass Disclimax.—Over a large portion of the mixed prairie, especially where rainfall and evaporation are less favorable, the mid grasses are usually inconspicuous or even absent.   As a consequence, such stretches were long regarded as a distinct climax, under the name of short-grass plains.   During the last decade, evidence has been accumulated from various sources, which makes it clear that the dominance of the short grasses is a result of overgrazing.   This greatly handicaps the taller grasses and correspondingly favors the short grasses; it has been so widespread and serious as to justify the impression that the short-grass plains are the most xerophytic climax of the grassland formation.   Three sources of evidence have, however, combined to prove that it is a modified form of the mixed prairie. In all protected places, as well as in those where sandy soil or broken topography increases the water available, the mid grasses still persist. Even more convincing evidence has been secured from exclosures fenced against cattle, in which the mid grasses return in a few years. Further, when the pressure of grazing is offset by normal or excess rainfall, the taller grasses are also able to compete with the short ones on equal terms or even to dominate them more or less completely. Finally, photographs taken by the Hayden Expedition in 1870 prove beyond any question that the undisturbed cover of the Great Plains was dominated by mid grasses. Under overgrazing, the subdominant forbs may suffer as much as the mid grasses, and the short-grass plains are often an almost unbroken sod of *Bouteloua* and *Buchloe* (Figs. 234 and 238).

The Desert Plains.—This is the most xerophytic association of the grassland, stretching as it does from southwestern Texas through southern New Mexico and Arizona and northern Mexico. This is reflected in the stature, the true climax dominants being almost wholly species of *Bouteloua* and *Aristida*. In consequence, it most nearly resembles the short-grass disclimax of the Great Plains and is hardly to be distinguished from it in appearance when overgrazed. Its major dominants are *Bouteloua eriopoda, B. rothrocki, B. filiformis, B. gracilis,* and *B. hirsuta; Aristida divaricata, A. purpurea, A. californica,* and *A. arizonica;* and *Hilaria cenchroides.* The only mid grass that belongs definitely to this group is *Muhlenbergia porteri,* but there are a number of similar species that are found in sand, in depressions, or on rough slopes and are, hence, somewhat postclimax in nature. Of those the most important are *Bouteloua curtipendula, Andropogon scoparius, A. saccharoides, Panicum lachnanthum, Heteropogon, Sporobolus cryptandrus, Eragrostis, Leptoloma,* etc. Most abundant of all, though to be regarded partly as a subclimax, is *Hilaria mutica,* which dominates extensive depressions or "swags" throughout the association, usually with a short grass, *Scleropogon,* as its associate (Fig. 264).

The chief contact of the desert plains is with the mixed prairie through its entire length on the north, and the two are mixed over a broad ecotone. Along the escarpment that rises from the Colorado Desert, it sweeps northward and replaces the mixed prairie in this region of low rainfall. At its eastern limit it touches the coastal prairie and contributes to it most of its short grasses. The northern boutelouas, together with *Andropogon* and *Hilaria cenchroides,* constitute the upper belt in the foothills at 4,000 to 5,000 feet, where they regularly form a savanna with several species of oaks. Owing to the dry subtropical climate, the major portion of this association is dotted with desert shrubs of the genera *Larrea, Prosopis,*

Acacia, Celtis, Ephedra, Flourensia, Opuntia, etc., which are often so increased by overgrazing as to simulate a scrub climax.

Intensive overgrazing has also produced a disclimax of annual grasses chiefly of the genera *Bouteloua* and *Aristida,* and of annual forbs, which develop during the summer rains and cover most of the area at the lower elevations. Even more striking are the vast societies of winter annuals, which often stretch for many miles in successive pure stands. The perennial societies of midsummer are represented largely by undershrubs. such as *Haplopappus, Gutierrezia, Psilostrophe,* and *Zinnia.*[367]

Fig. 264.—Desert plains grassland with *Yucca radiosa,* Empire Valley, Ariz.

The Pacific Prairie.—This association consists of mid grasses of the bunch life form and, hence, has much the same general appearance as the mixed and true prairies. This is enhanced by the fact that it has one dominant, *Stipa pulchra,* which far overshadows all the others. Several other mid grasses occur with it in sufficient abundance to serve as dominants, and to the north and along the seacoast *Stipa* becomes secondary or is entirely lacking. The most important of these are *Stipa eminens, Koeleria cristata, Poa scabrella, Melica imperfecta, Elymus sitanion,* and *E. triticoides,* with species of *Danthonia, Bromus,* and *Festuca* under moister and cooler conditions, as along the coast, in the north, and at higher levels (Fig. 265).

The native bunch-grass prairie of California has been so largely destroyed by overgrazing and fire that its reconstruction has required persistent search for relict areas. This has been so successful that it is now possible to determine its original area and composition and, in consequence, its contacts and relationships. Within the historical period, this grassland has been entirely confined to California and

Lower California. Its closest affinities are with the bunch-grass community of the Palouse, with which it forms an ecotone in northern California. Today it is completely separated from the mixed prairie by the Sierra Nevada and the deserts of the southwest, but relicts of *Bouteloua, Andropogon, Hilaria,* and *Aristida* in southern California and the presence of *Stipa eminens* and *S. speciosa* in Arizona and New Mexico attest a former connection through the Mohave and Colorado deserts. This is also supported by the presence of many of its species as relicts in the mountains in and about Death Valley, and the certainty of this connection is evidenced likewise by a large number of California forbs and shrubs that still persist in the mountains of Arizona.

FIG. 265.—*Stipa pulchra* consociation characteristic of the original bunch-grass prairie of California.

The native bunch grasses once occupied all of the Great Valley of California as well as the valleys and lower foothills of the Coast and cross ranges and of the Sierra Nevada. They have been more or less completely dispossessed by annual grasses introduced from Europe, as a consequence of overgrazing in a region with a long, dry season. This has resulted in making and maintaining a disclimax of annuals of such permanence as to simulate a climax, composed chiefly of *Avena fatua, Bromus rigidus, B. rubens,* and *B. hordeaceus; Hordeum maritimum, H. murinum,* and *H. pusillum;* and *Festuca myuros* and *F. megalura.* In the case of *Avena* especially, the cover is so tall and dense as to have suppressed many of the perennial forbs, and the societies of the grassland are largely winter annuals, the species more numerous than in Arizona but many of them identical. Among the most important genera are the following: *Eschscholtzia, Baeria, Orthocarpus, Lupinus, Lotus, Mimulus, Gilia, Phacelia, Nemophila, Layia, Hemizonia,* and *Madia,* while the perennials belong to *Brodiaea, Calochortus, Allium, Delphinium, Dodecatheon, Sisyrinchium, Pentstemon,* etc.

The Palouse Prairie.—This resembles the Pacific prairie in the life form of the grasses and in its relation to winter precipitation, but the major dominants are different. These are *Agropyron spicatum*, *Festuca idahoensis*, and *Elymus condensatus*, while it possesses *Poa scabrella*, *Koeleria cristata*, and *Elymus sitanion* in common with the Pacific and mixed prairies, and *Stipa comata* and *A. smithii* in common with the latter.[696] In composition, it resembles the latter more nearly, and this is reflected in the fact that they alternate and mingle along a wide zone of contact. On the other hand, this association stands close to the bunch-

FIG. 266.—Bluebunch wheat grass (*Agropyron spicatum*) in the Palouse prairie of eastern Washington.

grass prairie of California in its water relations and in the absence of short grasses, and the two lie in touch through the valleys of northern California. It attains its best development on the rugged hills of the great wheat-producing region known as the Palouse but is characteristic, in general, of eastern Washington and Oregon, southern Idaho, and northern Utah[964] (Fig. 266).

Over most of its area, this prairie has been replaced by two communities that owe their advantage to overgrazing and, in the case of the annuals, to fire also. So abundant is the sagebrush throughout the major portion that this whole region has been assigned to the sagebrush climax, but the study of relict and protected areas, especially experimental exclosures, proves that the grasses are climax and that they again assume dominance when grazing is much reduced or eliminated. A more recent change has been the replacement of the grasses by annuals, with results similar to those found in California. The most important invader is *Bromus tectorum*, frequently with other species of the same genus, while two annual forbs, *Sisymbrium altissimum* and *Lepidium perfoliatum*, are often of equal and sometimes greater importance. The societies of this association are drawn largely from the two adjacent prairies, but a number of them are peculiar to it. Especially characteristic ones are constituted by the composites, among which *Balsamorrhiza sagittata*, *Wyethia amplexicaulis*, *Gaillardia aristata*, *Achillea millefolium*, and *Agoseris grandiflora* are the more important.

THE WOODLAND CLIMAX

Extent and Nature.—The woodland formation is composed of small trees capable of forming a canopy and, hence, of constituting a real though low forest under the proper conditions. Typically, the woodland consists of small trees 20 to 40 feet high and belonging to the three genera, *Juniperus*, *Pinus*, and *Quercus*. While these vary widely in leaf character, they agree in being evergreen and xerophytic as well as more or less subtropical in temperature relations. They form fairly dense crowns and in favorable situations make a continuous canopy and a fairly dense shade. Practically all the species may vary from trees 30 to 50 feet tall to shrubs of 10 to 20 feet and, in some cases, to bushes of even smaller stature. As trees they often give the appearance of being integral parts of the forest communities in which they occur, while in the form of shrubs and bushes they are equally at home in chaparral. The consequence is that the same species may appear as an important if not abundant constituent of forest, woodland, or chaparral, and its proper role becomes difficult of determination.

The woodland formation is essentially southwestern, xeric, and subtropical, though at the upper altitudes of 6,000 feet or more it extends into the region of winter snow. It finds its best expression on the high plateaus of the Colorado Basin, but it occurs from the Edwards Plateau and the Davis and Guadalupe Mountains of western Texas through northern Mexico to Lower California. It extends northward along the foothills in New Mexico and Colorado to southwestern Wyoming and thence westward through Utah and Nevada to northern California, its outposts reaching the outer Coast Range in the south-central part of the state. At its lower limit it lies in touch with the grassland formation and especially the sagebrush savanna, while in California it is in contact with the chaparral, with which it forms extensive mixtures. Along its upper margin it meets the ponderosa pine consociation of the southern Rocky Mountains and the desert ranges.

As an essentially forest community in a warm, dry region, the woodland formation has suffered more from climatic desiccation than any other. In consequence, perhaps less than a fourth of it remains today in the climax condition with a closed canopy and a proper ground cover. Throughout most of its area it is a more or less open savanna in climatic mixed or bunch-grass prairie or, more rarely, in the desert plains. The true climax areas are found only at the upper altitudes, especially on the Colorado Plateau and in the higher ranges of southern Arizona and northern Mexico.[838] Over much of the lower region it is reduced to a single species of *Juniperus*, which appears as a low shrub or bush. This type of savanna has been greatly extended in the last half century in

Fig. 267.—Pine-oak woodland of the foothill region of California.

consequence of overgrazing and the carriage of the seeds by sheep an'l birds (Fig. 267).

The woodland climax falls into three divisions or associations, *viz.*, the *Quercus-Juniperus*, the *Pinus-Juniperus*, and the *Pinus-Quercus*. The first of these is southern and southeastern in position and probably represents the original mass of the formation. The second is central and typical, while the last is found in California and Lower California. The first two are in contact with each other over a long distance but are readily distinguished by the presence of *Juniperus pachyphloea* and the evergreen oaks in the former. The California association is separated from the other two by the Colorado and Mohave deserts and the Sierra Nevada, and the dominants mix but slightly, the contact being maintained only by *Pinus cembroides monophylla* and *Juniperus californica*. The major dominants of the oak-juniper woodland are *Quercus reticulata, Q. hypoleuca, Juniperus pachyphloea, J. occidentalis monosperma, J. sabinoides, Pinus cembroides,* and *P. cembroides edulis.* The piñon-juniper association is dominated by *Juniperus occidentalis monosperma, J. californica utahensis, Pinus cembroides edulis*, and *P. cembroides monophylla*, while the pine-oak woodland is essentially all savanna today, in which the important trees are *Pinus sabiniana, Quercus douglasii, Q. wislizeni, Juniperus californica* and its variety *utahensis, J. occidentalis, Pinus cembroides*, and *P. cembroides edulis*, often single or combined in groups of two or three.

THE CHAPARRAL CLIMAX

Extent and Nature.—The chaparral formation is characterized by shrubs of the same general life form and, for the most part, of similar systematic relationship. In comparison with forest it is xeric in character but less so than sagebrush and desert scrub, which resemble it in physiognomy. Climatically, it represents the intermediate condition between grassland and forest, and it actually occupies this position between these two climaxes along much of their line of contact. It is better developed in the south than the north and attains its best expression in subtropical regions that incline toward desert in nature. It is peculiarly responsive to fire, which has left an impress on its form at the same time that it has modified its area. Practically all species of the chaparral, as of the scrub generally, produce sprouts readily from the roots when the tops have been burned or cut. As a consequence, frequent burning reduces their stature and modifies their form by the production of several stems in place of a single trunk. An effect of even greater significance is the fact that fire, which is the great enemy of forest, regularly favors chaparral in its competition with grassland, except where it occurs practically every year.

Geographically, chaparral is a western formation, reaching its typical development on the foothills of the southern Rocky Mountains, the interior ranges in Utah and Arizona, and on those of the Sierra Nevada, Coast Ranges, and Cascade Mountains of the Pacific slope.[186] In reduced form it extends northwestward from the Black Hills to the Blue Mountains, and, as a narrow subclimax band, it borders much of the western edge of the deciduous forest. Somewhat similar postclimaxes of dwarf oaks, called *shinnery*, cover considerable areas of sand hills and river dunes through the southern portion of the mixed prairie.

This climax resembles forest in the wide range of rainfall in which it occurs, its correlation with the latter being much affected by relatively high temperatures and evaporation. In the Rocky Mountains the chaparral lies between 15 and 20 inches of rainfall; in southern California it ranges from 10 to 20 inches; and in northern California and adjacent Oregon it occurs on dry slopes under 50 to 60 inches. The occurrence of chaparral under 10 inches of rainfall is possible only where evaporation is reduced by the proximity of the ocean, and under 50 inches only where insolation greatly increases water loss. This community reaches its greatest height and density where the summer temperatures are high and, in particular, under a winter rainfall with no protracted cold period.

The lower contact of chaparral is typically with grassland, but in the southern half of California, as well as some parts of the Great Basin, it is with sagebrush. The upper portion touches woodland or the ponderosa pine consociation and because of their open nature often forms a layer beneath them. Its constituent shrubs invade talus slopes or rocky soils more readily than grasses and in such situations it may long persist as a postclimax in grassland.

The Petran Chaparral.—This association reaches its best development in Colorado, northern New Mexico, and eastern Utah, where most of the climax areas are to be found. As a subclimax much poorer in species and reduced in stature, it may be found along foothills from South Dakota to Texas and from the north to the south of the Great Basin. The association attains its best development between 5,000 and 8,000 feet, and the climax portions are restricted to this zone.

The major dominants of the widest extent are *Quercus gambelii, Q. undulata, Cercocarpus parvifolius, Rhus trilobata, Prunus demissa,* and *Amelanchier alnifolia.* In the southwest, *Robinia neomexicana, Fendlera rupicola, Cercocarpus ledifolius, Peraphyllum ramosissimum,* and *Philadelphus gordonianus* are often of equal or even greater importance, while in the mountains of central Arizona, *Arctostaphylos pungens* and *Ceanothus cuneatus* appear as dominants that mark the transition to the Sierran chaparral.

The Coastal Chaparral.—This association is much more massive than the Petran but covers a smaller territory. It differs, also, in consisting chiefly of evergreen or sclerophyll shrubs, only one of the major dominants, *Quercus dumosa,* being deciduous. The number of dominants and the continuity of the cover are greatest in California and adjacent Lower California, and both features diminish to the north. Apart from the fact that the one is typically evergreen and the other deciduous, the two associations resemble each other closely in the form, height, and general relations, in the genera of the dominants, and in the essential character of the community.

The coastal association is best developed on the Coast and cross ranges of middle and southern California and in northern Lower California. Though much reduced in species, it is still an important community as far north as southern Oregon. It extends eastward to the lower slopes of the Sierra Nevada and thence to southeastern California and adjacent Nevada and Arizona. Here it is reduced to *Ceanothus cuneatus greggii* and *Arctostaphylos pungens,* which range still farther eastward where they become merged in the Petran association. The climax proper is restricted chiefly to California, though even here extensive areas at the lower altitudes are subclimax (Fig. 51).[186] Subclimax chaparral also occurs in the lower portion of the montane zone as a fire community, but the species of the dominants are almost wholly different and the two subclimaxes are not closely related (Fig. 268).

The major dominants are *Adenostoma fasciculatum, Ceanothus cuneatus, C. oliganthus, C. spinosus, C. divaricatus, Arctostaphylos pungens,*

Fig. 268.—Sierran chaparral climax, composed chiefly of species of *Ceanothus.* Santa Barbara, Calif.

A. tomentosa, Quercus dumosa, Prunus ilicifolia, and *Rhamnus crocea.* There is a much larger number of minor and regional dominants belonging to the same genera, as well as *Rhus, Cercocarpus, Amelanchier,* and *Holodiscus,* which likewise occur in the Petran chaparral, where they are largely represented by the same species. In addition, the chaparral includes several species that properly belong to the coastal sagebrush of the next zone below.

THE SAGEBRUSH CLIMAX

Extent and Nature.—The sagebrush, *Artemisia tridentata,* is so striking in color and form as to give the appearance of a climax to wide stretches that belong climatically to the grassland formation. As a distinctive feature of the landscape, it is more or less abundant from the Black Hills to southern British Columbia, southeastern California, and northern Arizona. As a climax, however, it is confined essentially to the central portion of the Great Basin, from middle Utah to western Idaho and adjacent Oregon, northeastern California, and Nevada.[367,919]

The sagebrush climax owes its character to the dominance of low shrubs or bushes, and is to be regarded as a desert scrub that has migrated widely since its early development in the southwest. It differs from desert scrub, mesquite, and chaparral, however, in the fact that the dominants are practically all shrubby adaptations of families predominantly herbaceous, particularly the asters and goosefoots. This fact explains, in large measure, the success the sagebrush has experienced in its invasion of the contiguous formations—grassland, desert scrub, chaparral, and woodland. The bush life form with herbaceous branches is peculiarly fitted to adjust itself to a wide range of conditions, and while the climax is confined to a region of 5 to 10 inches of precipitation, *Artemisia tridentata* thrives in a rainfall of 20 inches when the grass competition is eliminated. Over the climax area especially, the rainfall is lowest in summer and the heaviest precipitation comes as snow during three or four winter months.

Owing to the barrier interposed by the Sierra Nevadas, the two associations differ somewhat more than is usually the case. The ecological unity of the formation is marked, as well as its general climatic harmony, but the two communities have no major dominant in common throughout. *Artemisia tridentata* is found in the eastern edge of the coastal sagebrush and *Eriogonum fasciculatum* in the xeric variety, *polifolium*, extends well into Nevada and Arizona, while *Chrysothamnus nauseosus* also occurs in both. *Salvia, Pentstemon, Isomeris, Atriplex,* and *Grayia* are important genera found in both, but abundant in one and only relict in the other.

The Basin Sagebrush.—As a climax, this extends over the central portion of the Great Basin as already indicated, while the outstanding dominant, *Artemisia tridentata*, constitutes a low, shrubby savanna, due in large part to overgrazing, over nearly all the Palouse prairie and the intermontane portions of the mixed prairie. It often mingles with the Petran chaparral on equal terms and pushes upward into the woodland and open pine forest as a dense undergrowth. The other dominants of major importance are *Atriplex confertifolia, A. canescens, Chrysothamnus nauseosus, Grayia spinosa,* and *Tetradymia spinosa*. With these are a number of undershrubs, often abundant or even controlling, such as *Artemisia trifida, A. arbuscula, A. spinescens, Eurotia lanata,* and *Chrysothamnus viscidiflorus*. Practically all the dominants withstand more or less alkali and, hence, are often associated with the dominants of dry saline soil, such as *Atriplex nuttallii* and *A. corrugata* or of moist saline lowlands, such as *Sarcobatus vermiculatus*[465] (Figs. 239 and 240).

The Coastal Sagebrush.—As the name indicates, this community is largely confined to the Coast and cross ranges of central and southern California and to Lower California. It is characteristic of the dry or rocky slopes of the lower foothills and is probably to be regarded as preclimax to the chaparral or as forming a postclimax savanna with the bunch-grass prairie over two-thirds or more of its area. The major

Fig. 269.—Coastal sagebrush of *Artemisia californica*, *Salvia*, and *Encelia*. Point Sal, Calif.

dominants possess gray herbage for the most part, and, hence, this community looks much like the Basin sagebrush. The most important species are *Artemisia californica*, *Salvia mellifera*, *S. apiana*, and *Eriogonum fasciculatum*, but a large number of other shrubs play a considerable part, *viz.*, *Pentstemon antirrhinoides*, *Eriodictyon crassifolium*, *Isomeris arborea*, *Rhus integrifolia*, and *Encelia californica* (Fig. 269).

THE DESERT-SCRUB CLIMAX

Extent and Nature.—The desert scrub is more or less intermediate between chaparral and sagebrush in character, but it resembles the latter more closely in its climatic relations. As the name indicates, it is distinctly the most xerophytic of the three, the climax development taking place in a rainfall of 3 to 6 inches. The dominants are bushy shrubs, 3 to 6 feet high, as a rule, and possess the ability to produce root sprouts, to which they owe the many-stemmed habit as well as much of their dominance. The characteristic feature that distinguishes the desert scrub from the two similar formations is the open structure of the community. The bushes stand 20 to 50 feet apart in climax portions and never form a canopy, except in the case of postclimax species like *Prosopis* and *Acacia*. The spacing is evidently a consequence of low rainfall and a correspondingly low holard, rendering a large area necessary for adequate absorption. With this is correlated the root habits of the major dominants, *Larrea*, in particular, possessing a shallow, wide-spreading system[842,844,871] (Fig. 270).

Fig. 270.—*Cereus-Encelia* postclimax on a lava ridge with *Larrea* below, Tucson, Ariz.

Like the sagebrush, the desert scrub is characterized by one great dominant, the creosote bush, *Larrea mexicana*. This further resembles *Artemisia tridentata* in extending over an area several times greater than the climax portion, forming savanna with the desert-plains grassland at the lower levels from western Texas to the Colorado Valley. The climax proper is much more restricted in area, the general limit being the isohyet of 5 inches, which coincides fairly well with the boundaries of the Gila-Sonoran, the Colorado, Mohave, and Death Valley deserts.[557] Here the characteristic dominants are but two, *Larrea* and *Franseria dumosa*, the former 2 to 4 feet tall and evergreen, the latter a bushy undershrub, 1 to 2 feet high and with drying persistent leaves. In the numerous washes, *Hilaria rigida*, a shrubby grass, is a typical dominant that often takes part in the full climax, while *Acacia, Prosopis, Parkinsonia, Dalea*, and *Chilopsis* mark the deeper and less arid valleys (Fig. 271).

Subclimaxes of the Desert Scrub.—It was formerly supposed that this formation comprised two associations, an eastern and a western, but the former has been proved to be a desert-plains savanna in which the shrubs *Larrea, Flourensia, Franseria deltoides, Ephedra, Condalia, Opuntia, Acacia*, and *Prosopis* have largely replaced the grasses in consequence of overgrazing and of fire, also, to some extent. Protected places usually exhibit *Bouteloua, Aristida*, and their associates as dominants, and wet seasons when the grazing pressure is lessened serve to reconstruct the desert plains in graphic fashion. Where the rainfall is regularly 12 to 15 inches, the dominant role of the grasses is beyond question, and the spacing of the low shrubs becomes much more open, a result also significant of protection against grazing.

FIG. 271.—*Fouquiera* postclimax in *Larrea* plain, Tucson, Ariz.

In addition to the bronze scrub or *Larrea-Flourensia* associes is a taller and more massive proclimax found in southwestern Texas and adjacent Mexico. This consists of *Acacia, Condalia, Celtis*, and *Prosopis* as major dominants and has all the appearance of a true climax. A study of the effects of fire and grazing, however, and of the course of succession makes it clear that this so-called *mesquite*, no matter how luxuriant and controlling, is really a proclimax associes that has greatly increased in extent during the historical period. In nature, it is probably post-climax, and other postclimaxes occur on escarpments, talus slopes, and rocky hills from western Texas to Mexico and eastern California. In western Texas this is known as *sotol*, an associes of *Agave, Dasylirion, Nolina, Yucca*, and *Opuntia*, while in Arizona and Mexico it comprises the thorn scrub, consisting of *Cereus, Fouquiera, Parkinsonia, Acacia, Opuntia*, and similar spiny shrubs[838] (Figs. 245 and 271).

Climax Map of North America.—This map is diagrammatic to a high degree, with the object of emphasizing the general relations and extent of the various climaxes. No attempt has been made to delimit these with accuracy, partly because of the small scale, but also because most of the information from remote regions especially has not taken the climax and subclimax into account. The scale has likewise made it necessary to exaggerate the width of narrow strips, such as the alpine tundra, and to ignore the many isolated peaks with this climax. Furthermore, the same color has not only been employed for the montane and subalpine climaxes, but the woodland and chaparral have necessarily been included in this. Savanna has been regularly included in the grassland climax, and the areas of sagebrush and desert scrub correspondingly reduced. The intimate relations of the several mountain climaxes, the position and extent of the associations within each formation, and the approximate boundaries of the many communities involved can only be exhibited by means of a large chart, such as is not practicable for the present book.

BIBLIOGRAPHY

1. AALTONEN, V. T. On the space arrangement of trees and root competition. *Jour. For.*, 24: 627–644. 1926.
2. ADAMS, C. C. The economic and social importance of animals in forestry with special reference to wild life. *Roosevelt Wild Life Bull.*, 3: 509–676. 1926.
3. ADAMS, J. The effect on certain plants of altering the daily period of light. *Ann. Bot.*, 37: 75–94. 1923.
4. ADAMS, J. The germination of the seeds of some plants with fleshy fruits. *Amer. Jour. Bot.*, 14: 415–428. 1927.
5. ADAMS, W. R. Effect of spacing in a jack pine plantation. *Vt. Agric. Exp. Sta., Bull.* 282. 1928.
6. ADAMS, W. R. Changes resulting from thinning in young pine plantations. *Jour. For.*, 34: 154–159. 1936.
7. ADDOMS, R. M. The effect of the hydrogen ion on the protoplasm of the root hairs of wheat. *Amer. Jour. Bot.*, 10: 211–220. 1923.
8. AIKMAN, J. Distribution and structure of the forests of eastern Nebraska. *Univ. Neb. Studies*, 26: 1–75. 1926. (1929.)
9. ALBERTSON, F. W. Ecology of mixed prairie in west central Kansas. *Ecol. Mono.*, 7: 481–547. 1937.
10. ALBRIGHT, W. D. Gardens of the Mackenzie. *Geog. Rev.*, 23: 1–22. 1933.
11. ALBRIGHT, W. D. Crop growth in high altitudes. *Geog. Rev.*, 23: 608–620. 1933.
12. ALDOUS, A. E. The effect of burning on Kansas bluestem pastures. *Kans. Agric. Coll. Exp. Sta., Tech. Bull.* 38. 1934.
13. ALDOUS, A. E., and H. L. SHANTZ. Types of vegetation in the semiarid portion of the United States and their economic significance. *Jour. Agric. Res.*, 28: 99–128. 1924.
14. ALLARD, H. A. Length of day in relation to the natural and artificial distribution of plants. *Ecology*, 13: 221–234. 1932.
15. ALTER, J. C. Crop safety on mountain slopes. *U. S. Dept. Agric., Yearbook*, 1912: 309–318. 1913.
16. ALWAY, F. J. Studies on the relation of the non-available water of the soil to the hygroscopic coefficient. *Neb. Agric. Exp. Sta., Res. Bull.* 3. 1913.
17. ALWAY, F. J., and P. M. HARMER. Minnesota glacial soil studies: II. The forest floor on the late Wisconsin drift. *Soil Science*, 23: 57–80. 1927.
18. ALWAY, F. J., J. KITTREDGE, and W. J. METHLEY. Composition of the forest floor layers under different forest types on the same soil type. *Soil Science*, 36: 387–398. 1933.
19. ALWAY, F. J., and P. R. McMILLER. Interrelationships of soil and forest cover on Star Island, Minnesota. *Soil Science*, 36: 281–295. 1933.
20. ALWAY, F. J., W. J. METHLEY, and O. R. YOUNGE. Distribution of volatile matter, lime, and nitrogen among litter, duff, and leafmold under different forest types. *Soil Science*, 36: 399–407. 1933.
21. ALWAY, F. J., *et al.* Relation of minimum moisture content of subsoil of prairies to hygroscopic coefficient. *Bot. Gaz.*, 67: 185–207. 1919.

22. ANDERSON, D. B. Relative humidity or vapor pressure deficit. *Ecology,* 17: 277–282. 1936.

23. ARBER, A. Water plants. A study of aquatic angiosperms. Cambridge University Press, London. 1920.

23a. ARNDT, C. H. Water absorption in the cotton plant as affected by soil and water temperatures. *Plant Physiol.,* 12: 703–720. 1937.

24. ARRHENIUS, O. Influence of soil reaction on earthworms. *Ecology,* 2: 255–257. 1921.

25. ARTHUR, J. M. Red pigment production in apples by means of artificial light sources. *Contr. Boyce Thompson Inst.,* 4: 1–18. 1932.

26. ARTHUR, J. M. Plant growth in continuous illumination. In DUGGAR, Biological effects of radiation. Vol. 2. Pp. 715–725. McGraw-Hill Book Company, Inc., New York. 1936.

27. ARTHUR, J. M., J. D. GUTHRIE, and J. N. NEWELL. Some effects of artificial climates on the growth and chemical composition of plants. *Amer. Jour. Bot.,* 17: 416–482. 1930.

28. ASHBY, E. The quantitative analysis of vegetation. *Ann. Bot.,* 49: 779–802. 1935.

29. ASHBY, E. Statistical ecology. *Bot. Rev.,* 2: 221–235. 1936.

30. AUSTIN, C. L. Influence of pruning upon top and root development. *Calif. Agric. Exp. Sta. Rept.* 1923. P. 210. 1923.

31. AUTEN, J. T. Porosity and water absorption of forest soils. *Jour. Agric. Res.,* 46: 997–1014. 1933.

32. BAILEY, I. W. The "spruce budworm" biocoenose. *Bot. Gaz.,* 80: 93–101. 1925.

33. BAILEY, V. Beaver habits, beaver control and possibilities in beaver farming. *U. S. Dept. Agric., Bull.* 1078. 1922.

34. BAKER, F. S. Theory and practice of silviculture. Pp. 212–213. McGraw-Hill Book Company, Inc., New York. 1934.

35. *Ibid.* P. 234.

36. BAKER, F. S., and C. F. KORSTIAN. Suitability of brush lands in the intermountain region for the growth of natural or planted western yellow pine forests. *U. S. Dept. Agric., Tech. Bull.* 256. 1931. Review in *Ecology,* 13: 197–200. 1932.

37. BAKER, O. E. A graphic summary of American agriculture. *U. S. Dept. Agric., Yearbook,* 1921: 407–506. 1922.

38. BAKER, O. E. The agriculture of the Great Plains region. *Ann. Assoc. Amer. Geog.,* 13: 109–167. 1923.

39. BALLS, W. L. The cotton plant in Egypt. Macmillan & Co., Ltd., London. 1919.

40. BARTON, L. V. Storage of some coniferous seeds. *Contr. Boyce Thompson Inst.,* 7: 379–404. 1935.

41. BARTON, L. V. Germination of some desert seeds. *Contr. Boyce Thompson Inst.,* 8: 7–11. 1936.

42. BATCHELOR, L. D., and F. L. WEST. Variation in minimum temperatures due to the topography of a mountain valley in its relation to fruit growing. *Utah Agric. Coll. Exp. Sta., Bull.* 141. 1915.

43. BATES, C. G. Windbreaks: their influence and value. *U. S. Dept. Agric., Forest Service, Bull.* 86. 1911.

44. BATES, C. G. The role of light in natural and artificial reforestation. *Jour. For.,* 15: 233–239. 1917.

45. BATES, C. G.   Physiological requirements of Rocky Mountain trees.   *Jour. Agric. Res.*, 24: 97–164.   1923.

46. BATES, C. G.   Relative resistance of tree seedlings to excessive heat.   *U. S. Dept. Agric., Dept. Bull.* 1263.   1924.

47. BATES, C. G.   The relative light requirements of some coniferous seedlings.   *Jour. For.*, 23: 869–879.   1925.

48. BATES, C. G.   The forest influence on stream flow under divergent conditions.   *Jour. For.*, 34: 961–969.   1936.

49. BATES, C. G., and R. G. PIERCE.   Forestation of the sandhills of Nebraska and Kansas.   *U. S. Dept. Agric., Forest Service, Bull.* 121.   1913.

50. BATES, C. G., and J. ROESER.   Light intensities required for growth of coniferous seedlings.   *Amer. Jour. Bot.*, 15: 185–194.   1928.

50a. BATES, C. G., and O. R. ZEASMAN.   Soil erosion—a local and national problem.   *Univ. Wis., Res. Bull.* 99.   1930.

51. BATES, C. G., and R. ZON.   Research methods in the study of forest environment.   *U. S. Dept. Agric., Bull.* 1059.   1922.

52. BAYLES, B. B., and J. F. MARTIN.   Growth habit and yield in wheat as influenced by time of seeding.   *Jour. Agric. Res.*, 42: 483–500.   1931.

53. BEALL, H. W.   The penetration of rainfall through hardwood and softwood forest canopy.   *Ecology*, 15: 412–415.   1934.

54. BECQUEREL, P.   Recherches sur la vie latente des grains.   *Ann. Sci. Nat. Bot.*, ser. 9, 5: 193–311.   1907.

55. BENNETT, H. H.   Dynamic action of rains in relation to erosion in the humid region.   *Trans. Amer. Geophysical Union*, part 2: 474–488.   1934.

56. BENNETT, H. H., and W. R. CHAPLINE.   Soil erosion a national menace.   *U. S. Dept. Agric., Circ.* 33.   1928.

57. BERGMAN, H. F.   The relation of aeration to the growth and activity of roots and its influence on the ecesis of plants in swamps.   *Ann. Bot.*, 34: 13–33.   1920.

58. BERGMAN, H. F.   The effect of cloudiness on the oxygen content of water and its significance in cranberry culture.   *Amer. Jour. Bot.*, 8: 50–58.   1921.

59. BERGMAN, H. F., and H. STALLARD.   The development of climax formations in northern Minnesota.   *Minn. Bot. Studies*, 4: 333–378.   1916.

60. BEWS, J. W.   On the survey of climatic grasslands, based on experience in South Africa.   In TANSLEY and CHIPP, Aims and methods in the study of vegetation.   Pp. 341–348.   Published by the British Empire Vegetation Committee and the Crown Agents for the Colonies, London.   1926.

61. BEWS, J. W.   The study of forest vegetation in South Africa.   In TANSLEY and CHIPP, Aims and methods in the study of vegetation.   Pp. 314–317.   Published by the British Empire Vegetation Committee and the Crown Agents for the Colonies, London.   1926.

62. BEWS, J. W., and R. D. AITKEN.   The measurement of the hydrogen ion concentration in South African soils in relation to plant distribution and other ecological problems.   *South African Jour. Sci.*, 19: 196–206.   1922.

63. BICKFORD, C. A.   A simple, accurate method of computing basal area of forest stands.   *Jour. Agric. Res.*, 51: 425–433.   1935.

64. BIRD, R. D.   Biotic communities of the aspen parkland of central Canada.   *Ecology*, 11: 356–442.   1930.

65. BIRGER, S.   Über endozoische Samenverbreitung durch Vögel.   *Svensk Bot. Tidskr.*, 1:1–31.   1907.

66. BISWELL, H. H.   Effects of environment upon the root habits of certain deciduous forest trees.   *Bot. Gaz.*, 96: 676–708.   1935.

67. Biswell, H. H., and J. E. Weaver. Effect of frequent clipping on the development of roots and tops of grasses in prairie sod. *Ecology*, 14: 368–390. 1933.
68. Blackman, F. F. The longevity and vitality of seeds. *New Phytol.*, 8: 31–36. 1909.
69. Blackman, V. H. Light and temperature and the reproduction of plants. *Nature*, 137: 971–973. 1936.
70. Blake, A. K. Viability and germination of seeds and early life history of prairie plants. *Ecol. Mono.*, 5: 405–460. 1935.
71. Blanchard, V. F. Depressing effects of wind on growth and yield of citrus trees. *Calif. Citrograph*, 19: 206. 1934.
72. Blaney, H. F. Consumptive use of water by native plants growing in moist areas in southern California. *Calif. Div. Water Resources, Bull.* 44. Part I. 1933.
73. Bonnier, G. Nouvelles observations sur les cultures expérimentales à diverses altitudes. *Rev. Gén. Bot.*, 32: 305–335. 1920.
74. Bortner, C. E. Toxicity of manganese to Turkish tobacco in acid Kentucky soils. *Soil Science*, 39: 15–33. 1935.
75. Bouyoucos, G. J. An investigation of soil temperature and some of the most important factors influencing it. *Mich. Agric. Exp. Sta., Tech. Bull.* 17. 1913.
76. Bouyoucos, G. J. Degree of temperature to which soils can be cooled without freezing. *Jour. Agric. Res.*, 20: 267–269. 1920.
77. Bradford, F. C. Orchard cover crops. *Mich. Agric. Exp. Sta., Circ. Bull.* 69. 1925.
78. Braid, K. W. The measurement of light for ecological purposes. *Jour. Ecol.*, 11: 49–63. 1923.
79. Brandon, J. F., and A. Kezer. Soil blowing and its control in Colorado. *Colo. Exp. Sta., Bull.* 419. 1936.
80. Braun, E. L. The physiographic ecology of the Cincinnati region. *Ohio Biol. Surv., Bull.* 7. 1916.
81. Braun, E. L. The undifferentiated deciduous forest climax and the association-segregate. *Ecology*, 16: 514–519. 1935.
82. Braun, E. L. The vegetation of Pine Mountain, Kentucky. *Amer. Midland Nat.*, 16: 517–565. 1935.
83. Braun, E. L. Forests of the Illinoian till plain of southwestern Ohio. *Ecol. Mono.*, 6: 89–149. 1936.
84. Braun, E. L. Notes on root behavior of certain trees and shrubs of the Illinoian till plain of southwestern Ohio. *Ohio Jour. Sci.*, 36: 141–146. 1936.
85. Braun-Blanquet, J. Plant sociology. Translated by G. D. Fuller and H. S. Conard. McGraw-Hill Book Company, Inc., New York. 1932.
86. Bray, W. L. The development of the vegetation of New York state. *N. Y. State Coll. For., Tech. Pub.* 3. 1915.
87. Brenchley, W. E. Buried weed seeds. *Jour. Agric. Sci.*, 9: 1–31. 1918.
88. Brenchley, W. E. Effect of weight of seed upon the resulting crop. *Ann. Appl. Biol.*, 10: 223–240. 1923.
89. Brenchley, W. E. The essential nature of certain minor elements for plant nutrition. *Bot. Rev.*, 2: 173–196. 1936.
90. Brenchley, W. E. Boron and the control of plant disease. *Nature*, 139: 536–537. 1937.
91. Brenchley, W. E., and K. Warington. The role of boron in the growth of plants. *Ann. Bot.*, 41: 167–187. 1927.

92. BRENCHLEY, W. E., and K. WARINGTON. The weed seed population of arable soil. I. Numerical estimation of viable seeds and observations on their natural dormancy. *Jour. Ecol.*, 18: 235–272. 1930.

93. BRENCHLEY, W. E., and K. WARINGTON. The weed seed population of arable soil. II. Influence of crop, soil and methods of cultivation upon the relative abundance of viable seeds. *Jour. Ecol.*, 21: 103–127. 1933.

94. BRENCHLEY, W. E., and K. WARINGTON. The weed seed population of arable soil. III. The re-establishment of weed species after reduction by fallowing. *Jour. Ecol.*, 24: 479–501. 1936.

95. BREWBAKER, H. E., and G. W. DEMING. Effect of variations in stand on yield and quality of sugar beets grown under irrigation. *Jour. Agric. Res.*, 50: 195–210. 1935.

96. BRIGGS, L. J., and J. E. BELZ. Dry farming in relation to rainfall and evaporation. *U. S. Dept. Agric., Bur. Plant Ind., Bull.* 188. 1911.

97. BRIGGS, L. J., and H. L. SHANTZ. The wilting coefficient for different plants and its indirect determination. *U. S. Dept. Agric., Bur. Plant Ind., Bull.* 230. 1912.

98. BRIGGS, L. J., and H. L. SHANTZ. Relative water requirement of plants. *Jour. Agric. Res.*, 3: 1–64. 1914.

99. BRIGGS, L. J., and H. L. SHANTZ. Hourly transpiration rate on clear days as determined by cyclic environmental factors. *Jour. Agric. Res.*, 5: 583–650. 1916.

100. BRIGGS, L. J., and H. L. SHANTZ. Daily transpiration during the normal growth period and its correlation with the weather. *Jour. Agric. Res.*, 7: 155–212. 1916.

101. BRIGGS, L. J., and H. L. SHANTZ. The water requirement of plants as influenced by environment. Second Pan-American Scientific Congress, Wash., D. C., Dec. 27, 1915—Jan. 8, 1916. Government Printing Office, Washington. 1917.

102. BRIGHT, D. N. E. The effects of exposure upon the structure of certain heath-plants. *Jour. Ecol.*, 16: 323–365. 1928.

103. BROMLEY, S. W. The original forest types of southern New England. *Ecol. Mono.*, 5: 61–89. 1935.

104. BROWN, B. A. Spacing of potato hills. *Storrs Agric. Exp. Sta., Bull.* 119. 1924.

105. BROWN, H. T., and F. ESCOMBE. Researches on some of the physiological processes of green leaves, with special reference to the interchange of energy between the leaf and its surroundings. *Proc. Roy. Soc. London*, ser. B, 76: 29–111. 1905

106. BROWN, P. E. A study of bacteria at different depths in some typical Iowa soils. *Centralbl. f. Bakt.*, II, 37: 497–521. 1913.

107. BROWN, W. H. The relation of the substratum to the growth of Elodea. *Philippine Jour. Sci.*, ser. C, Botany, 8: 1–20. 1913.

108. BRUNER, W. E. The vegetation of Oklahoma. *Ecol. Mono.*, 1: 99–188. 1931.

109. BRUNER. W. E., and J. E. WEAVER. Size and structure of leaves of cereals in relation to climate. *Univ. Neb. Studies*, 23: 163–199. 1924.

110. BURD, J. S., and J. C. MARTIN. Secular and seasonal changes in soils. *Hilgardia*, 5: 455–509. 1931.

111. BURGES. A. On the significance of mycorrhiza. *New Phytol.*, 35: 117–131. 1936.

112. BURKHOLDER, P. R. The role of light in the life of plants. *Bot. Rev.*, 2: 1–52. 1936.

113. *Ibid.* Pp. 97–172.

114. BURNS, G. P. Heterophylly in Proserpinaca palustris, L. *Ann. Bot.*, 18: 579–587. 1904.

114a. BURNS, G. P. Studies in tolerance of New England forest trees. *Vt. Agric. Exp. Sta., Bull.* 178. 1914.

115. BURNS, G. P. Studies in tolerance of New England forest trees. *Vt. Agric. Exp. Sta., Bull.* 193. 1916.

116. BURNS, G. P. Measurement of solar radiant energy in plant habitats. *Ecology*, 4: 189–195. 1923.

117. BURNS, G. P. Studies in tolerance of New England forest trees. *Vt. Agric. Exp. Sta., Bull.* 235. 1923.

118. BUSHNELL, J., and F. A. WELTON. Some effects of straw mulch on yield of potatoes. *Jour. Agric. Res.*, 43: 837–845. 1931.

119. BUSSE, W. F. Effect of low temperatures on germination of impermeable seeds. *Bot. Gaz.*, 89: 169–179. 1930.

120. BUTCHER, R. W. Studies on the ecology of rivers. I. On the distribution of macrophytic vegetation in the rivers of Britain. *Jour. Ecol.*, 21: 58–91. 1933.

121. BUXTON, P. A. The temperature of the surface of deserts. *Jour. Ecol.*, 12: 127–134. 1924.

122. CAIN, S. A. Airplane photography and ecological mapping. *Proc. Ind. Acad. Sci.*, 36: 269–272. 1927.

123. CAIN, S. A. Ecological studies of the vegetation of the Great Smoky Mountains of North Carolina and Tennessee. *Bot. Gaz.*, 91: 22–41. 1931.

124. CAIN, S. A. Studies on virgin hardwood forest: II. A comparison of quadrat sizes in a quantitative phytosociological study of Nash's Woods, Posey County, Indiana. *Amer. Midland Nat.*, 15: 529–566. 1934.

125. CAIN, S. A. Studies on virgin hardwood forest: III. Warren's Woods, a beech-maple climax forest in Berrien County, Michigan. *Ecology*, 16: 500–513. 1935.

126. CALDWELL, J. S. The relation of environmental conditions to the phenomenon of permanent wilting in plants. *Physiol. Res.*, 1: 1–56. 1913.

127. CAMPBELL, E. Wild legumes and soil fertility. *Ecology*, 8: 480–483. 1927.

128. CANNON, W. A. The root habits of desert plants. *Carnegie Inst. Wash., Pub.* 131. 1911.

129. CANNON, W. A. A note on a chaparral-forest relation at Carmel, California. *Plant World*, 16: 36–38. 1913.

130. CANNON, W. A. On the relation of root growth and development to the temperature and aeration of the soil. *Amer. Jour. Bot.*, 2: 211–224. 1915.

131. CANNON, W. A. Soil temperature and plant growth. *Plant World*, 20: 361–363. 1917.

132. CANNON, W. A. The evaluation of the soil temperature in root growth. *Plant World*, 21: 64–67. 1918.

133. CANNON, W. A. The influence of the temperature of the soil on the relation of roots to oxygen. *Science*, n. s., 58: 331–332. 1923.

134. CANNON, W. A. Physiological features of roots, with especial reference to the relation of roots to aeration of the soil. *Carnegie Inst. Wash., Pub.* 368. 1925.

135. CANNON, W. A. Studies on roots. *Carnegie Inst. Wash., Year Book*, 25: 317–325. 1926.

136. CANNON, W. A., and E. E. FREE. The ecological significance of soil aeration. *Science*, n. s., 45: 178–180. 1917.
137. CATES, J. S., and H. R. Cox. The weed factor in the cultivation of corn. *U. S. Dept. Agric., Bur. Plant Ind., Bull.* 257. 1912.
138. CHANDLER, W. H. The killing of plant tissue by low temperature. *Mo. Agric. Exp. Sta., Res. Bull.* 8. 1913.
139. CHANDLER, W. H. Sap studies with horticultural plants. *Mo. Agric. Exp. Sta., Res. Bull.* 14. 1914.
140. CHAPMAN, R. N., *et al.* A comparison of temperatures in widely different environments of the same climatic area. *Ecology*, 12: 305–322. 1931.
141. CHILCOTT, E. C. The relations between crop yields and precipitation in the Great Plains area. *U. S. Dept. Agric., Misc. Circ.* 81. 1927.
142. CLAPHAM, A. R. The form of the observational unit in quantitative ecology. *Jour. Ecol.*, 20: 192–197. 1932.
143. CLAPHAM, A. R. Over-dispersion in grassland communities and the use of statistical methods in plant ecology. *Jour. Ecol.*, 24: 232–251. 1936.
144. CLAPP, E. H., *et al.* The western range. Senate Document 199. 1936.
145. CLARK, W. M. The determination of hydrogen ions. Williams & Wilkins Company, Baltimore. 1925.
146. CLARKE, S. E. Pasture investigations on the short grass plains of Saskatchewan and Alberta. *Sci. Agric.*, 10: 732–749. 1930.
147. CLARKE, S. E., and E. W. TISDALE. Range pasture studies in southern Alberta and Saskatchewan. *Herbage Rev.*, 4: 51–64. 1936.
148. CLAYTON, E. E. The relation of temperature to the Fusarium wilt of the tomato. *Amer. Jour. Bot.*, 10: 71–88. 1923.
149. CLEMENTS, E. S. The relation of leaf structure to physical factors. *Trans. Amer. Microsc. Soc.*, 26: 19–102. 1905.
150. CLEMENTS, F. E. Research methods in ecology. University Publishing Company, Lincoln. 1905.
151. CLEMENTS, F. E. Plant physiology and ecology. Henry Holt & Company, New York. 1907.
152. CLEMENTS, F. E. The life history of lodgepole burn forests. *U. S. Forest Service, Bull.* 79. 1910.
153. CLEMENTS, F. E. Climax formations of North America. In Plant succession. *Carnegie Inst. Wash., Pub.* 242. 1916. Pp. 184–237. Gives a summary of successions in North America.
154. CLEMENTS, F. E. Plant succession. *Carnegie Inst. Wash., Pub.* 242. 1916.
155. CLEMENTS, F. E. Plant indicators. *Carnegie Inst. Wash., Pub.* 290. 1920.
156. *Ibid.* P. 80.
157. CLEMENTS, F. E. Aeration and air-content. *Carnegie Inst. Wash., Pub.* 315. 1921.
158. CLEMENTS, F. E. Plant succession and indicators. H. W. Wilson Company, New York. 1928.
159. CLEMENTS, F. E. Experimental methods in adaptation and morphogeny. *Jour. Ecol.*, 17: 356–379. 1929.
160. CLEMENTS, F. E. The relict method in dynamic ecology. *Jour. Ecol.*, 22: 39–68. 1934.
161. CLEMENTS, F. E. Experimental ecology in the public service. *Ecology*, 16: 342–363. 1935.
162. CLEMENTS, F. E. Nature and structure of the climax. *Jour. Ecol.*, 24: 252–284. 1936.

163. CLEMENTS, F. E., and R. W. CHANEY. Environment and life in the Great Plains. *Carnegie Inst. Wash., Suppl. Pub.* 24. 1936.

164. CLEMENTS, F. E., and E. S. CLEMENTS. Flower families and ancestors. H. W. Wilson Company, New York. 1928.

165. CLEMENTS, F. E., and G. W. GOLDSMITH. The phytometer method in ecology. *Carnegie Inst. Wash., Pub.* 356. 1924.

166. CLEMENTS, F. E., and H. M. HALL. Experimental taxonomy. *Carnegie Inst. Wash., Year Book,* 20: 395–396. 1921.

167. CLEMENTS, F. E., and F. L. LONG. Experimental pollination. *Carnegie Inst. Wash., Pub.* 336. 1923.

168. CLEMENTS, F. E., and F. L. LONG. Factors in elongation and expansion under reduced light intensity. *Plant Physiol.,* 9: 767–781. 1934.

169. CLEMENTS, F. E., and E. V. MARTIN. Effect of soil temperature on transpiration in Helianthus annuus. *Plant Physiol.,* 9: 619–630. 1934.

170. CLEMENTS, F. E., and V. E. SHELFORD. Bioecology. (In press.)

171. CLEMENTS, F. E., and J. E. WEAVER. Experimental vegetation. *Carnegie Inst. Wash., Pub.* 355. 1924.

172. CLEMENTS, F. E., J. E. WEAVER, and H. C. HANSON. Plant competition. *Carnegie Inst. Wash., Pub.* 398. 1929.

173. CLEMENTS, F. E., C. WHITFIELD, and L. GARDNER. Adaptation. *Carnegie Inst. Wash., Year Book,* 26: 306–312. 1927.

174. CLEMENTS, F. E., et al. Experimental adaptation. *Carnegie Inst. Wash., Year Book,* 29: 233–234. 1930. Adaptation and origin. 35: 221–223. 1936.

175. CLUM, H. H. The effect of transpiration and environmental factors on leaf temperatures I. Transpiration. *Amer. Jour. Bot.,* 13: 194–216. 1926.

176. COCKAYNE, L. The importance of plant ecology with regard to agriculture. *New Zealand Jour. Sci. & Tech.,* 1918: 70–74. 1918.

177. COCKAYNE, L. An economic investigation of the montane tussock-grassland of New Zealand. *New Zealand Jour. Agric.,* 18: 1–9, 321–331. 1919.

178. CONRAD, J. P., and F. J. VEIHMEYER. Root development and soil moisture. *Hilgardia,* 4: 113–134. 1929.

179. CONWAY, V. M. Studies in the autecology of Cladium Mariscus R. Br. III. The aeration of the subterranean parts of the plant. *New Phytol.,* 36: 64–96 1937.

180. COOK, O. F. The origin and distribution of the cocoa palm. *Contr. U. S. Nat. Herb.,* 7: 257–293. 1902.

181. COOK, O. F. History of the coconut palm in America. *Contr. U. S. Nat. Herb.,* 14: 271–342. 1912.

182. COOPER, W. S. Alpine vegetation in the vicinity of Long's Peak, Colorado. *Bot. Gaz.,* 45: 319–337. 1908.

183. COOPER, W. S. The ecological succession of mosses, as illustrated upon Isle Royale, Lake Superior. *Plant World,* 15: 197–213. 1912.

184. COOPER, W. S. The climax forest of Isle Royale, Lake Superior, and its development. *Bot. Gaz.,* 55: 1–44, 115–140, 189–235. 1913.

185. COOPER, W. S. Redwoods, rainfall and fog. *Plant World,* 20: 179–189. 1917.

186. COOPER, W. S. The broad-sclerophyll vegetation of California. *Carnegie Inst. Wash., Pub.* 319. 1922.

187. COOPER, W. S. The recent ecological history of Glacier Bay, Alaska. *Ecology,* 4: 93–128, 223–246, 355–365. 1923.

188. COOPER, W. S. An apparatus for photographic recording of quadrats. *Jour. Ecol.,* 12: 317–321. 1924.

189. COOPER, W. S.   The fundamentals of vegetational change   *Ecology*, 7: 391–413. 1926.

190. COOPER, W. S.   Seventeen years of successional change upon Isle Royale, Lake Superior. *Ecology*, 9: 1–5. 1928.

191. COOPER, W. S.   A third expedition to Glacier Bay, Alaska. *Ecology*, 12: 61–95. 1931.

191a. COOPERRIDER, C. K., and B. A. HENDRICKS.   Soil erosion and stream flow on range and forest lands on the upper Rio Grande watershed in relation to land resources and human welfare. *U. S. Dept. Agric., Tech. Bull.* 567. 1937.

192. CORBETT, L. C., *et al.*   Protecting fruits and vegetables from frost.   *U. S. Dept. Agric., Yearbook*, 1925: 207–211. 1926.

193. CORMACK, R. G. H.   Investigations on the development of root hairs.   *New Phytol.*, 34: 30–54. 1935.

194. CORMACK, R. G. H.   The development of root hairs by Elodea canadensis. *New Phytol.*, 36: 19–25. 1937.

195. COSTANTIN, J.   Études sur les feuilles des plantes aquatiques.   *Ann. Sci. Nat. Bot.*, ser. 7, 3: 94–162. 1886.

196. COTTLE, H. J.   Studies in the vegetation of southwestern Texas. *Ecology*, 12: 105–155. 1931.

197. COULTER, J. M., C. R. BARNES, and H. C. COWLES.   A textbook of botany: II, ecology. Pp. 651 *ff.* American Book Company, New York. 1911.

198. COVILLE, F. V.   The agricultural utilization of acid lands by means of acid-tolerant crops. *U. S. Dept. Agric., Bull.* 6. 1913.

199. COVILLE, F. V.   Directions for blueberry culture, 1916. *U. S. Dept. Agric., Bull.* 334. 1915.

200. COVILLE, F. V.   The influence of cold in stimulating the growth of plants. *Jour. Agric. Res.*, 20: 151–160. 1920.

201. COWLES, H. C.   The ecological relations of the vegetation on the sand dunes of Lake Michigan. *Bot. Gaz.*, 27: 95–116, 167–202, 281–308, 361–391. 1899.

202. COWLES, H. C.   The physiographic ecology of Chicago and vicinity; a study of the origin, development, and classification of plant societies. *Bot. Gaz.*, 31: 73–108, 145–182. 1901.

203. COWLES, H. C.   The causes of vegetative cycles. *Bot. Gaz.*, 51: 161–183. 1911.

204. COWLES, H. C.   A fifteen-year study of advancing sand dunes. *Rept. British Assoc. Adv. Sci.*, 1911: 565. 1912.

205. COX, C. F.   Alpine plant succession on James Peak, Colorado. *Ecol. Mono.*, 3: 299–372. 1933.

206. CRAIB, I. J.   Some aspects of soil moisture in the forest. *Yale Univ., School For., Bull.* 25. 1929.

207. CRIST, J. W., and G. J. STOUT.   Relation between top and root size in herbaceous plants. *Plant Physiol.*, 4: 63–85. 1929.

208. CRIST, J. W., and J. E. WEAVER.   Absorption of nutrients from subsoil in relation to crop yield. *Bot. Gaz.*, 77: 121–148. 1924.

209. CROCKER, W.   Mechanics of dormancy in seeds. *Amer. Jour. Bot.*, 3: 99–120. 1916.

210. CROCKER, W.   Seeds: their tricks and traits. *Jour. N. Y. Bot. Gardens*, 26: 178–187. 1925.

211. CROCKER, W. Harvesting, storage and stratification of seeds in relation to nursery practice. *Florists Rev.*, 65: 43–46. 1930.

211a. CROCKER, W. Effect of the visible spectrum upon the germination of seeds and fruits. In DUGGAR, Biological effects of radiation. Vol. 2. Pp. 791–827. McGraw-Hill Book Company, Inc., New York. 1936.

212. CROCKER, W., and L. V. BARTON. After-ripening, germination, and storage of certain rosaceous seeds. *Contr. Boyce Thompson Inst.*, 3: 385–404. 1931.

213. CROCKER, W., and W. E. DAVIS. Delayed germination in seed of Alisma plantago. *Bot. Gaz.*, 58: 285–321. 1914.

214. CROCKER, W., and G. T. HARRINGTON. Catalase and oxidase content of seeds in relation to their dormancy, age, vitality, and respiration. *Jour. Agric. Res.*, 15: 137–174. 1918.

215. CROXTON, W. C. Revegetation of Illinois coal stripped lands. *Ecology*, 9: 155–175. 1928.

216. CULLEY, M. J., R. S. Campbell, and R. H. CANFIELD. Values and limitations of clipped quadrats. *Ecology*, 14: 35–39. 1933.

217. CURTIS, O. F. Leaf temperatures and the cooling of leaves by radiation. *Plant Physiol.*, 11: 343–364. 1936.

217a. CURTIS, O. F. Comparative effects of altering leaf temperatures and air humidities on vapor pressure gradients. *Plant Physiol.*, 11: 595–603. 1936.

218. CUTLER, D. W., and L. M. CRUMP. Problems in soil microbiology. Longmans, Green & Company, New York. 1935.

219. DACHNOWSKI, A. Peat deposits of Ohio: their origin, formation and uses. *Geol. Surv. Ohio, Bull.* 16. 1912.

219a. DACHNOWSKI-STOKES, A. P. Peat deposits in United States of America: their characteristic profiles and classification. Handbuch der Moorkunde, 7: 1–140. Borntraeger, Berlin. 1933.

220. DANA, S. T. Farms, forests, and erosion. *U. S. Dept. Agric., Yearbook*, 1916: 107–134. 1917.

221. DANA, S. T. Timber growing and logging practice in the northeast. *U. S. Dept. Agric., Tech. Bull.* 166. 1930.

222. DARLINGTON, H. T. Dr. W. J. Beal's seed-vitality experiment. *Amer. Jour. Bot.*, 9: 266–269. 1922.

223. DARLINGTON, H. T. The 50-year period for Dr. Beal's seed viability experiment. *Amer. Jour. Bot.*, 18: 262–265. 1931.

224. DARROW, G. M. Tomatoes, berries and other crops under continuous light in Alaska. *Science*, 78: 370. 1933.

225. DARWIN, C. The effects of cross and self fertilization in the vegetable kingdom. D. Appleton and Company, New York. 1885.

226. DAUBENMIRE, R. F. The "big woods" of Minnesota: Its structure, and relation to climate, fire, and soils. *Ecol. Mono.*, 6: 233–268. 1936.

226a. DAVIS, C. A. Peat. *Rept. Geol. Surv. Mich.*, 1906: 93–395. 1907.

227. DAY, P. C. Relative humidities and vapor pressures over the United States, including a discussion of data from recording hair hygrometers. *Monthly Weather Rev., Suppl.* 6. 1917.

228. DAYTON, W. A. Important western browse plants. *U. S. Dept. Agric., Misc. Pub.* 101. 1931.

229. DEAN, B. E. Effect of soil type and aeration upon root systems of certain aquatic plants. *Plant Physiol.*, 8: 203–222. 1933.

230. DEMAREE, D. Submerging experiments with Taxodium. *Ecology*, 13: 258–262. 1932.

231. DENNY, F. E. Hastening the sprouting of dormant potato tubers. *Amer. Jour. Bot.*, 13: 118–125. 1926.

232. DENNY, F. E.   Field method for determining the saltiness of brackish water. *Ecology*, 8: 106–112.   1927.

233. DENNY, F. E.   Chemical treatments for controlling the growth of buds of plants. *Jour. Ind. & Eng. Chem.*, 20: 578–581.   1928.

234. DENNY, F. E., and L. P. MILLER.   Storage temperatures and chemical treatments for shortening the rest period of small corms and cormels of gladiolus. *Contr. Boyce Thompson Inst.*, 7: 257–265.   1935.

235. DENNY, F. E., and E. N. STANTON.   Chemical treatments for shortening the rest period of pot-grown woody plants. *Amer. Jour. Bot.*, 15: 327–336. 1928.

236. DEN UYL, D.   The zone of effective windbreak influence.   *Jour. For.*, 34: 689–695.   1936.

237. DEXTER, S. T.   Studies of the hardiness of plants: a modification of the Newton pressure method for small samples.   *Plant Physiol.*, 7: 721–726.   1932.

237a. DEXTER, S. T.   Decreasing hardiness of winter wheat in relation to photosynthesis, defoliation, and winter injury.   *Plant Physiol.*, 8: 297–304.   1933.

238. DEXTER, S. T., W. E. TOTTINGHAM, and L. F. GRABER.   Investigations of the hardiness of plants by measurement of electrical conductivity. *Plant Physiol.*, 7: 63–78.   1932.

239. DICKSON, J. G.   Influence of soil temperature and moisture on the development of the seedling-blight of wheat and corn caused by Gibberella saubinetii. *Jour. Agric. Res.*, 23: 837–870.   1923.

240. DICKSON, J. G., et al.   The nature of resistance to seedling blight of cereals. *Proc. Nat. Acad. Sci.*, 9: 434–439.   1923.

241. DIEBOLD, C. H.   Some relationships between soil type and forest site quality. *Ecology*, 16: 640–647.   1935.

242. DILLER, O. D.   The relation of temperature and precipitation to the growth of beech in northern Indiana. *Ecology*, 16: 72–81.   1935.

243. DILLMAN, A. C.   The water requirement of certain crop plants and weeds in the Northern Great Plains. *Jour. Agric. Res.*, 42: 187–238.   1931.

243a. DITTMER, H. J.   A quantitative study of the roots and root hairs of a winter rye plant (Secale cereale). *Amer. Jour. Bot.*, 24: 417–420.   1937.

244. DOCTEURS VAN LEEUWEN, W. M.   1936.   Krakatau, 1883–1933.   *Ann. Bot. Buitenzorg*, vol. 46–47, pp. 506.   Review by A. W. Hill in *Nature*, 139: 135–138.   1937.

245. DORE, W. G.   Pasture studies X.   Succession and variation in the botanical composition of permanent pastures.   *Sci. Agr.*, 16: 569–590.   1936.

246. DOUGLASS, A. E.   A method of estimating rainfall by the growth of trees. In HUNTINGTON, The climatic factor as illustrated in arid America.   *Carnegie Inst. Wash., Pub.* 192.   1914.

247. DOUGLASS, A. E.   Evidence of climatic effects in the annual rings of trees. *Ecology*, 1: 24–32.   1920.

248. DOUGLASS, A. E.   Climatic cycles and tree-growth.   *Carnegie Inst. Wash., Pub.* 289.   1919. Vol. 2.   1928.

249. DOUGLASS, A. E.   Tree rings and their relation to solar variations and chronology.   *Ann. Rept. Smithsonian Inst.* 1931: 304–312.   1932.

250. DOUGLASS, A. E.   Climatological researches.   *Carnegie Inst. Wash., Year Book*, 34: 215–219.   1935.

251. DRUDE, O.   Die Ökologie der Pflanzen.   F. Vieweg & Sohn, Braunschweig. 1913.

252. DULEY, F. L.   Controlling surface erosion of farm lands.   *Mo. Agric. Exp Sta., Bull.* 211.   1924.

253. DUNCAN, W. H. Root systems of woody plants of old fields of Indiana. *Ecology*, 16: 554–567. 1935.

254. DUREAU de la MALLE, A. J. C. A. Mémoire sur l'alternance ou sur ce problème: la succession alternative dans la reproduction des espèces végétales vivant en société, est-elle une loi générale de la nature. *Ann. Sci. Nat.*, ser. 1, 5: 353–381. 1825.

255. ECKERSON, S. A physiological and chemical study of after-ripening. *Bot. Gaz.*, 55: 286–299. 1913.

256. ECKERT, J. E. The flight range of the honeybee. *Jour. Agric. Res.*, 47: 257–285. 1933.

257. EGGINTON, G. E., and W. W. ROBBINS. Irrigation water as a factor in the dissemination of weed seeds. *Colo. Agric. Exp. Sta., Bull.* 253. 1920.

258. EHLERS, J. H. The temperature of leaves of Pinus in winter. *Amer. Jour. Bot.*, 2: 32–70. 1915.

259. EISELE, H. F., and J. M. AIKMAN. The development and survival of species and varieties in planted pastures. *Ecology*, 14: 123–135. 1933.

260. ELLETT, W. B., and L. CARRIER. The effect of frequent clipping on total yield and composition of grasses. *Jour. Amer. Soc. Agron.*, 7: 85–87. 1915.

261. ELLIOTT, G. R. B. Relation between the downward penetration of corn roots and water level in peat soil. *Ecology*, 5: 175–178. 1924.

262. ELLIS, M. M. Erosion silt as a factor in aquatic environments. *Ecology*, 17: 29–42. 1936.

263. EMERSON, F. W. Subterranean organs of bog plants. *Bot. Gaz.*, 72: 359–374. 1921.

264. EMERSON, F. W. The tension zone between the grama grass and piñon-juniper associations in northeastern New Mexico. *Ecology*, 13: 347–358. 1932.

265. EMERSON, R. The chlorophyll factor in photosynthesis. *Amer. Nat.*, 64: 252–260. 1930.

266. EMERSON, R. A. Cover-crops for young orchards. *Neb. Agric. Exp. Sta., Bull.* 92. 1906.

267. ENNIS, B. The life forms of Connecticut plants and their significance in relation to climate. *Conn. Geol. & Natural Hist. Surv., Bull.* 43. 1928.

268. ERDTMAN, G. New methods in pollen analysis. *Svensk Bot. Tidskr.*, 30: 154–164. 1936.

269. ERNST, A. The new flora of the volcanic islands of Krakatau. University Press, Cambridge, England. 1908.

270. ERRINGTON, P. L., and F. N. HAMERSTROM. The northern bob-white's winter territory. *Iowa Agric. Exp. Sta., Res. Bull.* 201. 1936.

271. EVANS, M. W. Relation of latitude to time of blooming of timothy. *Ecology*, 12: 182–187. 1931.

272. EVANS, M. W., and H. A. ALLARD. Relation of length of day to growth of timothy. *Jour. Agric. Res.*, 48: 571–586. 1934.

273. EWART, A. J. On the longevity of seeds. *Proc. Roy. Soc., Victoria*, n. s., 21: 1–210. 1908.

274. EWING, J. Plant successions of the brush-prairie in north-western Minnesota. *Jour. Ecol.*, 12: 238–266. 1924.

275. FABRICIUS, L. (1929) Neue Versuche zur Festellung des Einflusses von Wurzelwettbewerb und Lichtentzug des Schirmstandes auf den Jungwuchs. *Forstwiss. Centralbl.*, 51: 477–506. 1929. Reviewed in *Jour. For.*, 28: 992–994. 1930.

276. FARR, C. H. Studies on the growth of root hairs in solutions. *Amer. Jour. Bot.*, 14: 446–456. 1927.

277. FARRIS, N. F. Root habits of certain crop plants as observed in the humid soils of New Jersey. *Soil Science*, 38: 87–111. 1934.

278. FARROW, E. P. Plant life on east Anglian heaths. Cambridge University Press, London. 1925.

279. FINK, B. The rate of growth and ecesis in lichens. *Mycologia*, 9: 138–158. 1917.

280. FINNELL, H. H. Effect of wind on plant growth. *Jour. Amer. Soc. Agron.*, 20: 1206–1210. 1928.

281. FISHER, R. T. Soil changes and silviculture on the Harvard forest. *Ecology*, 9: 6–11. 1928.

282. FITTON, E. M., and C. F. BROOKS. Soil temperatures in the United States. *Monthly Weather Rev.*, 59: 6–16. 1931.

283. FIVAZ, A. E. Longevity and germination of seeds of Ribes, particularly R. rotundifolium, under laboratory and natural conditions. *U. S. Dept. Agric., Tech. Bull.* 261. 1931.

284. FLEISCHER, W. E. The relation between chlorophyll content and rate of photosynthesis. *Jour. Gen. Physiol.*, 18: 573–597. 1934–1935.

285. FLORY, E. L. Comparison of the environment and some physiological responses of prairie vegetation and cultivated maize. *Ecology*, 17: 67–103. 1936.

286. FLOWERS, S. Vegetation of the Great Salt Lake region. *Bot. Gaz.*, 95: 353–418. 1934.

287. FOISTER, C. E. The relation of weather to fungous and bacterial diseases. *Bot. Rev.*, 1: 497–516. 1935.

288. FOLLANSBEE, R. Evaporation from reservoir surfaces. *Proc. Amer. Soc. Civil Eng.*, 59: 258–262. 1933.

289. FOLSOM, D. The influence of certain environmental conditions, especially water supply, upon form and structure in Ranunculus. *Physiol. Res.*, 2: 209–276. 1918.

290. FORBES, R. D. Timber growing and logging and turpentining practices in the southern pine region. *U. S. Dept. Agric., Tech. Bull.* 204. 1930.

291. FORSLING, C. L. A study of the influence of herbaceous plant cover on surface run-off and soil erosion in relation to grazing on the Wasatch plateau in Utah. *U. S. Dept. Agric., Tech. Bull.* 220. 1931.

292. FORSLING, C. L., and W. A. DAYTON. Artificial reseeding on western mountain range lands. *U. S. Dept. Agric., Circ.* 178. 1931.

293. FOWLE, F. E. Smithsonian Physical Tables. *Smithsonian Misc. Collections* 88, *Pub.* 3240. 1934.

294. FOXWORTHY, F. W. Forest reconnaissance in Malaya. *Empire For. Jour.*, 3: 78. 1924.

295. FRICKE, K. "Licht- und Schattenholzarten," ein wissenschaftlich nicht begründetes Dogma. *Centralbl. f. d. gesamte Forstwesen*, 30: 315–325. 1904.

296. FRIESNER, R. C., and J. E. POTZGER. Studies in forest ecology. I. Factors concerned in hemlock reproduction in Indiana. II. The ecological significance of Tsuga canadensis in Indiana. *Butler Univ. Bot. Studies*, 2: 133–149. 1932.

297. FROLIK, A. L., and F. D. KEIM. Native vegetation in the prairie hay district of north central Nebraska. *Ecology*, 14: 298–305. 1933.

298. FROTHINGHAM, E. H. The northern hardwood forest: Its composition, growth, and management. *U. S. Dept. Agric., Bull.* 285. 1915.

299. FRY, E. J.   The mechanical action of crustaceous lichens on substrata of shale, schist, gneiss, limestone, and obsidian. *Ann. Bot.*, 41: 437–460. 1927.

300. FULLER, G. D.   Evaporation and soil moisture in relation to the succession of plant associations. *Bot. Gaz.*, 58: 193–234. 1914.

301. FULLER, G. D.   Peat bogs and postglacial vegetation. *Bot. Gaz.*, 87: 560–562. 1929.

302. FULLER, G. D.   The plant communities of the dunes. *Sci. Monthly*, 38: 444–451. 1934.

303. FULLER, G. D.   Postglacial vegetation of the Lake Michigan region. *Ecology*, 16: 473–487. 1935.

304. FULLER, G. D., and A. L. BAKKE.   Raunkiaer's "life forms," "leaf-size classes," and statistical methods. *Plant World*, 21: 25–37, 57–63. 1918.

305. FULTS, J. L.   Blue grama grass for erosion control and range reseeding in the Great Plains and a method of obtaining seed in large lots. *U. S. Dept. Agric., Circ.* 402. 1936.

306. GABRIELSON, I. N.   The correlation of forestry and wildlife management. *Jour. For.*, 34: 98–103. 1936.

307. GAIL, F. W.   Photosynthesis in some of the red and brown algae as related to depth and light. *Pub. Puget Sound Biol. Sta.*, 3: 177–193. 1922.

308. GAIL, F. W.   Osmotic pressure of cell sap and its possible relation to winter killing and leaf fall. *Bot. Gaz.*, 81: 434–445. 1926.

309. GARDNER, V. R., F. C. BRADFORD, and H. D. HOOKER.   The fundamentals of fruit production. P. 79. McGraw-Hill Book Company, Inc., New York. 1922.

310. GARDNER, W. A.   Effect of light on germination of light-sensitive seeds. *Bot. Gaz.*, 71: 249–288. 1921.

311. GARNER, W. W.   Comparative responses of long-day and short-day plants to relative length of day and night. *Plant Physiol.*, 8: 347–356. 1933.

312. GARNER, W. W.   Photoperiodism. In DUGGAR, Biological effects of radiation. Vol. 2. Pp. 677–713. McGraw-Hill Book Company, Inc., New York. 1936.

313. GARNER, W. W.   Recent work on photoperiodism. *Bot. Rev.*, 3: 259–275. 1937.

314. GARNER, W. W., and H. A. ALLARD.   Effect of the relative length of day and night and other factors of the environment on growth and reproduction in plants. *Jour. Agric. Res.*, 18: 553–606. 1920.

315. GARNER, W. W., and H. A. ALLARD.   Further studies in photoperiodism, the response of the plant to relative length of day and night. *Jour. Agric. Res.*, 23: 871–920. 1923.

316. GARNER, W. W., and H. A. ALLARD.   Localization of the response in plants to relative length of day and night. *Jour. Agric. Res.*, 31: 555–566. 1925.

317. GARNER, W. W., and H. A. ALLARD.   Duration of the flowerless condition of some plants in response to unfavorable lengths of day. *Jour. Agric. Res.*, 43: 439–443. 1931.

318. GARNER, W. W., C. W. BACON, and H. A. ALLARD.   Photoperiodism in relation to hydrogen-ion concentration of the cell sap and the carbohydrate content of the plant. *Jour. Agric. Res.*, 27: 119–156. 1924.

319. GARNER, W. W., and W. M. LUNN.   Effects of crops on the yields of succeeding crops in the rotation, with special reference to tobacco. *Jour. Agric. Res.*, 30: 1095–1132. 1925.

320. GATES, F. C.   Winter as a factor in the xerophily of certain evergreen ericads. *Bot. Gaz.*, 57: 445–489. 1914.

321. GATES, F. C.   Evaporation in vegetation at different heights.   *Amer. Jour. Bot.*, 13: 167–178.   1926.

322. GATES, F. C.   Aspen association in northern lower Michigan.   *Bot. Gaz.*, 90: 233–259.   1930.

323. GEVORKIANTZ, S. R., and E. I. ROE.   Photoperiodism in forestry.   *Jour. For.*, 33: 599–602.   1935.

324. GIÖBEL, G.   The relation of the soil nitrogen to nodule development and fixation of nitrogen by certain legumes.   *N. J. Agric. Exp. Sta., Bull.* 436. 1926.

325. GLEASON, H. A.   Botanical observations in northern Michigan.   *Jour. N. Y. Bot. Garden*, 24: 273–283.   1923.

326. GODWIN, H.   Pollen analysis: an outline of the problems and potentialities of the method.   I. Technique and interpretation.   *New Phytol.*, 33: 278–305. 1934.   II. General applications of pollen analysis.   *Ibid.*, 325–358.

327. GOEBEL, K.   Einleitung in die experimentelle Morphologie der Pflanzen. Leipzig.   1908.

328. GOFF, E. S.   The Russian thistle.   *Wis. Agric. Exp. Sta., Bull.* 37.   1893.

329. GORDON, R. B.   A unique raised bog at Urbana, Ohio.   *Ohio Jour. Sci.*, 33: 453–459.   1933.

329a. GORKE, H.   Über chemische Vorgänge beim Erfrieren der Pflanzen.   *Landw. Versuchs-Stationen*, 65: 149–160.   1906.

330. GOSS, R. W.   Temperature and humidity studies of some Fusaria rots of the Irish potato.   *Jour. Agric. Res.*, 22: 65–80.   1921.

331. GOSS, W. L.   The vitality of buried seeds.   *Jour. Agric. Res.*, 29: 349–362. 1924.

332. GOURLEY, J. H.   The effect of shading some horticultural plants.   *Proc. Soc. Hort. Sci.*, 17: 256–260.   1920.

333. GOURLEY, J. H., and G. T. NIGHTINGALE.   The effects of shading some horticultural plants.   *N. H. Coll. Agric. Exp. Sta., Tech. Bull.* 18.   1921.

334. GRABER, L. F.   Injury from burning off old grass on established bluegrass pastures.   *Jour. Amer. Soc. Agron.*, 18: 815–819.   1926.

335. GRABER, L. F., N. T. NELSON, W. A. LEUKEL, and W. B. ALBERT.   Organic food reserves in relation to the growth of alfalfa and other perennial herbaceous plants.   *Wis. Agric. Exp. Sta., Res. Bull.* 80.   1927.

336. GRANDFIELD, C. O.   The trend of organic food reserves in alfalfa roots as affected by cutting practices.   *Jour. Agric. Res.*, 50: 697–709.   1935.

337. GREENE, S. W.   Relation between winter grass fires and cattle grazing in the longleaf pine belt.   *Jour. For.*, 33: 338–341.   1935.

338. GRIFFITH, B. G., E. W. HARTWELL, and T. E. SHAW.   The evolution of soils as affected by the old field white pine-mixed hardwood succession in central New England.   *Harvard For. Bull.* 15.   1930.

339. GRIGGS, R. F.   The colonization of the Katmai ash, a new and inorganic "soil."   *Amer. Jour. Bot.*, 20: 92–113.   1933.

340. GRIGGS, R. F., *et al.*   Scientific results of the Katmai expeditions of the National Geographic Society.   I–X. *Ohio State Univ., Bull.* 24 (no. 15).   1920.

341. GRINNELL, J.   The burrowing rodents of California as agents in soil formation.   *Jour. Mam.*, 4: 137–149.   1923.

342. GRINNELL, J., and T. I. Storer.   Animal life in the Yosemite.   University of California Press, Berkeley, Calif.   1924.

343. GRISBORNE, H. T.   Measuring fire weather and forest inflammability.   *U. S. Dept. Agric., Circ.* 398.   1936.

344. GRISWOLD, S. M.   Effect of alternate moistening and drying on germination of seeds of western range plants. *Bot. Gaz.*, 98: 243–269.   1936.

345. GUPPY, H. B.   Observations of a naturalist in the Pacific.   2 vols.   Macmillan & Company, Ltd., London.   1903–1906.

346. GUPPY, H. B.   Studies in seeds and fruits.   Williams & Norgate, London.   1912.

347. GUPPY, H. B.   Plants, seeds, and currents in the West Indies and Azores. Williams & Norgate, London.   1917.

348. HAAS, P., and T. G. HILL.   The hydrogen ion concentration.   In An introduction to the chemistry of plant products.   Vol. 2.   Pp. 4–9.   Longmans, Green & Company, New York.   1922.

349. HAASIS, F. W.   Frost heaving of western yellow pine seedlings.   *Ecology*, 4: 378–390.   1923.

350. HAASIS, F. W.   Germinative energy of lots of coniferous-tree seed, as related to incubation temperature and to duration of incubation.   *Plant Physiol.*, 3: 365–412.   1928.

351. HABERLANDT, F.   Die oberen und unteren Temperaturgrenzen für die Keimung der wichtigeren landwirtschaftlichen Sämereien.   *Landw. Versuchs-Stationen,* 17: 104–116.   1874.

352. HABERLANDT, G.   Physiological plant anatomy.   Pp. 165–197.   Macmillan & Company, Ltd., London.   1914.

353. *Ibid.*   P. 377.

354. *Ibid.*   P. 432.

355. HADWEN, S., and L. J. PALMER.   Reindeer in Alaska.   *U. S. Dept. Agric., Bull.* 1089.   1922.

356. HAIG, I. T.   Accuracy of quadrat sampling in studying forest reproduction on cut-over areas. *Ecology*, 10: 374–381.   1929.

357. HAIG, I. T.   Premature germination of forest seed during natural storage in duff. *Ecology*, 13: 311–312.   1932.

358. HAIG, I. T.   Factors controlling initial establishment of western white pine and associated species.   *Yale Univ., School For., Bull.* 41.   1936.

359. HALL, A. D.   The book of the Rothamsted experiments.   P. 36.   John Murray, London.   1905.

360. HALL, A. G.   Lightning storms and fires on the National Forests of Oregon and Washington.   Review of mimeographed article by W. G. Morris.   *Jour. For.*, 32: 897–898.   1934.

361. HALL, H. M., and F. E. CLEMENTS.   The phylogenetic method in taxonomy. *Carnegie Inst. Wash., Pub.* 326.   1923.

362. HALL, H. M., and J. GRINNELL.   Life-zone indicators in California.   *Proc. Calif. Acad. Sci.*, ser. 4, 9: 37–67.   1919.

363. HALLIDAY, W. E. D.   A forest classification for Canada.   *Dominion of Canada Dept. Mines and Resources, For. Serv., Bull.* 89.   1937.

364. HALLSTED, A. L., and O. R. MATHEWS.   Soil moisture and winter wheat with suggestions on abandonment.   *Kans. Agric. Exp. Sta., Bull.* 273.   1936.

365. HAMLY, D. H.   Softening of the seeds of Melilotus alba.   *Bot. Gaz.*, 93: 345–375.   1932.

366. HANSON, H. C.   Leaf-structure as related to environment.   *Amer. Jour. Bot.*, 4: 533–560.   1917.

367. HANSON, H. C.   A study of the vegetation of northeastern Arizona.   *Univ. Neb. Studies*, 24: 85–94.   1924.

368. HANSON, H. C.   A comparison of methods of botanical analysis of the native prairie in western North Dakota.   *Jour. Agric. Res.*, 49: 815–842.   1934.

369. HANSON, H. C., and L. D. LOVE. Comparison of methods of quadratting. *Ecology*, 11: 734–748. 1930.

370. HANSON, H. C., and L. D. LOVE. Size of list quadrat for use in determining effects of different systems of grazing upon Agropyron smithii mixed prairie. *Jour. Agric. Res.*, 41: 549–560. 1930.

371. HANSON, H. C., L. D. LOVE, and M. S. MORRIS. Effects of different systems of grazing by cattle upon a western wheat-grass type of range. *Colo. Agric. Exp. Sta., Bull.* 377. 1931.

372. HARMER, P. M. Prevention of wind injury to crops on muck land. *Mich. Agric. Exp. Sta., Circ. Bull.* 103. 1927.

373. HARRINGTON, G. T. Optimum temperatures for flower seed germination. *Bot. Gaz.*, 72: 337–358. 1921.

374. HARRINGTON, G. T., and B. C. HITE. After-ripening and germination of apple seeds. *Jour. Agric. Res.*, 23: 153–161. 1923.

375. HARRINGTON, J. B. Varietal resistance of small grains to spring frost injury. *Jour. Amer. Soc. Agron.*, 28: 374–388. 1936.

376. HARRIS, F. S. Soil alkali, its origin, nature, and treatment. John Wiley & Sons, Inc., New York. 1920.

377. HARRIS, J. A. The tissue fluids of Egyptian and upland cottons and their F_1 hybrid. *Jour. Agric. Res.*, 27: 267–328. 1924.

378. HARRIS, J. A., and J. V. LAWRENCE. The osmotic concentration of the tissue fluids of Jamaican montane rain-forest vegetation. *Amer. Jour. Bot.*, 4: 268–298. 1917.

379. HARRIS, J. A., *et al.* The osmotic concentration, specific electrical conductivity and chlorid content of the tissue fluids of the indicator plants of Tooele valley, Utah. *Jour. Agric. Res.*, 27: 893–924. 1924.

380. HARRISON, C. M. Effect of cutting and fertilizer applications on grass development. *Plant Physiol.*, 6: 669–684. 1931.

381. HARSHBERGER, J. W. Phytogeographic survey of North America. G. E. Stechert & Company, New York. 1911.

382. HARSHBERGER, J. W. The vegetation of the New Jersey pine-barrens. Christopher Sower Company, Philadelphia. 1916.

383. HARSHBERGER, J. W. Preliminary notes on American snow patches and their plants. *Ecology*, 10: 275–281. 1929.

384. HARTLEY, C. Damping-off in forest nurseries. *U. S. Dept. Agric., Dept. Bull.* 934. 1921.

385. HARTWELL, B. L., *et al.* Lime requirement as determined by the plant and by the chemist. *Soil Science*, 7: 279–282. 1919.

386. HARVEY, R. B. Hardening process in plants and developments from frost injury. *Jour. Agric. Res.*, 15: 83–112. 1918.

387. HARVEY, R. B. Relation of the color of bark to the temperature of the cambium in winter. *Ecology*, 4: 391–394. 1923.

388. HARVEY, R. B. An annotated bibliography of the low temperature relations of plants. Burgess Publishing Company, Minneapolis. 1935.

389. HASSELBRING, H. The effect of shading on the transpiration and assimilation of the tobacco plant in Cuba. *Bot. Gaz.*, 57: 257–286. 1914.

390. HATCH, A. B. The role of mycorrhizae in afforestation. *Jour. For.*, 34: 22–29. 1936.

390a. HATCH, A. B. The physical basis of mycotrophy in Pinus. *The Black Rock Forest, Bull.* 6. 1937.

390b. HATCH, A. B., and K. D. DOAK. Mycorrhizal and other features of the root systems of Pinus. *Jour. Arnold Arboretum*, 14: 85–98. 1933.

391. HATTON, R. G., and W. S. ROGERS. The importance of the root system. Empire Marketing Board. (Imperial Fruit Show Leaflet.) 1929.

392. HAVILAND, M. D. Forest, steppe and tundra. Cambridge University Press, London. 1926.

393. HAYDEN, A. The ecologic subterranean anatomy of some plants of a prairie province in central Iowa. *Amer. Jour. Bot.*, 6: 87–105. 1919.

394. HAYWARD, H. E. Studies of plants in the Black Hills of South Dakota. *Bot. Gaz.*, 85: 353–412. 1928.

395. HAZARD, H. E. Plant indicators of pure white pine sites in southern New Hampshire. *Jour. For.*, 35: 477–486. 1937.

396. HEALD, F. D., and R. A. STUDHALTER. Birds as carriers of the chestnut-blight fungus. *Jour. Agric. Res.*, 2: 405–422. 1919.

397. HEALD, F. D., *et al.* Air and wind dissemination of ascospores of the chestnut-blight fungus. *Jour. Agric. Res.*, 3: 493–526. 1915.

398. HEIN, M. A., and H. N. VINALL. Persistence of grass and legume species under grazing conditions. *Jour. Amer. Soc. Agron.*, 25: 595–602. 1933.

399. HELM, C. A. Corn in Missouri. *Mo. Agric. Exp. Sta., Bull.* 185. 1921.

400. HENDRICKSON, A. H. The common honey bee as an agent in prune pollination. *Calif. Agric. Exp. Sta., Bull.* 291. 1918.

401. HENRICI, M. The chlorophyll-content of grasses of Bechuanaland. Reports of the Director of Veterinary Education and Research, 11 and 12: 259–271. 1926–1927.

402. HEYWARD, F. The root system of longleaf pine in the deep sands of western Florida. *Ecology*, 14: 136–148. 1933.

403. HIBBEN, S. G. Some light reflecting properties of flowers and foliage. *Trans. Illum. Eng. Soc.*, 24: 752–769. 1929.

404. HILGARD, E. W. The recognition of character of soils from their native vegetation. In Soils, Pp. 487–526. The Macmillan Company, New York. 1911.

405. HILGARD, E. W. Soils. P. 315. 1911.

406. HILL, R. R. Charting quadrats with a pantograph. *Ecology*, 1: 270–273. 1920.

407. HILL, T. G. Observations on the osmotic properties of the root hairs of certain salt marsh plants. *New Phytol.*, 7: 133–142. 1908.

408. HOAGLAND, D. R. The plant as a metabolic unit in the soil-plant system. Essays in geobotany. Pp. 219–245. University of California Press, Berkeley, Calif. 1936.

409. HOAGLAND, D. R., and J. C. MARTIN. Effect of season and crop growth on the physical state of the soil. *Jour. Agric. Res.*, 20: 397–404. 1920.

410. HOFFMAN, M. B., and G. R. SCHLUBATIS. The significance of soil variation in raspberry culture. *Mich. State Coll. Agric. Exp. Sta., Spec. Bull.* 177. 1928.

411. HOFMANN, J. V. Natural reproduction from seed stored in the forest floor. *Jour. Agric. Res.*, 11: 1–26. 1917.

412. HOFMANN, J. V. The importance of seed characteristics in the natural reproduction of coniferous forests. *Univ. Minn., Studies Biol. Science, No. 2.* 1918.

413. HOFMANN, J. V. The establishment of a Douglas fir forest. *Ecology*, 1: 49–53. 1920.

414. HOFMANN, J. V. The natural regeneration of Douglas fir in the Pacific northwest. *U. S. Dept. Agric., Dept. Bull.* 1200. 1924.

415. HOLCH, A. E. Development of roots and shoots of certain deciduous tree seedlings in different forest sites. *Ecology*, 12: 259–298. 1931.

416. HOLE, R. S. Plant oecology and its bearing on problems of economic importance in India. *Jour. & Proc. Asiat. Soc. Bengal*, 14: clvi–clxvii. 1918.

417. HOPKINS, E. S., *et al.* Soil drifting control in the prairie provinces. *Dominion of Canada, Dept. Agric. Bull.* 179 (n.s.). 1935.

418. HORTON, R. E. Rainfall interception. *Monthly Weather Rev.*, 47: 603–623. 1919.

419. HOUGH, A. F. A climax forest community on east Tionesta creek in northwestern Pennsylvania. *Ecology*, 17: 9–28. 1936.

420. HOWARD, A. The influence of soil factors on disease resistance. *Ann. Appl. Biol.*, 7: 373–389. 1921.

421. HOWARD, A. The economic significance of root-development. In Crop-production in India. Oxford University Press, London. Pp. 54–60. 1924.

422. HOWARD, A. The effect of grass on trees. *Proc. Roy. Soc. London*, ser. B, 97: 284–320. 1925.

423. HOWE, C. G. Pectic material in root hairs. *Bot. Gaz.*, 72: 313–320. 1921.

424. HUBERMAN, M. A. The role of western white pine in forest succession in northern Idaho. *Ecology*, 16: 137–151. 1935.

425. HULBERT, H. W., C. A. MICHELS, and F. L. BURKART. Border effect in variety tests of small grains. *Idaho Agric. Exp. Sta., Res. Bull.* 9. 1931.

426. HUMPHREY, R. R. Thorn formation in Fouquieria splendens and Idria columnaris. *Bull. Torrey Bot. Club*, 58: 263–264. 1931.

427. HUNTER, C., and E. M. RICH. The effect of artificial aeration of the soil on Impatiens balsamina L. *New Phytol.*, 24: 257–271. 1925.

428. HUNTINGTON, E. The climatic factor as illustrated in arid America. *Carnegie Inst. Wash., Pub.* 192. 1914.

429. HUNTINGTON, E. Civilization and climate. 3d ed. Yale University Press, New Haven. 1924.

430. HUNTINGTON, E. Marginal land and the shelter belt. *Jour. For.*, 32: 804–812. 1934.

431. HUTCHINGS, S. S. Light in relation to the seed germination of Mimulus ringens L. *Amer. Jour. Bot.*, 19: 632–643. 1932.

432. IKENBERRY, G. J. The relation of hydrogen-ion concentration to the growth and distribution of mosses. *Amer. Jour. Bot.*, 23: 271–279. 1936.

433. ILJIN, V., P. NAZAROVA, and M. OSTROVSKAJA. Osmotic pressure in roots and in leaves in relation to habitat moisture. *Jour. Ecol.*, 4: 160–173. 1916.

434. ILJIN, W. S. The point of death of plants at low temperatures. *Protoplasma*, 23: 288–289. 1935.

435. ILJIN, W. S. The relation of cell sap concentration to cold resistance in plants. *Bulletin de l'association russe pour les recherches scientifiques à Prague* 3 (8). Sections des sciences naturelles et mathématiques, no. 13: 35–55. 1935.

436. Imperial Bureau of Plant Genetics. Vernalization and phasic development of plants. *Bull.* 17. 1935.

437. Imperial Bureau of Soil Science. Soil, vegetation and climate. *Tech. Com.* 29: 1–40. 1934.

438. INGOLD, C. T. Spore discharge in the ascomycetes. *New Phytol.*, 32: 175–196. 1933.

439. INGRAM, D. C. Vegetative changes and grazing use on Douglas fir cut-over land. *Jour. Agric. Res.*, 43: 387–417. 1931.

440. ISAAC, L. A. Life of Douglas fir seed in the forest floor. *Jour. For.*, 33: 61–66. 1935.

441. JACKSON, C. V. Seed germination in certain New Mexico range grasses. *Bot. Gaz.*, 86: 270–294. 1928.

442. JACOT, A. P. Soil structure and soil biology. *Ecology*, 17: 359–379. 1936.
443. JEAN, F. C. Root inheritance in peas. *Bot. Gaz.*, 86: 318–329. 1928.
444. JEAN, F. C., and J. E. WEAVER. Root behavior and crop yield under irrigation. *Carnegie Inst. Wash., Pub.* 357. 1924.
445. JEFFREYS, H. On the vegetation of four Durham coal-measure fells. *Jour. Ecol.*, 5: 129–154. 1917.
446. JEFFS, R. E. The elongation of root hairs as affected by light and temperature. *Amer. Jour. Bot.*, 12: 577–606. 1925.
447. JEMISON, G. M. Beaufort scale of wind force as adapted for use on forested areas of the northern Rocky Mountains. *Jour. Agric. Res.*, 49: 77–82. 1934.
448. JEMISON, G. M. The significance of the effect of stand density upon the weather beneath the canopy. *Jour. For.*, 32: 446–451. 1934.
449. JENNY, H. A study of the influence of climate upon the nitrogen and organic matter content of the soil. *Mo. Agric. Exp. Sta., Res. Bull.* 152. 1930.
450. JENSEN, C. A. Relation of inorganic soil colloids to plowsole in citrus groves in southern California. *Jour. Agric. Res.*, 15: 505–519. 1918.
451. JOHANSEN, F. General observations on the vegetation. *Rept. Canadian Arctic Exped.* 1913–1918, 5: 3–580. 1926.
452. JOHNSON, C. Demonstration of peristome teeth movements. *New Phytol.*, 30: 218–219. 1931.
453. JOHNSON, J., and R. E. HARTMAN. Influence of soil environment on the rootrot of tobacco. *Jour. Agric. Res.*, 17: 41–86. 1919.
454. JOHNSON, L. An instrument for list charting. *Ecology*, 8: 282–283. 1927.
455. JOHNSTON, E. S. An index of hardiness in peach buds. *Amer. Jour. Bot.*, 6: 373–379. 1919.
456. JONES, J. S., and G. A. MITCHELL. The cause and control of yellow berry in turkey wheat grown under dry-farming conditions. *Jour. Agric. Res.*, 33: 281–292. 1926.
457. JONES, L. R. Soil temperature as a factor in phytopathology. *Plant World*, 20: 229–237. 1917.
458. JONES, L. R. The relation of environment to disease in plants. *Amer. Jour. Bot.*, 11: 601–609. 1924.
459. JONES, L. R., and W. B. TISDALE. Effect of soil temperature upon the development of nodules on the roots of certain legumes. *Jour. Agric. Res.*, 22: 17–31. 1921.
460. JONES, L. R., and W. B. TISDALE. The influence of soil temperature upon the development of flax wilt. *Phytopathology*, 12: 409–413. 1922.
461. JONES, L. R., *et al.* Fusarium resistant cabbage. *Wis. Agric. Exp. Sta., Res. Bull.* 48. 1920.
462. JONES, L. R., *et al.* Wisconsin studies upon the relation of soil temperature to plant disease. *Wis. Agric. Exp. Sta., Res. Bull.* 71. 1926.
463. JOSEPH, H. C. Germination and vitality of birch seeds. *Bot. Gaz.*, 87: 127–151. 1929.
464. KEARNEY, T. H., and C. S. SCOFIELD. The choice of crops for saline land. *U. S. Dept. Agric., Circ.* 404. 1936.
465. KEARNEY, T. H., *et al.* Indicator significance of vegetation in Tooele valley, Utah. *Jour. Agric. Res.*, 1: 365–417. 1914.
466. KEEN, B. A. The physical properties of the soil. P. 93. Longmans, Green & Company, New York. 1931.
467. *Ibid.* P. 334.

468. KELLERMANN, K. F. A review of the discovery of photoperiodism: the influence of the length of daily light periods upon the growth of plants. *Quarterly Rev. Biol.*, 1: 87–94. 1926.

469. KELLEY, W. P., and S. M. BROWN. Principles governing the reclamation of alkali soils. *Hilgardia*, 8: 149–177. 1934.

470. KELLOGG, C. E. The place of soil in the biological complex. *Sci. Monthly*, 39: 46–51. 1934.

471. KELLOGG, C. E. Soil blowing and dust storms. *U. S. Dept. Agric., Misc. Pub.* 221. 1935.

472. KELLOGG, C. E. Development and significance of the great soil groups of the United States. *U. S. Dept. Agric., Misc. Pub.* 229. 1936.

473. KENDEIGH, S. C. A study of Merriam's temperature laws. *Wilson Bull.* 44: 129–143. 1932.

474. KENOYER, L. A. General and successional ecology of the lower tropical rainforest at Barro Colorado Island, Panama. *Ecology*, 10: 201–222. 1929.

475. KERNER, A., and F. W. OLIVER. The natural history of plants. Vol. 2. Henry Holt & Company, New York. Undated.

476. KIDD, F. The controlling influence of carbon dioxid in the maturation, dormancy, and germination of seeds. *Proc. Roy. Soc. London*, ser. B, 87: 408–421, 609–625. 1914. 89: 136–156. 1917.

477. KIESSELBACH, T. A. Studies concerning the elimination of experimental error in comparative crop tests. *Neb. Agric. Exp. Sta., Res. Bull.* 13. 1917.

478. KIESSELBACH, T. A., A. Anderson, and J. C. RUSSEL. Subsoil moisture and crop sequence in relation to alfalfa production. *Jour. Amer. Soc. Agron.*, 26: 422–442. 1934.

479. KIESSELBACH, T. A., J. C. RUSSEL, and A. ANDERSON. The significance of subsoil moisture in alfalfa production. *Jour. Amer. Soc. Agron.*, 21: 241–268. 1929. Review in *Ecology*, 11: 452–454. 1930.

480. KIESSELBACH, T. A., and R. M. WEIHING. The comparative root development of selfed lines of corn and their F_1 and F_2 hybrids. *Jour. Amer. Soc. Agron.*, 27: 538–541. 1935.

481. KIMBALL, H. H. Intensity of solar radiation at the surface of the earth, and its variations with latitude, altitude, season, and time of day. *Monthly Weather Rev.*, 63: 1–4. 1935.

482. KINCER, J. B. Temperature influence on planting and harvest dates. *Monthly Weather Rev.*, 47: 312–323. 1919.

483. KINCER, J. B. Precipitation and humidity. *U. S. Dept. Agric., Atlas of American Agriculture*. Pp. 1–48. 1922.

484. KINCER, J. B. The relation of climate to the geographic distribution of crops in the United States. *Ecology*, 3: 127–133. 1922.

485. KIRKPATRICK, T. W. The climate and eco-climates of coffee plantations. The Crown Agents for the Colonies, London. 1935. Review in *Jour. Ecol.*, 23: 542–543. 1935.

486. KITTREDGE, J. Evidence of the rate of forest succession on Star Island, Minnesota. *Ecology*, 15: 24–35. 1934.

487. KITTREDGE, J., and A. K. CHITTENDEN. Oak forests of northern Michigan. *Mich. Agric. Exp. Sta., Spec. Bull.* 190. 1929.

488. KITTREDGE, J., and S. R. GEVORKIANTZ. Forest possibilities of aspen lands in the Lake States. *Univ. Minn. Agric. Exp. Sta., Tech. Bull.* 60. 1929.

489. KLUGH, A. B. Ecological photometry and a new instrument for measuring light. *Ecology*, 6: 203–237. 1925.

490. KNIGHT, R. C.   The response of plants in soil- and in water-culture to aeration of the roots. *Ann. Bot.*, 38: 305–325. 1924.
491. KNOTT, J. E.   Further localization of the response in plant tissue to relative length of day and night. *Proc. Amer. Soc. Hort. Sci.*, 23: 67–70. 1926.
492. KNUCHEL, H.   Spectrophotometrische Untersuchungen im Walde. *Mitt. Schweiz. Central Anst. Forst. Vers.*, 11. 1914.
493. KNUDSON, L.   Hydrogen-ion concentration and plant growth. *Jour. Amer. Soc. Agron.*, 17: 711–716. 1925.
494. KNUTH, P.   Handbook of flower pollination. 3 vols. Clarendon Press, Oxford, 1906, 1908, 1909.
495. KOLKUNOV, V.   On the question of working out drouth-resistant races of cultivated plants. Kiev, Russia. 1905.
496. KOLMORGEN, W.   Rainmakers of the plains. *Sci. Monthly*, 40: 146–152. 1935.
497. KORSTIAN, C. F.   The indicator significance of native vegetation in the determination of forest sites. *Plant World*, 20: 267–287. 1917.
498. KORSTIAN, C. F.   Density of cell sap in relation to environmental conditions in the Wasatch mountains of Utah. *Jour. Agric. Res.*, 28: 845–907. 1924.
499. KORSTIAN, C. F.   Some ecological effects of shading coniferous nursery stock. *Ecology*, 6: 48–51. 1925.
500. KORSTIAN, C. F.   Factors controlling germination and early survival in oaks. *Yale Univ., School For., Bull.* 19. 1927.
501. KORSTIAN, C. F., and F. S. BAKER.   Forest planting in the intermountain region. *U. S. Dept. Agric., Dept. Bull.* 1264. 1925.
502. KORSTIAN, C. F., and N. J. FETHEROLF.   Control of stem girdle of spruce transplants caused by excessive heat. *Phytopathology*, 11: 485–490. 1921.
503. KORSTIAN, C. F., and P. W. STICKEL.   The natural replacement of blight-killed chestnut in the hardwood forests of the northeast. *Jour. Agric. Res.*, 34: 631–648. 1927.
504. KRAEBEL, C. J.   Erosion control on mountain roads. *U. S. Dept. Agric., Circ.* 380. 1936.
505. KRAMER, J., and J. E. WEAVER.   Relative efficiency of roots and tops of plants in protecting the soil from erosion. *Conservation Dept. Univ. Neb., Bull.* 12. 1936.
506. KRAMER, P. J.   Effect of variation in length of day on growth and dormancy of trees. *Plant Physiol.*, 11: 127–137. 1936.
506a. KRAMER, P. J.   Photoperiodic stimulation of growth by artificial light as a cause of winter killing. *Plant Physiol.*, 12: 881–883. 1937.
507. KRAMER, P. J., and J. R. JESTER.   Further investigations of the effect of length of day on the length of growing season of woody plants. *Amer. Jour. Bot.*, 23: 693. 1936.
508. KRASSOVSKY, I.   The competition of primary and secondary crops in mixed cultures. *Bull. Appl. Bot., Gen. and Plant-breeding*, 25: 318–323. 1930–1931.
509. KROODSMA, R. F.   The permanent fixation of sand dunes in Michigan. *Jour. For.*, 35: 365–371. 1937.
510. KURZ, H.   Hydrogen ion concentration in relation to ecological factors. *Bot. Gaz.*, 76: 1–29. 1923.
511. KURZ, H.   Influence of sphagnum and other mosses on bog reactions. *Ecology*, 9: 56–69. 1928.
512. KURZ, H.   The relation of pH to plant distribution in nature. *Amer. Nat.*, 64: 314–341. 1930.

513. Kurz, H., and D. Demaree. Cypress buttresses and knees in relation to water and air. *Ecology*, 15: 36–41. 1934.

514. Lagerheim, G., and H. Witte. Stratiotes aloides L. funnen in Sveriges postglaciala aflagringar. *Geol. Fören. Förh.*, 27: 443. 1905.

515. Larsen, J. A. Natural reproduction after forest fires in northern Idaho. *Jour. Agric. Res.*, 30: 1177–1197. 1925.

516. Larsen, J. A. Relation of leaf structure of conifers to light and moisture. *Ecology*, 8: 371–377. 1927.

517. Larsen, J. A. Fire and forest succession in the Bitterroot Mountains of northern Idaho. *Ecology*, 10: 67–76. 1929.

518. Larsen, J. A. Forest types of the Northern Rocky Mountains and their climatic controls. *Ecology*, 11: 631–672. 1930.

519. Larsen, J. A. Natural spreading of planted black locust in southeastern Ohio. *Jour. For.*, 33: 616–619. 1935.

520. Laurie, A., and G. H. Poesch. Photoperiodism—the value of supplementary illumination and reduction of light on flowering plants in the greenhouse. *Ohio Agric. Exp. Sta., Bull.* 512. 1932.

521. Lauritzen, J. I., and L. L. Harter. The relation of humidity to infection of the sweet potato by Rhizopus. *Jour. Agric. Res.*, 33: 527–539. 1926.

522. Leding, A. R., and L. R. Lytton. Effects of plant spacing and irrigation on number of locks in cotton bolls. *Jour. Agric. Res.*, 47: 33–52. 1933.

523. Lee, B., and J. H. Priestley. The plant cuticle. *Ann. Bot.*, 38: 525–545. 1924.

524. Lees, R. D. Root development in wheat. *Agric. Gaz. New South Wales*, 35: 609–612. 1924.

525. Lehenbauer, P. A. Growth of maize seedlings in relation to temperature. *Physiol. Res.*, 1: 247–288. 1914.

526. Lehmann, E. W., and F. P. Hanson. Saving soil by the use of Mangum terraces. *Ill. Agric. Exp. Sta., Circ.* 290. 1924.

527. Leukel, W. A. Deposition and utilization of reserve foods in alfalfa plants. *Jour. Amer. Soc. Agron.*, 19: 596–623. 1927.

528. Levitt, J., and G. W. Scarth. Frost-hardening studies with living cells. I. Osmotic and bound water changes in relation to frost resistance and the seasonal cycle. *Canadian Jour. Res. C.*, 14: 267–284. 1936.

529. Levitt, J., and G. W. Scarth. Frost-hardening studies with living cells. II. Permeability in relation to frost resistance and the seasonal cycle. *Canadian Jour. Res. C.*, 14: 285–305. 1936.

530. Levy, E. B., and E. A. Madden. The point method of pasture analysis. *New Zealand Jour. Agric.*, 46: 267–279. 1933.

531. Lewis, F. J., and E. S. Dowding. The vegetation and retrogressive changes of peat areas ("muskegs") in Central Alberta. *Jour. Ecol.*, 14: 317–341. 1926.

532. Lewis, F. J., and G. M. Tuttle. Osmotic properties of some plant cells at low temperatures. *Ann. Bot.*, 34: 405–416. 1920.

533. Lewis, F. J., *et al.* The vegetation of Alberta. II. The swamp, moor and bog forest vegetation of Central Alberta. *Jour. Ecol.*, 16: 19–70. 1928.

534. Li, Tsi-Tung. Soil temperature as influenced by forest cover. *Yale Univ., School For., Bull.* 18. 1926.

535. Lipman, C. B., and G. N. Lewis. Tolerance for liquid-air temperatures by seeds of higher plants for sixty days. *Plant Physiol.*, 9: 392–394. 1934.

536. Livermore, J. R. A critical study of some of the factors concerned in measuring the effect of selection in the potato. *Jour. Amer. Soc. Agron.*, 19: 857–896. 1927.

537. LIVINGSTON, B. E.   Physiological temperature indices for the study of plant growth in relation to climatic conditions.   *Physiol. Res.*, 1: 399–420.   1916.

538. LIVINGSTON, B. E.   Atmometers of porous porcelain and paper, their use in physiological ecology.   *Ecology*, 16: 438–472.   1935.

539. LIVINGSTON, B. E., and E. E. FREE.   The effect of deficient soil oxygen on the roots of higher plants.   *The Johns Hopkins Univ., Circ.* 1917: 380.   1917.

540. LIVINGSTON, B. E., and F. W. HAASIS.   The measurement of evaporation in freezing weather.   *Jour. Ecol.*, 17: 315–328.   1929.

541. LIVINGSTON, B. E., and F. SHREVE.   The distribution of vegetation in the United States, as related to climatic conditions.   *Carnegie Inst. Wash., Pub.* 284.   1921.

542. LODEWICK, J. E.   Effect of certain climatic factors on the diameter growth of longleaf pine in western Florida.   *Jour. Agric. Res.*, 41: 349–363.   1930.

543. LOEHWING, W. F.   Physiological aspects of the effect of continuous soil aeration on plant growth.   *Plant Physiol.*, 9: 567–583.   1934.

543a. LOEHWING, W. F.   Root interactions of plants.   *Bot. Rev.*, 3: 195–239.   1937.

544. LOFTFIELD, J. V. G.   The behavior of stomata.   *Carnegie Inst. Wash., Pub.* 314.   1921.

545. LOOMIS, W. E.   Studies in the transplanting of vegetable plants.   *Cornell Univ. Agric. Exp. Sta., Mem.* 87.   1925.

546. LOVELL, J. H.   The flower and the bee.   Charles Scribner's Sons, New York.   1918.

547. LOWDERMILK, W. C.   Factors affecting reproduction of Engelmann spruce.   *Jour. Agric. Res.*, 30: 995–1009.   1925.

548. LOWDERMILK, W. C.   Factors influencing the surface run-off of rain waters.   *Proc. Pan-Pacific Sci. Congr., 3rd Congr., Tokyo*, 1926 (1928).

549. LOWDERMILK, W. C.   Influence of forest litter on run-off, percolation, and erosion.   *Jour. For.*, 28: 474–491.   1930.

550. LUNDEGARDH, H.   Environment and plant development.   Translated by E. Ashby.   Edward Arnold & Company, London.   1931.

551. LUTE, A. M.   Impermeable seed of alfalfa.   *Colo. Agric. Exp. Sta., Bull.* 326.   1928.

552. LUTZ, H. J.   Trends and silvicultural significance of upland forest successions in southern New England.   *Yale Univ., School For., Bull.* 22.   1928.

553. LUTZ, H. J.   Effect of cattle grazing on vegetation of a virgin forest in northwestern Pennsylvania.   *Jour. Agric. Res.*, 41: 561–570.   1930.

554. LUTZ, H. J.   The vegetation of Heart's Content, a virgin forest in northwestern Pennsylvania.   *Ecology*, 11: 1–29.   1930.

555. LUTZ, H. J.   Ecological relations in the pitch pine plains of southern New Jersey.   *Yale Univ., School For., Bull.* 38.   1934.

555a. LUTZ, H. J., J. B. ELY, and S. LITTLE.   The influence of soil profile horizons on root distribution of white pine (Pinus strobus L.).   *Yale Univ., School For., Bull.* 44.   1937.

556. LYON, C. J.   Tree ring width as an index of physiological dryness in New England.   *Ecology*, 17: 457–478.   1936.

557. MACDOUGAL, D. T.   Botanical features of North American deserts.   *Carnegie Inst. Wash., Pub.* 99.   1908.

558. MACDOUGAL, D. T.   The reactions of plants to new habitats.   *Ecology*, 2: 1–20.   1921.

559. MACDOUGAL, D. T., and E. S. SPALDING.   The water-balance of succulent plants.   *Carnegie Inst. Wash., Pub.* 141.   1910.

560. MacDougal, D. T., and H. A. Spoehr. The origination of xerophytism. *Plant World*, 21: 245–249. 1918.

561. MacDougal, D. T., *et al.* Basis of succulence in plants. *Bot. Gaz.*, 67: 405–416. 1919.

562. MacKinney, A. L. Effects of forest litter on soil temperature and soil freezing in autumn and winter. *Ecology*, 10: 312–321. 1929.

563. MacKinney, A. L. Increase in growth of loblolly pines left after partial cutting. *Jour. Agric. Res.*, 47: 807–821. 1933.

564. Magness, J. R. Status of orchard soil moisture research. *Proc. Amer. Soc. Hort. Sci.*, 32: 651–661. 1934.

565. Mallery, T. D. Rainfall records for the Sonoran Desert. *Ecology*, 17: 110–121. 1936.

566. Malmsten, H. E. Combination of list and chart quadrat methods for grazing studies. *Ecology*, 11: 749–751. 1930.

567. Marbut, C. F. Soils of the Great Plains. *Ann. Assoc. Amer. Geog.*, 13: 41–66. 1923.

568. Marbut, C. F. Soils of the United States. U. S. Dept. Agric., Atlas of American Agriculture, part 3. 1935.

569. Marloth, R. Results of further experiments on Table Mountain for ascertaining the amount of moisture deposited from the south-east clouds. *Trans. South African Phil. Soc.*, 16: 97–105. 1905.

570. Marshall, R. Influence of precipitation cycles on forestry. *Jour. For.*, 25: 415–429. 1927.

571. Martin, E. V. Effect of solar radiation on transpiration of Helianthus annuus. *Plant Physiol.*, 10: 341–354. 1935.

572. Martin, E. V., and F. E. Clements. Studies of the effect of artificial wind on growth and transpiration in Helianthus annuus. *Plant Physiol.*, 10: 613–636. 1935.

573. Martin, J. H. Comparative studies of winter hardiness in wheat. *Jour. Agric. Res.*, 35: 493–535. 1927.

574. Martonne, E. de. Traité de géographie physique. 4th ed. Paris. 1925.

575. Mattoon, W. R. Long leaf pine. *U. S. Dept. Agric., Bull.* 1061. 1922.

576. Maximov, N. A. Internal factors of frost and drought resistance in plants. *Protoplasma*, 7: 259–291. 1929.

577. Maximov, N. A. The plant in relation to water. Pp. 249–283. George Allen & Unwin, Ltd., London. 1929.

578. Maximov, N. A. The physiological significance of the xeromorphic structure of plants. *Jour. Ecol.*, 19: 273–282. 1931.

579. Maximov, N. A. The theoretical significance of vernalization. *Imp. Bur. Plant Genetics, Herb. Pub. Series, Bull.* 16. 1934.

580. McArdle, R. E. The relation of mycorrhizae to conifer seedlings. *Jour. Agric. Res.*, 44: 287–316. 1932.

581. McAtee, W. L. The relation of birds to woodlots in New York state. *Roosevelt Wild Life Bull.*, 4: 7–148. 1926.

582. McClelland, T. B. Studies of the photoperiodism of some economic plants. *Jour. Agric. Res.*, 37: 603–628. 1928.

583. McColloch, J. W. The role of insects in soil deterioration. *Jour. Amer. Soc. Agron.*, 18: 143–150. 1926.

584. McColloch, J. W., and W. P. Hayes. Soil temperature and its influence on white grub activities. *Ecology*, 4: 29–36. 1923.

585. McComb, A. L. The relation between acorn weight and the development of one year chestnut oak seedlings. *Jour. For.*, 32: 479–484. 1934.

586. McDougall, W. B.   On the mycorhizas of forest trees.   *Amer. Jour. Bot.*, 1: 51–74.   1914.

587. McDougall, W. B.   Thick-walled root hairs of Gleditsia and related genera. *Amer. Jour. Bot.*, 8: 171–175.   1921.

588. McDougall, W. B.   Mycorhizas of coniferous trees.   *Jour. For.*, 20: 255–260.   1922.

589. McDougall, W. B., and M. C. Jacobs.   Tree mycorhizas from the central Rocky Mountain region.   *Amer. Jour. Bot.*, 14: 258–266.   1927.

590. McDougall, W. B., and W. T. Penfound.   Ecological anatomy of some deciduous forest plants.   *Ecology*, 9: 349–353.   1928.

591. McGinnies, W. G.   The quadrat.   *Jour. For.*, 28: 23–27.   1930.

592. McHargue, J. S.   The occurrence of copper, manganese, zinc, nickel, and cobalt in soils, plants and animals, and their possible function as vital factors. *Jour. Agric. Res.*, 30: 193–196.   1925.

593. McIntosh, A. C.   The botanical survey of the Black Hills of South Dakota. *Black Hills Engineer*, 19: 157–276.   1931.

594. McKay, E.   Photosynthesis in Grimmia montana.   *Plant Physiol.*, 10: 803–809.   1935.

595. McLean, R. C.   Studies in the ecology of tropical rain-forest.   *Jour. Ecol.*, 7: 5–54.   1919.

596. McQuilkin, W. E.   Root development of pitch pine, with some comparative observations on shortleaf pine.   *Jour. Agric. Res.*, 51: 983–1016.   1935.

597. Meier, F. C.   Collecting micro-organisms from the arctic atmosphere, with field notes and material by Charles A. Lindbergh.   *Sci. Monthly*, 40: 5–20. 1935.

598. Meinzer, O. E.   Plants as indicators of ground water.   *U. S. Geol. Surv., Water-supply Paper* 577.   1927.

599. Melin, E.   Untersuchungen über die Bedeutung der Baummykorrhiza.   Eine ökologische-physiologische Studie.   Gustav Fischer, Jena.   1925.   Review in *Jour. Ecol.*, 14: 164–167.   1926.

600. Merriam, C. H.   Life zones and crop zones of the United States.   *U. S. Dept. Agric., Div. Biol. Surv., Bull.* 10.   1898.

601. Metcalf, W.   The influence of windbreaks in protecting citrus orchards. *Jour. For.*, 34: 571–580.   1936.

602. Mevius, W.   Reaktion des Bodens und Pflanzenwachstum.   In Naturwissenschaft und Landwirtschaft, edited by Boas, Neuberg, and Rippel, Vol. 11. F. P. Datterer & Co., Freising-München.   1927.

603. Meyer, B. S.   Seasonal variations in the physical and chemical properties of the leaves of the pitch pine, with especial reference to cold resistance.   *Amer. Jour. Bot.*, 15: 449–472.   1928.

604. Meyer, B. S.   Further studies on cold resistance in evergreens, with special reference to the possible rôle of bound water.   *Bot. Gaz.*, 94: 297–321.   1932.

605. Miller, E. C.   Comparative study of the root systems and leaf areas of corn and the sorghums.   *Jour. Agric. Res.*, 6: 311–332.   1916.

606. Miller, E. C.   Plant physiology.   Pp. 362–365.   McGraw-Hill Book Company, Inc., New York.   1931.

607. Miller, E. C., and A. R. Saunders.   Some observations on the temperature of the leaves of crop plants.   *Jour. Agric. Res.*, 26: 15–43.   1923.

608. Miller, M. F.   The soil and its management.   Ginn and Company, Boston. 1924.

609. Miller, M. F.   Cropping systems in relation to erosion control.   *Mo. Agric. Exp. Sta., Bull.* 366.   1936.

610. MILLER, M. F., and H. H. KRUSEKOPF. The influence of systems of cropping and methods of culture on surface runoff and soil erosion. *Mo. Agric. Exp. Sta., Res. Bull.* 177. 1932.

611. MITCHELL, E. Germination of seeds of plants native to Dutchess county, New York. *Bot. Gaz.,* 81: 108–112. 1926.

611a. MITCHELL, H. L., R. F. FINN, and R. O. ROSENDAHL. The relation between mycorrhizae and the growth and nutrient absorption of coniferous seedlings in nursery beds. *Black Rock Forest Papers,* 1 (10): 58–73. 1937.

612. MITCHELL, J. W. Effect of atmospheric humidity on rate of carbon fixation by plants. *Bot. Gaz.,* 98: 87–104. 1936.

613. MOCHKOV, B. S. To the question of photoperiodism of certain woody species. *Bull. Appl. Bot., Gen. and Plant-breeding,* 23: 509–510. 1929–1930.

614. MOHAMMAD, A., and R. B. DESHPANDE. Studies in Indian chillies. II. The root-system. *Agric. Jour. India,* 24: 251–258. 1929.

615. MOOERS, C. A. The effect of spacing on the yield of cotton. *Jour. Amer. Soc. Agron.,* 20: 211–230. 1928.

616. MOORE, B. Reproduction in the coniferous forests of northern New England. *Bot. Gaz.,* 64: 149–158. 1917.

617. MOORE, B. The scope of ecology. *Ecology,* 1: 3–5. 1920.

618. MOORE, B. Humus and root systems in certain northeastern forests in relation to reproduction and competition. *Jour. For.,* 20: 233–254. 1922.

619. MOORE, B. Influence of certain soil and light conditions on the establishment of reproduction in northeastern conifers. *Ecology,* 7: 191–220. 1926.

620. MOORE, B. Biological forest types in the Adirondack region. *Ecology,* 16: 648–651. 1935.

621. MOORE, B., and N. TAYLOR. Vegetation of Mount Desert Island, Maine, and its environment. *Brooklyn Bot. Garden Memoirs,* 3: 1–151. 1927.

622. MOSIER, J. G., and A. F. GUSTAFSON. Soil moisture and tillage for corn. *Ill. Agric. Exp. Sta., Bull.* 181. 1915.

623. MOSS, E. H. The vegetation of Alberta. IV. The poplar association and related vegetation of central Alberta. *Jour. Ecol.,* 20: 380–415. 1932.

624. MUELLER, D. Die Kohlensäureassimilation bei arktischen Pflanzen und die Abhängigkeit der Assimilation von der Temperatur. *Planta Arch. Wiss. Bot.,* 6: 22–39. 1928.

625. MUENSCHER, W. C. Seed germination in Lobelia, with special reference to the influence of light on Lobelia inflata. *Jour. Agric. Res.,* 52: 627–631. 1936.

626. MUENSCHER, W. C. Storage and germination of seeds of aquatic plants. *Cornell Univ. Agric. Exp. Sta., Bull.* 652. 1936.

627. MÜLLER, H. The fertilization of flowers. Macmillan & Company, Ltd., London. 1883.

628. MUNGER, T. T. Western yellow pine in Oregon. *U. S. Dept. Agric., Bull.* 418. 1917.

629. MUNGER, T. T., and W. B. GREELEY. Timber growing and logging practice in the Douglas fir region. *U. S. Dept. Agric., Dept. Bull.* 1493. 1927.

630. MUNNS, E. N., and I. H. SIMS. Forests in flood control. *Suppl. Rept. Com. Flood Control.* H. R. 12517. 1936.

631. MURRAY, S. M., and P. GLOVER. Some practical points regarding the detailed botanical analysis of grass-veld or other pastures by the list quadrat method. *Jour. Ecol.,* 23: 536–539. 1935.

632. MYERS, H. E. The differential influence of certain vegetative covers on deep subsoil moisture. *Jour. Amer. Soc. Agron.,* 28: 106–114. 1936.

633. NEDROW, W. W. Studies on the ecology of roots. *Ecology,* 18: 27–52. 1937.

634. NELSON, E. W.   Methods of studying shrubby plants in relation to grazing. *Ecology*, 11: 764–769.   1930.
635. NELSON, N. T.   The effects of frequent cutting on the production, root reserves, and behavior of alfalfa.   *Jour. Amer. Soc. Agron.*, 17: 100–113.   1925.
636. NEWTON, R.   The nature and practical measurement of frost resistance in winter wheat.   *Univ. Alta., Coll. Agric., Research Bull.* 1: 1–53.   1924.
637. NEWTON, R., and J. A. ANDERSON.   Respiration of winter wheat plants at low temperatures.   *Canadian Jour. Res.*, 5: 337–354.   1931.
638. NEWTON, R., and W. R. BROWN.   Frost precipitation of proteins of plant juice.   *Canadian Jour. Res.*, 5: 87–110.   1931.
639. NEWTON, R., and W. M. MARTIN.   Physico-chemical studies on the nature of drought resistance in crop plants.   *Canadian Jour. Res.*, 3: 336–427.   1930.
640. NICHOLS, G. E.   The vegetation of northern Cape Breton Island, Nova Scotia. *Trans. Conn. Acad. Arts & Sci.*, 22: 249–467.   1918.
641. NICHOLS, G. E.   The vegetation of Connecticut.   *Torreya*, 13: 89–112; 199–215; 14: 167–194.   1913, 1914.   *Bull. Torrey Bot. Club*, 42: 169–217; 43: 235-264; 47: 89–117.   1915, 1916, 1920.
642. NICHOLS, G. E.   A working basis for the ecological classification of plant communities.   *Ecology*, 4: 11–23; 154–179.   1923.
643. NICHOLS, G. E.   The terrestrial environment in its relation to plant life.   In Organic adaptation to environment.   Pp. 1–43.   Yale University Press, New Haven.   1924.
644. NICHOLS, G. E.   The influence of exposure to winter temperatures upon seed germination in various native American plants.   *Ecology*, 15: 364–373. 1934.
645. NICHOLS, G. E.   The hemlock-white pine-northern hardwood region of eastern North America.   *Ecology*, 16: 403–422.   1935.
646. NIGHTINGALE, G. T.   Effects of temperature on metabolism in tomato.   *Bot. Gaz.*, 95: 35–58.   1933.
647. NIGHTINGALE, G. T.   Effects of temperature on growth, anatomy, and metabolism of apple and peach roots.   *Bot. Gaz.*, 96: 581–639.   1935.
648. NIKIFOROFF, C. C.   General trends of the desert type of soil formation.   *Soil Science*, 43: 105–131.   1937.
649. NORMAN, A. G.   The natural decomposition of plant materials.   *Sci. Prog.*, 27: 470–485.   1933.
650. OHGA, I.   The germination of century-old and recently harvested Indian lotus fruits, with special reference to the effect of oxygen supply.   *Amer. Jour. Bot.*, 13: 754–759.   1926.
651. OSTENFELD, C. H.   Skildringer af vegetationen i Island.   *Bot. Tidskr.*, 22: 227–253.   1899.
652. OSVALD, H.   Untersuchungen über die Einwirkung des Grundwasserstandes auf die Bewurzelung von Wiesenpflanzen auf Moorboden.   *Fühling's Landw. Zeitschr.*, 68: 321, 370.   1919.
653. PACK, D. A.   After-ripening and germination of Juniperus seeds.   *Bot. Gaz.*, 71: 32–60.   1921.
654. PALLADIN, V. I.   Plant physiology. 2d ed.   P. 14.   P. Blakiston's Son & Company, Philadelphia.   1923.
655. PALMER, A. H.   The agricultural significance of sunshine as illustrated in California.   *Monthly Weather Rev.*, 48: 151–154.   1920.
656. PALMER, L. J.   Progress of reindeer grazing investigations in Alaska.   *U. S. Dept. Agric., Dept. Bull.* 1423.   1926.

657. PARKER, K. W., and A. W. SAMPSON. Growth and yield of certain Gramineae as influenced by reduction of photosynthetic tissue. *Hilgardia*, 5: 361–381. 1931.

658. PARKER, R. L. The collection and utilization of pollen by the honeybee. *Cornell Univ. Agric. Exp. Sta., Mem.* 98. 1926.

659. PAVLYCHENKO, T. K. Quantitative study of the entire root systems of weed and crop plants under field conditions. *Ecology*, 18: 62–79. 1937.

660. PAVLYCHENKO, T. K. The soil-block washing method in quantitative root study. *Canadian Jour. Res. C*, 15: 33–57. 1937.

661. PAVLYCHENKO, T. K., and J. B. HARRINGTON. Competitive efficiency of weeds and cereal crops. *Canadian Jour. Res.*, 10: 77–94. 1934.

662. PAVLYCHENKO, T. K., and J. B. HARRINGTON. Root development of weeds and crops in competition under dry farming. *Sci. Agric.*, 16: 151–160. 1935.

663. PEARSALL, W. H. The statistical analysis of vegetation; a criticism of the concepts and methods of the Upsala school. *Jour. Ecol.*, 12: 135–139. 1924.

664. PEARSE, C. K., and S. B. WOOLLEY. The influence of range plant cover on the rate of absorption of surface water by soils. *Jour. For.*, 34: 844–847. 1936.

665. PEARSE, K. An area-list method of measuring range plant populations. *Ecology*, 16: 573–579. 1935.

666. PEARSON, G. A. Studies in artificial reseeding. *U. S. Dept. Agric., Rev. Forest Service Invest.*, 2: 9–13. 1913.

667. PEARSON, G. A. Factors controlling the distribution of forest types. *Ecology*, 1: 139–159, 289–308. 1920.

668. PEARSON, G. A. Natural reproduction of western yellow pine in the southwest. *U. S. Dept. Agric., Dept. Bull.* 1105. 1923.

669. PEARSON, G. A. The other side of the light question. *Jour. For.*, 27: 807–812. 1929.

670. PEARSON, G. A. Light and moisture in forestry. *Ecology*, 11: 145–160. 1930.

671. PEARSON, G. A. Studies of climate and soil in relation to forest management in the southwestern United States. *Jour. Ecol.*, 18: 139–144. 1930.

672. PEARSON, G. A. Forest types in the southwest as determined by climate and soil. *U. S. Dept. Agric., Tech. Bull.* 247. 1931.

673. PEARSON, G. A. A twenty year record of changes in an Arizona pine forest. *Ecology*, 14: 272–285. 1933.

674. PEARSON, G. A. Some observations on the reaction of pine seedlings to shade. *Ecology*, 17: 270–276. 1936.

675. PEARSON, G. A. Why the prairies are treeless. *Jour. For.*, 34: 405–408. 1936.

676. PEARSON, G. A., and R. E. MARSH. Timber growing and logging practice in the southwest and in the Black Hills region. *U. S. Dept. Agric., Tech. Bull.* 480. 1935.

677. PEASE, V. A. Duration of leaves in evergreens. *Amer. Jour. Bot.*, 4: 145–160. 1917.

678. PECHANEC, J. F., and G. D. PICKFORD. A comparison of some methods used in determining percentage utilization of range grasses. *Jour. Agric. Res.*, 54: 753–765. 1937.

679. PEIRCE, G. J. The dissemination and germination of Arceuthobium occidentale, Eng. *Ann. Bot.*, 19: 99–113. 1905.

680. PELTIER, G. L. Distribution and prevalence of Ozonium root rot in the shelter-belt zone of Texas. *Phytopathology*, 27: 145–158. 1937.

681. Peltier, G. L., and H. M. Tysdal. A method for the determination of comparative hardiness in seedling alfalfas by controlled hardening and artificial freezing. *Jour. Agric. Res.*, 44: 429–444. 1932.

682. Peralta, F. de. Some principles of competition as illustrated by Sudan grass, Holcus sorghum sudanensis (Piper) Hitch. *Ecol. Mono.*, 5: 355–404. 1935.

683. Peren, G. S. Data on the lateral spread of the roots of fruit trees. *Jour. Pom. and Hort. Sci.*, 3: 96–102. 1923.

684. Pessin, L. J. Epiphyllous plants of certain regions in Jamaica. *Bull. Torrey Bot. Club*, 49: 1–14. 1922.

685. Pessin, L. J. Forest associations in the uplands of the lower gulf coastal plain (longleaf pine belt). *Ecology*, 14: 1–14. 1933.

686. Phillips, J. The biotic community. *Jour. Ecol.*, 19: 1–24. 1931.

687. Phillips, J. Succession, development, the climax, and the complex organism: an analysis of concepts. I. *Jour. Ecol.*, 22: 554–571. 1934.

688. Phillips, J. Succession, development, the climax, and the complex organism: an analysis of concepts. II. Development and the climax. *Jour. Ecol.*, 23: 210–246. 1935.

689. Phillips, J. Succession, development, the climax, and the complex organism: an analysis of concepts. III. The complex organism: conclusions. *Jour. Ecol.*, 23: 488–508. 1935.

690. Phillips, J. F. V. Experimental vegetation: the use of South African indigenous tree seedlings as phytometers. *South African Jour. Sci.*, 22: 197–214. 1925.

691. Phillips, J. F. V. Rainfall interception by plants. *Nature*, 118: 837–838. 1926.

692. Phillips, J. F. V. The behavior of Acacia melanoxylon R. Br. ("Tasmanian Blackwood") in the Knysna forests: an ecological study. *Trans. Roy. Soc. South Africa*, 16: part I, 31–43. 1928.

693. Pickford, G. D. The influence of continued heavy grazing and of promiscuous burning on spring-fall ranges in Utah. *Ecology*, 13: 159–171. 1932.

694. Pickford, G. D., and G. Stewart. Coordinate method of mapping low shrubs. *Ecology*, 16: 257–261. 1935.

695. Pipal, F. J. Red sorrel and its control. *Ind. Agric. Exp. Sta., Bull.* 197. 1916.

696. Piper, C. V. Flora of the state of Washington. *Contr. U. S. Nat. Herb.*, 11. 1906.

697. Plummer, F. G. Lightning in relation to forest fires. *U. S. Dept. Agric., Forest Service, Bull.* 111. 1912.

698. Plummer, F. G. Forest fires; their causes, extent and effects, with a summary of recorded destruction and loss. *U. S. Dept. Agric., Forest Service, Bull.* 117. 1912.

699. Polunin, N. The vegetation of the Akpatok Island. I. *Jour. Ecol.*, 22: 337–395. 1934. II. 23: 161–209. 1935.

700. Pond, R. H. The biological relation of aquatic plants to the substratum. *U. S. Com. Fish & Fisheries, Rept.* 1903: 485–526. 1905.

701. Pool, R. J. A study of the vegetation of the sandhills of Nebraska. *Minn. Bot. Studies*, 4: 189–312. 1914.

702. Pool, R. J. The invasion of a planted prairie grove. *Proc. Soc. Amer. For.*, 10: 1–8. 1915.

703. Pool, R. J. Xerophytism and comparative leaf anatomy in relation to transpiring power. *Bot. Gaz.*, 221–240. 1923.

704. Popp, H. W., and F. Brown. A review of recent work on the effect of ultra-violet radiation upon seed plants. *Bull. Torrey Bot. Club*, 60: 161–210. 1933.

705. Popp, H. W., and F. Brown. The effect of ultra-violet radiation upon seed plants. In Duggar, Biological effects of radiation. Vol. 2. Pp. 853–887. McGraw-Hill Book Company, Inc., New York. 1936.

706. Post, L. V. Einige südschwedischen Quellmoore. *Bull. Geol. Inst. Upsala*, 15: 219–278. 1916.

707. Pound, R., and F. E. Clements. The phytogeography of Nebraska. 1898. 2d ed. Jacob North & Company, Lincoln. 1900.

708. Priestley, J. H. Light and growth. I. The effect of brief light exposure upon etiolated plants. *New Phytol.*, 24: 271–283. 1925.

709. Priestley, J. H. The biology of the living chloroplast. *New Phytol.*, 28: 197–217. 1929.

710. Priestley, J. H., and L. M. Woffenden. Physiological studies in plant anatomy. *New Phytol.*, 21: 252–268. 1922.

711. Pulling, H. E. Root habit and plant distribution in the far north. *Plant World*, 21: 223–233. 1918.

712. Quayle, E. T. Local rain-producing influences under human control in South Australia. *Proc. Roy. Soc. Victoria*, 24: 89. 1922.

712a. Raber, O. Water utilization by trees, with special reference to the economic forest species of the north temperate zone. *U. S. Dept. Agric., Misc. Pub.* 257. 1937.

713. Ramaley, F. Influence of supplemental light on blooming. *Bot. Gaz.*, 96: 165–174. 1934.

714. Ramsbottom, J. Orchid mycorrhiza. *Trans. British Mycol. Soc.*, 8: 28–61. 1923.

715. Rathbun-Gravatt, A. Germination loss of coniferous seeds due to parasites. *Jour. Agric. Res.*, 42: 71–92. 1931.

716. Raunkiaer, C. The life forms of plants and statistical plant geography. Oxford University Press, New York. 1934.

717. Rayner, M. C. Mycorrhiza in the Ericaceae. *Trans. British Mycol. Soc.*, 8: 61–66. 1923.

718. Rayner, M. C. Mycorrhiza, an account of non-pathogenic infection by fungi in vascular plants and bryophytes. *New Phytol.* reprint 15. Weldon & Wesley, London. Reviewed in *Jour. Ecol.*, 16: 169–170. 1928.

719. Rayner, M. C. The mycorrhizal habit in relation to forestry. *Forestry*, 10: 1–22. 1936.

720. Redington, G. The effect of the duration of light upon the growth and development of the plant. *Biol. Rev. and Proc. Cambridge Phil. Soc.*, 4: 180–208. 1929.

721. Reitz, L. P., M. A. Bell, and H. E. Tower. Crested wheatgrass in Montana: comparisons with slender wheatgrass and brome grass. *Mont. Agric. Exp. Sta., Bull.* 323. 1936.

721a. Renner, F. G. Conditions influencing erosion on the Boise River watershed. *U. S. Dept. Agric., Tech. Bull.* 528. 1936.

722. Ridley, H. N. On the dispersal of seeds by wind. *Ann. Bot.*, 19: 351–363. 1905.

723. Ridley, H. N. The dispersal of plants throughout the world. L. Reeve & Company, Ltd., Ashford, England. 1930.

724. Rigg, G. B. Growth of trees in Sphagnum. *Bot. Gaz.*, 65: 359–362. 1918.

725. Rigg, G. B., and C. T. Richardson. The development of sphagnum bogs in the San Juan Islands. *Amer. Jour. Bot.*, 21: 610–622. 1934.

726. ROBBINS, W. J.   Precipitation and the growth of oaks at Columbia, Mo. *Mo. Agric. Exp. Sta., Res. Bull.* 44. 1921.
727. ROBBINS, W. R.   Relation of nutrient salt concentration to growth of the tomato and to the incidence of blossom-end rot of the fruit.   *Plant Physiol.,* 12: 21–50. 1937.
728. ROBBINS, W. W.   Native vegetation and climate of Colorado in their relation to agriculture.   *Colo. Agric. Exp. Sta., Bull.* 224. 1917.
729. ROBERTS, E. A.   The epidermal cells of roots.   *Bot. Gaz.,* 62: 488–506. 1916.
730. ROBERTS, H. H., and B. E. STRUCKMEYER.   The effect of temperature upon the responses of plants to photoperiod.   *Science,* 85: 290. 1937.
731. ROBERTSON, D. W., and A. M. LUTE.   Germination of the seed of farm crops in Colorado after storage for various periods of years.   *Jour. Agric. Res.,* 46: 455–462. 1933.
732. ROBERTSON, J. H.   Effect of frequent clipping on the development of certain grass seedlings.   *Plant Physiol.,* 8: 425–447. 1933.
733. ROBINSON, G. W.   Soils—Their origin, constitution, and classification. 2d ed. P. 224.   Thomas Murby & Co., London. 1936.
734. ROBINSON, R. R., W. H. PIERRE, and R. A. ACKERMAN.   A comparison of grazing and clipping for determining the response of permanent pastures to fertilization.   *Jour. Amer. Soc. Agron.,* 29: 349–359. 1937.
735. ROGERS, W. S.   Soil factors in relation to root growth.   *Trans. Third Internat. Congr. Soil Science,* 1: 249–253. 1935.
736. ROGERS, W. S.   Some observations on the roots of fruit trees.   *Ann. Rept. East Malling Res. Sta.*   (Kent, England.) 1935. Pp. 210–212. 1936.
737. ROMELL, L. G.   Luftväxlingen i Marken som ekologisk faktor.   *Medd. Fran. Stat. Skogsförsöks,* 19: 125–127, 334–335. 1922.
738. ROMELL, L. G.   L'aeration du sol.   *Rev. Int. de Renseign. Agric.,* 1 (n.s.): 300–315. 1923.
739. ROSA, J. T.   Investigations on the hardening process in vegetable plants.   *Mo. Agric. Exp. Sta., Res. Bull.* 48. 1921.
740. ROSE, R. C.   After-ripening and germination of seeds of Tilia, Sambucus, and Rubus.   *Bot. Gaz.,* 67: 281–308. 1919.
741. RÜBEL, E.   Geobotanische Untersuchungsmethoden.   Borntraeger, Berlin. 1922.
742. RUDOLF, P. O., and S. R. GEVORKIANTZ.   Shelterbelt experience in other lands. In Possibilities of shelterbelt planting in the Plains Region.   *U. S. For. Serv.* 1935.
743. RUNYON, E. H.   Ratio of water content to dry weight in leaves of the creosote bush.   *Bot. Gaz.,* 97: 518–553. 1936.
744. RUSSEL, J. C.   Organic matter requirements of soils under various climatic conditions.   *Jour. Amer. Soc. Agron.,* 19: 380–388. 1927.
745. RUSSEL, J. C., and W. G. McRUER.   The relation of organic matter and nitrogen content to series and type in virgin grassland soils.   *Soil Science,* 24: 421–452. 1927.
746. RUSSEL, J. C., et al.   The temperature and moisture factors in nitrate production.   *Soil Science,* 19: 381–398. 1925.
747. RUSSELL, E. J.   The micro-organisms of the soil.   Longmans, Green & Company, New York. 1923.
748. RUSSELL, E. J.   Plant nutrition and crop production.   University of California Press, Berkeley, Calif. 1926.
749. RUSSELL, E. J.   Soil conditions and plant growth.   Pp. 150–248.   Longmans, Green & Company, New York. 1932.

750. *Ibid.* P. 402.
751. *Ibid.* P. 406.
752. *Ibid.* Pp. 445–452.
753. *Ibid.* P. 487.
754. *Ibid.* P. 502.
755. RUSSELL, E. J., and A. APPLEYARD. The atmosphere of the soil: its composition and the causes of variation. *Jour. Agric. Sci.,* 7: 1–48. 1915.
756. SALISBURY, E. J. The significance of the calcicolous habit. *Jour. Ecol.,* 8: 202–215. 1920.
757. SALISBURY, E. J. Stratification and hydrogen-ion concentration . . . with special reference to woodlands. *Jour. Ecol.,* 9: 220–240. 1921.
758. SALISBURY, E. J. The soils of Blakeney Point: a study of soil reaction and succession in relation to the plant covering. *Ann. Bot.,* 36: 391–431. 1922.
759. SALISBURY, E. J. The geographical distribution of plants in relation to climatic factors. *Geog. Jour.,* 67: 312–335. 1926.
760. SALISBURY, E. J. On the causes and ecological significance of stomatal frequency, with special reference to the woodland flora. *Phil. Trans. Roy. Soc. London,* ser. B, 216: 1–65. 1927.
761. SALISBURY, E. J. The biological equipment of species in relation to competition. *Jour. Ecol.,* 17: 197–222. 1929.
762. SALISBURY, E. J. Soil structure in relation to vegetation. *Sci. Prog.,* 29: 409–425. 1935.
763. SALISBURY, E. J. The light climate of woodlands. *Ber. schweiz. bot. Ges.,* 46: 1–11. 1936.
764. SALMON, S. C. The relation of winter temperature to the distribution of winter and spring grains in the United States. *Jour. Amer. Soc. Agron.,* 9: 21–24. 1917.
765. SALMON, S. C. Seeding small grain in furrows. *Kans. Agric. Exp. Sta., Tech. Bull.* 13. 1924.
766. SALMON, S. C. Resistance of varieties of winter wheat and rye to low temperature in relation to winter hardiness and adaptation. *Kans. Agric. Exp. Sta., Tech. Bull.* 35. 1933.
767. SAMPSON, A. W. The reseeding of depleted grazing lands to cultivated forage plants. *U. S. Dept. Agric., Bull.* 4. 1913.
768. SAMPSON, A. W. Natural revegetation of range lands based upon growth requirements and life history of the vegetation. *Jour. Agric. Res.,* 3: 93–148. 1914.
769. SAMPSON, A. W. Climate and crop growth in certain vegetative associations. *U. S. Dept. Agric., Bull.* 700. 1919.
770. SAMPSON, A. W. Effect of grazing upon aspen reproduction. *U. S. Dept. Agric., Bull.* 741. 1919.
771. SAMPSON, A. W. Plant succession in relation to range management. *U. S. Dept. Agric., Bull.* 791. 1919.
772. SAMPSON, A. W. Range and pasture management. John Wiley & Sons, Inc., New York. 1923.
773. SAMPSON, A. W. Native American forage plants. John Wiley & Sons, Inc., New York. 1924.
774. SAMPSON, A. W., and H. E. MALMSTEN. Grazing periods and forage production on the national forests. *U. S. Dept. Agric., Dept. Bull.* 1405. 1926.
775. SAMPSON, A. W., and L. H. WEYL. Range preservation and its relation to erosion control on western grazing lands. *U. S. Dept. Agric., Bull.* 675. 1918.

776. SAMPSON, H. C.   An ecological survey of the prairie vegetation of Illinois. *Ill. Natural Hist. Surv.*, 13: 523–577.   1921.

777. SANFORD, F. H.   Michigan's shifting sands: their control and better utilization. *Mich. Agric. Exp. Sta., Spec. Bull.* 79.   1916.

778. SARGENT, C. S.   Report on the forests of North America, exclusive of Mexico. Tenth Census.   1884.

779. SARVIS, J. T.   Composition and density of the native vegetation in the vicinity of the northern Great Plains field station. *Jour. Agric. Res.*, 19: 63–72. 1920.

780. SARVIS, J. T.   Effects of different systems and intensities of grazing upon the native vegetation at the northern great plains field station. *U. S. Dept. Agric., Dept. Bull.* 1170.   1923.

781. SAVAGE, D. A.   Methods of reestablishing buffalo grass on cultivated land in the Great Plains. *U. S. Dept. Agric., Circ.* 328.   1934.

782. SAVAGE, D. A.   Drought survival of native grass species in the central and southern Great Plains, 1935. *U. S. Dept. Agric., Tech. Bull.* 549.   1937.

783. SAYRE, J. D.   Physiology of stomata of Rumex patientia. *Ohio Jour. Sci.*, 26: 233–266.   1926.

784. SAYRE, J. D.   A recording atmometer. *Ecology*, 9: 123–125.   1928.

785. SCARTH, G. W.   Stomatal movement: its regulation and regulatory rôle, a review. *Protoplasma*, 2: 498–511.   1927.

786. SCARTH, G. W.   Mechanism of the action of light and other factors on stomatal movement. *Plant Physiol.*, 7: 481–504.   1932.

787. SCARTH, G. W., and J. LEVITT.   The frost-hardening mechanism of plant cells. *Plant Physiol.*, 12: 51–78.   1937.

788. SCARTH, G. W., J. WHYTE, and A. BROWN.   On the cause of night opening of stomata. *Roy. Soc. Canada, Trans. and Proc.*, 27: 115–117.   1933.

789. SCHAFFNER, J. H.   Sex reversal and the experimental production of neutral tassels in Zea mays. *Bot. Gaz.*, 90: 279–298.   1930.

790. SCHAFFNER, J. H.   The fluctuation curve of sex reversal in staminate hemp plants induced by photoperiodicity. *Amer. Jour. Bot.*, 18: 424–430. 1931.

791. SCHANDERL, H., and W. KAEMPFERT.   Über die Strahlungsdurchlässigkeit von Blättern und Blattgeweben. *Planta Arch. Wiss. Bot.*, 18: 700–750. 1932.

792. SCHENCK, H.   Ueber das Aërenchym, ein dem Kork homologes Gewebe bei Sumpfpflanzen. *Jahrb. Wiss. Bot.*, 20: 526–574.   1889.

793. SCHERMERHORN, L. G.   Sweet potato studies in New Jersey. *N. J. Agric. Exp. Sta., Bull.* 398.   1924.

794. SCHIMPER, A. F. W.   Die indo-malayische Strandflora. Jena.   1891.

795. SCHIMPER, A. F. W.   Plant-geography upon a physiological basis. Clarendon Press, Oxford.   1903.

796. SCHOMER, H. A.   Photosynthesis of water plants at various depths in the lakes of northeastern Wisconsin. *Ecology*, 15: 217–218.   1934.

797. SCHÜBELER, F. C.   The effects of uninterrupted sunlight on plants. *Nature*, 21: 311–312.   1880.

798. SCHWARZ, F.   Die Wurzelhaare der Pflanzen. *Untersuch. Bot. Instit. Tübingen*, 1: 135–188.   1883.

799. SEARS, P. B.   The natural vegetation of Ohio. *Ohio Jour. Sci.*, 25: 139–149. 1925; 26: 128–146, 213–231.   1926.

800. SEARS, P. B.   A record of post-glacial climate in northern Ohio. *Ohio Jour. Sci.*, 30: 205–217.   1930.

801. SEARS, P. B. Types of North American pollen profiles. *Ecology*, 16: 488–499. 1935.

802. SEARS, P. B. Deserts on the march. University of Oklahoma Press, Norman, Okla. 1935.

803. SEELEY, D. A. Relation between temperature and crops. *Monthly Weather Rev.*, 45: 354–359. 1917.

804. SELLARDS, E. H., *et al.* Investigations on the Red river made in connection with the Oklahoma-Texas boundary suit. *Univ. Tex., Bull.* 2327. 1923.

805. SELLSCHOP, J. P. F., and S. C. SALMON. The influence of chilling, above the freezing point, on certain crop plants. *Jour. Agric. Res.*, 37: 315–338. 1928.

806. SETCHELL, W. A. Temperature and anthesis. *Amer. Jour. Bot.*, 12: 178–188. 1925.

807. SETON, E. T. The arctic prairies, 1911. Charles Scribner's Sons, New York. 1937.

808. SHANTZ, H. L. Natural vegetation as an indicator of the capabilities of land for crop production in the great plains area. *U. S. Dept. Agric., Bur. Plant Ind., Bull.* 201. 1911.

809. SHANTZ, H. L. Plant succession in Tooele valley, Utah. In CLEMENTS, Plant succession. *Carnegie Inst. Wash., Pub.* 242. Pp. 233–236. 1916.

810. SHANTZ, H. L. Plant succession on abandoned roads in eastern Colorado. *Jour. Ecol.*, 5: 19–42. 1917.

811. SHANTZ, H. L. The natural vegetation of the Great Plains region. *Ann. Assoc. Amer. Geog.*, 13: 81–107. 1923.

812. SHANTZ, H. L. Drought resistance and soil moisture. *Ecology*, 8: 145–157. 1927.

813. SHANTZ, H. L., and R. L. PIEMEISEL. Fungus fairy rings in eastern Colorado and their effect on vegetation. *Jour. Agric. Res.*, 11: 191–246. 1917.

814. SHANTZ, H. L., and R. L. PIEMEISEL. Indicator significance of the natural vegetation of the southwestern desert. *Jour. Agric. Res.*, 28: 721–802. 1924.

815. SHANTZ, H. L., and R. ZON. Natural vegetation. *U. S. Dept. Agric., Atlas of American Agriculture*, part 1, sec. E. 1924.

816. SHARP, L. T., and D. R. HOAGLAND. Acidity and adsorption in soils as measured by the hydrogen electrode. *Jour. Agric. Res.*, 7: 123–145. 1916.

817. SHAW, C. F. The normal moisture capacity of soils. *Soil Science*, 23: 303–317. 1927.

818. SHELFORD, V. E., editor. Naturalist's guide to the Americas. Williams & Wilkins Company, Baltimore. 1926.

819. SHERFF, E. E. The vegetation of Skokie Marsh, with reference to subterranean organs and their interrelationships. *Bot. Gaz.*, 53: 415–435. 1912.

820. SHIMEK, B. The prairies. *Bull. Lab. Nat. Hist., State Univ. Iowa*, 6: 169–240. 1911.

821. SHIRLEY, H. L. The influence of light intensity and light quality upon the growth of plants. *Amer. Jour. Bot.*, 16: 354–390. 1929.

822. SHIRLEY, H. L. Light sources and light measurements. *Plant Physiol.*, 6: 447–466. 1931.

823. SHIRLEY, H. L. Light intensity in relation to plant growth in a virgin Norway pine forest. *Jour. Agric. Res.*, 44: 227–244. 1932.

824. SHIRLEY, H. L. Observations on drought injury in Minnesota forests. *Ecology*, 15: 42–48. 1934.

825. SHIRLEY, H. L. Light as an ecological factor and its measurement. *Bot. Rev.*, 1: 355–381. 1935.

826. SHIRLEY, H. L. Lethal high temperatures for conifers, and the cooling effect of transpiration. *Jour. Agric. Res.*, 53: 239–258. 1936.

827. SHIRLEY, H. L. The effects of light intensity upon seed plants. In DUGGAR, Biological effects of radiation. Vol. 2. Pp. 727–762. McGraw-Hill Book Company, Inc., New York. 1936.

828. SHIRLEY, H. L. Direct seeding in the Lake States. *Jour. For.*, 35: 379–387. 1937.

829. SHORT, C. E. Observations on the botany of Illinois. *West. Jour. Med. Surg.*, 3: 185–198. 1845.

830. SHOW, S. B., and E. I. KOTOK. The rôle of fire in the California pine forests. *U. S. Dept. Agric., Dept. Bull.* 1294. 1924.

831. SHOW, S. B., and E. I. KOTOK. Cover type and fire control in the national forests of northern California. *U. S. Dept. Agric., Dept. Bull.* 1495. 1929.

832. SHREVE, E. B. Seasonal changes in the water relations of desert plants. *Ecology*, 4: 266–292. 1923.

833. SHREVE, F. The influence of low temperatures on the distribution of the giant cactus. *Plant World*, 14: 136–146. 1911.

834. SHREVE, F. Establishment behavior of the palo verde. *Plant World*, 14: 289–296. 1911.

835. SHREVE, F. A montane rain-forest; a contribution to the physiological plant geography of Jamaica. *Carnegie Inst. Wash., Pub.* 199. 1914.

836. SHREVE, F. Rainfall as a determinant of soil moisture. *Plant World*, 17: 9–26 1914.

837. SHREVE, F. The role of winter temperatures in determining the distribution of plants. *Amer. Jour. Bot.*, 1: 194–202. 1914.

838. SHREVE, F. The vegetation of a desert mountain range as conditioned by climatic factors. *Carnegie Inst. Wash., Pub.* 217. 1915.

839. SHREVE, F. The weight of physical factors in the study of plant distribution. *Plant World*, 19: 53–67. 1916.

840. SHREVE, F. The establishment of desert perennials. *Jour. Ecol.*, 5: 210–216. 1917.

841. SHREVE, F. Soil temperature as influenced by altitude and slope exposure. *Ecology*, 5: 128–136. 1924.

842. SHREVE, F. Ecological aspects of the deserts of California. *Ecology*, 6: 93–103. 1925.

843. SHREVE, F. Changes in desert vegetation. *Ecology*, 10: 364–373. 1929.

843a. SHREVE, F. Rainfall, runoff and soil moisture under desert conditions. *Ann. Assoc. Amer. Geog.*, 24: 131–156. 1934.

844. SHREVE, F. The plant life of the Sonoran Desert. *Sci. Monthly*, 42: 195–213. 1936.

845. SHREVE, F., and W. V. TURNAGE. The establishment of moisture equilibrium in soil. *Soil Science*, 41: 351–355. 1936.

846. SHULL, C. A. The rôle of oxygen in germination. *Bot. Gaz.*, 57: 64–69. 1914.

847. SHULL, C. A. Measurement of the surface forces in soils. *Bot. Gaz.*, 62: 1–31. 1916.

848. SHULL, C. A. A spectrophotometric study of reflection of light from leaf surfaces. *Bot. Gaz.*, 87: 583–607. 1929.

849. SHULL, C. A., and W. B. DAVIS. Delayed germination and catalase activity in Xanthium. *Bot. Gaz.*, 75: 268–281. 1923.

850. SHULL, G. H. The longevity of submerged seeds. *Plant World*, 17: 329–337. 1914.

851. SIEVERS, F. J., and H. F. HOLTZ. The silt loam soils of eastern Washington and their management. *Wash. Agric. Exp. Sta., Bull.* 166. 1922.

852. SIGGINS, H. W. Distribution and rate of fall of conifer seeds. *Jour. Agric. Res.*, 47: 119–128. 1933.

853. SILCOX, F. A., W. C. LOWDERMILK, and M. L. COOKE. The scientific aspects of flood control. *Occasional Publications* 3, A.A.A.S. Science Press, Lancaster, Pa. 1936.

854. SINGH, B. N., and G. V. CHALAM. Unit of quantitative study of weed flora on arable lands. *Jour. Amer. Soc. Agron.*, 28: 556–561. 1936.

855. SINGH, B. N., and G. V. CHALAM. A quantitative analysis of the weed flora on arable land. *Jour. Ecol.*, 25: 213–221. 1937.

856. SKENE, M. The biology of flowering plants. Sidgwick & Jackson, London. 1924.

857. SMITH, A. Daily seasonal air and soil temperatures at Davis, California. *Hilgardia*, 4: 77–112. 1929.

858. SMITH, A. M. On the internal temperature of leaves in tropical insolation. *Ann. Roy. Bot. Gardens Peradeniya*, 4: 229–298. 1909.

859. SMITH, J. G. Grazing problems in the southwest and how to meet them. *U. S. Dept. Agric., Div. Agrost., Bull.* 16. 1899.

860. SMITH, J. W. Agricultural meteorology. The Macmillan Company, New York. 1920.

861. SMITH, S. D. Forestation a success in the sand hills of Nebraska. *Proc. Soc. Amer. For.*, 9: 388–395. 1914.

862. SMYTH, E. S. A contribution to the physiology and ecology of Peltigera canina and P. polydactyla. *Ann. Bot.*, 48: 781–818. 1934.

863. SNOW, L. M. The development of root hairs. *Bot. Gaz.*, 40: 12–48. 1905.

864. SNOW, L. M. Contributions to the knowledge of the diaphragms of water plants. *Bot. Gaz.*, 58: 495–517. 1914. 69: 297–317. 1920.

865. SNYDER, E. F. Methods for determining the hydrogen-ion concentration of soils. *U. S. Dept. Agric., Circ.* 56. 1935.

866. Society of American Foresters. Forest cover types of the eastern United States. *Jour. For.*, 30: 1–48. 1932.

867. SOMMER, A. L. Studies concerning the essential nature of aluminum and silicon for plant growth. *Univ. Calif. Pub. Agric. Sci.*, 5: 57–81. 1926.

868. SOMMER, A. L., and C. B. LIPMAN. Evidence on the indispensable nature of zinc and boron for higher green plants. *Plant Physiol.*, 1: 231–249. 1926.

869. SPAETH, J. N. A physiological study of dormancy in Tilia seeds. *Cornell Univ. Agric. Exp. Sta., Mem.* 169. 1934.

870. SPALDING, V. M. Biological relations of desert shrubs. *Bot. Gaz.*, 41: 262–282. 1906.

871. SPALDING, V. M. Distribution and movements of desert plants. *Carnegie Inst. Wash., Pub.* 113. 1909.

872. SPERRY, T. M. Root systems in Illinois prairie. *Ecology*, 16: 178–202. 1935.

873. SPOEHR, H. A. The origin and role of pentose sugars. In The carbohydrate economy of cacti, pp. 75–79. *Carnegie Inst. Wash., Pub.* 287. 1919.

874. SPOEHR, H. A. Photosynthesis. P. 34. Chemical Catalog Co., New York. 1926.

875. SPOEHR, H. A., and J. H. C. SMITH. The light factor in photosynthesis. In DUGGAR, Biological effects of radiation. Vol. 2. Pp. 1015–1058. McGraw-Hill Book Company, Inc., New York. 1936.

876. STAKER, E. V. The effect of dry heat on alfalfa seed and its adulterants. *Jour. Amer. Soc. Agron.*, 17: 32–40. 1925.

877. STAKMAN, E. C., *et al.* Spores in the upper air. *Jour. Agric. Res.*, 24: 599–607. 1923.

878. STAMP, L. D. The aerial survey of the Irrawaddy delta forests (Burma). *Jour. Ecol.*, 13: 262–276. 1925.

879. STEIGER, T. L. Structure of prairie vegetation. *Ecology*, 11: 170–217. 1930.

879a. STEINBAUER, G. P. Dormancy and germination of Fraxinus seeds. *Plant Physiol.*, 12: 813–824. 1937.

880. STEINBERG, R. A., and W. W. GARNER. Response of certain plants to length of day and temperature under controlled conditions. *Jour. Agric. Res.*, 52: 943–960. 1936.

881. STEINMETZ, F. H. Winter hardiness in alfalfa varieties. *Minn. Agric. Exp. Sta., Tech. Bull.* 38. 1926.

882. STEVENS, C. L. Root growth of white pine (Pinus strobus L.). *Yale Univ., School For., Bull.* 32. 1931.

883. STEVENS, O. A. The number and weight of seeds produced by weeds. *Amer. Jour. Bot.*, 19: 784–794. 1932.

884. STEWART, G. R. A study of soil changes associated with the transition from fertile hardwood forest land to pasture types of decreasing fertility. *Ecol. Mono.*, 3: 107–145. 1933.

885. STEWART, G., and S. S. HUTCHINGS. The point-observation-plot (square-foot density) method of vegetation survey. *Jour. Amer. Soc. Agron.*, 28: 714–722. 1936.

886. STEWART, G. R., E. C. THOMAS, and J. HORNER. Some effects of mulching paper on Hawaiian soils. *Soil Science*, 22: 35–39. 1926.

887. STICKEL, P. W. Forest fire damage studies in the Northeast. II. First-year mortality in burn-over oak stands. *Jour. For.*, 33: 595–598. 1935.

888. STICKEL, P. W., and H. F. MARCO. Forest fire damage studies in the Northeast. III. Relation between fire injury and fungal infection. *Jour. For.*, 34: 420–423. 1936.

889. STILES, W. Photosynthesis. P. 175. Longmans, Green & Company, New York. 1925.

890. STOA, T. E. Persistence of viability of sweet clover seed in a cultivated soil. *Jour. Amer. Soc. Agron.*, 25: 177–181. 1933.

891. STOBER, J. P. A comparative study of winter and summer leaves of various herbs. *Bot. Gaz.*, 63: 89–109. 1917.

892. STOCKER, O. Über die Assimilationsbedingungen im tropischen Regenwald. *Ber. deutsch. bot. Ges.*, 49: 267–273. 1931.

893. STODDART, L. A. Osmotic pressure and water content of prairie plants. *Plant Physiol.*, 10: 661–680. 1935.

894. STRAUSBAUGH, P. D. Dormancy and hardiness in the plum. *Rot. Gaz.*, 71: 337–357. 1921.

895. STUART, W., and E. H. MILSTEAD. Shortening the rest period of the potato. *U. S. Dept. Agric., Tech. Bull.* 415. 1934.

896. SWEET, A. T. Soil profile and root penetration as indicators of apple production in the lake shore district of western New York. *U. S. Dept. Agric., Circ.* 303. 1933.

897. TANSLEY, A. G. The classification of vegetation and the concept of development. *Jour. Ecol.*, 8: 118–149. 1920.

898. TANSLEY, A. G. Practical plant ecology. Dodd, Mead & Company, Inc., New York. 1923.

899. TANSLEY, A. G., and T. F. CHIPP. Biotic factors. In Aims and methods in the study of vegetation. Pp. 140–151. Published by the British Empire

Vegetation Committee and the Crown Agents for the Colonies. London. 1926.

900. TANSLEY, A. G., and T. F. CHIPP. Classification of mature soils according to climatic soil types. In Aims and methods in the study of vegetation. Pp. 131–135. Published by the British Empire Vegetation Committee and the Crown Agents for the Colonies. London. 1926.

901. TAUBENHAUS, J. J., and W. N. EZEKIEL. Acid injury of cotton roots. *Bot. Gaz.*, 92: 430–435. 1931.

902. TAYLOR, N. The vegetation of Long Island. *Brooklyn Bot. Garden Mem.*, 2: 1–107. 1923.

903. TAYLOR, R. F. Available nitrogen as a factor influencing the occurrence of sitka spruce and western hemlock seedlings in the forests of south-eastern Alaska. *Ecology*, 16: 580–602. 1935.

904. TAYLOR, W. P. Significance of extreme or intermittent conditions in distribution of species and management of natural resources, with a restatement of Liebig's law of minimum. *Ecology*, 15: 374–379. 1934.

905. TAYLOR, W. P. Significance of the biotic community in ecological studies. *Quarterly Rev. Biol.*, 10: 291–307. 1935.

906. TAYLOR, W. P. Some animal relations to soils. *Ecology*, 16: 127–136. 1935.

907. TAYLOR, W. P., and J. V. G. LOFTFIELD. Damage to range grasses by the Zuni prairie dog. *U. S. Dept. Agric., Dept. Bull.* 1227. 1924.

908. TAYLOR, W. P., *et al.* The relation of jack rabbits to grazing in southern Arizona. *Jour. For.*, 33: 490–498. 1935.

909. TEHON, L. R. Epidemic diseases of grain crops in Illinois, 1922–1926. *Ill. Natural Hist. Surv.*, 17: 1–96. 1927.

910. THARP, B. C. Structure of Texas vegetation east of the 98th meridian. *Univ. Tex., Bull.* 2606. 1926.

911. THODAY, D. The significance of reduction in the size of leaves. *Jour. Ecol.*, 19: 297–303. 1931.

912. THOMAS, M. Plant physiology. Pp. 79–81. P. Blakiston's Son & Company, Philadelphia. 1935.

913. THOMPSON, H. C. Experimental studies of cultivation of certain vegetable crops. *Cornell Univ. Agric. Exp. Sta., Mem.* 107. 1927.

914. THOMSON, G. M. The naturalisation of animals and plants in New Zealand. P. 273. Cambridge University Press, London. 1922.

915. THORNTON, H. G. The present state of our ignorance concerning the nodules of leguminous plants. *Sci. Prog.*, 31: 236–249. 1936.

916. THORNTON, N. C. Carbon dioxide storage. V. Breaking the dormancy of potato tubers. *Contr. Boyce Thompson Inst.*, 5: 471–481. 1933.

917. THORNTON, N. C. Factors influencing germination and development of dormancy in cocklebur seeds. *Contr. Boyce Thompson Inst.*, 7: 477–496. 1935.

918. THORNTON, N. C. Carbon dioxide storage. IX. Germination of lettuce seeds at high temperatures in both light and darkness. *Contr. Boyce Thompson Inst.*, 8: 25–40. 1936.

919. TIDESTROM, I. Flora of Utah and Nevada. *Contr. U. S. Nat. Herb.*, 25. 1925.

920. TILLOTSON, C. R. Reforestation on the national forests. *U. S. Dept. Agric., Bull.* 475. 1917.

921. TILLOTSON, C. R., and W. B. GREELEY. Timber growing and logging practice in the central hardwood region. *U. S. Dept. Agric., Dept. Bull.*, 1491. 1927.

922. TINCKER, M. A. H.   The effect of length of day upon the growth and chemical composition of the tissues of certain economic plants.   *Ann. Bot.*, 42: 101–140. 1928.

923. TISDALE, W. H.   Relation of temperature to the growth and infecting power of Fusarium lini.   *Phytopathology*, 7: 356–360.   1917.

924. TITCOMB, J. W.   Aquatic plants in pond culture.   *Rept. U. S. Com. Fish.*, 1923, app. 2: 1–24.   1924.

925. TOUMEY, J. W.   Foundations of silviculture upon an ecological basis.   Vol. 1. P. 52.   John Wiley & Sons, Inc., New York.   1928.

926. *Ibid.*   P. 60.

927. *Ibid.*   Pp. 137–141.

928. TOUMEY, J. W.   Initial root habit in American trees and its bearing on regeneration.   *Proc. Internat. Congr. Plant Sci.*, 1: 713–728.   1929.

929. TOUMEY, J. W., and R. KIENHOLZ.   Trenched plots under forest canopies. *Yale Univ., School For., Bull.* 30.   1931.

929a. TOUMEY, J. W., and C. F. KORSTIAN.   Foundations of silviculture upon an ecological basis.   Pp. 97–102.   John Wiley & Sons, Inc., New York.   1937.

929b. *Ibid.*   Pp. 136–145.

930. TOUMEY, J. W., and E. J. NEETHLING.   Insolation a factor in the natural regeneration of certain conifers.   *Yale Univ., School For., Bull.* 11.   1924.

931. TOUMEY, J. W., and P. W. STICKEL.   A new device for taking maximum and minimum soil temperatures in forest investigations.   *Ecology*, 6: 171–178. 1925.

932. TRANSEAU, E. N.   On the development of palisade tissue and resinous deposits in leaves.   *Science*, n.s., 19: 866–867.   1904.

933. TRANSEAU, E. N.   Forest centers of eastern America.   *Amer. Nat.*, 39: 875–889.   1905.

934. TRUOG, E.   Soil acidity: I. Its relation to the growth of plants.   *Soil Science*, 5: 169–195.   1918.

935. TURNER, H. C.   The effect of planting method upon growth of western yellow pine.   *Jour. For.*, 16: 399–403.   1918.

936. TURNER, L. M.   Root growth of seedlings of Pinus echinata and Pinus taeda. *Jour. Agric. Res.*, 53: 145–149.   1936.

937. TURRELL, F. M.   The area of the internal exposed surface of dicotyledon leaves.   *Amer. Jour. Bot.*, 23: 255–264.   1936.

938. TUTTLE, G. M.   Induced changes in reserve materials in evergreen herbaceous leaves.   *Ann. Bot.*, 33: 201–210.   1919.

939. TYSDAL, H. M.   Influencing of light, temperature, and soil moisture on the hardening process in alfalfa.   *Jour. Agric. Res.*, 46: 483–515.   1933.

940. U. S. Forest Service.   When fire is banished from the land of the white oak. *U. S. Dept. Agric., Misc. Circ.* 53.   1925.

941. U. S. Forest Service.   Possibilities of shelterbelt planting in the Plains region. Government Printing Office, Washington.   1935.

941a. U. S. Forest Service.   Range plant handbook.   1937.

942. VEIHMEYER, F. J.   Some factors affecting the irrigation requirements of deciduous orchards.   *Hilgardia*, 2: 279.   1927.

943. VEIHMEYER, F. J., and A. H. HENDRICKSON.   Soil-moisture conditions in relation to plant growth.   *Plant Physiol.*, 2: 71–82.   1927.

943a. VEIHMEYER, F. J., and A. H. HENDRICKSON.   Some plant and soil-moisture relations.   *Amer. Soil Surv. Assoc., Bull.* 15: 76–80.   1934.

944. VENKATRAMAN, R. S., and U. V. RAO.   Coimbatore seedling canes.   *Agric. Jour. India*, 23: 37–38.   1928.

945. VISHER, S. S.   Indiana regional contrasts in temperature and precipitation. *Ind. Acad. Sci.*, 45: 183–204.   1936.

946. VORHIES, C. T., and W. P. TAYLOR.   Life history of the kangaroo rat.   *U. S. Dept. Agric., Bull.* 1091.   1922.

947. WAHLENBERG, W. G.   Reforestation by seed sowing in the northern Rocky Mountains. *Jour. Agric. Res.*, 30: 637–641.   1925.

948. WAHLENBERG, W. G.   Modification of western yellow pine root systems by fertilizing the soil at different depths in the nursery. *Jour. Agric. Res.*, 39: 137–146.   1929.

949. WAKSMAN, S. A.   The micro-biological complexes of the soil and soil deterioration. *Jour. Amer. Soc. Agron.*, 18: 137–142.   1926.

950. WAKSMAN, S. A.   Humus—Origin, chemical composition, and importance in nature.   Pp. 3–9.   Williams & Wilkins Company, Baltimore.   1936.

951. *Ibid.*   P. 328.

952. WAKSMAN, S. A., and K. R. N. IYER.   Contribution to our knowledge of the chemical nature and origin of humus: IV. Fixation of proteins by lignins and formation of complexes resistant to microbial decomposition. *Soil Science*, 36: 69–82.   1933.

953. WAKSMAN, S. A., and F. G. TENNEY.   Composition of natural organic materials and their decomposition in the soil: III. The influence of nature of plant upon the rapidity of its decomposition. *Soil Science*, 26: 155–171.   1928.

954. WAKSMAN, S. A., *et al.*   The role of microorganisms in the transformation of organic matter in forest soils. *Ecology*, 9: 126–144.   1928.

955. WALKER, J. C., and L. R. JONES.   Relation of soil temperature and other factors to onion smut infection. *Jour. Agric. Res.*, 22: 235–262.   1921.

956. WALKER, L. B., and E. N. ANDERSEN.   Relation of glycogen to spore-ejection. *Mycologia*, 17: 154–159.   1925.

957. WALTER, H.   Über den Wasserhaushalt der Mangrovepflanzen. *Ber. schweiz. bot. Ges.*, 46: 217–228.   1936.

958. WARMING, E.   Oecology of plants.   Oxford University Press, London.   2d impr.   1925.

959. WARMING, E., and P. GRAEBNER.   Lehrbuch der ökologischen Pflanzengeographie.   Borntraeger, Berlin.   1933.

960. WATENPAUGH, H. N.   The influence of the reaction of soil strata upon the root development of alfalfa. *Soil Science*, 41: 449–468.   1936.

961. WATT, A. S.   On the ecology of British beechwoods with special reference to their regeneration. *Jour. Ecol.*, 11: 1–48.   1923.

962. WATT, R. D.   The influence of phosphatic fertilizers on root development. *Rept. Australian Assoc. Adv. Sci.*, 1913, 14: 661–665.   1914.   (Abs. in *Exp. Sta. Rec.*, 33: 526.   1915.)

963. WEAVER, J. E.   Evaporation and plant succession in southeastern Washington and adjacent Idaho. *Plant World*, 17: 273–294.   1914.

964. WEAVER, J. E.   A study of the vegetation of southeastern Washington and adjacent Idaho. *Univ. Neb. Studies*, 17: 1–133.   1917.

965. WEAVER, J. E.   The ecological relations of roots. *Carnegie Inst. Wash., Pub.* 286.   1919.

966. WEAVER, J. E.   Root development in the grassland formation. *Carnegie Inst. Wash., Pub.* 292.   1920.

967. WEAVER, J. E.   Plant production as a measure of environment. *Jour. Ecol.*, 12: 205–237.   1924.

968. WEAVER, J. E.   Investigations on the root habits of plants. *Amer. Jour. Bot.*, 12: 502–509.   1925.

969. WEAVER, J. E. Root development of field crops. McGraw-Hill Book Company, Inc., New York. 1926.

970. WEAVER, J. E. Methods of studying root development. In Root development of field crops. McGraw-Hill Book Company, Inc., New York. 1926.

971. WEAVER, J. E. Some ecological aspects of agriculture in the prairie. *Ecology,* 8: 1–17. 1927.

972. WEAVER, J. E., and F. W. ALBERTSON. Effects of the great drought on the prairies of Iowa, Nebraska, and Kansas. *Ecology,* 17: 567–639. 1936.

973. WEAVER, J. E., and W. E. BRUNER. Root development of vegetable crops. McGraw-Hill Book Company, Inc., New York. 1927.

974. WEAVER, J. E., and J. W. CRIST. Direct measurement of water loss from vegetation without disturbing the normal structure of the soil. *Ecology,* 5: 153–170. 1924.

975. WEAVER, J. E., and T. J. FITZPATRICK. Ecology and relative importance of the dominants of tall-grass prairie. *Bot. Gaz.,* 93: 113–150. 1932.

976. WEAVER, J. E., and T. J. FITZPATRICK. The prairie. *Ecol. Mono.,* 4: 109–295. 1934.

977. WEAVER, J. E., and G. W. HARMON. Quantity of living plant materials in prairie soils in relation to run-off and soil erosion. *Univ. Neb. Conservation & Surv. Div., Bull.* 8. 1935.

978. WEAVER, J. E., and W. J. HIMMEL. Relation between the development of root system and shoot under long- and short-day illumination. *Plant Physiol.,* 4: 435–457. 1929.

979. WEAVER, J. E., and W. J. HIMMEL. Relation of increased water content and decreased aeration to root development in hydrophytes. *Plant Physiol.,* 5: 69–92. 1930.

979a. WEAVER, J. E., V. H. HOUGEN, and M. D. WELDON. Relation of root distribution to organic matter in prairie soil. *Bot. Gaz.,* 96: 389–420. 1935.

980. WEAVER, J. E., and J. KRAMER. Root system of Quercus macrocarpa in relation to the invasion of prairie. *Bot. Gaz.,* 94: 51–85. 1932.

981. WEAVER, J. E., and W. C. NOLL. Comparison of runoff and erosion in prairie, pasture, and cultivated land. *Univ. Neb. Conservation & Surv. Div., Bull.* 11. 1935.

982. WEAVER, J. E., L. A. STODDART, and W. NOLL. Response of the prairie to the great drought of 1934. *Ecology,* 16: 612–629. 1935.

983. WEAVER, J. E., *et al.* Development of root and shoot of winter wheat under field environment. *Ecology,* 5: 26–50. 1924.

984. WEAVER, J. E., *et al.* Transect method of studying woodland vegetation along streams. *Bot. Gaz.,* 80: 168–187. 1925.

985. WEIHING, R. M. The comparative root development of regional types of corn. *Jour. Amer. Soc. Agron.,* 27: 526–537. 1935.

986. WEISS, F. E. The dispersal of fruits and seeds by ants. *New Phytol.,* 7: 23–28. 1908.

987. WELCH, P. S. Limnology. Pp. 67–81. McGraw-Hill Book Company, Inc., New York. 1935.

988. WELLS, B. W. Major plant communities of North Carolina. *N. C. Agric. Exp. Sta., Tech. Bull.* 25. 1924.

989. WELLS, B. W. Plant communities of the coastal plain of North Carolina and their successional relations. *Ecology,* 9: 230–242. 1928.

990. WHERRY, E. T. Soil acidity and a field method for its measurement. *Ecology,* 1: 160–173. 1926.

991. WHERRY, E. T.   A new method of stating hydrogen-ion (hydrion) concentration. *Wagner Free Inst. Sci. Philadelphia, Bull.* 2: 59–64. 1927.

992. WHERRY, E. T.   Divergent soil reaction preferences of related plants. *Ecology,* 8: 197–206. 1927.

993. WHITAKER, E. S.   Root hairs and secondary thickening in the Compositae. *Bot. Gaz.,* 76: 30–58. 1923.

994. WHITE, J. W.   Concerning the growth and composition of clover and sorrel as influenced by varied amounts of limestone. *Pa. Agric. Exp. Sta., Rept.* 1913–1914: 46. 1916.

995. WHITE, W. N.   A method of estimating ground-water supplies based on discharge by plants and evaporation from soil. *U. S. Dept. Int. Geol. Surv., Water-Supply Paper* 659-A. 1932.

996. WHITFORD, H. N.   The genetic development of the forests of northern Michigan; a study in physiographic ecology. *Bot. Gaz.,* 31: 289–325. 1901.

997. WHITFORD, H. N.   The forests of the Flathead valley, Montana. *Bot. Gaz.,* 39: 99–122, 194–218, 276–296. 1905.

998. WHITNEY, M.   Growing Sumatra tobacco under shade in the Connecticut valley. *U. S. Dept. Agric., Bur. Soils, Bull.* 20. 1902.

999. WIEGAND, K. M.   Some studies regarding the biology of buds and twigs in winter. *Bot. Gaz.,* 41: 373–424. 1906.

1000. WIESLANDER, A. E.   First steps of the forest survey in California. *Jour. For.,* 33: 877–884. 1935.

1001. WIGGANS, C. C.   The effect of orchard plants on subsoil moisture. *Proc. Amer. Soc. Hort. Sci.,* 33: 103–107. 1936.

1002. WIGGANS, R. G.   Variations in the osmotic concentration of the guard cells during the opening and closing of stomata. *Amer. Jour. Bot.,* 8: 30–40. 1921.

1003. WILDE, S. A.   The relation of soils and forest vegetation in the Lake States region. *Ecology,* 14: 94–105. 1933.

1004. WILDE, S. A.   Soil reaction in relation to forestry and its determination by simple tests. *Jour. For.,* 32: 411–418. 1934.

1005. WILLIAMS, A. B.   The composition and dynamics of a beech-maple climax community. *Ecol. Mono.,* 6: 317–408. 1936.

1006. WILLIAMS, C. G., and F. A. WELTON.   Corn experiments. *Ohio Agric. Exp. Sta., Bull.* 282. 1915.

1007. WILSON, C. P.   The artificial reseeding of New Mexico ranges. *N. M. Agric. Exp. Sta., Bull.* 189. 1931.

1008. WILSON, J. D.   Environmental factors in relation to plant disease and injury: a bibliography. *Ohio Agric. Exp. Sta., Tech. Ser., Bull.* 9. 1932.

1009. WILSON, K.   The production of root-hairs in relation to the development of the piliferous layer. *Ann. Bot.,* 50: 121–154. 1936.

1010. WILSON, L. R.   Lake development and plant succession in Vilas County, Wisconsin. I. The medium hard water lakes. *Ecol. Mono.,* 5: 207–247. 1935.

1011. WILSON, W. P.   The production of aerating organs on the roots of swamp and other plants. *Proc. Acad. Nat. Sci. Phil.,* 1889: 67–69. 1890. Abstract in *Bot. Centralbl.,* 43: 148. 1890. *Just's Bot. Jahrb.,* 1889: 682. 1891.

1012. WODEHOUSE, R. P.   Pollen grains. McGraw-Hill Book Company, Inc., New York. 1935.

1013. WOLFANGER, L. A.   The major soil divisions of the United States. John Wiley & Sons, Inc., New York. 1930.

1014. WOOD, J. G.   The physiology of xerophytism in Australian plants.   *Jour. Ecol.*, 22: 69–87.   1934.

1015. WOODHEAD, T. W., and M. M. BRIERLEY.   Development of the climbing habit in Antirrhinum majus.   *New Phytol.*, 8: 284–298.   1909.

1016. WOODROOF, J. G., and N. C. WOODROOF.   Pecan root growth and development.   *Jour. Agric. Res.*, 49: 511–530.   1934.

1017. WRIGHT, K. E.   Effects of phosphorus and lime in reducing aluminum toxicity of acid soils.   *Plant Physiol.*, 12: 173–181.   1937.

1018. WRIGHT, R. C., and G. F. TAYLOR.   Freezing injury to potatoes when undercooled.   *U. S. Dept. Agric., Dept. Bull.* 916.   1921.

1019. WRIGHT, R. C., and G. F. TAYLOR.   The freezing temperatures of some fruits, vegetables, and cut flowers.   *U. S. Dept. Agric., Dept. Bull.* 1133.   1923.

1020. WURSTEN, J. L., and W. L. POWERS.   Reclamation of virgin black alkali soils.   *Jour. Amer. Soc. Agron.*, 26: 752–762.   1934.

1021. WYLIE, R. B.   The pollination of Vallisneria spiralis.   *Bot. Gaz.*, 63: 135–145.   1917.

1022. YAPP, R. H.   On stratification in the vegetation of a marsh, and its relations to evaporation and temperature.   *Ann. Bot.*, 23: 275–319.   1909.

1023. YAPP, R. H.   Spiraea ulmaria L., and its bearing on the problem of xeromorphy in marsh plants.   *Ann. Bot.*, 26: 815–870.   1912.

1024. YAPP, R. H.   The concept of habitat.   *Jour. Ecol.*, 10: 1–17.   1922.

1025. YEAGER, A. F.   Root systems of certain trees and shrubs grown on prairie soils.   *Jour. Agric. Res.*, 51: 1085–1092.   1935.

1026. YOCUM, W. W.   Development of roots and tops of young Delicious apple trees with different cultural treatments in two soil types.   *Neb. Agric. Exp. Sta., Res. Bull.* 95.   1937.

1027. ZALENSKI, V.   Transpiration from upper and lower leaves of plants.   *Bull. Univ. Saratov.*   1923.   Review by N. A. Maximov in The plant in relation to water.   Pp. 328–336.   1929.

1028. ZEASMAN, O. R.   Control soil erosion.   *Exten. Service Coll. Agric. Wis., Circ.* 249.   1931.

1029. ZEDERBAUER, E.   The light requirements of forest trees and the methods of measuring light.   Review in *For. Quarterly*, 6: 255–262.   1908.

1030. ZILLICH, R.   Über den Lichtgenusz einiger Unkräuter und Kulturpflanzen.   *Fortsch. Landw.*, 1: 461–470.   1926.

1031. ZIMMERMAN, P. W.   Recent investigations regarding seeds, seed germination, and root growth in cuttings.   *Florists Exchange*, Aug. 7, 14.   1926.

1032. ZIMMERMAN, P. W., and A. E. HITCHCOCK.   Root formation and flowering of dahlia cuttings when subjected to different day lengths.   *Bot. Gaz.*, 87: 1–13.   1929.

1033. ZIMMERMAN, P. W., and A. E. HITCHCOCK.   Tuberization of artichokes regulated by capping stem tips with black cloth.   *Contr. Boyce Thompson Inst.*, 8: 311–315.   1936.

1034. ZON, R.   Forests and water in the light of scientific investigation.   Appendix V.   *Final Rept. Nat. Waterways Com.*, 2d ed.   1927.

1035. ZON, R., and H. S. GRAVES.   Light in relation to tree growth.   *U. S. Dept. Agric., Forest Service, Bull.* 92.   1911.

INDEX

Boldface type indicates pages on which illustrations appear.

A

Abies, **237**, 370
 concolor (see *White fir*).
 lasiocarpa, **494, 496**
Absorption, in saline soil, 226
 in subsoil, 290
Acalypha, **1**
Acer, 294, 381, **386, 511**
Acid soils, 229–233
 adaptation of roots, 303, 304
 effect upon plants, 232, 233, 304
 in relation, to altitude, 230
 to topography, 230
 tolerant plants, 232
Aconitum, 266
Adansonia, **258**
Adaptation, to decreased water supply,
 446–453
 by osmotic pressure, 451
 by other changes, 453
 by succulence, 446
 by thickened walls, 449
 to water, 424–453
 types produced, 424
Aeration, in relation, to decay, 183
 to plant distribution, 52
 to root development, 298–301
 to root-hair development, 322
 to root response, **306**
 to seedbed preparation, 307
 to soil temperature, 308
 to tree growth, **45**
 in swamps, 298, 299
 temperature and growth, 308
Agents, of migration, 124
 of pollination, 263
Aggregation, 4, 145–147
 mixed, 147, **147**
 simple, 145, **145**
Agricultural regions, **377**
Agropyron, **20**, 41, 87, 315
 smithii, **170**, 249, **450**, **461**, 462

Agropyron, spicatum, 318, **528**
Agrostis, **127**
Air reactions, 249–254
Airplane view, **55**
Alfalfa, absorbing area, 296
 and aeration, 306
 dormancy, 136
 frequent cutting, 21
 root depth, 206, 301
 and salinity, 303
 and soil-moisture depletion, 206
 stomatal movement, **389**
Alisma, 136
Allenrolfea, 467
Allionia, **383**
Allogamy, 262
Almond, 312
Aloe, **447**
Alternation, **8**
Alternes, 7, **8, 80**
Altitude, effect on light, 400
 and temperature, 362
Ambrosia, 4, **133**, 154 (see also *Ragweed*).
Ammonification, 326
Amorpha, 207
Amphibious plants, 431–436
Andropogon, 315, 458, 459
 furcatus, **315**, 460, **521**
 hallii, **319**
 scoparius, **16, 315**
Anemometers, **349**
Animal coactions, **271**
Animal reactions, 247
Animals, as barriers, 172
 cycles of abundance, 284
 in migration, 127
 numbers of, 284
 and pollination, 263, **264**
Annual rings, 43–47, **43**
 and aeration, **45**
 in relation to rainfall, **44, 44**
 and succession, 43, 44

Deciduous forest, extent and nature, 508–510
Delayed germination, 133
Dendrobium, **173**
Denuded quadrats, 11, 29, 30
twigs of shrubs, 30
Deposit, **108,** 109–111
Desalinization, 225
Desert, 440, 445
Desert plains, 525, **526**
Desert scrub climax, 535–537
Desert scrub postclimaxes, **455, 536, 537,** 537
Desert soils, 195
Development, of soils (see *Soils*).
of vegetation, 9, **90**
Dew, 211
Dichogamy, 257
Diclinism, 257
Dioecious plants, 257
Direction of migration, 130
Disclimax, 86, 88
Disease, brown rot, 378
cabbage yellows, 328, **329,** 379
chlorosis, 328
clubroot of cabbage, 329
dry rot of potato, 378
fire blight, 377
flax wilt, 328
onion smut, 329
potato blight, 378
potato scab, 329
relation, to acidity, 329
to environment, 376–379
to nutrients, 328
to soil temperature, 328, 329
to water content, 328
russeting, 377
rusts, 378
tobacco root rot, 328, 379
tomato wilt, 328
wheat scab, 329
wheat smut, 329
yellow berry, 328
Dissemination, 120, **121**
Disseminules, 124
Distance of migration, 122
Distichlis, **225,** 227, 467
Disturbance climax, 86, 88
Dog's-tooth violet, **98,** 137, 368
Dominance, and competition, 149
and stabilization, 237, 238

Dominants, 7, 91, 94, 95, 478
of mixed prairie, 460
of true prairie, 458
Dormancy, 133
in conifers, 139
and delayed germination, 133
embryos requiring acidity, 137
external causes, 134
imperfect embryos, 137
impermeable seed coats, 135, 136
internal causes, 135
mechanically resistant seed coats, 136
Douglas fir, **8,** 92, **135,** 139, **406,** 406 **502**
osmotic pressure, **370**
root habits, 291
Drainage, 299, 301
Dropseed, **141**
Drought-enduring plants, 441
Drought-escaping plants, 441
Drought-evading plants, 441
Drought-resisting plants, 441, **442**
Dry rot of potatoes, 378
Duff, 184
Dunes, 74, **75, 250,** 250, 484
Duration of light, 410
Dust cloud, **248**

E

Earthworms, 180, 232
Ecballium, **129**
Ecesis, 3, 131–145
in aquatics, 132
in bare areas, 144
in deserts, 143
in forests, 142
and migration, 131
modified by temperature, 375, 376
of ragweed, **133**
Echard, 203
Echinocactus, **448**
Ecotone, 27, 104, **338**
Eichhornia, **429**
Eleocharis, **64**
Elm, **100**
Elodea, **425, 426**
Elymus, 315
Embryonic dunes, **74,** 74
Emersed plants (see *Amphibious plants*).
Encelia, **535, 536**
Enclosure, 37–39
Engelmann spruce, **45, 365,** 406, **494**
Environment, and disease, 376–379
measured by plants, 418–423